Gustav Mahler's
American Years
1907 - 1911

A Documentary History

Frontispiece. Gustav Mahler (photograph published in *MA* on December 18, 1909).

T.M

Gustav Mahler's
American Years
1907 - 1911

A Documentary History

by
Zoltan Roman

PENDRAGON PRESS
STUYVESANT, NY

To Anna Mahler
(1904-1988)

Musicological Series by Pendragon Press

Aesthetics in Music
Annotated Reference Tools in Music
Dance and Music
Festschrift Series
French Opera in the 17th and 18th Centuries
Giovanni Battista Pergolesi: The Complete
    Works/Opere Complete
The Historical Harpsichord
The Juilliard Performance Guides
Monographs in Musicology
Musical Life in 19th-Century France
RILM Retrospectives
The Sociology of Music
Thematic Catalogues

Library of Congress Cataloging-in-Publication Data

Gustav Mahler's American years, 1907-1911 : a documentary history /
    [compiled] by Zoltan Roman.
    544 p.   cm. —
    Includes index.
    ISBN 0-918728-73-8 : $62.00
    1. Mahler, Gustav, 1860-1911. 2. Composers—Austria—Biography.
3. Music—New York (N.Y.)—20th century—History and criticism.
4. New York (N.Y.)—Social life and customs. I. Roman, Zoltan,
1936-   . II. Series.
ML410.M23G95   1988
780'.92'4—dc19
[B]   88-18639
                                                              CIP
                                                              MN

Copyright 1989, Pendragon Press

Contents

List of Illustrations

Abbreviations

AME   Alma Mahler, *Gustav Mahler - Erinnerungen und Briefe,* Amsterdam, Allert de Lange, 1940.

AMM   Alma Mahler, *Gustav Mahler - Memories and Letters* (3. ed., revised and enlarged, ed. by Donald Mitchell, tr. by Basil Creighton; Appendix and Chronology by Knud Martner and Donald Mitchell; Appendix for the 1975 American Edition by Donald Mitchell), Seattle, University of Washington Press, 1975.

ANYP   Archives of the New York Philharmonic

BRM   Kurt Blaukopf (mit Beiträgen von Zoltan Roman), *Mahler - Sein Leben, sein Werk und seine Welt in zeitgenössischen Bildern und Texten*, Wien, Universal Edition, 1976.

BRM(E)   Kurt Blaukopf, comp. and ed. (with contributions by Zoltan Roman), (tr. by Paul Baker, Susanne Flatauer, P.R.J. Ford, Daisy Loman, Geoffrey Watkins), *Mahler - A Documentary Study*, London, Thames and Hudson, 1976.

COS   James Camner, ed., *The Great Opera Stars in Historic Photographs*, New York, Dover, 1978.

ELM   Alma Mahler, "Ein Leben mit Gustav Mahler". Typescript, in The Charles Patterson Van Pelt Library, University of Pennsylvania, Philadelphia; it served as the basis for *AME*. Permission to publish excerpts and documents from this typescript (as well as all other letters and photographs by and of Mahler included in this book) had been graciously granted by the late Anna Mahler.

                    The pagination, given in square brackets with the documents, was added to the typescript in Philadelphia; it serves the purpose of an approximate location guide.

GMB   *Gustav Mahler - Briefe* (Neuausgabe erweitert und revidiert von Herta Blaukopf), Wien, Hamburg, Zsolnay, 1982 (Bibliothek der Internationalen Gustav Mahler Gesellschaft).

HLG3   Henry-Louis de La Grange, *Gustav Mahler - Chronique d'une Vie* III (Le Génie Foudroyé, 1907-1911), Paris, Fayard, 1984.

KBM   Kurt Blaukopf, *Gustav Mahler, oder der Zeitgenosse der Zukunft* (2. ed.), Wien, *etc.*, Fritz Molden, 1969.

KBM(E)   Kurt Blaukopf, *Gustav Mahler* (tr. Inge Goodwin), London, Allen Lane, 1973.

LCE   Louis C. Elson, *The History of American Music*, New York, Burt Franklin, 1925 (reprint 1971).

MA   *Musical America*

MC   *The Musical Courier*

MSL   *Selected Letters of Gustav Mahler*, ed. Knud Martner (tr. Eithne Wilkins, Ernst Kaiser, Bill Hopkins), London, Boston, Faber and Faber / New York, Farrar, Straus, Giroux, 1979.

MUB   *Gustav Mahler - Unbekannte Briefe*, ed. Herta Blau-kopf, Wien, Hamburg, Zsolnay, 1983 (Bibliothek der Internationalen Gustav Mahler Gesellschaft).

MUB(E)   *Mahler's Unknown Letters* [revised], ed. Herta Blau-kopf (tr. Richard Stokes), London, Gollancz, 1986.

NALT   Music Division, The New York Public Library, Astor, Lenox and Tilden Foundations (also known as the Library and Museum of the Performing Arts at Lincoln Center).

NYH   *New York Herald*

NYS   *The [New York] Sun*

NYT   *The New York Times*

NYTrib   *New-York Daily Tribune*

NYW   *The [New York] World*

ÖNB-BA   Osterreichische Nationalbibliothek, Bildarchiv or
or -HS   Handschriftensammlung, Vienna.

RSM   Richard Specht, *Gustav Mahler*, Berlin, Leipzig, Schuster & Loeffler, 1913.

S.a., s.a.   See/see also

SFM   The Society of the Friends of Music, *Gustav Mahler - The Composer, the Conductor and the Man*, New York, 1916.

Foreword

When Zoltan Roman approached me with the suggestion to provide a few introductory remarks for his work I was immediately attracted to the idea—partly because, through a concatenation of circumstances, I was forced to come to this country in 1937, thirty years after Gustav Mahler. At that time I thought I had reached a point of no return, which he was spared. What similarities, what contrasts in the reactions of the two travelers!

Apart from this, I was in 1922 to 1925 a member of Alma Mahler's entourage when I was briefly married to Mahler's daughter Anna (to whose memory this book is dedicated.) I was also marginally involved with Alma's idea of having Mahler's unfinished Tenth Symphony completed. A short investigation of the sketches proved this to be impossible because substantial portions of the work would have to be newly invented and would remain recognizable as the latecomer's sheer guesswork. I edited only the first movement, which had been left by Mahler in a reasonably complete, although possibly preliminary version. This book shows that Mahler worked on the symphony during his first New York season and reports the incident when Mahler, watching a fireman's funeral on Fifth Avenue from his hotel window, heard a solitary beat on the bass drum when the cortege stopped for a minute. And in the sketches there is at the end of the Scherzo the lonely beat on the muted bass drum. (I heard Alma telling the story too.)

The attentive reader of this book will become aware that Mahler's original enthusiasm for America gradually gave way to increasing disenchantment. He had arrived, after the unpleasant departure from the hostile atmosphere of Vienna, with a very generous contract with Conried in his pocket and a relatively modest workload in sight. His authority, based on ten years of directorship at the Vienna Opera House, was well established and hardly doubted. But it wore off as time went by, and after his second season as one of the conductors of the Metropolitan Opera he changed over to the New York Philharmonic Orchestra. The thorough documentation of this book, which quotes practically all newspapers and magazines reporting on Mahler's conducting, shows clearly how eventually even small details like his use of the baton were scrutinized and criticized. A sick man, with the doctor's death warrant in his pocket, he left New York in April of 1911, never to return.

One can see that Mahler as a composer was acknowledged from the beginning, well distinguished from some of his "Kapellmeister" colleagues who through experience had acquired enough orchestral know-how to occasionally put together some symphonic exercises. But we can read that the few symphonies which he introduced personally to the American public did not meet with unqualified enthusiasm. It is amusing to read how several critics attacked Mahler for denying the existence of any "program" behind his music although he originally had stressed the opposite, thus causing a confusion of his own making. As seen from a present vantage point, the whole question is, of course, irrelevant.

In an interview, Mahler points out that new music should essentially emanate from folk music, such as it does in many of his own works. He mentions the syncopations so characteristic of what he calls American folk music and ventures that they are somehow related to those of Hungarian music. (He has no inkling of the esoterica of Jazz, and also does not know that the Hungarian music that had become world famous through Franz Liszt was really Gipsy music, as revealed through Béla Bartók's research, at that time just in progress.)

Since Gustav Mahler was born in a village near Jihlava (a medium-sized city in today's Czechoslovakia), some critics praised his rendition of Smetana's opera *The Bartered Bride* as particularly congenial—typically Bohemian. He protested, pointing out that he was the offspring of a German family and that his music was German music (of course, the Volkston that reverberates in his music is at home in German folklore.) It did not occur to him to call himself and his ancestors Jewish. This too is typical of the period. At that time

Jewishness was only a matter of religious convictions. A Jew that had been baptized had changed his faith and was converted. Only Hitler and his minions introduced the concept of race and stigmatized the Jews as *Untermenschen*, inferior human beings.

It remains to be mentioned that this account of Mahler's last four years throws a generally unfavorable light upon Alma. In New York, where her beauty was frequently praised, she stayed much of the time in bed, supposedly affected by what then was called angina (a sort of sore throat). During the summers, which the Mahlers had planned to spend in their newly acquired vacation home in the (then) Austrian Dolomites, she had to retire on her own to other resorts in order to attend to her ailments. It appears that Mahler's marital successor, the architect Walter Gropius, was already waiting in the wings. These conditions must have overshadowed Mahler's final time to the extent that he even felt like consulting Sigmund Freud, the psychoanalyst.

These and many more fascinating details of the last years of the great composer may be learned from this meticulously documented and annotated volume which also presents a vivid panorama of New York's artistic life of eighty years ago. I hope that a faithful reader will experience as much satisfaction as I did when perusing it.

Palm Springs, CA   Ernst Krenek
December 1987

Introduction

The years between 1907 and 1911, although brief in chronological terms, represented a rich and significant period in the life of Gustav Mahler, as well as in certain areas of the cultural history of the United States, especially of New York. For the approximate equivalent of four artistic seasons, the orbit of an exceptional human destiny, deeply rooted in the "Old World", overlapped with the panorama of musical-cultural development unfolding in a young, brash and inexhaustibly energetic "new" nation. In this book I have attempted to chart their essential points of intersection, and to reflect the rich and variegated colours which resulted from the cross-fertilization and from the clash of what were in some respects vastly differing traditions, experiences, values and expectations.

The bulk of the literature devoted to Mahler's "American" years consists of proportionally brief segments of general biographies;[1] periodical articles, mostly anecdotal in nature;[2] and personal accounts which tend to be highly subjective.[3] Three works, however, deserve to be mentioned as exceptions.

---

[1]*E.g.*, in *KBM/KBM(E)*.

[2]*E.g.*, John Ardoin, "A Genius of the Baton, Mahler Led a Conducting Career Marked by Paradoxes," *MA*, February 1960, pp. 13, 162.

[3]The outstanding example of such an account is, of course, found in Alma Mahler's memoirs. Since their first publication in 1940 (*AME*), these memoirs have gone through a number of confusing, and at times conflicting, German and English editions. The most recent, reliable and best annotated edition (used for the purposes of this study) is *AMM*.

The first two sizeable and scholarly studies of Mahler's life during the period in question saw the light of day as a Master's thesis by Philip T. Ventre, "Gustav Mahler in America, 1907-1911," and as a Doctoral dissertation by Marvin Lee von Deck, "Gustav Mahler in New York: His Conducting Activities in New York City, 1908-1911".[4] Within the natural limitations imposed by their respective genres, both provide fine surveys of contemporary musical life in the United States (especially New York), and of the main body of the music criticism of the time.

The book that stands alone in the depth and breadth of its coverage of the last four years of Mahler's life is the recently published third volume of Henry-Louis de La Grange's monumental biography.[5] It is an inexhaustible storehouse of information, as well as an invaluable touchstone.

In the area of documentary literature, a concentrated (if necessarily limited) textual and pictorial impression of Mahler's American years is captured in Kurt Blaukopf (mit Beiträgen von Zoltan Roman), *Mahler - Sein Leben, sein Werk und seine Welt in zeitgenössischen Bildern und Texten.*[6] In fact, the present study is an outgrowth of that volume. Due to considerations of space and proportions, only about ten per cent of the textual material I had collected on Kurt Blaukopf's commission could be included in our documentary. With his kind encouragement, I made use of the rest of that material for the purposes of this work.

It follows from the foregoing that the focus of this study, too, is a documentary one. The material is divided into four sections, corresponding to Mahler's four seasons in the United States. Each section of documents is preceded by an essay which provides a brief narrative account of the season in question. Additionally, the second, third and fourth essays fulfill a linking function: they contain essential information on Mahler's activities during the off-season. The first and fourth essays also incorporate material relating to, respectively, the events leading to Mahler's American engagement, and the circumstances of his death.

The bulk of the documentary material is comprised of a wide-ranging selection of reports, critiques and commentary from the daily

[4]Master of Music, New England Conservatory of Music, 1972; and Doctor of Philosophy, New York University, 1973.
[5]*HLG3.*
[6]*BRM/BRM(E).*

and weekly press. In an age without television, when even commercial broadcasting was an unrealized dream, the omnipresence and singular power of the press can hardly be overestimated. In Mahler's time Greater New York possessed nearly three dozen major daily and weekly newspapers; Boston and Philadelphia had no fewer than a dozen each. What is more, the circulation figures clearly indicate that their readership likely embraced a very high percentage of the population, at least in the urban areas. For example, even though it was to attain its present-day stature only during the first World War, the *New York Times* had reached a daily circulation of 200,000 copies by 1903—and this in spite of its conservative, non-sensationalist posture. It is, then, not surprising to find that Joseph Pulitzer's flamboyant *World* sold in the neighborhood of one million copies daily by the turn of the century.[7] In general, the daily circulation of American papers doubled in the years between 1892 and 1914.[8]

While by no means all of these newspapers carried music reportage, several of them did so on a regular basis. An examination of the New York papers during the period under investigation reveals the presence of an impressive number of writers on music who, through their critiques and columns, were able to shape public opinion and attitudes. For present purposes (taking into account also the need for a representative cross-section of the press) the chief ones among them were: Richard Aldrich of the *Times,*[9] Reginald de Koven of the *World,*[10] William J. Henderson of the *Sun,*[11] and Henry E. Krehbiel of the *Daily Tribune.*[12] That Henry T. Finck and James G. Huneker are not included in this group is due as much to the need for selectivity as to any other criterion.

[7]Willard Grosvenor Bleyer, *Main Currents in the History of American Journalism*, Boston, *etc*, Houghton-Mifflin, 1927, pp. 408 and 342.
[8]Frank Luther Mott, *American Journalism - A History: 1690-1960* (3. ed.), New York, Macmillan, 1962, p. 547.
[9]Richard Aldrich (1863-1937) - A graduate of Harvard University. After 10 years as assistant to Krehbiel on the *Tribune*, he was music critic of the *Times* from 1902 to 1924.
[10]Reginald de Koven (1859-1920) - Studied music in Europe; music critic on a number of American newspapers. He was also a prolific composer who enjoyed considerable success.
[11]William James Henderson (1855-1937) - Studied music privately. Author of several opera libretti and books on music, he preceded Aldrich at the *Times*; wrote for the *Sun* from 1902 to 1937.
[12]Henry Edward Krehbiel (1854-1923) - A critic and author of prodigious productivity, he was the *Tribune*'s critic for some 40 years. He also edited and published the English version of Thayer's *Beethoven*.

INTRODUCTION

To illustrate the fact that New Yorkers, while undoubtedly in a privileged position, were not alone in having access to professional music criticism, it is sufficient to mention Charles W. Cadman in Pittsburgh[13] and Philip Hale in Boston.[14]

While the daily press was unquestionably the most powerful medium in the continuity of cultural arbitration, a number of weekly magazines were able to contribute substantially to this process, for a variety of reasons. *Harper's Weekly*, for instance, although it was a general interest magazine, had on its staff the music critic Lawrence Gilman,[15] who was then at the beginning of a brilliant career. On the other hand, the two specialized music weeklies, *Musical America* and *The Musical Courier*, while they did carry selected criticism of varying quality, were most influential as purveyors of news, 'inside' information (by no means always reliable!), and downright gossip (frequently of a polemical intent).

In addition to demonstrating the breadth of critical coverage available to the reader—especially in New York—a survey of the work of a majority of American music critics reveals some striking and important characteristics. These can be described as a freshness and flexibility of attitude, an unspoilt—if at times naive—willingness to accentuate the positive, a desire to learn and to transmit newly acquired knowledge and insight. These characteristics are especially impressive when they are compared to the dogmatic, partisan, *ex cathedra* attitude and posture of many of their Continental colleagues. Even Krehbiel, who later became an obsessively polemical, irrationally unrelenting foe, must be acknowledged for his initial, commendably open-minded attempts to understand and interpret Mahler's music and music-making.

In order to attain as complete and rounded a view as possible of Mahler's American years, the press material is combined with items selected from a number of other sources. Aside from the few surviving official documents of the relevant organizations, the most important among these are what may be termed 'first person'

[13]Charles Wakefield Cadman (1881-1946) - Well educated in music, gained prominence primarily as a composer and teacher. He was the music critic of the *Pittsburgh Dispatch* from 1908 to 1910.
[14]Philip Hale (1854-1934) - Studied music in the United States and in Europe; organist and conductor. Wrote for several Boston papers; critic of the *Herald* from 1903 to 1933.
[15]Lawrence Gilman (1878-1939) - Eminent American music critic and writer on music, wrote for *Harper's Weekly* from 1901 to 1913.

documents: Mahler's own letters written from, or relating to his activities in, the United States, and letters written about him by other persons. Inevitably, the dating and interpretation of some of this material is made quite difficult by the fact that replies had been preserved only in the rarest instances.

Next in order of importance are the contemporary "eye-witness" accounts: Alma's memoirs, and the reminiscences of colleagues and musical collaborators. To be sure, the extreme subjectivity of some of this material presents the historian with many pitfalls, and thus with a need for judicious pruning and interpretation.

Finally, no documentary biography would be complete if it did not provide the reader with a sense of the time and place, of the *milieu* in which its subject lived and worked. In addition to the obvious aids, such as photographs, the excerpts from contemporary and later works of a socio-cultural nature serve this purpose, as do the press clippings which do not concern Mahler himself.

As a rule, annotations identifying people, places and objects, and elucidating events where necessary, appear in the documentary sections. Since no single work of this kind can or should attempt to be more than a compendium of the data most relevant to its own personal and historical focus, the time span covered by the annotations is generally restricted to the period dealt with here. For instance, while Arturo Toscanini is mentioned more than once, the reader should not expect to find a full exposition on his career in this study. In a few places, annotations which would have been necessary or desirable are missing because I was unable to find the required information.

For ease of reference (especially in the narrative essays), written documents and illustrations are numbered consecutively throughout the volume, the former with boldface Arabic numerals. Frequently cited sources are abbreviated; a comprehensive list of Abbreviations is found immediately after the list of Illustrations. For quotes from sources which appear in translation in the main text, the location of the original-language excerpt is included in the label pertaining to the given document.[16]

---

[16]In the case of previously published documents, only excerpts most relevant to the subject of this study are quoted. For documents published here for the first time, in part or in whole, an English translation is given in the main text, and the corresponding original text is given in the Appendix. Unless otherwise indicated, the translations are mine.

I am indebted to a number of persons and institutions for their moral and material assistance and permission to secure and use documents and illustrations. These are:

Bayerische Staatsbibliothek, Munich

Bibliothèque der Internationalen Gustav Mahler Gesellschaft

Bibliothèque Musicale Gustav Mahler, Paris

Dover Publications, Inc., New York

Faber and Faber Limited, London

Farrar, Straus & Giroux, Inc., New York

Mr. Péter Fülöp, Budapest

Gesellschaft der Musikfreunde, Vienna

Mr. Morton Glantz, New York

Victor Gollancz Limited, London

David Higham Associates Limited, London

Internationale Gustav Mahler Gesellschaft, Vienna

Dr. W.G.W. Kurz, Saskatoon, Canada

M. Henry-Louis de La Grange, Paris

Miss Anna Mahler, Spoleto

The Metropolitan Opera Archives, New York

Prof. Donald Mitchell, London

The New York Historical Society

The New York Philharmonic-Symphony Society Archives

The New York Public Library, Astor, Lenox and Tilden Foundations, Music Division

Österreichische Nationalbibliothek, Vienna

Paul Zsolnay Verlag, Vienna

The Pierpont Morgan Library, New York

Prof. Edward R. Reilly, Poughkeepsie, New York

Staatliche Landesbildstelle, Hamburg

Thames and Hudson Limited, London

To those copyright owners I may have inadvertently neglected— or was unable—to contact, I offer my apologies and the undertaking to make appropriate amends upon notification.

Special thanks are due to two people without whose encouragement, advice and help my task would have been infinitely more difficult and far less enjoyable. Frau Dr. Herta Blaukopf, Vienna, in addition to painstakingly checking my transcriptions and translations, provided unflagging support and tactful, erudite counsel. Mr. Robert Kessler of Pendragon Press was kind enough to listen to my proposal for this book; he also guided it to its completion with unequalled patience and good humour.

Finally, I wish to express my gratitude to the University of Calgary, whose generous award of a Killam Resident Fellowship enabled me to complete this work.

Calgary, August, 1986.

CHAPTER I

The 1907-1908 Season

Commentary

Mahler made his first appearance at the Metropolitan Opera in New York on January 1, 1908. His first season in the United States was a partial one, lasting less than four months. Such simple facts of history, however, often hide more than they reveal. So it was with Mahler's complex and at times circuitous road to America.

Before I outline the circumstances and events immediately relevant to Mahler's first appearance in New York, it will be of interest to recount three earlier instances which demonstrate a long-standing interest in such a venture on both sides of the Atlantic.

In February of 1887 Mahler was second conductor at the City Theatre (Opera) in Leipzig. Unhappy with his position there, he was considering a number of other posts that had been offered to him around that time. As we learn from a letter to his friend Friedrich Löhr, one of those offers came from New York:

> [...] I have received an offer from New York, an invitation to replace Anton Seidl. [...][1]

[1]*MSL*, p. 107; original German in *GMB*, p. 62. - As so many of Mahler's letters are, this letter is undated; it is assigned the date of February 18th in *MSL*.

The Hungarian-born Seidl, at that time 37, was only in his second year as conductor of the German repertoire at the Metropolitan. It is interesting to note that Mahler, not yet 27, was already considered good enough to replace him. Regrettably, nothing more is known about the circumstances of this invitation.

Only brief mention need be made of the second occasion on which Mahler's move to the United States had been rumoured. In a letter published by Alma, Mahler wrote to Arnold Berliner:

> [. . .] I have read in several newspapers including the *Hamburger Fremdenblatt*, that I have been engaged to go to *Boston*.
> For various reasons it is *extremely important* that this report should be *denied*. [. . .] The *démenti* should be quite brief, *without any further remarks*.
> [. . .]²

As will be seen, Mahler appears to have been offered the conductorship of the Boston Symphony once again shortly after his arrival in the United States.

The third time New York appears as a potential place of employment for Mahler, the offer is a most intriguing one; until quite recently, it has defied satisfactory interpretation. Among Mahler's extant letters to Lilli Lehmann, the great coloratura and dramatic soprano, one reads, in part, as follows:

> [. . .] I have just received an invitation from New York, as a conductor of 50 concerts per season, and as director of the "National Conservatory of Music of America" - 7 months each year. -
> [. . .]
> As I gather from your letter, I can thank you for this offer. - It is so dear of you to have thought of me [. . .].
> [. . .] As director of the Conservatory I would not have to teach, only direct and [?] approximately 7 hours per week.
> [. . .]³

---

²*MSL*, p. 150; original German in *GMB*, p. 110. - Alma Mahler's original edition (1924) implies that this letter bore the date June 21, 1893 in Mahler's hand. Knud Martner (*MSL*, p. 415) questions this date: apparently, the rumour concerning Mahler's Boston engagement was published in the Hamburg paper on June 17th, while his denial appeared on June 19th.
³Zoltan Roman, "Gustav Mahler und Lilli Lehmann," in *MUB*, pp. 105f.

As is so often the case, this letter by Mahler is undated. For its first publication, even the most painstaking analysis of its contents and their implications did not enable me to date it with any degree of certainty. The period around April of 1906 emerged as the most likely (or the least unlikely) one, although other possibilities ranged as far back in time as Mahler's years in Hamburg (*i.e.*, 1891-1897)!

The solution for the puzzle was found—quite unexpectedly, given the separation in time—during my reading through Alma Mahler's typescript memoirs (*ELM*) in search of materials for this book. It is contained in a letter to Mahler from an American impresario, written in May of 1907. As it has not been published before, and since—in addition to throwing light on an early plan for Mahler's removal to America—its subject will resurface, in various guises, in later years, the letter is given here in its entirety:

Concert Agency
Chas. Loewenstein

Founder of the former
Waldorf-Astoria Subscr. Concerts
  New York
    and
The Permanent Orchestra
  of New York
Anton Seidl, Conductor

New York address: Berlin, May 25, 1907
Waldorf-Astoria Hotel   Jägerstrasse 47/48
Fifth Avenue, 34th St.

    To the
    Director of the Imperial and Royal Court
      Opera in Vienna
    Herr Gustav Mahler
                Vienna.

Most esteemed Herr Director!

I hope that you will recall our correspondence of some years ago when I approached you to assume the leadership of my former grand subscription concerts here [sic!], from which you were prevented by the illness and death of your conductor Herr Dr. Fuchs.[4] As you will

---

[4] Johann Nepomuk Fuchs (1842-1899) - Conductor at the Imperial Opera from 1879 to his death.

remember, I was also indebted to Frau Lilli Lehmann's intervention for your having declared your willingness. To be sure, later I had to drop the concerts.

Today, most esteemed Herr Director, I come to you with an offer that will top by far the sumtotal of all things which you may have heretofore encountered in your sphere of activity. I have been called upon to head a committee that will, within a short time, build a grand Concert-Theatre in the capital of the empire, under the patronage of His Majesty the German Emperor, and that does not wish to take a single step before I had a chance to confer with you briefly concerning the musical directorship of this enterprise. Unfortunately, it is not possible for me to go into details with respect to the overall undertaking; let it be said here only that the financing has been assumed by a large syndicate. The pertinent prospectus is already in press, so that soon I shall be able to send you one of these. It should be mentioned here only that the exterior as well as the interior makeup of this Concert-Theatre will be the grandest and most pleasing that this continent has to offer anywhere.

For further information, I can tell you that the capacity of the house exceeds 3,000 people on main floor, loges and balconies, the orchestra-podium or stage will accommodate 800 people, and the lowered orchestra pit 150.

In addition, the house has a large concert organ, so that all artistic demands can be satisfied.

Now, most esteemed Herr Director, I believe that I am also acting in keeping with your intentions, when I am contacting you as the first person, knowing very well that there is no more qualified a master who can head such a musical undertaking fully and completely, as it should be.

The only request that I attach to this communication is that you should grant me your discretion over this matter.

Would you please let me know by return post when and where I may speak with you very soon about this matter? I would be most happy to come to Vienna, possibly; please let me know about this.

> Yours faithfully,
> Ch. Loewenstein[5]

As concerns our immediate interest, it is clear from this letter that the offers from New York—referred to in his undated letter to Lilli

[5]*ELM*, pp. [798f]; for the German text, see Appendix, A1.

Plate 1. Gustav Mahler in 1907. (ÖNB-BA)

Plate 2. Gustav Mahler in 1907. (ÖNB-BA)

Plate 3. Alma Mahler. (*BRM*, Illustration 203)

Lehmann, who evidently mediated them—must have been made to Mahler in the Spring of 1898. Anton Seidl died suddenly on March 28th (just around the time when the plans for a Permanent Orchestra of New York had been finalized); the National Conservatory had been, it would seem, without a permanent director since Dvořák's departure in 1895;[6] and it is likely that Lilli Lehmann was in New York briefly in March and April, when she could have personally recommended Mahler for the dual post. Why Mahler did *not*, in the end, go to New York in 1898 or 1899 (Fuchs's death was probably little more than a convenient way out) is a complicated subject, and is clearly beyond present concerns. More fascinating, and clearly indicative of the strength of the "siren song" of the New World is the fact that he *had* been prepared to go, a mere few months after attaining the pinnacle of his ambitions by becoming the all-powerful director of the Imperial Opera in Vienna!

This brings us to the year 1907, undoubtedly the most fateful year of Mahler's life in every respect. After nearly ten years at the helm of the world's most famous opera theatre, that spring he felt obliged to resign his position in Vienna. In July, the Mahlers lost their oldest daughter, Maria Anna, to scarlet fever and diphtheria, with the cruel suddenness then characteristic of such diseases. In the same month, Mahler's heart disease was diagnosed. To be sure, the decision to go to America had been made prior to the last two events. In retrospect it is clear that Mahler had been motivated, initially at least, simply by a desire to provide his family with economic security in a way which would least interfere with his freedom to compose and to satisfy personally the ever-growing demand for performances of his works. Following the tragic month of July, however, the chance for a complete change of *milieu*, the opportunity to begin what was in

---

[6]The history of the National Conservatory needs—and deserves—further study. The sources which I have been able to consult are either silent on the matter, or indicate a hiatus in the directorship between Dvořák and Paur (who was appointed—as a substitute for Mahler, it would seem—both as Conservatory director, and as conductor of the New York Philharmonic - the idea of the Permanent Orchestra having been dropped by then). A telegram, sent on August 25, 1897 by Dvořák to Mrs. Jeannette M. Thurber (founder of the Conservatory), also implies this: in it he gives permission for the use of his "name as director of National Conservatory"! (A facsimile of the telegram is found in Merton Robert Aborn, "The Influence on American Musical Culture of Dvořák's Sojourn in America," Ph.D. dissertation, Indiana University, 1965, p. 312.)

many respects a new existence,must have been welcomed by both Gustav and Alma for more than financial reasons.

Precisely when Heinrich Conried first contacted Mahler with a view to engaging him for the Metropolitan Opera is not known. As is shown by the surviving sketches of a letter dated September 24, 1906, Mahler and Conried had had prior dealings on a "director to director" basis. Apparently, Conried arranged the appearance of Caruso and Titta Ruffo at the Imperial Opera for a benefit performance of *Rigoletto* on October 6th of the same year.[7]

Curiously (since otherwise it deals in great detail with his successes in attracting European opera stars to New York), Conried's biography contains but a brief mention of his hiring of Mahler.[8] Certainly, once he had set his sights on him, Conried pursued Mahler relentlessly, bombarding him with cables and letters.[9] The first series of extant telegrams (see Documents **1** to **3**) originated in May; they show an early stage in the negotiations. Judging from **4**, the basic agreement was concluded in short order. That it did not prove to be "perfect", after all, is clear from subsequent events and documents.

Mahler's evolving plans for America, as well as the fact that he was confronted with a number of choices at the time, are evident from a letter to the impresario Norbert Salter. He wrote:

> I am at present so overwhelmed with projects and offers that— especially as no successor to me has yet been found—I cannot yet reply to any of them. [. . .] we shall discuss the matter when I come to Berlin in the very near future. I dare say America will be inevitable for me.[10]

Although the letter is undated, the trip to Berlin "in the very near future" was, in all likelihood, the same one he had been planning for the purpose of completing his contract with Conried.

Together with a number of other telegrams, Mahler's letter to Alma on June 5th from Berlin illustrates the progress of the ongoing negotiations:

[7]*BRM(E)*, p. 245.
[8]Montrose J. Moses, *The Life of Heinrich Conried*, New York, T.Y. Crowell, 1916, p. 321.
[9]*AMM*, p. 124.
[10]*BRM(E)*, p. 249; original German in *BRM*, p. 253.

> [. . .] [Conried] was full of projects - all fire and fervour. First and foremost, wanted me on exactly the same footing as Caruso. - Then 8 months (180,000 crowns) - then 6. Finally we got to this: 3 months (15th January to 15th April) for which 75,000 crowns guaranteed, journey and all expenses paid (first class hotel)! We have not yet come to an agreement about the length of the contract. He wants four years, I want only one. [. . .] I am to conduct Wagner and Mozart at the Opera and about 6 concerts (to include my C Minor with chorus). [. . .][11]

That negotiations with Conried did not always go smoothly is seen from another letter Mahler wrote to his agent:

> Dear Salter!
> It is possible that I will not come to an agreement with Conried! Is *Hammerstein*, in actual fact, considering me? In that case please make me a definite offer! *Perhaps by telegram.*
>> In the greatest hurry
>> Mahler[12]

The letter is undated, but it could well have been written while Mahler was actually negotiating with Conried in Berlin. At any rate, it is intriguing to think that—but for some contractual details— Mahler could have ended up with the "other" opera house in New York.

The financial details of the eventual contract with Conried show that Mahler's aim of combining immediate economic security with a great deal of freedom had been a realistic one: his 3-month salary of 75,000 crowns (then *ca.* $15,000) was more than five times his *yearly* salary (not including directorial and other honoraria) of 14,000 crowns in Vienna. (To be sure, upon his retirement from the Imperial Opera he was to receive 20,000 crowns as severance pay, and thereafter draw a pension of 14,000 crowns a year.)[13]

Mahler's bitterness at what must have at times appeared to him as an inescapable decision surfaces in a letter to Arnold Berliner, postmarked on June 17th:

---

[11]*AMM*, pp. 289f.; original German in *AME*, p. 377.
[12]For the German text, see Appendix, A2.
[13]Franz Willnauer, *Gustav Mahler und die Wiener Oper*, Wien, Jugend und Volk, 1979, pp. 300, 303f.

> It is all quite true. I am going because I can no longer endure the rabble. I am not leaving for America until the middle of January, and I shall stay until the middle of April. [. . .]¹⁴

Interviews given in Vienna as late as the end of August (for example, see **19**) testify to the fact that Mahler's sense of disillusionment remained largely unaffected by his plans for the future.

In the end Mahler bowed to Conried's wishes, and on June 21, 1907 signed a contract for four years. Towards the end of September, when an earlier departure for North America became possible for Mahler, the contract was amended in the form of an *addendum*. As the contract, a copy of which forms part of Alma's transcript memoirs, has never been published in its entirety, it and its *addendum* are reproduced in Documents **10** and **21**.

Perhaps the most fascinating clause of the contract is Article XII. It shows that Mahler must have been aware of the fact that *Parsifal* had already had a considerable history of "illegal" performances in New York. Clearly, he was anxious enough to preserve his good standing with the Wagner family (and to distance himself, as it were, from the *persona non grata* Conried) that he felt it necessary to make an explicit disclaimer a part of his contract with the director of the Metropolitan.

Although the Lord Chamberlain, Prince Montenuovo, had requested that neither Conried nor Mahler make their contract public until the latter's successor at the Opera had been appointed, the press was not left uninformed for long. There can be no doubt that Conried had leaked the news of Mahler's engagement, at least to the American press. On June 12th and 15th, respectively, both *The Musical Courier* and *Musical America* were able to report (even if not accurately) Mahler's signing—*before* the actual contract had been signed! For the next two months, the provisions of the contract and the high expectations placed on Mahler's coming activities at the Metropolitan were frequently aired in the press. Finally, on August 14th *Musical America* "confirmed" its earlier report, even though, once again, its description of Mahler's position in New York (or his position in Vienna) was not entirely correct.¹⁵ The "official confir-

---

¹⁴*MSL*, p. 301; original German in *GMB*, p. 320.

¹⁵Equally carelessly, the magazine featured a Mahler-photo from 1898 (acquired from the *World*) on the first page of its "Special Fall Issue" on September 28th. In fact, a photograph of Mahler had been published already on June 12th in *The Musical Courier* (p. 23) - but this one was from 1892!

mation" had no doubt been made possible by Montenuovo's permission—given after the fact, as it were—to release the news of Mahler's engagement. He wrote to Mahler on August 10th:

> I did not until yesterday receive the definite and official intimation [. . .] that Weingartner consented to take up the appointment on 1st January 1908.
> [. . .]
> Conried need now delay no longer making your engagement public. Please inform him of this. [16]

In light of the interest, and of the detailed information evidently available to the American press, an article in the *New York Times* on August 18th, under the heading "Conried plans many new operas", makes for curious reading. It does not even mention Mahler, even though plans for a "late season" mounting of *Fidelio*, in which "the staging will itself make the production a noteworthy one", are discussed. [17]

Even in Vienna, though, at least one newspaper had had early knowledge of the negotiations, if not of the details of the contract. On June 16, 1907, the *Neue Freie Presse* published a *feuilleton* with the title "Unmusical comments on the Mahler case" (see **8**). Together with later, similar articles, it speaks eloquently of the sense of loss many Viennese—artists, intellectuals, and common people—felt in anticipation of Mahler's final departure.

Following the sorrowful summer of 1907, Mahler returned briefly to his conducting duties in Vienna. He chose *Fidelio* as his last assignment at the Opera on October 15th. He bade Vienna farewell with a performance of his Second Symphony at the Gesellschaft der Musikfreunde on November 24th. The Mahlers left Vienna on December 9th and sailed from Cherbourg on the 12th, arriving in New York on December 21, 1907. [18]

Almost immediately after their arrival, the Mahlers faced their first Christmas in New York. The still-fresh sorrow of their daughter's

---

[16]*AMM*, pp. 301f.; original German in *AME*, pp. 401f.
[17]*NYT*, August 18, 1907, p. 7.
[18]Although it is identified as the SS America in Alma's memoirs (*AMM*, p. 127), reports of their arrival in New York name the SS Kaiserin Augusta Victoria as the ship on which the Mahlers crossed the Atlantic for the first time (see Document **25**).

Plate 4. Gustav Mahler in the Dolomites, August 1907. (ÖNB-HS)

Plate 5. The ocean liner *Kaiserin Augusta Victoria.*
(Staatliche Landesbildstelle, Hamburg)

Plate 6. New York from Governor's Island. Oil painting by
Carlton T. Chapman, 1904. (The New-York Historical Society)

death and the inevitable apprehensions concerning life in a foreign land combined to make this a devastatingly lonely occasion, one which is described in a touching manner (although elaborated with her ever-present snide remarks about secondary characters) in Alma's memoirs (see **33**).

Amidst such private cares and sorrows, Mahler doubtless welcomed the sustained distraction of the preparations for his debut at the Metropolitan Opera. This took place on New Year's Day, 1908, when he conducted *Tristan und Isolde*. His success was very great; audience and critics alike recognized in him a conductor under whose hand long-familiar scores would acquire new life and vitality. The high expectations raised by his *Tristan* were fulfilled by Mahler's productions of *Don Giovanni* on January 23rd and of *Die Walküre* on February 7th.

In the meantime Mahler had been approached by the shareholders of the Metropolitan to take over the theatre's management from the ailing Conried. As this would have been altogether contrary to his original reasons for coming to the United States, Mahler declined "quite decisively" (see **50**). Subsequently, a major reorganization of the administrative structure did take place: the theatre was to be run jointly by an artistic director (Giulio Gatti-Casazza) and an administrative manager (Andreas Dippel), under the control of a holding company presided over by Otto H. Kahn. It appears that while Mahler signed a new contract with this company, his fond plans to bring Alfred Roller to the Metropolitan came to nothing in the end (see **95 & 96**).

On February 19th, Mahler conducted *Siegfried* for the first time in New York. Although the performance was well received in general, some of the critics expressed reservations about Mahler's interpretation. In retrospect this attitude, though isolated at first, appears to foreshadow the increasingly numerous and specific attacks on certain aspects of Mahler's performances (operatic at first, orchestral later) that were to follow, beginning with his last major production of the season, *Fidelio*, on March 20th. Once again, the production as a whole (staged with the sets designed by Roller for Vienna) was greeted with enthusiasm. However, almost all of the critics noted (some mildly, some pointedly) that Mahler often "refuses to be bound [. . .] by the letter of the text" (*i.e.,* the score).

While the focus of Mahler's first season in the United States was, as had been intended, his work at the Metropolitan Opera, his reputation as a concert conductor made him a desirable catch for orchestral organizations from the beginning. Sometime during the early months of 1908 he was offered the conductorship of the Boston Symphony. Although he declined the offer, recommending Willem Mengelberg in his stead (see **92 & 93**), rumours of this offer were still circulating a year later (see **230**).

As recently published documents show (see **115** to **121**), another organization apparently had had more success in convincing Mahler to appear on the concert podium in America. The New York Symphony Society (then under the leadership of Walter Damrosch) had negotiated a number of concerts with Mahler for the spring of 1908. This agreement was probably made before Mahler's arrival in New York. These concerts were postponed in the end, and rescheduled for the autumn of 1908 (see *1908-1909*). The delay was due, at least in part, to Conried's refusal to sanction such "outside" activities by Mahler. It is also evident from some of these documents that Mahler's interest in the blandishments of another group of sponsors (which culminated eventually in his engagement by the New York Philharmonic) also played a role in these events. This impression is confirmed in the press: only a few days after the announcement of his rescheduled concerts with the Symphony, the "other" group of backers let it be known that Mahler would present four "festival concerts" with an "independent" orchestra in the spring of 1909 (see **136 & 138**).

Even during their first season in the United States, the Mahlers had opportunities to visit other cities with the touring Metropolitan Opera. Several single performances were given in Philadelphia in the course of the season, and in April the company moved to Boston for a full week of performances.

And now all that remained for Mahler to do was to say farewell to New York after his first season. A fitting opportunity was provided by the Metropolitan's gala performance of the complete *Ring* cycle upon their return from Boston. Mahler conducted *Die Walküre* (April 14) and *Siegfried* (April 16). One week after the latter performance, the Mahlers embarked for Europe.

The growing eagerness with which Mahler had been awaiting the return to Europe is clear from two letters he wrote around this time (see **131 & 132**). Unquestionably, his first season in the United States had been a very successful one, and he carried three new contracts in his pocket for the 1908-1909 season. Nonetheless, the months ahead held many joys in store for him: reunion with his little daughter, his family and friends; several conducting assignments and performances of his own works (including a première); and, last but not least, a well-deserved holiday.

Plate 7. Heinrich Conried. (The New-York Historical Society)

19

Plate 8. Otto H. Kahn. (Metropolitan Opera Archives)

1907-1908
Documents

1

[May 1907]

Mahler would agree to a two-year contract, four months per year, $5,000 per month [...] If agreed, he expects notification binding on your part, while for his own definite acceptance [...] he requests time to consider until June 8th [...][19]

(Telegram to Heinrich Conried,[20] presumably from Rudolf Winternitz;[21] *ELM*, p. [796])

2

[May 1907]

Naturally, I attach very great importance to engaging Mahler [...] for six months. [...] Should America not please him, or circumstances not agree with him, I am willing to guarantee mutual giving of notice up to

---

[19]For the German text, see Appendix, A3.

[20]Heinrich Conried [Cohn] (1848-1909) - Following an early acting career in Vienna, he managed various theatre enterprises in Europe and America. During his term at the Metropolitan, he was responsible for engaging such artists as Caruso, and for introducing *Parsifal* and *Salome* to New York (see Notes 128 and 129, pp. 120 and 121). By the 1906-1907 season, Conried's hold on matters at the Metropolitan had been badly shaken by ill health, as well as by the increasing competition from Hammerstein's Manhattan Opera House. Virtually his last important act as manager of the Metropolitan Opera was to secure the services of Mahler.

[21]Rudolf Winternitz - According to *HLG3* (pp. 53 and 105), he was director of the Atelier Blaschke, suppliers of costumes to the Vienna Opera. His role in the negotiations is unclear.

a date to be agreed upon. I am willing to arrange concerts in which his works would be performed [. . .] Should Mahler prefer a guest-engagement of four to six weeks, I am also agreeable to that. Such a guest-engagement could be repeated yearly.

Conried

(Telegram from Heinrich Conried, presumably to Rudolf Winternitz; *ELM*, p. [795])[22]

3

[May 1907]

Mahler's definitive proposal is for eight weeks [. . .] . Mahler would come for the eight weeks even if he should not be released here. If he is released, he reserves the right to return to your first offer concerning six months [. . .]

(Telegram to Heinrich Conried, presumably from Rudolf Winternitz; *ELM*, p. [794][23]

4

[May 26 or 27, 1907]

I herewith declare our agreement as perfect. Again, I ask for secrecy until official release accomplished. I am truly happy that we have got together, and hope to accomplish great things with you. Early in June I shall come to Berlin with Winternitz in order to draw up our battle-plan. [. . .]

Mahler

(Telegram from Mahler to Heinrich Conried; *ELM*, p. [792][24]

5

June 10, [1907]

[. . .] Mahler must be convinced that he is the musical head of the whole, and I will take any action only after consultation with him. To make Mahler's engagement public officially, in keeping with the wishes of the Prince I must wait until his release has been approved. Until then it must remain a rumour. [. . .]

Conried

[22]For the German text, see Appendix, A4.
[23]For the German text, see Appendix, A5.
[24]For the German text, see Appendix, A6.

(Telegram from Heinrich Conried, presumably to Rudolf Winternitz; *ELM*, p. [788][25]

6

THE MUSICAL COURIER was the first newspaper to report that Gustav Mahler had resigned from the Vienna Opera. Now comes the cabled report from Europe that the great conductor has been signed for the Wagner performances at the Metropolitan next season. This ought to be good news to the American musical world, for Mahler is noted as an adamant disciplinarian and a tooth and nail foe of the pernicious "star" system of opera. In Vienna, Mahler made the conductor's word law over the singers. If he succeeds in doing the same thing here he will deserve a monument higher than Trinity steeple. From a purely musical standpoint Mahler is the most important conductor the Metropolitan ever has had, for, besides being an authority on operatic style and stage management, he also is one of the foremost composers in Europe, albeit not one of the most popular ones.

(*MC* 54, no. 24, June 12, 1907, p. 20)

7

A report that was circulated in New York early in the week to the effect that Heinrich Conried had secured Gustav Mahler, the noted conductor of the Royal Opera in Vienna, for next season, was confirmed on Tuesday, when a cable received from Mr. Conried at the Metropolitan Opera House stated that the contract had been signed on Monday. [...]

Besides being the principal conductor at the Metropolitan, in which position he will have complete control of the orchestra, he will also have much to do with the producing of operas. [...]

(*MA* 6, no. 5, June 15, 1907, p. 1)

8

Unmusical Comments on the Mahler Case

Some European countries have legal safeguards against the unauthorized exporting of art works. Thus, Italy has her *lex* Pacca [...]

It has often been said that we in Austria could also use a *lex* Pacca [...] Only, another kind of law would be even more necessary for us,

[25]For the German text, see Appendix, A7.

Plate 9. Metropolitan Opera House, *ca.* 1912. (The Library of Congress)

24

Plate 10. Interior of the Metropolitan Opera. This photograph, although
taken some years later, shows the auditorium as it was in Mahler's day.
(Irving Kolodin, *The Metropolitan Opera 1883-1966*, New York,
Knopf, 1967, following p. 166)

[. . .] a law against the exporting of artists, that would be incomparably more valuable and to the point, for who is unaware of the fact that the exporting of creative artistic forces has long ago assumed critical proportions with us.

[. . .]

Hardly has the old world loosened its hold on Mahler than the New World reaches out for him. The well-known siren song, accompanied by an astute impresario on a golden lyre with golden strings, sounds from across the water, tempting, tempting, and probably not tempting in vain. And we let him go. With an easy mind we let the man go, for it is time to prove once again how carelessly we husband our cultural resources.

[. . .]

The comment that Mahler was, in fact, not dismissed but left voluntarily, is hardly worth refuting. One knows such "voluntariness". That is the accepted expression.

[. . .]

An opera director is leaving us after ten years, and they don't even deign to say openly, why. Why should the public concern itself with the true reasons for this departure? But more caution would be in order. The Opera had known times when the auditor was a rare bird in the house, and those times can return. A strike by the public – one should be wary of such a possibility.

[. . .]

(*Neue Freie Presse*, June 16, 1907, Morning edition, pp. 1 ff.;
excerpt in *KBM(E)*, p. 215, additional translation by Z. Roman)

9

June 18, [1907]

[. . .] I have telegraphed the Prince for his permission to make the engagement public. Expect his agreement. [. . .]

Conried

(Telegram from Heinrich Conried to Mahler; *ELM*, p. [787][26]

10
AN AGREEMENT,

made and entered into on the day given hereunder between Herr Director GUSTAV MAHLER in Vienna on the one hand, and Herr Director

[26]For the German text, see Appendix, A8.

Plate 11. Title page of the Conried Metropolitan Opera Company's
prospectus for the 1907-1908 season.

Plate 12. New York from Jersey City, 1908. (U.S. History, Local History & Genealogy Division, The New York Public Library, Astor, Lenox and Tilden Foundations)

Plate 13. Hotel Majestic, New York. (The New-York Historical Society)

HEINRICH CONRIED, President of the CONRIED
METROPOLITAN OPERA COMPANY on the other hand, as
follows:

I.

Herr Director HEINRICH CONRIED hereby engages Herr Director
GUSTAV MAHLER for the UNITED STATES of NORTH
AMERICA as a conductor of opera and concerts for a duration of 3
(three) months each for the years 1908 (eight) to 1911 (eleven).

The three-month engagement of Herr Director GUSTAV MAHLER
begins in each of the given four years on the second day following his
arrival in New York and runs for 90 (ninety) consecutive days thereafter.

Herr Director GUSTAV MAHLER undertakes to embark on his
journey in a timely manner each year, so as to allow him to arrive in New
York between the 20th and 25th of January.

II.

During the period of time specified in Article I, for the four years
named in Article I, Herr Director GUSTAV MAHLER undertakes to
conduct operas and concerts in the UNITED STATES of NORTH
AMERICA wherever Herr Director HEINRICH CONRIED desires,
subject to the condition that the productions in question have an artistic
character. Herr Director GUSTAV MAHLER is not, however, obliged
to conduct more often than three times per week. Should Herr Director
GUSTAV MAHLER at any time find himself exhausted by his earlier
activities in the United States of North America, so that he is unable to
conduct more often than twice per week, the reduction of the obligation
to twice per week for the week so affected is hereby agreed.
Reciprocally, Herr Director GUSTAV MAHLER declares himself
ready to conduct more often than three times when he is able to do so,
without expected additional compensation for same.

III.

Herr Director GUSTAV MAHLER undertakes to work exclusively
for the CONRIED METROPOLITAN OPERA COMPANY in the
UNITED STATES of North America from the day of the signing of this
agreement until its expiry, that is until the end of the three-month period
specified in Article I in the year 1911, and not to appear as a musical
performing artist in either public or private places without the express
permission of Herr Director HEINRICH CONRIED.

Herr Director Gustav MAHLER'S activities are not subject to
restriction in any other country.

IV.

For his three-month service more specifically described in Article II,

Herr Director Gustav MAHLER is to receive an honorarium of 75,000 (seventy-five thousand) crowns each year, for a total of 300,000 (three hundred thousand) crowns in four years. In addition, each year Herr Director GUSTAV MAHLER is to be reimbursed for his travel expenses, to and from New York in first-class cabin, also first-class railway sleeping car or day-coach, as well as transportation to and from the railway station. The same applies to travel costs in the United States of North America, when and if Herr Director Gustav MAHLER is required to conduct outside New York.

Further, Herr Director Gustav MAHLER is to be reimbursed for the total cost of his stay in the United States of North America—that is, the costs of accommodation and meals suited to a normal life-style—according to the cost of maintenance in first-class hotels.

Further, Herr Director Gustav MAHLER will be entitled to receive reimbursement of travel- and maintenance costs for his wife in one of the four years chosen by him.

V.

No later than on the 1st of December preceding the commencement of his activities in each year (that is, on December 1, 1907 in the first instance, and on December 1, 1908, 1909 and 1910 in the second, third and fourth instances) Herr Director Gustav MAHLER's honorarium of 75,000 crowns is to be secured with the k.k. priv. Austrian Boden-Kredit-Anstalt in Vienna (or with another banking institution acceptable to Herr Director Gustav MAHLER) in such a manner that the said banking institution agrees to extend to Herr Director Gustav MAHLER credit equivalent to the amount of the honorarium.

No later than on the 1st of December preceding the commencement of his activities in each year Herr Director Gustav Mahler is to be paid an advance of 25,000 (twenty-five thousand) crowns on his honorarium, with the guarantee of the bank being reduced by the same amount. The balance of the honorarium remaining after the deduction of the 25,000-crown advance is to be paid to Herr Director Gustav MAHLER in three equal instalments at the end of each month, provided that Herr Director Gustav MAHLER had discharged, or had been ready to discharge, his obligations as outlined in Article II.

Together with the instalments of the honorarium, Herr Director MAHLER is to be reimbursed for the expenses enumerated in Article IV, insofar as these had not been assumed directly by the CONRIED METROPOLITAN OPERA COMPANY.

VI.

In the case of illness during the time period stipulated in Article I, Herr Director Gustav MAHLER is not entitled to the honorarium—or to the instalment of the honorarium—specified in Article IV for the time during which he is inactive for such a reason, and the appropriate portion of the honorarium is to be deducted at the time of payment. However, even in this case Herr Director Gustav MAHLER is entitled to full reimbursement of his travel and maintenance costs in keeping with the provisions of Article IV, including return travel, and to such portion of the honorarium as he may have earned before or after the illness.

VII.

Herr Director Heinrich CONRIED and the CONRIED METROPOLITAN OPERA COMPANY are joint participants in this contract, and have joint interest in and obligations under it.

VIII.

It is understood that the legal provisions of this agreement are governed exclusively by Austrian law.

IX.

The costs of making this contract are to be assumed by the CONRIED METROPOLITAN OPERA COMPANY and/or Herr Director HEINRICH CONRIED, or are to be reimbursed to Herr Director Gustav Mahler.

X.

This contract is made in one original copy which is the common property of the two parties, and which is to be held by a joint trustee. Both parties receive a certified copy of the contract.

XI.

Should Herr Director Heinrich CONRIED retire, for whatever reason, from the directorship of the METROPOLITAN OPERA, Herr Director Gustav MAHLER has the right to cancel this contract in all its parts.

XII.

Herr Director Gustav MAHLER is not obligated to conduct Richard Wagner's "Parsifal".

With the concluding of this contract all prior agreements, insofar as they are in conflict with this contract, are rendered null and void.
NAUHEIM

WIEN, 21. June 1907

Director Heinrich Conried   Gustav Mahler m.p.
President of the Conried Metro-
politan Opera Co., New York

Ernest Goerlitz, as Witness   Alfred Roller, as Witness

I.C. Coppicus, as Witness   Rudolf Winternitz, as Witness

(*ELM*, pp. [287-292])[27]

11

Mahler seems to be very much the right sort. To a Vienna interviewer he said recently that he recognized Cosima Wagner's moral right to the monopoly of "Parsifal" until 1913, and that he would not conduct it at the Metropolitan or anywhere else until that time. [...]

(*MC* 54, no. 26, June 26, 1907, p. 20)

12

With the coming of Gustav Mahler next Fall the Metropolitan Opera House will enter upon a new era of its existence and if the new conductor lives up to his reputation as a man who has the courage of his convictions - one of vital significance to the future development of its art principles.

Mahler is one of the most imposing personalities in the art world of today. As a composer he is one of the most aggressive spirits in the "modern German" school. As a conductor he has high ideals and insists upon having them adhered to by all in any way concerned in a performance given under his baton. Thoroughly imbued with a sense of the importance of every detail, he is said to be intolerant of failure on the part of anyone to confirm with his ideas in seeking excellence of ensemble. The "star" system is offensive to his artistic sensibilities, a fact that augurs well for the influence he will exert upon the policy of the Metropolitan Opera House.

According to the terms of his contract, he will have much more authority than has fallen to the lot of any of his predecessors, and as his claims to distinction as an interpreter are based pre-eminently upon his readings of Wagner, Mozart and Beethoven, it is safe to predict that German opera will come into its own next season at the Metropolitan and that all the productions made will be on a higher level than heretofore.

(Editorial in *MA* 6, no. 6, June 22, 1907, p. 10)[28]

---

[27]For the German text, see Appendix, A9.
[28]The editor of *MA*, John Christian Freund (1848-1924), although British by birth and education, was an American nationalist; he founded the magazine in 1898.

13

According to private advices received in New York this week, it seems that Heinrich Conried will depend upon Gustav Mahler, who was recently engaged as principal conductor, for the active direction of affairs at the Metropolitan Opera House. [. . .]

Mahler, as a matter of fact, was not disposed at first to consider the offer made him to come to New York, and stipulated, it is understood, that if he came he should be given absolute power, such as he had been accustomed to at the Vienna Court Opera, of which he has been director for the last ten years.

By the agreement which Mr. Conried is reported to have made with the noted German composer and conductor, the latter will exercise supreme sway and therefore be able with the forces at hand to carry into effect the lofty art principles he champions. Mr. Conried, on his part, will be able to keep his finger on the Metropolitan's pulse and give his new associate the benefit of the managerial wisdom his experience has taught him. [. . .]

(*MA* 6, no. 7, June 29, 1907, p. 1)

14

Richard Heuberger,[29] conductor of the Vienna Male Chorus, which visited America last month, has the following to say in the "Neues Wiener Tageblatt" concerning music in this country:

"What heretofore was music to the American? This most subtle, immaterial, most soul inspiring of all arts was to him a noise which pleased him only if it was loud, very loud. The clashing of symbals [sic], orchestra tuttis, were the indispensable conclusion effects of music pieces designed to 'please'. Gentle, soft, sweet music was not considered music at all. The creation of large orchestras and choirs, which dates back only a few decades in the United States, has made a beginning for something better. First class instrumental associations, like the Gericke[30] Orchestra in Boston, have prepared the ground and accustomed the American at least to pay for the best. In time, haply, they will also learn to understand the best.

[29]Richard Franz Joseph Heuberger (1850-1914) - Austrian conductor, composer and critic. He wrote for the leading Viennese dailies, and conducted the Männergesangverein from 1902 to 1909.

[30]Wilhelm Gericke (1845-1925) - Well known Austrian conductor; he was a member of the Vienna Conservatory jury which failed to award Mahler the Beethoven-Prize in 1881. He was the conductor of the Boston Symphony from 1884 to 1889 and from 1898 to 1906.

"One of the principal reasons why there is so little musical understanding in America is probably to be sought in the preponderance of the English race, so little gifted in the matter of music. The Germans, for whom the day brings so much labor that there is little time and money for joyful festivities - these Germans are too small a fraction of the population to exert a decided influence. [. . .]"

Commenting on these statements, H.E. Krehbiel, writing in the New York "Tribune", says in part:

"The insinuation that thus far the Boston Orchestra has taught Americans only to pay for music, not how to enjoy it, is too silly, and it is too contemptible for comment. How long has Vienna been paying for orchestral music of the same character? Longer than Boston, truly, but not so long as New York. [. . .]"

(*MA* 6, no. 7, June 29, 1907, p. 13)

15

Mahler, with the London Symphony Orchestra, was to have made a ten days' trip to the United States to give eight concerts within a week and return here [London].[31] The concerts were to be in New York, Boston, Philadelphia, etc. The guarantees had been secured and the arrangements nearly perfected when Mahler notified the London managers who were engaged in this, that his contract with the Metropolitan Company prevented him from going. In the meantime that contract with the Metropolitan is, according to late accounts, still pending. There are those who doubt that Mahler and the Metropolitan will live together as congenially as two doves.

("Reflections", *MC* 55, no. 7, August 14, 1907, p. 5)

16

The engagement of Gustav Mahler, the famous conductor of the Vienna Imperial Opera House as musical director of the Metropolitan Opera House in New York, was officially confirmed this week. [. . .]

Otto H. Kahn,[32] of the Metropolitan Opera Board of Directors [. . .], expressed the opinion that Herr Mahler's predilection for the works of

---

[31] I have been unable to find any evidence for such a plan.
[32] Otto H. Kahn (1867-1934) - German-born banker, emigrated to the United States in 1893. There he was connected with many artistic and educational enterprises (*e.g.*, president and chairman of the board of the Metropolitan Opera until 1931; vice president of the Philharmonic Symphony Society).

Wagner and Mozart would not materially effect the number of French and Italian operas usually given at the Metropolitan.

Herr Mahler is spending the Summer months in a small town some distance from Vienna, keeping himself in seclusion, owing to depression over the recent loss of his little daughter. [. . .]

(*MA* 6, no. 14, August 17, 1907, p. 1)

17

Although to this moment there is no official confirmation of the news that Felix Weingartner[33] will assume the directorship of the Viennese Court Opera as Mahler's successor, and although in official circles any knowledge of negotiations with the Berlin conductor is as good as denied, there can be no doubt whatever that the talks with Weingartner are rather far advanced, and that the formal conclusion of a contract is, if nothing unforeseen comes up, only a matter of days. [. . .]

About Director Mahler's plans for the future, we have received the following information: initially, Mahler wishes to completely withdraw from Vienna. Berlin was brought into the picture. But he dropped this idea and will, it is now definite, retain his permanent residence in Vienna. At first, Mahler will devote himself entirely to composition. [. . .] At the end of January, Director Mahler will sail to America, to commence his engagement with Director Conried at the Metropolitan Opera House. At this time, it is not yet certain whether Director Mahler's family will travel with him to America. [. . .]

(*Neue Freie Presse*, August 20, 1907, Morning edition, p. 9)

18

Director Mahler arrived here yesterday and resumed the directorial activities at the Court Opera. He was kind enough to grant an interview to one of our correspondents. [. . .]

"What are your plans for the immediate future at the Opera?" [. . .]

"I have made a commitment to continue working at the Opera until my successor arrives." [. . .]

"And your plans for the future?"

"There are several plans. As of now, however, nothing other than my

[33]Felix von Weingartner (1863-1942) - Eminent Austrian-born conductor. Active mainly in Berlin, Munich and Vienna, where he succeeded Mahler as director of the Imperial Opera. He appeared as guest conductor with the New York Philharmonic between 1905 and 1907.

trip to America is certain; if I am in good health, I will leave on that at the end of January. [. . .]"

"What commitments do you have in America, Herr Director?"

"As concerns my sojourn in America, I have undertaken to conduct some operas and several concerts between the end of January and the middle of April."

"Is it true, Herr Director, that you will conduct only Wagner and Mozart operas?"

"It is only agreed that I will not conduct 'Parsifal', otherwise I will also conduct works by other composers. I have made it a condition that performances I will conduct must be artistically thoroughly prepared, though I have committed myself only as a conductor."

"Will you only conduct your own works in concerts?"

"I will conduct not only my own symphonies, but also works by others. I can, in fact, tell you this: it gives me more pleasure to conduct a symphony by Beethoven or by Schumann than one of my own. In general, I have renounced concert conducting until now. I have attended or led the performance of one of my works only when my presence has been unquestionably necessary. It was never a pleasure for me. I have travelled to conduct only out of necessity. Now it is different. Now I am free, I can again take on concerts, and so it is all the same to me whether my name is on the programme, or that of another modern composer. [. . .]"

(*Neue Freie Presse*, August 26, 1907, Evening edition, p. 9)

19

In an interview with one of our correspondents, Director Mahler spoke about the reasons for his resignation. "That people in general ignore the faults of our theatre operations today," said Director Mahler, "must lie in the fact that the public has become thoroughly accustomed to them. Consider the programme of our Opera. Works in the most diverse styles follow one upon the other. And there must be a performance every day. That thus not all performances can be equally good, goes without saying. There is no time for a sufficient number of rehearsals. This results, in the first place, in an inadequate preparation of the whole, but also in the uncertainty of individual singers. Some of them drift along, while others attempt to win applause for details of their presentations by aggressively exceeding the artistic limits. Is an artistically unblemished performance possible at all, then? Ten years ago, I was bold enough to answer that question in the affirmative, I thought in my youthful enthusiasm to be able to improve the world. But in this last ten years, it has become increasingly clear to me that under current conditions it is impossible to produce only good performances. The means for this are not available. But if the purpose of an artistic institution is good performances, then there is an incongruity between means and purpose that can be rooted only in the weakness of the institution's organization. It is ridiculous to want to make the director responsible for that. But it is up to the director to decide for himself whether he wishes to pursue his higher artistic goals, or to brand the institution he leads as a commercial undertaking. I have elected the former and resigned my post, as I could no longer reconcile it with my artistic conscience. Perhaps other circumstances have contributed to a speeding up of my decision. But I want to stress this: I am leaving voluntarily."

(*Neue Freie Presse*, August 27, 1907, Morning edition, p. 11)

20

September 27, 1907

My very dear Director,

[. . .]

The Herr Director will see what the artistic value of the fact will be that Mahler goes to America four weeks earlier. That is quite impossible to foreshadow today, and will show itself in the quality of the performances following upon this artistic preparatory work.

Certainly, Mahler will gain no material advantage from going over four weeks early. He stated quite honestly that at the honorarium of 25,000 crowns for these four weeks, he will make 2,000 florins more than he would have earned in Russia and Holland.

Quite aside from the fact that Director Mahler says that any artist in America will earn at least double that in the same period, one must also weigh the fact that through his concerts in Russia and Holland an important field of future activity would, indeed, have opened to him; yet, he is sacrificing that advantage in the interest of your joint endeavours, and wishes only to achieve great and perfect things.

[. . .]

He is approaching your joint undertaking with great enthusiasm, he is practicing "Isolde" with Fremstad[34] in such a way that Fräulein von Mildenburg[35] and Fremstad work together in the morning in Mahler's

---

[34]Olive Fremstad (1871-1951) - Swedish-born soprano, celebrated interpreter of Wagnerian roles. She sang her first Isolde in Mahler's debut performance at the Metropolitan.

[35]Anna von Mildenburg (1872-1947) - Celebrated Austrian soprano. She began her career in Hamburg, and was hired for the Vienna Opera in 1899 by Mahler, with whom she is presumed to have had an intimate relationship earlier.

rehearsal studio. He is quite charmed by Fremstad, and wishes you to know that "Tristan" will quite certainly be a great success.

He is also practicing with Fräulein La Fornia.[36]

The new tenor Martin[37] interests him very much, and appeals to him exceptionally, and he congratulates you on this acquisition. He is also practicing diligently with this gentleman. He says that you, Herr Director, will be amazed at how much the work over there will be simplified by such artistic preparation.

Finally, Director Mahler asks you to confirm that the established programme remains valid, to wit: 1. performance "Tristan", 2. performance "Fidelio". Despite his arrival four weeks earlier, he is very much for staying with this order.

[. . .]

(To Heinrich Conried, presumably from Rudolf Winternitz;
ELM, pp. [295ff.])[38]

21
ADDENDUM

As an addition to the contract concluded on June 21, 1907 between the CONRIED METROPOLITAN OPERA COMPANY through its President Herr HEINRICH CONRIED on the one hand, and Herr Director GUSTAV MAHLER on the other hand, the following agreements are made:

Herr Director GUSTAV MAHLER commences his journey *circa* 4 (four) weeks earlier than was stipulated in the contract, to wit, Herr Director MAHLER will sail from Cherbourg to America on the 12th of December.

For this extension of four weeks Herr Director Gustav MAHLER receives an honorarium of 25,000 (twenty-five thousand) crowns, in return for which he undertakes to conduct 2 (two) times weekly during the four weeks.

These additional agreements are made subject to the condition that Herr Director Gustav MAHLER succeeds in freeing himself from the obligations he had entered into for this time in Russia and Holland, to

---

[36]Rita Fornia-Labey (née Newman) (1878-1922) - American mezzo-soprano, well known for her Wagner-roles. Following her debut in Germany, she sang at the Metropolitan from 1907 to her death.
[37]Riccardo [Hugh Whitfield] Martin (1874-1952) - American tenor and singing teacher, at the Metropolitan Opera from 1907 to 1915, and 1917-1918.
[38]For the German text, see Appendix, A10.

which end Herr Director Gustav MAHLER has taken the immediate and necessary steps.

This addendum is again prepared in one original copy which, signed by both parties and jointly owned by both parties, remains with the trustee, while both contracting parties receive a copy of the addendum.

As for the rest, all conditions stipulated in the main contract (including also those pertaining to maintenance, etc.) are valid for this addendum without exception, and this honorarium of 25,000 (twenty-five thousand) crowns will be paid to Herr Director MAHLER at the end of these first FOUR weeks.

Wien, 27. September 1907   Gustav Mahler m.p.
  as Witness: Alfred Roller m.p.
  as Witness: Rudolf Winternitz m.p.

(*ELM*, pp. [293f.])[39]

22

Full plans for the long and active season which the Symphony Society of New York will inaugurate on Nov. 2 at Carnegie Hall include the first performance in America of Tschaikowsky's greatest opera, "Eugen Onegin", the only appearance in concert of Mme. Emma Eames, the first reappearance of four other distinguished soloists, and a Beethoven cycle comprising six concerts. There will also be initial performances of symphonic works by Chadwick, d'Indy and Mahler.

[...]

The biggest subscription series ever given in New York City is the fact which should interest the general public. To bring this about, and to promote the welfare of the New York Symphony Orchestra, the organization was placed under contract last Spring for this entire season by the Symphony Society of New York, following a fruitful meeting at the residence of Harry Harkness Flagler, one of the trustees of the orchestra fund. Walter Damrosch[40] was appointed musical director and conductor and awarded charge of all matters artistic. The result was that New York now has an orchestra of ninety-five disciplined artists who are to work together during at least seven months of the year solely for the cultivation of symphonic music - a circumstance which promises to have an influence on the musical life of the city that can hardly be overestimated.

[39]For the German text, see Appendix, A11.
[40]Walter Damrosch (1862-1950) - Son of Leopold Damrosch, founder of the Symphony Society. He conducted the New York Oratorio Society, and was musical director of the Symphony Society from 1903 to 1927.

The large number of concerts in the subscription series will give Mr. Damrosch broader opportunities in the arrangement of programmes [. . .]

Three symphonies brand new to New York are announced. Mahler's Symphony No. 7 will be conducted by the composer,[41] if the Society's plans in this respect do not miscarry. [. . .]

(*NYT*, October 6, 1907, Part Six, p. 7)

23

[At the performance of Mahler's Second Symphony yesterday] the scene was transformed into one of such a loving farewell in the concert hall, the likes of which has hardly ever been extended to an artist who has not been working on the stage. People were honouring the composer, the director, the conductor - the complete genial personality of Mahler, who has now been lost to Vienna. [. . .]

(*Neue Freie Presse*, November 25, 1907, Evening edition, p. 10)

24

There have been many inquiries at the Metropolitan Opera House of late as to when Mme. Olive Fremstad's name would reappear in the bills. This singer [. . .] has usually been brought forward soon after the opera house opened. This year her appearance has been deferred until the arrival of Gustav Mahler, director of the Royal Court Theatre [sic] in Vienna. [. . .] Yesterday she saw a *Times* reporter and talked with him: "Gustav Mahler's greatness cannot be overestimated. I heard a performance of 'Fidelio' at his theatre in Vienna, and it made me cry to watch him. He is a small man, but his force is tremendous and he absolutely hypnotizes his men and his singers. [. . .] I am sure that [. . .] the New York public will make the acquaintance of a great man".

(*NYT*, December 9, 1907, p. 7)

25

Gustav Mahler, composer and conductor of the Royal Court Theatre [sic] in Vienna, arrived yesterday on the Augusta Victoria to conduct

---

[41]Although rumours kept surfacing concerning plans for such a performance, the Seventh Symphony was never performed in the United States under Mahler (s.a. **292, 293**, Note 56, p. 280).

works of Wagner, Beethoven, Mozart and Weber at the Metropolitan Opera House.

"I have been looking forward with pleasure to my engagement in America," said Mr. Mahler, when seen at his apartment in the Hotel Majestic. "I am thoroughly in sympathy with the season which Mr. Conried has planned, and I hope to be able to contribute something in an artistic way. I shall make my first appearance here [...] with Wagner's music drama 'Tristan und Isolde'. [...] The Mozart and Beethoven operas will be staged and presented exactly as they are in Vienna.

[...] Later in the season I shall probably conduct some concerts at which I hope to present one or two of my own symphonies".

(*NYT*, December 22, 1907, p. 9)

26

The arrival in New York—the harbour and all the sights and scenes and human bustle—so took our breath away that we forgot all our troubles. But not for long.

[...]

We had a suite of rooms on the eleventh floor [of the Hotel Majestic], and, of course, two pianos. So we felt at home.[42]

[...]

At first we lived almost in solitary confinement. Mahler was so shattered by the verdict on his heart that he spent the greater part of the day in bed. When he was not having a meal, he was reading; and he got up only for rehearsals or for the performance at night, if he was conducting.

(*AMM*, pp. 128, 137; original German in *AME*, pp. 158, 168)

27

There is an island surrounded by rivers, and about it the tide scurries fast and deep. It is a beautiful island, long, narrow, magnificently populated, and with such a wealth of life and interest as no island in the whole world before has ever possessed. Long lines of vessels of every description nose its banks. Enormous buildings and many splendid mansions line its streets.

It is filled with a vast population, millions coming and going, and is the

---

[42]In the original draft of her memoirs (*ELM*, p. [187]), Alma described their suite in greater detail: "On the eleventh floor, two large bedrooms, two bathrooms, an enormous corner salon - an instant home."

scene of so much life and enthusiasm and ambition that its fame is, as the sound of a bell, heard afar.

And the interest which this island has for the world is that it is seemingly a place of opportunity and happiness. If you were to listen to the tales of its glory carried the land over and see the picture which it presents to the incoming eye, you would assume that it was all that it seemed. Glory for those who enter its walls seeking glory. Happiness for those who come seeking happiness. A world of comfort and satisfaction for all who take up their abode within it - an island of beauty and delight.

(Theodore Dreiser,[43] *The Color of a Great City*, New York, 1923, p. 284 [essays written between 1900 and 1915])

28

This millionaire leader of Tammany Hall[44] was by no means an unpleasant man to meet. He had a certain diffidence and he was not a good talker. [. . .] He had none of the ordinary vices [. . .] He attended Mass every Sunday, and gave liberal donations to the church. [. . .] He was accessible to anybody who wanted to talk to him [. . .] a dictator in fact, yet preserving all of the tokens of democratic accessibility. [. . .]

By the period when Charles F. Murphy[45] became "chief", the "business-man" type of leader had evolved. Under this plan—a plan that afforded the most plausible opportunities for explaining the sudden acquisition of wealth—Tammany men became open and secret partners in contracting firms, using the pressure of political power to have large contracts awarded to their concerns. [. . .] None could now fail to note the great transition from the previous period when Tammany leaders used only the vulgar and criminal methods of stealing money out of the city treasury. Under Murphy's leadership the obvious methods used were those of "honest graft" - the making of millions from contracts with public service corporations [. . .]

(Gustavus Myers, *The History of Tammany Hall*, New York, Burt Franklin, 1917, pp. 302f., 310f., 318f.)

---

[43]Theodore Dreiser (1871-1945) - A novelist and essayist, he was one of the most eloquent and significant chroniclers of American life and social conditions in his time.

[44]Tammany Hall - The Society of St. Tammany, or Columbian Order, was formed in the 18th century as a patriotic, anti-aristocratic organization. Although initially it was dedicated to the widest democratization of political life, by the beginning of the 19th century Tammany Hall secured control of New York City.

[45]Charles Francis Murphy (1858-1924) - Son of Irish immigrants, he had limited formal education. Saloon and hotel owner after 1878; New York dock commissioner in 1898. He was the absolute boss of Tammany Hall from 1902 to 1924.

29

Broadway, at Forty-Second Street, on the spring evenings when the city is crowded [. . .] when the doors of all shops are open, the windows of nearly all restaurants wide to the gaze of the idlest passer-by. Here is the great city, and it is lush and dreamy. [. . .] A hundred, a thousand electric signs will blink and wink; [. . .] the taxis and private cars fluttering about like jeweled flies. [. . .] Life bubbles, sparkles: chatters gay, incoherent stuff. Such is Broadway.

And then Fifth Avenue, that singing, crystal street, on a shopping afternoon, winter, summer, spring or fall. [. . .] its windows crowded with delicate effronteries of silks and gay nothings of all description, it greets you in January, February and March [. . .]; as early as November [. . .] it sings of [. . .] the lesser or greater joys of the tropics and the warmer seas [. . .]; in September [. . .] the haughty display of furs and rugs, in this same avenue, and costumes deluxe for ball and dinner. [. . .] One might think, from the picture presented and the residences which line the upper section, that all the world was inordinately prosperous and exclusive and happy.

[. . .]

New York City has one hundred thousand people who, under unfavourable conditions, work with their fingers for so little money that they are understood, even by the uninitiated general public, to form a class by themselves. [. . .] In a general sense, the term, tenement workers, includes them all. They form a great section in one place, and in others little patches.

[. . .] In any one of these areas you will encounter a civilization that is as strange and un-American as if it were not included in this land at all. [. . .] Push carts and marketstalls [. . .] little stores and grimy windows are characteristic of these sections. There is an atmosphere of crowdedness and poverty [. . .]

The people themselves are a strange mixture of all races and creeds. There are Greeks, Italians, Russians, Poles, Syrians, American, Hungarians and Jews [. . .] All are poverty stricken. [. . .] In the same hundred thousand, and under the same tenement conditions, are many who are not foreign-born. [. . .] Thousands of children born and reared in New York City are growing up under conditions which would better become a slum section of Constantinople.

[. . .] Working as these people do, they have very little time for education. [. . .] Parents have to struggle too hard. Their ignorant influence upon the lives of the young ones is too great.

[. . .] Nearly the only ideal that is set before these strugglers is the one of getting money. [. . .] They are inoculated in infancy with the doctrine that wealth is all—the shabbiest and most degrading doctrine that can be impressed upon anyone. [. . .] They are infatuated with the rush and soar of a great metropolis. They are fascinated by the illusion of pleasure. Broadway, Fifth Avenue, the mansions, the lights, the beauty. A thirst [. . .] for excitement is burning them up. For this they labour. For this they endure a hard, unnatural existence. For this they crowd themselves in stifling, inhuman quarters, and for this they die.

(Dreiser, *op. cit.*, pp. 2f., 85, 87f., 98f., 275)

30

Opera first struck deep roots in social New York at the Academy of Music[46] [. . .] opened in 1854. In the beginning it contained six large proscenium boxes; [. . .] after the fire of 1866 the boxes were increased to eighteen. [. . .] By the year 1880 it was seen that the number of possible boxholders had [. . .] been outgrown by ambitious wealth; crusty oligarchs refused as much as $30,000 for a box. Parvenues, led by William K. and Cornelius Vanderbilt, did the inevitable and built their own house, the Metropolitan Opera.[47]

[. . .] There were two rows of boxes, held to be of equal social prominence, called the Golden Horseshoe by reporters, who estimated the wealth there represented at $540,000,000. After the fire of 1892 the inner circle of the Metropolitan Opera [. . .] decided to consolidate its gains by reducing the double-horseshoe to thirty-five luxurious parterre boxes at $60,000 each, soon styled the Diamond Horseshoe. The grand tier and stall boxes [. . .] were [. . .] socially second-class—which in society means worse than nothing, so that if one loved prestige more than music he would do better to stay at home.

After the reduction in the number of stockholders, a box at the Metropolitan—which was either hereditary or else the result of purchase from an original investor—remained up to the [First World War] the most luscious of social plums.

---

[46]The Academy of Music (14th Street and Irving Place) was devoted specifically to music; it had a regular opera season until 1886. When it was opened in 1854, it had the largest stage in the world and seated 4,600 people.

[47]The Metropolitan Opera House was opened on October 22, 1883. For the next twenty years, it was managed on behalf of the stockholders, with varying degrees of success, by Henry E. Abbey, Leopold Damrosch and Maurice Grau. Upon Grau's retirement in 1903, the Metropolitan Opera and Real Estate Company (a group of 35 stockholders formed in 1892) decided (on a vote of seven to six!) to lease the Opera House to the Conried Metropolitan Opera Company, a producing company headed by Heinrich Conried.

(Dixon Wecter, *The Saga of American Society*, New York, Scribner, 1937, pp. 463f.)

31

The narrow margin[48] by which Heinrich Conried and his associates became the successors of Maurice Grau[49] [. . .] at the Metropolitan foreshadowed the rather troubled time they had in the next five years. [. . .] As an opera impresario Conried was as ill equipped as he was well equipped to run a theatre. He had scant technical knowledge of voices, little grasp of the problems of operating an international repertory, rather limited acquaintance with music itself. To be sure, he saw clearly the theatrical shortcomings of Grau's productions and could well see how they could be improved - by overhauling the chorus and orchestra, providing more rehearsal time and [. . .] abolishing the star system.

(Irving Kolodin, *The Metropolitan Opera 1883-1966*, New York, Knopf, 1967, pp. 159f.)

32

Gustav Mahler began his first rehearsal at the Metropolitan Opera House yesterday with an exercise of authority. He stopped the orchestra after a few bars of the prelude to "Tristan und Isolde," and said:

"All other rehearsals in this theatre must be stopped. I can't hear my orchestra."

And immediately the chorus rehearsal which was going on in the lobby ceased. Other conductors at the Metropolitan have attempted to effect the same result, but less successfully.

Mr. Mahler was introduced to the orchestra by Mr. Conried. The orchestra played a "tusch" in honour of the new conductor and then went to work. After three-quarters of an hour with the score Mahler shut up his big book and said he was satisfied.

(*NYT*, December 24, 1907, p. 7)

33

Our saddest evening of all was Christmas Eve, the first we had spent separated from our children and in a foreign country. Mahler did not

---

[48]See Note 47, p. 45.
[49]Maurice Grau (1849-1907) - Czech-born impresario and theatre director; managed the Metropolitan Opera from 1897 to 1903.

want to be reminded that it was Christmas and in the desolation of loneliness I wept without ceasing all day.

Towards evening there was a knock. It was Baumfeld,[50] that good but clumsy Samaritan, whose obsession was a German theatre for New York. He read the whole truth in my face and would not rest until we agreed to go with him to where we could see a Christmas tree and children and friendly faces. It took us out of ourselves at once; but we were driven away after dinner when some actors and actresses came in. One of these was a raddled female called 'Putzi'. This renewed our grief, for Putzi was the pet name for the child we had lost.

(*AMM*, pp. 129f.; original German in *AME*, 159f.)

34

Conried resigned twice last week and was dismissed once; Hammerstein gave up the Manhattan and built a magnificent opera house in Brooklyn; Mary Garden had pneumonia; Mahler succeeded Conried at the Metropolitan; Caruso will have to leave that Opera if the director does, etc. - at least, according to the local dailies last week.[51]

(*MC* 55, no. 26, December 25, 1907, p. 22)

35

Gustav Mahler, the celebrated composer and conductor, [. . .] reached New York last Saturday [. . .] to enter upon his engagement with Heinrich Conried as conductor-in-chief at the Metropolitan Opera House. [. . .] He began rehearsals with the orchestra on Monday.
[. . .]

The new conductor is of small stature, with dark hair, and a somewhat nervous manner. He has brought with him his wife, a pretty blonde woman, attractively Viennese in appearance.

His arrival has inspired new rumors, or revivified old ones, to the effect that he is to be Mr. Conried's successor at the Metropolitan. [. . .]

(*MA* 7, no. 7, December 28, 1907, pp. 1 and 4)

---

[50]Maurice Baumfeld (1868-1913) - Austrian-born journalist. Beginning in 1907, he was a theatre director in New York (Irving Place Theatre).
[51]As will be seen in many excerpts, Marc A. Blumenberg (1861-1913), founder and first editor-in-chief of *MC*, had a running feud with the music critics (as much as with the general editorial policies) of the daily newspapers.

36

The coming of Gustav Mahler [...] will be an important event in this musical season [...] . For Mr. Mahler is at the present time one of the most distinguished personalities in the world of music. He is admittedly one of the greatest and most individual of conductors. He is also conspicuous as a composer; but here his achievements are still subject to great debate and contention, as, in fact, are those of almost all who at the present day produce music.

[...]

It must be confessed that his acceptance of the appointment in New York was a surprise to all who knew of Mahler's personal qualities, his ideals and methods as a conductor, and the conditions that prevail at the Metropolitan Opera House, that necessarily must prevail there as long as it remains what it is in the musical and social life of this community. In Vienna he was a dictator, with funds almost unlimited, with power to enforce all his wishes as to casts, rehearsals, scenic decoration, interpretation, and he had no hesitation in enforcing them to the utmost. It is, perhaps, needless to say that whatever may be given him nominally in New York, he will, in actual practice, have no such free hand. But such an iron will as Mahler's, joined to such a genius for conducting and for organization, as all accounts agree that he possesses, will accomplish much.

[...]

Mr. Mahler's coming to New York as conductor may be expected to offer much of the same sort of absorbing interest that has been felt in the appearance here of the numerous great conductors who have made recent musical seasons notable - Weingartner, Mottl,[52] Strauss,[53] Colonne,[54] Henry Wood,[55] and the others.

(*NYT*, December 29, 1907, Part Six, p. 2)

---

[52]Felix Mottl (1856-1911) - Prominent Austrian conductor. Active mainly in Karlsruhe, Bayreuth and Munich, he was regarded as one of the greatest Wagner conductors of his time.
[53]Strauss - presumably, Richard Strauss.
[54]Edouard Colonne (1838-1910) - French violinist and conductor, founder of the *Concerts du Châtelet* (later known as the *Concerts Colonne*) in Paris.
[55]Sir Henry Wood (1869-1944) - Distinguished English opera and concert conductor. Founder of the "Promenade" concerts in London. Conducted the New York Philharmonic in 1904.

Plate 14. Olive Fremstad was Mahler's first Isolde, Sieglinde and Brünnhilde (in *Siegfried*) in New York. (*COS*, Illustration 103)

Plate 15. Anton van Rooy sang Kurvenal, Wotan and The Wanderer
in Mahler's American productions. (*COS*, Illustration 99)

37

The German works have had scant showing at the Metropolitan Opera
House so far this winter. Their time has come now, however, with the
coming of Gustav Mahler to occupy the chief place in the conductor's
chair. He made his first appearance before a New York audience last
evening, conducting the first performance given there this season of
"Tristan und Isolde."[56]

[. . .] There was enough here to key up the interest of the lovers of
Wagner's great tragedy to a high pitch, and there was the promise of a
performance remarkable in many respects. The promise was kept, and
more than kept. The performance was indeed a remarkable one. [. . .]
The influence of the new conductor was felt and heard in the whole spirit
of the performance. [. . .] His tempos were frequently somewhat more
rapid than we have lately been accustomed to; and they were always such
as to fill the music with dramatic life. They were elastic and full of subtle
variations.

Most striking was the firm hand with which he kept the volume of
orchestral sound controlled and subordinated to the voices. These were
never overwhelmed; the balance was never lost, and they were allowed to
keep their place above the orchestra and to blend with it always in their
rightful place. And yet the score was revealed in all its complex beauty,
with its strands of interwoven melody always clearly disposed and united
with an exquisite sense of proportion and an unerring sense of the larger
values. Delicacy and clearness were the characteristics of many
passages, yet the climaxes were made superbly effectual. Through it all
went the pulse of dramatic passion and the sense of fine musical beauty.

(*NYT*, January 2, 1908, p. 9)

38

Features of the occasion were the debut of Fremstad as Isolde and the
first appearance before an American audience of the celebrated Viennese
conductor, Gustav Mahler, to both of whom eminent success must be
credited. [. . .] Mahler caught his audience at once, and I predict for him
the popularity and influence which his great talent should demand. His

[56]The complete cast was as follows: Isolde - Fremstad; Brangäne - Homer; Tristan -
Knote; Kurvenal - Van Rooy; King Marke - Blass; Melot - Mühlmann; Shepherd
and Sailor's Voice - Reiss; Steersman - Bayer. Except for a performance on
February 3, when Gadski sang Isolde, Mahler's cast remained stable for this season.
   (Unless otherwise specified, all information on casting is taken from William H.
Seltsam, *Metropolitan Opera Annals*, New York, H.W. Wilson, 1949.)

conducting is marked by the authority and restrained force bred of great artistic knowledge and experience, and a firm facile beat. In his reading great lucidity and balance of tonal effect, strong rhythmic quality and a remarkable feeling for romance and dramatic contrast and climax are noticeable.

(*NYW*, January 2, 1908, p. 9)

39

[Significantly], the house was as large as it might have been on a Caruso night. [. . .] The applause was general and prolonged. Many stood up and cheered. Mr. Mahler looked happy. [. . .] There was no doubt as to the impression he and the performers made upon the auditors.

[. . .] it was a notably good performance, filled with vitality and voicing a conception of high beauty. The guiding hand of Mr. Mahler was discernible in every musical detail of the interpretation; [. . .] he read the score with refinement, with poetic feeling and with an artist's consideration for the ensemble. [. . .] Tempi familiar in late years were changed here and there. Accelerations and retardations of high value were employed. But best of all, the eloquent variety of Wagner's instrumentation was displayed by the simple process of bringing out clearly every solo phrase, while the harmonic and contrapuntal background was never slighted. Mr. Mahler knows well how to hunt Wagner's melody [. . .] and let the auditors hear it.

(*NYS*, January 2, 1908, p. 7)

40

Herr Mahler [. . .] is a newcomer whose appearance here, while full of significance, is not likely to excite one-half the interest in New York that his departure from Europe did on the other side of the water. This will seem paradoxical in Germany, where the density of ignorance of what musical conditions are outside of the environs of German cities which enjoy opera houses supported by municipal or national subsidies, is a phenomenon of a character simply incomprehensible to a public that has been familiar with all that is best in operatic art for a quarter of a century.

But this raises a question that can better be discussed at some other time and in some other place. It is enough for the present that it was easy to recognize in Herr Mahler's work last night that he is master of his art whom New Yorkers will take particular delight to honour. He was welcomed with an unusual and cordial demonstration last night [. . .] There can be no question of the amiability of such a proceeding on the

Plate 16. William J. Henderson, critic of the *Sun* from 1902 to 1937. (*LCE*, Figure 90)

Plate 17. Henry E. Krehbiel, critic of the *Tribune*. (*LCE*, Figure 89)

part of the public, though there might of the New York public's judgment and knowledge, of which our foreign friends, and even our self-conceited native artists, profess at times in other climes to have a poor opinion. Nevertheless, Mr. Mahler did honour to himself, Wagner's music and the New York public. It was a strikingly vital reading which he gave to Wagner's familiar score [. . .] but those who expected new things from him in the way of stage management, which has been a feature of his administration of the Imperial Opera in Vienna, must have been woefully disappointed. There were some changes in the first stage picture from that which has for years been equally familiar and absurd, but the changes only accentuated the absurdities. We have at last attained a mastless ship, with shrouds running up into nothingness and illustrating a score of other absurdities.

(*NYTrib*, January 2, 1908, p. 7)

41

The orchestra, the singing, the house itself - all was wonderful, and even if the settings, which Conried kept in his own hands, were often—though not always—abominable, Mahler did not care. Fremstad sang Isolde, Knote[57] Tristan. For the first time in my life I heard the second act as pure music. Mahler swam in bliss.

[. . .]

His triumph was immediate. Americans are very critical and do not by any means receive every European celebrity with favour. They really know something about music.

(*AMM*, p. 129; original German in *AME*, pp. 158f.)

42

Last week's performance of "Tristan und Isolde" was doubly interesting from the disclosure made of the powers of two artists, Gustav Mahler and Olive Fremstad. Mr. Mahler's conducting resulted in a reading of the score that is comparable with the best that New York has known - the readings of Anton Seidl[58] and of Felix Mottl. It was on the whole, a finer reading that Mottl's, conceived in a larger mold, with all its finesse and subtlety, and with a greater power in the dramatic climaxes. Refinement

[57]Heinrich Knote (1870-1953) - German tenor. One of the most sought after Wagnerian tenors in the early decades of the twentieth century.
[58]Anton Seidl (1850-1898) - Hungarian-born conductor. Following engagements in Leipzig, Bremen and Prague, he succeeded Leopold Damrosch as head of German opera at the Metropolitan in 1885.

and poetic insight were the salient characteristics of it. In the old days of Seidl there used to be complaint from the boxes, so it is said, that the music of "Tristan" was too soft, that it was not possible to converse comfortably without arousing anger in the pit. It was this kind of reading that Mr. Mahler achieved.

It seemed likely last Friday night that he was a man who will give New York music lovers some interesting experiences. His methods in the conductor's chair are straightforward and direct. His beat is uncommonly sharp, decided, and angular, and his attention is alertly directed at all points, seemingly, at once. It is significant that his left hand was almost constantly used in the "Tristan" performance to check and subdue. He gives the unmistakable impression of a man commanding authority and of keen insight.

It was noted in this journal that Mr. Mahler's tempi in "Tristan" are in some passages somewhat more rapid than we have been accustomed to - whereby he is differentiated at once from the prevailing Baireuth [sic] school of conductors upon whom the influence is always toward deliberation and even dragging of the movement. Mr. Mahler's tempi in "Tristan" are made for the enhancement of the dramatic effect, to keep the blood of life pulsing in the score; yet there was nothing subversive in them or destructive of the musical values. The skilful and elastic modification of tempo is one of the touchstones of fine dramatic conducting, and in this respect Mr. Mahler showed himself a master. There were innumerable instances of it through the score; take, for instance, the approach to the climax of the prelude. How often is this driven on with an obvious hurrying of the beat! Mr. Mahler made an acceleration that was well nigh imperceptible as it advanced, yet when he arrived at the climax the beat was materially increased.

It followed from the poetic subtlety and refinement of Mr. Mahler's reading that the voices were given rights of which it is certain Wagner never intended them to be deprived. Chief of these is to be heard, and (if the singers' diction is of the true kind) understood. The orchestral part had all its beauty, all its dramatic power and effectiveness; it had all the contrast and variation of power, of accent, of crescendo and climax. Yet it did not drown the voices, and here, too, was an added beauty brought into prominence that has not always been heard in Wagnerian performances, that of the blending of voices with the orchestral tone. How beautiful was the sound of Brangaene's warning song from the tower in the second act, as sung by Mme. Homer[59] - who, it should be said, has seldom sung this part with a more opulent beauty of voice.

[59]Louise Homer [Beatty] (1871-1947) - Born in the United States, she was the Metropolitan's leading alto from 1900 to 1919. She was also a successful concert singer.

Mr. Mahler is a conductor after Wagner's own heart in his instinctively right feeling for the pervasive melody of the orchestral score. He seeks what Wagner called the "melos" and never lets it sink from its position of preeminence.

Altogether he is a man that has some very high ideals and some deeply cherished memories of great conductors at their work.

(*NYT*, January 5, 1908, Part Six, p. 4)

43

[. . .] Hardly a single critic on our dailies omitted to inject a mention of Seidl in the report of last Wednesday's "Tristan und Isolde" performance at the Metropolitan. [. . .]

What has the dead and gone Seidl to do with the vital and present Mahler? [. . .]

Seidl was an excellent leader, but he lacked the individuality, personality and mentality of a man like Mahler. The latter lives in a time when the orchestral boundaries and their application are considerably wider than in the day of Seidl, and the musician who wielded the baton last Wednesday has made himself a master of the modern orchestra not only by conducting it, but also by writing for it music which exhausts the possibilities of every instrument in the body orchestral. Mahler's conducting of "Tristan und Isolde" was a tremendous achievement, and revealed the score in absolutely new aspects, intellectual, poetical and musical. [. . .][60]

(*MC* 56, no. 2, January 8, 1908, pp. 21 f.)

44

In its account of the second performance of "Tristan und Isolde", under Mahler, the Press says:

"Many persons who heard the last act of 'Tristan und Isolde' [. . .] wondered whether Mahler would have dared to present Wagner's score in such abbreviated form abroad, or whether he had reserved this slashing for the 'musical barbarians' of New York. [. . .]"

On the other hand, the Tribune finds Mahler's adjustments very satisfactory and says so [. . .] .

---

[60]Most of the full reviews in *MC* were written by Leonard Liebling (1874-1945), an American pianist and critic who joined the magazine in 1902, and became its editor-in-chief in 1911. From the very beginning, the critical stance of *MC* was pro-Mahler; it remained so until the end, 'deviating' only on very rare occasions.

In spite of the length of the Press arguments, its critic is wrong this time, and THE MUSICAL COURIER awards the decision to the Tribune critic.[61] As Mahler gives "Tristan und Isolde", the work appears at its best, shorn of much useless detail and musical tautology. There is nothing important or essential left out in the Mahler reading, and it is in all respects the best this town has experienced.

(MC 56, no. 3, January 15, 1908, p. 22)

45

[. . .] In his native land Mr. Mahler is an exceedingly distinguished and influential person, and his fame has spread to the four corners of the artistic world. [. . .] He is, in fact, one of the most illustrious of living conductors, and he is a composer of great skill, amazing endurance, and boundless ambition [. . .]

The manner in which Mr. Mahler's conception of the "Tristan" score was made known conveyed, it may be said at the start, a suggestion of portentousness that was somewhat unfortunate [. . .]

Mr. Mahler possessed, seemingly, the order of mind that is called analytical. [. . .] His attitude is detached, rigorously objective. [. . .] His reading is indescribably lucid, exquisitely calculated, extraordinary in its finesse, its poise, its distinction and dignity of plan.

But Mr. Mahler fails, in considerable measure, to lay bare the heart of this music. [. . .] It is not extravagant to say that so tame, so ineffectual, a performance of the last act of this music drama as that achieved by Mr. Mahler has not been heard in New York [. . .]

In the matter of tempo, Mr. Mahler does not appear to have that sure and instinctive sense of what is appropriate and inevitable which, as Wagner conceived, is the ultimate test of fitness in a conductor. [. . .]

It should be said, in conclusion of this brief discussion, that Mr. Mahler sees fit to cut the music of "Tristan" with ruthlessness and a lack of regard for its dramatic relationships that are, one must confess, a little shocking. [. . .]

(Lawrence Gilman in Harper's Weekly 52, January 25, 1908, p. 30)

---

[61]Among the critics on the dailies, Krehbiel had the dubious distinction of being attacked and ridiculed most often and most mercilessly in *MC* (that is, by Blumenberg). This praise, therefore, however faint, represented a notable exception. (Concerning the question of operatic cuts, s.a. **45**, **145**, Note 18, Chapter II, **146** and **147**.)

46

[. . .] In ordering fifteen rehearsals[62] for "Don Giovanni", Mahler [. . .] is following the precedence of the legitimate school of opera of the Continent of Europe, and proving what respect he has for Mozart's profound work, which is usually thrown aside in New York as an evidence of what a few "stars" can do.

(*MC* 56, no. 2, January 8, 1908, p. 20)

47

"New York's musical public—especially the opera going public— comprises the most highly educated audiences in the world".

This statement was made by Mr. Heinrich Conried, and it came frankly and without any qualifications. [. . .] A HERALD reporter had gone to interview the impresario of the Metropolitan Opera House a couple of days ago on the subject of operatic conditions prevailing here, and to ask his view of the attitude of the opera going public of the present season.

[. . .]

"[. . .] Mr. Conried, do you find that in the matter of operatic novelties the public is as eager and as responsible as it ought to be, if it is, as you say, 'the most highly educated audience in the world'?"

"It is probably as eager as any in the world and doubtless more appreciative than the public of most other cities".

[. . .]

"When I succeeded Maurice Grau it was my ambition to rescue the patrons of this institution from repetitions of 'Faust' and 'Romeo et Juliette'[63] and the like. I built ambitious plans and remodelled the répertoire so that after my first season there was little danger of falling back into the old rut."

[. . .]

"The sum and total of my experiences [. . .] taught me that once a satisfying répertoire is formed as a nucleus, it is only possible to add a reasonable amount of new works each season, and these must be fully rehearsed before the season begins. [. . .].

---

[62]In the essay that precedes the documents for the 1909-1910 season, I mention the fact that we are relatively uninformed as to the amount of rehearsing Mahler was allowed (or was expected to do) at the Metropolitan. This document is rare in that it contains quantitative information (s.a. Note 10, p. 252).

[63]*Faust* and *Roméo et Juliette* - operas by Charles Gounod, the first one premièred in 1859, the second one in 1867.

"Any other scheme is impossible so long as it is necessary to give opera performances every day in the week, twice on Saturday and a Sunday concert."

[...]

"The way to please the public [is] to let it consult its own pleasure in the matter of opera. [...] Gradually the public gets to hear the novelties and from them it chooses its favorites and adds them mentally to its beloved operas.

"I can give you a good example [...] You will admit that today Puccini's 'La Boheme' is one of the most popular of operas here. Well, it took years for the public to wake up to its beauties. At first it drew hardly at all; then gradually its friends increased, until today I have but to announce 'La Boheme' in order to assure myself of a sold out house."

[...]

"Is there any way of finding out what the New York operatic public desires?"

"No", admitted the impresario, "for the public's taste changes in opera as it does in books and plays. The best you can do is to hope to please and continue trying until you succeed in doing so."

[...]

"If the foreign success of an opera or of a singer could always be duplicated in this country the trials of the impresario would be minimized tremendously - then all I would have to do would be to watch the public operatic barometer in Vienna, Berlin, Paris and London in order to secure successes for the Metropolitan. But the New York public claims the right to choose and judge for itself. That is absolutely its privilege, and since it pays for its opera, it has the right to select what it pays for."

[...]

"Do you think the native public is spoiled in the matter of great singers?"

"It is thoroughly spoiled in that respect. It wants nothing but the best that the world affords."

"Then there is no hope of ever again gathering an ensemble without a sprinkling of great stars?"

"No, I see no such possibility, for New York opera lovers demand the best that is to be heard, and they show more interest in singers, frequently, than they do in the operas themselves."

[...]

"The present operatic conditions," said Mr. Conried, as though he were totalling up the sum of his experiences, "is the result of giving the public what it demands. When I first began to direct the affairs of the opera house the subscription amounted to about $280,000; now, before the opening of the present season, the subscription was more than

$500,000 - it had doubled within four years.

"That is the conclusive proof of my theory - namely, to give the public what it wants. You cannot force the public to like certain operas any more than you can force it to like certain dishes. Both are matters of taste. Knowing that the opera impresario has but to give the public what he thinks it will like, not what he thinks it ought to hear, I have tried to do the former, and I am perfectly satisfied with the manner in which the public has supported my efforts. Should I not be?"

With this unanswered query the interview was concluded. And as the HERALD reporter went out into the sunlit Broadway he asked himself, Does any one really know what the public wants, either in matters operatic or theatrical? Nor did there seem to be any use in asking the public what it wants on the stages of its theatre and opera house, for does the public know? The least an impresario can do, anyhow, is to find out by experimenting extravagantly; and the most he can do is to be monumentally patient about it all.

(*NYH*, January 5, 1908, 3. Section, p. 12)

48

Gustav Mahler [. . .] is the man who just now is most likely to be chosen for the place of Heinrich Conried when he vacates it at the close of the present season.

A week ago, in fact up to the very day he made his debut, Mr. Mahler was not viewed as a serious contender for the position [. . .] But he has so completely upset advance reports concerning his methods—which were to the effect that he was a musical despot, obtaining results in the harshest ways—that he stands today in a light which many others vainly have endeavored to reach.

Foreign reports recently received here mentioned Gatti-Casazza,[64] director for ten years of La Scala at Milan, as the probable new head of the Metropolitan.

[. . .] One member of the Metropolitan Opera Company, though asking not to be directly quoted, said that it certainly looked as though it were not necessary to go much further to find the future artistic head of the organization. [. . .]

(*NYW*, January 5, 1908, 2. edition, Want Directory, p. W1.)

---

[64]Giulio Gatti-Casazza (1869-1940) - Italian impresario and opera director. He was artistic director of La Scala of Milan from 1898, and artistic director of the Metropolitan Opera from 1908 to 1935.

49
HOTEL MAJESTIC, NEW YORK

[Early 1908]

Dear Herr Gutmann,[65]

As a result of Conried's resignation and my refusal to take his place, I'm afraid everything here is now in a state of flux, so I do not yet know whether and, if so, for how long I am to return here next season. [. . .]

(*MSL*, p. 311; original German in *GMB*, p. 335)

50
HOTEL MAJESTIC, NEW YORK

Evening of 20. January [1908]

Dear [Roller],[66]

This in great haste to give you notice (quite official) of the imminent visit of Mr. *Cottenet*,[67] an influential member of the *management* of the Metropolitan Opera, who is tomorrow embarking for Italy, whence he will proceed, a few days after you receive this letter, to Vienna. - He is going to Vienna for the sole purpose of seeing you, in the hope of obtaining your services for the opera here.

The following for your guidance.

In general.

As a result of the *absolute* incompetence and fraudulent activities of those who have for years had control over the stage in matters of business and art (managers, producers, stage managers, etc.), almost all of whom are immigrants, the situation at the Opera is bleak. -

The audiences here, and all the factors affecting the artist—not least the board themselves (most of whom are multimillionaires)—though corrupt and misguided are—in contrast with 'our people'[68] in Vienna

---

[65]Emil Gutmann (1877-19??) - German concert agent. At this time he was situated in Munich, where he organized the first performance of Mahler's Eighth Symphony in 1910.

[66]Alfred Roller (1864-1935) - Painter, important figure in the Vienna Secession. From 1903, he was chief of stage design at the Vienna Opera, where he remained until 1909.

[67]Rawlins Lowndes Cottenet (1866-1951) - Socialite, member of the Metropolitan Board from 1908 to 1950. Friend of many famous musicians (*e.g.*, Kreisler, Hofmann, Heifetz), he was also an amateur composer.

[68]'our people' - according to a translator's note in *MSL*, this expression is "sometimes" used by Jews in reference to other Jews."

(among whom I also include the Aryan gentry)—*unsophisticated*, hungry for novelty, and in the highest degree eager to learn. -

The position here is as follows: *Conried* has long been quite discredited here. - He has put himself beyond the pale mainly by being unfair and tactless. - The management (i.e. the millionaire board) has sacked him. - At the same time it was planned to appoint me in his place - this even before I arrived. - My (to me incomprehensible) resounding success evidently gave the whole affair impetus. - As you have guessed, I quite decisively refused. But I expressed my willingness to continue assisting the management, in some capacity, in artistic matters, and in any case to continue conducting and producing. - I'm afraid in these circumstances I have little influence on future developments. - The management plan, first of all, to appoint the present director of *La Scala*, manager of the Metropolitan Opera, and to appoint *Toscanini,* [69] a *very well-thought-of* conductor, to take charge of Italian opera, and hand, as it were, German opera over to me. - But this is all still in the air. For my part, I shall first have to decide how it all appeals to me. -

But now the main thing!

I have proved to the management (or rather, to one of them, the prime mover) beyond doubt that it is *above all* the *stage* here that needs a new master, and that I know only one man with the artistic and personal ability to clear up the mess. - At the same time I assured them (and I am still working on these lines) of the necessity of handing over the stage, and everything to do with it, lock, stock and barrel, to this man. Rather the way I always saw our position in Vienna. - I could write much more about this. Personally, I must tell you you will find here the *most ample* funds and the finest company—no intrigues—no red tape. - In a word, the most splendid sphere of activity I could wish for you. If I could take over the directorship, I shouldn't waste a word. But since you would have to deal with someone about whom I know nothing at all (the Italian from La Scala - or whoever it may be), I must advise caution. - Above all, should you receive an official offer—which is not yet certain—you must secure yourself complete freedom of action and authority over everything concerning the *stage*.

At least the position you have in Vienna.

You must above all insist on coming over here as soon as possible to see to everything for yourself and inform yourself while the season is still on. (The management will meet your every wish, if they see you are serious about it.)

---

[69] Arturo Toscanini (1867-1957) - Celebrated Italian conductor. After 10 years as conductor at La Scala, he joined the Metropolitan Opera in 1908.

For your information, you would have a season of approximately five months here - and could use some of the holiday for your preparations. **Last not least** - I think you can demand a salary of 15,000 dollars (75,000 marks). But to be on the safe side - in all these matters plead ignorance of the conditions and ask for time to think things over. You could perhaps ask the management to conduct all negotiations, on your behalf, with me personally here, since I am by now thoroughly familiar with conditions here and also with your needs and expectations. - Regarding the 15,000 dollars - if this point is raised, do not be too *firm*. The fact is I don't yet know exactly how far we can go, because the position you must demand does not yet exist at this opera house. - It would be best if you could arrange to hand over negotiations on this matter *to me* on the grounds that only I am *in a position* to deal impartially with both your interests and conditions - and that you know too little of conditions here.

Seize the opportunity, my dear fellow, if you receive an offer and if there is nothing to detain you in Vienna. - The people here are tremendously unspoilt - all the crudeness and ignorance are - *teething troubles*. *Spite* and hypocrisy are found only among our dear immigrant compatriots. Here the dollar *does not reign supreme* - it's merely easy to earn. Only one thing is respected here: *ability* and *drive*! Well, I hope I've now given you all the information you need on that score.

Everything here is generous and healthy - but ruined by the immigrant *canaille* - I am writing in wild haste - it is only half an hour ago that I was authorized to write this letter, and the ship leaves tomorrow morning.

My wife has been confined to bed for the last week (poor thing). She sends her affectionate regards. We received your card today. Very best wishes, old friend, and keep a very cool head when Mr. Cottenet comes. What impresses these people most is what you have in high degree: *resolution* - calmness without chill.

Yours,
Mahler

I almost forgot something *important*. You have been given a bad name by those dubious gentry who guessed I was going to propose you. They say you "squander millions and there would not be enough for you in New York". -

I explained to the management that you spent great sums of money in the *right place*, which in fact meant you were *very economical*.

The (*very munificent*) board found this entirely plausible.

But in discussion it is essential to present yourself as *shrewd and capable* in financial matters. This will put their minds at rest, and then here it will be all the easier for you to ask for whatever you need.

Once again: None of this is yet settled. My own refusal may yet bring about some quite unforeseen situation.

But *in any case*, before tying yourself down in any way in *Vienna*, let me know *first*.

(*MSL*, pp. 309ff.; original German in *GMB*, pp. 324-327)

51
HOTEL MAJESTIC, NEW YORK

4 February 1908

Dear Herr Reitler,[70]

[...]

That I turned down the offer here you will of course have realized from my having once told you my main reasons for giving up my position in Vienna. And I am so firm in this belief that I must not tie myself down that even the incredible allurements that New York has to offer— *unlimited* funds and a salary that would sound fantastic in Vienna (300,000 crowns for six months plus some extras)—could not sway me.

[...]

(*MSL*, p. 313; original German in *GMB*, p. 328)

52

Mme. Nordica[71] was hostess at a large musicale last night in Sherry's, which was remarkable for the number of celebrated men and women who accepted the diva's invitation. [...] After the musicale, supper for almost 400 guests was served.

[...] Mme. Nordica's supper partner was Joseph H. Choate, ex-Ambassador to Great Britain. Stuyvesant Fish escorted Mrs. Choate and William K. Vanderbilt took in Mrs. Fish. Mrs. Vanderbilt's partner was Mark Twain. [...] Among Mme. Nordica's guests [was] [...] Gustav Mahler [...]

(*NYT*, January 13, 1908, p. 7)

---

[70]Josef Reitler (1883-1948) - Austrian music critic (*Neue Freie Presse*) and music educator. He emigrated to the United States in the 1930's.

[71]Lillian Nordica [Norton] (1857-1914) - American-born dramatic soprano; especially valued for her interpretation of Wagnerian roles. Starred at the Metropolitan from 1891 to 1910.

53

That Gustav Mahler interests conductors was shown yesterday afternoon, when at least four—Alfred Hertz,[72] Walter Damrosch, Frank van der Stucken,[73] and Victor Herbert[74]—went to hear his interpretation of "Tristan und Isolde" at the Metropolitan Opera House. [. . .]

(*NYT*, January 19, 1908, Part Three, p. 4)

54

Official announcement of the selection of Heinrich Conried's successor as directing manager of the Metropolitan Opera House is expected soon. It is understood that Gatti-Casazza, head of La Scala at Milan, will be the choice of the board of directors.

Rawlins L. Cottenet, a member of the board, sailed yesterday for Italy, where, it is presumed, he will confer with Gatti-Casazza. [. . .]

"We have decided not to discuss for publication anything bearing on the conduct of the opera house next season", said one of the board members. [. . .]

"We want to give better opera than any one else, and it is our aim to make the Metropolitan a sort of national house. For that reason we shall do all we can to make our directing heads as strong as possible."

[. . .]

With Gatti-Casazza as artistic head of the Metropolitan, Gustav Mahler as one of the chief musical directors and an American skilled in operatic business methods, it is pointed out a foundation for an institution such as is the aim of the present board would be secured.

(*NYW*, January 22, 1908, 2. edition, p. 7)

---

[72]Alfred Hertz (1872-1942) - German conductor, he was engaged by the Metropolitan Opera in 1902, where he remained until 1915. He conducted the first American performances of *Parsifal*, *Salome*, and *Der Rosenkavalier*.

[73]Frank van der Stucken (1858-1929) - American composer and conductor; studied with Grieg and Liszt. He conducted in Cincinnati and directed the College of Music from 1895 to 1907.

[74]Victor Herbert (1859-1924) - Irish-born American composer, cellist and conductor. He founded his own orchestra in 1904. He was one of the earliest American composers of film music.

Plate 18. Alfred Roller. (*RSM*, "Bilder," p. 26)

Plate 19. Alfred Hertz, conductor at the Metropolitan Opera from 1902
to 1915. (Kolodin, *op. cit.*, following p. 614)

55

Mozart's "Don Giovanni" was given for the first time this season at the Metropolitan Opera House last evening.[75] [. . .] Much was expected of Mr. Mahler's direction of the performance, which he controlled and dominated with results that were in many ways admirable. The most significant feature of it was in the matter of tempo, which in several places differed from what lovers of Mozart's masterpiece here are accustomed to. [. . .] The result [in some cases] did not carry conviction. He presented the opera in two acts, as the composer wrote it, instead of dividing it into four, as is usually done. [. . .] Mr. Mahler himself played the accompaniments of the secco recitatives as the conductor was expected to do in Mozart's day.[76] [. . .] there was much that was delightful in the finish and point of the phrasing and the elasticity of much of the orchestra's playing.

(*NYT*, January 24, 1908, p. 7)

56

Though Mozart's "Don Giovanni" as performed under the direction of Mr. Mahler [. . .] was not an unalloyed delight, it came near to that, and even more, in some of its features, notably those in which the distinguished conductor could give expression to his wishes unhampered by the shortcomings of the stage folk. [. . .] Mr. Mahler, it was plain, attempted to recreate the opera as it was in the period of the composer, both in spirit and in matter [. . .] [although] he refused to follow the traditional tempi in a few instances, generally to the grievous disappointment of his hearers.

[. . .] This notice must not close without a word of praise, which cannot be made warm enough for Mr. Mahler's treatment of the orchestral part. The Metropolitan's walls have never echoed to anything so exquisite as last night's instrumental music. Mr. Mahler used the full string complement of the Metropolitan Orchestra, but the Mozartean list of wood and brass wind instruments. But the volume of tone was that

---

[75]The complete cast was as follows: Donna Anna - Eames; Donna Elvira - Gadski; Zerlina - Sembrich; Don Giovanni - Scotti; Don Ottavio - Bonci; Leporello - Chaliapine; Masetto - Dufriche; Commandant - Blass. The changes in this cast were somewhat more extensive than had been the case with *Tristan*. On April 3, for example, Zerlina was sung by Farrar, Donna Elvira by Fornia, Leporello by Blass, Masetto by Baracchi, and the Commandant by Mühlmann.
[76]Mahler had revived this practice as early as 1890 when he was director of the Royal Hungarian Opera in Budapest. His "innovation" had a mixed reception then.

appropriate to the ideal house for which also the singers sang. The effect was ravishing.

(*NYTrib*, January 24, 1908, p. 7)

57

Mr. Mahler is known in Europe as a great interpreter of Mozart, and much was expected of him. Much was received. Doubtless Mr. Mahler would himself be the first to declare that the performance was not ideal; but it was made in the spirit of an ideal which has hitherto been as far from Metropolitan Opera House presentations of "Don Giovanni" as the equator from the poles. [. . .] Mr. Mahler treated "Don Giovanni" not as a collection of set pieces for singers, but as a drama in music. [. . .] The beauty of [the singers'] arias was enhanced by the exquisite sense of proportion which was present in the interpretation, and the interest of the audience in them was heightened by the restoration of the continuity of the dramatic thought.

(*NYS*, January 24, 1908, p. 7)

58

It would be [. . .] a trial of patience to discuss the Leporello of Mr. Chaliapine,[77] who seems to conceive all his characters as if they had been dug out of the muck of Gorky's[78] stories of Russian low life. Such a vulgarism the companion (for companion though servant he is) of a Spanish nobleman!

(*NYTrib*, January 28, 1908, p. 7)

59

To the Editor of the Tribune.

Sir: If you would enter a protest against the reengagement of Mr. Chaliapine another season I am sure you would have many supporters. The coarseness and vulgarity of his representations are an insult to the patrons of the Metropolitan Opera House. And that our dainty Mme.

[77]Feodor Chaliapine (1873-1938) - Celebrated Russian-born bass baritone. He became known early for his realistic acting.
[78]Maxim Gorky [Peshkov] (1868-1936) - Significant Russian writer, best known for the stark realism of his stories and novels.

Sembrich[79] should be compelled to appear on the stage with him is an insult to her as well. [. . .]

An indignant subscriber.

(*NYTrib*, February 9, 1908, Part Five, p. 4)

60

[Postmark: New York, 17 February 1908]

Dear [Hammerschlag],[80]

It is rather awful of me not to have given any sign of life before this. After a performance of *Don Giovanni* with Italian singers, among whom you probably know only Bonci[81] (Ottavio) and Sembrich (Zerlina), I thought of you intensely, regretting not having the faithful companion of my Mozart experiences beside me. *And in spite of the fact* that the singing was almost unsurpassable, I yearned for my Vienna production, which Mozart too, I think, would have liked better.

But if I were young and had the energy I squandered during the ten years in Vienna, something might perhaps be brought about here that we groped for, as an ideal, in Vienna: the exclusion of any commercial consideration whatsoever. For the decisive bodies here are *so* fair and the means at their disposal are so unlimited. You will already have heard that the stockholders (i.e. the owners of the Opera) offered me the directorship with absolute authority, and that I firmly rejected it. I have not changed my views on the nature of the whole institution. Five years ago, however, I should not have been able to resist such an alluring offer. The climate, the people and the extremely generous conditions suit me extraordinarily well. [. . .]

(*MSL*, p. 316; original German in *GMB*, p. 330)

61

Two facts became apparent yesterday in the question of the Directorship of the Metropolitan Opera House - that Mr. Conried's health will not

---

[79]Marcella Sembrich [P. Marcelline Kochańska] (1858-1935) - Polish-born American soprano. Following her peak years as a celebrated member of the Metropolitan Opera (1902-1909), she became a sought after teacher.
[80]Paul Hammerschlag (1860-1933) - Viennese banker and business man, he was one of the founders of the Wiener Konzertverein.
[81]Alessandro Bonci (1870-1940) - Celebrated Italian tenor, he was considered Caruso's chief rival early in the century. From 1906 on, he appeared frequently in the United States.

permit him to remain at his post much longer, and that Gustav Mahler will not work under an Italian Director.

[...]

The Directors of the opera company are said to have held a secret meeting in one of the uptown hotels to which Gustav Mahler was invited. The proposition of a new Directorship was broached to him, and it was suggested to him, it is said, that he and Toscanini, the Italian conductor at La Scala, should divide the orchestra.

The German conductor is said to have flatly refused this offer, as he has made a contract with the Conried Metropolitan Opera Company. He is said to be willing at present to work under no new Director, although he does not care for the Directorship himself.

Mr. Mahler could not be seen last night, and most of the Directors, acting on their recent decision to keep still, would say nothing. [...]

(*NYT*, January 30, 1908, p. 1)

62

"Tannhäuser", Paris version, was sung for the first time this season at the Metropolitan last night. [Conductor Alfred] Hertz should take a few lessons in artistic restraint from his confrere, Mahler. His idea of a Bacchanale effect was to let loose the brass and percussion to do their worst. And they did. He fairly hurled himself at the orchestra and led with such a heavy hand that some of his climaxes were positively brutal.

(*NYW*, January 31, 1908, p. 7)

63

[...] Mme. Emmy Raabe-Burg[82] chose a varied and well made list of songs for her first New York concert last evening at Mendelssohn Hall, in support of her title, as given on the house bill, of coloratura soprano. [After Rossini, Spohr, Schumann, Schubert, Mozart and Brahms, the newcomer offered] a series of modern songs, by composers ranging from Richard Strauss to Raff[83] and from Gustav Mahler to Mrs. Beach.[84]

---

[82]Krehbiel's low opinion of this singer, and the fact that her name does not appear in any reference work known to me, imply that she was an amateur. In the review, she is identified as the wife of the stage director (also an "admired comedian") of the Irving Place German Theatre. - No programme or review known to me identifies the song (or songs) by Mahler included on this recital.

[83]Joseph Joachim Raff (1822-1882) - Prolific Swiss composer, member of the Liszt-Bülow circle.

[84]Amy Mary Beach (1867-1944) - American composer and pianist.

[...]

Despite [her] natural gifts the singer's performances last evening were often disappointing. Her sustained tones were uneven in quality and her attacks were slovenly. Fluent and agreeable in rapid passages, her singing failed of conviction and authority. There is a great gulf between the mere possession of a pretty voice and the acquirement of the art that makes its disclosure a source of musical pleasure. [...]

(NYTrib, February 2, 1908, p. 9)

64

To the Editor of the New York Times:

In view of the widespread interest taken by the opera-going public in the present state of affairs concerning a change in the management of the Metropolitan Opera House, I beg leave to call your attention to the following:

The Metropolitan Opera House is in a way a National institution, and the music-loving public looks to it as an institution in which only the best singers, orchestra and chorus should be heard. As it now appears settled that Conried will retire, his administration could be dismissed as a thing of the past, were he alone to blame for all the errors. How can certain Directors of the Conried Opera Company explain their action a short time ago in signing a statement given to the press, in which they state that New York never has had better opera than under Conried, and that they were satisfied with him; when it would now appear that these same men were then contemplating getting rid of him for the head of an Italian music publishing house! Conried may be to blame for many things, but certain Directors of his opera company are nearly as much to blame as he is. The head of the Italian publishing house would naturally have tried to give those operas in which his house was interested, not to speak of certain other well-known disqualifications.

These same Directors up to this time seemed to think that the destiny of the Metropolitan was entirely in their hands, and that they could engage any man for Director in Chief they wished to; that they could push to the front at the expense of the public any particular favorite of theirs, and that they could absolutely dictate what operas should be given and how they should be cast. Fortunately the Italian publisher has been eliminated from the field, not through the foresight of these Directors, but through the efforts of the Metropolitan Real Estate Company that owns the Opera House.

Now that the owners of the Metropolitan Opera House have exerted their authority in regard to a betterment in the management, it is to be hoped that they will keep the Directors of the so-called Conried Opera Company under their careful observation, and compel them to give New York the best. In doing so they would force certain of the Directors who are now running the Conried Opera Company to desist from their present practice of often producing poor operas with a great tenor and sometimes a great baritone, with the rest of the cast unfit to be heard.

AN OLD METROPOLITAN OPERA HOUSE HABITUE.
New York, Feb. 1, 1908.

(*NYT*, February 2, 1908, p. 8)

65

In the gossip about a forthcoming change in the management of the Metropolitan Opera House there has been some talk of the establishment of a dual directorship. There is reason to believe that this plan has been seriously considered and may be put into effect. [...]

It is well known that the melody and grace of Italian opera are more highly appreciated by many of the supporters of the Metropolitan than the best qualities of the German music drama. The success of Mr. CAMPANINI[85] as a conductor in the rival house has led to negotiations for the services of the most renowned of all Italian conductors, Mr. TOSCANELLI [sic]. That Mr. GUSTAVE [sic] MAHLER will conduct all the German performances, and those of some other modern works, next season, is no longer a secret. There will be nothing new in this employment of different orchestral conductors for different operas.

The wisdom of the two directors, however, one whose taste, skill and training are supposed to best fit him for selecting the artists to sing in the German and French operas, and attending to the details of their production, while the other devotes himself to the Italian works, seems dubious to an outsider. There is always danger in divided authority. One competent director, who thoroughly understands the operatic requirements of New York, who has had ripe experience in the musical field, who is known to be enterprising and tactful, ought to be able to produce better results than two directors with opposing views.

But it cannot be doubted that the gentlemen who control the destinies of the Metropolitan Opera House are the best judges of the needs of the institution they support. If the dual directorship is decided upon it will only be after patient and intelligent consideration of every problem the

[85]Cleofonte Campanini (1860-1919) - Italian conductor. Having estabished his reputation in Italy, from 1906 he conducted in the United States, first at the Manhattan Opera, later in Chicago.

plan suggests. Mr. CONRIED's retirement after this season is inevitable. That ill-health compels an impresario so variously competent as he to retire to private life will be a cause for general regret. We have no doubt that the high standards observed in his term of management will be maintained.

(Editorial, *NYT*, February 2, 1908, p. 8)

66

ROME, Feb. 2 - Despite statements to the contrary, Signor Puccini, the composer, thinks Arturo Toscanini, director of the orchestra at La Scala, Milan, has been engaged as the successor of Heinrich Conried, director of the Metropolitan Opera House in New York.

(*NYT*, February 3, 1908, p. 1)

67

Heinrich Conried's relations to the Metropolitan Opera House remain unchanged, and this probably will be the case for a long time to come. Such was the deduction drawn from the results of the meeting of the board of directors of the Metropolitan Opera and Real Estate Company, held yesterday afternoon [. . .] A proposition for an extended lease of the opera house was presented to the board by a committee of directors of the Conried Metropolitan Opera Company. After a conference of almost two hours the matter was laid over until the next meeting, which will be called within a week.

[. . .] The present lease by which the Conried Metropolitan Opera Company rents the house from the Metropolitan Opera and Real Estate Company is personal in that it is framed to be operative only during the regime of Mr. Conried. The lease which is for a five years' term, was drawn two years ago, and, therefore, is to run, unless altered by agreement, until 1911.

It was reported yesterday that the proposed new lease would be binding even if Mr. Conried should cease to be the managing director. This report, coming as it does after so many rumors regarding a change in the directorship, is most significant. The fact that after a prolonged meeting the board of directors gave out only a brief report stating that action was deferred is interpreted by persons familiar with the situation to mean that Mr. Conried's friends are standing by him and will refuse to consider any change that might look toward eliminating him from the Metropolitan.

(*NYTrib*, February 8, 1908, p. 7)

68

Mr. Gustav Mahler, German conductor at the Metropolitan Opera House, has proved himself to be a wit and a diplomatist. At the Vienna Imperial Opera he was tsar, and all of his friends and those who opposed him as well predicted he would find the artistic arrangement of things at the Metropolitan Opera House so impossible that he would pack bag, baggage and baton and return to Europe in less than ten days after his arrival in New York.

But they were mistaken; for he has handled his singing and orchestral forces so deftly here that, instead of finding him a dictator, they are eager to do his bidding, and that is a remarkable feat, for every one knows that singers and snakes cannot be charmed too easily.

Occasions for his ready tact have arisen from time to time. One arose at a rehearsal of "Die Walkuere" recently. The chorus of the Valkyries is a difficult one, and it is usually filled by as many principals as the ensemble of an opera house can spare for it. When the Metropolitan Valkyries were assembled, Mr. Mahler heard them sing the chorus, and at its close he said: -

"Ladies, I must pay you the complement that never before have I heard such voices assembled for the Valkyries chorus - not even in Vienna!"

At this the singers fairly beamed with delight. Then Mr. Mahler held up his hand and motioned that he was about to continue: -

"And now ladies, finding that you are possessed of such wonderful voices, I must ask you to use them."

That was all, but its subtlety escaped none of the singers. And when the chorus was repeated it sounded different.

(*NYH*, February 9, 1908, 3. Section, p. 10)

69

"Die Walküre" was given for the first time this season[86] [. . .] under the direction of Mr. Gustav Mahler [. . .] The spirit of the drama had taken on a new embodiment. This was, of course, most notable in the orchestral

---

[86]The complete cast was as follows: Brünnhilde - Gadski; Sieglinde - Fremstad; Fricka and Waltraute - Kirkby-Lunn; Gerhilde - Alten; Ortlinde-Weed; Schwertleite - Wöhning; Helmwige - Fornia; Siegrune - Mattfeld; Grimgerde - Langendorff; Rossweisse - Jacoby; Siegmund - Burgstaller; Wotan - Van Rooy; Hunding - Blass. Some later performances had Leffler-Burkhard as Brünnhilde, Morena as Sieglinde, and Burrian or Dippel as Siegmund.

score. This Mr. Mahler infused with a new and exquisite sort of beauty. Like that of "Tristan", as he conceives it, it was much subdued, reduced to a lower plane of dynamics. But on this plane everything had a projection of outline and phrasing, clearness, and incisiveness of modelling, depth and richness of colour, intensity and dramatic expression. [. . .] Mr. Mahler's tempos are free and full of the subtlest variations; they are spurred to dramatic life and potency, yet how lovingly can he linger over certain passages charged with a special emotion and fill them with a rich expressiveness!

(*NYT*, February 8, 1908, p. 7)

70

Last night Gustav Mahler doubtless learned some of the reasons why his journey from Vienna to New York was likely to result in disappointment to himself and wonder to many operagoers. In the Imperal Opera of Vienna Mr. Mahler was in a position to dictate. He was the intendant [sic] and his word was law. At the Metropolitan Opera House he is the principal conductor of German operas and he has only the prerogatives of the conductor. And he cannot always exercise those to his own satisfaction. [. . .] His conducting was finely planned and finely carried out. [. . .] If everything else in the performance had been as good as the orchestral part the sum of results would have been to the fame of Wagner and the peace of Mr. Mahler's mind.

(*NYS*, February 8, 1908, p. 8)

71

[. . .] There was a new element in the treatment of the orchestra under the hands of Mr. Mahler. His influence was less noticeable on the stage, where there were pictures and doings which reminded the audience [. . .] of the unhappy rut into which the Wagnerian representations have been permitted to fall at the Metropolitan [. . .]

(*NYTrib*, February 8, 1908, p. 7)

72

The retirement of Heinrich Conried, director of the Metropolitan Opera House, to be succeeded by the joint management of M. Giulio Gatti-

Casazza and Herr Andreas Dippel,[87] was officially verified yesterday afternoon. [. . .] Herr Dippel would assume the management of the business details immediately, and M. Gatti-Casazza would arrive in this country in March, to arrange for assuming his duties as artistic manager. The engagement of Gustav Mahler, the leader whose success during a brief season here has rivalled that of Campanini at the Manhattan, and of Arturo Toscanini of La Scala, Milan, is announced as conductors.

The reason for Herr Conried's retirement was given as ill health.

But more important than the announcement of the sweeping change of management is the decision on the part of the wealthy directors of the Metropolitan Company to remove the opera house from the realm of an institution for art. [. . .] The Metropolitan [. . .] now becomes [. . .] a national organization operated without a sense of profit.

(*NYW*, February 12, 1908, p. 1)

73

According to present arrangements, Mr. Otto H. Kahn will be president of the new Metropolitan Grand Opera Company, which succeeds the Conried Metropolitan Opera Company [. . .] at the end of the season.

(*NYH*, February 13, 1908, p. 10)

74

With the acceptance of Heinrich Conried's resignation as director, the Executive Board of the Metropolitan Opera and Real Estate Company, representing the Conried Metropolitan Opera Company, announced this week that in the future the policy of the institution will be to give opera for art's sake only and that all profits which may accrue from the undertaking will be devoted to a pension fund for the advancement of the opera house as an art institution.

(*MA* 7, no. 14, February 15, 1908, p. 1)

75

The introduction to New York of grand opera in English is now a certainty for next season, according to a statement made yesterday by

---

[87]Andreas Dippel (1866-1932) - German-born tenor, highly regarded for his Wagnerian roles in Vienna (1893-1898), Bayreuth, London and New York. Administrative manager of the Metropolitan Opera from 1908 to 1910.

Otto H. Kahn, chairman of the executive committee of the Metropolitan Opera Company. [. . .]

"It has been a dream of ours," said Mr. Kahn yesterday, "to produce English opera. Somehow the impression has been made that we intend to give translations of Italian, French and German opera. This is not so. We want to produce English opera as an addition to and not as a substitute for the operas that have heretofore been sung here. [. . .] It is likely that we will begin with Weber's 'Oberon'. It is not generally known that this was composed to an English libretto, so it will not be a translation, although it is more familiar in German.[88]

"It has been the idea of a number of directors for a long time now that the Metropolitan Opera House would be more truly a national institution if English opera were given there. Mr. Dippel, Mr. Mahler and I have discussed this recently and we believe that such a course would be an improvement. Of course, the details are not yet completed and the change in repertoire will be gradual. It will, moreover, aid native American talent, of which there will be no scarcity. [. . .] As opera in English becomes more frequently produced the inducements for native singers will increase. All this will add to the national educational value of the Metropolitan Opera House."

[. . .] Although the directors of the opera company are continuing to make additions to the corps of singers, Mr. Kahn said he wished it understood that Mr. Gatti-Casazza and Mr. Dippel would have full charge next season.

"We do not care to have people think", he said, "that the business men who are directors are to interfere in any way with the musical directors. [. . .]"

(NYTrib, February 14, 1908, p. 7)

76

HOTEL MAJESTIC

New York, 15 February 1908

My dear [Roller],

Meanwhile events here have been taking their inexorable course. The new management has been set up and the situation has clarified to the extent that those whose views will be immediately decisive in future, i.e. the representatives of the proprietors of the Opera House (millionaires), then Dippel, to whom the administration has been entrusted, and yours truly, who has so far been hovering as a kind of spirit over the waters and

---

[88]Carl Maria von Weber's opera had its première in 1826 in London, under the title *Oberon or the Elf King's Oath.*

will probably continue to do so in the future if circumstances remain unchanged, are now seriously discussing your appointment. I hope you will be receiving a telegram within the next few days, i.e. even before this letter arrives, suggesting that you should, to begin with, come here on an exploratory visit in the near future, that is, as soon as you can get away. During this visit everything is to be discussed and, I hope, also settled. First of all, whether you are willing and able to accept the position, what attitude you take towards the sitution you find here, and what influence you can exercise over future developments. It has been agreed between me and the powers that be that you should be engaged as *chief stage manager* in charge of all stage and theatrical matters, with complete authority within your own sphere - responsible only to the board. - From the way negotiations have been going I hope to get you a salary of 12,000 dollars (60,000 crowns) per annum. To judge from all the inquiries I have made, you will easily be able to save 7,000 dollars a year. - Whatever arrangements Mr. Cottenet is meanwhile making with you are already superseded, and you should act solely on this information from me. The best thing would be for you to take your holidays in April, arranging your trip to America so that you could return to Europe with us on 23 April, spending at least a *fortnight* here seeing exactly what your appointment will involve. - But what about your Vienna contract? Have you received it yet? If so, what are its terms? You will, of course, have to take that into consideration. - Let me know about that by return of post so that I know just where I stand! Fräulein Uchatius,[89] who lives here and often visits us, says she could not imagine a more splendid place for you and that you would find it immensely stimulating and satisfying here. I think so too. There is still everything to be done here, and you will be coming at just the right moment. It would be delightful if we could be together again, yet I cannot conceal from you that I shall be able to enjoy your company for only a short time. I do not intend to stay here long; but at least for next season, if I am still in good health. - However, this is *just between ourselves*! Very best wishes (in great haste) also to your wife, who, as far as I can judge, would be very happy here.

Yours as ever,
Mahler

(*MSL*, pp. 314f.; original German in *GMB*, pp. 328f.)

---

[89]Marie Uchatius (1882-1958) - She was a graphic artist; as a student of Roller, she graduated from the Kunstgewerbeschule.

Plate 20. Alma and Anna Mahler in 1909. (*HLG3*, Illustration 53)

77

HOTEL MAJESTIC, NEW YORK

Sunday, 16 February 1908

My dear Karl![90]

Many thanks for your kind letter. My conscience assaults me daily that I have not yet replied to it. - But you will understand if I tell you that I have absolutely no time here; for I am constantly loafing. - That is work one never sees the end of. My working schedule is of uncommon simplicity. When I arise, I have breakfast. Hereafter my conscience assaults me for a time (always depending on the weather). Afterwards I idle away my chores. Then comes lunch. Thereupon I must rest for a few hours on doctor's orders. When I get up, it is snack time. From then until dinner I would have some time. But those wretched habits are so difficult to conquer. Right - now and then I also conduct and hold rehearsals. -

When a letter arrives from Mama or you, it is a festive occasion for us (for me merely dimmed a bit by the blows [?] which I receive from conscience). -

We must chat about America a great deal during the summer. I now regard it as an awkward youth, whose incivilities one gladly overlooks as excesses of a driving life-force. - Whether the attractive youngster may not turn into a disgusting philistine later on, I will leave untouched. But certainly one finds here, as in Europe, that very small group of people because of whom life seems worth living. - Furthermore, we especially get to know everything from the most pleasant side, which is what people instinctively show the distinguished foreigner. - To spend a few weeks each year here will be, if it is granted to me, always pleasant for me; and I am determined that you, too, must one day experience first hand this life which is so extraordinarily exuberant and refreshing for a European. - Like all young peoples, the Americans are exceptionally grateful (regrettably, they gulp everything down, like children, with uncritical enjoyment - that is to say, strictly speaking there are consumers here for everything, the good as well as the bad). - If I were still theatre-oriented, I would have found here, as never before, the arena for my restless energies. Now I must be satisfied, however, with "stocking the larder" for Almschi and Gucki as well as I can. - You are no doubt kept informed about these things by Almsch.

It is quite new for me—after the Viennese wilderness—to find sympathy and thanks everywhere for the little bit that I am able to

[90]Carl Moll (1861-1945) - Austrian painter, one of the founders of the Vienna Secession. He was Alma Mahler's step father.

contribute. I live like a prima donna, am constantly preoccupied with my own person, and thus hope that this feared America will not harm me. -

The new developments at the Metropolitan Theatre will perhaps also bring Roller over. He would discover a field of activity the likes of which he could not have imagined in his wildest dreams. All the stories about America which circulate among us originate with that disgusting type of German you know as well as I do. The dregs of our society, who ascribe all misfortunes, which arise from their own incompetence and indolence, to "circumstances", and who, at the same time, make it more difficult for those who come after by causing the mistrust of foreigners to increase more and more. - This also appears to me as the chief danger to the young society here. - A truly *native* American is a *high-minded* and *capable* person. Make a note of this in any case, dear friend. What among this type is made to appear laughable to you out there, is always to be blamed on the immigrants who constantly bring everything native into disrepute. - As yet, the native soil is strong enough to overcome everything foreign. For how long? - that I cannot judge. - Almschi, who was rather miserable in every respect for the first 4 weeks, has been quite recovering for the past 2 weeks, thank God, and is—*touch wood!*—quite lively; and I intend to see to it that she remains so.

I cannot place Elizza[91] *here*. All specialities are overstaffed. I am truly sorry about it.

Now I must to rehearsal. - Perhaps I will soon overcome my idleness, and write more. For now, a thousand greetings for you and Mama, and thank you for your love.

Your old
Gustav[92]

78

The directors of the Metropolitan Opera Company—which succeeds the Conried Opera Company at the close of the present season—expect to close shortly a formal contract with Mr. Gustav Mahler for his services as conductor at the Metropolitan next winter.

By the terms of his contract with the Conried Opera Company, Mr. Mahler reserved the right to resign at the close of the present season in case Mr. Conried retired. Yesterday he availed himself of the rights of this clause and formally handed in his resignation.

This does not mean that Mr. Mahler is not to officiate as conductor at

[91]Elise Elizza (1870-1926) - Soprano at the Vienna Opera. Highly regarded by Mahler, she was a soloist at the première of *Das klagende Lied* (1901).
[92]For the German text, see Appendix, A12.

the Metropolitan next winter. On the contrary, it is verbally settled that
he will remain, although the final contract between him and the directors
of the new company has not yet been signed and sealed. It is expected
that this will be done in a few days, and then the matter of his return next
year will be absolutely settled.

(*NYH*, February 16, 1908, p. 13)

79

"The game is not worth the candle" [. . .] Just one week ago the
HERALD foretold exclusively what would happen and when it would
happen, and now that everything had occurred according to the
programme outlined in the HERALD, and the resignation of Mr.
Conried had been regretfully accepted by his directors and the
Metropolitan owners, the man who is soon to seek retirement and
health—at least for a period—sat at his desk and repeated: -

"The game is not worth the candle."

He did not say this in a spirit of regret, but it was uttered as by a man
who was taking inventory of his days and nights spent in the toils of his
duties.

"Which means," queried a HERALD reporter, "that if you had to do
it all over again you would not be persuaded into accepting the position
of director of this big opera institution?"

"I certainly would not. It is a post that is ruthless in the demands of its
exacting duties. No one—save he who has been unfortunate enough to
try to fill it—can know what its demands are."

[. . .]

"Then your principal sentiment on contemplating retirement is one of
relief, is it not?"

"I feel relieved to think the burden is about to be lifted and that then I
can regain my health. But there are other circumstances that make my
heart heavy. I hate to part company with the faithful heads of the various
business departments who have stood by me so devotedly; with the artists
who have surrounded me, and who have done so much and so well to
maintain and lift higher the Metropolitan's artistic standard. Many of
them have come to me with tears in their eyes and have expressed their
regret at my leaving. And last, but not least, I hate to part with the great
public who have never faltered in their encouragement, and whom it has
been my delight as well as my duty to serve. I hope they are satisfied with
my stewardship.

"There is compensation," concluded the director, "for all these years
of labor if that great public says 'Well done' and there is a note of

happiness as well as one of sadness in the parting, for my family and near friends smile at me once more, for they know that my worries are over. And, what is more, I am able to smile back at them, for now there is something else in my life besides directing an opera house. I retire as opera director to become [. . .] once more a human being. [. . .]"

(NYH, February 16, 1908, 3. Section, p. 11)

80

Respect for the verities of history seems to call for a few corrective observations on the information published in the newspapers yesterday, including The Tribune, concerning the personality, labors and achievements of the Milanese gentlemen, Giulio Gatti-Casazza and Arturo Toscanini, into whose hands the Metropolitan Opera Company has placed much of the future destiny of New York's chief lyrical establishment. [. . .]

Why indeed should it be thought necessary to give a certificate of good character to the director and conductor who are coming from Milan? No one ever asked the gentlemen who employ them to excuse themselves or offer explanations of their conduct. The wisdom or folly of their choice will be made manifest in time [. . .] It is therefore doubly unfortunate that an inspection of the certificate shows it to be invalid.

[. . .] Mr. Conried sold the Metropolitan's birthright for the Puccini pottage last year; there are no indications that there will be a change in the situation when the new directors take hold.

We are told of the skill of Signor Toscanini as a conductor of Wagner's operas and of the achievement of Signor Gatti-Casazza in creating a love for those operas in Italy. He found Wagner proscribed when he took charge of La Scala in 1898, and now Wagner is popular. This the strange tale; but historical records show that Wagner's operas and lyric dramas, nearly all of them, were performed in Italy for from ten to twenty years before Signor Gatti-Casazza came to the surface in Milan. [. . .] Wagner's works seem to have got along pretty well without the services of the present managers of the Teatro della Scala. Besides, the popular understanding of the case thus far has been that the German repertory at the Metropolitan next year was to be the concern of Messrs. Dippel and Mahler, and the Italian of Messrs. Gatti-Casazza and Toscanini. Under such circumstances it ought not to signify greatly that the director is the creator of the Wagner cult in Italy, and that the conductor can hum "Salome" without the book. [. . .]

(NYTrib, February 22, 1908, p. 7)

81

Under the head "Conried's Successor", the Milan correspondent of the "Tageblatt" of Berlin introduces Signor Gatti-Casazza to the readers of that journal, prefacing his account with the statement that he is less well known than Toscanini outside of Italy. His story of the manager's administration of La Scala is highly flattering to Signor Gatti-Casazza, though he makes some statements which cannot bear the test of inquiry. For instance, he says that Caruso,[93] Bonci, Storchio[94] and Tetrazzini[95] first demonstrated their ability at La Scala under his administration, whereas all four were well advanced in their career before they sang at La Scala, and Bonci, at least, was a member of the troupe before Gatti-Casazza appeared on the scene. [...]

(*NYTrib*, March 1, 1908, p. 9)

82

Neither of the two performances [of *Tristan* and *Die Walküre*] [...] was in any sense revolutionary, but it is quite otherwise with [...] "Don Giovanni", [...] since [Mahler] treats the opera in what is to modern opera goers an entirely novel and extraordinary manner. [...] Mahler has [...] restored the original score and in every way he has sought to produce the opera as Mozart wrote it [...]

(*The Philadelphia Inquirer*, February 16, 1908, p. 7a)

83

Don Giovanni in Philadelphia - Donna Elvira was to come on for her great aria, but she could not, because she was shut up in a little stage-property-room on the stage and the door had been forgotten. Mahler made one fermata after another, looked round to me with a charming smile and we both enjoyed the delightful impasse to the full. At last

---

[93]Enrico Caruso (1873-1921) - Celebrated Italian tenor. He was a regular member of the Metropolitan Opera ensemble from 1903 to 1920, although he continued to sing widely as a guest at other opera houses.
[94]Rosina Storchio (1876-1945) - Famed Italian soprano; made her debut in 1893 in Milan. She created the role of Madama Butterfly.
[95]Luisa Tetrazzini (1871-1940) - World renowned Italian soprano; made her debut in 1890 in Florence. At this time she was a member of Hammerstein's Manhattan Opera Company.

Gadski[96] burst boldly from one corner of the chamber in which she was enclosed after the whole structure had heaved and quivered. For a moment the back of the stage was revealed; then the corner was hurridly closed up behind her and the aria began. She sang it beautifully, far more beautifully than it was ever sung in our Ministry of Music, as we used to call the Opera in Vienna, with all its hundreds of rooms and corridors. Here it was different. It was a feast for the ear, not the eyes. Don Giovanni, Scotti;[97] Donna Anna, Fremstad; Elvira, Gadski; Zerline, Farrar;[98] Ottavio, Bonci; Leporello, Chaliapin.

(*AMM*, pp. 132f.; original German in *AME*, p. 163)

84

It was my honor and good fortune to have sung "Don Giovanni" and "Le Nozze di Figaro" under Maestro Mahler's direction. This gave me opportunities of judging the great musician's genius at close range. Suffice it to say that in all my career I remember no incidents with more delight nor any conductor with greater respect. [. . .]

(Antonio Scotti in *SFM*, p. 29)

85

Last night's performance of "Don Giovanni" [. . .], while it had its good points and was excellent and enjoyable in some important respects, left upon the whole a good deal to be desired [. . .] Mr. Mahler conducted with sympathy and skill, although he might advantageously have given the orchestra a looser rein; but why did he exclude the chorus from the stage at the close of the first act in the "trema, scellerato" number? That this innovation was an improvement is more than can be admitted.

(*The Philadelphia Inquirer*, February 19, 1908, p. 2)

---

[96]Johanna Gadski (1872-1932) - Renowned German dramatic soprano, one of the greatest Wagner-singers at the turn of the century. She was at the Metropolitan from 1900 to 1917. It appears that Alma's recollection of this performance was in error in respect to the cast: according to the review in the *Philadelphia Inquirer* (February 19, 1908, p. 2), Elvira was sung by Rita Fornia and Donna Anna by Marion Weed.
[97]Antonio Scotti (1866-1936) - Italian baritone, became famous after he joined the Metropolitan Opera. His most celebrated roles were Don Giovanni, Falstaff and Scarpia.
[98]Geraldine Farrar (1882-1967) - American soprano, pupil of Lilli Lehmann. Although she sang all over Europe, she spent the greatest part of her career (1906-1922) at the Metropolitan Opera.

86

Marie Uchatius, a young art-student, paid me a visit one day in the Hotel Majestic. Hearing a confused noise, we leaned out the window and saw a long procession in the broad street along the side of Central Park. It was the funeral cortège of a fireman, of whose heroic death we had read in the newspaper. The chief mourners were almost immediately beneath us when the procession halted, and the master of ceremonies stepped forward and gave a short address. From our eleventh-floor window we could only guess what he said. There was a brief pause and then a stroke on the muffled drum, followed by a dead silence. The procession then moved forward and all was over.

The scene brought tears to our eyes and I looked anxiously at Mahler's window. But he too was leaning out and his face was streaming with tears. The brief drum-stroke impressed him so deeply that he used it in the Tenth Symphony.[99]

(*AMM*, p. 135; original German in *AME*, p. 166)

87

Claude Debussy's opera "Pelléas et Mélisande," was produced for the first time in America last evening at the Manhattan Opera House.[100] [...] There has been a great curiosity on the part of the music-loving public not only in New York but in other musical centres as well to become acquainted with this remarkable product of twentieth century art [...]

The production was generally acknowledged to be a highly important one, on account of the position that Debussy has taken as the leader and most original exponent of a new departure in music; in the eyes of his admirers it was an importance comparable to the productions of "Parsifal" and "Salome". [...]

[99]The funeral in question was that of Charles W. Kruger, Deputy Chief of the Fire Department of the City of New York, who had been fatally injured while fighting a fire; the date of the funeral was February 16, 1908 (*AMM*, p. 384).

In the Tenth Symphony's performing version, reconstructed by Deryck Cooke, the muffled drum-strokes occur at the end of the second scherzo and at the beginning of the last movement.

[100]The Manhattan Opera House, built by Oscar Hammerstein on West 34th Street, was opened on December 3, 1906, with a seating capacity of 3,100. For four seasons it provided the Metropolitan Opera with competition so great that in the spring of 1910 the Metropolitan was forced to buy out Hammerstein (see *1909-1910*).

[Conductor Campanini] found the innermost secret of this most elusive of all music, and his rendering of the score was a marvel of sympathy, of subtle appreciation of the composer's purpose [. . .] Never, indeed, has the commanding genius of this great artist so completely established itself as in this achievement.

[. . .]

[The drama] is fascinating; and its fascination is now, and is likely long to be, inseparable from the music through which Debussy has heightened and deepened its significance. [The opera's] beauty is almost indefinable, strange and unaccustomed; but it is very real. It may be said to be, for the opera goer accustomed to all the wide gamut of musical expression from Gluck and Mozart to Wagner and even Strauss, almost a complete negative of all that has been hitherto accepted as music. It is a complete stranger to traditional art.

[. . .]

Debussy in this music is as original as it is given any creative artist to be in an art that is built upon the achievements of those who have gone before. It is comparable with no other music but his own. It is easy to say that but for Wagner and César Franck the score could not exist as it is, but that is scarcely more than to say that Debussy comes after those two masters in point of time. There are indeed a few traces of "Tristan", of "Parsifal", but they are not important. It is an artistic phenomenon that, as far as may be, begins with this composer. Whether it will end with him is something for the future to discover. [. . .]

(*NYT*, February 20, 1908, p. 7)

88

Mahler and I attended the New York première of Debussy's "Pelléas et Mélisande" at the Hammerstein Opera House.[101] It was an outstanding performance, quite in the spirit of the two authors Maeterlinck and Debussy. The decorations were fantastically created in grey and gold by

[101]As both the première of *Pelléas* at the Manhattan Opera and the opening night of Mahler's *Siegfried* at the Metropolitan took place on February 19th, the Mahlers could not have been in the first-night audience at the Manhattan. Given the coincidence of the two performances, and the relatively greater importance of the *Pelléas*-première, one may assume that the reviews of *Siegfried* were not written by the 'first-line' critics of the various papers.

Plate 21. Oscar Hammerstein. (*HLG3*, Illustration 13)

Plate 22. Mary Garden, the Manhattan Opera's prima donna.
(*COS*, Illustration 138)

a disciple of Puvis de Chavannes.[102] Périer,[103] Dufranne,[104] Mary Garden[105] sang. I asked Mahler about his impression of the music. "It is harmless", came the answer.

(Alma Mahler-Werfel, *Mein Leben*, Frankfurt a.M., S. Fischer Verlag, 1960, p. 48)

89

Last night [. . .] was the first time that Gustav Mahler conducted "[Siegfried]" here.[106] [. . .] He evidently gives the best that is in him to this score. The orchestra played as if fired with the spirit of the work. The forest music of the second act was played with the most exquisite nuances, and the love music in the last act mounted to mighty climaxes. There were times when Mr. Mahler did not hold in his orchestra. He urged his men to huge crescendos. The effect of these, following his usual moderation of tone, was tremendous.

(*NYT*, February 20, 1908, p. 7)

90

The centre of gravity in last night's doings [. . .] lay [. . .] in Mr. Gustav Mahler's conducting of the score. [. . .] After "Tristan" and "Die Walküre", it was no surprise to hear [. . .] a superbly vital and influential performance of "Siegfried".

[. . .] Carefully as the conductor avoided submerging the singers in floods of orchestral sound, he never left them stranded [. . .] by the too sudden or violent ebbing of the tonal tide. [. . .] Mr. Mahler's part in this "Siegfried" performance was both controlling and memorable.

(*NYTrib*, February 20, 1908, p. 7)

---

[102]Pierre-Cécile Puvis de Chavannes (1824-1898) - He was the leading French mural painter of his time, admired for his monumental, decorative, fresco style.
[103]Jean Périer (1859-1954) - Well known French baritone; created the role of Pelléas. He was also successful as a singer-actor on stage and in films.
[104]Hector Dufranne (1872-1951) - Belgian-born French baritone. He was especially successful in France and in America; he was celebrated for his character acting (*e.g.*, Mephistopheles).
[105]Mary Garden (1877-1967) - Celebrated Scottish soprano; she created the role of Mélisande. She joined the Chicago Opera in 1910, and directed it between 1921 and 1923.
[106]The complete cast was as follows: Brünnhilde - Fremstad; Erda - Kirkby-Lunn; Forest Bird - Alten; Siegfried - Burgstaller; Wanderer - Van Rooy; Alberich - Goritz; Mime - Reiss; Fafner - Blass. Beginning with the next performance, Siegfried was sung by Burrian.

91

[In] Mr. Mahler's [. . .] reading of the score [. . .] intellectual and temperamental traits, which in the music of "Tristan und Isolde" were perfectly paired with the more refined and subtle qualities of the work, failed to achieve a perfect exposition of the tremendous elemental force of the purely physical expression of "Siegfried".

Mr. Mahler was more scholarly than passionate in his reading. It was admirable, but it was not stirring. [. . .] It was immensely interesting, but it never overwhelmed.

(*NYS*, February 28, 1908, p. 5)

92

HOTEL MAJESTIC, NEW YORK

[Postmark: 24 February 1908]

My dear [Mengelberg],[107]

You will soon (I hope) be receiving from Boston a letter asking you to take over that (splendid) orchestra, as successor to Muck.[108] Schnelling,[109] with whom I discussed the matter yesterday, did say you were not very inclined to accept the position. As I can easily imagine your reasons, it is perhaps as well if I give you a little information, so that you get a clear picture of the conditions here, to avoid making too onesided a decision.

The position in Boston is the finest any musician could wish for. - It is the *first and highest* in this whole continent. A first-class orchestra which is only equalled by the *Viennese* one. A position of absolute authority. A social position that no musician can ever attain in Europe. - A public more eager to learn and more grateful than any European can imagine. Your New York experiences are no criterion. Here in New York the theatre is the centre of attraction, and concert-going is confined to a small minority.

---

[107]Willem Mengelberg (1871-1951) - Dutch conductor, one of the greatest of his age. He led the Amsterdam Concertgebouw Orchestra from 1895 to 1945.
[108]Carl Muck (1859-1940) - Eminent German conductor, especially celebrated for his Wagner interpretations. He led the Boston Symphony Orchestra from 1906 to 1908, and from 1912 to 1914.
[109]Ernest (Henry) Schelling (1876-1939) - Well-respected American pianist, conductor and composer.

Plate 23. Gustav Mahler in Amsterdam, October 1909. To the right stand Willem Mengelberg and Alphons Diepenbrock. (W.G.W. Kurz Collection)

And now to what must also help to tip the scales for you: the salary. - If you are approached, ask for *20,000* dollars (approximately *50,000* guilders, indeed, slightly more). You can live very comfortably indeed on 6,000 to 8,000 dollars, putting the rest aside. If I were you I should not hesitate to accept the offer, for the most important thing for an artist is the instrument at his disposal and the response that his art awakens. - Please let me know by return what you think about it plus if you wish me to go on using my influence in the matter. I shall be meeting *Higgins*[110] at the end of March (I have only had correspondence with him so far) and could then discuss everything on your behalf, perhaps settling a number of things that are difficult to deal with by letter. - It would be wonderful for me to have you nearby again. I shall probably also be spending the next few years here in America.

I am quite entranced with this country, even though the artistic satisfaction to be got out of the *Metropolitan* is very far from what it might be. [. . .]

(*MSL*, pp. 313f. (incomplete); original German in *GMB*, pp. 331f.)

93

[Postmark: Vienna, 1 November 1908]

My dear [Diepenbrock],[111]

[. . .] Last winter I had hoped so much that a fortunate coincidence would land [Mengelberg] close to me in Boston. And just why nothing came of this business which seemed as good as done to me, I don't know.

It seems to me that perhaps he did the right thing, now that his star is rapidly ascending, not to leave his sphere of activity. [. . .]

(Original German in Eduard Reeser, *Gustav Mahler und Holland* * *Briefe*, Wien, Internationale Gustav Mahler Gesellschaft, 1980, p. 94)

94

"To the Subscribers of the season 1907-1908: -

"Dear Sir or Madam: - The subscription season comes to a close Saturday, March 21. In compliance with many demands and owing to

---

[110]Actually Higginson, Henry Lee (1834-1919) - A banker and philanthropist, he had studied music in Vienna as a young man. He founded and personally endowed the Boston Symphony in 1881.
[111]Alphons Diepenbrock (1862-1921) - Dutch composer, he was mainly self-taught. His music was greatly influenced by Mahler, whose life-long admirer and supporter he remained.

the prosperity of the season in my house I will add one more week of opera. [. . .]

"I take pleasure in offering you the courtesy of the house for the additional week - March 23-28. The tickets for the seats or boxes you are occupying now and subscribed for for your respective evenings or matinees will be mailed to you in a few days. No charge whatsoever will be made for them. Respectfully,

Oscar Hammerstein."[112]

(*NYH*, February 29, 1908, p. 10)

95
HOTEL MAJESTIC, NEW YORK

[Postmark: 27 February 1908]

Dear [Roller],

Things have taken a turn that I cannot yet entirely assess. This much seems clear to me: that someone has put a spoke in my wheel. - What is striking is that the change I think I observe has occurred since *Cottenet's* visit to Vienna. - What happened there? Did he come and see you? And did he see anyone else? I have not yet been able to find out anything about it (which in itself is very suspicious), but have noticed a considerable cooling off on the part of the powers that be. I thought I could trump all their aces, hoping to have you here for Fidelio. Unfortunately this is not possible, as I see from your telegram. And so we have lost the only opportunity of presenting positive grounds to strengthen our cause. - I no longer believe an offer will be made to you. The only thing I have been able to achieve is that you should be sent an invitation to spend one or two weeks here in *April* (at the company's expense, of course) to discuss this very matter (which I regard as settled in the negative). - I am putting this so bluntly so that you should have no illusions. If you think there is any point in coming here to have a look around—as an artist you would find it tremendously stimulating—let me know at once and I shall arrange everything. [. . .]

I am convinced that Mr. Cottenet—a very feeble character and an adherent of the Italians—has been thoroughly 'informed' about you and me by our dear compatriots. -

I advise the following: if you are interested in seeing America and can *disguise* your holiday *so well* that no one can in *any* circumstances

[112]Oscar Hammerstein (1846-1919) - German-born theatre director and writer. He founded the Manhattan Opera in 1906, and organized the opera in Philadelphia in 1908 (s.a. Note 100, p. 88).

interpret or construe it as an unsuccessful attempt to find a position here, accept the offer and let us know at once when you will be arriving. [. . .]

(*MSL*, pp. 317f.; original German in *GMB*, pp. 333f.)

96

[Vienna] 11 March 1908

My dear Director,

Your very welcome letter arrived yesterday, and I cabled to you today to say that I was not coming to New York. In the light of what you tell me, it would be no more than a pleasure-trip. [. . .] I cannot imagine what is responsible for the turn the affair has taken. You will have had my letter meanwhile (or was it two?), written since Mr. Cottenet's arrival in Vienna, and therewith the answers to most of your questions. I do not know whom he saw in Vienna. [. . .] Maybe I made a bad impression on him. I can only speak English fluently on the most elementary topics, and of what he said I never understood more than a part, and sometimes nothing at all. It may also be that Dippel's more recent appearance in Vienna, of which I heard later, has something to do with it. I cannot tell you what it costs me to see this beautiful dream fade away. The summons to New York would have been particularly welcome now, when I feel that my position at the Opera is coming to an end. [. . .]

I [. . .] now [. . .] will add a few more details of my talk with Mr. Cottenet. It was very short. After he had broached the question I said: 'I know too little about the state of affairs in New York to be able to make any detailed reply. I can only say that I am ready to go to America on condition that only serious work is asked of me and that I have a position of complete independence in all matters of stage décor. I cannot say anything, even approximately, about the salary. I suggest that Herr Mahler might say something on this point, as he alone can properly speak for both sides. In any case, I count on something considerable. I should come over before the contract was concluded to see everything for myself on the spot'. He said I should have to be over there throughout the entire season; I should have to mount German opera in cooperation with you, and Italian in cooperation with Toscanini; further, he was raising the question merely for purposes of information and what he said was not binding. I noted this and expressed agreement. That was all. [. . .] I have told you already that when I asked him what Gatti-Casazza and Toscanini would have to say to my prospective engagement, he replied that they would welcome it gladly. The most likely explanation in my opinion is that the difficulties are made by Gatti-Casazza. [. . .] I must add to the account of may talk with Cottenet that when he spoke of the vast resources deployed in New York I said: 'I have been hauled over the coals here for extravagance. Actually, however, I have not a great deal of money at my disposal, and to spend little is not, in my opinion, always a saving. The point is to spend effectively; then money is spent well. Money spent to no effect is lost. It is the same with housekeeping'. That is what I said, or, rather, tried to say. Cottenet nodded his head and said Yes, yes; but whether he understood my broken English I really do not know. [. . .]

Always wholly yours,
Roller

(*AMM*, pp. 313-316; original German in *AME*, pp. 420-424)

_____

97

R.L. Cottenet, a director of the Conried Metropolitan Company [. . .] arrived here yesterday [. . .] Soon after, a statement was issued at the Metropolitan Opera House that there are no unsettled conditions or differences regarding the engagement of Gatti-Casazza and that he has already signed the contract.

Asked if he had met the director of La Scala in a business way or had discussed with him the offer from the Metropolitan Opera House, Mr. Cottenet said he had not.

"I simply went abroad for pleasure", he said, "and visited the opera at Paris, Vienna and Milan. All the questions I have been asked today concerning the Metropolitan Opera House negotiations are new to me. I assure you I made no business arrangements at Milan. There is really nothing for me to say apart from the fact that I went abroad for pleasure and visited the opera in the three cities."

[. . .]

The statement given out at the Metropolitan Opera House in contradiction of rumors about the terms of Mr. Gatti-Casazza's engagement is as follows:

'In an article published yesterday in a morning newspaper it was stated that Mr. Gatti-Casazza had refused to accept the directorship of the Metropolitan Opera House, unless he be allowed to bring with him his entire stage staff from La Scala at Milan. There is not the slightest foundation of truth in this statement, which is only calculated to disturb the stage personnel of the Metropolitan Opera House, and to create an impression highly prejudicial to Mr. Gatti-Casazza.

As a matter of fact, so far from there being any unsettled question, conditions or differences between Mr. Gatti-Casazza and the

Metropolitan Opera House, it is authoritatively announced that he has already signed the contract for his engagement as general director. [. . .]'

(*NYTrib*, March 7, 1908, p. 7)

98

Albany, March 2. - According to the ruling of Secretary of State Whalen, the name of Heinrich Conried cannot be dropped from the Metropolitan Opera Company just yet and the designation remains The Conried Metropolitan Opera Company. [. . .]

(*MA* 7, no. 17, March 7, 1908, p. 23)

99

Opera enthusiasts who peep into the orchestra pit at the Metropolitan Opera House on the nights when Mr. Gustav Mahler conducts have noticed that he seems to pay a great deal of attention to the score open before him. This subject was recently discussed between some dyed-in-the-wool Wagnerites, and one declared that if his memory served him aright years and years ago Mr. Mahler conducted in Germany and that he did not consult the score at all, but conducted from memory.

One was deputized to ask the conductor if this were true, and a few days afterward he encountered Mr. Mahler at rehearsal and asked him the question.

"Oh, yes," answered the conductor. "That was years ago - when I was very young. I remember distinctly I not only refused to use a score, but I also took care to take it off my desk with a certain bravado so that the audience might see it and say to themselves: -

"What a devil of a fellow he is!"

"But I have grown older since then, and those tricks of happy youth are not any longer for me. Now I need the score—not to follow the music, for I know that by heart—but I need it to hold my attention. If I did not have it I would be tempted to make life miserable for those singers up on the stage, for I would pursue them with look and gesture and would give them obvious cues until they would loathe the sight of me."

So that explains why Mr. Mahler employs a score when conducting Wagner opera.

(*NYH*, March 8, 1908, 3. Section, p. 10)

100

Among conductors, the question of whether or not one should conduct from memory is always being discussed. Do you know what Mahler's opinions on this subject were?

He conducted from memory because it was becoming the fashion, the "mode", but I can tell you that he preferred to have the score before him. He used to say that one could forget details and endanger the composition unnecessarily. Of course, with works that he knew very well—a Beethoven symphony, let us say—it might be more trouble to turn the pages than to conduct from memory. In Vienna, after all, not only Mahler but everyone knew the Beethoven symphonies by heart.

(From "Conversation Piece: Mahler as Conductor - An Interview with Mrs. Alma Mahler Werfel", in Howard Shanet, "Notes on the Programs" [of the New York Philharmonic], February 4-7, 1960, p. 3)

101

"The two most wonderful things I have experienced in New York are the opera house and Mahler. [. . .] I never had the delight [of singing under him] in Germany, but had to come here to experience it. He makes the orchestra sing with the singer. At the same time it is a wonderful support to the singer, and he suggests things in the music that have never been suspected before. Of course he is a strict master, but it is only right that he should be. He knows what is in the score, and naturally he desires to have it brought out and works himself until it is perfect. [. . .] The simplicity of great art [. . .] - it is easy enough to make striking effects by bizarre or studied readings, but the great classic perfection of any art work rests on naturalness."

(Berta Morena,[113] quoted in *NYS*, March 15, 1908, 3. Section, p. 8)

102
AS OTHERS SEE US

The "Neue Freie Presse" of Vienna informs its readers on the strength of a private letter received by an unmentioned person in Vienna from an unmentioned person in New York that the directorship of the Metropolitan Opera House was offered to Herr Mahler and declined by

---

[113]Berta Morena [Meyer] (1878-1952) - German soprano; she was world renowned for her interpretation of Wagnerian roles.

him, although extraordinary means for carrying out his artistic aims were offered him, to say nothing of a salary of 600,000 crowns (in round numbers $120,000) for six months of service.

On Herr Knote's arrival in Munich last month he was promptly interviewed by a reporter of the "Münchener Zeitung." A portion of the interview was to this effect:

"What have you to say about Gustav Mahler? It is said that it is not always pleasant to work with him: that he is inconsiderate and almost impolite."

"Yes, that is the report: but it is not correct. I'll permit nothing to be said against Mahler. He came and captured the entire orchestra by storm at his first rehearsal. He made the most thorough rehearsals in the shortest time imaginable. Nothing was lost, and yet every syllable of the singers was understood in the audience room. He breathed with the singers. We had a performance of "Tristan" of unheard-of greatness. It was the most powerful representation that I ever experienced and an unexampled triumph for German art in New York. All the "Tristan" performances which followed—I sang in the work six more times under Mahler—were sold out. "Don Giovanni," too, under Mahler has created a sensation. The greatest stars, spoiled prima donnas all of them, gave breathless attention to the explanations of this man. He made all his arrangements in extraordinary quietness and with unusual knowledge, but protested against shortcomings with equal energy. There was no arguing with him. He gave instructions in the scenic department with the same accuracy. His opinions were absolutely convincing. Formerly there was a good deal of sinning in the matter of accompanying the singers. The conductor plunged ahead, the public understood never a word and was bored. Now, all at once, we were heard, and interest followed, as a matter of course. On the other hand, Mahler was delighted with the singers. To me he said: "You have the most beautiful tenor voice that I ever heard, nor did I ever hear the third act of "Tristan" as you sing it. At last I have heard it sung not declaimed."

Here solemn comment would be too bad. [. . .] Five performances at which the smallness of the attendance grieved the souls of the lovers of Wagner, grown to seven at which the house was sold out! The first intelligible and intelligent performances of "Tristan und Isolde" that were ever vouchsafed to New York; yet we have know the drama over twenty years, and have heard it sung by Lehmann[114] and Niemann[115], [etc.], and

[114]Lilli Lehmann (1848-1929) - Celebrated German soprano of the opera and concert stages, she later became a famous teacher. Following their first acquaintance in Budapest in 1890, she became one of Mahler's most influential supporters.
[115]Albert Niemann (1831-1917) - German heroic tenor, mostly active in Berlin. He was celebrated for his Wagner-roles.

101

conducted by Seidl and Mottl and Hertz and Damrosch. Mahler never heard so beautiful a tenor voice as Knote's; how diligently he must have closed his ears to Caruso! But it must be so, for Knote—he himself—has said it. Verily, the German proverb is correct: Paper is patient.

(*NYTrib*, March 17, 1908, p. 7)

103
William and Pine Streets

Kuhn, Loeb & Co.   New York, March 18, 1908
Honoured Herr Mahler!

Sincere thanks for your letter of 16th instant. I presented it to our 'Executive Committee', who are in complete agreement with the proposed arrangements, and wish to make only the following, relatively unimportant additions to the contractual points mentioned by you:

1. The choice of the stateroom is yours, but the outlay to which we are thereby committed should not exceed $500 for the outward journey, and the same sum for the return one (as I understand it, the cabin that was arranged by Conried for your outbound trip cost under $200).

2. In order to avoid unpleasant discussions as to what is to be understood under "costs of the New York sojourn" in the sense of the contract, we propose to fix a sum that we pay to you for taking care of such costs; specifically, $200 per week would appear to us as equitable.

3. During the three months of your engagement, we shall have the right to arrange a few concerts for you, precisely as it had been envisioned in your contract with Conried. We also hope to have you agree that you will conduct nowhere in America before 1-7th of January; naturally, after 1-7th of April you are completely free.

As soon as I receive your response concerning these points, I shall have the contract drawn up in legal form. Perhaps you will be kind enough to send me your current contract, so that I may use it as a model.

It gives all of us great pleasure to hear from you that you "look forward to developments under the new regime with confidence". From everything that the two Italian gentlemen have said and done, it is clear how genuinely and highly they value your artistry. How gratifying it is to me to know that your genial talent will continue to be at the service of our cause, I don't have to tell you.

With best regards,
Your most devoted
Otto Kahn

(*ELM*, pp. [383f.])[116]

Plate 24. Roller's design painting for Act I, Scene 1 of the Vienna (1904) and New York (1908) productions of *Fidelio*. (*RSM*, "Bilder", p. 30)

Plate 25. Photograph of the stage for Act I, Scene 2 of the Roller-Mahler production of *Fidelio*. (Metropolitan Opera Archives)

104

Beethoven's "Fidelio" was produced [. . .] last evening for the first time
in more than three years[117] - and for the first time in many more years
than that, if by "production" is meant an adequate, well-considered, and
thoroughly prepared treatment of the great master's only opera. [. . .]
This careful and in many respects remarkably fine representation of
"Fidelio" [. . .] was [. . .] one of the missions [Mahler] came to New
York to fulfill. [. . .] The performance [. . .] was one of uncommonly
vivid dramatic effect and consistency and of much musical beauty. [. . .]
Mr. Mahler is a man of strong original ideas of his own [. . .] He makes
no fetich of great masterpieces, and refuses to be bound by tradition, or
even by the letter of the text. How far such an attitude is justified on the
part of a conductor [. . .] may be open to question. It is certain that in
"Fidelio" Mr. Mahler makes a number of changes from accepted
traditions. [. . .] Significant is the division which Mr. Mahler makes of
the opera. He drops the curtain once and makes but two acts as the score
directs. The quick march that precedes Pizarro's arrival becomes a sort
of intermezzo for the change that the new setting makes necessary
between the first and second scenes of the first act. Instead of playing the
great "Leonore" overture, No. 3, as many do, after the first act, Mr.
Mahler uses it during the change of scene in the second act [. . .] This
performance of the overture, it may be said, was a remarkable one, the
achievement of a great conductor: wonderfully thrilling, subtle in its
nuances, imposing in its climaxes, and eloquent of the dramatic
exposition that Beethoven makes in it.

(*NYT*, March 21, 1908, p. 9)

---

[116]This letter, **108**, and **134** are evidently concerned with the new contract between
Mahler and the administration that was replacing Heinrich Conried at the
Metropolitan Opera. - For the German text, see Appendix, A13.
[117]The complete cast was as follows: Leonore - Morena; Marzellina - Alten; Florestan -
Burrian; Pizarro - Goritz; Rocco - Blass; Jaquino - Reiss; Don Fernando - Van
Rooy. At the next performance on March 26th, Leonore was sung by Leffler-
Burkhard.

105

A few years ago Mr. Mahler brought "Fidelio" out in Vienna,[118] with the help of Professor Roller, who designed new scenery for it and certain mechanical devices which Mr. Mahler wished to introduce to enhance the dramatic effect of the work. [. . .] Nearly all of them were duplicated with painstaking care in the representation at the Metropolitan last night. [. . .] A word must be said of the music [at the opening the second act], which has undergone a change that alters its character completely. Mr. Mahler has transposed the clarinet parts an octave upward in the dissonant chords and exaggerated the dynamics in both directions. The result is to give a colour to the music not to be found elsewhere in the opera or in any other of Beethoven's scores, and when the drum taps are heard it is found that they have become sinister instead of mournful, as the cries of the horns and woodwinds, raised from *forte* to *fortissimo* have been changed from utterances of pain to shrieks of something akin to rage. There is harmony between the reading and the scene as Professor Roller has modelled it, but as yet we cannot find it between the score and the book as they left the hands of Beethoven.

(*NYT*, March 21, 1908, p. 9)

106

Mr. Mahler's conception of the moods of the drama, which governed and characterized the entire performance, was one of the profoundest sympathy. In his treatment of the score he showed that keen perception of relative tonal values, of significant instrumental phrases, of general colour and of the proportion between orchestra and voices which was a repetition of that which he displayed in his production of "Don Giovanni." [. . .] The chief credit for last night's performance must go to the musical director. "Fidelio" and "Don Giovanni" have been his best achievements.

(*NYS*, March 21, 1908, p. 3)

---

[118]Their production of *Fidelio* in Vienna (public première on October 7, 1904) was one of the most celebrated (and debated) instances of Mahler's and Roller's collaboration. Apparently, Roller's sets were reproduced precisely for the production at the Metropolitan. - It was also in connection with the Vienna production (and partly in order to accommodate Roller's technical requirements) that Mahler initiated the custom of opening the performance of the opera with the short E major overture, and playing the great C major overture (Leonore No. 3) during the scene change in the second act.

Plates 26 and 27. Two costume designs for *Fidelio* by Roller.
(*RSM*, "Bilder", pp. 37, 38)

106

107

As an introduction to the last scene of "Fidelio", [. . .] Gustav Mahler played the No. 3 "Leonora" overture. The orchestra was the Metropolitan Opera Orchestra, consisting of New York musicians. It is doubtful if ever a performance of that kind was heard before in this city. [. . .] It made an exceedingly deep impression on the audience which is not accustomed to the classical overture.

After hearing that, can any one blame THE MUSICAL COURIER for paying no attention to the orchestral concerts given in this city by men like Safonoff[119] and Damrosch? Is there any use to go to hear those Beethoven concerts given by Mr. Damrosch with a New York orchestra also? Does not this prove conclusively that it is not the New York musician, not the New York orchestral player, but that it is the conductor who is responsible for all this chaotic conducting? [. . .] We were convinced again on Friday night that the attention, with knowledge and idealism as a basis, will produce results with New York musicians. [. . .]

These musicians all love to play well, but they cannot do it in these concerts in New York City under these conductors that are well known. It is impossible, because they do not respect the conductors themselves. [. . .] The lackadaisical manner in which the musician attacks these works under these conductors is in itself the direct proof of their indifference to the whole scheme, and consequently we can get no good orchestral music here. [. . .] It was a magnificent performance on Friday night, that No. 3 "Leonora". Magnificent! There is no use going to New York concerts after that.

("Reflections", *MC* 56, no. 13, March 25, 1908, p. 23)[120]

108

William and Pine Streets

Kuhn, Loeb & Co.   New York, March 23, 1908
Honoured Herr Mahler!

Please excuse the delay in the response to your letter of March 18th. The reason is that I had to ascertain the views of our 'Executive

---

[119]Wassily Safonoff (1852-1918) - Highly regarded Russian pianist and conductor. In addition to his conducting, he taught at the St. Petersburg Conservatory, and became director of the Moscow Conservatory. He had conducted the Philharmonic since 1906.
[120]"Reflections" was the *MC*'s equivalent of editorials. - In this column, Blumenberg's habitual antagonism towards the Damrosch brothers receives relatively mild expression.

Committee' on both of the points brought up by you, and I could not get them together sooner.

Re 1. - We had thought that $200 per week for rooms, meals, etc., was adequate compensation; nonetheless, the 'Executive Committee' is prepared to raise this sum to $225 per week. I will add personally that if, nevertheless, you hold out for $250 per week, I will have this sum put into your contract without wasting another word on it, and assume the responsibility for obtaining the agreement of the 'Executive Committee'.

Re 2. - With all the artistic enthusiasm in the world, we must see to it that our expenditures remain within the bounds of our income. When, at our first discussion of the matter, the 'Executive Committee' was taken aback by the idea of compensation that amounted to $22,000 (including travel costs and *per diem*) for three months' work, it was countered that we could probably recoup $3,000 to $5,000 of this amount through the concerts that you would conduct. Now the 'Executive Committee' thinks that if you undertake several concert engagements on your own account prior to January 1st, our placing of you in concerts will be made considerably more difficult, and will be of reduced commercial value. Therefore, to do both sides justice, we should like to propose that you restrict your concerts *prior to January 1st* to two. In our discussion the question also came up incidentally whether you would be willing—if you are in New York already before January 1st, and *in case you have free time*—to devote part of this time to preparatory rehearsals for your opera season - without additional financial obligation on our part, but also without any commitment from you, and only in so far as it suits you, in the interest of the artistic results.

In case you prefer to respond to this letter verbally, rather than in writing, it will be my pleasure to visit you in the afternoon on Wednesday.

I was very sorry that my dumb chauffeur made you wait last Saturday; I had instructed him to be there for you at 2.30, but he claims to have understood it as 3.30.

With best regards,
Your most devoted,
Otto H. Kahn

(*ELM*, pp. [880f.])[121]

---

[121]See Note 116, p. 104; for the German text, see Appendix, A14.

109
HOTEL MAJESTIC, NEW YORK

24 March [1908]

Dear [Adler], [122]

[...]

The people have responded to G. with open arms. *Fidelio* with the Roller sets was a couple of days ago - and it was an *unprecedented* success. Gustav is just about to sign for next year. On the whole we both feel ourselves immensely well. Not least we are indebted to the dear warm people who all strive to make the stay as lovely as possible for one. We Viennese had no idea of an American winter with its *eternal* sunshine. [...]

Alma Mahler

(Edward R. Reilly, *Gustav Mahler and Guido Adler - Records of a Friendship*, Cambridge, etc., Cambridge University Press, 1982, pp. 105f.)

110
HOTEL MAJESTIC, NEW YORK

[after 20 March 1908]

Dearest Mama,

In frantic haste as usual.

Here I am sending you a 'news-paper'. Not only because it really lays itself out (and you enjoy that, I know), but because it gives a very clear picture of the present situation. Fidelio was a total success, completely altering my prospects from one day to the next. I am moving, or rather 'things' are moving, towards the formation of a Mahler Orchestra entirely at my own disposal, which would not only earn me a good deal of money, but also give me some satisfaction. Everything now depends on the New Yorkers' attitude to my work. - Since they are completely unprejudiced I hope I shall here find fertile ground for my works and thus a spiritual home, something that, for all the sensationalism, I should never be able to achieve in Europe. A tree needs such ground if it is not to die. I feel this very strongly. [...]

(*MSL*, p. 319; original German in *GMB*, p. 337)

---

[122]Guido Adler (1855-1941) - Eminent Austrian musicologist, professor of the University of Vienna from 1898 to 1927. He was a life-long admirer and influential supporter of Mahler.

111

A Viennese newspaper has gravely given vent to the information that Gustav Mahler was offered the neat sum of $120,000 a year to be the director of the Metropolitan Opera House and refused it. The same newspaper did not explain how it was that he became a party to the four cornered arrangement of direction, the great Gatti-Casazza-Dippel-Toscanini-Mahler quartet, in which the salary allotted to him is quoted at $25,000 a season.

It is always instructive to read European newspapers on American affairs. It gives us the much needed opportunity to see ourselves as others see us - with their eyes shut. If one of the returning singers were to assert that the new managers of the Metropolitan Opera House would be paid a million for their services, this flamboyant fable would be gravely disseminated through Europe as another evidence of the gross and vulgar wealth of the Americans.

It would not occur to a European newspaper man to sit down with pencil and paper and calculate how much money could be taken in at the Metropolitan box office in the course of a season of twenty weeks and set that over against the staggering cost of conducting opera when directors were to receive a million and respectable German singers $90,000 a season.

But after all even such a calculation would not convince a European journalist that the story was false, for what are millions to us? Do we not all reek with malodorous lucre? Are we not a nation of tradesmen? Are not our foremost financiers merely opulent malefactors? Suppose then that at the end of the season the balance sheet showed half a million? Would there be weeping and wailing and gnashing of teeth? Not at all. Mr. Morgan or Mr. Vanderbilt would dash off a check for the amount, more German singers would be engaged at twelve times their usual salaries and the brave work of making propaganda for German art would continue, while Mr. Caruso and Mr. Morgan paid the freight.

It is most instructive to study the logic of the European intellect when it is engaged in its favorite amusement, that of demonstrating that the American is the product of a distinctly inferior order of the dust of the earth. In one sentence it writes us down a nation of moneymaking merchants and in the next charges us with business methods fit only for the ravings of an asylum.

For the amusement of the Viennese newspapers, which will, of course, not believe the plain facts, let it be here recorded that Mr. Mahler up to the present time has not refused either the exclusive direction of the Metropolitan Opera House nor $120,000 for the sufficient reason that neither has been offered to him. Mr. Mahler is not going to be the manager of the Metropolitan next season; this is indeed true, but not because too much money was offered to him.

The inference to be drawn from the statement of the Vienna newspaper is that Mr. Mahler refused the princely sum because its acceptance would have required some sacrifice of his artistic standards. And yet at this writing Mr. Mahler seems to be tolerably well satisfied with the conditions surrounding his performances at the Metropolitan - much better satisfied, indeed, than many who pay for the precious privilege of attending them.

Doubtless the Viennese observer of American barbarism might find a deeper conviction of our benighted condition in the indisputable fact that the artistic cataclysm which separated Mr. Mahler from the Imperial Opera in the Austrian capital and brought him to this city has not been measured here by the yardstick of European pride. The coming of the new interpreter of German operas was awaited with interest and received with pleasure, but there was no public excitement.

The stock market was not affected. This comment is made because it would naturally be expected of us in Europe. It would be quite useless to remark in passing that we do not grow excited over the arrival of new interpreters from Europe, for the sufficient reason that we have already heard many of the best Europe has ever known, and we are fully informed that the present generation of operatic impersonators is distinctly inferior to that which enlightened us. Pretty much the same thing is the state of affairs in respect of conductors.

Mr. Mahler came and the flowing tides of the experienced bay bore him with equanimity. He conducted "Tristan und Isolde", and he did it beautifully. It was a refined, polished, intellectual interpretation, more like Seidl's in its continence than many others which we have had, but lacking the flaming passion of the other conductor, who taught us our first "Tristan" lessons. The disclosure of the delicate details of the score by Mahler was masterly, but we have sighed for something more overmastering than "these wrought riddles of the night and day".

Naturally this will be interpreted by Vienna to mean that Mr. Mahler is too scholarly for the American barbarians. If such a comment is made we shall be delighted to leave the office of answering it to one Carl Muck, who may possibly make some claims himself to the possession of musical scholarship and appreciation in the money grubbing metropolis of the sordid Western nation. Meanwhile certain facts are indisputable. The Wagner drama is today less popular than it has been for some years, and that too despite the arrival from Vienna of the great conductor. Thus it is all the more astonishing that Mr. Mahler has refused $120,000 to be the whole direction next season.

But for the further information of the usual Vienna journalist, let us hasten to declare that the comparatively smaller popularity of the Wagner drama at the present moment is in no way due to Mr. Mahler. It is principally due to the patent fact that the interest of the public is entirely centered upon beautiful vocal interpretation and that its hero is Mr. Caruso. The most interesting singers, the most magnetic personalities, are found in the works of the French and Italian schools. [...]

(NYS, March 22, 1908, 3. Section, p. 8)

112

A correspondent of "The Daily Telegraph" of London devotes a column and a half in that journal to an article on Signor Gatti-Casazza and Signor Toscanini and gives an interview with the former on his career as an impresario and the purposes which he will carry with him to his new field of labor. Says the correspondent:

'The offer of the great New York theatre toward which are now directed the eyes of Italian artists, from the chorister to the diva, was not only a splendid diploma granted by a unanimous vote. It was accompanied by a goodly pile of dollars - 30,000 a year for Gatti-Casazza, and for Toscanini 6,000 a month for the six months of the season. [...]'

The interview was as follows:

"And now you are soon departing for New York, but surely not without some regret. I think you will be sorry to abandon a theatre to which you have given the full maturity of your genius. Ten years of assiduous care at the Scala cannot but have left you some pleasant remembrances. . . .

"Many, many remembrances", Gatti-Casazza interrupted, "but not all happy. Yet the progress which the Scala has made under the direction of myself and Toscanini is sufficient to console us for any bitterness. We have always proceeded with complete unity of thought and action, so that we have overcome every obstacle. As soon as we came to the Scala— which at that time, I may tell you, had nothing but its walls—we set ourselves to form a first class orchestra and chorus, and to give great importance to the mise-en-scène, which in Italy had always been neglected."

[...]

"With what programme", I asked, "are you going to New York?"

"We intend", he replied, "to maintain at the Metropolitan such high artistic endeavors as will correspond with those which Toscanini and I have displayed in the management of the Scala. At the end of the present season I shall make my first journey to America, and shall consider on the spot what is best to be done. For the moment my only preoccupation is to acquire the English language."

(*NYTrib*, March 22, 1908, Part Five, p. 4)

113

It is probable that Gustav Mahler, who yesterday signed his contract for the next season at the Metropolitan Opera House, will give in this city next winter a series of symphonic concerts preceding his term of directorship at the Metropolitan. Mr. Mahler under the terms of his new contract will for three months conduct the German operas at the Metropolitan. [. . .]

"It is not intended to form a new orchestra," said one of the organizers of the concerts, "as that would be too difficult and would not be thought of until the scheme in its original form had proved a success. There are a great many music lovers in this city who would like to hear such a famous conductor as Mr. Mahler in a symphony concert.

"To that end ample funds have been subscribed and we are waiting only the consent of Mr. Mahler to the plan. We desire to have the concerts before the period of the conductor's engagment at the Metropolitan."

(*NYS*, March 25, 1908, p. 7)

114

Mr. Heinrich Conried's annual benefit performance took place last night, and if the size of the audience could have been taken as measuring solely the esteem in which the manager is held it would be only just to write him down as a veritable phenomenon of popularity. Doubtless there was an expression of public good will to be read in the presence of so fine a gathering of spectators. [. . .]

The bill comprised excerpts from half a dozen popular operas and also the performance of the "Leonore" overture, No. 3, under the direction of Mr. Mahler, which, it may be said at once, provided the musical culmination of the evening and was received with as much acclaim as anything on the entire list. [. . .][123]

(*NYTrib*, March 25, 1908, p. 7)

---

[123]This reviewer claims that Mahler also conducted an excerpt from Act 3 of *Die Meitersinger*. However, it is clear from the *Herald*'s review (March 25, 1908, p. 11), as well as from Seltsam's list (*op. cit.*) that this excerpt was conducted by Hertz.

115
HOTEL MAJESTIC, NEW YORK

16 March 1908

Dear Herr Damrosch,

I did not have the opportunity yesterday to also tell you personally how sorry I am that I cannot conduct for you this year, and how much I regret the inconvenience that was caused you by my "Chef's" lack of understanding.

But I would like to make up for the omission at least next season; and since at the upcoming renewal of my contract it is now incumbent upon me to ensure a free hand in this direction, I am now enquiring of you whether you wish to have me next year; and if so, I would like to discuss the specifics with you verbally, so that we may avoid all difficulties. [. . .]

(Original German in Edward R. Reilly, "Gustav Mahler und Walter Damrosch", *MUB*, pp. 35f.)

116
HOTEL MAJESTIC, NEW YORK

[Date in another hand, probably by Damrosch: 18 March 1908]

Dear Herr Damrosch,

[. . .]

My engagement with the Metropolitan begins on January 7. - Would it be possible to arrange with you for 2 concerts in quick succession to precede this. The first one with a classical programme and the 2. with my choral symphony?

That would suit me the best. I could devote myself entirely to my task, as I would not yet have obligations at the Opera; and in this way I could present myself to New York in a meaningful way before taking up my not very invigorating post. [. . .]

(Original German in *op. cit.*, p. 36)

117
HOTEL MAJESTIC, NEW YORK

[Dated by Damrosch: 26 March]

Dear Herr Damrosch,

Some difficulties have cropped up at the last moment which, although I hope to overcome them, oblige me to beg your indulgence a little while longer as concerns our affair.

Please be so kind and await my next message before we consider the matter as settled. [. . .]

(Original German in *op. cit.*, p. 38)

118
HOTEL MAJESTIC, NEW YORK

[28 March 1908]

Dear Herr Damrosch,

I regret that once again I will be unable to take advantage of your kindness tomorrow, since at 3:30 I must be at a meeting of the "Executive Comittee [sic]", where they will also make the final decision concerning my affairs. [. . .]

(Original German in *op. cit.*, p. 39)

119
HOTEL MAJESTIC, NEW YORK

[31 March 1908]

Dear Herr Damrosch,

Kahn has, of course, given me a free hand. But with that the matter is resolved only for the Metropolitan Company, for I must give up $3000 of my income in return for this release. Accordingly, I must first see now how I can make that up; and the connections I am forming are also [. . .] as yet unclarified. - I have asked Kahn for 10 days to think it over; and I would also ask you to bear with me for that long.

That a relationship with you appeals to me most strongly, I have already indicated to you. But you will appreciate that under the circumstances I must also take other points of view into account. [. . .]

(Original German in *op. cit.*, p. 40)

120
DAVE H. MORRIS[124]
COUNSELLOR AT LAW
68 BROAD ST., N.Y.

1 April 1908

My dear Mr. Damrosch,

A Committee of ladies have retained me to take charge of the legal

---

[124]Dave Hennen Morris (1872-1944) - Prominent New York lawyer (later diplomat). He was an accomplished amateur violinist, and was involved in many facets of New York musical life.

formalities in relation to certain concerts they desire to give next fall under the direction of Gustav Mahler. Among other things, they wanted my opinion as to whether or not Mr. Mahler was free to make a contract with them. After hearing what they had to say, and after interviewing Mr. Mahler, I have come to the conclusion that Mr. Mahler is free to make any contract he pleases, as I cannot discover that he has bound himself to anyone except the Conried Opera Company, and with them he has certain arrangements which enable him to make concert contracts with others. In making this Conried Contract, he was obliged to give a certain concession to obtain the concert privilege, and I understand from him that he was willing to make this concession on account of the proposition made by the Committee of ladies which I represent, which proposition he has accepted in writing, and a contract has been duly entered into.

Both Mr. Mahler and the Committee have suggested my seeing you, as they know me to be a friend and personal admirer of yours, for the purpose of stating the case to you so that you may understand just what has transpired. I should like very much to hear from you your views of your tentative negotiations with Mr. Mahler, as it would grieve me extremely to express an opinion not warranted by the facts in the case, which would in any way adversely affect your interests. I am sure that both the Committee and Mr. Mahler feel similarly disposed, and though they have stated facts to me as carefully and conscientiously as possible, they feel, nevertheless, they may have omitted something and desire that you should correct, or fill in any omission on their part.

Will you not, therefore, make an appointment with me at your earliest convenience in the event that you care to take up the matter with me?

Yours sincerely,
Dave H. Morris

(The original text is published here with the kind permission of NALT; German translation in *op. cit.*, pp. 41f.)

121
HOTEL MAJESTIC, NEW YORK

[Between 2 and 7 April 1908]

Dear Herr Damrosch,

Your new proposal was passed on to me by Herr Kahn yesterday. Yet, much to my regret, this cannot alter the situation. - Personally, this makes me extremely unhappy. [. . .]

Still, I have just thought of a way out which would help both sides. I will discuss this, and find an opportunity in a few days to consult you about it personally. [. . .]

(Original German in *op. cit.*, pp. 42f.)

122

Gustav Mahler, who is to be entrusted next year with the task of restoring the popularity of Wagner at the Metropolitan [. . .] believes that the public can be brought back when the works are done in ideal fashion.

"There must be a perfect ensemble," he said, "because the German operatic stage offers no such stars as exist now in the Italian field.

"With Mme. Sembrich and Signor Caruso, for instance, the problem of an Italian performance is settled. But in the Wagner dramas we have no such powerful personalities.

"The substitute must be a perfectly trained ensemble, faultless mise en scène and orchestra. In that way Wagner opera may once more be brought into the position it formerly held here.

"But this ensemble can only be created by having the same singers in every rehearsal and at every performance. That must be arranged at the Metropolitan if Wagner operas are to be sung in a way to make the public love them again.

"I had many rehearsals of "Don Giovanni", and the same cast but twice. I also had two Sieglindes for "Die Walküre" in the two performances. That is no way in which to secure a perfect ensemble. The operas must be rehearsed and sung by the same artists time and time again, that they may be performed as the Wagner operas should in order to have success with the public.

"When these conditions exist there is no doubt that the Wagner operas will attract the public as much as ever."[125]

(*NYS*, March 29, 1908, 3. Section, p. 8)

---

[125]In spite of the critical success of Mahler's productions, the decline in the size of the audiences for Wagner operas—increasingly worrisome for the Metropolitan's management with the passing years—continued during the 1907-1908 season. In order to try to determine the cause for this phenomenon, a number of New York's leading musical personalities, among them Mahler, were interviewed by the press. His remarks, beyond their topical interest, also shed light on the Metropolitan Opera's problems in general.

123

```
Mr. and Mrs. New York,

    To MUSIC, Dr.
    Season of 1907-08

TO 20 weeks and 125 operas at the
    Manhattan Opera-House..................... $1,000,000
21 weeks, 131 operas, Metropolitan
    Opera-House............................... $1,310,000
Season's music at Carnegie Hall .............. $  680,000
Miscellaneous concerts ....................... $1,000,000
                                               $3,960,000


Received payment,
    HAMMERSTEIN, CONRIED & CO.
```

New York's Musical Salary List:
   [. . .] Tetrazzini $40,000 [. . .] Caruso $56,000 [. . .] Mahler
$20,000 [. . .] Paderewski[126] $60,000 [. . .] Kreisler[127] $30,000 [. . .]
   These figures are supplied by persons prominently connected with
music in New York. The World does not vouch for them.

(*NYW*, March 29, 1908, Metropolitan Section, p. M1)

124

With this season ends Mr. Heinrich Conried's period of management
after five years' incumbency. [. . .] This season has been, even more
than those that have immediately preceded it, under the Italian
ascendancy. [. . .] Not till Mr. Mahler came in January did the German
element in the repertory come to the front. [. . .] Mr. Mahler's
engagement has been one of the most interesting features of recent years
at the Metropolitan. Measured in numerical terms, what he has done here
does not loom large. Under him new studies have been made of "Tristan
und Isolde", "Don Giovanni", "Die Walküre", "Siegfried" and
"Fidelio". These studies brought a new spirit into the performances and

---

[126]Ignac Jan Paderewski (1860-1941) - Born in Poland, he was perhaps the greatest
pianist of his time. He was also a composer and a statesman.
[127]Fritz Kreisler (1875-1962) - World renowned Austrian violinist and composer. In
addition to several, extensive tours of the United States, he was a resident of New
York for many years.

revealed a kind of beauty that has not been enjoyed in these works for a long time.

(*NYT*, April 5, 1908, Part Six, p. 4)

125

The retirement of Heinrich Conried from the direction of the Metropolitan Opera House is made in conditions so painful that they almost forbid the publication of certain obvious comments. Mr. Conried commands sympathy and his return to the seclusion of the estate which he occupied before he was thrust into the fierce publicity of operatic management must be respected. He is entitled to all the peace and quiet he can get. He has thoroughly earned them.

That he made many mistakes in his direction of the Metropolitan Opera House will be conceded by most persons, including probably himself. It would have been one of the marvels of the young twentieth century if he had not. In the fulness of a wisdom passing the understanding of common mortals a body of expert business men selected as the managing director of an artistic enterprise a man who had absolutely no acquaintance with its methods or its traditions.

[. . .] Mr. Conried's one radical blunder was his refusal from the beginning to admit that he knew nothing about opera and to accept advice or suggestions from those of his assistants who did. But the greatest blunder was that made in selecting as director a man ignorant of music in all its departments and equally innocent of knowledge of opera, even as it is known to the casual operagoer.

[. . .] The Metropolitan Opera House has steadily gone down hill since the first foam of excitement over the "Parsifal" production[128]

[128]Conried's first *coup* as the new manager of the Metropolitan Opera was his production there of *Parsifal* on December 24, 1903. This was the first stage production of the music drama outside Bayreuth; it was undertaken against the express prohibition of the Wagner family. (European opera houses were to stage the work only some ten years later, following the expiration of the copyright.)

Although it inevitably generated a certain amount of controversy (chiefly on religious grounds), the production (conducted by Hertz, with Burgstaller as Parsifal) was received with high critical praise. For example, Aldrich wrote in his review (*NYT*, December 25, 1903, pp. 1f.):

"[. . .] At the very outset it may be said that yesterday's production went far to justify the bold undertaking of Mr. Heinrich Conried, the new director [. . .] The artistic value of the production was of the very highest. It was in many respects equal to anything done at Bayreuth, and in some it was superior. It was without doubt the most perfect production ever made on the American lyric stage. Those who wish to quarrel with the performance on aesthetic, moral or religious grounds have still as much upon which to stand as before; artistically it was nothing less than triumphant. [. . .]"

120

subsided. Even the cheap sensationalism of the "Salome" incident[129] did not help it. The performances of the season of 1906-07 were bad. Those of 1907-08 have been worse. If the system now in vogue in the house were to be continued another year they would be still worse. [. . .]

Mr. Conried, retiring into the peace and repose of private life, need not trouble himself to recall his promise to remove from the cosmos of the Metropolitan Opera House the pernicious star system and to substitute for it a beautiful and artistic ensemble.[130]

He has got rid of many stars, but not of the star system, and the ensemble has not at any time been as good in the course of his management as it was in that of his predecessor, Maurice Grau [. . .]

The part of the public which generously supports the Metropolitan by subscribing to its performances has had some interesting experiences. It has been obliged to endure casts such as Mr. Grau would have thought of offering only at reduced prices on Saturday nights [. . .]

In the planning of the season's répertoire more than anything else has the director's lack of skill in managing an opera house been demonstrated. [. . .]

[129]On January 22, 1907—some 13 months after its première in Dresden—the Metropolitan Opera presented the first American performance of *Salome* (Hertz conducted, Fremstad sang the title role). The subject and its presentation on the stage created a furor of such a magnitude that the directors of the Metropolitan holding company forced Conried to take the opera off the programme after its single performance. *Salome* was next performed at the Metropolitan only in 1933.

While a few of the critics attempted to assess the work on its own merits, most of them were of a mind with Krehbiel, who wrote as follows (quoted in Seltsam, *op. cit*, pp. 172f., from the review in the *Tribune*):

"[. . .] What shall be said [. . .] when music adorns itself with its loveliest attributes and leads them to the apotheosis of that which is indescribably, yes, inconceivably, gross and abominable? [. . .] There is not a whiff of fresh and healthy air blowing through 'Salome' except that which exhales from the cistern [. . .] Salome is the unspeakable; Herodias [. . .] is a human hyena; Herod, a neurasthenic voluptuary. [. . .]"

In order to put the reactions of New Yorkers in 1907 into proper perspective, it may be mentioned here that in 1905 Mahler was prevented from staging *Salome* in Vienna by the edict of the Court censor.

[130]The elimination of the "pernicious star system" seems to have been the dream— largely unrealized—of most opera directors at least since the end of the nineteenth century. Mahler himself had made this his chief goal during his three-year reign of the Budapest Opera between 1888 and 1891. Even though he did not succeed completely, his achievement was regarded highly enough to merit this evaluation by an historical observer: "When the young Gustav Mahler was opera director in Budapest [. . .] he found the energy to oppose himself to the system, the star-mania, the greed of the singers. After a few years, his example bore fruit everywhere." (Hans H. Stuckenschmidt, "Charakteristika des modernen Musiklebens," in Joachim E. Berendt and Jürgen Uhde, ed., *Prisma der gegenwärtigen Musik*, Hamburg, Fuche-Verlag, 1959, p. 105).

The outlook for the coming season is by no means so rosy as the members of the Metropolitan Opera Company would have us believe. It is true that we are to have new blood in the management and that the direction is to pass into the hands of men who know the opera game from one end to the other. But the directors of the company behind Mr. Conried have failed signally in one detail.

They allowed to remain in the hands of Mr. Conried the power to engage singers for next season. The result is that the expenses of the Metropolitan Opera House will be larger than ever and that a lot of useless lumber will be retained.

At the risk of offending several great dignitaries in the world of "art" this commentator is impelled to say that the secret of the present want of interest in the Wagnerian works is to be found in the unattractiveness of the interpreters. The Metropolitan Opera House does not possess a single tenor capable of any charm in such roles as Tristan and Siegfried.

The impersonators of these parts are honest, industrious, well schooled performers, without any poetic imagination and without any eloquence for the public. The same thing might be said of singers of some other roles. What the house needs worse than anything else in its German department is new singers.

It is useless to bring over men like Mahler and to expect them to solve the problem in spite of the drawbacks on the stage.[. . .]

It is useless for the opponents of Wagner to tell us that [the] dulness is in the works themselves, because those of us who began to go to the opera before 1900 know better. [. . .]

One other fact of significance in the present conditions of opera in this city cannot have escaped the notice of any old observer of musical doings here, and that is that the taste of the public today is far below that of the public which used to attend the performances in the old Academy of Music twenty-five years ago.[. . .]

In [the Metropolitan Opera House] thunders of applause are bestowed on doings which can be nothing but grievous to lovers of chaste and honest art. Let us hope that with the advent of managers who have some acquaintance with traditions of opera we shall witness the beginning of a movement in the opposite direction.

But candor compels the admission that there is abundant room for doubt. Whether the active members of the opera company which has engaged Messrs. Dippel and Gatti-Casazza will remain in the background and permit these impresarios to conduct the opera according to their wisdom and knowledge is something that at present seems entirely problematic. These men say that they will not interfere in any way with the management, but up to the present time they have taken a very active part in all the proceedings. When are they going to stop?

Have they set a date on which they will cease to meddle in things of which they know just as much as any other box occupants?

[. . .] The writer frankly confesses that he is not at all sanguine as to the future of opera in this city. The public steadily and with irrestible power refuses to regard it as an art form. The managers, who are in the business for business reasons, all proclamations to the contrary notwithstanding, strive to give the public what it desires.

The singers are all overcome with a sense of their own importance. Rarely for a moment do they forget that they are singing to an audience or lose themselves in the drama. They invite plaudits in the most open and unhesitating manner. The whole thing has become a show, and so the public seems bent on viewing it.

Every effort to raise it above that level meets with the unconquerable hostility of cold indifference. Witness the public attitude towards the "Don Giovanni" and "Fidelio" performances. What the outcome of all this is to be no man may say, but the promise is not inspiring.

[. . .]

(*NYS*, April 5, 1908, 3. Section, p. 6)

126

The whole opera migrated in a body to Boston as soon as the New York season came to an end. [. . .]

Boston itself was dull and sedate compared with other American towns. Here too we lived in isolation for the few days were were there.

(*AMM*, p. 131; original German in *AME*, pp. 161f.)

127

The most striking feature of the performance [of *Die Walküre*] was the conducting of Mr. Mahler. [. . .] He exerted a remarkable authority over his men; this authority was maintained quietly, without distressing pantomimic show. [. . .] His interpretation was eloquent [and] poetic [. . .] under [his] beat, this orchestra seems a different body of players from that with which we have been familiar.

(*The Boston Herald*, April 9, 1908, p. 14)

128

The theatre was crowded last night for the performance of [*Don Giovanni*]. [. . .] Mr. Mahler [. . .] fully sustained his reputation as the

Plate 28. Boston Theatre, *ca.* 1875 (woodcut published in the
Boston Illustrated).

Plate 29. Symphony Hall, Boston. (*LCE*, Figure 12)

best interpreter of Mozart; he always had the orchestra under control and [. . .] he used the harpsichord in accompanying most of the recitatives.

(*Boston Daily Globe*, April 10, 1908, Morning edition, p. 9)

129

It should not be forgotten that Mme. Fremstad was greatly assisted by Mr. Mahler's inspired reading of the score [of *Tristan und Isolde*] and marvellous control over the orchestra.

(*The Boston Herald*, April 12, 1908, p. 7)

130

Like [Alessandro] Bonci, Gustav Mahler, the conductor, is a little man: not so small as Bonci and more troubled looking. I saw him the night of his arrival while the brand of travel was still upon him. His face is a composite of Richard Wagner and Beethoven. [. . .] His hair is tousled, his eyes peer strainedly through his glasses, his mouth in repose tells of work, of sorrow, and of sympathy. He seems more the man to write music than to conduct public performances. He can do both in a masterly fashion.

The conducting of an orchestra he likened to riding a spirited horse; sometimes you spurred him on, again, you curbed him. But the rider should not try to make himself conspicuous. Mr. Mahler abhors pyrotechnical conducting. The leader is there to interpret the composer, not trying to flag a train; and an excess of energy is distracting to the auditors. "Many great composers were poor conductors; many of them were poor pianists or violinists."

I asked Mr. Mahler if, in giving himself to the interpretation of other works, he lost power as a creator. He thought not, but admitted that while the season was on he didn't give himself to composition.

(*The Boston Herald*, April 12, 1908, Special Section, p. 2)

131

[Philadelphia and New York
end of March-early April 1908][131]

My dear [Zemlinsky],[132]

A completely unexpected quarter of an hour of leisure and solitude during a 'guest'-tour gives me a chance to send at least a cordial greeting in reply to your delightful and interesting letter. [. . .]

This scrap of a letter has been in my dress-coat pocket for a week now—the coat in which I conducted the matinée in Philadelphia and into which I put the envelope when I was interrupted in the middle of writing—and I am only posting it because it illustrates the life I lead here better than anything I could say.

I live literally from day to day, conducting, rehearsing, dining, going for walks - according to the dictates of the timetable that my wife keeps beside her. I am not exerting myself at all, am doing very little, and have never had so little time as now. You will know this from your own experience. - I am eagerly looking forward to seeing Vienna and my old friends again. Next winter I shall be back here. We have both come to like this country very much; we are very much attracted by all the freshness, soundness and straightforwardness of the way things are done. There is a future in everything. [. . .]

(*MSL*, pp. 353f.; original German in *GMB*, pp. 337f.)

132

[New York, 17 April 1908]

My very dear Countess [Wydenbruck],[133]

[. . .] By the time you receive this letter I shall be happily afloat, and

[131]This letter is undated in Alma's edition of the letters (1924), while it is assigned to March, 1910 in *MSL*. However, the tone of the letter, both in its references to America, as well as in Mahler's reference to the "new regime" of Weingartner in Vienna (not quoted here) indisputably mark it as a letter written during Mahler's first season in the United States. On March 24, 1908, the Metropolitan Opera presented a matinée performance of *Siegfried* in Philadelphia; the letter was probably begun then.

[132]Alexander von Zemlinsky (1871 or 1872)1942) - Austrian composer, conductor and teacher. Mahler had one of his operas produced at the Vienna Opera. His pupils included Alma Mahler.

[133]Misa Esterhazy-Widenbruck (1859-1926) - Although she appears to have been a good friend of the Mahlers, little of substance is known about her relationship with Mahler. Apparently, she was a member of the Singverein chorus at the première of the Eighth Symphony (*HLG3*, p. 831).

even at this very moment I no longer have any peace: either for sitting down or for writing. The homesickness that has tormented me all the time (I'm afraid I shall never be anything but a dyed-in-the-wool Viennese) is changing into that excited yearning which you too doubtless know. [. . .]

(*MSL*, p. 319; original German in *GMB*, p. 339)

133

Gustav Mahler, it was announced last night, will conduct three concerts for the New York Symphony Society next season on Sunday afternoons, Nov. 29 and Dec. 13, and on Tuesday evening, Dec. 8.

Walter Damrosch invited Mr. Mahler to conduct during this season, but owing to his engagement at the Metropolitan Opera House he could not accept. His contract for next year, however, allows for a few outside appearances, and the concerts of the New York Symphony Society will be his first and only appearances before the beginning of his duties with the opera.

(*NYT*, April 14, 1908, p. 9)

134

New York, April 15, 1908

Dear Herr Director!

I have thought of another solution with respect to the pending question of the period of your engagement, one that would spare us the need to trouble Herr Kahn once again, and would avoid having to submit the matter to the 'Board' yet again. It is and, indeed, remains only a question of money, and it is already painful for me that, because of the time lost on this tiresome matter, we are quite unable to get to the point of discussing in detail certain necessary artistic questions. Once I had been given a free hand to come to an understanding with you concerning the dates of your engagement, I wanted to satisfy your wishes fully and completely, but I run into difficulties because of the repertoire of the 'Festival Performances'. Please meet me halfway, therefore, and agree to letting your contract commence on December 17th and terminate on March 16th. This could perhaps assist me with the planning of the repertoire, and it would avoid having to reopen the question all over again. There would be only three free days following your concert in December. On the 14th you should rest, in any case; Philadelphia is on the 15th, and you know yourself that one cannot rehearse there properly.

Concerning the difference between 3 and 4 days off for concerts, let us perhaps put into the contract "three, possibly four days", which will also exclude any further discussion. As you ask, in your letter of March 16th, for a paid trip for your wife (with her maid) and yourself from Vienna to New York and return, and for reimbursement of sundry travel expenses, it is certainly more practical for you to hand in a composite bill for these expenses later, rather than to insist on a fixed sum now, which will once again lead to drawn out consequences.

As I am very busy throughout the day, I would like to ask you most kindly to advise me as soon as possible whether you are in agreement with the above proposals.

With best regards,

Your devoted
A. Dippel

(*ELM*, pp. [385f.])[134]

135

New York, April 24, 1908.

An informal meeting was held at the residence of Mrs. George R. Sheldon, 24 East 38th Street, on April the 15th, 1908, to consider the plan of giving four Festival Concerts, to be conducted by Mr. Gustav Mahler next season at Carnegie Hall. It met with such enthusiastic approval, that it has been arranged with Mr. Mahler to give these concerts.

A guarantee fund of $17,000 is found necessary to cover all expenses, of which $11,000 have already been subscribed.

Mr. Mahler is to have the selection of the musicians for these concerts and he has the assurance from the Committee of their support in obtaining the very best material possible.

At this meeting, it was decided that these concerts should be but the beginning of a permanent orchestra. We recognize that this is a great undertaking, but the enthusiasm of those interested in the highest development of orchestral music, is sufficient to warrant this venture.

We feel that it is an inopportune moment to urge subscriptions of large sums of money, we therefore want those who are interested in this most important movement, to express their views in the matter. In the autumn our first aim will be to work for a permanent fund. Unless this fund is forthcoming within a reasonable time after the meeting in November, the question of a three years' guarantee fund will have to be considered.

The orchestra is not being formed for any one conductor, but we consider ourselves fortunate in being able to secure Mr. Mahler's

[134]See Note 116, p. 104; for the German text, see Appendix, A15.

128

services for the founding of a permanent organization. Heretofore, when attempts have been made to organize a permanent orchestra, the cry has been that there was no able conductor. Mr. Mahler has given his promise to enter into no negotiations whatsoever with any musical project in America before consulting with this Committee.

Mr. Mahler has expressed his confidence in his ability to form such an orchestra here and the ambition of the musicians in their desire to be associated with a really great organization, should point to its ultimate success.

The Board of Directors will have the power of engaging the conductor and we feel that a man of Mr. Mahler's eminence who has entered so wholly into the spirit of training a really fine orchestra for this City, will have trained the men to such a degree of perfection, that, if in the future, another conductor should have to be considered, this orchestra already formed, shall be of such a standard of excellence as to appeal to other eminent conductors should the moment arise to engage them.

Mr. Mahler sees the promise of the very best in orchestral development in this country and it only rests with us to determine whether we will support the best. It certainly seems as if Manhattan and Brooklyn should unite in forming an orchestra.

"The Greater New York Orchestra," excelled by none other.

This letter is sent to you with the hope that you give it your earnest and careful consideration. We feel that the opportunity has come to establish something which stands for the very highest in musical art and that it would be an irreparable loss to our City, to allow the formation of this orchestra to fall through when one of the most eminent conductors is here willing and anxious to undertake the great work of organizing.

A meeting will be held early in November, when it will be necessary for final action to be taken and we sincerely trust that you will make every effort to secure the co-operation of all music lovers for its furtherance.

An expression of your opinion as to this plan is desired.

Committee for the Four Festival Concerts.

Miss Charlotte B. Arnold.
Mrs. William T. Bull.
Mrs. William P. Douglas.
Mrs. William H. Draper.
Mrs. Foxhall P. Keene.
Mrs. H. Van Rensselear Kennedy.
Mrs. George R. Sheldon, *Chairman.*
Mrs. George Montgomery Tuttle.
Mrs. Samuel Untermeyer.
Mr. Alexander Lambert.

Mr. Dave Hennen Morris, *Treasurer.*
Mr. Patrick A. Valentine.
Mr. Felix Warburg. [135]

136

An arrangement has been made with Gustav Mahler, it was learned last night, by which that conductor will give a series of four festival concerts at Carnegie Hall in March and April, 1909, with a specially selected orchestra. [. . .] These festival concerts are to be given without the cooperation of any symphony society. Mr. Mahler is to select his own men.

Mrs. George R. Sheldon[136] is responsible for the plan, and has interested several of her friends in the scheme. She had the whole idea worked out before any announcement was made.

"Mr. Mahler's influence has been deeply felt at the Metropolitan Opera House this Winter," said Mrs. Sheldon last evening, "and we have to thank Mr. Conried for bringing him over. While he is here it would be a pity if he should not have a chance to conduct purely orchestral music with an orchestra of his own.

"Since the idea first came to me I have talked it over with many of my friends, and all of them have been extremely enthusiastic."

(*NYT*, April 19, 1908, p. 9)

137

In spite of the present alleged unpopularity of Richard Wagner, the Metropolitan Opera House was crowded at last night's performance of "Siegfried" in the present "Ring" cycle, and after the final act there were ten curtain calls, an ovation which involved Olive Fremstad and Gustav Mahler, both of whom said farewell to New York for the season.

Whether it is due to the Festival spirit or some other cause, the fact remains that the present performances of the "Ring" at the Metropolitan are being given much better than any of the Wagner performances of the regular season, and last night's "Siegfried" was notable in every sense of the word.

---

[135]This is a circular letter, presumably sent to potential supporters of the 'new' Philharmonic. The original was printed on three sides and folded; this copy is in the Damrosch Collection, NALT.
[136]Mrs. George Rumsey Sheldon (née Mary R. Seney) - wife of the leading financier (banking, *etc.*) and powerful Republican.

Gustav Mahler's reading of this score has already been praised highly, but last night the orchestra fairly sang under his baton. [. . .]

Altogether, it was an extraordinary performance, as the unprecedented enthusiasm at the end testified. Mr. Mahler, Mme. Fremstad, and Mr. Burrian[137] combined to make the final scene the culmination of a very notable evening.

(*NYT*, April 17, 1908, p. 6)

138

New York is to have another permanent symphony orchestra next season. While no public announcement has been made yet by the promoters, it is known in music circles that another organization is being founded to compete [. . .] for the favor of the metropolitan public.

The name of the conductor chosen for the regular concerts of the new orchestra has not been divulged, but it has been made known that Gustav Mahler has been engaged to conduct four concerts. [. . .]

It is understood that the new orchestra is being organized by a number of the former promoters of the New York Symphony Society, this step being the outcome of an attitude of disgruntlement toward former associates in the directorate of the organization conducted by Walter Damrosch. [. . .]

(*MA* 8, no. 2, May 23, 1908, p. 1)

---

[137]Carl Burrian [Karel Burian] (1870-1924) - Bohemian-born tenor, sang at the Metropolitan from 1906 to 1913.

Plate 30. Fifth Avenue, New York. Oil painting by Colin Campbell, 1907.
(The New-York Historical Society)

Plate 31. Hotel Savoy, New York, *ca.*, 1910.
(The New-York Historical Society)

CHAPTER II

The 1908-1909 Season

Commentary

Considering the shortness of the time Mahler spent in the United States each year, it is not surprising that the months he spent in Europe (nearly seven in all in 1908) were very full ones. While it is not my main purpose in this work to give a comprehensive account of the events of the times Mahler spent in Europe during these years, the desirability of a certain degree of biographical continuity justifies a brief survey of these months.

Although Mahler was only too aware of the need for a thorough rest during the summer months, the demand for performances of his own works (old and new), as well as for his appearance with various orchestras in general, made it unavoidable that he should travel widely for concerts between May and November. Thus, a few days after arriving back in Europe, he headed to Wiesbaden to conduct a performance of his First Symphony on May 8th. On May 23rd, he conducted the first one of a series of ten concerts mounted by the Czech Philharmonic in Prague to celebrate Emperor Franz Joseph's diamond jubilee. Nearly four months later, Mahler was back in Prague; on September 19th, the first performance of his Seventh Symphony constituted the closing concert of the jubilee series. In the autumn, he conducted the Seventh in Munich on October 27th, and led a concert in Hamburg on November 8th.

It was equally important that Mahler take advantage of the relative freedom and flexibility of the European months to devote time and energy to his creative work. As their previous summer residence in Maiernigg reminded them too much of their dead child, from 1908 to 1910 the Mahlers took a house in Toblach in the south of Tyrol (today Dobbiaco in Italy). It was here that Mahler composed most of *Das Lied von der Erde* during the summer of 1908.

As the excerpts from *Musical America* and *The Musical Courier* illustrate, some segments of the New York press sought to overcome the summer doldrums in the arts by keeping alive the intrigues relating to the future of orchestral music in the city. Not surprisingly, the rumours concerning Mahler's negotiations with operatic interests in Berlin provided additional fuel for speculation and innuendo.

In fact, as Documents **143** and **144**—among others—clearly show, Mahler was unable to put New York out of his mind during the summer. The planning for the next Metropolitan season—and that under new management—was a time-consuming, and in some respects a vexatious process. Although he had had to give up the idea of having Roller at his side permanently at the Metropolitan, he continued his efforts to make use of Roller's stage designs on a work-to-work basis. Uppermost in Mahler's mind during this summer, however, was the matter of his own position at the Metropolitan, especially in relation to Toscanini. It was seen in the previous section that the latter's arrival in New York had been preceded by glowing reports about his prowess as a Wagner conductor. Wishing to capitalize on this reputation, and considering that Mahler was not to appear at the Opera until well into the season, the management had proposed that Toscanini should conduct some performances of *Tristan* in the autumn. As one would expect, Mahler defended his rights to *Tristan*, the vehicle of some of his greatest triumphs both in Vienna and in New York, adamantly. It was probably because of Mahler's attitude that Toscanini's first performance of *Tristan* at the Metropolitan did not take place until a year later, after Mahler had severed his formal ties with the theater (see *1909-1910*).[1]

[1]Nonetheless, on March 26, 1909 (p. 7) the *Sun* published the following report: "Signor Toscanini has been suffering from such a severe attack of inflammation of the eyes that it was impossible for him to prepare the orchestra scores for his production of 'Tristan und Isolde'. [. . .] he has handed over the performances [. . .] to Mr. Hertz."

This year the Mahlers (complete with daughter and governess) sailed from Hamburg (Cuxhaven), and arrived in New York on November 21, 1908. For this season (as well as for the next two) they took rooms at the Hotel Savoy.

As had been arranged during the spring, Mahler began his second season in the United States by leading the New York Symphony Orchestra in three concerts. It is clear from the reviews that the first and third concerts (on November 29th and December 13th) were received most enthusiastically by the audience; the critical reactions ranged from unreserved praise to complaints about interpretation and execution. The overall impression gained from these critiques is perhaps best summed up by citing one of Krehbiel's comments from his review of the third concert: Mahler's first and third concerts with the Symphony were found to be "more inciting and exciting than satisfying."

Important and revealing as Mahler's interpretations of other composers' works may have been for himself and the critics, his introduction to New York as a composer-conductor with his Second Symphony on December 8th undoubtedly made this, the second concert the most significant one of the series. While some of his works had been heard in America before (such as the Fourth and Fifth Symphonies—see **177**), this was his first work to be conducted by Mahler himself. Although the critics were quick to note the audience's warm reception of the Symphony, their own reactions are unmistakably coloured by a certain inability (if not actual reluctance) to come to grips with the infinitely variegated riches, the overwhelming proportions and expressive range of the work.

While Mahler was occupied with his guest-appearances with the Symphony, the long-rumoured reorganization of the Philharmonic was well underway. Reading the press reports, one is struck by the apparent reluctance of the sponsors to confirm Mahler's place in their scheme of things. Yet, as was seen in the preceding section, in his personal correspondence Mahler had mentioned plans for an orchestra of his own as early as the spring of 1908. And already in January, 1909, he was engaged in a search for a new concert master (see **206**). At the same time, there was an evident desire on the part of the sponsors of the reorganization to keep Mahler's name firmly connected with the Philharmonic: the plans for two spring concerts with that orchestra were advertised in no less curious a place than the programme of the December 13th concert of the Symphony, their rival organization! In any case, Mahler's appointment by the Philharmonic was confirmed officially only in the middle of February.[2]

Once he had discharged his long-standing obligation to the New York Symphony, it was time for Mahler to take up his duties at the Metropolitan Opera. One cannot but wonder about the state of mind in which he must have approached the resumption of his work there. Although we are uninformed of the extent to which Mahler followed the New York press, it is unlikely that he could have remained ignorant of the growing tensions and administrative problems at the theatre. Above all, he must have apprehended the inevitability of increasing comparisons between himself and Toscanini as Wagner conductors, especially after the latter's triumphant Wagner debut with *Götterdämmerung* on December 10th. Even though it is no longer possible to reconstruct the programming process, it was probably not an accident that Mahler made his first Metropolitan appearance of the season on December 23rd with *Tristan*, the work with which he had initially conquered New York. As may be expected, the praise of the critics was warm and unstinting; equally unavoidably, most reviews incorporated overt or implied references to Toscanini.

Mahler's first new production of the season was one that neither called for nor occasioned comparisons. Quite simply, *Le Nozze di Figaro* on January 13, 1909 (its first production at the Metropolitan in four years) was acclaimed by the critics as incomparable. So great was the success of this opera under Mahler that a post-season European tour of it was hastily announced "as a specimen of what the forces at the Metropolitan are capable of accomplishing" (see **226**). For unknown reasons, this tour did not take place; the Metropolitan went to Paris for a month-long engagement at the conclusion of the 1909-1910 season.

One of the chief musical-social events of the current New York season was the retiring of Marcella Sembrich, the Suzanna of Mahler's memorable production of *Figaro*, after twenty-five years at

[2]Even though the fact that Mahler's appointment became "official" around this time is clearly evident from the multitude of press reports, his contract with the Philharmonic was approved only at the end of March. The minutes of the "Meeting of the Committee of Guarantors" on March 30, 1909 includes this paragraph: "Contract for Mr. Gustav Mahler was read and it was resolved to have the contract executed by the proper officers of the Society in the form presented." (The Minutes are in ANYP; this excerpt is published with their kind permission.)

the Metropolitan. It was eminently fitting that the Mahlers figured prominently in the whirl of concerts, dinners and balls in her honour during the first week of February.

On February 19th, Mahler conducted the American première of Smetana's *The Bartered Bride*. It is clear from the reports and reviews that no expense had been spared to mount this unusual work in a colourful and stylistically suitable manner. As a result, it brought not only critical acclaim, but also wholesale approval from an audience "not especially prejudiced in favour of peasant operas".

As the management of the Metropolitan had intended to safeguard itself against the possible failure of an exotic novelty like *The Bartered Bride*, a performance of *Fidelio*, the previous year's great success, was scheduled for the following night. Even some of the critics noted with surprise that this was to be the work's only performance in the current season. For that reason, perhaps, the production was apparently a less polished one than had been the norm, although Mahler received the usual critical praise.

During February and March, rumours continued to circulate that Mahler would remain with the Metropolitan on a contractual, if part-time, basis for the 1909-1910 season. It is clear from his letter to Roller (see **242**), however, that he had already decided to make the conductorship of the Philharmonic his sole occupation for the following year. In point of fact, the Metropolitan's management did prevail on Mahler to conduct one of its new productions in the spring of 1910 (see *1909-1910*).

As Mahler's letters to Roller (see above), Anna Moll (see **171**) and Carl Moll (see **250**) show, sometime during the early months of 1909 the Mahlers were visited in New York by "Mama," Alma's mother. Somewhat surprisingly, Alma's memoirs make no mention of this event.

The season at the Metropolitan was slowly drawing to a close for Mahler. On March 12th, he conducted the work to which he returned again and again as his *tour de force, Tristan und Isolde*. According to one critic, on this occasion he performed with uncharacteristic abandon, hurling "all petty restraints to the four winds of heaven." For his last appearance as a regular conductor at the Metropolitan on March 26th, Mahler chose *Le Nozze di Figaro*, the opera which brought him the most undivided and sustained critical acclaim in New York. Although he had by now lost Sembrich from the cast, this performance did nothing to blemish Mahler's record of success with *Figaro*.

The final brief but very important chapter of the 1908-1909 season for Mahler was centered entirely on the New York Philharmonic Orchestra. Through much of the season, beginning in earnest in December, scarcely a day could go by without a report or comment in the press concerning some aspect of the ongoing reorganization. A nasty and persistent undercurrent in the public discussion and debate was represented by the real or imagined (in any case, exploited) animosities between supporters and officials of the Symphony and of the Philharmonic. Inevitably and naturally, the rumours and reports concerning the dismissal of some Philharmonic musicians and the hiring of others—even if these often proved to be less fact than fiction—also provided the public with interesting reading. In fact, the changes that were to take place in the orchestra personnel for the 1909-1910 season were fairly extensive; they were also to continue into the season after that. (For a full discussion, see the next essay.)

After much anticipation, the day of the first of two concerts announced in the autumn arrived. The "conservative" programme chosen by Mahler for March 31st was generally well received by the critics. Some of them expressed their appreciation of the evident improvements in the orchestra's precision, tone and ensemble, while others greeted the concert as a promising indication of the standards to be established in the new season. Most reviewers remarked on the differences they noted in Mahler's interpretation of Beethoven's Seventh Symphony; all did so briefly and mildly.

Very little of this mildness was still evident in the reviews of the second Philharmonic concert on April 6th. As if some of the writers had lost patience with what they perceived as Mahler's transgressions against Beethoven's music, disputed points concerning his treatment of the "text" of the Ninth Symphony were catalogued at length. For the first time, one can make a clear distinction between the attitudes of Aldrich and Krehbiel, the two critics who were to remain most consistently pro- and anti-Mahler from now on.

It is interesting to note in the reviews of both Philharmonic concerts that there was nearly unanimous disapproval of Mahler's use (or, in the critics' view, misuse) of the timpani. Except for the fact that such complaints were to recur regularly, the blame could have more likely fallen on the available instruments and player than on the conductor. At any rate, Mahler was authorized to buy a new set of timpani in Europe during the summer (see **264** and **276**). Furthermore, the recruiting of a competent timpanist was to be one of his chief concerns during the off-season (see *1909-1910*).

As was the custom, the major New York papers published articles which surveyed the season just ending, and incorporated the writers' hopes and expectations for the coming season. In most cases, the prognostication centered on the plans of the reorganized Philharmonic and its increased role in New York's musical life. Detailed concert calendars were published, and the opportunity to enjoy Mahler's "supreme ability as an orchestral conductor" was welcomed enthusiastically. In general, the reader gains the impression that most interested observers looked forward to the anticipated reduction of what one writer described as "the enormous preponderance of opera over music of every other kind, sort and description."

By the time most of these season's-end columns appeared, the Mahlers were on the high seas; they had sailed from New York on April 10th. Because of the schedule of concerts set for the Philharmonic's 1909-1910 season, and due to the need for finalizing certain aspects of the orchestra's staffing, the summer of 1909 was to be somewhat shorter and more occupied with overseas affairs for Mahler than the previous one had been. Nevertheless, he was once again looking forward to a time of rest, composing, and general rejuvenation.

1908-1909
Documents

139

Vienna, June 10, 1908

Most esteemed Herr Director!

Last year, the general management of the Teatro Colón in Buenos Aires could not reach agreement with you for the following reasons:

I. because Salome and the Ring were omitted and were to be given only in the Summer of 1909;

II. because the theatre was completed too late and insufficient time was left to negotiate between New York and Europe.

Now the general management has authorized me to make you, esteemed Herr Director, an offer already for 1909 that would be finalized upon the arrival of the general management in August.

The theatre will present next year, in the Italian language, the following operas that are reserved for the German conductor.

Parsifal - Tristan - Tannhäuser - Lohengrin - Salome - Elektra - Rheingold - Siegfried - Walküre - Götterdämmerung and some other operas. You asked for 20,000 dollars for three months and the general management will be pleased to grant you 80,000 Frs or 16,000 dollars. Departure on April 28, return arrival in Europe middle of September. As these days the trip requires 15-16 days from Genoa to Buenos Aires and 6 days from New York to Cherbourg, it is more advantageous to effect the return trip via Europe.

Awaiting your kind affirmative response,
with all due respect,
yours truly,
Wilh[elm] Minkus
[Theatrical Agent][3]

140

Interesting facts concerning the manner in which Giulio Gatti-Casazza was engaged as Heinrich Conried's successor in New York, have just come to light in an interview obtained by a MUSICAL AMERICA correspondent abroad. It appears that the Milan impresario received his first invitation to compete in the contest for the directorship of the Metropolitan Opera House one year ago last Saturday. This fact is of more than passing interest, when it is recalled that the board of directors of the opera company and Mr. Conried himself declared throughout last Summer that the rumors regarding a proposed change in the control of the Metropolitan were entirely without foundation.

[. . .]

Regarding the relations which will exist between Gatti-Casazza and Andreas Dippel, it is reported that the former made the following statement to the latter while they were both in New York: "Listen, my dear Dippel, here I am the director, and do what I wish; you, too, may do what you wish, but only—after having asked my permission!"

That there will be no friction between Gustav Mahler, the distinguished German conductor, and Toscanini is made clear in another statement, attributed to the new director:

"When Toscanini knew that Mahler was to be his associate, he said to me: 'I am content. I am certain that we shall agree, for he is a great *maestro*. Only the small, incompetent ones are contrary and captious.'"

(*MA* 8, no. 7, June 27, 1908, p. 1)

---

[3]The 'new' Teatro Colón, seating 3,950, opened in 1908; it replaced one that had been in use from 1857 to 1888. - *ELM* contains three more communications to Mahler concerning this subject. A telegram and a letter from Minkus—dated June 30th and July 1st, respectively—conveyed to Mahler a final offer from Buenos Aires; quite probably, these brought the negotiations concerning the summer of 1909 to an end. The third item is a telegram to Mahler, dated July 7th, this time directly from the Milan agents of the Società Teatrale Italo-Argentina, asking for Mahler's conditions for an engagement for the "following summer." If this clause is understood to refer to the summer of 1910, this communication provides an explanation for the otherwise somewhat baffling resurfacing of the subject in the summer of 1909 (see **277**). - For the German text, see Appendix, A16.

141

[Vienna, June 1908]

Dear [Roller],

If Dippel keeps his word he will be calling on you in the next few days, asking you to take over *Tristan* and *Figaro* for New York. I should like to discuss the matter with you in detail. [. . .]

For today I want merely to draw your attention to the fact that in any discussion with Dippel it would be quite in order for you to bring up the matter of the fee that is still outstanding for your production of Fidelio. [. . .][4]

(*MSL*, p. 320; original German in *GMB*, p. 339)

142

SIGNOR GATTI-CASAZZA, Herr Andreas Dippel, Signor Toscanini and Herr Gustav Mahler have been all week in Vienna,[5] arranging the repertory of the Metropolitan season. They expect to separate today, and further than that no news.

(*MC* 57, no. 2, July 8, 1908, p. 20)

143

Kaltenleutgeben, Rudolfshof,
July 9, 1908.

Dear Herr Director!

I have returned from my trip, and had hoped to find an opportunity within the next week to look you up in your summer retreat and discuss with you in person the various questions that concern the coming season. Unfortunately, I still have much urgent work to take care of, also to make yet another few business trips so that, to my great regret, I must yet again postpone for a time my planned excursion to you. I spent six days with Gatti-Casazza in Vienna, and together we have worked out the repertoire for the season, partly in specific detail and in part along general lines. We also gave out a brief press communiqué, but this was considerably distorted through some commentary added by various papers on their own initiative. Accordingly, I consider it appropriate to send you here the precise text in the form of the item in the Neuer Wiener Tagblatt which

[4]See Note 118, p. 105.
[5]**141**, **143** and **144** prove beyond a doubt that this 'summit conference' included Mahler only in the imagination of the magazine's source.

contains the true wording of our release. From it, you can see that I had at once acceded to your wishes concerning the engaging of Spetrino,[6] in that immediately after your last visit I notified Herr Gatti and appraised him of your favorable recommendation. I had also hoped to be able to give you good news concerning your wish with respect to Tristan in a brand new production by Professor Roller, but I have encountered difficulties here, in that Herr Gatti has acquired by purchase a part of the Milanese stock, which also includes Tristan. Although I expressed my sincere regret that questions concerning the staging of Tristan in New York are not solved conclusively with this experiment, considering that I was faced with an accomplished fact, I did not believe that I should continue to protest. As a division of the German opera from the Italian, that we had both expected, will not take place under the regime that has been created, it is the view of the Board of Directors, and it is also only right and proper, that Herr Gatti be given the chance to show what he can do. I myself had also held out for this privilege and, for example, have been contractually guaranteed freedom of action with respect to the novelties "Tiefland", "Verkaufte Braut", "Königskinder" (which we will produce as our first opera in English, and as a world première). After you told me that you would gladly conduct the "Bartered Bride", I have taken quite special pains to see that all your wishes and requests should be honoured, and ask only that you let me know as soon as possible what more I can do on my part to do justice to your intentions. I have ordered the set from Kautsky,[7] the costumes from Blaschke,[8] have sought out all the materials according to Lefler's[9] renderings with his personal assistance, so that I am certain that we shall avoid the usual theatrical cliches in this case and will create a stylish production. For the role of Hans I have expressly engaged Jörn[10] from Berlin, Destinn[11] will sing

[6]Francesco Spetrino (1857-1948) - Italian conductor and composer. He conducted at the Imperial Opera in Vienna from 1903 to 1908, and went from there to the Metropolitan, on Mahler's recommendation. He remained there only for 1908-1909.

[7]Johann Kautzky (1827-1896), Carlo Brioschi (1826-1895) and Hermann Burghart (1834-1901) set up a joint studio/workshop in Vienna to supply sets and decorations to the Opera. It continued in this role after the deaths of the original principals and, for this reason, continued to be referred to by one or another of their names.

[8]See Note 21, p. 21.

[9]Heinrich Lefler (1863-1919) - Painter. He was the head of stage design at the Vienna Opera from 1900 to 1903, and thus Roller's immediate predecessor.

[10]Karl Jörn (1873-1947) - Latvian-born tenor. Following engagements in Germany, he sang at the Metropolitan from 1908 to 1914. He later became a highly regarded teacher.

[11]Emmy Destinn [Kittl] (1878-1930) - World renowned soprano of Czech extraction; she joined the Metropolitan in 1908. Puccini created the role of Minnie in *La fanciulla del West* expressly for Destinn.

Plate 32. Alessandro Bonci sang Don Ottavio under Mahler.
(*COS*, Illustration 102)

Plate 33. During his first season at the Metropolitan, Leo Slezak created the role of Hermann in Mahler's production of *Pique Dame*.
(*COS*, Illustration 127)

147

Marie, and we had already agreed on Goritz[12] as Kezal. The rest of the parts we will double and triple cast from the beginning so that you will, indeed, be able to select the best performers yourself. I have ordered the musical material from Bote & Bock in Berlin, and since you said to me that you would like to perform the overture in one of your concerts, I have right away ordered the string parts in sufficient numbers (10 first violin stands, etc.), so that the correct material for the concert is immediately at your disposal.

As concerns "Pique Dame", which you and I would also like to present, you yourself should decide whether you wish to entrust the directing to the stage manager of the Italian-French opera, Herr Speck (a good German name, by the way), or whether you wish to come to an agreement with me, in which case, with the help of Schertel[13] and several stage managers, we will undertake to produce the thing to your satisfaction. To keep everything orderly, I should mention that I have not yet brought up this question with Herr Gatti, and do so only today in order to learn your main thoughts on it. For the time being, I have acted in this matter only to the extent of ordering the sets from Burghart[14] in Vienna, and the costumes (about 200 of them new, the rest we can easily supply from stock) from Blaschke; all of it with the help, and based on the personal instructions of Lefler, who will also provide me with all important details of the production, as far as he can recall them. We will perform the opera in Italian, for we can best cast it in that language, and chiefly because we are counting on Caruso for the tenor part. Do you think that Morena could fit the part of Lisa? We would gladly give her a new part, to keep her busy. As the Countess, Maria Gay receives first consideration; beside her we also have Fremstad and Homer, as well as Madame Flauhaut. However, I will send you complete casting proposals for both operas in the very near future. I am looking after the acquisition of the musical materials. This is not such a simple matter. Italian vocal scores are found only in Russia; from there they will not re-deliver to Germany, and the German score is to be had only in Leipzig. Now I am trying to acquire the material from Moscow via Riga because, as the work is not under copyright in America, we want to avoid paying royalties. In general, I am of the opinion that royalties should accrue only to the composer and not to the publisher.

---

[12]Otto Goritz (1873-1929) - German baritone; following early engagements in Breslau and Hamburg, he sang at the Metropolitan Opera between 1903 and 1917; he did not, however, sing the role of Kezal in the first performance of *The Bartered Bride* see Note 79, p. 220).

[13]Anton Schertel's name appears on contemporary playbills as "Stage Manager."

[14]See Note 7, p. 145.

I have spoken with Herr Schmid in the Hofoper; he himself will arrange the material according to the Viennese production. If you have further wishes, I must ask you to let me know them at the earliest.

"Marriage of Figaro". According to the repertoire-plan, this could be the first new opera that you would conduct, and the première is scheduled for December 19th. Cast, as we had discussed it before: Eames - Countess (Gadski arrives only in February), Sembrich - Suzanna, Farrar - Cherubino, Sparkes (a young American with a powerful voice) - Bärbchen, Amato or Scotti - Count (perhaps also Feinhals, Munich, whom I have only recently engaged, if he can learn the part in Italian), Campanari or Didur - Figaro, Marcellina - Frau Matja van Niessen or Woehning, Basilio and Don Curzio - Reiss-Delvary-Tecchi-Bada, Bartolo - Paterna, Antonio - Missinao, etc., etc. You will find a slew of new names, but you will see, it will be a brilliant cast, and the performance itself will give you pleasure and grant you artistic satisfaction. If only I could now solve the question of sets and costumes satisfactorily, I would be a very happy man. Unfortunately, Herr Professor Roller upset my plans badly: quite aside from claiming that he can no longer deliver the drawings and renderings (a point that could have been solved easily by the Vienna Hofoper lending us the things with Roller's permission), he demands the well nigh unheard of sum of 6,000 crowns for the drawings, renderings, etc., etc. I cannot take on the responsibility for such a financial sacrifice for our Board of Directors, especially since, for example, Professor Lefler asks for 1,000 crowns for the three drawings and the renderings for Humperdinck's "Königskinder", and even that may possibly be paid by the publisher. I should have thought that, in the first instance, Roller should wish to be accommodating to you, who have personally done so much for him, and, secondly, that in order to establish firm connections with the Metropolitan Opera, he would have made at least somewhat negotiable demands. But it seems that artists of all types loose their power of clear reasoning as soon as the word 'America' is pronounced. That I remain true to Vienna, I have proved with the commissions that I have made to the workshops here, and the execution of which must be to my credit, in order to be able to face up to the competition that is definitely getting stronger this year. Therefore, I should have been only too happy if this year we could have also boasted of the artistic collaboration of Herr Professor Roller. Under these circumstances, I must naturally do my best to bring about a production as stylish visually as possible, even without Herr Professor Roller. Herr Lefler is most delighted to be of assistance to me in word and deed; his presence in Vienna several times a week, and the fact that I am in regular contact with him, are also of the greatest importance. To this is added the fact that already today we are projecting

an enormous deficit for the coming season, and so cannot order haphazardly but must work within the budget. As we must go all out for Pique Dame, to present it in a brilliant setting, if the opera is to succeed, Herr Professor Lefler suggested that one may very well save on Figaro in various ways if one acquires much for Pique Dame. For example, even at the Vienna Hofoper the ballroom from Pique Dame is used in Figaro; this was also confirmed by Brioschi.[15] As long as you do not place special emphasis on it, one could perhaps omit the scene interpolated by you into the 3. act (I mean the garden-scenery, where the letter-duet takes place); then completely newly built must be: the Countess's room, and the room for the first act and the closing scene. We must, in any case, alter the room for the first act for New York, that much you have confirmed yourself during our last meeting. On the other hand, I believe that we must retain the idea for the last act that the scene of action is removed to a terrace from where one looks down to the castle. The room of the Countess is simply a question of money: one can create it more cheaply or more expensively, and personally I am for creating something really solid, even if we must be very careful with life-like sets, given the stage and storage conditions in New York. Other than that, the room can be arranged similarly to that in Vienna, and I will also order the appropriate furniture, and so on, in Vienna. If you have any other special wishes for Figaro, please let me know as soon as possible, for at the moment there is still sufficient time to take these into account, whereas it may be too late in a couple of weeks.

Fidelio and Don Giovanni will come later in the season, and then most likely as extraordinary productions outside the subscription, so that these performances should not be attended by that public which desires merely distraction, rather than artistic challenge, from opera. Incidentally, I think that under certain circumstances we may well let our German chorus (which otherwise has little to do) sing in Italian in Don Giovanni and Nozze di Figaro; if you agree with this suggestion, I will speak about it with Gatti-Casazza at our next meeting.

Further, I must address yet another question to you, to which you should respond in principle first before we make our definite plans. You had most obligingly declared yourself ready to share the Wagner operas with Toscanini and Hertz, and we have interpreted this in such a way that you would not object if one of the conductors would conduct one or another of the Wagner operas before you. We will even be forced to produce three or four Wagner operas before you take up your engagment and, in all likelihood, those operas will be produced first for which the

---

[15]Anton Brioschi (1855-1920) - A scene painter at the Court Opera since 1886, he designed the sets for most of the productions until Roller's engagement in 1903. Son of Carlo (see Note 7, p. 145).

new German chorus, which must be thoroughly trained first, is not needed. Moreover, Parsifal will be given on November 26, 'Thanksgiving Day'; we must concentrate the full force of the new chorus on this. Lohengrin will not be given at all in the season, and Tannhäuser, Meistersinger and Götterdämmerung only later. Walküre is right in the first week with Hertz, and I think that you will not make it into a federal question if Toscanini conducts a few Tristan performances before your arrival, in the Milanese *mis-en-scène* familiar to him. It is generally known that for a foreigner, who wishes to show that he can also conduct Wagner in addition to the Italian repertoire, it is easier to make his debut with Tristan than with another opera, and that especially because of the soloists, with whom it is relatively simpler to come to an understanding in such a work. Also, in comparison with Siegfried, Walküre and so on, Tristan is a complete work, whereas the other music dramas are only parts of a larger whole. It goes without saying that during the span of your engagement Tristan is available for you to conduct whenever you wish; please let me know also whether, or which of the other operas in question, such as Götterdämmerung, Tannhäuser or Meistersinger, you may wish to take on, or whether you are sufficiently occupied with the proposed work schedule. Incidentally, during our conference I also brought up the question whether you, who have always demonstrated a great liking for light opera, might not be interested in preparing a work like Elisir d'Amore or Don Pasquale. Would you please let me know when convenient whether you are thinking of such a work? We would then, naturally, select the one that we could best cast.

Please forgive me that I am bombarding you with such a long letter in your summer retreat. As I have already said, I would have been much happier to talk about it all in person.

I am looking forward to an early reply to the questions posed, and remain with heartiest greetings,

Your devoted,
A. Dippel[16]

144

Dear Director [Dippel],

Allow me, in the first place, to reply to two points in your kind letter.

1. *Nozze di Figaro* on 19th December[17] is not possible. I shall

[16]For the German text, see Appendix, A17.
[17]Because of his three concerts with the New York Symphony, Mahler's Metropolitan contract for the 1908-1909 season was to come into effect only on December 17th (see **134**). It is clear from the reviews of *Figaro* that Mahler's extensive, carefully planned rehearsal schedule bore the desired results.

certainly keep my promise to be at the disposal of the theatre for rehearsals before the commencement of my engagement, in so far as this is practicable. I must, however, presumably devote the whole time that I reserve for this purpose, namely from 30th November to 17th December, to the piano rehearsals. As neither I, nor the personnel as an ensemble, will be continuously available, the number of rehearsals we can reckon on will, besides, be a limited one; and I shall have to rest content if rehearsal with piano, which with a *whole cast* is extremely difficult and tedious, can be got through before the commencement of my engagement. But then on top of that there would be the *director's rehearsals* and the *orchestra rehearsals*, to which I must give quite as much time and care as Conried let me give last year to *Don Giovanni*.

2. It is inconceivable to me that a new production of *Tristan* should be put on without my being consulted in any way, and I cannot give my consent. Further, I expressly stated when the contract was being discussed, *as you yourself can witness*, that I wished to keep in my hands for the ensuing season those works which I had already rehearsed and conducted in New York. I was given every assurance that this would be so, and it was only at your request and desire that I abstained from having it put in writing in the contract. If recently—out of consideration for the wishes of my colleague—I gave a free hand to the new Director, it was with the express exception of *Tristan*. - I took very special pains with *Tristan* last season and can well maintain that the form in which this work now appears in New York is my spiritual property. If Toscanini, for whom, though unknown to me, I have the greatest respect, and whom I consider it an honour to be able to salute as a colleague, were now to take over *Tristan* before my arrival, the work would obviously be given an entirely new character, and it would be quite out of the question for me to resume my performances in the course of the season. I must therefore urgently request that it shall be reserved for me to conduct and not be put in the repertory until after 17th December. [. . .]

(*AMM*, pp. 316f.; original German in *AME*, pp. 424f.)

145

"Mahler also conducts 'Tristan', and he has—which should be of especial interest in Vienna right now—effected certain cuts. It is our intention that next year the Wagner operas, the conducting of which will be shared by Mahler, Hertz and Toscanini, will be presented uncut in cyclic performances, but with cuts in single presentations."[18]

(Interview with Dippel, published in the *Neue Freie Presse* on July 2, 1908. Quoted in Stephen E. Hefling, "Gustav Mahler und Leo Slezak", in *MUB*, p. 191)

146
TOBLACH, VILLA ALTSCHLUDERBACH

[Summer, 1908]

Dear [Slezak],[19]

[. . .]

As concerns the "cutting affair" [. . .], I do not wish to get caught up in a controversy in this matter any more than in any other. The situation in Newyork [sic] and Vienna cannot be compared. - I go for 3 months to a theatre enterprise which, considering it in its entirety for 5 months of the year, in its total organization resembles more an Italian *stagione*. And in fact the Italian opera is in reality the focal point of the entire undertaking and German opera is at present more tolerated than established. So, without following the famous example of Don Quixote, I cannot hope to reform the personnel, the public, etc. in these few weeks and I must first accommodate myself to the cutting practices customary over there. Especially since the primary concern is to convince the public—which stays away disgusted from the careless performances—through convincing efforts to attend again and to stay to the end of the performances. -

That is what I did also when I came to Vienna; I first raised the general standard of the productions, and only gradually, without saying much about it, did I restore the cuts. [. . .]

Should I be called upon to be active in New York for a longer period, I do not doubt that with the gradual improvement in the artistic conditions

---

[18]The question of cutting Wagner's music dramas (and not only *Tristan*!) has always been a vexed one for opera houses. As this and the following two documents show, Mahler himself was not adverse to this practice, whether in Vienna or in New York (in fact, there is evidence of it already during his Budapest years), and the attempt at rationalization in **146** notwithstanding. And what strikes one as a typical exaggeration by Alma in **147** ("He not only introduced all the usual cuts, but invented new ones [. . .]") at first glance, gains considerable credence in light of **255** (s.a. **44** and **45**).

[19]Leo Slezak (1873-1946) - Celebrated Austrian tenor of Czech extraction. His flexible voice and great acting ability made him equally at home in all genres. He was a frequent guest at the Metropolitan between 1909 and 1913.

I will also prevent the quite *unjustified* (and at a *German opera theatre* downright *unforgivable*) mutilation of the Wagnerian works. [. . .]

(Original German in *op. cit.*, pp. 195f.)

147

Mahler in Vienna, whether as Director of the Opera or conductor of the orchestra, was intransigent in the extreme. He permitted no cuts in Wagner and imposed five or six hours' performances on the public. [. . .] [He] was very different in New York. He not only introduced all the usual cuts, but invented new ones in order to abbreviate the operas. He was merely amused, too, by lapses in the settings which in Vienna would have roused him to fury. It was not because his mind was distracted by the anxiety his illness caused him, nor that he did not take the New York public seriously - on the contrary, he found the public there entirely of his own way of thinking. The reason was that his whole attitude to the world and life in general had changed. The death of our child and his own personal sorrow had set another scale to the importance of things.

(*AMM*, pp. 135f.; original German in *AME*, pp. 166f.)

148

[Toblach, Summer 1908]

Dear Herr Lambert![20]

Many thanks for your kind lines. We have rented a farmhouse in Toblach, and hope very much to be able to greet you there before your departure. -

I will approach Herr Mildenberg's[21] opera with the greatest goodwill. When you speak with Wolfsohn,[22] please don't let on *in any way* that we have not considered *him* for manager for the coming years. He is counting on it very much, and would certainly embroil himself in the intrigues this year if he should find out how things stand.

---

[20]Alexander Lambert (1862-1929) - Polish-born American pianist and teacher. After studying with Liszt and Julius Epstein (Mahler's teacher), he moved to America in 1884; he directed the New York College of Music from 1887 to 1905.
[21]Albert Mildenberg (1878-1918) - American composer, conductor and teacher; in his operas, he was strongly influenced by Massenet.
[22]Henry Wolfsohn (*ca.* 1842-1909) - The German-born Wolfsohn became one of the first and most successful American agents and managers. At various times, he had such luminaries as Joseffy, Lhévinne and Richard Strauss under his wing.

Plate 34. Contemporary photograph of the "Komponierhäuschen", Mahler's studio-hut at Toblach. (W.G.W. Kurz Collection)

Plate 35. Carl Moll's drawing of the "Häuschen" at Toblach. (*RSM*, "Bilder", p. 50)

Cordial greetings and hoping to see you soon in Toblach.

Your devoted
Mahler[23]

149

A cable dispatch received in New York from Paris this week announced that Wassily Safonoff, the Russian conductor, has been re-engaged by the New York Philharmonic Society for a term of three years. Mr. Safonoff's present contract expires next April, so that his connection with the musical life of New York is now guaranteed until 1912, at least.

This announcement sets at rest the many rumors of the disagreement in the Philharmonic camp as to whether Mr. Safonoff should be re-engaged or a new conductor sought in his stead. M. Colonne, [. . .] Henry Wood, [. . .] and several conspicuous Germans and Russians had been mentioned in the discussion of a possible successor. Another story shown to be worthless by this development is the report that had reached Europe and gained credence in some quarters that the charter of the Philharmonic Society had been offered to a new orchestral organization, of which Mrs. George Sheldon was to be the head, and for which Gustav Mahler was to be secured at the termination of his duties at the Metropolitan Opera House.

(*MA* 8, no. 12, August 1, 1908, p. 1)

150

The New York Philharmonic Society is in serious trouble owing to the resignation of a number of its best players. [. . .] [They] have left the Philharmonic and signed contracts with the Metropolitan Opera House for its "extra" orchestra.[24] The reason given by some of the players for the defection of the malcontents is dissatisfaction with general Philharmonic conditions and with its conductor.

(*MC* 57, no. 6, August 5, 1908, p. 20)

---

[23]*HLG3* (p. 782) implies that this letter was written during the summer of 1910. Aside from the evidence of the second sentence, in which Mahler appears to announce the rental of their summer house at Toblach as something new, the fact that Wolfsohn died suddenly on May 31, 1909 almost definitely places this letter in the summer of 1908. - For the German text, see Appendix, A18.
[24]See **267** and Note 91, p. 237.

151

The "news" spread about some weeks ago, that Safonoff had been re-engaged by the Philharmonic Society to serve another three years after the expiration (next spring) of his present contract, was premature and now turns out to have sprung from inspired sources. The Russian leader has not been re-engaged by the Philharmonic, and THE MUSICAL COURIER is informed by one of the influential members of the organization that the coming season will in all likelihood be Safonoff's last in New York.

(*MC* 57, no. 7, August 12, 1908, p. 19)

152

Patrons of orchestra music in New York City are discussing with no little interest the report from Paris, on Sunday, to the effect that Mrs. George R. Sheldon is devoting her time to the institution of a new orchestra for the metropolis, with Gustav Mahler, of the Metropolitan Opera House as conductor. [. . .]

In orchestral circles there is a general belief that the plan has been conceived as an opposition force to the New York Symphony Orchestra, of which Mrs. Sheldon was formerly a member of the board of directors. In her announcement from Paris she is quoted as declaring that there is at present no worthy orchestra in New York, and the organization she purposes forming will be of a standard that will supply the need.

[. . .]

Mrs. Sheldon intends to cooperate with Richard Arnold,[25] of the Philharmonic Society, in forming the proposed orchestra, but there is no definite assurance on the part of Mr. Arnold [. . .] that the Philharmonic is willing to undergo a reorganization such as she suggests.

(*MA* 8, no. 16, August 29, 1908, p. 1)

153

Walter Damrosch [. . .] has given out a statement in regard to the plans of Mrs. George R. Sheldon, to establish another orchestra in New York.

[25]Richard Arnold (1845-1918) - German-born American violinist; studied in Leipzig. He played in the Theodore Thomas orchestra between 1869 and 1876 and was concert master of the New York Philharmonic from 1880 to 1909 (see also Note 81, p. 305).

Mr. Damrosch says that the agitation for the new orchestra seems to have been started by "two or three restless women with no occupation, and more money than they seem to know what to do with."

He points out the stability of the symphony society, which has been placed on a permanent basis [. . .] .

(*MA* 8, no. 17, September 5, 1908, p. 1)

154
Mahler Summoned to Berlin
(An Interview with Mahler)

We noted a dispatch of the "Neue Freie Presse" yesterday, whereby it is intended in Berlin to divide the directorship of the Royal Court Theatre, following the Viennese example, and to hand the directorship of the Royal Opera to Gustav Mahler. Mahler would then have the overall artistic leadership of the Berlin Opera, as he once did in Vienna. This news was calculated to occasion sensation and interest in the world of theatre, and as Gustav Mahler has been in Prague for some days now in order to lead the rehearsals for the première of his new symphony, we sent one of our correspondents to him to learn more about the Berlin plans.

Mahler was, of course, already aware of the news, but stated that he has no personal knowledge about the situation. Only his wife, who is staying in Vienna, notified him by telegram that rumours are circulating about his being called to Berlin. Much as his name may have come into play in Berlin, and given rise to such press reports, he, in any case, has not yet been approached in this affair. Also, as things stand in Berlin, it does not seem very likely to him that he should be summoned there, for there are three first conductors working there at the moment, Muck, Dr. Richard Strauss and Blech.[26] For the present, Mahler has also not considered a European engagement. He will go to America in November. [. . .].

(*Prager Tagblatt*, September 14, 1908, p. 5)

155
(Cable to THE MUSICAL COURIER)
PARIS, September 22, 1908.

---

[26]Leo Blech (1871-1958) - Eminent German opera conductor and composer. He was at the Berlin Opera 1906-1923 and 1926-1936.

"Mahler negotiating for the directorship of the Royal Opera in Berlin
[...]."

(*MC* 57, no. 13, September 23, 1908, p. 25)

156

From the New York Tribune (isn't that real earthy?) the following item
may be reprinted without offending any Democrats:

"If Mrs. George Sheldon was correctly reported," said Walter
Damrosch, conductor of the New York Symphony Society, yesterday,
"in saying that New York has no great orchestra, and therefore needs the
formation of one, she is wilfully and maliciously ignoring the actual
conditions." [...]

"This agitation," he said, "seems to have been started by two or three
restless women with no occupation and more money than they know
what to do with. There are people to whom music is merely food for
nervous excitement [...].

"The New York Symphony Orchestra [...] is on a permanent basis
[...]."

[...] New York has no permanent orchestra. This is a definite
statement which this paper is prepared to prove, if challenged. [...]

"Two or three restless women," according to Mr. Damrosch, are
agitating. This paper has been agitating for years past, so that New York
might finally enjoy what is known as a permanent orchestra headed by
what we call a competent conductor. [...] The restlessness is the
manifestation of an unsatisfied desire. That is the reason this paper has
been so restless. That is the reason thousands of musical people have
been so restless, and that is the reason an orchestra is going to be devised
and organized and a renowned conductor like Gustav Mahler put at its
head by "restless" elements, because there is no such combination, so
necessary to culture, here in New York. Mr. Damrosch is unhappy in the
choice of his language if the Tribune, whose music critic is an associate
of Damrosch, quotes him correctly [...]. Mr. Mahler [...] has done
work for a season at the Metropolitan Opera House that made us wonder
how it ever could have been possible for our critics to have reported as
favorably as they did on the conducting of most opera conductors at that
house. His direction of the "Leonora No. 3" overture on a "Fidelio"
night last winter was one of the events of our local musical history, and
told us of the horrible butchery of Beethoven for years past in our city,
the to us unintelligible performance under Damrosch of the ninth
symphony being merely one item in a long list of offenses against that
sacred memory committed by any number of men who had the insolence
to subject the works of Beethoven to their sacrilegious treatment. [...]

It is a wonder that there is no "restless" community to put an end to the present New York orchestral administration. And Damrosch says—if the words are his—that "there are people to whom music is merely food for nervous excitement," making this a reply to the honest and disinterested effort of certain music lovers of New York to create a competent orchestra under a recognized conductor who has already proved, in our own city, his superiority to most orchestral conductors that have ever appeared here. [. . .]

New York music must get out of its slough of despond. The orchestral situation has been one of despair, hopeless at times, seemingly incorrigible. It is about time for "restless" women and others and men with courage and quiet determination to get together and retrieve the situation. [. . .] Thanks to "restless" women, for whom music is "food for nervous excitement," and not "boodle," we are going to have some orchestral music in New York during the winter made by our own players under a conductor who will show us what music conveys. He will also give the negative evidence of what has been lost through the local conditions of the past. The committee of "restless" women will not stop until the task has been permanently performed; they will never be satisfied with a temporary success. Conditions of the past have made them entirely too "restless," particularly as they have not had sufficient and proper "food for nervous excitement."

Does it come with good grace from Damrosch that he discourages orchestral organizations? Is he not in favor of as much good music as a community can possibly furnish? Where is that much vaunted public spirit? Why decry an effort for more good orchestral music? Because one is running his own orchestral machine? The noble art of music is supposed to produce a different effect, particularly on the cultured twentieth century musical mind. Or is the noble art merely there for business? It would not be a bad idea to cultivate some of these "restless women" and get their ideas of the noble art: it might help along. A city like ours can support any number of good orchestras. So far it has refused to support one orchestra, exactly for that reason.

("Reflections", *MC* 57, no. 13, September 23, 1908, pp. 21f.)

157

ALWIN SCHROEDER,[27] the well known Boston cellist, who retired to Europe a year ago, and now has returned to make his permanent home in

[27]Alwin Schroeder (1855-1928) - Born in Germany, he was first cellist of the Gewandhaus Orchestra in Leipzig. He joined the Boston Symphony in 1891; also played in the Kneisel Quartet for a time.

this country, is credited with the appended statement in the Evening Post column of Henry T. Finck: "There is more 'musical atmosphere' here than there is abroad. I was very much disappointed with my return to Germany. The musical life here is much broader and more cosmopolitan." We hear the reverse asserted so often that it is a pleasant change to read an encouraging word about the musical culture of America, even if we feel in our heart of hearts that the compliment is more kindly than correct. We have better opera and better opera singers in New York than at Frankfurt, where Mr. Schroeder spent his year abroad, and Boston has a better orchestra than the conservative old German banking town, but those two circumstances in themselves do not constitute "musical atmosphere." Whether a country possesses that elusive quality or not usually is determined by the degree of musical culture found in the average inhabitant. Making a rude guess, we will venture to say that there are in Frankfurt many more business men who can play second violin in a quartet than in Boston or New York (to say nothing of those cities here which are the same size as Frankfurt in point of population), and we feel sure that the same ratio applies also to those business men and average citizens of Frankfurt, Boston and New York who might be able to tell offhand the name of Beethoven's only opera, the composer of "Les Huguenots," the story of "Götterdämmerung," and to enumerate three compositions each of Schubert, Schumann, Haydn, Mendelssohn, Verdi, Mozart, Chopin, Liszt, Brahms and Strauss. Then, too, there are more mechanical pianos and 65 note rolls[28] in Boston and New York than in all Germany, or possibly all Europe, and that suffices to stamp our two centers of culture as places lacking in the truest kind of "musical atmosphere."

(*MC* 57, no. 13, September 23, 1908, p. 20)

158

That the formation of new orchestras by the Metropolitan and the Manhattan has resulted to a certain extent in the depletion of the ranks of New York's principal symphony organizations, is shown by the membership lists of the leading orchestras of the city for the new season. The expansion of the opera campaign, combined with other minor causes, has necessitated practically a reorganization in one or two instances; in short, intrumentalists of the first rank are probably in greater demand in the metropolis this Fall than ever before.

---

[28]For some time, *MC* had been conducting a relentless campaign against player-pianos in general, and against the 65 (as distinct from the 88) note roll in particular.

[. . .]

Speaking of the withdrawal of so many of the Philharmonic players, Richard Arnold [said]: "You cannot blame men if they go where they can get a good permanent salary. A man's first duty is to his family. Some of the men who are leaving have been with the orchestra from twenty-five to thirty years, and you may be sure that they gave the matter much consideration before taking the step [. . .]"

(*MA* 8, no. 20, September 26, 1908, p. 1)

159

A rather ominous rumor is making the rounds. For some time past it has been whispered that the managements of the Theater and Opera at Berlin [. . .] are to be separated in [their] functions [. . .] and that negotiations are pending with Gustav Mahler for the place of director of the Opera at Berlin—that is, the Royal Opera. [. . .]

The likelihood of a Mahler diversion became apparent with the appointment of Toscanini for the Metropolitan conductorship [. . .] . Meanwhile Mahler [. . .] writes to the Prague Bohemia [. . .] that he is in negotiation with the Berlin Royal Opera and so far, or so good, as the case may be.

The very fact that Mahler could, at the present stage of affairs at the Metropolitan, when some results of his first season's work could find a more definite expression under his own control, even [. . .] consider [. . .] any proposition from any source, discloses a polity which may have been presaged by some, but hardly considered serious by most [. . .] . It has been suggested by the Mahler enthusiasts of New York, most justifiably, that at last the proper man had been found for the permanent enthronement of the ideal reality in the midst of us. Mahler's confirmation of the fact that negotiations are pending with Berlin does, however, not signify that we shall be without Mahler this season, and, let us hope, many other seasons.

("Reflections", *MC* 57, no. 14, September 30, 1908, p. 22)

160

Mrs. George Sheldon, whose plan to organize a new symphony orchestra with Gustav Mahler as director has already been described in MUSICAL AMERICA, has encountered a setback in the action of Alexander Lambert, the pianist, who has resigned from the committee which had the matter in charge.

Mrs. Sheldon has written to Richard Arnold, of the Philharmonic

Society, to say that she had no share in starting the report that the Philharmonic Society was to be used as the basis of the permanent orchestra. It is believed that Mr. Mahler will not return to America after the present season, as he is said to be negotiating for the directorship of the Royal Opera in Berlin for a period of five years.

(MA 8, no. 22, October 10, 1908, p. 6)

161

[ca. October 1908]

Dear Friend![29]

Just a brief greeting, and the announcement that we sail on the "Amerika" on the 12th of November, and expect to arrive in New York on approximately the 20th or 21st. If you would be so kind to advise *Mr. Damrosch* (both brothers) of my arrival, and as you will no doubt find yourself in the Hotel Savoy on occasion, also let Herr Ries know, so that he may have our suite ready for us.

We look forward very much to be able to chat with you again soon, and send you our cordial greetings,

Your devoted
Gustav Mahler

162

During Gustav Mahler's stay in New York it was my privilege to hold many intimate conversations with him which enabled me to obtain a deeper knowledge of his inner feelings and thoughts than casual acquaintance would have permitted. His extreme nervousness, his tremendous concentration upon his work and his artistic purposes frequently made him appear to the casual observer as unsociable and sometimes even rude, but those who knew him best recognized that this resulted from no intent to give offence. Mahler liked to live his own life in his own way and felt that social amenities should not be expected of him. He was hypersensitive, and things which would have left a less nervous organism untouched irritated him deeply.

Mahler was a great musician and a sincere artist. His brief activity in

---

[29]*HLG3* (p. 406) assumes that this letter was addressed to Alexander Lambert. - For the German text, see Appendix, A19.

163

Plate 36. Frank Damrosch. (*LCE*, Figure 98)

Plate 37. Walter Damrosch. (*LCE*, Figure 22)

New York will ever be remembered by understanding music lovers and musicians as a stimulating and inspiring experience.

(Frank Damrosch[30] in *SFM*, p. 9)

163

The last time I met Mahler was when I was director of the Opera at Hamburg. [. . .] [He] had just returned from his first American tour and we were very eager to hear from him what he had to say about the New World. He was very talkative about the American life, which he liked so much. He praised the practical sense of the American people and told us that the American orchestras were beginning to be equal to those of Europe. It appeared to me that he was not disappointed to have given up his throne in Vienna.

(Joseph Stransky[31] in *The New York Herald Tribune*,
March 22, 1931, 8. Section, p. 9)

164

We met in Hamburg and went on board at Cuxhaven. [. . .]

We had our three-year-old child with us for the first time and I had engaged an elderly Englishwoman as nurse,[32] who was always inculcating the stoicism of a Samurai in her charge. When we were on the tender and the large ship loomed up, the little girl gave a cry of delight, whereupon this lady advanced, held her tightly by the hands and said sternly: 'Don't get excited - don't get excited!' Mahler heard this and instantly snatched her up and sat her on the taffrail with her feet dangling over the water. 'There you are, and now be as excited as you like. You shall be excited.' She was.

We did not go back to the Majestic but stayed this year and the next year at the Savoy, where nearly all the stars of the Metropolitan, Caruso, Sembrich, etc., stayed also.

---

[30]Frank (Heino) Damrosch (1859-1937) - Conductor and teacher, Walter's brother. He was chorus master at the Metropolitan Opera from 1885 to 1891, and conducted the Oratorio Society, as successor to Walter, from 1898 to 1912.

[31]Josef Stransky (1872-1936) - Born in Bohemia, Stransky had a successful career in Prague, Hamburg and Berlin before he came to the United States in 1911, as Mahler's successor at the head of the New York Philharmonic, whom he was to lead until 1923.

Mahler conducted a concert in Hamburg in November, 1908, immediately prior to embarking for America.

[32]This is no doubt the "Miss Turner" mentioned in **265**.

(AMM, pp. 144f.; original German in *AME*, p. 178)

165

Gustav Mahler, conductor of the Metropolitan Opera Company, arrived yesterday with his wife on the Hamburg-American liner Amerika. Mr. and Mrs. Mahler have been abroad since Spring, and the conductor, when he stepped ashore last night and received a welcome from his friends, said that he had had a very good time abroad.

(NYT, November 22, 1908, p. 11)

166

In view of the many conflicting reports published from time to time in regard to the connection between the plans of Mrs. George Sheldon and the New York Philharmonic Society, a representative of MUSICAL AMERICA called on Richard Arnold, the vice-president of the society and concert-master of the orchestra, and obtained from him [an] interview, which will definitely dispose of the many rumors now current:
  "[. . .]
  "The plan in a nutshell is this: To raise an endowment for the Philharmonic Society sufficient to make possible the playing of symphonic music only, to guarantee a sufficient number of rehearsals, and to make it a permanent orchestra in every sense of the term.
  "The plan was evolved by Mrs. George Sheldon and myself after many conversations, and had its origin in a desire to make this society a permanent organization: there is not, and never has been, the slightest intention of antagonizing any other local orchestra.
  "While these plans are not without a possibility of failure, yet they have progressed so far, and have met with so little opposition (absolutely none, I may say), that it has been possible to approach Gustav Mahler with an offer of the directorship of the permanant orchestra. There is no contract between us, but there is a very clear understanding as to the offer of the post of director and its acceptance, and the amount of salary, when the plan materializes.
  "[. . .]"

(MA 9, no. 3, November 28, 1908)

167

Gustav Mahler, who is to conduct three of the New York Symphony Society's concerts [. . .] has had a very interesting career as a theatre

Plate 38. Giulio Gatti-Casazza in 1908. (U.S. History, Local History & Genealogy Division, The New York Public Library, Astor, Lenox and Tilden Foundations)

Plate 39. Richard Arnold, concertmaster of the New York Philharmonic from 1880 to 1909. (Howard Shanet, *Philharmonic—New York's Orchestra*, Garden City, Doubleday, 1975, Illustration 33)

and symphonic conductor in Austria, Germany, England and America. Not only is he notable as a conductor, but he has been a most active composer.

Besides his eight symphonies, two of which, the seventh and eighth, are still in the manuscript and have never been performed,[33] Gustav Mahler has written mainly songs. [...]

Mr. Mahler's versatile genius has applied itself not only to music, but to literature as well. The "songs of the road"[34] were written on his own words as was the choral[e] of his second symphony[35] [...]

(*NYW*, November 29, 1908, Metropolitan Section, p. M5)

168

Mr. Gustav Mahler began yesterday afternoon in Carnegie Hall[36] the series of three concerts in which he is to conduct the New York Symphony orchestra. [...] It was not one of the least of Mr. Mahler's achievements yesterday that he divested himself so far as he did of the qualities of a dramatic conductor in music that is opposed to the dramatic character - music represented especially on his programme by Schumann's first symphony. The rest of the programme was on the other side - Beethoven's "Coriolanus" overture, Smetana's overture to "The Bartered Bride", and Wagner's "Meistersinger" overture.

No conductor is less concerned with the pictorial impression he makes upon his listeners, or is more concentrated upon the business of the orchestra than Mr. Mahler. He has absolutely none of the graces, none of the poses or ornate and unnecessary gestures of the "prima donna"

---

[33]The writer of this item was clearly unaware of the première of the Seventh Symphony during the preceding September in Prague.

[34]*Lieder eines fahrenden Gesellen* (Songs of a Wayfarer). In point of fact, only the texts of the last three songs are original verses by Mahler; the text of the first song is unmistakably from *Des Knaben Wunderhorn*, even though it was modified by Mahler (for details, see Zoltan Roman, ed., *Lieder eines fahrenden Gesellen*, London and Vienna, Weinberger and IGMG, 1982, pp. viiif. [*Gustav Mahler-Sämtliche Werke-Kritische Gesamtausgabe*, vols. XIII and XIV, fascicle 1]).

[35]Again, this is not entirely correct. Approximately the first quarter of Mahler's text (not to mention the inspiration for it) was taken (in a slightly modified form) from Friedrich Klopstock's poem "Die Auferstehen," one of his *Geistliche Lieder*.

[36]Carnegie Hall, seating 2,784, was built in 1891 by Andrew Carnegie (at first it was simply known as Music Hall). Tchaikovsky was the guest of honour at the opening ceremonies.

conductor[37] as he stands upon the platform, short in stature, without distinction of figure or of manner, with the left hand occasionally thrust into his pocket. His beat is usually short and decisive, very clear; his motions all for the orchestra, without graphic or picturesque significance for the eye of the listener. But the intense energy, the keenness and penetration, the force and authority of the man were as an electric stimulus to the players.

Mr. Mahler has a strong and sensitive feeling for the essential characteristics of the music he is interpreting - the characteristics that make it what it is and that differentiate its spirit from other music. He has the unfailing power of seizing upon them and molding his interpretation in accordance with them. He has the vision of a poet, but it is clear and never obscured by the mists of sentimentality. Health and strength are in him, and with them fine and subtle qualities of intellect, poignant intensity of spirit.

Mr. Mahler is not one of the ostentatiously "subjective" conductors. He is one who seeks always sincerely for the spirit of the composer and for its expression through a natural and eloquent utterance. And while this expression is necessarily conditioned by nature and temperament and sympathies of the conductor, it is the composer who is interpreted, not the conductor who is exploited. Thus Mr. Mahler had no new "readings" of any of the music he put upon his programme. There were no inner instrumental voices brought into prominence strangely to overlay familiar passages with a new suggestion. His tempi for the most part seemed natural, inevitable, not ostentatiously modified with the changing expression, nor obstructed with rubatos. There was no anxious

---

[37]This is one of a number of American descriptions of Mahler's deportment on the podium; in all of them, his calm, economical movements and lack of superfluous gestures is emphasized (see also **130, 258**). Yet, in his earlier years he was often the target of censure and ridicule because of his volatile, excessively gesticulative conducting. Some ten years earlier, for example, he was described thus in Vienna:

"Herr Mahler's manner of conducting is not above criticism. [...] It often happens that Herr Mahler's left hand does not know what the right is doing. [...]

Mahler's left hand often jerks convulsively, marking the Bohemian magic circle, digging for treasure, fluttering, snatching, strangling, thrashing the waves, throttling babes-in-arms, kneading, performing sleights of hand - in short it is often lost in *delirium tremens*, but it does not conduct." (*Deutsche Zeitung*, November 4, 1898; quoted in *BRM(E)*, p. 217, *BRM*, p. 220)

Even if one takes into account that the writer of the above lines was decidedly anti-Mahler, the many surviving caricatures from this and earlier times tend to lend credence to his description. Evidently, Mahler's physical exuberance on the podium had moderated considerably by the time he made his first appearance in America. In part, this was undoubtedly due to an increase in maturity and experience; at the same time, his illness may well have hastened the process.

seeking after "expression", no rhetorical phrasing or extravagant modelling in high relief, to the detriment of the symmetry of the larger outline. But there were warmth and sincerity of expression, abounding life and vitality, an exquisite and unfailing rhythmic quality. There was the clear delineation of the melody wherever it was manifest, and there was skillful and unerring adjustment of the instrumental values in the orchestration.

Schumann's symphony was played with splendid verve and buoyancy that expressed the Springtime joyousness of the composer's mood; there was poetry in the slow movement, and there were some especially delightful touches in the trios of the scherzo. Mr. Mahler's finest achievement was in the "Coriolanus" overture of Beethoven. His playing of it was truly in the grand style, expounding the profound tragedy of the music, with its contrasting tenderness beautifully sung in the second theme. The music tempts to exaggeration of the moods that are expressed in it; but the tragedy in Mr. Mahler's reading was not rhetorical nor the tenderness sentimental.

The overture to Smetana's opera "The Bartered Bride"—an opera which Mr. Mahler expects to conduct at the Opera House later in the season—has been often played, but rarely at so breathless a pace or with so whispered a pianissimo in the fugato in which the strings unite with so deliciously witty an effect. The conception and performance of the piece were as of an actual prelude to a comedy to follow, and they were marked by the utmost vivacity and humour. [...]

The prelude to "Die Meistersinger" closed the concert. It was played with a most stirring effect, and the performance was as finished and ornate in detail as it was splendid and sonorous in its larger proportions. [...]

(*NYT*, November 30, 1908, p. 9)

169

Herr Mahler has already been acclaimed here, as elsewhere, [as a conductor of opera] but the audience yesterday enjoyed the first opportunity of judging his work in a new and even more exacting field of artistic effort.

Herr Mahler, as I hear, was reported to have said that his conducting yesterday was something of a farce, as the members of the orchestra neither came to nor stayed at rehearsals, as he wished them to, and I am inclined to believe the report as accounting for the lack of quick response from the orchestra to his beat, specially noticeable in the first movement of the symphony. For all this the orchestra played yesterday so much better than usual, with so much more precision, sonority, colour and unity of orchestral feeling.

[. . .] There can be no question that the dramatic and forcible in music, rather than the romantic and tender appeal first to this really great conductor. This is probably owing to his operatic training, and to this also it is doubtless due that three dramatic overtures proved the most effective and satisfactory portion of the programme yesterday. Not that the symphony was not well played, for it was; but I deem it hardly dignified to play tricks with the classical masters as Mahler did with the tempi of Schumann's most beautiful work. Convention and tradition may at times bind too fast, but the tempi set by the experience of nearly seventy years [. . .] may not be lightly upset, especially when the results are decidedly questionable.

The introduction marked andante maestoso lost in nobility by being taken too fast, while the andantino tempo at which Mahler played the heavenly larghetto robbed the movement of half its beauty and romantic charm. The somewhat rubato interpretation given the tempi in the scherzo was justified by the admirable effect of variety of movement and colour thereby obtained; but I can but deprecate the almost amateurish ritards in the opening theme of the finale and in the flute solo at the reprise which made Schumann sound like Delibes in "Silvia". [. . .]

(*NYW*, November 30, 1908, p. 7)

170

It has leaked out that after the Sunday concert of the New York Symphony Society, at Carnegie Hall last Sunday, at which Gustav Mahler appeared for the first time in this country as a conductor, that Herr Mahler complained bitterly of the orchestra and said that, as many of the members of the orchestra neither came to rehearsals nor, if they did come, stayed as he wished them to, his conducting was reduced to more or less of a farce, and as he was to be held responsible he wished the fact known.

This, it will be remembered, is one of the reasons why a movement is on foot to make a permanent orchestra in New York City out of the Philharmonic - that is, to raise money enough to pay the members of the orchestra sufficiently so that they will attend rehearsals and not send substitutes and thereby reduce conducting to a farce, as Herr Mahler says.

(*MA* 9, no. 4, December 5, 1908, p. 4)

171

[New York, late 1908]

My dearest little Mama,

[...]

We are eagerly looking forward to your arrival, for you really are coming, aren't you? Arrange things so as to make the return trip with us in grand style, in your own state-room.

[...]

[added by Alma:] No, *I'd* rather it was in February - then I'd see you sooner, or mid-January. [...]

(*MSL*, pp. 328f.; original German in *GMB*, p. 350)

172

Outwardly at the temple of music at 39th Street and Broadway all has been harmony, though patrons of the opera have noted that there has been a superabundance of productions of works from the Italian repertory in comparison with those of the German and French composers,[38] and have drawn their own conclusions as to whose is the final authority in the conduct of the Metropolitan.

[...]

Many reasons, it is said, have contributed to the friction that has already arisen in the management at the Metropolitan. The chief cause of the trouble, however, is said to be the failure of the board of directors to indicate the spheres of Mr. Gatti-Casazza, the general manager, and Mr. Dippel, the administrative manager, although that failure was predicted when the first announcement was made that two men—one an Italian with no American experience, and the other a German, for years the

---

[38]Such a statement (most often in the form of a complaint) is found quite frequently in the press and in other records. It seems from the statistical evidence that it was not entirely without foundation: during the 1908-1909 season, there were 79 Italian performances, 45 German, and 19 French. In the following season, the management's promises notwithstanding, the imbalance grew worse: 79 Italian, 34 German, 13 French (H.E. Krehbiel, *More Chapters of Opera*, New York, H. Holt, 1919, pp. 426, 428).

The implication that this imbalance was due to the preferences of the new management of the Metropolitan—an implication that often forms part of such complaints—does not, however, stand up to close scrutiny. An analysis of season-end statistics published by the *Times* (April 5, 1908, Part Six, p. 4) shows that during the 1907-1908 season there had been 78 Italian, 41 German, and 11 French performances.

most useful and reliable tenor in the Metropolitan cast—had been selected to share the responsibility of putting the Metropolitan on a new and higher plane.

(*NYTrib*, December 5, 1908, p. 7)

173

Giulio Gatti-Casazza, at the last meeting of the Board of Directors of the Metropolitan Opera House, was re-engaged as General Manager for the next three years. The Directors failed to take similar action regarding Andreas Dippel, the present administrative manager. Mr. Toscanini will be retained as Italian conductor.

[. . .] [In a] letter sent to the Board of Directors by Messrs. Caruso and Scotti, and Mesdames Eames,[39] Farrar and Sembrich, [. . .] the board was asked to extend the contract of Andreas Dippel, [. . .] at the same time that it extended that of Mr. Gatti-Casazza [. . .] This was the reply sent to the singers [. . .] :

New York, Dec. 2, 1908.
Ladies and Gentlemen: We beg to acknowledge receipt of your communication of Nov. 25, to which we have given due consideration, with particular reference to your expression as to the protection of your own artistic interests. [. . .] The board and the management are grateful to you, and sincerely appreciate that you are entitled to every consideration and courtesy. Your interests and theirs are identical - namely, to achieve for the performances at the Metropolitan Opera House the highest possible level of artistic excellence. [. . .] on the other hand, we are entirely convinced that your own experience and intelligent appreciation of the facts must lead you to realize that, however great the individual artists, the greatest artistic success can only be accomplished if there exists a spirit of willing co-operation with and submission to the management, and a recognition of the necessity of centralized authority, together with mutual confidence and good will.

It is not possible to administer an organization like the Metropolitan Opera under two heads, and it was never intended that it should be so administered. We do full justice to the excellent qualities of the Administrative Manager, Mr. Dippel, and to his intelligent and zealous labors. [. . .] but there can be no divided artistic authority, and [. . .]

---

[39]Emma Eames (1865-1952) - American soprano; active chiefly at the Metropolitan and Covent Garden between 1891 and 1909. She was especially prized by Puccini for her representation of Tosca.

Mr. Dippel's functions are, and must be, subordinate to those of the General Manager [. . .]

Very truly yours,
Otto H. Kahn [etc.]

(*NYT*, December 6, 1908, p. 1)

174

Mr. Gatti-Casazza [stated] that he would be only too happy to give the New York public Opera in German. He thinks, however, the New York public is lacking in appreciation of German opera, but hopes to amend this fault by the presentation of the operas with the best singers and in the best possible manner. In explanation of Mr. Mahler's late appearance in the season, it was stated yesterday that his contract at the Metropolitan Opera House did not begin until December 15.

(*NYTrib*, December 8, 1908, p. 7)

175

The announcement that Heinrich Conried, former director of the Metropolitan Opera House, intends to sue the Conried Metropolitan Opera Company for breach of contract, estimating his loss at $90,000, does not come as a surprise to those who have been in touch with operatic affairs in New York City, nor will it arouse as much interest as it would have done were Mr. Conried still in power.

[. . .]

To-day, the situation at the Metropolitan is rapidly tending to duplicate the situation in the latter part of Mr. Conried's term. We have [. . .] the same conditions in the front of the house with regard to the imposition on the public in the way of seats. We have had unquestioned deterioration in the performances that are being given, for while there has been undoubted improvement in the way of orchestra, chorus and *mise-en-scene*, many of the artists who are appearing in the operas are certainly not up to the standard of former years, for which there should certainly be no excuse, if Messrs. Dippel and Gatti-Casazza have had the resources which, it is understood, were placed at their disposal.

One of the causes for this would appear to be the fact that the powers behind the management of the Opera House are less concerned in promoting musical culture and satisfying the public, than they are concerned in maintaining a certain social prestige. There are men connected with large financial institutions who are either interested in the directorship or allied with it, who appear to think that because they have been able to float large amounts of questionable securities on the public—as recent revelations have shown us—they will be also able to float singers of questionable ability on the musical public as well!

The results of this will be that the public will gradually lose interest, or will confine itself to sustaining Mr. Hammerstein, who is doing splendid work at the Manhattan, and before long, in spite of the enormous subscription which the Metropolitan directors have, amounting to over a million dollars, including Brooklyn and Philadelphia, the managers will be face to face with a very considerable deficit.

(Editorial, *MA* 9, no. 5, December 12, 1908, p. 16)

176

After a sharp dispute between Hugo Colombini,[40] one of Oscar Hammerstein's new tenor singers and Cleofonte Campanini, musical director of the Manhattan Opera House, the status of Signor Colombini [. . .] is in doubt.

[. . .]

"Colombini threatened to kill me at the rehearsal", said the Maestro, "because he was very excited, believing it was through me that he had been cast for the part of Cassio in 'Otello'. I told him that Mr. Hammerstein had selected the artists [. . .].

" [. . .] He said angrily he had been engaged to sing first-class roles and Cassio was a second part."

[. . .]

Colombini was engaged for the season by Mr. Hammerstein in Milan last Summer. [. . .] Mr. Hammerstein says that if he likes he may go back there.

(*NYT*, December 6, 1908, p. 1)

177

At the second of the concerts in which he will conduct the New York Symphony Orchestra [. . .] Gustav Mahler will perform only one work - his own second symphony in C minor, which will then be heard for the first time in America. This is noted as one of the most ambitious and

---

[40]This incident must have ended Colombini's career, certainly in New York. His name does not occur in the cast lists, or as a member of the company, in a detailed history of the Manhattan Opera (John Frederick Cone, *Oscar Hammerstein's Manhattan Opera Company*, Norman (Okl.), Oklahoma University Press, 1966), nor is it found in standard reference sources.

certainly one of the longest and most colossal of modern symphonic works. [. . .]

Music of Mr. Mahler is still fresh in the recollection of the New York musical public. On Nov. 6, 1904, Walter Damrosch performed his fourth symphony for the first time in this country, and on Feb. 15, 1906, Mr. Gericke had the Boston Symphony Orchestra play his fifth here. [. . .] In recent years Mr. Mahler has come to take an important place among contemporaneous composers, and his work, like that of most other modern composers of mark, has aroused controversy and has called forth a passionate propaganda on its behalf. This propaganda is carried on in Germany, where it seems to be one of the necessities of intellectual life to champion militantly somebody with something to say in music new, or at least unusual, strange, and to some repellant. [. . .] Mr. Mahler himself, however, is not much concerned about such things. Neither the passionate zeal of self-appointed partisans nor the abuse of the hostile seems to affect him greatly, and he goes his own way [. . .] He occupies a curious and rather anomalous position in the field of modern orchestral music. He is no follower of the modern idea of the "programme" in music [. . .] What he writes he calls symphonies, though they are symphonies often in only a rather loose acceptance of the term. [. . .] Yet he does not intend them to be listened to as the interpretation of any prearranged programme; he objects to having any programmes laid down for his music, or even to permitting any thematic analyses to appear in the concert room where it is played. [. . .]

Yet Mahler himself has given in many of his works hints, and more than hints, of underlying poetic ideas outside and beyond the music itself - wherein is to be found much of the essence of the programme music idea. [. . .] The second symphony [. . .] has also a soprano and an alto solo, a mixed chorus and a bird's voice (represented instrumentally), all with various superscriptions. [. . .]

In the second symphony Mahler has striven for the expression of huge ideas on a large scale, joined with other ideas simple, Schubertian, almost naive; a union that often appears in his works. He has a liking for tunes of a folk song character as students of his music soon discover. He calls for an extraordinary orchestral apparatus [. . .]

The composer has withheld any title or any suggestion of a significance of this symphony, other than the inscriptions at the head of the last two movements and the verses sung by the singers. The suggestions that have been made in explanation of it are, therefore, to be taken only as individual conjectures; as that by Ernest [sic] Otto Nodnagel, in his book, "Jenseits von Wagner und Liszt" [. . .][41]

[41]Ernest Otto Nodnagel, *Jenseits von Wagner und Liszt*, Königsberg, Ostpreußische Druckerei, 1902.

Mr. Mahler, who wrote explanatory titles and mottoes to the movements of his first symphonies, ended by publishing them without any, to be listened to as purely absolute music. And he has called attention to the diametrical opposition of his aims in music to such descriptive programme music, for instance, as Strauss's. "My music arrives at the programme, at last, as the final, idealistic interpretation in words, while with Strauss the programme is as a task set to be fulfilled."[42] Another statement of the composer's that bears on this subject is quoted in The Bulletin of the Symphony Society, as follows: "I, for one, know well that, so long as my life happenings can be conveyed fitly through words, I will not use them as a musical theme. The longing to express myself musically comes over me only in the realm of obscure feelings, at the threshold of the world beyond, the world in which the categories of time and space rule no more."

(*NYT*, December 6, 1908, Part Six, p. 8)

178

[Postmarks: New York, 8 December 1908;
Munich, 18/19 December 1908]

My dear [Ritter],[43]

[. . .] I am in the middle of rehearsals for my II., unfortunately with completely inadequate forces. America really does not even know yet what to do with me (in my view, it doesn't know what to do with any art at all, and perhaps it is not at all part of the universal scheme of things that it should). [. . .]

(Eleonore and Bruno Vondenhoff, "Gustav Mahler und William Ritter", in *MUB*, pp. 150f.)

---

[42]One can only wonder about Aldrich's source for this quote. Today we know it from one of Mahler's letters, written on February 17, 1897 to Arthur Seidl (1863-1928), a German critic and music educator in Leipzig, who was one of his early champions. The letter (*MSL*, pp. 212ff.; original German in *GMB*, pp. 199-202) is an important document with respect to the genesis of the Second Symphony and, in general, for the insight it provides into Mahler's creative ideals. The sentence in Aldrich's column is actually *quoted* by Mahler, evidently from a letter by Seidl to which his is a reply.

[43]William Ritter (1867-1955) - French novelist and essayist of wide-ranging cultural interests. Although skeptical at first, he eventually became an ardent champion of Mahler as conductor and composer. In appreciation, Mahler made him a gift of the manuscript of the piano version of "Um Mitternacht" in 1908.

179

Though the patrons of the New York Symphony Society doubtless looked upon Mr. Gustav Mahler as their guest last evening, when he conducted the second of his eight symphonies at Carnegie Hall, it was by demonstrations of far more than mere politeness that the large audience found vent for its feelings of interest and pleasure in this new music and its author.[44] [. . .] Whatever the relationship between the composer's lofty aim and his actual accomplishment in this symphony, it is a pleasure to record the quick and evidently sincere expression of a New York audience of representative character in its favour.

[. . .] The composer has distinctly asserted that he seeks expression in music only when no other medium will convey his thought, and this declaration comes with all the more weight from Mr. Mahler, since he has given proof of some eloquence as a writer in words.

[. . .] Beyond all doubt Mr. Mahler was deeply in earnest when he wrote this music, and of the beauty and insight of certain episodes there can be no doubt.

(*NYTrib*, December 9, 1908, p. 7)

180

In place of a criticism, THE MUSICAL COURIER presents to its readers the criticisms of some of the daily press on Mahler's second symphony [. . .] THE MUSICAL COURIER [. . .] accepts as sympathetic and in accordance with its own views the criticism of the New York Sun. There is no necessity to repeat this. [. . .] But this opinion is utilized for the purpose of illustrating, more than anything else, the utter vapidity of the Tribune's remarks, which are not, of course, critical, and the absence of all declaration. As usual, the paper is on the fence, unable to declare for itself what the Mahler symphony means. As we have stated years ago, it is a combination of words, words, words, in the Tribune, meaningless, without giving the reader anything but a generalization adapted for the purpose of evading any decisive statement. Particular attention is called to such expressions, for instance, as "portentiously insignificant," "proclamations from invisible brass choir," "Mr. Mahler was deeply in earnest when he wrote this music," as if he

[44]According to the reports, the performing forces consisted of 115 orchestral players, the 200-strong chorus of the Oratorio Society, the soprano Laura Combs and the alto Gertrude Stein-Bailey.

could have been joking or indifferent, and, finally, the conclusion that the work is too large to be passed upon at the first performance.

[. . .]

We would advise the musical people who are interested in these matters to make a collection of Tribune criticisms and find one in which there is a declaration of opinion. That would also be original.

(*MC* 57, no. 25, December 16, 1908, p. 38)

181

In spite of the warnings of example Mr. Mahler elected to utilize forces which might have easily crushed the imaginations of his hearers when injudiciously used, and this is precisely what took place in passages where the reaching out after infinite detail of expression issued in herculean effort and nothing more. There are several such passages in this huge second symphony, and they are emphasized by the persistent employment of the penetrating tones of a solo trumpet written in its high register. There have been few successes indeed in the use of this instrumental utterance since Bach.

It is owing to the presence of these portions of the symphony that the composition fails in its entirety to make the impression of absolute mastery. For this is indeed a work of splendid imagination, a creation always interesting, for the most part beautiful, and frequently inspiring. The programme was furnished with some confusing notes by Richard Specht,[45] which might better have been replaced by half a dozen sentences from the composer himself, setting forth briefly his general purpose. [. . .] On the whole [the symphony] is one of the noteworthy productions of this time and establishes for Mr. Mahler a position among important musicians of this period.

(*NYS*, December 9, 1908, p. 5)

182

The past week witnessed the successful production for the first time in America of an important symphonic work. Gustav Mahler [. . .] at once establishes himself as a writer in the symphonic form, whose ability hereafter must be reckoned with in any consideration of the modern development of the symphony. [. . .] The Fourth and Fifth [symphonies]

---

[45]Richard Specht (1870-1932) - Prolific Austrian writer on music. His works include two books on Mahler, and analytical guides to a number of his symphonies, among them the Second.

have already been heard in this country without creating any very marked impression. The second, heard on Tuesday, however, created an impression so marked that it must be set down as a triumph for its composer.

(*NYW*, December 13, 1908, Metropolitan Section, p. M5)

183

Mr. Gustav Mahler may not inaptly be regarded as the Prometheus of modern music. Let it be added at once that it is Mahler the composer, the maker of symphonies, to whom reference is made, not Mahler the conductor. As a conductor, Mr. Mahler is not wholly above reproach (for example, he reads Wagner, at times, as if he were reading Brahms); but he is, on the whole, an interpreter of remarkable powers, and his achievements in this capacity are often superb and always engrossing. His conceptions may cause violent disagreements [. . .] yet as a conductor he never fails to command respect and to provoke interest. But Mr. Mahler [. . .] is also a composer; and in this aspect, alas! he is a far less impressive phenomenon. [. . .] He is at the moment principally conspicuous by reason of the performance on December 8 [. . .] of his extraordinary second symphony (in C-minor) - an event the reverberations of which are still perceptible in the local music world.

[. . .]

Mr. Mahler is known to be an unrepentant denigrator of programme-music. Yet in his practice he is curiously inconsistent. He believes it to be an entirely proper and logical proceeding to write music associated with certain definite concepts and ideas—pictorial, dramatic, symbolical—and then to offer it to his hearers without giving them any adequate clue to his purposes.

[. . .]

There is [. . .], in the exterior of the music as well as in its inspirational basis, something Promethean, heaven-storming, magnificently audacious; and properly so. It should be conceded by any candid mind that you cannot describe the Judgment Day in music written for a quartette of mandolins, or even for the ordinary symphonic orchestra [. . .] It is one of the fallacies of the blander kind of criticism that simplicity is a *sine qua non* of artistic greatness. Mr. Mahler has dared to objure simplicity [. . .] His fault is that he has neglected to provide himself with the requisite outfit of original, potent, and noble musical ideas. [. . .] If iron purpose and inflexible determination were all that is needed for the writing of eloquent music, Mr. Mahler would be a composer whose sway his contemporaries would find it difficult to dispute. As a matter of fact, he has, in the evangelical phrase, no true "vocation" as a music maker. [. . .] To be precise, his music is not original, it is not individual, it is not imaginative. [. . .] Its lack is in that which no purpose can assure and no determination compel: the wind of inspiration, which blows at the behest of no man's will, however imperious and indomitable, though it may fill with splendor the casual page of the humblest slave of beauty.

(Lawrence Gilman in *Harper's Weekly* 52, December 26, 1908, p. 27)

184

[. . .] [Mahler] gave the impression to outsiders of being a very reserved man, but I shall always remember with rare pleasure the first time I spoke with him, when the veil was lifted from the earnest, grave and careworn face, and for one moment there was a fleeting glimpse of the rare and sympathetic inner nature of the man. It was after a Kneisel Quartette concert,[46] and I asked Franz Kneisel[47] to introduce him to me. I had heard only a few days previously his remarkable Second Symphony, with the wonderful finale. [. . .] I was still glowing under the inspiration of all this when I met him and said impulsively: "Mr. Mahler, in these days of cheap pessimism and materialism, which we find so much of in modern art, it is a rare inspiration to meet a composer who has great ethical ideas." He grasped my hand and said warmly: "It is a comfort to meet musicians who appreciate what one has been striving for", and then we parted. [. . .]

(Henry Holden Huss[48] in *SFM*, pp. 19f.)

185

Reports that the Philharmonic Society was to be rehabilitated were confirmed yesterday by Mrs. George R. Sheldon, wife of the banker and treasurer of the Republican national committee. [. . .] The reports have had it that Gustav Mahler is to be the new leader of the orchestra after it has been reorganized. This is one of the details that Mrs. Sheldon is not quite ready to give out.

(*NYS*, December 9, 1908, p. 5)

[46]This was, in all likelihood, the concert on December 15th in which Ossip Gabrilovitch (see Note 90, p. 489), a good friend of Mahler's, also played.
[47]Franz Kneisel (1865-1926) - Austrian violinist. Following several years as concertmaster of the Boston Symphony, from 1903 on he taught, and led his own quartet, in New York.
[48]Henry Holden Huss (1862-1953) - American pianist and composer; he studied with Rheinberger.

186

Although the executive committee, in its reply to the five singers who wrote the famous letter asking that Mr. Dippel be retained indicated that Mr. Gatti-Casazza was the head of the institution, neither of the managers of the opera house is as yet assured that the committee's letter is the final word on the matter. On the surface things appear harmonious, but at today's meeting of the executive committee Mr. Dippel will make appearance in person and ask that body to define his status in the Metropolitan.

Despite statements to the contrary, Mr. Dippel has as yet made no formal application to the executive committee [...] to have his contract renewed after March 1 next, the date when it expires, but it is entirely probable that he will do so today.[49] At any rate, it is certain that Mr. Dippel will ask for an explanation of his position in connection with the various assurances and statements made at the time of his retention last spring. [...]

(*NYTrib*, December 10, 1908, p. 7)

187

The Directors of the Metropolitan Opera Company are to hold one of their frequent meetings today, and when this meeting is over several of them will know more about the inside working of the present régime at the Opera House than they did before. Among other things they will learn why Andreas Dippel has felt secure in insisting upon his rights as the "co-director" of opera at the Metropolitan.

[...] There will be laid before the directors before they separate, a formal demand by Mr. Dippel for recognition of his rights and to back this demand there will be produced a contract of the existence of which most of the Directors are ignorant. It is understood to have been made with Mr. Dippel early in the proceedings which followed the termination of the Conried régime [...]

The contract, of the existence of which the public knew no more than some of the Directors, is understood to contain the word "co-director", as applied to Mr. Dippel. It further gives him large and far-reaching powers. [...]

A TIMES reporter who accidentally stumbled on the secret asked Mr. Dippel about the contract last night. Mr. Dippel declined to discuss the

---

[49]Dippel left the Metropolitan after the 1909-1910 season (s.a. **188**).

matter, but did not deny that such a contract was in existence, nor that its time had not expired, nor that it would be made known to the Directors today. [...]

(*NYT*, December 10, 1908, p. 1)

188

For more than three hours yesterday afternoon the Executive Committee of the Metropolitan Opera Directors [...] was in conference [...] with Mr. Gatti-Casazza and Andreas Dippel, who has been directing the productions of German operas at the Metropolitan and whose contract for three years had not been confirmed.

After the conference [...] Mr. Dippel handed out this statement:

"I am deeply appreciative of the many manifestations of kindly interest and good will which have come to me.

"Any unfortunate misunderstandings which have arisen in the Metropolitan Opera House have been vastly exaggerated, but the slight differences which really exist will, I am confident, be adjusted to the satisfaction of all concerned, although this adjustment will be made the more difficult of accomplishment if the subject continues to be publicly ventilated.

"As to the future, I am not worrying, but am devoting to the work of the present within the sphere of my duties at the Metropolitan Opera House my most loyal and earnest endeavors to assist in the aim of the Board of Directors and the General Manager of giving to New York the best opera possible and to achieve the most artistic results.

ANDREAS DIPPEL
Administrative Manager."

[...]

The New York Times is informed on unquestionable authority that the statement which was printed in its issue of yesterday as to a secret contract having been signed last Spring is without any basis in fact whatever.

(*NYT*, December 11, 1908, p. 1)

189

Wagner's "Götterdämmerung" was produced at the Metropolitan Opera House last evening, and a performance in many respects of remarkable quality was given. Not one of the least remarkable facts about it was that, though the Opera House has distinguished German conductors upon its staff, at least one of them one of the most

distinguished, this production was intrusted to the Italian, Mr. Toscanini.
Indeed, it had been much heralded in advance as one of his most
noteworthy achievements; he has conducted it in Italy, and has made of it
one of the cornerstones of his reputation.

[...]

It cannot be said that he made a new revelation of this score to the
lovers of Wagner in New York who have heard interpretations of
supreme authority; but he presented a performance of remarkable energy
and dramatic power, as well as one of great musical beauty. It was not in
every respect ideal, even so far as the conductor's work could make it so.

[...]

NYT, December 11, 1908, p. 8)

190

The plans for the placing of the New York Philharmonic Society on a
new musical and financial basis are again creating much discussion.

[...]

The only authentic announcements in regard to the new plans are that
Gustav Mahler will direct three concerts in the Spring, with men selected
from the Philharmonic and elsewhere, and that the money is already
gotten for these concerts.

Dr. Frank Damrosch, on the other hand, declares that the scheme for a
new orchestra had its beginning in a desire to injure his brother Walter
and the New York Symphony Society. He also predicts interesting
experiences for the parties back of the new organization if they attempt to
run it on an endowment of $100,000.

(*MA* 9, no. 5, December 12, 1908, p. 25)

191

To the Editor of the New York Times:

There has been a good deal of mistaken comment, based on
misinformation, about the movement now in progress to effect a
reorganization of the Philharmonic Society. May I, through your
columns, correct some of these misapprehensions?

The plans that are now under way contemplate only making possible
the continued existence of the Philharmonic Society, the oldest orchestral
organization in the country, and one that can pride itself justly on having
a most honorable history of achievement. It is now in its sixty-seventh
year, and its record is one that may properly be compared with that of
any similar organization in the world. Its record and its achievements

have endeared it to very many musical people in New York, to whom it would be a bitter regret to see its existence come to an end and its record closed. But the society itself and, I think, most of its friends, have come to recognize that it cannot go on much longer under its present organization and methods. Those were proper and sufficient for the time and conditions that prevailed when the society was formed; they are entirely outgrown now.

The society itself has requested, co-operated in, and given its willing consent to the plans that have been formed for its benefit. It is proposed to change its organization, giving up its co-operative basis, and making its discipline and methods such as are now recognized to be necessary in a modern orchestra. It is proposed to have the orchestra under the absolute control of a conductor, he having been appointed by a Board of Trustees composed of both professional and non-professional men. We are working to raise a fund sufficient to have this body of musicians play constantly together during a period of about twenty-five weeks and even to extend their work elsewhere.

Why this plan should have aroused opposition and severe criticism, as it seems to have, is not easy to understand. It is not proposed to add another to the number of orchestral organizations in New York. It is not intended to crowd anybody out. Nobody has thought of "eliminating" any one. There will be no more of a competitive struggle in the orchestral world of New York than there is now. There is only one purpose in view, and that is to rehabilitate the Philharmonic Society. If there is room for the Philharmonic Society now in New York, if there has been room for the society to make the record of which we are so proud, in the last sixty-six years, there will be room for it under its new organization. So far as we can see there is nothing "hysterical" about this plan, but a plain and commonsense attempt to save something that is very well worth saving, and benefiting thereby the musical life of New York.

Nor is it, I may say, an attempt to form an orchestra for the benefit of any one conductor. It is, naturally, intended to procure the best conductor that is available; but the principal concern is to establish the old Philharmonic Society on a living and substantial basis.

I submit that this is not an ignoble purpose, that our plans are not hasty or ill-considered, and that every provision has been made for wise, conservative, and properly centralized management.

Mary R. Sheldon
New York, Dec. 11, 1908.

(*NYT*, December 13, 1908, p. 12)

192

The club-women of New York are the objects of a severe rebuke for their treatment of musicians in an article entitled "The Worst Parasites of the Musicians", published in "der Barde",[50] a German magazine devoted to the musical interests of this country. The author is Signor di Pirani,[51] an Italian composer and pianist, who has spent the Winters in this city for the last few years.

All clubs and societies, no matter what their purpose, the writer declares, expect to have their programmes varied with music, and when one considers how many clubs exist, he begins to realize the great abundance of music demanded. Instead of thus affording a large opening for artists, the writer says, the societies have become the worst parasites, for they expect their entertainment without pay.

[. . .]

"It is astonishing," says Signor di Pirani, "how slyly these rich women go to work to escape paying a few dollars from their well-filled pockets for music. The 'coup' is carefully planned, especially when the artist, man or woman, is of considerable note. A close friendship is struck up and the unsuspicious musician feels immensely flattered. Soon, however, the explanation appears. The splendor of the next evening-company is to be increased by the 'masterly playing' or 'moving singing' of the artist friend."

[. . .]

"Would any one dare," Signor di Pirani asks, "use a physician, architect, or lawyer that way? Large sums are paid out by these same women's clubs for flowers, dinners, room rent, service, and elegantly printed programmes, but for the genial performance of the musicians, the centre of attraction in the affair, not one cent is paid. Worse than all, the artist who is contributing his or her services is criticized for not having the technique of Liszt or Rubinstein, or because the abilities of the singer do not equal Sembrich or Patti.

"Finally, the woman artist comes in for the reproach that her gown was not tasteful, or, perhaps, not sufficiently elegant, or horrors! - it was the same one she wore recently at another club."

When this article was pointed out to a well-known clubwoman interested along educational lines, she immediately replied, "Guilty, guilty on every score. We don't pay the musicians, and sometimes we

---

[50]The full title of this short-lived magazine (2 volumes, New York, 1908-09), published in German, was *Der Barde: Devoted to Art, Music, Literature.*
[51]Eugenio di Pirani (1852-1939) - Italian pianist and composer. After teaching in Germany, and concertizing in several European countries, he moved to the United States in 1905.

don't even treat them politely. But it's a perfectly well-understood game. They come for the sake of the possible advertising or pupils they may get out of it."

[. . .]

(*NYT*, December 13, 1908, p. 8)

193

"There would be fewer divorces if there were more high-grade music in the home, and the little love god would stay longer were he nourished on the elevating strains of good music as well as upon discussions of the price of bacon and eggs."

Walter Damrosch, director of the New York Symphony Orchestra, gave utterance to these sentences [. . .] .

"There is more domestic discord in the American home than in that of any other country on the globe, and I believe it is because there is not enough cultivation of the finer things of life. There is little family music or art of any kind, and there is small wonder that elements of discord enter when there is nothing more diverting than calculation on the cost of butter, eggs and bacon.

"[. . .]

"This fact is better recognized in the homes of other countries, where there is a greater companionship between members of the family, and where the day's routine is not rehearsed for the evening's entertainment. There is not so apt to be a violent disagreement over Beethoven's symphonies as there is over the price of beefsteak.

"I believe every child, boys as well as girls, should be reared in the atmosphere of music, so that the best part of their natures may fully develop."

(*MA* 9, no. 5, December 12, 1908, p. 17)

194

Mr. Mahler conducted [. . .] the Symphony Society in Carnegie Hall yesterday afternoon. [. . .]

Without notice to the public, except on the house bill, the symphony had been changed from Beethoven's Seventh to the same composer's Fifth - probably because Mr. Mahler fancied that since Miss Duncan[52] has taken to dancing the A major symphony, or rather dancing to its

---

[52]Isadora Duncan (1877-1927) - Famous American dancer, pioneer of modern dance. She made it a principle to dance to "good" music.

music, more respect could be shown to the composer by the production of a work which has not yet been enlisted in the service of Terpsichore. The overtures were the one which Wagner carefully designated "one to 'Faust' " [. . .] and that to Weber's "Oberon".

Without presuming to descant in any way by the remark upon the manner in which the music of the concert was played, it may be said that the most remarkable feature of the afternoon was the enthusiasm which greeted Mr. Mahler and all that he did. Applause almost frenetic filled all the pauses and endured a long time after the concert was over. As for the interpretation which the compositions received, a reviewer, mindful of an obvious play upon words which is more effective in German than English, might say that it was more inciting and exciting than satisfying. There was more crudeness and impurity of intonation in the orchestra than usual and less precision of attack and utterance; but it was not always plain that this was the fault of the players. Mr. Mahler conducted at times as if he were in a highly nervous state. [. . .]

(NYTrib, December 14, 1908, p. 7)

195

Beethoven the beginning, von Weber the continuation, and Wagner the conclusion of a line of musical development, all on a single programme which Gustav Mahler [. . .] played [. . .] yesterday afternoon before a large audience.

[. . .] In the "Faust" overture [. . .] Mahler in his most thoughtful reading emphasized [. . .] intellectuality somewhat at the expense of what little of romantic feeling the work possesses. But in the "Oberon" overture [. . .] everything was changed and [. . .] we heard [. . .] a bit of brilliant virtuosity in which the orchestra fairly surpassed themselves.

[. . .] Mahler closed the programme [. . .] with Beethoven's "Fifth Symphony" [. . .]

I must confess I did not entirely admire either Mr. Mahler's conception or execution of this most sublime of all symphonic works, save only the immortal "mirth", as I found it lacking in subtlety, inward feeling and emotion.

(NYW, December 14, 1908, 2. edition, p. 7)

196

The advertisements in yesterday afternoon's programme contained the announcement that Mr. Mahler will conduct two concerts of the

Philharmonic Society on the evenings of March 31 and April 6.

(*NYS*, December 14, 1908, p. 7)

197

There have been various attempts in former times to place the Philharmonic Society on a permanent financial basis, one in connection with the late Anton Seidl, under whose able direction the Society reached its floodtide of prosperity, another where Walter Damrosch's name was brought forward as a permanent conductor, with a promise of solid financial backing if accepted. But the trouble with these former attempts, as also with the present one, lies in the attempt to tie a string to each plan for the reorganization of the society by making such reorganization depend on some one particular conductor. Anton Seidl died, the Walter Damrosch scheme did not materialize, and now the name of Gustav Mahler is brought forward as a necessary adjunct to any rehabilitation of the finances of the Philharmonic.

The only proper plan for those having the matter at heart would be to first secure the necessary funds, which the past history of the Philharmonic Society ought to secure, for the reorganization of the society on the more modern and less communistic basis which present conditions point out as desirable, and then secure a competent conductor, preferably by public trial of his ability, to direct its destinies for the future.

(*NYW*, December 20, 1908, Metropolitan Section, p. M5)

198

The Philharmonic Society, in its sixty-seventh year, has come to the conclusion that it must suffer a sea change into something new, if not strange, in order to prolong its honorable career. Six years ago the society seemed for a time convinced of this, and there was a proposal made by friends outside its ranks to raise a guarantee-fund of $25,000 a year for four years.[53] [. . .] The society, after deliberation, rejected this proposition, on the ground that it would "so change its nature and interfere with the control of its affairs by its members, which has always been its vital principle, that the future of the society would be thereby imperiled." [. . .]

[53] Walter Damrosch, in his autobiography, claims the credit for initiating the funding proposal in January, 1903. According to him, the aim of the would-be guarantors (one of whom was Samuel Untermeyer) was to create a fund of $50,000 a year for four years (*My Musical Life*, New York, 1926, pp. 207f.).

191

The experiences of the last six years seem to have brought conviction that the future of the society will be still more imperiled by a continuance of the present conditions, which, to put it mildly, are not favorable to either the best artistic achievements or the necessary pecuniary results. Representatives of the Philharmonic have reopened the negotiations that were abandoned with the rejection of the former proposals, and, freely recognizing the present critical position of affairs and the underlying causes of them, have gone much further than the friends of the Philharmonic dared to suggest when they formed their plan six years ago. [. . .] It is proposed to have a Board of Trustees manage the affairs of the society, composed of both professional and non-professional men; to have the orchestra under the absolute control of a conductor to be selected by that board, with unquestioned power of removal and appointment. [. . .]

It remains, naturally, for the people interested in the present movement to raise the great amount of money that will be necessary. An annual guarantee fund is only a makeshift and a temporary expedient. There should be a sufficient endowment, if, as it seems, there is no counterpart to Henry L. Higginson in New York to take the charges of such an organization upon himself. There is much wealth in New York that might be turned into this channel to serve the cause of music and to preserve this ancient and honorable body with all its prestige. But the possessors of this wealth have always had a strange and obstinate disinclination to let other people spend it for them. [. . .]

(NYT, December 20, 1908, Part Six, p. 8)

199

[. . .] *Tristan und Isolde* was performed last night at the Metropolitan Opera House for the first time this season,[54] and Gustav Mahler, who has been in town for some weeks, made his first appearance in the conductor's chair. Doubtless this event will arouse in inquisitive minds a profound desire to know who conducts Wagnerian works better, Toscanini or Mahler. The asking of such momentous questions is the futile practice of indolent minds. [. . .]

Of Mr. Mahler's interpretation of the score nothing can be said now that was not said last season. It is a deeply appreciative reading, and its noble reposefulness is by no means the least of its excellences.

But last night's performance served to renew the conviction that Mr. Mahler respects most fully Wagner's purpose to permit the dialogue of

[54]This was the same cast as on January 1, 1908 (see Note 56, p. 51), except Schmedes sang Tristan, and Feinhals Kurvenal.

his drama to be heard. He demonstrates anew that the colours of this score are rich but not dazzling, that the splendours of the orchestration can be displayed without occultation of the voices. [. . .] Mr. Mahler deserves and gets admiration for the skill with which he causes his orchestra to sing every significant phrase of its music while permitting the voices to be heard singing theirs.

(*NYS*, December 24, 1908, p. 5)

200

Since conductors play leading roles at the opera houses and in concert rooms nowadays [. . .] let praise for a performance of Wagner's great love-drama, which was full of thrilling moments and always moved on a lofty plane, go to the conductor. How completely he can make its multitudinous agencies proclaim its most tumultuous passions as well as its tenderest and languorous utterances the Metropolitan public learned last season. Last night was only a delightful reminder which awakened again the gratitude of the public and its rapturous expression after each act and the final closing of the curtain.

(*NYTrib*, December 24, 1908, p. 7)

201

Mr. Mahler's remarkable performance of "Tristan und Isolde" [. . .] again delighted the lovers of Wagner's drama. It is full of noteworthy points of excellence that denote the fine feeling and the strongly musical qualities of the conductor, as well as his dominating instinct [for the dramatic aspect] of the score.

There was a certain disappointment felt last season by some of the Wagnerians—were they not younger ones?—in Mr. Mahler's reading, and there will doubtless be again this season, since his reading has not changed. They complained that it was not "dramatic" enough, that he did not let loose the power of the orchestra in places where the superlative climaxes come. Some of the "thrills", so it was declared, and may be again, were missed. The ebb and flow of the great orchestral tide, it was thought, was too much in miniature.

But Mr. Mahler has a very definite and distinct purpose in presenting the orchestral score in the light he does. It is really for a higher dramatic purpose, not a lesser one. That purpose is that the voices of the singers may come to their fullest rights upon the stage. [. . .]

[His] ideal is that every word of the singers, every phrase of the text, should be intelligible to the listeners; or that it may be so. [. . .] Wagner founded his reform of the lyric drama on the dictum, printed in large type, that "the error in the art genre of opera consists herein: that a means of expression, music, has been made the end, while the end of expression, drama, has been made the means". It too often seems as if the conductors of Wagner's works were losing sight of this principle as much as the older composers of the flimsy Italian opera.

[...]

Is it possible that some of our Wagner lovers have lost their sense of proportion through the love of certain conductors for sonorous and crashing orchestral tones? In the older days of Seidl there used to be complaint from the boxes that the music of "Tristan und Isolde" was so soft that it was not possible to converse comfortably without arousing anger in the pit. That, after all, implies a certain ideal.

(NYT, December 27, 1908, Part Six, p. 8)

202

Wholly without promptings of prejudice or inimical feeling of any kind, and as a simple statement of fact uncolored by personal or individual judgment or inclination, it may be stated that there is a present and evergrowing opinion and sentiment in the minds of the public at large that opera at the Metropolitan is not what it should be or what the public who pay their money to support it have the right to expect. [...]

I have heard from regular subscribers to both seats and boxes expressions of opinion as to the positive inadequacy of many of the performances given so far this season, so radical and so sweeping in condemnation that no critic having the best interests of opera in New York at heart would care to print them. Yet I hear rumors of an impression among those most nearly connected with and interested in the present management of the Metropolitan that the critical opinions of opera published in the New York press emanate from a body of men who in spite of their long experience and special training for the work in hand know nothing, and are banded together in open hostility to the present management; a condition of affairs which I can state with confidence does not obtain and which moreover is absurd on the face of it.

[...]

But granting everything in the situation that may be urged pro and con, [...] there is another aspect to present operatic conditions, an aesthetic, temperamental and psychical one, which may not have occurred to many as a factor, but which is one which governs and influences the situation to a very considerable extent.

For years past and until very recently, the Metropolitan, as the only opera house in New York, has been necessarily its own standard of comparison. [. . .] But since the inception and the successful continuance of the Manhattan Opera House, the case has been altered and the whole situation changed. Now people have the opportunity of hearing opera in an auditorium unusually well adapted acoustically for that purpose [. . .] in a way that is impossible at the Metropolitan, because of the size and acoustic conditions of that house. [. . .] Thus a steady standard of comparison has been established which in my judgment is going to materially affect the future destinies of the Metropolitan [. . .] Personally I am of [the] opinion that [the] fact [. . .] that many an artist is adequate and to be enjoyed on the stage of the Manhattan who would be lost in the vast depths of the Metropolitan surroundings, is more accountable for the generally expressed discontent with recent performances at the Metropolitan than the possible artistic shortcomings of the performances themselves.

In conjunction with this conclusion, [. . .] the recent announcement made by Mr. Hammerstein that he proposed building another opera house, although since denied, is of real importance and significance. [. . .]

After the experience of opera-goers at the Manhattan, and in view of the definite effect of this experience, [. . .] the necessity of a new opera house in this opera-mad community may well be recognized and urged. In view of the many disabilities and disadvantages, acoustic and otherwise, attached at the Metropolitan as a place for opera-giving, [. . .] it can hardly be amiss at this time to point out to the owners of the Metropolitan the necessity which may at any time become imminent of a change of operatic quarters. For, should Mr. Hammerstein succeed [. . .], the Metropolitan might not inconceivably suddenly find itself bereft of its patronage and shorn of its artistic and social prestige. It would thus certainly be the part of prudence for the directors to consider well the possibilities of such an emergency and be prepared to meet it if and when it should arrive. The fact cannot be too strongly urged at the present moment that the present policy of the Manhattan seems more in accord with popular operatic sentiment and desire than that of the Metropolitan, for the principal reason that Mr. Hammerstein understands the American public, and local conditions and their necessities, far better than Mr. Gatti-Casazza does or seems to have any wish to do, and that the competition and concurrence which would obtain were Mr. Hammerstein to carry out his latest operatic plan would be far greater and wide-reaching in result and far more difficult to meet.

[. . .]

Legitimate competition is undoubtedly the soul of business, and the operatic competition which has existed thus far has undoubtedly been beneficial in raising the standard of opera-giving in New York, but [. . .] it is quite possible for such competition to reach a point where [. . .] expenses may well reach such a point as to destroy the hardly gained position of opera-giving as a paying financial possibility.

[. . .] there is little doubt that neither opera house is now making any money. [. . .] This would seem to point to the fact that competition has already reached a point where the continuance of opera on its present artistically satisfactory basis in New York is endangered [. . .] There can be no question [. . .] that if all personal prejudice could be laid aside and the situation considered on its merits and for the greatest good of the greatest number, a satisfactory adjustment could readily be reached. Such an adjustment I suggested just a year ago, as follows: "As it seems to me, the only possible outcome of the situation would be that the Metropolitan should remain the home of what is known as Grand Opera, and that the Manhattan should become the Opera Comique of New York, to be used as the home of lyric drama and opera comique, as it is known in France, for which its size and acoustic properties give it a suitability which the Metropolitan does not possess. It might also be possible to unite both houses under one general management and have one great ensemble attributed to both, members of which could be used indifferently at either one house or the other". Such a plan seems to me to be equally feasible at the present time and need not necessarily be affected were Mr. Hammerstein or the Metropolitan or both to build and dedicate new homes of opera in this city.

(*NYW*, December 27, 1908, Metropolitan Section, p. M3)

203

Carl Burrian, the Bohemian tenor [. . .] explained [to Dresden reporters] some features of the Wagner performances [in New York] that must have opened the eyes of the Germans.

"The Wagner performances," he said, "are the least patronized by the public. The whole business apparently bores the audiences to death. If one of these performances does interest the public, how do the most conspicuous—that is, the richest—express their feelings? The beginning of the performance is announced for 8 o'clock. 'They', however, come after 9. An usher with an electric light in his hands enters the box and shows the guests their seats. There is a constant coming and going; the spectators greet one another, look around them to see who is there. And the climax of the delight of the evening?

"You might think that it came in the supreme moment of the music drama. Not in the least. The principal thing is the long intermission

196

during which the gentlemen and ladies of society promenade about arm in arm to show their toilets and diamonds in their greatest beauty. After the long intermission one need only to glance in the boxes to see that by a few minutes after 11 there is a packing up of opera glasses in reticules and the start for home. What may happen on the stage after that interests nobody. It is true that in *Tannhäuser* the audience rises and flees from the opera house after Wolfram's song to the 'Evening Star'. The tenor who appears after Wolfram's song sings the closing music of his part to the barytone on the stage or the conductor. He might as well play cards with them on the stage so far as the public is concerned. I would like to bet that the fewest possible number of subscribers to the Metropolitan Opera House have the least idea how the story of Tannhäuser and poor Elisabeth ends".

(*NYS*, December 27, 1908, 3. Section, p. 8)

204

New Year's Eve came and the long expected party in Bitter's[55] studio; but Mahler had to go alone because I was not feeling well. A terrific blizzard blew up during the evening, and I was so anxious that in spite of a high temperature I could not leave the window. [. . .]

Mahler arrived at last at two o'clock, utterly exhausted. He had left Bitter just after twelve [. . .] [and] with much difficulty found a hansom. A few minutes later it was blown over and he had to creep from under it. [. . .] He was now two streets away and after clawing his way along for half an hour was blown into the entrance of the hotel.

(*AMM*, p. 147; original German in *AME*, pp. 181f.)

205

The weather last night worked well for the initial performance of 1909 in this town. By day it was clear and cold; by night it was still colder, which but added to the zest of the revelers. Any one who remained long on the streets last night was encouraged to do things to keep warm, and the things that presented themselves to most folks were noisy things. It was so cold that folks who could get into theatres the early part of the night did so. The restaurants and hotels were all thronged early.

(*NYT*, January 1, 1909, p. 1)

---

[55]Karl Bitter (1867-1915) - Austrian sculptor, emigrated to America in 1889. At first he was best known for his architectural decorative sculptures; later created a number of monuments in New York City.

206

HOTEL SAVOY

[Postmarks: New York, 6 January 1909
Essen, 27 January 1909]

Dear Herr Kosman,[56]

Please forgive me for answering your kind lines of 19 November only today. However, I wanted to be able to tell you something definitive right away.

The situation here is as good as settled. Beginning next year, a permanent orchestra will be formed here under my leadership. The season will last for approximately 6 months. For the rest of the year, you would be free! I am supposed to ask you about your conditions for joining our organization as 1. concert master. I need as detailed and precise an answer as possible, for a quick decision must be made here. At all events, here there would be a rich arena for your talents, and certainly also satisfaction for you. - I am writing in great haste, and will be in a position, when I have your reply in hand, to tell you more about the details.

With cordial greetings
your devoted
Mahler

207

If the present plans of the Philharmonic Society do not materialize, there is more than a probability that Hans Richter[57] may become its permanent leader. He has frequently said that he never would cross the ocean, but there is no telling what a foreign musician will or will not do when he hears the siren song of many of Uncle Sam's silver dollars.

(*MC* 58, no. 1, January 6, 1909, p. 20)

---

[56]Alexander Kosman (1872-1950) - Dutch violinist. Trained in Paris, he worked as concert master of several leading orchestras in France, Scotland, the United States (Philadelphia, 1903) and Germany. He did not join the New York Philharmonic.- For the German text, see Appendix, A20.
[57]Hans Richter (1843-1916) - The Hungarian-born Richter was one of the preeminent conductors of his age, especially in the Wagner-repertoire. From 1875 to 1900 he led the Vienna Philharmonic, and conducted at the Imperial Opera; from 1900 to 1911 he directed the Hallé Orchestra in Manchester, England.

208

Mr. Charles Dillingham,[58] who was asked by the directors of the Metropolitan Opera Company to take his executive staff and make a thorough business survey of the contracts and all other business matters at the Metropolitan Opera House, yesterday agreed to accept the offer. This afternoon he and Mr. Fred Latham,[59] his general manager, will take up their new duties.

[. . .]

Dillingham will, it was stated yesterday, devote his attention as a practical theatrical manager to looking after where the money comes from, where it goes to, and in fact everything pertaining to the business management of the opera house from the front door to the men who turn on and off the electric lights. Mr. Latham knows all about opera contracts, big and little, and he will devote most of his time to this important part of the company's affairs. [. . .]

(*NYH*, January 6, 1909, p. 12)

209

As cool and imperturbable as ever, Giulio Gatti-Casazza, the general manager of the Metropolitan Opera Company, was in his office yesterday and declined to become exercized over the announcement that Mr. Hammerstein would soon be in a position to give him directions how to run an opera house. The executive committee of the board of directors of the Metropolitan considered the report of the formation of the opera house chain, comprising the Metropolitan, Manhattan and Philadelphia opera houses, with Mr. Hammerstein as the directing mind, as too absurd to merit a denial.[60]

(*NYTrib*, January 10, 1909, p. 9)

---

[58]Charles Bancroft Dillingham (1868-1934) - American journalist and critic turned theatrical producer and agent. He opened the Globe Theatre in 1910.
[59]Fred G. Latham (1853-1943) - English-born theatre manager (managed the Drury Lane and Covent Garden Theatres in London). After emigrating to America, he was associated with Grau at the Metropolitan in 1903, and then with Dillingham as producer and director of plays and musical comedies.
[60]In point of fact, precisely at this time Hammerstein was in serious difficulties concerning the financing of his recently completed Philadelphia Opera House (see Cone, *op. cit.*, pp. 200-206).

210

Mozart's comedy, "Le Nozze di Figaro", was given at the Metropolitan Opera House last evening for the first time in four years.[61] It had been newly studied under the direction of Gustav Mahler; there were several new singers in the cast, there was a new and very becoming stage setting and new costumes. The performance was one of the most delightful and brilliant that can be easily recalled; not so much in the excellence of the individual singers, though here, too, there was much to enjoy; but most of all in the finished ensemble, the vivacity and gayety that were infused into every scene, the dramatic verisimilitude with which the intensions of the composer were realized.

It was a performance such as there have been few at the Metropolitan Opera House in the way of precision and the elaboration of the finer details of the action upon the stage, the exquisite and delicate beauty of the orchestral part, and the skillful co-ordination of these factors in one impression upon eye and ear. Such a performance shows the dominating influence of a master mind filled with the spirit of Mozart's music, as Mr. Mahler's is, with an opportunity to achieve the results that he wishes. This "Figaro" had evidently been prepared with much care, and it was one that reflected the greatest credit on all who were concerned in it. The potent authority of Mr. Mahler was evident in it from the beginning to the end.

(*NYT*, January 14, 1909, p. 7)

211

What Mr. Mahler did last season for "Don Giovanni" and "Fidelio" he has done again for "Le Nozze di Figaro;" and done it better. It was possible for those who know Mozart's music, as much as they admire it, to disagree profoundly with some of Mr. Mahler's ideas concerning the music of "Don Giovanni," especially with his sluggish tempi. Last night there was no chance for such a quarrel. All the vivacious music foamed and sparkled and flashed like champagne.

(*NYTrib*, January 14, 1909, p. 7)

---

[61]The complete cast was as follows: Almaviva - Scotti; Countess - Eames; Cherubino - Farrar; Figaro - Didur; Susanna - Sembrich; Marcellina - Mattfeld; Bartolo - Paterna; Basilio - Reiss; Antonio - Ananian; Barbarina - L'Huillier; Don Curzio - Tecchi; Maids of Honour - Sparkes, Snelling. The cast remained stable until the retirement of Sembrich (see **223**); then the roles of Susanna and the Countess were taken over by, respectively, de Pasquali and Gadski.

Plate 40. Emma Eames. (*COS*, Illustration 87)

Plate 41. Geraldine Farrar. (*COS*, Illustration 186)

Plate 42. Marcella Sembrich. (*COS*, Illustration 64)

Plate 43. Antonio Scotti (*COS*, Illustration 92)

These four singers appeared in both of Mahler's Mozart-productions in America (as did Johanna Gadski—see Plate 79.).

212

"Le Nozze di Figaro" is above all things an ensemble opera. It requires a complete and harmonious operation of all the elements in its performance and [. . .] this result was achieved last night. For this result surely every one of the artists concerned in the representation must be thanked, but the chief praise is assuredly due Gustav Mahler, the musical director, and Andreas Dippel, administrative director of the Metropolitan.

Mr. Mahler interpreted Mozart's artistic purposes in a masterly manner, and his careful and intelligent rehearsals of the opera, with the willing cooperation of the singers, brought about a happy issue. There was a fine unity of style in the treatment of the music, and the orchestral playing was clean, accurate, elastic and transparent. The accompaniment of the recitatives by an imitation harpsichord and in the proper places by a union of this instrument with the orchestral strings was excellent. [. . .] The entire production was a demonstration of what can be accomplished in an American opera house when knowledge and genuine artistic enthusiasm work in felicitous unison.

(*NYS*, January 14, 1909, p. 7)

213

Charming is the word that perhaps best characterizes last night's performance. [. . .] With Mahler in the chair, giving life and spirit to the whole, it could hardly have been otherwise than good. [. . .] There was no dry-as-dust classicism or musty tradition in his reading. Everything was spirited, sparkling and light hearted, with true appreciation of the inner meaning of the work, yet with no lack of classic elegance and becoming reverence.

(*NYW*, January 14, 1909, p. 5)

214

[. . .] Among the many great conductors with whom I have sung, I know of none greater than [Mahler]. He was a genius with an abstract ideal and great humanity. [. . .] In his simplicity and modesty he showed his true genius. [. . .]

I am very glad and very proud to number among the memories of my career the "Nozze di Figaro" and "Don Giovanni" under his leadership - a leadership so delicate and so considerate that it was collaboration and not dictatorship. [. . .]

(Emma Eames de Gogorza in *SFM*, p. 10)

215

Mr. Charles Dillingham has completed his investigation of the affairs of the Metropolitan Opera House and has handed in his report to the committee, consisting of Mr. Henry Rogers Winthrop, Clarence H. Mackay and Robert Goelet, appointed by the directors to inquire into matters. [...]

It is said that the report contains many suggested improvements for the present season and still more for future seasons. [...] It was said by a person familiar with opera affairs that nothing would be made public about [it]. [...]

(*NYH*, January 16, 1909, p. 12)

216

Smetana's *Die Verkaufte Braut* is to be sung for the first time at a Bohemian benefit, which insures a profit on the first production, whatever may happen to the others. [...] Gustav Mahler will conduct.

(*NYS*, January 17, 1909, 3. Section, p. 8)

217

In a circular sent out yesterday [Mr. Hammerstein] announced the beginning on August 16 next of a season of "educational grand opera for the masses" to last three months and to be preliminary to his regular season. [...]

In this new season [...] which [...] will be given every year [...] opera will be given in English as well as Italian. [...] In his determination to educate as much of the public as possible, Mr. Hammerstein is going to remove the boxes during the preliminary season and substitute seats. The boxes will be replaced, of course, for the regular season.

Mr. Hammerstein is explicit on the point that, though moderate prices will prevail during this season, it will not be "cheap opera, but real grand opera". The impresario's impelling motive, it would seem, is to educate a great part of the population to demanding something they have no opportunity now of obtaining.

(*NYTrib*, January 18, 1909, p. 7)

218

The Bohemians, a club composed of New York musicians, will give a dinner in honour of Gustav Mahler, conductor at the Metropolitan Opera House, at the Hotel Astor on Saturday evening.

(*NYTrib*, January 20, 1909, p. 7)

219

Richard Strauss as a dramatic composer seems still to be a most desirable ally for the operatic managers. His works have most useful qualities for advertising and for arousing public interest. Just as "Salome" is to be produced for the second time in New York, his "Elektra" is sending anticipated thrills through the musical people of Europe, who are "appealing" for tickets to the first performance at the Dresden opera tomorrow night.[62] There is a plenty of interest in Mr. Hammerstein's "Salome" production, which will attract great audiences, although the valuable preliminary protests and demonstrations which did so much good to Mr. Conried's business two years ago, and would have done so much more had he been allowed to go on, have been lacking.[63]

[...]

There were plenty of predictions two years ago that "Salome" would be a short-lived sensation, and that its career would be like those of Strauss's two previous operas, "Guntram" and "Feuersnot".[64] [...] But "Salome" has previously been given at various opera houses of Europe in various languages, and is still a subject of lively interest in the musical world.

There will be a better opportunity to arrive at a dispassionate estimate of the work now than there was two years ago, when so many exciting and extraneous considerations were forced into view. The very novelty of the composition, the vastness and complication of the music, bewildered and overwhelmed the listener. [...]

As a matter of fact, however, the novelty of Strauss's score is more apparent than real. "Salome" is only a new manifestation of the development that much of the current musical production has been making since Wagner, and his own in particular. [...] Vast orchestral complications, the use of a kind of polyphony that simply combines many

---

[62]*Elektra* was given for the first time on January 25, 1909 in Dresden.
[63]See Note 129, p. 121.
[64]*Guntram* was Strauss's first opera; it was premièred in 1894 at Weimar, and has completely disappeared from the repertoire. His second opera, *Feuersnot* (1901, Dresden) had a similar fate; it was, however, produced by Mahler in Vienna in January, 1902.

voices by main strength without regard to what used to be considered musical aptitude for combination and expertness in making such combination; the forcing together of incommensurable harmonies without consideration for what have hitherto been held to be the possibilities of the human ear [. . .] are characteristic of his score. [. . .] His inventive power is enormous as to devices, combinations, technique; but it is far more concerned with these matters than with the real essence of music itself, the subject matter of the art. Much of his musical thought is insignificant, short breathed, of little originality. What Strauss accomplishes with the material with which he has provided himself is truly wonderful, and the effects he makes are astonishing, stimulating, sometimes profoundly stirring. And that is in itself a wonderful achievement.

"Salome" is in reality not a work of revolutionary import. Since the single hearing that we had of it here two years ago there has been a lyric drama producted here of which it can truly be said that it is of revolutionary import: and that is Claude Debussy's "Pelléas et Mélisande". [. . .]

(*NYT*, January 24, 1909, Part Six, p. 7)

220

The Manhattan Opera, for a long time superior to the Metropolitan itself, was the creation of Hammerstein, the cigar merchant. We saw Mary Garden there as Salome [. . .]

(*AMM*, p. 162; original German in *AME*, p. 200)

221

[Vienna, May-June 1909]

My dear [Strauss],

[. . .] Your Salome received a decidedly *vulgar* performance, but due to a *wonderful* interpretation of the title role by Mary Garden, makes a *powerful impact*. Dalmores[65] as Herod is also great! [. . .]

(Original German in Herta Blaukopf, ed., *Gustav Mahler/ Richard Strauss - Briefwechsel 1888-1911,* Munich, etc., Piper, 1980, p. 125)

---

[65]Charles Dalmorès (1871-1939) - French tenor, especially renowned for his acting ability. Pelléas was one of his most celebrated creations.

222

While "La Wally"[66] was being sung in the Metropolitan Opera House other forces of the Metropolitan Opera Company were presenting Mozart's exquisite "Le Nozze di Figaro" in the Brooklyn Academy of Music.

It was a great night operatically across the bridge. Being Mme. Sembrich's operatic farewell in Brooklyn, she was singled out especially for honors. [...]

Mme. Eames, Miss Farrar, Mr. Scotti and Mr. Didur[67] filled their respective roles admirably and Mr. Mahler conducted. They were all called before the curtain many times by an audience that packed the beautiful new opera house.

(*NYH*, February 5, 1909, p. 19)

223

On the same stage where she made her first appearance in opera in New York, some twenty-five years ago last October, Mme. Marcella Sembrich [...] sang and said last night her formal farewell as an opera singer. [...]

After the [first] act of "La Traviata" [...] the curtain was rung down for a few moments, and then raised upon the same scene. [...] There was a thunder of applause as Mme. Sembrich was led on to the stage by Mr. Gatti-Casazza [to the accompaniment of the march from "Le Nozze di Figaro" conducted by Mahler][68] [...]

Later M. [William Stengel][69] and Mme. Sembrich entertained at supper in the ballroom of the Hotel Savoy. [...] Among those who accepted [their] invitation were [...] Mr. and Mrs. Gustav Mahler [...]

(*NYTrib*, February 7, 1909, p. 9)

---

[66]Alfredo Catalani's (1854-1893) last and most successful opera (introduced in 1892 at La Scala); it was especially admired by Toscanini.
[67]Adamo Didur (1874-1946) - Celebrated Polish-born bass; later he became a sought after teacher. He joined the Metropolitan Opera in 1909.
[68]Curiously enough, it appears that Mahler was a late addition to the company of artists who participated in the farewell concert (*NYS*, February 6, 1909, p. 5).
[69]Marcella Sembrich's husband.

224

The master musicians and some of those who have had the management of musical affairs greeted Mme. Sembrich at the reception and dinner [at the Hotel Astor last night].

[. . .] Among those whom Mme. Sembrich received and who dined with her later were [. . .] Mr. and Mrs. Gustav Mahler [. . .].

(*NYS*, February 8, 1909, p. 5)

225

Gustav Mahler, of whom I entertained a high appreciation not only as a symphonic composer but also as an operatic director, was equally wonderful in such widely varied music as that of Wagner and Mozart. I found it a great delight to sing under his leadership in the immortal works of Mozart, "Le Nozze di Figaro" and "Don Giovanni", whose musical and dramatic qualities Mahler so thoroughly enjoyed and interpreted. [. . .]

(Marcella Sembrich in *SFM*, p. 29)

226

The most notable production of the present season at the Metropolitan Opera House has been Mozart's "Le Nozze di Figaro," which has to its credit the greatest amount of critical praise as well as popular success. Now foreign cities are to have the opportunity to hear the work as a specimen of what the forces at the Metropolitan are capable of accomplishing. [. . .] So far as the arrangements have been settled there will be three performances in Paris [. . .] three in London and three in Berlin. Gustav Mahler will of course be the conductor.[70]

(*NYS*, February 14, 1909, p. 10)

227

Minnie Untermeyer[71] and Mrs. Sheldon, both leading lights in New York

[70]See the introductory essay to this season, p. 138.
[71]Mrs. Samuel Untermeyer (or Untermyer) (née Minnie Carl) (1858-1940) - wife of the eminent lawyer. - It was not only the Mahlers who wrote "Untermyer"; the contemporary usage of the family name seems to have been quite inconsistent. For example, while Walter Damrosch omitted the middle 'e' (*op. cit.*), *MA* used both forms of the name, just as both forms occur in the list of Philharmonic box-holders when these began to be included in the programme-booklets. Accordingly, here the name is given in its modern form or in the form in which it is found in the given source.

society, left [the Metropolitan] together after one of [the] performances. Both were full of enthusiasm, and on their way home they had an inspiration. They determined to put an orchestra at Mahler's disposal and within a few days they collected a hundred thousand dollars. This came in very opportunely for Mahler. His relations with the Metropolitan were no longer very good. Conried was at death's door. Gatti-Casazza, who had been sent for from the Scala, was now director of the Metropolitan, and he had brought Toscanini over with him. The glorious days of German supremacy were over. It is fair to say that Mahler was offered the post but declined it.

[. . .]

And so Mahler joyfully welcomed another outlet. A committee was formed immediately, the active members of which were Mrs. Draper,[72] Mrs. Untermeyer, Mrs. Sheldon and Mrs. Schelling.[73] The contract was signed before we left for Europe and the engagement which was to begin when we returned, was by no means exacting. He was to give a series of concerts with an orchestra of his own. This had always been his dream.

(*AMM*, pp. 145f.; original German in *AME*, pp. 179f.)

228

In the season of 1908-9, while Safonoff was still the conductor, Mrs. George R. Sheldon [. . .] and a number of other public-spirited citizens began to organize a group of so-called Guarantors of the Fund for the Permanent Orchestra of the Philharmonic Society of New York. [. . .] By the early part of 1909 large sums were being pledged by some of the old and a great many new supporters of the Philharmonic. [. . .] They came from a long list of people whose names meant wealth or position in New York's social and business circles - J.P. Morgan, Thomas Fortune Ryan, Joseph Pulitzer, John D. Rockefeller, E.J. de Coppet, Mrs. Harry Payne Whitney, Miss Dorothy Whitney, Alex Smith Cochran, Mrs. Samuel Untermeyer, Arthur Curtiss James, and many others.

On February 6, 1909, Mr. and Mrs. Sheldon and four of their friends,* acting for the Guarantors, were able to send the Philharmonic the following historic proposition—in effect an ultimatum—destined to revolutionize the orchestra's career:

¶ It was proposed to organize in New York an orchestra of the highest order, under the exclusive direction of a fine conductor, the members of the orchestra to devote their time to its work for at least twenty-three successive weeks a year.

---

[72]Mrs. William H. Draper - wife of the congressman and wealthy manufacturer.
[73]Mrs. Ernest Schelling (née Lucie How Draper) - wife of the pianist, conductor and composer.

211

¶ The corporate frame of the Philharmonic *could* be used for this purpose (the implication was that, if the Philharmonic did not cooperate, an orchestra might be formed without it), but this would require "radical changes in its organization and methods", especially in the commitment of every player to give his time to the orchestra for the full season, in return for a stated salary.

¶ The Guarantors would undertake to make good any deficits for the three seasons 1909-12, and hoped, moreover, in that period, to raise an endowment fund to give the orchestra a permanent basis, but they would insist on having the entire control of the affairs of the Society. The Philharmonic would no longer be governed by its democratically elected Board of Directors. Instead, a powerful Committee of the Guarantors would designate the Directors (of whom three, however, would always be orchestra men), and would control all their actions, including the choice of officers, conductor, and manager, and the making of contracts. Some of the present members of the Society might even be dismissed from the orchestra, for each player would have to be accepted by the new conductor, with the approval of the Guarantors' Committee.

¶ To underline the readiness of the project, a list of Guarantors and Donors was appended, with the actual amounts that each pledged.[#]

The Society acted swiftly to accept the proposition. On February 12, 1909, it suspended all bylaws that might conflict with the terms of the offer, stipulating only that no performer be paid less than $35 per week under the new system, and that all contracts be carried out in accordance with the rules of the New York musicians' union. By the end of the month a Guarantors' Committee, with Mrs. Sheldon as Chairman, was meeting regularly,[+] and the wheels of the Philharmonic's new machinery were beginning to turn.

[*]They were Ruth Dana Draper, Henry Lane Eno, Ernest H. Schelling, and Nelson S. Spencer.

[#]The letter on which this condensed summary is based is entered in the Minutes of the Annual Meetings of the Philharmonic Society of New York, 1904-32, pp. 84-91 (meeting of February 12, 1909). [Note 133, p. 445]

[+]The Guarantors' Committee included, in addition to [those under *] above], three members of the orchestra: Richard Arnold, Felix F. Leifels[74] [as Secretary], and Henry P. Schmitt.

(Howard Shanet, *Philharmonic - A History of New York's Orchestra*, Garden City, N.Y., Doubleday, 1975, pp. 207ff.)

---

[74]Felix F. Leifels played double bass in the orchestra. He was also Manager and Secretary of the Philharmonic Society until 1921 (he was briefly replaced as Manager by Loudon Charlton from 1910 to 1912) (Shanet, *op. cit.*, pp. 210, 220, 445). (S.a. Note 81, p. 305).

229

Mrs. George R. Sheldon has succeeded in raising the necessary
guarantee fund to rehabilitate the Philharmonic Society. The proposition
made to the members of the Philharmonic Society indicates the aims of
the guarantors of the new organization. The proposition says [amongst
other things]:

"It is proposed to organize an orchestra in New York for the
performance of the highest kind of music, under the exclusive and
absolute direction of a competent conductor, the members of which shall
devote their time to its work for a period of at least twenty-three weeks in
each year. [...] With the approval of the conductor the present
orchestra will be continued under existing conditions of assignment and
retirement."

The conductor may make changes and add to the membership of the
orchestra, subject to the approval of the guarantors' committee. [...]
The action of the guarantors was brought to a climax last week when Mr.
Mahler, who has been selected as conductor, was invited to become the
head of another organization.[75] The guarantors submitted their
proposition to the members of the Philharmonic Society, who
unanimously accepted it. Mr. Mahler was thereupon engaged for a period
of two years.

The members of the Philharmonic Society, instead of receiving a share
in the profits as their compensation, will get a regular salary, and the
business management of the organization will be in the hands of a
separate staff and not under the control of the members of the orchestra.
In return for the surrender of its old privileges of self-government the
Philharmonic Society has the payment of its deficiencies guaranteed for
three years, multiplies the number of its concerts and is freed from the
financial responsibility.

(*NYS*, February 16, 1909, p. 7)

230

Gustav Mahler was obliged to give the ladies who have charge of the new
Philharmonic organization quick notice that a decision had to come
immediately as to his future in this city in relation to orchestral concerts.
He had an offer from the Boston Symphony, unless things were greatly
misrepresented. [...] a meeting was rapidly called, and Mr. Mahler was
selected as the conductor of the Philharmonic for next season [...] .

[75]This is probably another reference to the lasting rumour that Mahler was being
courted by the Boston Symphony (see, for example, **230** and **246**).

[. . .] Mr. Mahler is understood to have accepted it under condition that he is to be permitted, during the first season, to weed out of the orchestra the incompetents; that it is to contain a strength of a hundred players on the average, and that rehearsing is to be systematized according to his rule. We probably shall have some concerts here next year by our local orchestra. It will be the first time that we will have concerts. [. . .] No one who believes in the righteousness of the cause of music for one moment would assume that these various concerts of the Damrosch Brothers represent any musical elevation as compared with what is done by the Boston Symphony Orchestra. It is an impossibility. Even if the Damrosch Brothers were the greatest conductors that were ever sent here by a divine Providence [. . .] the concerts could be of no consequence because they are not rehearsed. A few rehearsals are not rehearsing. [. . .] the same musicians do not play at the rehearsals that play at the concerts. These so called rehearsals here are farces, except at the opera. That is the reason the opera orchestra can produce results. [. . .]

(*MC* 58, no. 7, February 17, 1909, p. 23)

231

HOTEL SAVOY, NEW YORK

[Beginning of 1909]

My dear [Walter],[76]

[. . .]

The permanent orchestra here really seems to be in formation. If it does come to something, could you recommend a young musician of real talent as a conductor, and with general musical experience, who would come here as my "*assistent* [sic] conductor"?

For this would be the condition on which I should be prepared to enter into a contract for yet another year. I must have someone to do the preparatory work for my rehearsals and also take over a concert for me every now and then. [. . .]

(*MSL*, pp. 329f.; original German in *GMB*, pp. 351f.)

---

[76]Bruno Walter [Schlesinger] (1876-1962) - Celebrated German-born conductor. He was Mahler's protégé in Hamburg and Vienna, and conducted the posthumous performances of his Ninth Symphony and *Das Lied von der Erde.*

Plate 44. Bruno Walter. (*RSM*, "Bilder," p. 44)

232

[New York, February 1909]

My dearest [Walter],

In greatest haste! Please *find out* at once whether the *splendid* trumpeter of the Konzertverein, by whom we were so much struck that time, *is* still in *Vienna* and if so look him up and see if he would be willing to come to me in New York? If he is no longer in Vienna, find out where he is now and immediately *cable* me his *name, address*, and if he can come - just those essentials. - Be so kind as to go to this expense on my behalf. I shall definitely be taking over the orchestra in *New York*. More about that soon. If you receive an offer in the near future, don't do anything final without asking me.

Affectionate greetings,
Yours,
Mahler

Very urgent!

Ask *Dreyer* and *Schnellar*[77] whether they would be able to take up an offer from me. Perhaps even add it very briefly to the *cable*.

(*MSL*, p. 330; original German in *GMB*, p. 355)

233

The announcement [. . .] that a sufficient fund had been raised to put the Philharmonic Society on a secure financial basis [. . .] and the statements issued Monday drew fire yesterday from [. . .] the Symphony Society of New York [. . .]

Richard Welling, secretary of the society, yesterday sent the following communication to the newspapers:

'The announcement published in this morning's papers by the committee in charge of the proposed reorganization of a rival orchestral society contains a statement which it is my duty to correct as it appears misleading. The paragraph which reads as follows, "New York now possesses for the first time a permanent orchestra in the true sense of the word", is disingenuous, as for two years already the orchestra of the Symphony Society of New York has been on a "permanent basis". Our musicians are engaged at a regular salary for from thirty-one to forty-five weeks during the year, to devote themselves exclusively to the study and public performance of symphonic music. As in the opinion of the

---

[77]Franz Dreyer and Hans Schnellar were, respectively, trombonist and timpanist with the Vienna Philharmonic; they remained with that orchestra (concerning Schnellar, s.a. **277** and **283**).

promoters of the rival organization twenty-three weeks seems to be the term necessary to give an orchestra a "permanent character in the true sense of the word", we seem to be fully justified in asking you to correct this misstatement of our position.

Let me add that our annual outlay for orchestral salaries exceeds $96,000 [. . .]'

(NYTrib, February 17, 1909, p. 7)

234

The following statement concerning the attitude of the New York Symphony Society toward "guest conductors" was given to MUSICAL AMERICA at the offices of the society:

"The New York Symphony Society does not expect to repeat in the future its experiment of inviting European 'guest conductors' to officiate at any of their concerts, as their last experience with Herr Gustav Mahler, who conducted three of their concerts, was rather unsatisfactory. Special efforts were made to advertise the concerts in the dailies, the Carnegie Hall and Metropolitan Opera House programs. Over 12,000 Mahler bulletins, containing four pages of biographical and analytical notes, were printed and distributed. A large quantity of three-sheet posters were displayed. Large extra expenses were incurred by the engagement of extra musicians, necessary for the production of Mahler's second symphony.

"The entire expenses for the three concerts were over $10,000, while the box-office sales, including the pro rata subscription, amounted to only $4,300, making a deficiency of nearly $6,000. This deficiency was met by the private contributions of a few of the directors of the society, as it was felt that the regular fund of $35,000 yearly, which is used for maintaining the orchestra on a permanent basis throughout the year, should not be burdened with this extra expense.
[. . .]"

(MA 9, no. 15, February 20, 1909, p. 4)

235

The Metropolitan Opera House will fulfill another one of its promises of new opera on Friday next, when Smetana's comic opera, "The Bartered Bride", will be produced in German. [. . .] [The] opera is called one of the most truly Bohemian and popular in the spirit of any, and is compared in this respect with "Der Freischütz" of Weber. [. . .] The Metropolitan is fortunate in having a great Bohemian conductor who will

Metropolitan Opera House.

METROPOLITAN OPERA CO., LESSEE.

TELEPHONE BRYANT 1146.

GRAND OPERA

SEASON 1908-1909

GIULIO GATTI-CASAZZA
GENERAL MANAGER.

ANDREAS DIPPEL
ADMINISTRATIVE MANAGER.

FRIDAY EVENING, FEBRUARY 19, 1909,
at 8 o'clock

First Performance in America of

The Bartered Bride

(PRODANÁ NEVĚSTA)

BOHEMIAN OPERA IN THREE ACTS
By K. Sabina, German Text by Max Kalbeck.

MUSIC by BEDRICH SMETANA

(IN GERMAN)

KRUSCHINA, a peasant, ... ROBERT BLASS
KATHINKA, his wife, ... MARIE MATTFELD
MARIE, their daughter, ... EMMY DESTINN
MICHA, landowner, ... ADOLF MÜHLMANN
AGNES, his wife, ... HENRIETTA WAKEFIELD
WENZEL, their son, ... ALBERT REISS
HANS, Micha's son by first marriage, ... CARL JÖRN
KEZAL, marriage broker, ... ADAMO DIDUR
SPRINGER, director of a traveling circus, JULIUS BAYER
ESMERALDA, a dancer, . . . ISABELLE L'HUILLIER
MUFF, a comedian, ... LUDWIG BURGSTALLER

Peasants and Circus People.

CONDUCTOR . . . . GUSTAV MAHLER
STAGE MANAGER . . . . ANTON SCHERTEL
CHORUS MASTER . . . . HANS STEINER

Incidental Dances arranged by M. OTTOKAR BARTIK:

Act I.—Polka by M. Ottokar Bartik, Mlle. Gina Torriani and Corps of Bohemian Dancers.

Act II.—Furiant by M. Ottokar Bartik, Mlles. Gast and Pechfelder.

Act III.—Comedy: Mlles. Gina Torriani, Gast, Pechfelder, Bourgeau and Weidlich.

The Overture will be played between Acts I. and II.

Plate 45. From the programme booklet of the Metropolitan Opera for the première of *The Bartered Bride*.

produce the work - Gustav Mahler; and furthermore a great Bohemian singer, who will enact the chief part, Miss Emmy Destinn. And there will be another touch of national color put into the work by the engagement of a company of Bohemian dancers, who will show the opera-going public of New York for the first time what the national dances of Bohemia are like.

[...]

Smetana had the fierce and flaming nationalism that is the heritage of all Czechs. For them there is no union with Austria other than that which a superior power has forced upon them [...] Smetana started out to establish a national utterance for his country's art through music. The national dances and folksongs are mirrored in his compositions [...]

None of his operas, it is said, is more successful in this, or more wholly characteristic, than the one to be produced here on Friday [...] This was produced first in Prague in 1866 [...] In 1893 it was given in Vienna, and attracted much attention there - in fact, the musical public for a time went daft about it. [...][78]

"The Bartered Bride" roots deep in Bohemian soil. It is a fragment from the life of a Bohemian village, and the characters are animated by the Bohemian spirit, its gayety and passing shadows of melancholy, its simplicity and directness, its mixture of good sense and ludicrous folly. [...]

(*NYT*, February 14, 1909, Part Six, p. 7)

236

The authoritative statement issued on Monday last by the directors of the Metropolitan Opera House with regard to the present and future status of German opera at that institution will be read with a great deal of interest, and undoubtedly with satisfaction, by those who love German opera, support it and believe that it can be always made financially successful if properly presented.

[...]

MUSICAL AMERICA is in a position to state certain facts with regard to the situation at the Metropolitan which will throw a great deal of light on the situation, and which may be accepted as coming from an authoritative source.

[78]Mahler had had a long-standing love for Smetana's music. He conducted the Hamburg première of *The Bartered Bride*; in Vienna, his first new production as director of the Opera was the first Viennese performance of *Dalibor* (January 17, 1894, and October 4, 1897, respectively).

In the first place, it can be said with confidence that the men of prominence and wealth who are the directors of the Metropolitan Opera House Company, which is responsible for the productions, resent the tendency on the part of the press and the public to interfere with matters which they consider to be purely their own domestic concern. They do not consider the question as to whether there will be a deficit or a profit in the business to be the public's concern. They admit the right of criticism; they also admit that the public preference for the character of opera to be given should be given due weight.

[...]

Further, these gentlemen take the ground that, while it is true that there is a large public in this country enthusiastically well disposed to German opera, there is another public, and perhaps a larger one, which is more enthusiastically disposed to Italian and French opera, as shown by Mr. Hammerstein's success, and that, consequently, while German opera has a just right to be fully represented in the season's repertoire, the main dependence must, after all, be put upon Italian and French opera, for the plain reason that that is what is most popular with the general opera-going public.

(*MA* 9, no. 15, February 20, 1909, pp. 1, 5)

237

Smetana's opera, *The Bartered Bride*, [...] was produced last evening at the Metropolitan Opera House for the first time in America.[79] [...] The opera gave much pleasure, and was received with genuine enthusiasm, not only by the representatives of the Bohemian colony who were present, but also by the great body of the audience, perhaps more sophisticated in the matter of new productions, and not especially prejudiced in favour of peasant operas. [...]

In all and through all the master hand of Mr. Mahler was evident, whose performances all have a special quality of their own, in the finish and dramatic potency with which the music is presented, and all the factors of a vivid dramatic presentation are brought together and coordinated.

(*NYT*, February 20, 1909, p. 7)

---

[79]The complete cast was as follows: Kruschina - Blass; Kathinka - Mattfeld; Marie - Destinn; Micha - Mühlmann; Agnes - Wakefield; Wenzel - Reiss; Hans - Jörn; Kezal - Didur; Springer - Bayer; Esmeralda - L'Huillier; Muff - Burgstaller. All repetitions of this opera conducted by Mahler had the same cast.

Plate 46. Cast photograph of *The Bartered Bride*.
(Metropolitan Opera Archives)

221

238

The musical presentation of the opera last night was in every way admirable. The orchestra, under Mr. Mahler, in delicacy and finish, in phrasing and nuance, in that authority and precision bred alone of careful and competent rehearsal, was a constant delight. The choruses were well sung, the costumes and stage settings and groupings were picturesque and well ordered.

(*NYW*, February 20, 1909, p. 3)

239

How dear [*The Bartered Bride*] has become to the hearts of the Bohemian people had a present and vivid illustration in the fact that several weeks ago [. . .] over $2,000 had been sent to the opera house by members of New York's Bohemian colony for the purchase of seats for the first performance.
[. . .]
Local concertgoers have long been familiar with the overture to "The Bartered Bride". [. . .] Because Mr. Mahler [. . .] did not wish to waste the overture on late arrivals at the opera, he played it between the first and second acts. Then, though it was safeguarded from disturbance, it had no more meaning than it would have had at the beginning. If it were played between the second and third acts its effectiveness would be increased tenfold, for then it would serve one of the purposes of between-acts music, which it may be said ought to bridge over the moods with which one act or scene ends and the other begins. In neither place, however, is the overture an anticlimax like the third "Leonore" when played after the dungeon scene in "Fidelio". [. . .]
And the performance? Mr. Mahler is a Bohemian. Miss Destinn is a daughter of Bohemia's capital. The dancers were brought from the National Theatre at Prague, the home of Czechish music. They are to the Bohemian manner born. [. . .] Altogether, it was an evening of unalloyed delight, and the opera and its production were most unqualified and pronounced successes.

(*NYTrib*, February 20, 1909, p. 7)

240

The question whether there can be any sustained popularity for an opera of the character of "Die Verkaufte Braut" seemed to be swiftly answered by the public enjoyment of its novelty of style and colour. The author and composer invite us to enter fields unfamiliar to our operatic experience. [. . .] The production of last night was most excellent and added to the laurels already earned by the present management.

(*NYS*, February 20, 1909, p. 5)

241

It was decided yesterday that Gustav Mahler will not retire after all from the Metropolitan Opera House at the close of this season. In addition to his duties as conductor of the new Philharmonic Orchestra he will appear at the Metropolitan twenty times next season and will conduct his usual repertoire in addition to the novelties that may be performed.

(*NYS*, February 21, 1909, p. 7)

242
HOTEL SAVOY, NEW YORK

[End of February 1909]

My dear [Roller],

[. . .]

About myself I have only good news to send. I am in relatively good health, as also is my family. My work is at least not degrading and not completely distasteful. I staged a really rather good production of Figaro (entirely in the Lefler spirit) and a magnificent *Bartered Bride* (Lefler above, Mahler below); am definitely leaving the theatre this season and taking over a concert enterprise as from next year. [. . .]

Just now Mama Moll is with us; she really enjoys everything with an undiminished capacity for pleasure, and will no doubt have much to report on personally. [. . .]

(*MSL*, p. 332 (incomplete); original German in *GMB*, pp. 353f.)

243

The remarkably beautiful and eloquent interpretation of Beethoven's "Fidelio" that Mr. Mahler set before the New York music loving public last season was given again last evening at the Metropolitan Opera House.[80] [. . .] It will be a cause of regret to many that it was announced as the only performance of Beethoven's masterpiece this season. [. . .]

---

[80]The cast was almost identical with that of the performance on March 20, 1908 (see Note 117, p. 104), except that Mühlmann sang the role of Don Fernando, and Fornia that of Marzellina.

The performance was not in all respects as finished as those which were heard last season. It did not seem as if the preparation had been so careful. The orchestra at times played roughly and there were places in which the co-operation between the orchestra and the singers was not perfect. Yet in its spirit and in its larger outlines it was a performance of real eloquence.

(*NYT*, February 21, 1909, p. 7)

244

Once more a successful performance was largely due to Mahler's masterly work. His reading of the score was a constant delight; such force and delicacy, such clarity, such dramatic feeling, varied colour and contrast, together with such artistic restraint and authority, are seldom heard in combination. As usual, a spirited performance of the "Fidelio" overture preceded the opera, and the great "Leonora" overture played between the scenes of act two was superbly rendered.

(*NYW*, February 21, 1909, p. 6)

245

Concert Master Wendling,[81] a prominent member of the staff of the Hoftheater at Stuttgart and a favourite of the Stuttgart music world, has received an invitation from the New York Philharmonic Society to join its orchestra as first concertmaster.

(*NYT*, February 21, 1909, p. 7)

246

The reconstruction [of the Philharmonic Society] means [. . .] that for a period of two years at least New York is to enjoy the undoubted advantages and privileges accruing from the presence here as all powerful head of its principal orchestral society of a conductor of the eminence, authority and genius of Gustav Mahler who, it is said, declined to

[81]Karl Wendling (1875-1962) - An eminent pupil of Joachim, Wendling had had a brief tenure as concertmaster of the Boston Symphony during the 1907-1908 season. In 1909 he settled in Stuttgart, and had a long career as a solo and chamber violinist, as well as a teacher.

consider the possibility of a conductorship of the Boston Symphony Orchestra, to accept that of the Philharmonic.

(*NYW*, February 28, 1909, Metropolitan Section, p. M3)

247

The directors of the Metropolitan Opera House Company held an important meeting yesterday afternoon in their offices, at which the contracts of Mr. Giulio Gatti-Casazza, the general manager, and Mr. Andreas Dippel, the administrative manager, for next season were ratified. [. . .] no action toward the engagement of a business manager for the Metropolitan had been taken [. . .]

This statement was issued by the directors after the meeting: -

"It has been agreed between the Board of Directors of the Metropolitan Opera Company and Mr. Dippel, with the concurrence of the general manager, Mr. Gatti-Casazza, that Mr. Dippel's contract as administrative manager (which provided that either the company or himself might terminate the same upon notification on or before February 28) will remain in force unchanged. Mr. Gatti-Casazza, while preserving the authority inherent in his position as general manager, has willingly consented to the assignment to Mr. Dippel besides his administrative functions an important share in the artistic management. The division of activities thus arranged for will not be along the lines of the nationality of composers or conductors, but the management will bend their united efforts toward obtaining the highest standard of performances in whatever language and by whatever composer."

"Mr. Dippel's continuation as administrative manager meets with my cordial satisfaction", said Mr. Gatti-Casazza.

"It was but natural that at the beginning of the new régime there should have developed misunderstandings and even discord, and that it became necessary to clarify the situation by emphasizing the position of the general manager as head of the organization. However, that phase of affairs is fortunately behind us. There exists now between Mr. Dippel and myself perfect accord and amity, and a full understanding on all points covering our respective spheres of activity.

[. . .]"

"I indorse Mr. Gatti-Casazza's statement unqualifiedly [. . .]", said Mr. Dippel. "[. . .] Whatever differences of views may at one time have existed between [us]—and these differences have been greatly exaggerated in the public mind—have now been dissolved into complete harmony and unity of purpose. [. . .]

"I am particularly gratified that the unfortunately now prevalent idea of a division of the Metropolitan Opera forces into two antagonistic camps, one Italian and one German, cannot, under the arrangement provided for next season, retain even a semblance of reality. [. . .]"

(*NYH*, February 28, 1909, p. 14)

248

In the Tribune of last Sunday the critic of that paper speaks as follows about his own "program annotations" for the Philharmonic concert: "Of 'The Good Friday Spell' the commentator of the program has supplied the following interesting explanatory remarks." Hatters should try to secure orders to fit the size of the head that breeds such egotism.

(*MC* 58, no. 9, March 3, 1909, p. 20)

249

Gustav Mahler has already begun the organization of the new Philharmonic Society according to his ideas, and is now engaging the musicians whom he wishes to have when the orchestra goes regularly under his direction next year. One of the conditions on which the distinguished conductor accepted the post at the head of the new Philharmonic orchestra was the engaging of the best available musicians. This plan corresponded exactly with the intention of the guarantors, who will furnish the best material for the efforts Mr. Mahler has already under way.

(*NYTrib*, March 7, 1909, Part Five, p. 4)

250
HOTEL SAVOY, NEW YORK

[10 March 1909]

My dear Karl,
 [. . .]
 A thousand thanks for sending dear little Mama to us. It did all of us a world of good, and by now I suppose she is back with you, busily unpacking. [. . .]

(*MSL*, p. 333; original German in *GMB*, p. 356)

251
What was it that breathed the white heat into last night's performance [of

Plates 47 and 48. Two photographs (*ca.* 1905) taken in the garden of the Villa Moll; Carl Moll is in the centre above, while Anna Moll sits in the wicker seat below. (ÖNB-BA)

Tristan und Isolde]? There were no new singers in the cast.[82] The same
old ship was idle with her swelling sail upon the painted ocean. The same
horn echoed in the cut wood wings. The same shepherd's pipe crooned its
heartbreaking lament behind the same old wall. And Gustav Mahler
waved his hands over it all.

Yet it was all changed. Mr. Mahler hurled all petty restraints to the
four winds of heaven and turned loose such a torrent of vital sound as he
never before let us hear in "Tristan und Isolde." He has always polished
to perfection the gentler passages of the score. He has kept the orchestra
subject to the royal voices and adhered to a narrow but effectual range of
dynamics. But the barbaric, beating flood of the tragedy he has not felt as
he did last night. [. . .] In short, Mr. Mahler's reading last night had just
those elements of power and passion which have been wanting in his
previous interpretations.

(*NYS*, March 13, 1909, p. 5)

252

Gustav Mahler is endeavoring to have some certainty as to the operas he
will be called upon to conduct next year before signing his contract with
the Metropolitan Opera House. He does not care to repeat the
experience of the present season when he rehearsed "Le Nozze di
Figaro" frequently and then had but a few performances with the original
cast, two of the most important characters being afterward assumed by
singers who had none of the advantage of the original preparation. He
wants the assurance that he will be able to accomplish some artistic
contribution to the season's success before he agrees to divide his time
between the opera house and the Philharmonic Society.

(*NYS*, March 28, 1909, 3. Section, p. 8)

253

The concert of the Philharmonic Orchestra in Carnegie Hall last night
was a testimonial to Wasilly [sic] Safonoff, the retiring conductor, and to
Richard Arnold, who this year ends his services with the orchestra as
concert master. At the end of Tschaikowsky's Sixth Symphony, the
orchestra presented Mr. Safonoff with a wreath of silver laurel, in
recognition of his services to the orchestra.

---

[82]Same cast as that of January 1, 1908 (see Note 56, p. 51), except for the roles of
Tristan and Kurvenal, which were sung by Burrian and Goritz, respectively.

At the end of the concert, Andrew Carnegie,[83] President of the Philharmonic Society, stepped on the platform and after a short speech presented to Mr. Safonoff a diamond watch fob, and a book containing the names of the subscribers to the society. Mr. Carnegie then turned to Mr. Arnold, and after congratulating him on his twenty years' service with the society, presented to him a silver loving cup and a book identical with the one he had given to Mr. Safonoff.

In his address to Mr. Safonoff, Mr. Carnegie said:

"Your friends, whose names are legion, could not allow this occasion to pass without giving expression to their sorrow at your departure. Never did conductor more completely captivate his orchestra and his audiences as artist, nor attach himself more closely to those who have been privileged to know him as a man. You have delighted thousands of music lovers and made hosts of friends.

"This hall is to possess as among its most precious traditions the fact that Tschaikowsky led the opening performances,[84] revealing to us some of his masterpieces, and Safonoff for three years has held us under the weird spell of Slavonic music. We ask you to accept this token of our admiration for you as an artist and of appreciation as a man. You carry with you back to your home in Russia the grateful thanks of many thousands of music lovers, the deep regard of the Philharmonic Orchestra, and the friendship of many who rejoice in having made your acquaintance."

(*NYT*, March 28, 1909, p. 13)

254

Gustav Mahler's first appearance with the Philharmonic Society, at Carnegie Hall on next Wednesday evening, derives particular interest from the fact that he is to have permanent control of the orchestra for three seasons, beginning November next. Mr. Mahler's achievements in New York have been so closely identified hitherto with his triumphs in opera that his position as symphonic conductor has necessarily been subordinated to his duties at the Metropolitan Opera House. Mr. Mahler is one of the few famous conductors of Europe who has won equal laurels in the opera house and on the concert stage. His record at the Imperial Opera House in Vienna was no less notable in the history of musical

---

[83]Andrew Carnegie (1835-1919) - Scottish-born American industrialist and philanthropist. He is perhaps best known for the large number of public libraries he endowed in the United States and Great Britain, and for the Carnegie Foundation for the Advancement of Teaching (1905).
[84]See Note 36, p. 170.

affairs than his direction of the Vienna Philharmonic concerts, to which he was the first conductor to be elected by acclamation.[85] The number of musicians has been increased for the local concerts to one hundred. There has been, however, no change in the composition of the orchestra, which as the Philharmonic Society that has been known to New York for so many years will be heard for the last time at these two special concerts.

(*NYTrib*, March 28, 1909, Part Five, p. 4)

255

The sixth of the series of special performances at the Metropolitan Opera House was given yesterday. It was a performance of "Tristan und Isolde", that had certain parts of the score which have been cut out in the last two seasons in the representations under Mr. Mahler's direction restored to their places. It was not, however, a performance of the complete score, for there were still large omissions that have been customary in most opera houses where the work is given for the general public. [. . .]

The performance, which was under the direction of Mr. Hertz, was a beautiful one, and made a deep impression on the audience. [. . .]

(*NYT*, March 31, 1909, p. 11)

256

The Philharmonic Society gave last evening the first of the two concerts it has proposed for the close of the season under the direction of Gustav Mahler. [. . .] These two [concerts] are in the nature of an introduction of Mr. Mahler as the newly appointed conductor of the society. [. . .]

He is not a stranger to the concert platform in New York, having conducted concerts earlier in the Winter of the New York Symphony Society. His programme last evening was a conservative one, comprising Schumann's overture to "Manfred", Beethoven's Seventh Symphony, and Wagner's "Siegfried Idyll", and overture to "Tannhäuser". The playing of the orchestra was of a remarkable precision, rhythmic energy and elasticity and a pulsating vitality that have long been absent from it. Its various choirs seemed fused into a new cohesiveness, and the tone

---

[85]Mahler led the Vienna Philharmonic from 1898 to 1901.

gained a new intensity and value. The players were on their nettle [sic], and played with spirit and enthusiasm. The ensemble had a finish and accuracy such as the Philharmonic players have not often shown. Mr. Mahler's authority and stimulating force were shown at every point. [. . .]

Mr. Mahler's tempos [in the Beethoven symphony] carried conviction. He made abundant modifications, but they were so subtly managed as to be insensible as modifications, and seemed as the inevitable outcome of the musical development. Thus the symmetry and larger proportions of the work were preserved, with the richness and variety of detail that were brought out.

(*NYT*, April 1, 1909, p. 9)

257

[. . .] It would be misleading to regard this concert as a correct indication of what is to be expected of Mr. Mahler hereafter. The orchestra of next winter will without doubt not be that which has been heard during the last three years. The new conductor is to have power to reorganize it. Some of the players will go out. New ones will take their places. Doubtless there will be some rearrangement of the places among the strings which remain.

Mr. Mahler may perhaps discover the long lost wood wind players. Heaven send that he may, for the Philharmonic sadly needs them. [. . .]

Of Mr. Mahler's readings of the compositions much might be written. [. . .] We are inclined to think that close study of this director's readings of Beethoven may be deferred for the present. [. . .]

[. . .] It might not be far out of the way to conjecture that Mr. Mahler would take the tempi of the scherzo [of Beethoven's Seventh Symphony] [. . .] faster if he were perfectly certain of his instrument. [. . .]

On the whole it was a good performance of the symphony. The reading was dignified and sane. It had no tricks of interpretation, no points of sensationalism. It augered well for what will come in the future. [. . .]

Mr. Mahler is exceedingly enamored of the timpani. In the process of time he will discover that the acoustics of Carnegie Hall deal generously with the beat of the drum, and he will doubtless be merciful. Last night's concert achieved much [. . .] It promised more. That was its best feature. [. . .]

(*NYS*, April 1, 1909, p. 7)

258

[. . .] The men who form the Philharmonic band can play well; that everybody knows. [. . .] Whether they shall play well or ill rests generally with the conductor. Last night a quiet, undemonstrative, masterful man had them in hand, and they played as they have played when masters have called on them on rare occasions in the past. [. . .] In his reading of the symphony Mr. Mahler departed from tradition in being more moderate than Beethoven, as indicated by his metronome marks (except in the last movement), or any of the conductors with whom New Yorkers of this generation are familiar, but there was still abundance of life in the performance. [. . .] The audience, not numerous, was most cordial in its recognition of the excellences of the concert.

(*NYTrib*, April 1, 1909, p. 7)

259

The new management of the Philharmonic Society, which will give concerts next season under the direction of Gustav Mahler, has arranged the several series of performances to be given then and the dates. Besides the concerts that will be given in Manhattan, the society will give five in Brooklyn and five in Philadelphia. Near the end of February it will go on a short tour, giving concerts in Boston, Northhampton, New Haven, Hartford, and Springfield.[86]

In New York the concerts will comprise, first, the regular series of eight afternoon concerts, repeated on the evening of the following days, such as the society has given from time immemorial. [. . .]

There will be also a "historical cycle" of six evening concerts [. . .] Mr. Mahler also purposes a Beethoven cycle of five concerts [. . .] There will be, further, four Sunday afternoon concerts [. . .]

Finally there will be an extra concert on Christmas Day in the afternoon. All these concerts will be given in Carnegie Hall.

(*NYT*, April 4, 1909, Part Six, p. 9)

260

Mr. Mahler will depart for his summer home in Austria next Saturday [. . .] It is pleasant to contemplate the plans which have been formulated for the reorganized Philharmonic for next season. Mr. Mahler will have leisure during the summer to reflect upon the character of the offerings which he will make to the patrons of the society next season. In a general way the plans

---

[86]As will be seen in the next chapter (*1909-1910*), the actual tour stops were not identical with the ones announced.

have been laid out, and it is plain that they look toward the maintenance, at least, of some of the traditions of the past.

(NYTrib, April 5, 1909, p. 7)

261

The second of the two concerts given by the Philharmonic Society [...] under the direction of Mr. Gustav Mahler, its new conductor, took place last evening in Carnegie Hall. [...] Mr. Mahler's programme contained only Beethoven's Ninth Symphony, preceded by his overture to "Egmont." Conductors in these days regard this symphony as a touchstone of their highest powers, and it was not unnatural that Mr. Mahler should wish to give it in one of these concerts. [...]

It was an interesting and in parts a deeply stirring performance. It was conceived in a highly dramatic vein, with strong contrasts, an energetic movement, and insistent rhythms. [...]

The music was given an intense vitality and pregnant force by Mr. Mahler's treatment that was absorbing; and it was as true of the finesse and delicacy of his reading, with its unfailing rhythmic quality, its plastic treatment of phrase, its insistence upon the melodic line, its expressive modifications of tempo. [...]

Mr. Mahler, like many other modern conductors, does not hesitate to revise Beethoven's scoring, to reinforce it with a doubling of the instruments, to continue the melodic line in certain voices of the brass instruments where it is presumed the composer left them fragmentary because of the imperfections in their power of execution that have been remedied since Beethoven's day. His revision extends even to the omission of a few bars in the return of the theme of the scherzo that probably seem to him a mistake in the copying of the composer's manuscript. As to all such editorial procedures, there is much to be said on both sides. Mr. Mahler takes a position among the less conservative.

(NYT, April 7, 1909, p. 11)

262

Mr. Mahler [...] signed a contract last April for two concerts [with the Philharmonic Orchestra] which he intended to give last fall. After the terms of the contract had been agreed upon and all preliminary arrangements made it was discovered that the Symphony Society "had a prior claim upon his service, morally if not legally". Thereupon a change was made, and two spring concerts were arranged. [...] These concerts have now been given. [...]

Mr. Mahler made as free with the text of the [Ninth] symphony as modern conductors are in the habit of doing, and thereby achieved effects both good and bad [...] Obviously his purpose, like that of his predecessors who have done similar things, was to "make more definite and certain" (as the lawyers say) the thoughts of the composer, who is supposed, for several reasons, not to have been able to express himself as clearly as he ought or might. With many of them there is no inclination to quarrel. With one it would be a waste of time. Those who think Beethoven wished to have the ears of his auditors assaulted as they were last night by the kettledrum player must have been delighted by the bombardment to which they were subjected; others must have felt outraged. Traditions extending over two generations have not prepared New York's lovers of the symphony for such a reading.[87]

(*NYTrib*, April 7, 1909, p. 7)

263

Mr. Mahler's reading demonstrated conclusively that one feature of the symphony was particularly dear to his heart. We had occasion to note his penchant for the tympani [sic] in the seventh symphony; but what was then a fondness had by last night become an obsession. Tympani have often

---

[87]The raising of objections to Mahler's rescoring of Beethoven's music was by no means unique to American critics. Following his performance of the Ninth Symphony with the Vienna Philharmonic in 1900, Richard Heuberger (see Note 29, p. 24)—for long a strongly pro-Mahler critic—wrote this:

"On the paintings of old masters the art-lover may discover—with horror—traces of over-painting from many different eras. [...] Efforts are now being made everywhere to remove the traces of such senseless conceits, to allow the masters to speak to us as *they* saw fit. But in music it is in our age that attempts are being made to introduce the entirely irresponsible idea of 'touching-up' the works of the classics. What we were given yesterday under the name of 'Beethoven's Ninth Symphony' is a regrettable example of this aberration, this barbarism. A whole multitude of passages had been completely re-orchestrated, which means changed in their sound and thus also in their meaning, changed against Beethoven's clearly expressed will. [...]" (*BRM(E)*, p. 221; original German in *BRM*, pp. 224f.)

On that occasion, Mahler was sufficiently disturbed by the critical reaction that, for one of the very few times in his life, he defended himself in writing and publicly. A lengthy leaflet—citing Beethoven's deafness, improvements in modern wind instruments, and precedents set by Wagner—was distributed to the audience at the repetition of the above concert. (The two concerts took place on February 18 and 22, 1900. Mahler's leaflet is reproduced in *BRM*, p. 224; English translation in *BRM(E)*, pp. 221f.)

For a recent, even if brief discussion of this question, see Ernst Hilmar, "Mahlers Beethoven-Interpretation," in Rudolf Stephan, ed., *Mahler-Interpretation*, Mainz, *etc.*, Schott, 1985, pp. 29-44.

been beaten but last night they were castigated. They volleyed and thundered at times so that the melodic instruments could not be heard. [...]

This may seem in narration to be a small blemish, but there were times—and not a few of them—when it robbed the performance of its musical effect. This was notably the case in the first movement and the last. [...]

The performance as a whole must have left many questionings in the minds of Beethoven's worshippers, who love his music far more than they love conductors, no matter how distinguished.

(*NYS*, April 7, 1909, p. 7)

264

[...]

Resolved that Mr. H.E. Krehbiel be engaged to furnish the program annotations for the coming season, terms to be $25. for each concert at which annotations are required.

Resolved that Mr. Mahler be authorized to engage a Concertmeister [sic] in Europe for next season at a salary not to exceed $6,000.

Resolved that Mr. Gustav Mahler be authorized to engage a first flute player in Europe, providing none can be procured in this country that will be satisfactory to the requirements of Mr. Mahler, at a salary not to exceed $3,000.

Mr. Mahler was requested to order the necessary tympani [sic] for the use of the Orchestra.

(Excerpt from the Minutes of the Meeting of the Guarantors' Committee, April 7, 1909. The Minutes are in ANYP; this excerpt is published here with their kind permission.)

265
HOTEL SAVOY, NEW YORK

[April 8, 1909][88]

My dear Mr. Morris!

May I ask for your intervention in the following matter?

In my contract a "*State Cabin*" was granted me for the crossing. Such a cabin consists of a bed- and a living room and bath. Mr. Schelling, who was commissioned to make the necessary preparations for my October trip, has taken a *Luxury Cabin* for me and my wife. I must, in

[88]Although Mahler did not date the letter, its precise date can be established from the accompanying note with which Morris forwarded it to Leifels.

accordance with the arrangement, decline and request, as per my contract, a "State Cabin" (called a Suite on the "Kaiser Wilhelm") and a First Class Cabin for Miss Turner. I would like to receive the tickets *before my departure.*

2. In a meeting yesterday I made the suggestion, in order to do the Committee a favour, to make the arrangement with Mr. Dippel that the Metropolitan Opera assume the expense of my October trip, for which I promised to take upon myself two performances at the Metropolitan. Since, however, the time is already too far advanced and I wish to have my October trip arranged within the shortest possible time, I would like to modify my proposal to the effect that this arrangement be accepted for my *return trip to Europe* next April. We would then have time through the whole winter to make the arrangement with the Metropolitan.

I again repeat my proposal, to conduct two performances next winter at the Metropolitan to the benefit of the Guarantee Fund. - Since I shall depart already on Saturday, I would be infinitely obliged to you if you would settle both points in the course of today and tomorrow. With heartiest thanks,

your devoted
Mahler

The suites which appear suitable to me, are among the following:
130, 131, 132, 129
125, 126. -

The cabin for Miss Turner should be nearby.
My address in Europe is:

Director Mahler
Wien
III. Rennweg 5   *until 1st* June
after 1st June
Toblach a.d. Südbahn
Tyrol[89]

266

Quarantine N[ew] Y[ork] April 10 [1909]

Mrs. Untermyer, 675 5th Ave. N[ew] Y[ork]

A thousand thanks and our love, undying love. You are the only person who makes leaving difficult for us. We embrace you.

Gustav and Alma Mahler[90]

---

[89]For the German text, see Appendix, A21.
[90]For the German text, see Appendix, A22.

267

The final note of the season's opera in New York was sounded last evening at the Metropolitan Opera House. [...]

[...]

The season has been a stormy one in many ways, and the public still has fresh in mind such portions of the conflicts as have gotten into the press - and most of them seem to have gotten there sooner or later. Opera houses in all lands have always been the areas for teapot tempests, and operatic history is in large part a narrative of such disturbances. The Metropolitan this season has made an ample contribution to the record of them.

The artistic results obtained by the new management have unquestionably reached a higher level in many respects than has prevailed at the Metropolitan Opera House for years. This has been especially noticeable in the matters of stage management, in the creation of dramatic ensemble, in the care and intelligence with which most of the performances were prepared, in the finish and consistency with which they were set before the public, and in the effects of chorus and of orchestra. [...] It is perhaps neither necessary nor desirable to apportion from an outside view the merits and deserts of Mr. Gatti-Casazza and Mr. Dippel in securing the results that have been gained, or in laying the blame that should be borne for shortcomings.

[...]

The acquisition of Mr. Toscanini has brought musical enjoyment of a high order in the Italian works that he has conducted as well as in the fine performances of "Götterdämmerung" that are due to his labors. [...] The return of Mr. Mahler has been important for the season, and the performances that he has conducted have afforded some of its keenest delights. [...] A most important gain has been made in the orchestra. The great increase in its numbers, making possible the formation of two bodies,[91] has put less work on the men. They have played with less fatigue and there has been possible a greater attention, in some cases, at least, to rehearsal and proper preparation. There has been a great improvement in the chorus, and especially in the German division. [...]

In the matter of producing new works the season has not been remarkably brilliant, and it has seen about half the promises made at the beginning of the season unfulfilled at the end of it. [...] Only four of the promised new works were given.

---

[91]Apparently, the reorganization of the Metropolitan with the advent of Gatti-Casazza's administration included the enlarging of the pool of orchestral players to 135, as well as the establishing of two separate choruses (100 voices each) for the Italian-French and German repertoires (Kolodin, *op. cit.*, p. 200). (S.a. **150**.)

Of these the only one to make an unequivocal success was Smetana's "Bartered Bride", of which the melodic freshness, the merriment, the exuberant spirit, the new and unaccustomed charm of the Bohemian atmosphere, and the evident reality of the enthusiasm with which the music was sung, the action carried on, the dances danced, and the orchestral part played under Mr. Mahler's direction made an impression that was different from anything experienced at the Metropolitan in a long time. Seldom has a new production there been received with the obvious pleasure and sympathy that greeted the first production of "The Bartered Bride".

[. . .]

Interesting revivals were made of Mozart's "Le Nozze di Figaro", of which a performance of extraordinary brilliancy, finish, and sparkling spirit was given under Mr. Mahler's direction - a performance of unusual merit that was rewarded by unusual public interest. A pity that its central figure was lost in the departure of Mme. Sembrich and that an unsatisfactory substitute had to be accepted for later performances.

[. . .]

On the whole, [. . .] with all the disappointments of various kinds, and disregarding the factional feeling that has run high for and against various nationalities and personalities, [. . .] the season at the Metropolitan was marked by an advance to a higher level of artistic merit in some very important matters.

[. . .]

(*NYT*, April 11, 1909, Part Six, p. 7)

268

In looking back over the season as a whole, one is struck first by the enormous preponderance of opera over music of every other kind, sort and description. [. . .] In view of this somewhat curious disproportion, which surely proves conclusively that operatic music is what New York is chiefly interested in, perhaps the most important and significant musical happening in its probable effect on the future of music in this community has been the reorganization of the Philharmonic Society under Gustav Mahler. As the preliminary announcement of the plans of the society for the coming year provides for a number of concerts more than double what the society has ever before given in its history, and evidences have already been given by Mr. Mahler, and especially by his magnificent performance of the Ninth Symphony last week, of his supreme ability as an orchestral conductor, it is safe to assume that purely orchestral music will another season in New York attain a prominence and importance that it has never enjoyed before.

(*NYW*, April 11, 1909, Metropolitan Section, p. M5)

269

The recent reorganization of the Philharmonic Society, and the change from the share alike to the salary basis, is merely an experiment, and after its trial the old order may be restored to vogue. These are the prospects, according to Anthony Reiff,[92] chairman of the trustees, and for twenty-eight years a member of the orchestra.

[...]

Should the arrangement under which the Philharmonic will be reincarnated next season prove a failure, although financially that is hardly possible, with such an array of affluent backers, then, says Mr. Reiff, ho! for the Orchestral Republic!

[...]

Mr. Reiff deprecates the attitude of the New York public in belittling the local to the exaltation of the foreign, and the frenzied worship of the "star" executant. In his opinion it is in vain that metropolitans seem only able to enjoy imported ware, musically speaking, and taboo the idea that anything without the foreign label can be of acme brand. From the ranks of the orchestra itself should come the leader, he opines, allowing, of course, that there are men of merit in it.

(*MA* 10, no. 4, June 5, 1909, p. 2)

[92]Anthony Reiff, Jr. (*ca.* 1838-1916) - Son of one of the founders of the present Philharmonic in 1842, Reiff joined the orchestra at the age of 17 as a violinist; he later became Vice President of the Society. (He is the retired member of the Trustees, alluded to in Note 8, p. 248.)

CHAPTER III

The 1909-1910 Season

Commentary

Upon his arrival in Europe in the spring of 1908, Mahler had immediately embarked on a conducting tour. In 1909, the Mahlers began their European sojourn with a brief holiday in Paris. Their friends in the spring-time city welcomed them with open arms, and there followed a round of glittering social events. While Gustav usually felt impatient and ill at ease on such occasions, Alma's unquenchable thirst for, and unlimited pleasure in, the *grand monde* suffuses her description of some of these events. For example:

> Picquart, then Minister for War, gave us lunch in the Ministry, where he lived. His old friend, Madame Ramazotti, was hostess. Painlevé, the Clemenceaus, Baron L'Allemand and we were the guests. [...]
> When we drove up to the Ministry the gates opened, and a guard of honour drawn up to the left and right in full-dress uniform presented arms as we passed through. Picquart was standing at the top of the steps, as happy as a child over this idea of his.
> "It is the rule in the case of royalty. You are the same in my eyes", he called out to Mahler. [...][1]

[1]*AMM*, pp. 149, 150; original German in *AME*, pp. 184, 185.

Whatever pleasure Mahler may have derived from the social whirl, his stay in Paris in the spring of 1909 at least resulted in what is undoubtedly one of the best-known items in the Mahler iconography. According to Alma, it was Carl Moll who had commissioned the venerable French sculptor, Auguste Rodin, to do a bust of Mahler. Although the subject initially had to be tricked into the sittings, the result was the well-known bronze bust.[2]

From Paris the Mahlers went on to Vienna, where they were to stay for a while before proceeding to their summer home in Toblach. It is evident from the surviving documents that much of Mahler's time in Vienna was taken up with the affairs of the New York Philharmonic (for example, see **272** and **276**). Following what he described as an "unbelievably difficult" search, he engaged Theodore Spiering as the new concertmaster of the orchestra. Although he did not succeed in securing the services of a suitable (and, above all, 'importable') flautist, it appears that his wish for a better timpanist was to be fulfilled by the hiring of a man already resident in the United States (see **277**). In order to provide this new player with the best possible equipment, Mahler also took care of the purchasing of the two pairs of timpani that had been authorized by the Guarantors' Committee in April (see **264**).

During the summer of 1909 Mahler was also much occupied with the weighing of new opportunities in the operatic field. While in this instance we do not have the communications addressed to him, it seems from a number of his letters to Alma that he was once again actively considering an offer from Buenos Aires, presumably for the spring of 1910. More of a long-range prospect (one that was also reported in the New York press) was represented by an approach made to Mahler by the planners of a new opera house in Berlin. In a letter clearly central to this affair, Humperdinck to all intents and purposes offered to Mahler the directorship of what was tentatively designated as the Richard Wagner Theatre (see **274**).

Although some of the details are not as clear as one would wish, it seems that Mahler spent a considerable portion of the next few months apart from his family. As a letter dated June 13, 1909 tells us, he moved to Toblach on the 12th, and Alma and their daughter

---

[2]*AMM*, p. 148. - (François) Auguste (René) Rodin (1840-1917).

went to another spa for a "rest cure."[3] At Toblach, Mahler completed the Ninth Symphony, and probably began to sketch the Tenth. As his letters to Mengelberg, Walter, and especially Alma show, he also continued to be very busy with the ongoing planning for his first season with the New York Philharmonic. This activity culminated—at least in the sense of a diversion—in an extended visit to Toblach by Richard Arnold and his wife.

Early in September Mahler returned to Vienna,[4] although probably only briefly. It appears that Alma and Anna both had to undergo tonsillectomies. During this time Mahler seems to have gone to Göding (today Hodonin in Czechoslovakia), where he stayed with the industrialist Fritz Redlich. According to Alma, Mahler put the final touches to *Das Lied von der Erde* while at Göding.[5]

---

[3]*AMM*, p. 319; original German in *AME*, p. 429. - Even though it may seem like a digression, I must quote from Alma's memoirs at some length here. The following passages provide a very clear—if painful—insight into the sometimes happy, often troubled, always unlikely relationship of this unlikely couple; she - much younger, healthy, exceedingly self-centered; he - older and ill, worshipful of her, yet often supremely oblivious to the world around him, and thus to her needs:

"By the time we got back to Vienna my nerves were in a critical state and I was ordered a rest-cure at Levico. I first took Mahler to Toblach and then went to Levico with my child. I was in a state of profound melancholy. I sat night after night on my balcony, weeping and looking out at the crowd of gay and happy people, whose laughter grated on my ears. I longed to plunge myself into love or life or anything that could release me from my icy constraint. We exchanged letters daily on abstract topics. He got anxious about me and at last he came to see me.

I met him at Trient, but when he got out of the train I failed to recognize him. Wishing to look his best he had gone to the barber at Toblach before he left, and he had been given a close crop while he read the newspaper without giving a thought to what was going on. The sides of his head were shorn as close as a convict's and his excessively long, thin face, deprived now of all relief, was unrecognizably ugly. I could not get used to the transformation and after two days he sadly departed again." (*AMM*, p. 151; original German in *AME*, p. 187.)

[4]His intention to do so is stated in a letter he wrote to Bruno Walter in August (*GMB*, pp. 367f.; English translation in *MSL*, pp. 341f.). - The same letter allows us to conclude that the Ninth Symphony had been completed, even though, as was his usual practice, Mahler avoided referring to it by number, supposedly for superstitious reasons. A slightly later letter to Oscar Fried, written probably in September, confirms the completion of the Ninth. It may also be the only known occasion on which Mahler identified it at this early stage by its appropriate number; he wrote simply: "Die 9. ist fertig." (Rudolf Stephan, "Gustav Mahler und Oskar Fried," in *MUB*, p. 56).

[5]*AMM*, p. 153. - Presumably, because of Alma's small chronological slip, transposing the move from the apartment in Vienna (see in the following) and Mahler's trip, Donald Mitchell disputes the visit to Göding (see *AMM*, p. 365).

In anticipation of continuing, annual sojourns in America, the Mahlers decided to give up their long-term residence in Vienna. Mahler occupied the apartment at Auenbruggergasse 2 with Justine in 1898; following their respective marriages in 1902, it became the home he shared with Alma. Now, at the beginning of October, 1909 he went to Holland to conduct, while she looked after the removal from the apartment.[6]

In light of Mahler's world-wide reputation—well established as a conductor, and ever-growing as a composer—and his fondness for orchestral conducting, it is somewhat surprising to find that his European concert appearances in 1909 were restricted to those in October in Holland. Leading the Concertgebouw, which had been carefully rehearsed by Mengelberg, he now conducted his Seventh Symphony three times within six days: on the 2nd in The Hague, and on the 3rd and 7th in Amsterdam. In spite of the inevitable success of these performances with an orchestra, and before audiences, familiar with him, this prolonged immersion in its difficulties decided Mahler against "starting with" his Seventh Symphony in New York (see **293**). In fact, he was not to conduct this work at all in New York, even though rumours of its anticipated performance had persisted ever since the autumn of his first season in America (see **22**).

Following his final concert in Holland, Mahler went to Paris. He was met there on the 8th of October by his family, who had travelled directly from Vienna. They sailed for the United States on the 13th from Cherbourg, and arrived in New York on the 19th.

While an autumn arrival in America was becoming a routine affair for Mahler by 1909, this occasion differed significantly from the previous two in at least two areas.

As was seen in the first chapter, in 1907 Mahler arrived in the United States with all the respect and fanfare due the celebrated conductor and immediate past head of one of the world's preeminent operatic institutions. A year later he came back, his overseas reputation having been confirmed and enhanced by his achievements during his first season in New York. Yet, in both of those years he

---

[6]Apparently, as Alma makes it a point to assure us, such a "division of duties" was by no means exceptional:

"I always did my utmost to save Mahler all the drudgery of life. When we moved house or went away anywhere, he knew nothing of what went on behind the scenes," and so on. (*AMM*, p. 153; original German in *AME*, p. 189.)

came to the Metropolitan Opera not as the single, undisputed star in the firmament of the organization, but "merely" as *one* of its bright lights. Ironically, this was perhaps even more true in 1908, as Toscanini had also joined the Metropolitan by then.

Now, in October of 1909, Mahler returned to the United States as the all-powerful leader (at least in theory!) of a venerable musical organization, the New York Philharmonic Society. Aside from the personal satisfaction this gave him (and that it did is abundantly clear from the array of pertinent documents—letters, interviews, memoirs— in this and the preceding chapter), it also gave him powers which he had not possessed for the past two years. While his preferences regarding his own repertoire were very likely met, he had no say in the overall programming at the Metropolitan. Further, even if he could exercise a limited amount of control over the casting of his operas, he could almost certainly not influence the hiring or dismissing of singers and orchestral musicians employed by the Metropolitan. Now, in the autumn of 1909 (in every practical sense, in the spring of 1909) Mahler was once more in full control (as it appears in retrospect) of the programming and personnel of a major musical organization.

Since Mahler's programming, in an overall sense, reveals itself quite satisfactorily through the reviews and other documents presented for this season and the next, it needs no concentrated discussion here. Occasionally, particularly noteworthy aspects of it will be touched upon in the following chronological narrative, as well as in the essay which precedes the documents of the 1910-1911 season. As concerns the personnel changes in the Philharmonic Orchestra, however, a detailed discussion is justified at this point, especially since a great many contradictory statements and accounts had gained currency at the time and over the intervening years.[7]

From many of the contemporary references (both before and after the event) to the changes in the orchestra's membership effected by or because of Mahler, one gains the impression that the ensemble

---

[7] I do not wish to infer, of course, that my account is, in any sense, flawless or incontrovertible. For that, far too many of the essential contemporary documents are missing. At best, it is a piecing together of bits of information from a wide variety (and, inevitably, range of reliability) of sources. The lists of orchestra members regularly included in the programme booklets of the Society constituted my chief source of information.

Plate 49. Mahler and Anna at Toblach, Summer 1909. (ÖNB-BA)

Plate 50. Gustav Mahler at Göding (Hodonin), Summer 1909.
(*BRM*, Illustration 306)

eventually directed by him constituted what was virtually a new orchestra (for example, see **230** and Note 63). At the opposite end of the scale, the extent of the changes is downplayed in some historical accounts (see Note 63). In addition, we encounter vague anticipations of "some" changes, including a reseating of the string sections (*e.g.,* **257**), as well as fairly accurate reports of the changes in specific sections of the orchestra (*e.g.,* **297**). As may be expected, the extent of the actual changes constitutes a range which falls between the two extremes. Nevertheless, as the figures in the following demonstrate, the overall differences between Safonoff's and Mahler's orchestras may be described as quite large, especially in light of the already considerable power of the Musicians' Union.

Of the 102 players listed in the programme for one of the last concerts under Safonoff (March 5, 1909),[8] only 56 appear in the list for Mahler's opening concert on November 4th. Of the smaller orchestra of 92 listed in November, only 55 players had been members of the ensemble in March. The overall turnover was in the range of 40-45%. An analysis of the changes by choirs also produces some interesting results.

At least numerically, the string choir escaped the reorganization relatively unscathed: 43 (74%) of the 58 players in Mahler's orchestra had been members of the old ensemble. The various sections, however, did not fare equally well. While all eight contrabass players of the "new" orchestra were survivors, five of the 14 second violins (including the leader) were new members. The seating order was also rearranged quite extensively in some of the sections. For example, the 12 former members among the 16 first violins in Mahler's orchestra occupied the following chairs in the two ensembles: 2. chair in the new ensemble (2. chair in the old one); 3 (3); 4 (4); 5 (7); 6 (10); 7 (13); 8 (6); 9 (15); 11 (12); 13 (second violins, 6. chair); 14 (11); and 15 (14). In contrast, only one of the eight double bass players was in a new position in Mahler's orchestra in November of 1909.

---

[8]In addition to the complement of performers, the programmes prior to the reorganization also listed the Officers, Directors, and Pension Fund Trustees of the Society. These lists provide us with an interesting insight into the inherently conservative nature of the Philharmonic's old co-operative structure. Of the 12 orchestral musicians (one of them retired) included in the three groups of functionaries, no fewer than ten belonged to the string section, the traditional core of an orchestra.

Plates 51 and 52. Gustav Mahler in Amsterdam, October 1909.
(*BRM*, Illustration 307; W.G.W. Kurz Collection)

250

The situation was radically different among the performers in the various groups of the wind choirs. In total, woodwind and brass players had little more than half the chance of survival of their string-playing colleagues. Only 11 of Safonoff's 29 wind players show up in Mahler's orchestra; all but three of them had been demoted. While two out of the three former trumpet players were retained, not a single one of the four flute and piccolo players survived the reorganization. Among those wind players who stayed on, some suffered permanent and doubtless humiliating demotion: Safonoff's first oboist, for instance, never again rose higher than third chair.

Finally (and not unexpectedly in the light of continuing complaints in the press), the entire timpani and percussion section was staffed by newly engaged players in November, 1909.

Clearly, it was with some justification that Mahler and others occasionally referred to the New York Philharmonic as it appeared at the opening of the 1909-1910 concert season as a "new" orchestra. Yet in order to see the magnitude of the orchestra's reorganization in 1909 in the proper perspective, it must be compared briefly with the personnel changes that occurred in 1910 (Mahler's second season) and in 1911 (after Mahler's departure). The results support the contention that the restaffing of the orchestra in 1909 was, indeed, a major one; they also dispel the notion, however, that it was in any way excessive.

It is not surprising to find that the turnover apparent in the orchestra with which Mahler opened his second season on November 1, 1910 was of a smaller order than that a year earlier. The list of 83 players included 15 new members - an overall rate of only 18%. Some of the intrasectional changes, however, were quite extensive. Thus, four of the eight contrabasses were new; only one flautist remained (and he moved down from principal to second); and no fewer than 14 of the 16 first violins sat in chairs different from those in which they had concluded the 1909-1910 season.

Again not unexpectedly, a much higher number of players (27 out of 82, or 33%) were new to the orchestra listed for the first concert of the 1911-1912 season. It is interesting to note that a number of musicians who had been left out of the orchestra in either one of the preceding two seasons were now playing again. Similarly, formerly held positions were regained by a few players in every section of the orchestra.

Another area in which Mahler faced a substantially different situation upon his third return to the United States was in the type and size of his workload.[9]

As we saw in the first chapter, Mahler's contract with Conried committed him to the conducting of up to three performances a week for the Metropolitan Opera. It appears that he actually ended up conducting only 26 performances during the approximately 18 weeks he spent in America during the 1907-1908 season. Nineteen of these performances, of only five different operas, were given in New York. With the exception of a week in Boston at the end of the season, the other appearances away from New York required only day-trips to Philadelphia and Boston. Although we have no definite information on the frequency and number of rehearsals Mahler had to conduct, and even if we take into account his well-known zeal for preparing all phases of a new production personally, it seems reasonable to assume that at least some of the preparatory and most of the repertoire rehearsals were conducted by others.[10] During his second season at the Metropolitan, Mahler's workload appears even to have decreased. He conducted 15 times in New York; of the four operas in his charge, only two were new productions.

On the whole, then, Mahler's workload during his two seasons at the Metropolitan Opera was anything but excessive.[11] Certainly in comparison with it, the season's task with which he was faced upon assuming the leadership of the New York Philharmonic Orchestra was a much more extensive and taxing one. Over a period of approximately 24 weeks, he had originally been scheduled to conduct 43 concerts: 32 in New York, 5 in Brooklyn, and 6 in various

[9]Naturally, here we are again confronted with a situation where comparisons—for the want of a variety of documents—have to be based on "soft" numbers, and on information culled from a number of more or less reliable sources. Still, I am satisfied that the *relative* values which emerge make the exercise worthwhile.

[10]Apparently, there were as many as 20 rehearsals for the new production of *Le nozze di Figaro* in January, 1909 (Kolodin, *The Metropolitan Opera*, p. 205). In all likelihood, however, this was an unusually high number of rehearsals at the Metropolitan (but see **46**).

[11]Such a conclusion appears to be especially well justified when one compares this workload with Mahler's conducting activities at the Vienna Opera. During the 1897-1898 season, for instance, he conducted 108 performances of 23 operas. And in addition to this, he had his directorial duties to perform!

other cities. The concerts in New York were divided into four series: 8 pairs (Thursday evening, repeated Friday afternoon) of "regular" subscription concerts; 6 "historical" concerts; 5 Beethoven-concerts; and 5 Sunday concerts. In the end, the concerts totalled 46: two concerts were added to the Sunday-series, and the final Beethoven-concert was repeated as the "farewell" concert of the season.

Again, we have no reliable statistical information on the number of rehearsals Mahler held on a per-concert basis. Some of the contemporary reports and documents refer to (*e.g.,* **310**), or give the impression of (*e.g.,* **305**) a considerable number of rehearsals, at least for some of the concerts. At the same time, it seems reasonable to assume that concerts which had programmes consisting of all, or mostly familiar works (perhaps just played) were preceded by very few rehearsals, if any. However, the very fact that the programmes of the 1909-1910 season included no fewer than 97 works by 33 composers[12] implies that the 46 concerts would have needed at least two rehearsals per concert, on the average.

All in all, it is clear that Mahler's workload during his first season with the New York Philharmonic was of a magnitude which belies Alma's descriptions of it as "by no means exacting" (see **227**) and "child's play" (see **345**). Rather, it supports the impression of overwork created by his letters to Adler (his later, attempted disclaimer notwithstanding - see **313** and **353**) and Walter (see **346**). Inevitably, the load was unevenly distributed, with some of the weeks and months worse than others.

The greatest number of concerts (11) in this first season took place in January; the week of January 16th alone witnessed four of them: on Sunday, Thursday and Friday in New York, with a concert in Philadelphia wedged in on the Monday! In general, the travelling demanded during this season was also more onerous than it had been with the Metropolitan Opera. For example, in February (with a total

[12]Performance statistics for this, as well as for the next season are derived chiefly from James Gibbons Huneker, *The Philharmonic Society of New York and its Seventy-Fifth Anniversary - A Retrospect*, [New York], 1917, pp. 76-86; Irving Kolodin, "Mahler in America," *Saturday Review*, July 16, 1960, p. 45; *HLG3*; and Knud Martner, *Gustav Mahler im Konzertsaal - Eine Dokumentation seiner Konzerttätigkeit 1870-1911*, Kopenhagen, 1985.

Plate 53. The New York Philharmonic Orchestra, *ca.* 1902. (Shanet, *op. cit.*, Illustration 31)

of 10 concerts) concerts were given in four different cities on four consecutive days during the week of the 20th. [13]

Of course, as he somewhat ruefully acknowledged in his letter to Walter, Mahler was his own worst enemy at times. In addition to his nine Philharmonic concerts in March, he also prepared and conducted four performances of *Pique Dame* at the Metropolitan Opera.

And now, a brief chronological survey of some of the highlights of the 1909-1910 season. To begin with, it is instructive to look at the first concerts of each of the four series.

It is fair to say that Mahler's debut as the official leader of the New York Philharmonic Orchestra was awaited, greeted, and reviewed with even more interest than his first appearance in New York had been nearly two years earlier. The programme of the opening pair of concerts of the regular series on November 4th and 5th (see **291**), dominated by the music of Beethoven and Strauss, constituted a concentrated preview of the season to come. By the closing concert on April 2nd, more works of Beethoven had been conducted by Mahler than those of any other composer (even Wagner!). Similarly, Richard Strauss was established as the most often played "modern" composer under Mahler's baton. *Till Eulenspiegel* was heard no fewer than 10 times - the most of any single work in this first season.

If the programme of the opening concerts was a "representative" one, so was its reception by the critics. The reviews are dominated by a willingness to grant—and even advance, as it were—credit for the improvements in the playing of the orchestra. At the same time, Krehbiel's slightly sarcastic tone unmistakably points to the future: his was clearly an expectancy less benevolent than that of the other critics. Also, themes already familiar—some of which were to become increasingly strident in the next year and a half—appear in several reviews. Aldrich, for instance, clearly felt obliged to comment on what he felt was an "insistence on the loudest things" during much of the opening concert (see **307**).

---

[13] I should emphasize that these figures and comparisons are meaningful only for the period into which fall Mahler's four seasons in the United States. Indeed, many later conductors of the Philharmonic faced far greater workloads. Concerts on four (or even five) consecutive days soon became the norm. During one particular stretch of the 1953-1954 season, for example, Dimitri Mitropoulos conducted concerts on 18 consecutive days - 14 of them in a row in 14 different cities! (Shanet, *op. cit.*, p. 581.)

Judging from the tone of slight discomfort evident in a number of the reviews of the first "historical" concert on November 10th, its programme was somewhat less familiar to some of the critics. Even though historical concerts were not new to New York, Mahler's approach to some aspects of this material baffled, and in some instances upset critics and audiences alike. Chief among these were his combination of movements from two of Bach's orchestral Suites, and—perhaps to an even greater extent—his introduction of a modified piano as a substitute for the *continuo* harpsichord. Beyond the unfamiliar tone of this instrument, his auditors were evidently troubled by the fact that Mahler—regarded as one of the greatest among the many great virtuoso conductors of the age—would wish to voluntarily diminish his rightful position by conducting while seated at the keyboard!

The first concert of the Beethoven-series on November 19th was literally an invitation to most of the critics to recall their past grievances, and to rearm themselves in anticipation of a season-long battle over Mahler's "treatment" of Beethoven's music. For that concert, Aldrich found it sufficient to remark on the few "disconcerting," "insistent accents" in the Second Symphony (see **322**), while Henderson grumbled mildly about the doubling of the woodwinds (see **324**).

Finally, the opening concert of the last (Sunday) series was given on November 21st. Perhaps this was the series that Mahler had in mind when he voiced his desire in October to give "special concerts" at "popular prices" (see **301**). Judging from de Koven's review (see **326**), some of the critics would also have welcomed occasional "popular" concerts. In fact, his only complaint was directed against what he perceived as the "classic severity" of much of the programme of this first Sunday concert. Reading this review, one is reminded of the critic's eternal want of satisfaction: it was only in April that de Koven had welcomed with eager anticipation the announced increase in the number of Philharmonic concerts; seven months later (and less than three weeks into the new season), he considered it of "serious import and moment" to ask whether New York wanted symphony concerts "during the week and on Sundays too!"

Although he had ceased to be a member on permanent contract there with the end of the 1908-1909 season, the Metropolitan Opera (and operatic matters in general) continued to encroach—directly or indirectly—on Mahler's life and his consciousness for another year.

One wonders, for instance, what his state of mind was on November 27th, when Toscanini conducted *Tristan und Isolde* for the first time at the Metropolitan. Was Mahler, perhaps, at the performance? (He did not have a concert to conduct that day.) Did he read, or have read to him, the glowing tributes in which the critics declared Toscanini's success (although with reservations on the part of Aldrich - see **329**)? The letters, the memoirs are all silent on this subject.

Though Mahler's letter in April to the lawyer representing the Philharmonic's Guarantors (see **265**) seems to indicate quite clearly that an appearance by him at the Metropolitan in the 1909-1910 season was being contemplated, his letter to Bruno Walter in December (see **346**) implies that such arrangements were far from complete even then. By February, however, it was widely known that the vehicle with which Mahler had been tempted back to the Metropolitan for his only appearance of the season was nothing lesser than the first American stage production of a Tchaikovsky opera. (S.a. **287**, **290** and Note 51.)

The première of *Pique Dame* took place on March 5th; it was quickly followed by three more performances. It is an anomaly in the history of American musical life that, despite the great and lasting success of his orchestral music (already established for quite some time by 1910), Tchaikovsky's operas could not find even moderate success. Such an outcome for *Pique Dame* was foreshadowed by the tone of the reviews on March 6, 1910. Henderson, for example, while appreciative of Mahler's efforts, and admitting the "singularly insinuating musical power" of the opera, wondered whether it would "suit the taste of this public." Apparently, it did not: after the four performances in 1910, *Pique Dame* was not produced again at the Metropolitan until 1965.[14]

Far more successful with the public (although not unequivocally so with the critics) was a new operatic production of the season at the rival house. For present purposes, the intriguing sidelight of the American première of *Elektra* at the Manhattan Opera House on February 1st was that Mahler—an avowed and active champion of Strauss's music—apparently disliked this work intensely. So, at least, according to Alma (see **375**).

---

[14]*Eugen Onegin* has not fared much better: produced for the first time at the Metropolitan in 1919, it remained in the repertoire for one more year, and then disappeared until 1957 (Kolodin, *The Metropolitan Opera*, pp. 759, 755).

Whatever Mahler's actual reaction may have been to *Elektra*, he—along with hundreds of others in the opening-night audience—was probably aware of the possibility that this was to be the last operatic triumph mounted by Oscar Hammerstein. Ever since December, rumours had been circulating concerning negotiations between the Metropolitan Opera and Hammerstein which were aimed at resolving "a crisis in operatic affairs"—namely, an alarmingly high and mounting deficit at the Metropolitan. Clearly threatened by his popularity,[15] the businessmen-owners of the older theatre rid themselves of Hammerstein in the only way they knew: in April they concluded an agreement with him, buying his "silence" for one million two hundred thousand dollars (see **432**).

In the meantime, the power struggle at the Metropolitan, which had lasted for more than a year (see *1908-1909*), ended with a result that had been clearly foreseeable. Dippel, who had been loosing ground steadily against an increasingly powerful Italian faction, tendered his resignation as administrative manager in February. He went on to a successful stint as general manager of the Chicago Opera, while Gatti-Casazza was handed the sole control of the Metropolitan by its directors.

It may be recalled that Mahler had introduced himself to New York as a composer-conductor rather successfully in December of 1908 when he led the Symphony Society's orchestra in a guest-performance of his Second Symphony. Now, as full-time conductor of the Philharmonic, he had programmed two very different works: his earliest symphony, and his latest song cycle already performed, the *Kindertotenlieder*.

The First Symphony, played at the pair of regular subscription concerts on December 16th and 17th, was received with uniform disapproval by the critics. Condemnation ranged from Aldrich's relatively mild comment on the Symphony's "dangerous verging [. . .] upon the commonplace" to Krehbiel's description of the finale as the work of a "prophet of the ugly" (see **338** and **341**). It is evident from the reviews that not the least of Mahler's problems was

---

[15]The opening of the recently completed New Theatre in November as a branch-operation of the Metropolitan (see **321**) was an ill-conceived attempt at presenting New Yorkers with yet another alternative to the Manhattan Opera. Inevitably, it merely fragmented yet further the potential audience for opera; for this, and a number of other reasons, it proved to be a short-lived venture.

his stubborn refusal to provide an explanation of the work's "poetical, dramatic, or emotional contents" (see Note 89). At the very least, he had now ensured himself of Krehbiel's implacable hostility!

Judging from his letters written around this time, Mahler was certainly aware of the fact, if perhaps not of the extent, of the First Symphony's failure. Thus, the success in January of the *Kindertotenlieder*, though not undivided, must have been more than ordinarily welcome to him. (Incidentally, it throws interesting light on Mahler's conception of that term that he performed his song cycle in one of the "historical" concerts.)

Throughout the season, criticism of Mahler's interpretation of, and "tampering" with the music of others continued and in some quarters even intensified in the new year. Even Henderson indulged himself in a series of *feuilletons* (for example, see **357** and **360**) in which he gave vent to his discomfort and unhappiness with all things modern—whether composers, conductors, or their interpretations of the "classics." However, snide as Henderson's references to Mahler's "exploration" of Beethoven's music may have been, they fell far short of the vitriolic sarcasm that permeates Krehbiel's attack on, for example, Mahler's treatment of the Sixth Symphony (see **358**). In comparison, the admirably sensitive and open-minded review (regrettably, unsigned) of a performance of the Fifth Symphony in the *Philadelphia Inquirer* only a few days later makes for refreshing reading (see **364**).

It is difficult to gauge today the extent to which the critical reception of Mahler's first season as the Philharmonic's full-time conductor may have influenced the planning for 1910-1911. Conversely, it is safe to assume that the generally poor attendance record of the season was a worrisome matter for the directors of the Society (in effect, the Guarantors' Committee). Season's-end reports and interviews (for example, see **415** and **425**) indicate that one solution contemplated was a drastic reduction in the diversity (although certainly not in the overall number) of concerts. They also show Mahler as unwilling to be specific with regard to his plans for the following season. It is more than likely that this apparent reticence was caused chiefly by a beginning of the conflicts with the management which were to develop so rapidly over the next few months (see *1910-1911*).

The Mahlers sailed for Europe on April 5, 1910. Unaware of the brief time remaining to him, Mahler was looking forward to one of his busiest summers of late. Its professional highlight was certainly to be the first performance of his gigantic Eighth Symphony, an event for many months in the planning. On the personal plane, and as yet unbeknownst to him, he was to have an equally momentous encounter with Sigmund Freud.

1909-1910
Documents

270

Berlin, May 15. - According to a local dispatch, there is good reason to believe that Gustav Mahler will accept a leading conductorial position at the Richard Wagner Theatre to be newly established in Berlin. Appropriate negotiations are under way.

———————————

The Richard Wagner Theatre is expected to open in 1914, and to be dedicated chiefly to the performance of Richard Wagner's works.[16] The Berlin rumours which connect Gustav Mahler with this undertaking are not particularly credible. Gustav Mahler is under contract to the

---

[16]As was seen already in the first two chapters, Mahler's name had been coming up in connection with Berlin ever since his pending departure from the Vienna Opera became public knowledge in 1907. However, it was in the spring and summer of 1909 that such considerations appeared to assume concrete form. Rumours in the press (of which **270** is merely an example), as well as the extant substantive documents (*e.g.*, **274**) indicate quite clearly that steps were being taken in certain quarters to win Mahler for the directorship of a new opera theatre in Berlin. This was, in all likelihood, the opera house which eventually opened on December 7, 1912 at Charlottenburg (today it is the Deutsche Oper in West Berlin). The initial plans for this theatre called for one of a more 'popular' character; nevertheless, it was in this house that the German première of *La Fanciulla del West* took place (in 1913), as did the first German performance of *Parsifal* outside Bayreuth (1914).

Regrettably (and somewhat surprisingly), we know nothing about Mahler's reactions and plans with respect to this invitation. (Earlier rumours, such as that in **154**, may or may not have concerned this new theatre planned for Berlin.)

Metropolitan Opera in New York for a further two years; then Mahler may work in Paris, for persons of authority in Paris are endeavoring to win the eminent conductor for a certain artistic position in Paris[17] following the end of his engagement in New York.

(*Neue Freie Presse*, May 16, 1909, Morning edition, p. 17)

271

On the advice of Fritz Kreisler I had applied for the post of concertmaster of the New York Philharmonic Society, and [. . .] received a friendly invitation to present myself as soon as possible. By chance I met Mahler in the street [. . .] and he immediately took me on a walk [. . .] and told me straight away of his plans for the reorganization of the New York orchestra. Then at five in the afternoon I arrived punctually at his flat; Arnold Rosé[18] [. . .] had also come, presumably to help him with my audition. [. . .] Mahler asked me, more or less as soon as I arrived, whether I was ready to play. This impatience—or rather this businesslike approach—was something I later often observed in him. [. . .] My audition was to the satisfaction of both sides, and I was immediately engaged and made to feel heartily welcome. [. . .]

(Theodore Spiering[19] in the *Vossische Zeitung*, May 21, 1911; quoted in *BRM(E)*, p. 259; original German in *BRM*, p. 264)

272

[Summer 1909]

Dear Herr Arnold,

As of now I still haven't had a report from you on where things stand with the filling of the flute and timpani positions. My *cables* appear not to be received; for otherwise I cannot understand that they regularly go unanswered. - As I leave Vienna next week, to move to my summer residence, I do not know whether or not I can engage Herr Van Leeuwen.[20]-The fact that the timpanist is not yet secured also makes me

---

[17]I have not been able to find any other indication of such plans.
[18]Arnold (Josef) Rosé (1863-1946) - Distinguished Austrian violinist; he married Mahler's sister Justine in 1902. From 1881 to 1938 he was concertmaster of the Vienna Philharmonic, and led his own quartet from 1882 on.
[19]Theodore Spiering (1871-1925) - American-born violinist, conductor and teacher. Prior to this engagement by Mahler, he had held positions in Chicago and Berlin.
[20]Arie van Leeuwen (1875-?) - Dutch flautist, at the Vienna Opera from 1903. He later moved to the United States.

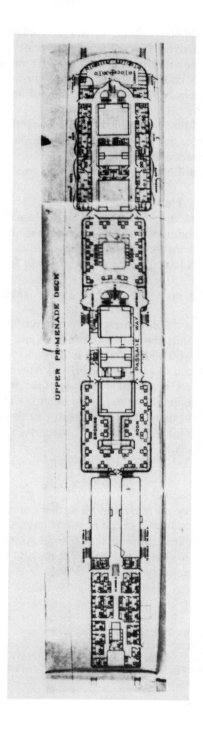

Plate 54. Plan of the Mahlers' shipboard "suite" for the crossing to New York in October, 1909. (ANYP, *The Bruno Walter Microfilm Collection*, vol. 21)

most uneasy. - My steamship tickets, which Herr Leifels promised to clear up, have also not yet arrived. Upon enquiring directly at the German Lloyd I learnt that there are reserved not a *suite* for me and one of those first class cabins for my child's governess - as is *expressly* stipulated in the contract, but rather the very same cabins to which I had already objected before I left New York.

You will understand that I find this also annoying. Be so kind and see to it that everything necessary is done in this matter and that the provisions of my contract are adhered to.

After unbelievably difficult negotiations with a number of candidates I have engaged

Herr *Theodore Spiering,*

a native-born American and a **member** of the *Chicago Union*, as concertmaster. The conditions you will see from the enclosed contract. Please be so kind as to ensure also that a first-class cabin is provided for Herr *Spiering* on the *Kaiser* Wilhelm II, which sails from Bremen on *12th* October.

This is the same ship on which I and my family leave from Cherbourg on the *13th.*

Since I have engaged a *Union member* for the post of concertmaster, and the Union had permitted me to import a foreigner for this *position*; and since furthermore you and I received permission to engage a foreigner for the flute and to get the timpanist in America wherever we could find one; then the **Union** will surely not object if I import the **flautist** and engage a timpanist from a town other than New York? Do please explain all this to them! And also the difficulties which we have already had with the timpanist in our April concerts.[21]

My summer address is

Toblach

Tyrol

Villa Altschluderbach.

Be so kind and address your reply and all further communications there.- I will send you the programmes in the next few days. -

A quite splended violinist, Herr Hammer,[22] an American and a Union member, has returned to America. Please engage him if possible. - Please be quite detailed in your reply.

---

[21]Presumably, the reference here is to the critics' complaints about what appears to have been the overpowering thunder of the kettledrums (see **257, 263**).

[22]Heinrich Albert Eduard Hammer (1862-1954) - German-American violinist, conductor and composer. He settled in the United States in 1908; he owned his own orchestra in Washington until 1921.

Greet Herr Leifels for me. He should excuse the fact that I do not respond to his letter separately. He will find everything in this letter to you. -

As to the guest-artists he had proposed: Herr Busoni[23]
Herr Wüllner[24]
Fräulein Tilly Koenen,[25]
I am in agreement. Only I must ask for a precise *indication* **of the dates**, and for programme proposals, so that I may arrange my own programme accordingly. Merely Mrs. *Powell*,[26] about whom he writes, do I not know! If she is truly *outstanding*, you may certainly engage her!

With hearty greetings, and the request that, together with Herr Leifels, you solve the problem of my crossing. Your most devoted

Gustav Mahler[27]

273

May 26, 1909

Dear Miss [Koenen]!

Would you please let me know the date for which I may set your first appearance? Further, I should be grateful if you could propose a programme. I am very much looking forward to working with you once again, and hope that the Americans wil be just as receptive to your grand artistry as are the Europeans.

Your most devoted
Gustav Mahler[28]

(Facsimile in *MC* 59, no. 1, July 7, 1909, and
in *MA* 10, no. 10, July17, 1909.)

---

[23]Ferruccio Benvenuto Busoni (1866-1924) - Celebrated Italian-German pianist; he was also highly regarded as a composer and theorist. Although he toured and taught widely, he resided chiefly in Berlin.
[24]Ludwig Wüllner (1858-1938) - Distinguished German actor and singer (baritone). He made extensive tours of America as a concert singer between 1908 and 1910.
[25]Tilly [Mathilde Caroline] Koenen (1873-1941) - Dutch mezzosoprano, best known for her concerts. She toured the United States in 1909-1910 and 1915-1916.
[26]Maud Powell (1868-1920) - American violinist, her concert career (from 1885 on) was limited mostly to the United States.
[27]For the German text, see Appendix, A23.
[28]This letter does not seem to be included in any modern publication of Mahler's letters, or mentioned anywhere in the literature. - Mahler's allusion to earlier collaboration with Koenen refers to concerts in Munich in 1906 and in Russia in 1907; the only previously known letter from Mahler to her, written in January, 1907, is published in Reeser, *op. cit.*, p. 80.
For the German text, see Appendix, A24.

274

May 30, 1909

Confidential!

Honoured Master!

You brother-in-law has kindly given me your present address, and I hasten to lay the following before you.

You have doubtless already learned from the newspapers of the proposal to establish a *second opera house* in Berlin [. . .] A building is to be erected as far as possible after the pattern of Bayreuth; negotiations have been initiated which will enable Wagner's works to be performed even before the expiry of the embargo. [. . .] The opening could take place in the spring of 1911.

We still, however, lack what is more important than all else: the *future Director* of our Richard Wagner Theatre, who must be not only a man of proved attainments and firm will, but above all a great artist; and, in short, combine all those qualities which are summed up in the name Mahler, a guarantee in itself of an artistic programme unsurpassable in its range and excellence. And as the bearer of this name is at the present time within reach, I venture, my dear Master, to ask whether you would be disposed to answer our call and to take this great work in hand. The position of general director would naturally in your case be furnished with which the most far-reaching powers - similar to those you had at your command in Vienna. I can therefore well believe that the task of giving life to a new and unique enterprise would perhaps have a charm for you.

[. . .] As soon as we hear that you are not in principle disinclined to consider the proposal, our managing director, Herr Delmar, will get in touch with you personally and in due course travel to Vienna, in order to arrange all business matters with you. [. . .]

Yours most sincerely,
E. Humperdinck[29]

(*AMM*, pp. 324f.; original German in *AME*, pp. 439f.)

275

GERMAN daily papers [. . .] say that negotiations are pending between Gustav Mahler and the owners of the projected Richard Wagner Theatre of Berlin for the engagement of Mahler as the chief conductor at that house. Furthermore, it is said that these negotiations appear now to reach

---

[29]Engelbert Humperdinck (1854-1921) - This prolific and celebrated German composer, critic and teacher was a champion and confidante of Wagner, and had assisted him in the preparation for publication of the score of *Parsifal*.

a successful conclusion. [. . .] Very few persons understanding the situation believe that Mahler looks upon America as a steady attraction. [. . .]

(*MC* 58, no. 23, June 2, 1909, p. 20)

276

[Summer 1909]

Dear Herr Leifels,

I have just arranged everything with Herr Schnellar (Court Musician, Vienna) concerning the timpani.[30]

He is immediately sending two pairs of his new timpani to the address of Mr. Arnold in New York. Be so good, when they have arrived, as to arrange the necessary for customs clearance and delivery and show them to the timpanist there (who by then will, I hope, already be on hand) so that he can get to know how to handle them. They cost: *2,700 crowns* (that is $540), and I beg you to be so kind as to arrange for this amount to be sent, on the arrival of the instruments, to Herr Hofmusiker Hans Schnellar

Vienna

I k.k. Hofoper.

As you know Mrs. Sheldon has kindly made the sum available. But the costs of the transportation and duties will be assumed, as is right and proper, by the Philharmonic?! Unfortunately, I still haven't received a reply to my last cablegram. - I can absolutely not understand this. I hope that I shall now get a detailed report on everything at my summer address: Toblach a.d. Südbahn

Tyrol.

I shall yet prepare and send you the programmes in the course of this month.

With heartiest greetings to you and
Herr Arnold
your devoted
Mahler[31]

---

[30]This is the Schnellar mentioned in **232** (s.a. Note 77, Chapter II). Apparently, he developed timpani that were particularly easy to tune and to operate (s.a. **283**).
[31]For the German text, see Appendix, A25.

277

Toblach, June 1909[32]

[Dear Alma],

[...] So I will begin the negotiations concerning Buenos Aires and will drag them out at least until your return, when we can discuss it all thoroughly in person. - Soon now Arnold will be arriving from New York; I am curious what he has to tell me. *The timpanist*, whom they seem to have acquired *from Pittsburgh*, is quite good. [...]

(Incomplete letter in *ELM*, p. [431])[33]

278

Toblach a.d. Südbahn, June 16, 1909

My dear [Mengelberg],

[...] I only wonder to myself how these gentlemen will go about being admitted over there; because there is a "*Union*" there which, through their rules, make it well nigh impossible to import musicians. [...][34]

(Original German in Reeser, *op. cit.*, p. 96)

---

[32]It is impossible to determine from *ELM* whether all or part of the dateline of a given letter had been part of the original, or was added to the typescript by Alma. Accordingly, datelines in *ELM*, given here as found, may convey only Alma's recollection of the place and date of the writing of a letter; editorial amendations are enclosed in square brackets.

As Mahler's seemingly inexhaustible store of nicknames for his wife is not susceptible to sensible translation, the stereotyped salutation used here serves merely as a label of convenience for present purposes.

For the German text, see Appendix, A26.

[33]For the reference to Buenos Aires, see **139** and Note 3, Chapter II. In another, presumably slightly earlier letter in *ELM* (p. [427]), Mahler describes the expectations stipulated in the new offer: "Fifty Wagner performances in three months; to be sure, no rehearsals in between up to the dress rehearsals."

For the reference to "the timpanist," see **272, 283, 287** and **294**.

[34]Although Mahler's reference to the "gentlemen" is an obscure one, the intrinsic interest of this letter lies in his mention of the "Union". As several other documents show (for example, see **272**), problems with the Musicians' Union in connection with the reorganization of the Philharmonic engaged Mahler almost to the point of obsession around this time, and on occasion also later (see **304** and **346**).

Sunday Mahler

1. 21. Nov
1. Beeth. Leonore III
2. Beeth. Eroica
3. Wagner a) Trist. u. Is. b) Meisters.

2. 12. Dez.
1. Weber Oberon
2. Schubert Unvoll.
3. Smetana Vltava
4. Strauss T. Eulenspiegel

3. 25. Dez (Christm.)
1. Beeth. IV
2. Strauss Tod u. Verkl.
3. Wagner Vorsp. Parsifal
4. Wagner Tannhäuser

Regular Series

I. Nov. 4 & 5 - 1909
1. Beeth. Ouv. Weihe d. Hauses
2 " Eroica
3. Liszt Mazeppa
4. R Strauss Till Eulenspiegel

II. Nov. 25-26-1909
1. Brahms 3. Symph.
2. Goldmark Sakuntala
3. Ducas L'Apprenti S.
4. Solo — Carreño

III. Dec-16-17-1909
1. Schubert - Unvollendete
2. Smetana Vltava
3. Mahler I. Symph.

IV. Jan 6 & 7-1910
1. Weber Euryanthe
2. Schumann IV. Symph.
3. R. Strauss Don Juan
4. Solo - Busoni

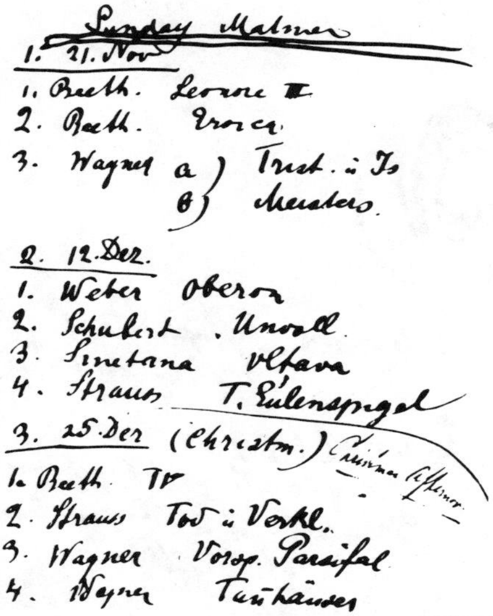

Plate 55. Mahler's program plans for the first three and four concerts of the "Sunday" and "Regular" series, respectively, of the 1909-1910 Philharmonic season. Judging from the annotations in a different hand, these are probably two of the pages Mahler sent to New York from Toblach (see **287**). (ANYP, *The Bruno Walter Microfilm Collection*, vol. 21)

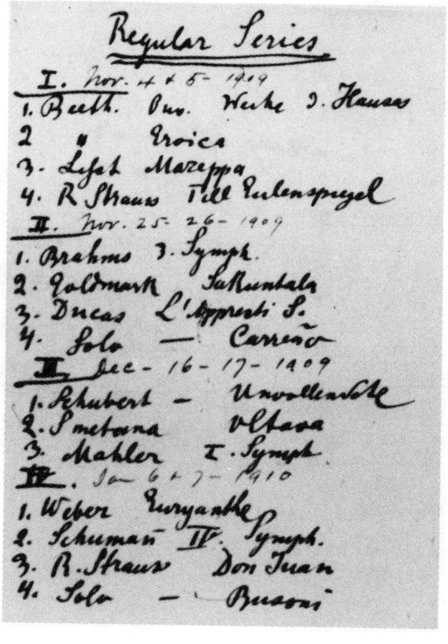

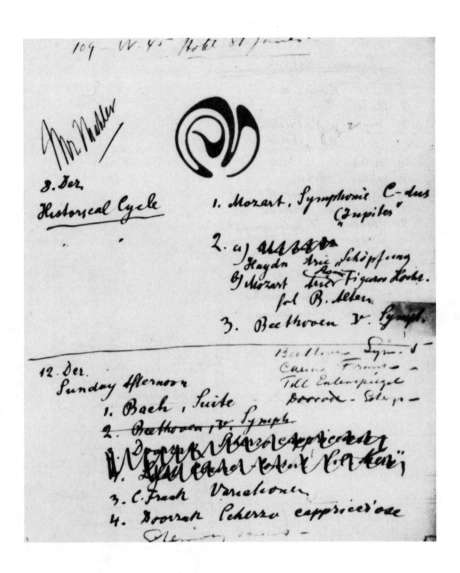

Plate 56. Despite the signs of haste and irresolution by Mahler, these two program plans are later (and all but final) versions of the programs seen in the preceding (December 12) and following (December 8) illustrations. (*loc. cit.*)

V. .... 21 - 1910
1. Mozart   g-moll Symph.
2. Schumann   Manfred
3. Berlioz   Phantastique

VI. ... ... - 1910
1. Beeth.   VII.
2. Solo   Koenen
3. Bizet   L'Arlesienne
4. Solo   Koenen
5. Chabrier   Espagne

VII. ... 17. 18. ...
1. Tschaikowski   "Romeo & Julia"
2. Weber   Oberon
3. Mahler   VII.

VIII.
1. Mendelssohn   A-moll Symph.
2. R. Strauss   Tod u. Verkl.
3. Beeth.   Leonore 3.
4. Solo   — Kreisler

I. Historical-Cycle
1. Händel   Concerto grosso 12 H-moll
2. Bach   Alte Jahrgang XXXI. 1.
(Orgelschwyle)   die großen Ausgabe Breitkopf u. Härtel
Auswahl aus   Ouverture H-moll
und   Ouverture D-dur
(1 zu Bearbeitung)
3. Solo — Ave Ryder — K
4. Rameau   Rigaudon
5. Solo   u. R.K.
6. Gluck   Iphigenie i. Aulis
und Schluß von Wagner

II.
1. Haydn   Symphonie D-moll
(Breitk. u. Härtel roter Band No. 2)
2. Mozart   Notturno - Serenade
3. Beeth.   V.

Plate 57. On the left side of this page Mahler continued his planning for the
"Regular" series, begun on the page forming part of Illustration 55. The two
"Historical" program plans on the right show his concern with the securing
of specific editions of the works by Bach and Haydn. (*loc. cit.*)

271

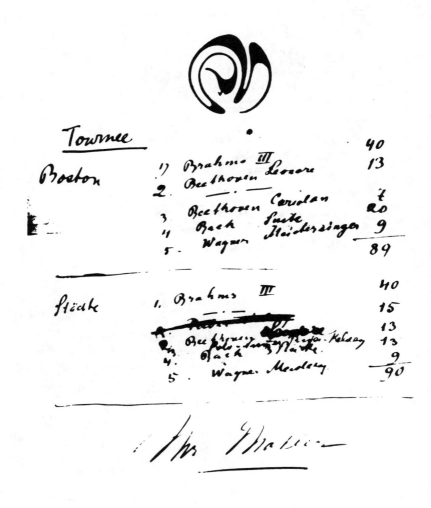

Plate 58. This is one of two extant program plans which shows Mahler's
timings for some works. The two plans—one for Boston, and a slightly
different one for the other "cities"—were intended for the inaugural tour
of the Philharmonic. (*loc. cit.*)

279

Toblach, [summer 1909]

My dear [Walter],

I have been put under extreme pressure, having to deliver 24 programmes for next season within a fortnight! Please *make something up* for me - and send it soon. [. . .][35]

(*MSL*, p. 331; original German in *GMB*, p. 363)

280

Toblach, June 17, 1909
[Dear Alma],

[. . .] I am working hard here, planning programmes - for, because of the rehearsals, it is really not so simple; so that, by the time Arnold arrives from New York, all will be in order. [. . .]

(*ELM*, p. [432])[36]

281

Toblach, June [18], 1909

[Dear Alma],

I have just been to the post office to get your letters - there comes Arnold in the other direction, straight from New York - quite friendly - so, I will certainly not get to writing any more today [. . .]

(*ELM*, p. [419])[37]

282

Toblach, June [19], 1909

[Dear Alma],

The unending dullness of the American couple has descended on this land. In the first moment, as I glimpsed the better half of my

---

[35]As **272** and **276** imply, Mahler must have procrastinated a great deal before he sat down to make up the Philharmonic programmes for the coming season. ANYP has some ten pieces of assorted paper on which he jotted down the initial outlines for the programmes in the various series to be given, as well as for the tours; these are, of course, undated (see Plates 55-58). It is clear that in the end Mahler felt forced to ask for Bruno Walter's help; whatever this may have amounted to may be incorporated in the sketches.
[36]For the German text, see Appendix, A27.
[37]For the German text, see Appendix, A28.

'management', it was clear to me that I am one of the most inhospitable of people, and relinquished to the [Hotel] Germania all the honour and pleasure that accommodating our 'distinguished foreigners' means. Freund[38] arrives tonight [. . .]

So, I am once again engulfed in orchestral affairs, thanks to the Arnolds. There is actually a great deal to do. - The Arnolds have most generously extended their stay at the Germania until Thursday. - Tomorrow (Sunday) I am having them to lunch. [. . .]

I have replied to Deckner's letter[39] to the effect that I am making the following demands:

18,000 dollars, stateroom, engaging of an assistant conductor who will share the conducting with me, engaging of van Rooy. - [. . .]

(ELM, p. [426])[40]

283

Vienna, June 18, 1909
13./2 Matznergasse 44.III.

Herr Director Gustav Mahler, Esq.

Toblach.

Honoured Sir!

It is my pleasure to bring to your kind attention the fact that one pair of timpani (such as you had seen in Munich) have been completed and—I am especially happy to say—have turned out extremely well. It went so quickly because all of the components were on hand. In contrast, the 2. pair (pedal-timp.) will take a long time because for this pair everything has first to be acquired; especially the here essential "Temper"-Gussteile will only be got in weeks and with difficulty from the factory (St. Pölten). It goes without saying that I will do everything to ensure that the instruments are in New York in good time. -

Transportation: To Hamburg, I definitely recommend express freight. Ship's cargo is reckoned on the basis of *volume*, on a fast steamer (7 days' crossing) $8 per cubic meter; on a freight steamer only $6, but it takes 12-14 days from Hamburg to New York. Entirely as you wish.

Duty: It is calculated on the basis of the value, ca. 20%; the shipment

---

[38]Emil Freund (1859-1928) - Freund had been Mahler's close friend since their school days in Iglau; later on he became Mahler's lawyer.

[39]Although I was unable to find any other trace of Deckner, in light of **277** it seems reasonable to assume—as *HLG3* does (p. 554)—that this concerns the negotiations with Buenos Aires.

[40]For the German text, see Appendix, A29.

must be accompanied by two identical invoices, certified by a local notary public and the American Consulate.

I would be happy to accommodate the generous lady donor of the timpani in this, and as a matter of form enter a lower price in the official invoice; yet, under certain circumstances there could be a slip-up or something similar, whereby I could in fact only demand the false price. I would also appreciate getting your instructions on this.

Spare skins are already on hand, packed in rolls. *When* and *where* should I bring (send) them?—

A humble request, by the granting of which you could relieve me of a great worry: I must pay out the accumulated expenses (wages, materials) weekly, as a rule. The already *completed* timpani (1200 Crowns) have nearly exhausted my (as of now not sufficient) working capital. Reluctant as I am to trouble you with such things, I ask you most kindly to let me have 600 Crowns on account; this is covered by the already completed and available timpani. -

The planned engagement really does not have to come to $3,000; at any rate, I do not consider this a condition; after all, the gentlemen may not wish to spend this on a timpanist (!), although I do not doubt their "ability" to do so for a moment. If the *Herr Director* wishes it, the above sum is as good as guaranteed. -[41]

Wishing most earnestly that the Herr Director enjoy an *excellent* summer for the sake of the upcoming great artistic endeavours, I await your kind reply and remain, your most devoted

Hans Schnellar.

(The above address is correct; this year I am not in Bayreuth.)[42]

284

Toblach, [June 20] 1909

[Dear Alma],

[. . .] Thus I saw [Emil Freund] only at lunch today in the most stimulating company of the Arnold couple; especially the wife is distinguished by a very piquant manner of expressing herself and by an accompanying sense of good humour, about which I had not the slightest idea, and is capable of immediate and decisive repartee [. . .] And so went today's lunch - doing appropriate honour to the occasion, [the cook]

---

[41]It seems clear from **277** that Schnellar's contemplated hiring by the New York Philharmonic was no longer a topical question by this time (s.a. **232** and Note 77, p. 216).
[42]For the German text, see Appendix, A30.

Agnes invented what was to her own mind an American, but in actual fact a Canadian menu. [...]

(Original German in *AME*, p. 433)

285

Toblach, June [21], 1909

[Dear Alma],

[...] In the meantime, I have gained deep insight into Mrs. *Arnold's* nature - it was yesterday while writing a postcard to friend Leifels. - Formerly I thought of her as wooden! But no! She is a wag. Her basic nature is playful. Yesterday, as I [thought of] her enthusiasm for nature— above all, she likes illustrated views— an idea suddenly came to me, curiously enough again in a chaise. Tomorrow (Tuesday instead of Thursday) they are going by carriage on the new Dolomite-road, to see all areas around here. - Wasn't that brilliant? [...]

(*ELM*, p. [454])[43]

286

Toblach, June 25, 1909

[Dear Alma],

[...] The Arnold couple are gone as of yesterday. - It was certainly high time. These people have got on my nerves - truly, I could *not* have stood it any longer. - Freund is staying until Saturday. [...]

(*ELM*, p. [436])[44]

287

[Toblach, June 25, 1909?][45]

My dear Herr Leifels!

I have mistakenly opened your letter to H[err] Arnold (who had departed for Leipzig yesterday), and have glimpsed its contents. -

I have sent off the programme to H[er]r Krehbiel's summer address. H[err] Arnold took a copy of it with him. - Please let me know whether

---

[43]For the German text, see Appendix, A31.
[44]For the German text, see Appendix, A32.
[45]As usual, this letter is undated. With its references to Arnold's departure, and to Mahler's completion of the programmes for the Philharmonic season, it seems reasonable to assign it to the same date as **286**.
    For the German text, see Appendix, A33.

H[er]r Krehbiel received my despatch, and please be good enough to comply with all his wishes in respect of the programmes. -[46]

H[err] Spiering's address reads:

Mr. Th. Spiering

Heppenheim

Germany   Bergstrasse

Despatches to him, though, should be *registered.*

I have as yet made no arrangement with H[err] Dippel; but have discussed it that when my time allows it, without it being to the detriment of the Philharmonic, I will conduct a few performances at the new theatre.[47] In that case, the Metropolitan Company would pay for my **return trip.** That is, the *journey there* must, in any case, be paid by the Philharmonic. Certainly, it is *too annoying* that H[er]r Schelling who, after all, had been most familiar with my contract, did not immediately take the state-cabin to which I am entitled. - Then we could have perhaps made a more advantageous arrangement. Please don't forget that, in addition to the state-cabin, I also need a first class cabin for our governess. -

If only we would encounter no difficulties with Herr *Friese*[48] at the last moment! Do you think that it is certain that they will release him in Pittsburgh? And if not - what happens then? - The flautist Scheers[49] is *mediocre*, as I am advised by H[er]r Mengelberg from Amsterdam! Also annoying!

With cordial greetings

your

Gustav Mahler

[46]Considering the general impression one gets of Mahler's relationship with Krehbiel during his American years as a whole, the second sentence of this paragraph is quite surprising. While it is understandable that Mahler should have wished (or should have been instructed) to send the programmes to the Philharmonic's official annotator (see **264**), the tone of this sentence suggests that, as the orchestra's new, 'permanent' conductor, he was anxious to ensure Krehbiel's goodwill. It is possible, then, that the final irreversible deterioration of the relations between the two set in only in December, and was brought about my Mahler's refusal to supply Krehbiel with a programmatic interpretation of his First Symphony (see **339, 341** and Note 89).

[47]See also **265, 290** and Note 51.

[48]Alfred Friese - He is undoubtedly the timpanist to whom Mahler referred in **277** (s.a. **272** and **294**). His name first appears in the list of orchestra members at the beginning of the 1909-1910 season. Following an unexplained absence of a year, his name reappears in the lists for 1911-1912.

[49]I was unable to trace Scheers. His name does not appear in the list of Philharmonic players between 1909 and 1912.

[Postscript, added above the salutation:]
For all I know, H[err] Spiering has already reserved a cabin on his own - in any case, I would be most grateful if you could take care of this matter.

288

[Postmark: July 3, 1909]

My dear Herr Spiering,

[. . .]

Please indicate which of the following concertos you would prefer.

1. Beethoven. 2. Mendelssohn. 3. Brahms. - Also what you would like besides (to start with). Only I must confess I regard it as essential for you to start with a true master, not a display piece in the style of Vieuxtemps, Bruch, etc.

Incidentally, I gather we are slightly restricted in our choice by the engagement of Herr Kreisler and of Maud Powell. I shall nevertheless seek to promote your interests in the matter, since I myself have no obligations to anyone. -

So I shall now draw up the programmes, letting you know the result. I too am glad to have you as a travelling-companion.

Please also be so good as to let me know—what I forgot to ask— whether you need an advance and whether I should see to having your passage paid from New York. - Please tell me frankly. We musicians are under no obligation to be capitalists - all we have to do is conduct well, play the fiddle well.

[. . .]

(*MSL*, pp. 338f.; original German in *GMB*, p. 364)

289

Toblach, July 11, 1909

[Dear Alma],

[. . .] Imagine, Leifels has already secured the ship's stateroom - but it costs *1800 dollars*! To Mrs. Sheldon, I have sent a nice letter and the complete programmes. She will really appreciate that. [. . .]

(*ELM*, pp. [448f.])[50]

---

[50]For the German text, see Appendix, A34.

290

Tschaikowsky's "Pique-Dame" and Auber's "Fra Diavolo"[51] are two of the operas Gustav Mahler is to conduct at the Metropolitan and the New Theatre next season. For each of the ten performances under his baton he will receive $500.

(*MA* 10, no. 14, August 14, 1909. p. 14)

291
[Postmark: Toblach, 15 August [?], 1909][52]

Dear Herr Spiering,
[. . .]
The first programme is:
Beethoven: *Weihe des Hauses*
— " — : *Eroica*
Liszt: *Mazeppa*
Strauss: *Till Eulenspiegel*
The second evening is for the first historical concert. - Do please play Bach's violin concerto. A piano part (continuo) would, however, have to be arranged for it, for I find one does really violate Bach's and Handel's works if one does not include a continuo.
Do you happen to know if such an arrangement exists?
[. . .]

(*MSL*, p. 342; original German in *GMB*, p. 367)

292

One of the new compositions to be played at the concerts of the New York Philharmonic Society in Carnegie Hall this season will be Gustav Mahler's seventh symphony. Publicly performed for the first time last

[51]Mahler only conducted Tchaikovsky's opera during this season (even that had been postponed, it appears, from the 1908-1090 season—see **143**). Nonetheless it seems quite possible that early plans may have included Auber's opera. It was, in fact, presented at the New Theater in January, 1910, and Mahler had conducted it in Vienna in 1899 and 1900 (Willnauer, *op. cit.*, p. 275). (S.a. **265** and **287**.)
[52]In her first edition of the letters (1924), Alma Mahler gave September as the month in the postmark. As Mahler wrote "I shall remain here until the end of August" later in the letter, her reading of the postmark must have been incorrect.

spring in Prague,[53] it comes to America now for its initial performance. One of the odd characteristics of the symphony is the instrumentation, which calls for the use of a mandolin and a guitar in addition to two harps. The first symphony of Mahler, written in 1891 [sic],[54] is also to be given.

(*NYTrib*, October 3, 1909, Part Four, p. 2)

293

Amsterdam, October 6, 1909[55]

My Almscherl!

[. . .] I have made up my mind not to start in New York with a performance of the Seventh, but the Fourth.[56] The Seventh is too complicated for a public which knows nothing of me.

In case the women give me no peace, they shall have their Tchaikovsky. (At least then they keep quiet.)

[. . .]

(*AMM*, p. 309; original German in *AME*, p. 414)

294

[Friese] best remembers rehearsals of Mahler's Seventh Symphony because of an altercation over the timpani solo starting the last movement.[57] He was asked to play it *piano* the first day the orchestra worked at the piece, and Mahler shouted at him to play it *forte* the next

---

[53]In fact, as was mentioned in the preceding chapter, the first performance of the Seventh Symphony took place on September 19, 1908.

[54]The First Symphony was, of course, performed for the first time already in 1889. As 1891 turns up regularly also in articles around the time of the New York performance in December, one must assume that this "information" came from Mahler himself! It is also interesting to note that no mention is ever made of the fact that the original version of the Symphony had five movements.

[55]Although Alma assigned this letter to the year 1908, its precise date of writing is easily determined from its contents.

[56]Although it is a matter of record that Mahler did not perform his Seventh Symphony in New York (the Fourth, incidentally, will have been performed only during the 1910-1911 season), **292** and the programme for Concert VII in Ill. 57 indicates that he had included it in his initial plans for his first season with the New York Philharmonic. Also—the change of mind signalled in **293** notwithstanding—**294** leaves little doubt that he must have at least rehearsed it with them at one time or another.

[57]The solo in question consists of an opening measure at *f*, and a second bar of four *sfp*'s.

280

day. "And if you'll decide tomorrow before the performance", Friese shouted back, "I'll do it whichever way you want it then too. The men got a good laugh at him over that, I tell you [. . .] and right away Mahler told me I was through. He called me back a few minutes later because he knew he had to have me play that part. And, you know, he was awfully nice to me after that." Friese still has the Philharmonic's timpani part at the studio where he teaches. "Sometimes I get it out and play it just as I did for Mahler".

(Joseph Roddy, "Mr. Mahler in Manhattan/Mr. Mahler - The Macabre Story of a Poet", *High Fidelity* 10, no. 7 (July 1960), pp. 33, 85)

295

Gustav Mahler sends word from abroad that he is anxious to try the new set of machine tuned tympani which Mrs. George R. Sheldon recently presented to the Philharmonic Society. With the set, which is ready for use during the coming season, it is expected that there will follow improved results from this department of the orchestra.

(*NYTrib*, October 10, 1909, Part Four, p. 2)

296

[Late Summer, 1909]

Dear [Mrs. Untermyer]![58]

I have received a letter (this time a fairly impolite one), demanding payment, for the third time already from the Viennese supplier of our new timpani (himself an orchestral musician quite without private means). He has still not received his money. I cannot imagine what sort of confusion lies behind this. I have appealed to Arnold innumerable times to settle the matter. Now I am turning to you, dear lady, our guardian angel, and ask for your kind intervention. - Both of us (my wife who, unfortunately, is in bed again with an attack of angina, and I) are very much looking forward already to seeing you again. My search for good musicians is

---

[58]As Mahler did not include a name in the salutation, the identity of the addressee is open to question. However, even though it was Mrs. Sheldon who gave the money needed for the timpani (see **276**), the content and tone of this letter allow for the reasonable assumption that it was addressed to Mrs. Untermeyer.

For the German text, see Appendix, A35.

progressing, and I hope soon to present you with favourable results. With best regards,

Your most devoted
Gustav Mahler

297

In the reorganization process which has taken place in the Philharmonic Society the chief changes are noticeable in the wind choirs. Gustav Mahler, the new conductor, is now on his way here from Bremen, whence he sailed October 12,[59] and he will soon be at work with his rehearsals. In the wood wind choir only two old members of the orchestra remain, all the newcomers being of the French or Belgian school. [...] Only three former players in the brass section [will remain]. [...] Theodor Spiering, who makes his first appearance as a concertmaster, has been for many years a first violin in a leading symphony orchestras of Europe.

(*NYTrib*, October 17, 1909, Part Four, p. 2)

298

The personnel of the orchestra has been entirely rejuvenated, and no expense spared to secure the best players. To what extent this policy has been carried may be inferred from the fact that the best horn player in America was enticed away from the Metropolitan.[60] It used to be the other way, the best Philharmonic players being enticed away by the offers of a bigger salary.[61]

[...]

The most important thing about the new Philharmonic, however, is that it has secured in Gustav Mahler one of the greatest living interpreters, a man whose every reading is of interest, and who will thrill as well as edify and educate the hearers.

---

[59]In fact, we know that the Mahlers met in Paris on the 8th, and boarded the ship at Cherbourg on the 13th.

[60]This was, in all likelihood, the horn-player Reiter mentioned in **408**. An X. Reiter appears as principal horn-player in the list of orchestra members at the beginning of the 1909-1910 season.

[61]This may well have signalled the reversal of the earlier trend which had caused serious problems for the symphony orchestras (see **150, 267** and Note 91, Chapter II). Following the financial losses of the 1908-1909 and 1909-1910 seasons, the management of the Metropolitan reduced their orchestral (as well as choral) forces (see Kolodin, *The Metropolitan Opera*, pp. 209, 221f.).

(Henry T. Finck[62] in the *Post*, November 6, 1909; quoted in
Frank Milburn, Jr., "Mahler's Four Last Winters, Spent in New York,
as Viewed Through the Eyes of the Press", *MA*, February 1960, p. 12)[63]

299

Among the passengers who arrived last night on the Kaiser Wilhelm II
were Gustav Mahler, the new leader of the Philharmonic Orchestra, and
Fritz Kreisler, the violinist. Mr. Mahler said that he was so engrossed in
his work with the Philharmonic that he could not say now whether he
would be able to conduct any operas at the Metropolitan. The
Metropolitan Opera Company in its announcement gave Mr. Mahler as
one of its conductors. Mr. Mahler brought with him a number of music
scores, among them a new symphony of his own. He was accompanied
by his wife and daughter.

(*NYTrib*, October 20, 1909, p. 7)

300

October found us in America once more. We could no more restrain our
tears now than the first time at the sight of the magnificent spectacle
which the arrival in the harbour of New York unfolds. No one who was
near and dear to us ever awaited us on the quay, and yet this scene,
unequalled of its kind in the whole world, moved us so deeply that our
knees shook as we walked down the gangway; and not even the highly

---

[62]Henry Theophilus Finck (1854-1926) - Educated at Harvard and in Europe,
Finck played the piano and the cello. He was the music critic of the *Post* from 1881
to 1924.

[63]As was mentioned already in the preceding chapter, the changes wrought by
Mahler in the makeup of the orchestra gave rise to a wide variety of claims and
counter-claims, both at the time and in historical accounts. *Musical America*, for
instance, commented at the time: "Mr. Mahler will be the first conductor of the
Philharmonic to have the final decision as to its make-up. [. . .] That he deemed a
sweeping change necessary is evident from the fact that of the 100 musicians [. . .]
about two-thirds are new men. To mention but one department, of the eleven players
in the wood wind division, nine are new" (October 30, 1909). On the other hand,
Howard Shanet writes: "Too much has been made, in general, of Mahler's hiring
new players for the orchestra. Most of the wind players were new, it is true, but the
strings were largely the same [. . .] at least twenty-six of the 'new' players in the
orchestra were the same New York musicians that the Philharmonic had hired in
1908-9 as extras [. . .]" (Shanet, *op. cit.*, p. 220). For a detailed discussion of this
question, see pp. 245, 248, 251.

unpleasant customs examination could dash the feeling of eager suspense.

(*AMM*, p. 154; original German in *AME*, p. 190)

301

Gustav Mahler [...] told a Tribune reporter yesterday [...] that he would try to give special concerts during the season at popular prices. [...]

"These concerts," said Mr. Mahler, "will be apart from those given in the regular season, but I hope to conduct them, as it is only right that all, no matter what their means, should have the chance of hearing the best music."

Mr. Mahler said that he intended to devote his time to his symphony work rather than to the opera, as he considered the symphony the basis on which the musical education of a people must stand.

"In my selection of programmes," said Mr. Mahler, "I shall play, besides selections of established merit, novelties that I may consider possess merit, and in my choice I shall be governed, to a large extent, by the wishes of the critics and the public."

(*NYTrib*, October 21, 1909, p. 7)

302

Tomorrow afternoon in Carnegie Hall Gustav Mahler will face the ninety-five men of his orchestra, the New York Philharmonic, for the first rehearsal of the season. [...] The conductor will put the musicians through a thorough test in all branches of their work before the afternoon is over. [...]

"There is much for us to do," said Conductor Mahler yesterday, "because we are all new to one another. We must become acquainted and learn that we are but part of one great instrument. We have before us a great work to do, and it can be done in only one way - the best. But, regardless of our individual abilities, the one and only way to secure finished results is by constant practice. That is why the Philharmonic Society was put on a permanent basis. Our rehearsals will be held regularly and often, and we shall endeavor to give the classic and best modern works in the manner expected of an orchestra of the first rank."

(*NYTrib*, October 24, 1909, Part Four, p. 2)

303

If Gustav Mahler follows out the policy he outlines to THE MUSICAL COURIER, then the Philharmonic Society will be an invaluable adjunct to the musical life of this city. [. . .] Speaking of the plans he has for the coming season Conductor Mahler said: "Although I have a well formed idea of the musical end I wish to reach I am not so particular about the methods of getting there that I am not open to suggestion. During the next few months I shall study the audiences of the Philharmonic with care. But I intend to let my public and the music critics of the press help me in picking out the musical way we should go. At the Opera the people cannot hear, and see, and think all at the same time. It is impossible. At the symphony concert it is different; the people have nothing to do but listen. It is the symphony concert which forms the basis of the musical development of the community and whatever standard that community reaches is the result of the education provided by symphonic music. I have already spoken, through the daily press, of the plan to give popular concerts for the masses. This plan, which will not be put in operation immediately, should make it possible for all workers and students who are not financially able to pay for seats at the regular concerts to hear the popular Sunday afternoon programs which will be conducted at prices barely enabling the Philharmonic Society to pay the expenses of these programs. But the general aim of our concerts of the coming season will be to educate and for that reason I have formed several series; four, to be exact. For the regular subscribers of previous years there will be the eclectic programs. The Beethoven cycle will be for the education of the lovers of classical music, for the education of my orchestra and for the students. The historical cycle, in which I shall try in six evenings to give an outline of the development of orchestral music from Bach to the modern composer, chronologically, also should have its interest." These be brave words, and Mahler is the sort of man to realize them when once spoken.

(*MC* 59, no. 17, October 27, 1909, p. 20)

304

"To raise popular musical standards and make the New York Philharmonic Orchestra the best in this country and the equal of any in the world is what I am striving for. If hard work can accomplish that ambition, accomplished it surely will be."

That is the epitomized plan of campaign outlined by Gustav Mahler, under whose baton the veteran orchestra began rehearsals on Monday for its sixty-eighth season [. . .].

"It will be my aim to educate the public," said Mr. Mahler, as he sat in his rooms in the Savoy Hotel, shortly after his arrival from Europe, "and that education will be made gradually and in a manner which will enable those who may not now have a taste for the best later to appreciate it. The basis of the season's programs will be classical music. [. . .] But we shall not forget to pay attention to the novelties. I am willing to play such of these as the public demands, provided the music is worthy, and even though I may not personally like the composition. But if the music is not worthy, then I shall not play it.

[. . .]

"The best orchestra in the world to-day," continued Mr. Mahler, "is, to my mind, that of Vienna. Munich, Dresden, Berlin and Paris have splendid organizations, but that of Vienna attained under Hans Richter a perfection that I know of nowhere else. My ambition is to make the Philharmonic performances as perfect and as inspiring as those of Vienna.

"There is really no reason why this cannot be done. The material is here. I wish that we could, in case of necessity, bring over some men from Europe, but that seems to be impossible, owing to the regulations of the musical union. Fortunately, there are good men in every department here, if we can only engage them. The great thing will be to weld the orchestra into an effective instrument. This can only be done by dint of constant practice in the best of the world's music, and that is what the reorganization will make possible."

[. . .]

Concerning his own new "Seventh" Symphony, which he conducted in Amsterdam shortly before his departure for this country, Mr. Mahler, with characteristic modesty, did not like to talk. He is fanatically conscientious in the performance of his manifold duties, of either a creative or interpretative nature, but superlatively prone to self-effacement the moment it becomes a question of reaping the rewards which his arduous labors have earned. Deficient in those mannerisms that are wont to be associated with genius, Herr Mahler at the same time does not fail to convey the impression of a philosopher and an idealist of lofty aspiration and stubborn determination to fight down obstacles in the way of all that is purest in art. With it all he is possessed of a personal charm and magnetism that none who encounters him, even casually, can escape.

[. . .]

(*MA* 10, no. 25, October 30, 1909, p. 31)

305

In New York the rehearsals began at once. Mahler threw himself into his work with enormous enthusiasm. There were most careful rehearsals every day. [. . .]

Our rehearsals were always interesting but not taxing. No particular duration was adhered to. They rarely exceeded the 3 1/2-hour limit set by the Union. Sometimes he was done in an hour and a half - or even an hour and a quarter.

Mahler always worked flat out. Every minute counted. There were no breaks. We almost never just played anything through. A constant struggle with recalcitrant matter until it was overcome.

(Spiering, *op. cit.; BRM(E)*, p. 261; original German in *BRM*, p. 267)

306

Kreisler's "Caprice Viennois" [smacks] of Strauss - but Richard, rather than Johann. [. . .] [This] is all the more remarkable inasmuch as Kreisler is heart and soul a Mahler man [. . .]. "I crossed the ocean with him," says Fritz, "and had occasion to spend hours and hours with him, going over his remarkable scores and hearing them explained by the composer. I can truthfully say that in certain effects of orchestration Mahler has no superior, nor does any writer of music exist who outdoes him in sincerity and in the desire to express only what is in him without the slightest conscious use of sensational or extraneous means. The whole world is bound to give him unreserved and enthusiastic recognition before long, and the signs of this attitude already are becoming visible in many cultured centers." Kreisler is a thinking musician and his opinions are not expressed lightly nor without undue deliberation. [. . .]

(*MC* 59, no. 18, November 3, 1909, p. 25)

307

The New York Philharmonic Society began its sixty-eighth season last evening with a concert in Carnegie Hall. The beginning of its new season is marked by radical changes in the ancient corporation, its methods and organization, if not its policy. Considering what a past the Philharmonic has, what it has accomplished and stood for, what it has been in the musical life of New York, and what a mark it has made in musical history, its new departure is a matter of much significance. [. . .]

The quality of the orchestra is probably not at present so good as it will be when Mr. Mahler has obtained what he wants and has secured a

Plate 59. Carnegie Hall. (U.S. History, Local History & Genealogy Division, The New York Public Library, Astor, Lenox and Tilden Foundations)

Plate 60. Interior of Carnegie Hall, 1891. (*Harper's Weekly* 35, May 9, 1891, p. 340)

greater homogeneity and blending of the different choirs and the several instruments of each choir. [...]

The general impression derived from the concert last evening even before the first number was finished, was that the orchestra was already something very different from what it has been for long years; in many respects better; in some respects perhaps a disappointment [...]. But there is every reason to expect that the orchestra will be, when its transformation is finished, an extremely fine one. [...]

Mr. Mahler's performance of the ninth symphony last season gave something of a forecast of his views as to playing Beethoven, and his performance of the Eroica amply confirmed it. He sought for a dramatic expression highly coloured, strongly emphasized, very free in tempo, into which he introduced many modifications; an exceedingly strenuous interpretation, in which there was much to arouse dissent, though there was also much that was fine, poetically expressive, noble, and authoritative.

But on the whole, the nobility and dignity, the Olympian poise, that are the fundamental qualities of the work, suffered from this kind of treatment. The bredth and sweep of the line are interrupted by the frequent insistence upon points of emphasis and of colour. [...]

There was a splendid rhythmical quality in Mr. Mahler's reading everywhere that was never lost, and there were many beautiful and expressive details in all four of the movements, especially in the last, the series of variations in which there is much opportunity for plastic modeling, of which he took the fullest advantage. There was perhaps too much insistence on the loudest things, on the strokes of the kettledrums, the blasts of trombones and trumpets.

This was the case with Strauss's "Till Eulenspiegel", which, of course, endures it much better, even if it does not require it. But the performance of this extraordinary work was an extraordinary one. Never has there been a more clear and brilliant setting forth of its complications, with such fluency and dexterity; it seemed more than ever impossible to believe that such cleverness could really exist.

(*NYT*, November 5, 1909, p. 9)

308

Bruno Labate, who was first oboist in the Philharmonic under Mahler,[64]

---

[64]Apparently, this is not entirely correct. Although Labate (1883?-1968) did play under Mahler, he became first oboist of the Philharmonic only in 1919.

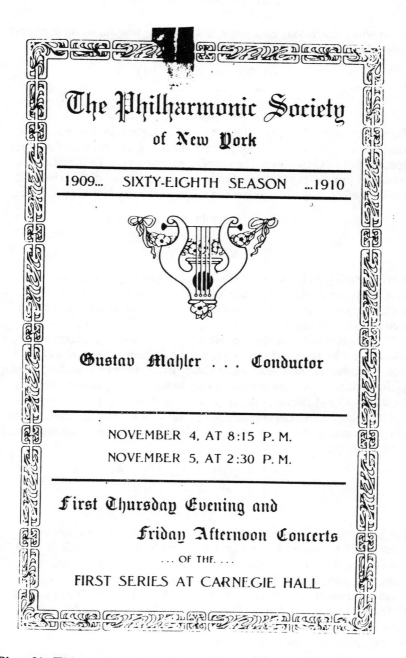

The Philharmonic Society

of New York

1909...   SIXTY-EIGHTH SEASON   ...1910

Gustav Mahler . . . Conductor

NOVEMBER 4, AT 8:15 P. M.

NOVEMBER 5, AT 2:30 P. M.

First Thursday Evening and

Friday Afternoon Concerts

. . . OF THE . . .

FIRST SERIES AT CARNEGIE HALL

Plate 61. Title page of the program booklet for Mahler's first concert as permanent conductor of the Philharmonic.

291

felt he was a marvelous conductor, but one who was eccentric in regard to dynamics, and firm in his interpretative convictions.

(Ardoin, *op. cit.*, p. 162)

309

There were many features of the concert last night which demand consideration, and they cannot all be disposed of in a review of the first meeting. [. . .] Geniuses in the art of conducting must be permitted to have their principles of interpretation and their canons of taste become familiar before they are condemned unduly or praised with enthusiasm.

(*NYTrib*, November 5, 1909, p. 7)

310

In commenting on the work of the orchestra last night one must remember that as Rome was not built in a day, neither is a first rate symphony orchestra made in one series of nine rehearsals, even under such a master as Mahler. [. . .]

The suave, homogeneous tone which marks orchestral personality can only come with time and rehearsal, but the present orchestral tone, though brilliant, is hard and rather sharp. But there was abundant power, spirit, good precision and plenty of that swing and enthusiasm which a conductor like Mahler can develop from the first. [. . .]

Altogether, there was encouraging promise of a brilliant future for the new orchestra, which, allowing for the fact of its newness, acquitted itself remarkably well.

(*NYW*, November 5, 1909, p. 6)

311

The ensemble playing, it is a pleasure to note, has emerged from the mists which surrounded it last season. It was not always distinguished last evening by perfect precision and there were passages in which unanimity was lacking, but on the whole there was an encouraging demonstration of the achievement of a good conductor in the matter of dynamics, attack and nuance. The orchestra has many gradations between a pianissimo and its uttermost forte and when it spoke in full power it did not cease to be musical.

There was a beautiful gain in clarity. The balance of tone not only among the three choirs but among the instruments of each one was far

292

better than it was last year. This too must be set down to the credit of Mr. Mahler. With so much that shows progress thus early in the season it is natural to expect still more advance before the winter is ended.

(*NYS*, November 5, 1909, p. 9)

312

With the first concert [. . .] Mahler was well satisfied. But when things did not go quite as well in the second concert he was deeply disappointed and cast down. Changes of mood of this kind recurred regularly as might be expected; I was almost always alone with him in the performers' room, and it was sometimes decidedly depressing for me.

(Spiering, *op. cit.*; *BRM(E)*, p. 261; original German in *BRM*, p. 267)

313

[New York, November-December, 1909]

Dear [Adler],

I received your letter this summer in the midst of the turmoil of my departure, which became particularly complicated this time because I gave up my Vienna residence.

[. . .]

Here real American turmoil prevails. I have daily rehearsals and concerts. Must conserve my strength a great deal, and after rehearsal generally go to bed, where I take my midday meal (here they call the abominable food "lunch"). - If I survive these two years without injury - then, I hope, I can also settle down to enjoying everything and perhaps also to creating "con amore".

(Reilly, *Gustav Mahler and Guido Adler*, pp. 108f.; original German in the author's *Gustav Mahler und Guido Adler*, Wien, Universal Edition, 1978, pp. 54f.)

314

It requires no apology for this paper to call attention to a journalistic victory that far exceeds any of the transitory victories achieved by daily papers in political campaigns or politics, for it is now a matter of a quarter of a century that this paper has directed attention to the colossal blunders of our orchestral situation in New York which have prevented us from enjoying classical concerts of a high character by our own local orchestral forces, until now, when, with the reconstitution of the

Philharmonic Society, we have finally found our own, as it is now fondly called [. . .].

The back files of this paper have been a constant request and demand that we should have an authoritative conductor for the Philharmonic, which is the nucleus of our orchestral work in New York, and that the Philharmonic could not consider itself capable of producing great works unless thoroughly rehearsed for each performance [. . .]. A man like Mr. Mahler is an artist who refused to identify himself with any concert unless the program has been definitely and properly put through rehearsals, as he knows that that is the secret of success in technical work and the interpretative work of the individual players brought together in order to make a unit of expression.

One of the great difficulties we have had to contend with in New York has been inflicted by a series of calamities that have placed at the head of some of our most important organizations two brothers who have been exceptionally successful in their commercial operations as conductors of musical work and of musical performances. They deserve, under the circumstances, the utmost consideration, from the very fact that they were compelled to commercialize their affairs in order to keep them alive; but from the point of view of THE MUSICAL COURIER, neither Walter Damrosch nor his brother, Frank Damrosch, has ever been justified, through his education or his standing in the musical world, to direct the destinies of this city from his podium or position. [. . .]

Chief [. . .] of all proof, cumulative in its effect, are the performances given under Mahler last week, for it was the first time that the Philharmonic in reality gave us a genuine orchestral concert that could compete with the concerts of the Boston Symphony Orchestra and other visiting orchestras such as the Philadelphia and those of the West. [. . .]

[. . .] What we have longed for and asked for, for years past, has been the establishment of an organization such as Mr. Mahler now has under his control and which he has succeeded in organizing, not withstanding Walter Damrosch's harangue this past spring against the ladies and the community who started out to bring about this revolution [. . .]. Unfortunately, we are still surrounded by a condition which will make Mr. Mahler's task a difficult one in the beginning, for he is faced by a situation which is altogether due to the indifference of the owners of the daily papers to the real conditions of art in New York City [. . .].

However, we are now on the road, musically, at least, to secure some advantages. We have the rival opera houses, a proposed introduction of the system of opera comique at the New Theatre, and this remarkable, unhoped for, but at last realized, Philharmonic organization under Mahler. Every musician of the City of New York, who means to dwell here for his own success as an artist, must support the Philharmonic concerts, not only for the sake of the artistic conscience as centered upon himself, but also for the benefit of the musical art in this city and its surroundings.

("Reflections," *MC* 59, no. 19, November 10, 1909, pp. 21f.)

315

At Carnegie Hall last night the first of a series of historical concerts [. . .] took place under the direction of Mr. Mahler. [. . .] There are to be six of these historical concerts, and their programmes have been planned to cover the field of music from the period of Bach down to today.[65] A large stride was made last night when the names of Bach, Handel, Rameau, Gretry and Haydn were on the scheme. [. . .] The first of the Bach pieces was a compages of movements from two of his suites. [. . .] Mr. Mahler took the Overture, Rondeau and Badinerie from the suite in B Minor and consorted with them the well known air and gavotte from the first of the two suites in D. To complete the old master's representation Mr. Theodore Spiering, the new concert master of the Philharmonic Orchestra, played the violin concerto in E major. [. . .]

Not only the music but also the manner of performance was in keeping with the period chosen for representation. Mr. Mahler conducted all the music except the [Haydn Symphony in D] seated at the clavier, which took the place of the harpsichord, and played the figured bass part [. . .] on it. [. . .] It was not a harpsichord but a Steinway pianoforte with hammer action modified to produce a twanging tone resembling that of the harpsichord but of greater volume. [. . .] The effect was not favourably received by the musicians in last night's audience, but was probably as near that heard in Bach's day as could be obtained, considering the vast difference in conditions. [. . .] Being occupied with the accompanment, Mr. Mahler had to do without the precision which he would have obtained had he given all his attention to directing the band. [. . .] Mr. Spiering created the impression of a refined, well equipped and sensitive musician, but an obvious nervousness robbed his

---

[65]It would be interesting to know more about the the genesis of these historical concerts. Was the series, for instance, Mahler's idea? Even if he could not often find a practical outlet for it, there is ample evidence throughout his life of an historical consciousness considerably greater than was general in his day. In all likelihood his life-long friendship with the pioneering musicologist Guido Adler played a significant role in this interest.

performance of the concerto of that supremely essential quality in all
art - repose.

(NYTrib, November 11, 1909, p. 7)

316

It was perhaps for the sake of contrast that Mr. Mahler did not give the
whole of any one of Bach's four suites for orchestra. [. . .] But sticklers
for accuracy might complain that in a historical concert the works should
be performed as they were made and not rearranged for the sake of
effect. [. . .]

Mr. Mahler's dissertation on the clavier was interesting because of its
remarkable vigour and he exhibited great dexterity in laying down and
picking up the baton.

(NYS, November 11, 1909, p. 9)

317

[. . .] In the original score [of the *Concerto for Violin*, No. 2 in E Major
by Johann Sebastian Bach] the accompaniment is written for strings and
a *continuo*—that is, a bass part with figures to indicate the harmonic
structure which was played upon the harpsichord by the leader. [. . .]
The manner in which the *continuo* was played is a lost art, and much
attention has been given by scholars to its restoration. One thing is very
obvious and that is that the harpsichord player provided something more
than a mere chordal support for the other instruments whose parts were
written out. [. . .] In the version of the present concerto played at a
concert of the Philharmonic Society on December 21, 1901, by Herr
Kreisler [. . .] the *continuo* was discreetly written out for organ by M.
Gevaert.[66] In the present case both harpsichord and organ are
employed.[67] [. . .]

(From Krehbiel's programme notes for
the November 10, 1909 concert, pp. 4f.)

---

[66]François Auguste Gevaert (1828-1908) - Eminent Belgian music historian and
teacher. He was one of the pioneers of systematic research in the history of earlier
music.

[67]It is stated on the inside title page of the programme booklet that "Mr. Mahler will
play the Bach Klavier in the compositions of Bach and Handel," and Arthur S.
Hyde is listed as organist. This statement also explains Mahler's reference to the
Bach concerto in his letter to Hammerschlag (see **320**).

318

In reading the so-called analytical pamphlets of the New York Philharmonic Society concerts one is struck by the advantage a writer has in the possession of a musical reference library. There is actually not one original idea or expression in those notes on the program; the material is all data taken from the usual works applying to the respective compositions. And the style of compilation is so labored, so overweighted with effort, so transparently appropriated, that it requires more than the usual patience to enter seriously into the perusal of the unnecessary document, a document that contrives to interfere with the rational consideration of the performances. It ought to be abolished.

(*MC* 59, no. 20, November 17, 1909, p. 20)

319

Mahler took four particularly lovely pieces from the Bach suites and strung them together for one of his concert programmes. He worked out the figured bass and played it marvellously on the harpsichord [sic], with his baton clipped tightly under his arm. [. . .] He played it at many of the concerts, more for us than for the audience.[68] He altered his continuo realization according to his fancy every time and crossexamined me afterwards about the effect of each. It was hardly likely that any change would be lost on me. The critics over there did not raise the cry of sacrilege. This was reserved for the pundits of Europe.

(*AMM*, pp. 154f.; original German in *AME*, pp. 190f.)

320

[Postmark: New York, November 19, 1909]

Dear [Hammerschlag],

[. . .] I am quite content with my position here. We have had many a concert that I would dearly have liked you to hear. I had great fun recently with a Bach concerto, for which I worked out the *basso*

---

[68]Mahler's arrangement was published by Schirmer in 1910, with the title and description: Johann Sebastian Bach, *Suite aus seinen Orchesterwerken* (Ouverture-Rondeau u. Badinerie-Air-Gavotte No. 1 u. 2) mit ausgeführtem Continuo zum Konzertvortrag bearbeitet von Gustav Mahler (1909).

Although she curiously mistakes the number of movements, Alma is correct about the frequency with which Mahler performed this work: of the wide variety and large number of works performed during the two seasons, only the *Meistersinger* overture was played as often as the Bach-arrangement.

continuo for organ, conducting and improvising—quite in the style of the old masters—from a very rich-toned spinet specially adopted by Steinway for the purpose. - This produced a number of surprises for me (and also for the audience). - It was as though a floodlight had been turned on to this long-buried literature. The result was intenser (also in terms of tone-colour) than any modern work. But I am dreadfully busy, worse than ever. [. . .]

(*MSL*, p. 345; original German in *GMB*, p. 371)

321

The Metropolitan Opera Company began its series of so-called "opera comique" at the New Theatre last evening, with a performance of Massenet's "Werther". There has been much interest manifested in this new scheme, and the beautiful house was quite filled with an appreciative audience. There was a long delay in beginning the performance [. . .] An apology that covered this and certain shortcomings in the lighting apparatus, other stage mechanicism and needed facilities was printed on the programme; it was also stated that it had been impossible to secure adequate stage rehearsals. For which reasons the opening performance was not presented in full accordance with the standards of the company. [. . .]

It was a fortunate idea to utilize the new house as a place for the production of works of this smaller genre for which the Metropolitan Opera House is entirely unsuited because of its size. There might be a quarrel to be picked with the name "opera comique", which in no accurate sense describes most of the works that are in view for performance there. It does not properly describe "Werther". But the fact is of more importance than the name. Those who consider these things have been very well aware for a quarter of a century of the unsuitableness of the Metropolitan for such works.[69] Mr. Hammerstein's Manhattan Opera House has given convincing proof to the eye and ear of how much more interesting and effective such operas are in a theatre of smaller, or at least different, dimensions, that will afford more intimate surroundings. The New Theatre is of a size that will increase the enjoyment of the works which it is proposed to present there.

[. . .]

This production was made by a new wing of the Metropolitan's forces,

---

[69]For an example of such views, see **202**.

on this occasion headed by Miss Geraldine Farrar. All the others were newcomers, including the conductor, Mr. Tango.[70]

[...]

It is a company from which excellent results ought to be forthcoming in the course of the season. [...]

(*NYT*, November 17, 1909, p. 9)

322

The Philharmonic Society began yesterday afternoon the Beethoven Cycle that is one of Mr. Mahler's cherished projects in connection with the enlargement of the Philharmonic's sphere of activity. The cycle is to consist of five concerts, in which will be performed all the nine symphonies except the first, and seven of the eleven overtures.[71] [...] In yesterday's concert [...] the second symphony was played together with the four overtures that Beethoven wrote at different times [...] for his opera now known as "Fidelio". [...]

The playing of the orchestra has improved. Its tone has gained in richness, smoothness, and beauty of quality, as well as in homogeneity. [...] There is still something for Mr. Mahler to do in perfecting the precision of ensemble of his band, for in this particular it is still far from an ideal state.

The second symphony was played with much life and vigour, and especially with an inspiring rhythmic vitality. Mr. Mahler read it sanely and soberly; a few of his insistent accents seemed a little disconcerting in the symphony.

(*NYT*, November 20, 1909, p. 7)

323

The making of the Philharmonic into an orchestral personality grows apace, for Mahler's training is evident in the improved playing of the orchestra, even since the first concert. [...]

Mahler evidently takes his Beethoven as the first great romantic composer, as his reading of the Second Symphony, which is often made

---

[70]Egisto Tango (1873-1951) - Eminent Italian opera conductor. His career spanned nearly 60 years, in such diverse places as Venice, Milan, Berlin, New York (1909-1910), Budapest, Vienna and Copenhagen.
[71]In the end, eight of the overtures were performed, while the Eighth Symphony was also omitted.

rather dry and Haydnesque, [had] poetic sentiment and romance, graceful charm and the joy and gayety which illuminates as with sunshine every bar of [the] work.

(*NYW*, November 20, 1909, p. 9)

324

The reading of the second symphony by Mr. Mahler was on the whole good, but sensitive worshippers of Beethoven may have wished that he had laid less stress on some of the accents. It reminded at least one hearer of some of Dr. von Bülow's[72] methodic demonstrations of the way in which Beethoven ought to be played.

The doubling of the wood winds produced good effects in some places and disturbing ones in others. But this has always been the case and it will probably continue to be a debatable question whether the doubling is to the glory of Beethoven or not.

(*NYS*, November 20, 1909, p. 5)

325

One day after Mahler had got his orchestra, a card arrived from Louis Tiffany[73] requesting permission to attend the rehearsals in concealment owing to his shyness. Shortly afterwards he invited us to his house and Mrs. Havemeyer,[74] the link between us, took us there. We stopped before a palatial building and ascended an imposing flight of steps; thence we proceeded upstairs. Sudanese native huts with all their furnishings were let into the walls all the way up on either side. At the top we entered a room so enormous it seemed to us immeasurable. Coloured lustres shed a soft, flowerlike light through the gloom. The prelude to *Parsifal* was being played on an organ. We were told later that the organist was a grandson of Shelley. [. . .]

Then a man with a remarkably fine head came up to us and murmured a few incomprehensible words. It was Tiffany, the man who spoke to no one; and before we could collect our wits, before Mahler, indeed, could

---

[72]Hans G. von Bülow (1830-1894) - One of the greatest pianists and conductors of his time, he was the foremost German exponent of the music of Liszt and Wagner. As a conductor he was revered by Mahler, who knew him briefly in Hamburg.
[73]Louis Comfort Tiffany (1848-1933) - American painter, designer, decorator, craftsman and philanthropist. He was a great and early force in the Art Nouveau movement. His luxurious estate on Long Island was much admired.

have had time to make any reply, he vanished. We heard afterwards that Tiffany was a hashish addict and never quite in his right senses. Like everything there, he made the impression of being enchanted. [. . .]

(*AMM*, p. 160; original German in *AME*, pp. 196f.)

326

The first of the series of Sunday concerts outlined by the Philharmonic Society as a part of their varied and extensive plans, which occurred at Carnegie Hall yesterday afternoon, raises to my thinking a question of serious import and moment. Do we, the New York music-loving public, want symphony concerts during the week and on Sundays too? Just as opera comique and light opera form a pleasant and needed relief from grand opera, so I believe that some music, lighter in type than that offered at yesterday's concert, would create an agreeable contrast as between symphony and Sunday concerts which the public would welcome with gratitude.

The programme yesterday was duly symphonic, even severely so; as besides the funeral march in the "Eroica" symphony, which opened the concert, we had the "Trauermarsch" from "Goetterdaemmerung", the prelude to "Die Meistersinger" being the only number in any way of a popular character.

M. Gilbert,[75] as soloist, tempered somewhat the classic severity of the proceedings by three vocal selections, the recitative and largo from Handel's "Xerxes", a spirited aria from Bizet's opera "La Jolie Fille de Perth" and the charming "Legend of the Sagebrush" from Massenet's "Le Jongleur", with all his usual finish, spirit and suavity of style [. . .]

In spite of some "yellow" notes from the horns, never as good as they should be, both [Wagner pieces] were well played with spirit and authority by the orchestra, the heavy brass in especial showing marked improvement in mellow sonority. This Philharmonic Orchestra certainly seems to improve with every hearing.

(*NYW*, November 22, 1909, p. 13)

---

[74]Mrs. Henry Osborne Havemeyer (née Louisine Waldron Elder) - widow of the wealthy industrialist.

[75]Charles Gilibert (1866-1910) - French concert and operatic baritone. He sang at the Metropolitan and Manhattan Opera Houses from 1900 to 1903 and from 1906 to 1910, respectively.

Plate 62. *Left,* Charles Gilibert. (*COS,* Illustration 94)

Plate 63. *Right,* Pasquale Amato. (*COS,* Illustration 165)

Two of the soloists who sang with the Philharmonic
in the 1909-1910 season.

327

Many patrons of the Philharmonic Society must have felt tempted to question the wisdom of Mr. Mahler's act, placing upon the programme of the second regular subscription concert the suite for orchestra by Bach with which he opened the society's historical series. But justification for the act came when last night the music was given with a brilliancy and beauty which were scarcely hinted at before. [. . .] The improvement was not confined to this performance, however. Nothing finer than the finale of Brahms's third symphony under Mr. Mahler's direction has been heard in our concert rooms for years. Mme. Carreño[76] kept the concert on [a] high plane [. . .] by a performance of Weber's "Concertstück" [. . .] The concluding number, a show piece for the band, was "L'Apprenti Sorcier", by Paul Dukas, which, though not new to our concert rooms, had a place for the first time on a Philharmonic programme. The enthusiasm of the audience grew with every number in the scheme.

(*NYTrib*, November 26, 1909, p. 7)

328

It may be stated without gratification that never in the history of this town has the Brahms F major symphony been performed by any local orchestra with due regard to its importance until last Thursday night (and the Friday afternoon following), when the reorganized Philharmonic Society, under Gustav Mahler, played it. Never had justice been done to it here until then, and all the preceding performances, previously lauded to the skies by our daily papers, with few exceptions, were characterized by the slovenly and careless methods that gradually fell to our lot in Philharmonic and New York Symphony concerts here. How could it be otherwise when, in the first place, we did not have the conductors competent for such works, and, in the next place, when we had no rehearsing?

[. . .]

The "Notes on the Program" were more interesting than usual because of their sublime absurdities. All that had sense was either quoted—one quotation from Apthorp,[77] the other from the late Sir Julius (meaning, in

---

[76](Maria) Teresa Carreño (1853-1917) - Although she was a musician of many talents, the Venezuelan-born Carreño became famous as a pianist. One of her pupils was Edward MacDowell.

[77]William Foster Apthorp (1848-1913) - American critic and prolific writer on music, very conservative in outlook. He also annotated the Boston Symphony's programme notes from 1892 to 1901.

plain terms, Julius Benedict)[78]—or taken from the handy musical reference books to be found everywhere. [. . .]

[. . .]

I ask, as a duty to musical propriety and progress, if the time has not come to put an end to these useless "notes," substituting for them, if they really are requisite for people of taste or culture, original notes by men of musical knowledge [. . .].

Besides, it is in the worst of bad taste to hire the services of a critic of a daily paper, whose duty it is to criticise in such a paper the very performances of the society. It has the color of a bribe. It appears, without using any casuistry at all, to prove it, like a purchase of good will. I do not know whether the Philharmonic pays for these useless "Notes," and that does not enter into the argument.[79] The society has started out with a dignified appeal to the musical world and it cannot afford to continue this old system of using, as its programatist, any critic on any paper criticising its performances.

("Reflections," *MC* 59, no. 22, December 1, 1909, pp. 21f.)

329

Mr. Toscanini last season showed that his biggest ambitions at the Metropolitan Opera House were directed toward conducting of the greatest and most exacting of Wagner's music-dramas, by claiming the performance of "Götterdämmerung". To this he has now added that of "Tristan und Isolde", and he conducted it yesterday afternoon for the first time in New York.[80] There was another very large audience, which revealed its own quality by the rapt attention paid to it. It was the kind of audience that refutes by its numbers, its understanding, and its silence the silly talk that occasionally is heard of the obsolescence of Wagner in New York.

The performance was one that might well rivet the attention of a gathering of intelligent and sympathetic listeners. Mr. Toscanini was, as he so often is in the performances he conducts, the dominating force; and this one differed from others of the same work chiefly in the respects in

---

[78]Julius Benedict (1804-1885) - German-born and educated (he was a pupil of Weber) conductor and composer (especially of operas).
[79]We do know, in fact, that Krehbiel was paid $25 per concert - not an inconsiderable sum in those days (see **264**). While Blumenberg disliked Krehbiel quite enough in general, his chief complaint stemmed from what he regarded as Krehbiel's 'conflict-of-interest' position as a critic on the one hand, and as annotator of the Philharmonic's programme notes on the other (s.a. **248**).
[80]See **144** and Note 1, Chapter II; also **189**.

which he made it. There was a spirit of indescribable exaltation and intense passion animating it throughout. His treatment of the orchestral score was remarkable for its wonderful euphony and richness of tone, the surge of emotion that swept through it, the unceasing elucidation of every dramatic detail, and the building up of overwhelming climaxes. [. . .]

But his reading of the score was a cruel one for the voices.

For Mr. Toscanini, as he has before made evident, the statue is very apt to stand in the orchestra and the pedestal on the stage. That, at least, is the ultimate result of his reading, and of the weight and emphasis that he throws on the orchestra. His climaxes were often, as we have said, overpowering; but it was sometimes difficult to tell by the ear alone whether or not there was a singer singing behind the orchestra. We have heard from Mr. Mahler how the orchestra in "Tristan" and others of Wagner's later music dramas can give eloquent utterance, can build up climaxes and can express the sum of all he attributes to it, and yet hide the tone and even the enunciation of no singer's voice. It is the logic and the necessity of the aesthetic theory of Wagner's music dramas that this must be the right proportion. There is evidence enough and to spare that this was what Wagner wished - and found that he seldom obtained. It is, indeed, much more difficult to obtain such a balance between orchestra and voices, and yet have the modelling and proportion of the orchestral part such as to express all its meaning, than it is to obtain from the orchestra all that it can give. But it is perhaps too much to expect that this way—of which Mr. Toscanini offered such a magnificent specimen— should not the more deeply impress the public.

[. . .]

(*NYT*, November 28, 1909, p. 11)

330

At last Brooklyn is really in New York. Last night the New York Philharmonic Orchestra, for the first time in its sixty-eight years [. . .] played in the Brooklyn Academy of Music.[81] [. . .]

Mahler is an intellectual conductor, as distinguished from the emotional sort. At the head of the latter stands Toscanini at the opera, who makes orchestra and chorus thrill with his own personal passion for the music he is leading. At the head of the other school once stood

---

[81]The names of both Richard Arnold and Felix F. Leifels appear on the front page of the concert programme, the former as "Administrative Manager," the latter as "Business Manager." After the Philharmonic's reorganization, this is one of the rare instances in which anyone other than Mahler is listed by name from among the functionaries of the Society (see also Notes 25 and 74, Chapter II).

Plate 64. Title page of the program booklet for the Philharmonic's
inaugural concert in Brooklyn.

306

Theodore Thomas,[82] the special and anointed prophet of Beethoven. So nearly as one man can represent another Mr. Mahler seems to be the heir to the Thomas ideals. He made a programme that would have filled Thomas with joy. It began with Beethoven's Fifth Symphony, included the "Leonore" No. 3 overture, Mendelssohn's concerto, with Maud Powell to play, and closed with the "Meistersinger" overture. [...]

The wonder was not that flaws could be found here and there with the work of an orchestra which has been under one conductor for only two months, but that such a high degree of precision and unanimity with such delicacy of balance could have been attained in that time. [...]

So far the concert had been like walking in a gallery of classic sculpture. There had been beauty at every turn, but perhaps the beauty had been a little cold, and to those with the dramatic temperament there had begun to be a little sense of monotony amid the perfection of line. With the "Meistersinger" music the walls were thrown open and the sunshine streamed in in life-giving floods. Sunshine, warmth, life and joy came with the overture. It brought a classic evening to a happy and human close.

(*The Brooklyn Daily Eagle*, December 4, 1909, p. 5)

331

[New York, Winter 1909-1910?]

My dear Karl,

[...]

On the whole, we are quite well. - Don't worry about my diet. I am blooming, my weight is normal, and I am handling the hard work splendidly. This year, things are **much** better also with Almschl. In the last few days (for the first time this year), she again has that certain weakened condition. But nowhere near as severely as last year. The little one has a cold right now but is, on the whole, also in good shape. My success as a conductor is as one would wish. (In fact, perhaps beyond

---

[82] Theodore Thomas (1835-1905) - German-born American conductor. As the leader of orchestras in New York and Chicago, he championed the music of Liszt, Wagner and Brahms in the United States.

that - for the more successful I am, the more difficult it is to get away
from here.) [. . .][83]

332

The second of the Philharmonic Society's series of historical concerts
took place at Carnegie Hall last night. The programme began with
Mozart's C major symphony and ended with Beethoven's in C minor.
Between these two works stood two vocal numbers [. . .] from Haydn's
oratorio "The Creation", and [. . .] from Mozart's opera "Le Nozze di
Figaro". The singer was Bella Alten,[84] soprano, of the Metropolitan
Opera House company.

[. . .]

It must be confessed that [Haydn] is not best studied in his vocal
music, in spite of the record of the high estimate placed on "The
Creation" in its day. There were more skilful and effective composers for
the voice—notably Mozart himself—and the great oratorio of Haydn has
historical importance rather by reason of the innovations in its
instrumental treatment than in its vocal writing.

[. . .]

Mozart's C major symphony, called the "Jupiter" in its own day, still
has its charm, though since the birth of Beethoven's works it does not
awe us with the Jovelike front which it presented over a century
ago. [. . .]

The playing of the orchestra last night showed progress in balance of
tone, in transparency and in smoothness. There were some moments
when precision was not perfect, but on the whole the concert deserves
praise.

(*NYS*, December 9, 1909, p. 9)

---

[83]Even an approximate dating of this letter is little more than an educated guess. It is
written on the same unique, decorative letterhead as the letter from April, 1910 to
Leifels (see **427**). Mahler's remark as to his "success as a conductor" may be a
reference to his first season at the head of the Philharmonic.

The rest of the letter (3 handwritten pages) is meaningless without Moll's letter to
which this is a reply, and is therefore not reproduced here.

For the German text, see Appendix, A36.

[84]Bella Alten (1877-1962) - Polish-born soprano, she sang at Leipzig, Braunschweig,
Cologne and Berlin, before making her debut at the Metropolitan in 1905, where she
sang until 1913.

333

The Philharmonic Society gave its second historical concert at Carnegie Hall on the evening of December 8. [. . .]

Mr. Mahler gave a very happy reading of [Mozart's] "Jupiter" [Symphony]. [. . .]

Miss Alten added to the pleasure and interest of the evening. [. . .]

But what shall be said of Mr. Mahler's Fifth Symphony? The concert was called a historical concert. If there was anything historical about any point of Mr. Mahler's interpretation it would have required a microscope to discover it. Liberties of tempo and accent are sometimes commendable in the interests of a modern, vital interpretation of the classics, and are justifiable when they do not thwart the very obvious message of the composer. Mr. Mahler's liberty with the Beethoven seemed to approach the domain of sheer license or even whimsicality, and at times to take him far from the spirit of Beethoven's intent. Mahler is a big man in the matter of outlines. He seems to have a clear perspective upon the great formal features of the works which he interprets, and this often lends a sense of mightiness to his reading even when one does not approve of his treatment of details.

[. . .]

All in all, this seems to have been the most disconcerting and extraordinary reading of Beethoven's Fifth Symphony ever heard in New York; and yet, withal, there were moments of extraordinary dramatic impressiveness. In fact, repose and mystery, two of Beethoven's greatest qualities, appeared to have been sacrificed on the altar of dramatic effect. The reading of this symphony was educational, perhaps, in many ways. Historical it certainly was not.

(Arthur Farwell[85] in *MA* 11, no. 6, December 18, 1909, p. 17)

334

The question as to whether a musical manager shall abide silently and without protest by the judgments passed by the newspaper musical critics, when he believes they have purposely and without reasonable cause "roasted" his artists, has been decided, so far as Robert E. Johnston is concerned, by the cutting from his press list of the name of Henry E. Krehbiel, of the New York TRIBUNE. Mr. Johnston has taken this step as the result of an article written by Mr. Krehbiel in the

---

[85]Arthur Farwell (1872-1952) - American composer and music educator. He was on the editorial staff of *MA* only in 1909, and spent his life teaching, and championing American music.

TRIBUNE on the debut of Pepito Arriola, the Spanish piano prodigy.
"After hearing only the first number of Pepito's program, the Beethoven Sonata op. 53, Mr. Krehbiel left the hall. His criticism of the entire performance was based purely upon the impression he gained from this one number [. . .]"

(*MA* 11, no. 5, December 11, 1909, p. 1)

335

The Philharmonic Society gave its second Sunday concert yesterday afternoon to a large audience with a programme that contained a repetition of Beethoven's Fifth Symphony and Strauss's "Till Eulenspiegel", which had recently been performed by the society, and included also Dvorak's "Scherzo Capriccioso" for orchestra and Liszt's A major concerto for piano, played by Yolanda Merö.[86] [. . .]

It was rather alarming to hear in Strauss's extravagant but enormously clever "Till Eulenspiegel", and, to a somewhat less degree, in Dvorak's Scherzo, the fearful beating of the kettledrums that was allowed by Mr. Mahler to go on unchecked and unrebuked. The orchestra is making continuous progress in its quality and homogeneity of tone, its precision of ensemble, its pliability under the conductor's hands, but the musical beauty of its performances is shivered and shattered by the violence of this and some other noise-making instruments of the orchestra, which Mr. Mahler will have to moderate, if he gauges correctly the force of sound that reaches the ears of his listeners.

[. . .]

Miss Merö played Liszt's concerto with great dash and verve.

(*NYT*, December 13, 1909, p. 9)

336

In this week's edition of MUSICAL AMERICA there appears, as an art supplement, the picture of Gustav Mahler.[87] Mr. Mahler can scarcely be said to require any extended introduction, as his work during the past two years at the Metropolitan Opera House, and during the present season as conductor of the reorganized Philharmonic, has thoroughly endeared him to all music lovers in this city.

---

[86]Yolanda Merö (1887-1963) - Hungarian-born American pianist.
[87]The photograph—taken as most of Mahler's American portraits, in the studio of Aimé Dupont—is inscribed by him: "Greetings to Musical America/Gustav Mahler" (see Frontispiece).

[...]

Mr. Mahler is a stern disciplinarian at rehearsals, but in private the charm and magnetism of his personality are most engaging. Excessive modesty is one of his chief characteristics, and he is strongly averse to ostentatious praise. Regarding the success of his own compositions he is generally silent, and on the conductor's stand he will never condescend to bow to any applause that has not the ring of genuine enthusiasm and sponteneity in it. At home he is the personification of courtesy, and seeks as much as possible to dispel the foolish idea that he is taciturn and disdainfully superior to less gifted mortals. Five minutes with Mr. Mahler serve forever to dispose of so palpable an error.

(*MA* 11, no. 6, December 18, 1909, p. 4)

337

Mahler, at the request of the ladies of the committee, gave a performance of his First Symphony. After thorough rehearsal he arrived with his mind at peace. He had a rude awakening. To do him honour these ladies had wreathed and also heightened the podium, distributed the strings in an outer circle around and beneath him, and massed the brass in a tight circle at his feet. He came on to the platform suspecting nothing and was so taken aback that he could only stand and gasp. The performance was a veritable martyrdom for him, and for me too. The brass was deafening and drowned all else. We were amazed at the audience who sat it out quietly and even applauded dutifully at the end, the credit for which must be divided between Mahler's prestige and their own insensibility to music.[88]

(*AMM*, p. 166; original German in *AME*, pp. 203f.)

338

Yesterday [evening] in Carnegie Hall [...] Mr. Mahler's [first symphony in D major was heard for the first time in this country, and it was the fourth of his symphonies to be heard here. [...] This one found, probably, less favour from its listeners than did the other three. [...]

Mr. Mahler is said to have declared that no one could understand the symphony who was not familiar with one period of his own life. It

---

[88]As there is not a single mention of this incident in the innumerable reviews of either of the two concerts at which the First Symphony was performed, there can be little doubt but that it is an outright fabrication by Alma.

obviously has a "programme" of some kind as a basis, and without a suggestion of what it is the music is not of itself wholly intelligible. There are matters in it that, as "absolute" music, have no evident significance, and that serve merely to puzzle and perplex.[89] [. . .]

To those who listen to this [work] as absolute music it seems less distinguished, less individual than the later music of Mr. Mahler's that is known here. The musical material has a less pregnant quality, less beauty and expressiveness. There is a dangerous verging more than once upon the commonplace. [. . .] The instrumentation is one of the least satisfactory elements of the work, and has not the skill and resource of the master that are in evidence in Mr. Mahler's later works. Much of it is without refinement and richness of colour. [. . .]

[In] the performance of Schubert's ["Unfinished" Symphony], was it wise for Mr. Mahler to double the wood-wind players in certain passages [. . .]? There is gain of sonority, but there is also change of quality, loss of some of the transparency that is so fascinating in Schubert's instrumentation.

(NYT, December 17, 1909, p. 11)

339

In deference to the wish of Mr. Mahler, the annotator of the Philharmonic Society's programmes refrains from even an outline analysis of the symphony which is performing for the first time in New York on this occasion, as also from an attempt to suggest what might be or has been set forth as its possible poetical, dramatic, or emotional contents. It is due to the composer, however, to say that when applied to for the score he placed it at the writer's disposition without hesitation or reservation. Mr. Mahler's conviction, frequently expressed publicly as well as privately, is that it is a hindrance to appreciation to read an analysis which with the help of musical examples lays bare the contents and structure of a composition while it is playing. All interest and attention should be concentrated on the music itself. "At a concert", he says, "one should listen, not look - use the ears, not the eyes". As to the exposition of the probable, possible, or likely poetic contents of the music

---

[89]Such a reaction, evident in virtually every review, is strongly reminiscent of the critical reaction on the occasion of the Symphony's first performance in Budapest two decades earlier. But whereas at that time Mahler was still insecure enough to fashion a programme after the fact (even though he withdrew it later), in 1909 he was confident enought to actually forbid Krehbiel to speculate "officially" on the "contents" of the work (see **399, 341**).

(the "programme" as it is called), the book, poem, picture, incident, or what not which prompted the work and influenced the composer in its construction, or the train of thought or emotion which may be called up by it in the minds of the hearers - all this, he thinks, should be left wholly to the imagination of each individual. All writings about music, even those of musicians themselves, he holds to be injurious to musical enjoyment. [. . .]

(From Krehbiel's programme notes for
the December 16-17, 1909 concerts, pp. 5f.)

340

Just wherein [Mahler's First Symphony] is entitled to claim a seat in the august assemblage of symphonies does not appear in the first, second or third movements. [. . .]

The fourth movement [. . .] is more perplexing than its forerunners. One feels that there are going to be difficulties when he sees the several drummers and the cymbal player girding themselves for the struggle. Nor is the expectant hearer disappointed. The movement is complex in its structure, and it seems to mean much that might have been happily explained had not the composer laid the ban of silence on the programme annotator. [. . .] At one place in the movement Mr. Mahler sang a cantabile theme of such rare beauty and emotional potency that it led the hearer to wonder that he did not bend his talents oftener in the direction of such art. [. . .] The conclusion of the movement reverts to the manner of its beginning [. . .] and suggests that when the weather is bad in Tyrol it is beyond the power of language to characterize.

(*NYS*, December 17, 1909, p. 9)

341

If Mr. Gustav Mahler were not the conductor of the Philharmonic Society, and if his programmes and performances were not significant of a tendency which has been foreign to concerts of that organization during the two generations in which it has cultivated high class music, the production of his symphony [No. 1] [. . .] could be disposed of with very few words indeed. But Mr. Mahler has been a considerable figure in the world of music for fifteen years or more; he has shown great seriousness of striving as a composer by devoting his attention almost exclusively to the large forms, and he has become a potent influence in the musical life of this city. His symphony cannot, therefore, be as summarily dismissed as we are inclined to think that it ought to be. [. . .]

313

Mr. Mahler is a composer of programme music, and his Symphony in D is of that class. The fact does not save it from criticism, but if it were not so the condemnation which would have to be meted out would be swift, summary and for the sake of the art, vigorous. There is abundant evidence in Mr. Mahler's compositions that in constructing them he follows extra-musical suggestions.

[. . .] New York's music lovers have heard enough of Mr. Mahler's symphonies to know their quality, both as programmatic and absolute music. The impression made on the writer at the first performance, and confirmed at the subsequent performances, was that Mr. Mahler is by instinct a naive though unoriginal melodist, who, had he not been drawn into the latter-day swirl by a desire to exploit new colours, new harmonies and new notions about form, would have become a true symphonist. There is no reason why he should be a prophet of the ugly, as he discloses himself in the last movement of the Symphony in D.

[. . .] The symphony has no justification without a programme. [. . .] More than the public the composer would have benefited had he told what train of thought, or sequence of emotions, he conceived to be at the basis of his symphony. It was not dignified by being left to make its appeal unaided; it would have not been degraded had an extra-musical purpose been ascribed to it. [. . .] Mr. Mahler's refusal to take advantage of his opportunity presents him in the light of a composer convinced that his music carries its own message; it compelled a multitude of his hearers to wonder what he bases his conviction upon.

(*NYTrib*, December 18, 1909, p. 7)

342

At the third set of concerts of its regular or major series [. . .] the Philharmonic Society played [. . .] Mahler's first symphony [. . .]. [Krehbiel's] notice of the Mahler symphony [. . .] was extremely unfavorable, and several knowing persons told the present writer that they considered the diatribes to represent the Tribune critic's petty manner of revenging himself for having been prohibited by Mr. Mahler from airing "notes" on the subject of the symphony. This seems hardly credible, however.

[. . .]

Considered as absolute music, the Mahler symphony offers a wide variety of interest, being filled with much picturesque detail in melody, harmony, and orchestration, all having cohesion and musical purpose, and revealing a strongly marked sense of form in technical construction. [. . .] Always it is excellent symphonic writing, based on the best models and executed with the sure mastery of a man whose vivid imagination is seconded ably by a technical ability of unfailing effectiveness.

[...] As a fledgling composer's first work in that form, this initial opus by Mahler is a truly remarkable achievement, foreshadowing accurately the bigger things since achieved by him. [...]

(*MC* 59, no. 25, December 22, 1909, p. 52)

343

The production of a new modern symphonic work, especially when the composer is a familiar and admired personality, is always a matter of musical moment and interest, but had Mr. Mahler made his debut here as a symphonist with his First Symphony, he could hardly be accorded the rank as a composer of this class of work which his Second Symphony undoubtedly gained for him. [...]

Strictly speaking, the work is not a symphony at all, but rather a characteristic orchestral suite, for while the ever insistent interval of the fourth dominates the work to a certain extent structurally, the four movements have no definite relation one to the other, and might be played independently, especially the two middle movements, without loss of effect.

(*NYW*, December 19, 1909, Metropolitan Section, p. M5)

344

Doubtless but few of those who betook themselves to Carnegie Hall on Thursday evening of last week for the purpose of attending the third regular concert of the Philharmonic were in any way prepared for the agreeable surprise that awaited them.

[...] the *pièce de résistance* of the occasion was [...] the early [work] of the Philharmonic's esteemed conductor. And as some persons may have harbored more or less unpleasant recollections of the Brobdingnagian dimensions of another work of the same composer presented last year, there may possibly have been less joy in the anticipation of this particular event than was enthusiastically manifested at its conclusion. The plain truth of the matter is that whereas Mr. Mahler's second symphony is, and will probably remain for a considerable time, caviare to the general public, his first is for the greater part endowed with such qualities as are destined to captivate its hearers, one and all.

Why this work should for almost twenty-three years have remained perfectly strange to this city is a mystery. [...]

Mr. Mahler has tacitly expressed himself as willing, and more than willing, to permit critics and industrious commentators to cudgel their brains for an appropriate "program," by declining to give forth analyses and explanations, and by declaring that the poetical contents of the work should be left wholly to individual imagination. [. . .] However, the essentially self interpreting, subjectively emotional nature of this symphony should tend to obviate excess of arduous labor in this direction. [. . .]

It is a symphony of youthful ardor and exuberance, an overflowing manifestation of the sheer joy of living. There is storm and stress in the close, to be sure, but it is physical conflict devoid of any trace of morbidness.

[. . .]

The difficulties in performance of this music are tremendous, but the Philharmonic players overcame all of them with flying colors. Mr. Mahler seemed heart and soul in the rendering of his music, and the result was a presentation of it that few organizations could have equalled and none surpassed. [. . .]

(Herbert F. Peyser[90] in *MA* 11, no. 7, December 25, 1909, p. 4)

345

Our box at the opera was the resort of many friends and acquaintances: Kneisel, leader of the best quartet in New York, Hassmann,[91] the loafing Viennese painter, Fränkel,[92] the beautiful Crosby, the Schellings—he an extremely gifted composer, she a charming woman—Prince Troubetzkoy,[93] brother of the sculptor, a wild, handsome Russian, whom one feared to meet in the streets of New York accompanied by his two

---

[90]Herbert Francis Peyser (1886-1953) - American music critic; studied in Germany, France and the United States. He was on the staff of *MA* from 1909 to 1920.
[91]Carl Hassmann (1869-1933) - Austrian historical painter, member of the Wiener Künstlerhaus from 1909.
[92]Joseph Fränkel (1867-1920) - Austrian-born physician. He befriended the Mahlers in New York, where he was practicing at the time, and attended Mahler through his last illness there.
[93]This was, in all likelihood, Prince Paul Troubetzkoy (1866-1938), brother of the sculptor Wladimir, and himself a sculptor. Paul was well known for his flamboyant lifestyle, as well as for his animal sculptures and his busts of society women.

wolves, Schindler,[94] a really gifted musician, always eager to manage us, and many others [. . .]

There was Poultney Bigelow,[95] too, an aristocratic Englishman, who had been brought up with Kaiser Wilhelm the Second. He was living in New York in princely style and introduced us to all the literary people there. We could not make much of this opportunity owing to the unsurmountable barrier of language; and even when we got to speaking English of a sort it did not help us to join in serious conversation [. . .]

We also knew Natalie Curtis[96] [. . .]

All these people were friends of ours. We were more at home than in Vienna. They loved Mahler over there and—with the exception of a malignant critic named Krehbiel—he was not harried by hostile criticism as in Vienna, where up to the very last he was always being rapped on the knuckles.

The work he was called upon to do was child's play compared with his official duties in Vienna. There were rehearsals only every other morning. I often picked him up afterwards and we walked home. He performed a great deal of music merely to hear it himself and to get to know it, without bothering whether it went down with the public or not. He conducted the overture to the *Flying Dutchman* and the Paris version of the *Tannhäuser* overture six times in succession, merely because he had fallen in love with them.

(*AMM*, pp. 166ff.; original German in *AME*, pp. 204f.)

346

[New York, December 18 or 19, 1909]

My dear [Walter],

I hope you have not been worried about my silence. The only reason for it is a tremendous burden of work (reminding me of Vienna days), which allows for only four things: conducting, writing music, eating and sleeping. I see by now that I am incorrigible. People of our kind cannot help doing thoroughly whatever they do at all. And that, as I have come

[94]Kurt Schindler (1882-1935) - German-born composer, conductor and writer on music. He conducted at the Metropolitan between 1905 and 1907, and from 1909 on directed the MacDowell Chorus.
[95]Poultney Bigelow (1855-1954) - American (Alma's description notwithstanding) lawyer, journalist and world traveller (he was the first to take a canoe through the then infamous Iron Gates on the Danube).
[96]Natalie Curtis (1875-1921) - She studied in Europe (amongst others, with Busoni), and became known for her pioneering writings on the music and lore of the North American Indian.

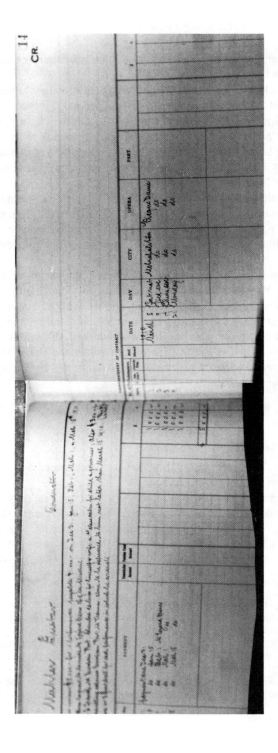

Plate 65. As this Metropolitan Opera ledger page for 1910 shows, Mahler's original contract had called for 10 performances of *Pique Dame* for a fee of $5,000; in fact, he conducted only four times for that fee and the additional emoluments! (Metropolitan Opera Archives)

to realize, means overworking. [...] My orchestra here is the true American orchestra. Untalented and phlegmatic. One fights a losing battle. I find it very dispiriting to have to start all over again as a conductor. The only pleasure I get from it all is rehearsing a work I haven't done before. Simply making music is still tremendous fun for me. If only my musicians were a bit better! [...]

The day before yesterday I did my First here! Apparently without getting much reaction.[97] However, I myself was pretty pleased with that youthful effort! [...]

Please send me Slezak's transposition in the *Queen of Spades* - from the passage leading up to it right to the end. - I am to conduct this opera at the Metropolitan, and they are paying so much money that I shall probably be unable to resist. Please also tell Hohmann[98] that I should awfully like to have him. But there are disgusting difficulties with the *union* here. - They don't allow musicians to be imported. That is, anyone who comes with his contract in his pocket *will be rejected*. There is therefore only one thing for Hohmann to do - that is, come *without* a contract, spend six solid months here, not breathing a word to *anyone* about working for me (people gossip terribly, and if a complaint is made he will be thrown out at once and will not be allowed to play - that happened to me last year with a timpanist). [...]

The audiences here are very lovable and relatively far better mannered than in Vienna. They listen attentively and sympathetically. The superiors[99] are the same as anywhere else. I don't read any of them, but sometimes receive reports of what they say. (*I can recommend the same practice to you* - what they write sounds far less aggressive when reported.) [...]

(*MSL*, pp. 345ff.; original German in *GMB*, pp. 371-374)

---

[97]As was seen earlier, there was, in fact, a great deal of critical reaction to the performance of the First Symphony - probably more than to any other work of his performed by Mahler in New York during his time there. Clearly, he was fully in earnest when he wrote at the end of this letter: "I don't read any of them ... ".

[98]Albert Hohmann - He was a percussionist with the Wiener Konzertverein between 1907 and 1910.

[99]According to a footnote by Alma, "the superiors" (*die Vorgesetzte* in German) was Mahler's term for the critics.

347

Newyork, January 1909 [sic]
[Postmark: New York, January 10, 1910]
My dear friend Schönberg!

[. . .] My First Symphony was pretty well a failure here - you can see from that that I exist here more or less incognito. And how I literally long for home (by which I actually mean the few people who may understand me and whom I treasure). [. . .]

(Original German in Stephen E. Hefling,
"Gustav Mahler und Arnold Schönberg," in *MUB*, p. 186)

348

[Winter 1909-1910?]
Dear [Frau Untermyer]!

Something you said yesterday ("I do nothing but give money") stayed on my mind. Yesterday I did not understand its full implication. But now I feel obliged to tell you that you *do a great deal more* than "give money"! (Which, in any case, is very much needed) - I am very much in need of you, and the Philharmonic is gratefully aware of your constant, kind interest in all our concerns, small and large, day in and day out. You underestimate your service to our cause greatly, and I had to tell you that before you left for the South, where I wish you a pleasant time.

Your most devoted
Gustav Mahler[100]

349

The Philharmonic Society's third historical concert, which took place last night at Carnegie Hall, offered for public delectation three numbers, namely Schubert's "unfinished" symphony, Mendelssohn's violin concerto and Schumann's symphony in D minor. The solo performer was Maud Powell, violinist. There was no note on the programme to convey to the audience just what period of the historical development of music the programme was intended to illustrate. But doubtless Philharmonic audiences know musical history too well to require instruction about the doings of the composers who immediately followed Beethoven along the path of instrumental progress.

[. . .] Mr. Mahler makes his points deliberately. There is no

---

[100]For the German text, see Appendix, A37.

possibility of mistaking his intent. Some conductors have been satisfied to let Schubert's music explain itself, but Mr. Mahler exposes in a bright light his own commentary on its design.

If this was the case with the Schubert work, which is one long and lovely song, it was still more so with the Schumann symphony, which has an architecture planned for the temptation and fall of analytic conductors. Furthermore there is a lurking trouble in every page of its instrumentation. On this point the words of an experienced director of symphonic music are not without their value.

Felix Weingartner asserted that Schumann "did not know how to handle the orchestra, either as director or composer [. . .]". [. . .]

If then the orchestration of Schumann is so deficient that a conductor must often find himself at a loss to bring about intelligibility, certainly neither exaggeration of accents nor hastening of tempi can achieve the much desired result. Clarity would better be secured by repressing those parts which tend to thicken the orchestral utterance, and by taking tempi in confused passages at a more deliberate pace.

[. . .]

Miss Powell's playing of the Mendelssohn concerto was a real delight. [. . .] Her performance was worthy of her high position among the artists of the violin.

(*NYS*, December 30, 1909, p. 7)

350

One million dollars is the price Oscar Hammerstein is said to have refused to retire from the opera business.

A few days ago, the rumour goes, the head of the Manhattan organization was approached on the question of leaving the operatic field clear to his adversary providing he was properly reimbursed. [. . .]

At the Metropolitan, it was vigorously denied that any offer, either directly or indirectly, had been or would be made to Hammerstein, to give up his operatic enterprises.[101] Nevertheless, it was conceded that a crisis in operatic affairs had been reached, [. . .] and that important changes of policy must soon be made by the Metropolitan directorate if the present season's apparent deficit of half a million dollars is not to be exceeded.

(*NYW*, December 31, 1909, p. 7)

---

[101]By the end of 1909, such rumours (as well as "vigorous" disclaimers) may be found in the press virtually every other day (see also **354** and **432**).

351

The Philharmonic Society, which lets no week go by now without one or two or three concerts in one or another of its series, gave yesterday afternoon the second of its Beethoven concerts. Upon the programme appeared two overtures, those to "Egmont" and "Coriolanus", the concerto for violin played by Miss Maud Powell, and the fourth symphony. The "Coriolanus" overture had been played at a recent concert of the society's regular season. The performance of all the orchestral pieces was such a one as Mr. Mahler's previous treatment of Beethoven had led his hearers to expect. [. . .]

Miss Powell's playing of the concerto was poetically conceived and artistically carried out. It was not, in some respects, quite so finely finished as her playing of Mendelssohn's a few days ago in the same place, but it had breadth and warmth of expression and nobility of style. Perhaps one reason why the total effect was less entirely satisfying than her previous performance was the rather unfinished manner in which the orchestral accompaniment was provided. [. . .]

(*NYT*, January 1, 1910, p. 9)

352

I worship the memory of Gustav Mahler, the man and the musician. I sensed his genius most keenly perhaps in the beautiful intimacy that exists between conductor and soloist in interpreting a master work like the Beethoven Violin Concerto. The sensitiveness, the inspirational vision, the forgetfulness of self in the searching appreciation of the composer's intent revealed a musical soul of ineffable sweetness coupled with the force we call genius. As a man he did not belong to our hurly-burly, materialistic age; he was a pathetic figure, sick, shy, often irritable, unworldly to the point of making enemies on all sides, completely in earnest, simple in taste and habits, and, like all sensitive souls, overjoyed when perchance he found some one who understood him. Certainly he was not understood in New York, and it is an ineffaceable blot on our musical history that the critical harassing he suffered at our hands undoubtedly hastened his death. [. . .]

(Maud Powell in *SFM*, pp. 24f.)

353

New York, January 1, 1910

My dear [Adler],

My last letter seems to have been badly misunderstood by you. I learn this from a quantity of letters that I have been getting from Vienna for several days; and from them it is apparent that most unjust and (I admit it) also vexing interpretations have been linked to it. Thus firstly, *ad vocem* letter: I often go the bed after rehearsals (I first heard of this hygiene from Richard Strauss) because it rests me splendidly and agrees with me excellently. In Vienna I simply had no time for that. - I have very much to do, but by no means too much, as in Vienna. On the whole I feel myself fresher and healthier in this activity and mode of life than in many years. -

Do you really believe that a man as accustomed to activity as I am could feel lastingly well as a 'pensioner'?

I absolutely require a practical exercise of my musical abilities as a counterpoise to the enormous inner happenings in creating; and this very conducting of a concert orchestra was my life-long wish. I am happy to be able to enjoy this once in my life (not to mention that I am learning much in the process, for the technique of the theatre is an entirely different one, and I am convinced that a great many of my previous shortcomings in instrumentation are entirely due to the fact that I am accustomed to hearing under the entirely different acoustical conditions of the theatre). Why has not Germany or Austria offered something similar? Can I help it that Vienna threw me out? - Further: I need a certain luxury, a comfort in the conduct of life, which my pension (the only one that I could earn in almost thirty years of directorial activity) could not have permitted. Thus it was a more welcome way out for me that America not only offered an occupation adequate to my inclination and capabilities, but also an ample reward for it, which soon now will put me in a position to enjoy that evening of my life still allotted to me in a manner worthy of a human being. And now, most closely connected with this situation, I come to speak of my wife, to whom you with your views and utterances have done a great injustice. You can take my word for it that she has nothing other than my welfare in view. [. . .] You certainly know her well enough! When have you noticed extravagance or egotism in her? [. . .] Once more I assure you that to me my wife is not only a brave, faithful companion, sharing in everything intellectually, but also (a rare combination) a clever, prudent steward, who, without regard for all the comfort of bodily existence, helps me put by money, and to whom I owe well-being and order in the true sense. [. . .] Forgive my scrawl and attribute my prolixity to the regard and friendship I preserve for you, and to the wish that you will not inflict a grievous injustice upon my wife, and hence upon me also [. . .]

(Reilly, *op. cit.*, pp. 110f; original German in *GMB*, pp. 374ff.)

354

Directors of the Metropolitan Opera Company at a meeting next
Tuesday will consider an arrangement with the Manhattan Opera
Company, whereby changes may be made in the conduct of opera to the
financial and artistic benefit of both companies. [. . .]

For several days, negotiations between Arthur Hammerstein,[102]
representing the Manhattan forces, and the director of the Metropolitan
Company have been underway. [. . .] Officers of the latter organization
today said that Hammerstein had made the advances.

(The Philadelphia Press, January 20, 1910, p. 1)

355

New York, January 6, [19]10

My dear [Roller],

[. . .]

It is the same here as it was there: every minute is chock-full, and the
hours are too few. - I see with satisfaction the distance that I still have to
cover here becoming less and less and, God willing, I hope that in about
a year I shall be able to achieve a human way of life. [. . .] I think—
especially as the America-enthusiasm of my wife is definitely beginning
to fade[103]—that we shall before long arrive somewhere not far from
Vienna, where the sun shines and beautiful grapes grow, and that we shall
not go away again. [. . .]

(MSL, pp. 349f. (incomplete);
original German in GMB, pp. 376f.)

356

The fourth concert of the regular series of the Philharmonic Society was
given last evening [. . .] Berlioz's "Symphonie Fantastique" was the
principal orchestral number on the programme, the only other one being
the prelude to Wagner's "Meistersinger". Mr. Ferruccio Busoni, pianist,
was the soloist. He played Beethoven's E flat major concerto, instead of

---

[102]Arthur Hammerstein, (1873?-1955) - The son of Oscar, he became his father's
representative in 1906, and had his own career as theatrical producer from 1912 to
1932.
[103]This clause is missing from Alma's original edition of the letter (1924) - not an
unusual instance of her suppression of materials she considered unfavourable—
however remotely, or merely potentially—to herself.

Plate 66. Ferruccio Busoni. (*HLG3*, Illustration 39)

Liszt's arrangement with orchestral accompaniment of Schubert's "Wanderer" fantasie, that had been announed.

Berlioz's symphony has had several performances in New York in the last few years, two of them being due to the fact that both Mr. Colonne and Mr. Weingartner have made the work one of their battle horses, and when they came to New York as "guest" conductors in the interregnum before the engagement of Mr. Safonoff, each, not unnaturally, wished to produce it, as something of which they stood as exponents of special authority. [...]

The performance under Mr. Mahler's direction was a wonderfully graphic, vivid, and powerful reading of the score, and let no detail in it escape its due presentation, in its proper proportion and significance. The reading was free, full of expressive nuance, intensely colored and brilliantly rhythmed. [...]

Mr. Busoni returns to America after several years of absence, and this was his first appearance. His art has undergone little change since he has last played here, apparently.

He is a pianist of consummate powers, of an eery finished style, of the most perfect and polished technique. His performance of Beethoven's concerto [...] was deeply interesting, but it was interesting in an analytical way rather than compellingly emotional, and it did not, on the whole, greatly warm the heart. [...]

(*NYT*, January 7, 1910, p. 7)

357

A friend of music and [of] *The Sun* writes a complaint of the bearing of Gustav Mahler against printed comment on music. [...] There are many [...] who passionately battle against criticism made on the performance of music. [...]

It is therefore somewhat interesting and perhaps instructive that Mr. Mahler, being a living composer, should set forth his view that writing about music is futile. He holds that music must make its own appeal to the hearer. The friend of music and [of] *The Sun* pertinently takes note that this position of Mr. Mahler was disclosed about the time that the hirelings of the press mildly wondered whether there was not some want of consideration on the part of the distinguished composer in refusing any information as to the purport of a symphony which plainly was built on a programmatic scheme and which without some hint of the composer's aims was entirely incomprehensible. [...]

A conductor is a performer just as much as a pianist or a violinist is. His instrument is the orchestra, and he plays upon it with his little stick.

[. . .] It makes no difference how he does it, he must play on the orchestra. The complaint of the friend of music and [of] *The Sun* is without doubt evoked by the contemporaneous custom of diversity in reading.

The error lies not in analytical interpretation of masterpieces *per se* but in the jealousy of conductors. They have become a body of prima donnas of the baton and each must have his own special reading of this or that composition and must endeavor to convince audiences and critics that it is better than any other reading. [. . .]

One of the first things that the prima donna conductor feels obliged to do is to take a movement at a tempo different from that employed by other conductors. In nine cases out of ten, it is only by this simple and ingenious process that he can produce any effect varying from those usually heard [. . .]

When Hans von Bulow was here, he gave us some slow tempi [. . .] Now we have in Mr. Mahler a conductor who seems to suspect shrewdly that we have been hearing everything too slow. At any rate, he has introduced us to some pretty lively tempi in the reposeful domain of the classics. [. . .]

Conductors will not only derange tempi but they will practice that device of which Wagner seemed not to have had even a suspicion, namely dragging out middle voices in the harmony and pushing them to the front as if they were solos. [. . .]

This trick, and others like it, are common among orchestra conductors. Mr. Mahler is only one of a small army.

(*NYS*, January 9, 1910, 3. section, p. 10)

358

The third concert of the Beethoven series [. . .] took place in Carnegie Hall yesterday afternoon. The audience was perhaps the smallest in number that ever gathered at a Philharmonic concert, but the weather furnished ample explanation for that fact. The programme consisted of two symphonies only—the "Pastoral" and the C minor—which were played in the order indicated, and as they were when they had their original production. [. . .]

To Mr. Mahler's treatment of [the Fifth Symphony] considerable space was given in this journal some weeks ago. His augmentations of its text, however, are inconsiderable compared with the additions which he has taken the liberty to make to the "Pastoral". Mr. Mahler is not satisfied with the thunder of Beethoven's kettledrum, so he has added another pair, with a part of their own. The fact that Beethoven was in his day an innovator in the use of the kettledrums, and might have written three parts or four if he had been so disposed, might be offered as a plea for the preservation of the purity of the classic text. But under present conditions it would be idle to offer it. We can only wonder that since a "thunder machine" has been added to the symphonic apparatus it was not enlisted. Very realistic lightning effects are also easily produced on every stage. They might not add to the impressiveness of the symphony from a musical point of view, but they might to its delineation. The symphony has also been done with the help of a moving panorama. Mr. Mahler's changes of accents in the accompaniment figure of the "Scene by the Brook" made the flow of the water strangely jerky, but for this reasons may have been found since the death of the composer by observations made in the valley between Heiligenstadt and Gringis,[104] which is the scene of the pretty musical drama which Beethoven gave us. But is it allowable to change the text of a master in cases where the medium of utterance was as perfect in his day as ours?

(*NYTrib*, January 15, 1910, p. 7)

359

The compelling fascination of the Mahler reading in the "Pastorale" symphony last Friday afternoon at Carnegie Hall had one notable and instantaneous result. After the first few measures, the auditors stopped reading the so called "notes on the program" and gave their entire attention to the actual rendering of the work. [. . .]

(*MC* 60, no. 3, January 19, 1910, p. 20)

360

Everyone sat up and rejoiced a few days ago when a sinfonietta by George Chadwick[105] was played [. . .] - a work in which there was no pitfall for the unwary, no concealed meanings, no pathological or other -ogical subtleties. [. . .]

If Mr. Chadwick had been a German, he doubtless would have felt it his solemn duty to scoff at diatonic harmonies and the shopworn custom of writing trombone parts for the trombones. In these days, we dally only

---

[104]Krehbiel (the man who considered himself the high priest of Beethoven's music in America) meant, of course, Grinzing.
[105]George Whitefield Chadwick (1854-1931) - American composer, highly regarded in his own day. He taught at, and later directed, the New England Conservatory of Music.

with exotic scales, and for trombones we write piccolo parts, while for trumpets we jot down suggestive little passages quasi-pizzicato or pen a rollicking conceit of muted contra-bass tubas doubled with sarrusophones and E Flat clarinets.

We know a lot more than the ancients, but sometimes we grow weary about ourselves [. . .] then the old masters come to our relief, but they do not rock us to sleep.

Why must such works be relegated to the programmes of concerts devoted to archaic specialities? Why could not some of them profitably appear in the regular concert programmes? They would not shrink from association with the works of Strauss and Reger. [. . .]

A few of us would like to hear some of the old things. We would for their sake even forego the unspeakable joy of listening to a symphony by D'Indy or observing Max Reger in the act of committing seven deadly variations.

It might also save some of us from having to observe conductors in the great act of interpreting Beethoven. This business of probing the depths of Beethoven's scores to find things which the master perversely concealed from the native eye grows apace. We used to think that Beethoven's scoring was tolerably simple and that most of it was purely harmonic or constructed on a rational distribution of the component parts of chords.

But we are rapidly learning that it is quite as contrapuntal as Bach's and that what he foolishly supposed were mere thirds or sixths in chord formations are in reality individual melodic voices which must be brought out by exploring conductors.

(*NYS*, January 16, 1910, 3. section, p. 8)

361

The Philharmonic Society [. . .] added still another concert to its already formidable list yesterday afternoon in Carnegie Hall. [. . .]

Sergei Rachmaninov, the Russian composer-pianist, was the soloist, playing his Third Concerto in D Minor. This concerto [. . .] was given its initial performance anywhere [. . .] in conjunction with the Symphony Society of New York on Sunday afternoon, November 28, 1909 [. . .] Yesterday was its third performance, and on this occasion the favourable impression it had made when it was played before was deepened. It is more mature, more finished, more interesting in its structure, and more effective than Rachmaninov's other compositions in this form. [. . .]

Rachmaninov gave it a sympathetic reading, if lacking in some of the brilliance which parts of the work demand. The orchestra played a fine accompaniment.

(*NYT*, January 17, 1910, p. 7)

362

At that time Mahler was the only conductor whom I considered worthy to be classed with Nikisch.[106] He touched my composer's heart straight away by devoting himself to my concerto until the accompaniment, which is rather complicated, had been practiced to the point of perfection, although he had already gone through another long rehearsal. According to Mahler, every detail of the score was important—an attitude which is unfortunately rare amongst conductors.

(Oskar von Riesemann, *Rachmaninov's Recollections*, London Allen & Unwin, 1934, p. 158)

363

Theodore Spiering, concertmaster of the Philharmonic Society, tells me that at a recent rehearsal of the organization Gustav Mahler said to his men: "When I lead music I try with heart and soul to feel it as the composer felt it; I give myself up to the task with all there is in me, and for the time being I have no other ambition in the world than to reproduce the art work in hand to the very best of my ability and to reflect the music and its spirit with no thought of selfish glory or individual gain. That man in my orchestra who does not feel as I do, and who does not do it as I do - that man I regard as my personal enemy."

(*MC* 60, no. 4, January 26, 1910, p. 24)

364

At the Academy of Music[107] last evening [. . .] the orchestra of the Philharmonic Society of New York made its first appearance in this city under the direction of Mr. Gustav Mahler. [. . .] The occasion was one

---

[106]Arthur Nikisch (1855-1922) - Born in Hungary, he was one of the greatest conductors of his age. Among many and varied positions, he conducted in Boston between 1889 and 1893.

[107]The American Academy of Music in Phildelphia was built in 1857, modelled on La Scala, to seat 2,900. Said to be the finest opera house in the country then, it later became the home of the Philadelphia Orchestra.

Plate 67. Academy of Music, Philadelphia. (*LCE*, Figure 99)

of the most noteworthy and enjoyable in a season which has been full of musical interest. [. . .] What rendered the occasion notable was the demonstration it afforded of Mr. Mahler's exceptional powers as an interpreter of such music as a symphony orchestra customarily plays. [. . .]

The programme [. . .] illustrated each principal phase of musical development since the opening of the nineteenth century. [. . .] It enabled Mr. Mahler to show himself equally at home in every school. [. . .]

His reading of the symphony [in C Minor by Beethoven] [. . .] showed [. . .] that the performance of a classic masterpiece does not need to be dull and dry and wholely impersonal for it to remain faithful to the period of the score. He gave one of the most highly coloured and strongly accentuated renderings of this familiar music that can be recalled, and yet it contained nothing that could give legitimate offence to the most sensitive stickler for the maintenance of the classical traditions. [. . .] Strength, sanity, virility, dignity, and lucidity, a total absence of self-consciousness, and an absolute freedom from any suggestion of insincerity or affectation, such were the salient elements of as fine a performance of the C Minor in all the features of truly interpreted greatness as has been heard here since Theodore Thomas laid the baton down.

(*The Philadelphia Inquirer*, January 18, 1910, p. 4)

365

The fifth concert of the Philharmonic Society's first series took place last night at Carnegie Hall. The programme consisted of three numbers. Tchaikowsky's sixth symphony, the vorspiel to "Tristan und Isolde" and the overture to Smetana's "Bartered Bride". Mr. Mahler's readings of the last two works are well known. [. . .]

Every one conducts the Tchaikowsky symphony known as the "Pathetic". Hence Mr. Mahler deserved to have his turn. But it is a pity that this composition cannot have a period of retirement. It is likely to suffer from over use. Without doubt there are some music lovers in whose minds the question arises just now whether all such music as this is not sadly overrated, especially by the enthusiastic young Walther von Stolzings[108] who believe that the laws of form in art wore themselves out

[108]This reference to the character Wagner created in *Die Meistersinger* to represent the age-old conflict between youthful, creative genius and petty conservative pedantry, provides a revealing glimpse of the fundamentally traditionalist viewpoint of most American critics, even if they were, much of the time, willing to give the new at least a fair hearing.

with such old fogies as Michael Angelo [sic], or perhaps a little later with pedants like Beethoven.

[. . .]

The performance of the symphony last night was in general good. [. . .] The solidity of tone, the richness of color and the sweep of attack in the performance showed that Mr. Mahler's instrument was in pretty good condition and that he was not afraid to play vigorously upon it.

(*NYS*, January 21, 1910, p. 9)

366

The fourth concert in the Philharmonic Society's historical series brought the programme last evening to [. . .] Mr. Mahler himself as a composer. [. . .]

Mr. Mahler's contribution to the programme—a set of five "Children's Death Songs", to verses by Rückert—belong to the class of songs with orchestral accompaniment that modern composers are cultivating with especial interest, and of which they are making almost a new genre.

They are something more and more elaborate than lyrics; and these of Mr. Mahler's, in fact, are in the nature of little dramas or dramatic scenes in miniature.[. . .] They are mournful, gloomy in tone, and they do not make an immediate appeal; but there is much beauty in them, and much poignant expressiveness. A large part of their importance resides in the orchestral part, which is much more than an accompaniment of the voice. There is here some striking and effective orchestration, skillful enhancement of the mood and though there are some passages which seem rather bald and others where the composer's inspiration failed him, the set is, as a whole, impressive.

(*NYT*, January 27, 1910, p. 9)

367

The poems [by Rückert] are for the most part of touching beauty.

[. . .]

The music that Mr. Mahler has written for these sombre verses is evidently sincere in its reflection of the text, but in spite of this fortunate quality and of numerous felicities in workmanship, it cannot be taken as sounding the note of original thought. Mr. Mahler feels but he does not create. Everyone of the five songs has some distinctive piece of good musical craftsmanship, such as the unisonal support of the voice by cellos and lower woodwinds in the second and third of the group, the unlooked for curve of the melodic line in the closing measures of the first and second stanzas of the first song and the prelude of grumbling strings in the last of the set. But they do not seem musically significant in the larger sense.

(*NYS*, January 27, 1910, p. 7)

368

If the Mahler songs had not spread an atmosphere of gloom over the occasion, they would not have served their purpose. They are weighted with grief of such poignant sincerity that one must conclude that they have an autobiographic significance.[109] We have not heard any music by Mr. Mahler which has so individual a note, or which is so calculated to stir up the imagination and the emotions.

(*NYTrib*, January 27, 1910, p. 7)

369

[Mahler] had not been long in America when the Charles Steinways[110] invited me to meet him and his wife at dinner. I was so excited over the prospect that I arrived a full half-hour too soon. Mrs. Steinway greeted me with the words:

"I am seating you beside Mahler at table tonight, but do not expect him to speak. He cannot be made to talk at dinner parties."

Mr. Steinway gallantly murmured something to the effect that "Olga ought to be able to draw him out", but Mrs. Steinway was not disposed to flattery. [. . .] "If my husband is right and you *do* make him talk, I will give you five dollars".

[. . .] When we sat down at dinner he never even glanced at me. [. . .]

Finally, [. . .] I boldly asked him if he did not consider *The Brothers Karamazoff* a much overrated book.

"Not at all", said Mahler fiercely, putting down his knife and fork. "You ask that because you do not understand it". He thereupon launched into a long discourse on the subject of Russian psychology and

---

[109]Once again, Mahler must have refused to provide Krehbiel with material of "autobiographic significance." The notes on the *Kindertotenlieder* in the programme booklet for this concert consist of a translation of Mahler's injunction against premature applause (printed on the first page of the score) and the texts of the songs.
[110]Charles Herman Steinway (1857-1919) - President from 1896 until his death of the famous German-American piano manufacturing firm, Steinway & Sons.

Dostoyevsky's supreme understanding of it, while I settled down to the enjoyment of my dinner (and my triumph!), only throwing in an occasional provocative question when Mahler paused to eat a mouthful.

The signals exchanged between me and the Steinways must have mystified anybody who saw them. Mr. Steinway kept looking at his watch and lifting his glass to me. [. . .]

Before I left, my crestfallen hostess presented me with six crisp new dollar bills. She felt that five would not be enought in view of the length of the conversation!

> (Olga Samaroff-Stokowski,[111] *An American Musician's Story*,
> New York, Norton, 1939, pp. 159f.)

370

> The
> STEINWAY
> VERTEGRAND
> is the embodiment of scientific research and musical progress of the Twentieth Century.
> GUSTAV MAHLER, the famous conductor of the Philharmonic Society, writes us as follows:
> "I never imagined that an upright piano could be constructed which would satisfy a musician's requirements in every respect."

> (*NYTrib*, January 30, 1910, Part Four, p. 2)[112]

---

[111]Olga Samaroff-Stokowski (née Hickenlooper) (1882-1948) - American pianist, critic and teacher. Following studies in Paris, Baltimore and Berlin, she toured widely in America and Europe as a soloist and chamber musician.

[112]It is clear that Steinway & Sons wished to capitalize on Mahler's 'market value' in the first flush of his popularity as conductor of the Philharmonic. Only three days after this advertisement, a full-page one—with photograph, and with the same quote—was published in *The Musical Courier*. Furthermore, the facing page featured Edward Elgar in the same 'role'; the full spread carries the heading: "Two Artistic Opinions on One Artistic Subject" (*MC* 60, no. 5, February 2, 1910, pp. 16f.).

371

Gustav Mahler [...] fell out with his soloist at a rehearsal [...] and the upshot was that the piano concerto had to be played at the concert in Carnegie Hall yesterday afternoon by a substitute.[113]

The soloist was to have been Josef Weiss[114] of Leipsig, whom Mr. Mahler brought to New York especially for the concert yesterday afternoon. Mr. Weiss and Mr. Mahler had been friends for a good while and even last night when Mr. Weiss was threatening to bring suit against the Philharmonic unless he got his pay for the appearance that he didn't make, he declared his lasting friendship for the conductor. He didn't think that it was spoiled a bit.

[...]

The trouble started on Saturday afternoon at rehearsal when Mr. Mahler offered some suggestions to Mr. Weiss about the way he wished the concerto played. Mr. Weiss retaliated in kind, suggesting that if the oboes played a little more pianissimo in the finale, the piano could be heard to better effect.

Mr. Mahler suggested at this point that he understood conducting pretty thoroughly, and Mr. Weiss replied that he thought he knew more about all there was to know about piano playing. Mr. Mahler said that if Mr. Weiss would play more and talk less that he would be pleased.

At this point, the angry pianist shut down the cover of the piano and walked out of the hall.

(Compiled from *NYS*, January 31, 1910, p. 7, and
NYT, January 31, 1910, p. 1)

372

We got to know Joseph Weiss, the pianist, through the painter, Groll[115] [...] Weiss had a square, bald skull, with the merest tuft in the middle, and brown eyes wedged in slits, which could only mean either insanity or genius. He was the greatest pianist Mahler, according to his own account, had ever heard.

---

[113]Apparently, Yolanda Merö was engaged as the substitute, but was supposed to have suffered an injury during rehearsal. The concert was eventually played (without a rehearsal, consequently not very well) by Paolo Gallico (1868-1955), the Italian-born American pianist and composer.

[114]Josef Weiss [Weisz] (1864-1940?) - Hungarian-born German pianist. Although he was mostly active in Berlin, he also played and taught extensively in Russia and America.

[115]Albert Lorey Groll (1866-1952) - Amerian landscape painter, he was a pioneer in painting the American West, and also Canadian winter landscapes.

[. . .]

In spite of warnings from all sides he agreed to let him play Schumann's piano concerto at his next concert. [. . .]

Weiss was starving and Mahler had induced the committee to pay him a big fee. Weiss appeared to be pleased and the rehearsals passed off unexpectedly well. Then came the dress-rehearsal. He was rather more nervous than usual, but he played the first movement well, even if without his true *élan*. This and a few wilfulnesses in his tempo annoyed Mahler, whereupon Weiss made some impertinent remarks under his breath, which Mahler purposely did not hear. He wanted to help him. Weiss recovered his self-control and began the second movement. Mahler called out to him: "Good!" This was the end of Weiss. He seized the music and hurled it on the floor at Mahler's feet. "As good as you any day", he shouted, raving like a lunatic. The orchestra, thinking Mahler was in need of protection, flung themselves on Weiss. Mahler begged them not to touch him, but now it had gone too far and Weiss had to leave the concert hall.

The rehearsal was broken off and Mahler came home, half-enraged and half-amused. But his strongest feeling was pity for Weiss. [. . .]

(*AMM*, pp. 164ff.; original German in *AME*, pp. 201ff.)

373

Strauss's "Elektra" now finally impends, the first American production being set down for Tuesday evening next at the Manhattan Opera House. The work has required the same sort of laborious preparation that was given to "Salome" last season, and the same sort of interest is expected to be aroused in it. [. . .] Strauss, with the practice and experience gained in his previous music drama, is said to have piled up the orchestral agony even higher. [. . .]

The theme of "Elektra" is deeply imbedded in Greek mythology and literature, and its whole connotation is characteristic of the Greek point of view. [. . .] The legend is gloomy, fraught with a dark terror.

There is gloom enough in the treatment of it made by Von Hofmannsthal;[116] but he has changed its aspect. His drama is lurid and passionate exposition of the play of convulsive emotion, the outbreak of distorted personality, of morbid and alienated intellects.

(*NYT*, January 30, 1910, Part Five, p. 15)

---

[116]Hugo von Hofmannsthal (1874-1929) - Austrian poet and playwright. Highly lyrical in tone, his works represent an exquisite late blooming of German Romanticism. He collaborated with Strauss on several operas.

374

Enormous pains and study had been spent upon the preparation of "Elektra", for the demands it makes upon the participating singers, the orchestral players, the conductor, as well as upon the nerves, patience and pecuniary resources of the manager, are of the greatest.[117] The Opera House was full last evening, and the new work was listened to with profound attention; though, lasting, as it does two hours without an intermission and straining the conscientious listener's senses to the uttermost, it is an exhausting experience.

[...]

Whatever the effect of the spoken drama may be, that of Strauss's setting has only at certain moments the direct and penetrating thrust of potent dramatic power. [...]

The long speeches give the musician endless opportunity for his minute delineation, in tones and in orchestral color, of the changing shades of emotion and passion that run through them, but leave little opportunity for action on the stage. For long stretches in the first part of the drama the attention of the listener is wearied by these interlocutions, of which it is impossible to hear and understand the words, and of which the potent effect is soon blunted and lost. In "Salome" something ominous, disastrous, terrible, was continually happening, or about to happen; and the feeling of the movement of events was communicated across the footlights, even if only in the sense of uneasy foreboding, realized by the result. Whatever may be in other respects the comparative merits of these two, it is undeniable that "Elektra" is less dramatically effective, that it makes more exacting demands upon the listener's attention.

The Strauss of "Elektra", however, is the Strauss of "Salome" and of the last symphonic poems. His ideals and intentions are the same, his methods the same. The reservoire from which his musical inspiration is drawn has neither broadened nor deepened. There may be a greater skill in the treatment of the musical material, a more adept manipulation of the complexities of texture in which the composer delights. But in its moments of greatest eloquence "Elektra" scarcely rises to the splendors that mark the great climaxes of "Salome".

[...] Strauss, in his later works, has become more and more indifferent to the purely musical quality of his material, to its potency for specifically musical development. He seeks only such as admits of plastic

---

[117]There is no doubt that financial risks taken by independent producers like Hammerstein were truly staggering in the monetary context of the times. Apparently, he had paid $10,000 to Strauss simply for the American rights to *Elektra*, plus an additional $18,000 in advance royalties, while the ten weeks of rehearsals cost $15,000 (Cone, *op. cit.*, p. 264).

or picturesque development, superficial suggestion, all sorts of ingenuities in manipulation, combination; bits that might serve for the purposes of a Chinese puzzle or that could be pieced together as a mosaic.

The music is written with a more reckless disregard for what has hitherto passed for tonal beauty and expressiveness than any other Strauss has produced. He puts his motives together with absolute unconcern as to harmony or the preservation of tonality. It has been said that Strauss seems to seek for a sort of neutral tonality, in which all keys may be found at will. It is, in other words, the negation of euphony, the acceptance, for all purposes, of any kind of cacophony.

[...]

Strauss clings even closer to the letter than the spirit in his dramatic illustrations, and he has again made his score teem with fantastic exaggerations of all sorts of verbal details. [...]

That with this material and with his use of orchestral effect Strauss is able to create an atmosphere that, for want of another name, may be called musical, and impose the mood of the drama is undeniable. The extraordinary complication of this orchestral part is the instant reflection of every aspect of the drama. In it Strauss's wonderful technical skill is shown at its highest. [...]

Much has been written about the overwhelming noise of this orchestration. Either the reports have been grossly exaggerated or Mr. de la Fuente[118] has exercised a restraint of his own upon his forces. [...] The vocal parts are unsingable, as can well be imagined. They have nothing melodic, nothing thematic, nothing that has any recognizable outline even as musical declamation. As one critic has remarked, Strauss uses the voices merely for a kind of characteristic shouting. [...]

Whether "Elektra" is an addition to the production of modern art that will live is even more doubtful than the question as to "Salome". [...]

(*NYT*, February 2, 1910, p. 7)

375

The première of Strauss's *Elektra* took place at this time at the Manhattan Opera House. Mahler disliked it so much that he wanted to go out in the middle. We sat it out, but agreed afterwards that we had seldom in our lives been so bored. The public decided against us. It was a success and some, very characteristically, described it as "awfully nice".

[118]Henriquez de la Fuente - Following a conducting career in Antwerp, he came to the United States in 1909.

The production was a brilliant success, as Hammerstein's always were. The youthful Labia,[119] the *décor* - all superb!

(*AMM*, pp. 168f.; original German in *AME*, p. 211)

376

In attempting to respond to a third recall at the close of the performance by the great audience that witnessed the first production in America of "Elektra" at the Manhattan Opera House last evening, Mme. Mazarin[120] fainted upon the stage. [...]

The final touch of a stricken artist was scarcely needed to make the opera the event of the musical season. The audience which gave $19,000 for the privilege of being present at the premiere was fairly representative of such an occasion. [...]

Among those present were [...] Gustav and Mrs. Mahler [...].

(*NYW*, February 2, 1910, p. 3)

377

Greeks of the city to the number of about 1,000 met last night in the Greek [...] Church, [...] and vigorously protested against the present production of the opera "Elektra" at the Manhattan Opera House. The principal speakers were Raymond Duncan, brother of Isadora Duncan, the dancer, who still clings to the traditional Greek manner of dress; Pope Lazaris, the priest of the church, and Michael F. Theodoropolas, L.L.D., editor of the Thermopylae, the Greek paper published in New York.

The objection to the opera as set forth by all the speakers is that it violates all the accepted canons of Greek dramatic structure, defames the Greek classics, and gives the American people an entirely erroneous idea of Greek literature and art. After the meeting a project was formed to teach Hellenic music in this city.

A school for this purpose will be started Monday evening in the basement of the Greek Church. [...] Next Saturday afternoon, as a further protest to the American method of presenting ancient Greek

---

[119]This is, apparently, another flight of fancy by Alma. Labia did not only not sing in *Elektra*, but appears to have left the Manhattan altogether at the end of the previous season!

[120]Mariette Mazarin (*ca.* 1883-?) - Born and trained in France, Mazarin earned fame at an early age in Europe in the title roles of *Aida*, *Carmen*, *Louise* (under Charpentier's tutelage), *Salome* and *Elektra* (both under the composer's direction).

dramas, the Greek colony in the city will give scenes from the original "Elektra" of Sophocles and from other ancient Greek dramas at Carnegie Lyceum.

The scene last night was picturesque. Dressed in flowing robes and sandals, with his long hair streaming over his shoulders, Mr. Duncan stirred his audience in the gas and candle lighted church to enthusiasm. [. . .] In the present opera, he said, Elektra was represented as a shrieking, howling maniac, while in the original she was just the opposite.

"[. . .] 'Elektra', which is one of the most wonderful and beautiful of the Greek works, has been mutilated and molded into one of the most vile and immodest plays ever put on the American stage. [. . .]"

The speaker told the audience to try and spread the knowledge in America of what real Grecian art and literature meant.

When he had finished several hundred excited Greeks announced their intention of attending the school of music as soon as it is started.

(*NYT*, February 10, 1910, p. 7)

378

Gustav Mahler and the Philharmonic Society players aroused the enthusiasm of an audience of rainy evening size last night by their performance of Schumann's D minor symphony, No. 4; the Strauss "Don Juan" fantasia and the overture to "Tannhäuser". All three compositions were presented in a way to reveal the technical prowess of the orchestra [. . .]

The soloist was Miss Tilly Koenen, the Dutch contralto. She sang Beethoven's scene and aria "Ah! Perfido", with a large tone and also a large style. Her voice, as has been observed before, is not one of sensuous beauty, but she sings with intelligence and earnestness. She was heard also in songs by Strauss, Fiedler[121] and Wolf, with orchestral accompaniment.

(*NYS*, February 4, 1910, p. 7)

379

Regarding the rumor that Gustav Mahler, director of the Philharmonic Orchestra, will not be re-engaged when his present contract expires, as the result of differences which have arisen between him and some of the

---

[121]A. Max Fiedler (1859-1939) - Prominent German conductor and composer. He led the Boston Symphony from 1908 to 1912.

society women who are interested in the project, a man high in the counsels of that organization authorizes MUSICAL AMERICA to state: "Mr. Mahler's contract does not expire until the end of next season, and no question has ever been raised as to its renewal. If it has been raised, the statements made in the report printed in this connection would not have been considered. Mr. Mahler has always been exceedingly ready to listen to any suggestions from the committee, and there has at no time been any lack of harmony between him and any member of the committee."

(*MA* 11, no. 13, February 5, 1910, p. 1)

380

Gustav Mahler will conduct the Philharmonic concerts next season and after that he will return to Europe permanently. His contract is for two years and will not be renewed, as he refuses to continue under present conditions as they exist in this city.

(*MC* 60, no. 6, February 9, 1910, p. 25)

381

Theodore Spiering, concert master of the Philharmonic Orchestra, [. . .] gave his first New York recital in Mendelssohn Hall on Thursday afternoon, February 10. [. . .]

Mr. Spiering had cause to be highly gratified because of the prominent musicians—Gustav Mahler, [. . .] Alfred Hertz, [. . .] Henry Holden Huss [. . .] being present. Mr. Spiering had his audience with him from the first number, and was recalled many times after each appearance.

[. . .]

The accompaniments were played by Kurt Schindler.

(*MA* 11, no. 15, February 19, 1910, p. 33)

382

It was doubtless merely a coincidence that the concerts given by the Philharmonic and Symphony societies yesterday afternoon were both memorial concerts. The date being the twenty-seventh anniversary of the death of Richard Wagner, Mr. Mahler [. . .] devoted the programme [. . .] to music composed by that master, and called in the aid of a singer—albeit an Italian—from the Metropolitan Opera House. At The New Theatre Mr. Walter Damrosch [. . .] set aside the second part of the concert for a performance of Brahms's symphony in C minor in memory of the late Samuel S. Sanford, who was the president of the society [. . .]

Aside from the two vocal numbers sung at the Philharmonic concert by Pasquale Amato[122] (Wotan's farewell to Brünnhilde from "Die Walküre" and Hans Sach's monologue, "Wahn! Wahn!" from "Die Meistersinger"), the programme contained the "Kaisermarsch", "Eine Faust Ouvertüre", the "Siegfried Idyl", the prelude to "Die Meistersinger" and overture to "Tannhäuser". [. . .] The first three received their first performance at the hands of the orchestra under the direction of Mr. Mahler. They were vividly read, with fine elasticity of melodic contour, a broad sweep, much warmth of color and poetical distribution of nuances. Signor Amato sang, to the obvious delight of the audience, though with not so advantageous an exhibition of his admirable qualities as he makes in Italian opera. His German diction is very faulty, as all operagoers know who have heard him in "Tristan und Isolde", yet he shows a large sympathy for the music of the German master.

(*NYTrib*, February 14, 1910, p. 7)

383

With Mahler's vividly dramatic and highly temperamental reading of Berlioz's individual work [the Fantastic Symphony] still fresh in my mind, I could not but feel that Mr. Damrosch's reading, though pictorial and appreciative, was rather tame in sonority and climax and lacking in incisive qualities - more fanciful than fantastic.

Perhaps the uncertain acoustics of the New Theatre mocked me, but I thought the ball scene banal, the scene in the country cold as if drenched with rain, the march more noisy than awesome, and that the first thrill and warmth or richness of color came with the finale. From a technical standpoint the execution of the work was well nigh faultless.

(*NYW*, February 14, 1910, p. 4)

384

The seventh concert in the Philharmonic Society's regular series was given last evening in Carnegie Hall. The programme was exceptional for

[122]Pasquale Amato (1878-1942) - Italian baritone, member of the Metropolitan from 1908 to 1921. He sang the role of Kurvenal in Toscanini's first *Tristan und Isolde* in New York (see **329**).

one of these concerts, in that it contained no symphony; but there was plenty of interesting and important matter. [...]

What was nearest to a new offering to the frequenters of the Philharmonic concerts was the set of three Nocturnes by Debussy [...]

It is not easy to imagine Mr. Mahler in full sympathy with music of this school, yet he obtained a remarkably beautiful performance of these pieces, full of subtle nuances and blending of the orchestral color; in the "'Fêtes" there were Debussy's "rhythm dancing in the atmosphere", the "bursts of brusque light", the dazzling vision of the procession. The chorus of women sang in the "Sirens" with fine tone and balance and with secure mastery of the music, a difficult task. It was the MacDowell Chorus,[123] directed by Mr. Kurt Schindler; and it reflected much credit on his work. [...]

(*NYT*, February 18, 1910, p. 7)

385

For the first time in the sixty-eight years of its existence, the Philharmonic Society is to make a tour to [...] New Haven [Connecticut], [...] Springfield [Massachusetts], [...] Providence [Rhode Island] and Boston. [...] Felix Leifels, business manager of the Philharmonic, will be in charge of the tour.

(*NYTrib*, February 20, 1910, Part Four, p. 2)

386

The New York Philharmonic Society concert in Woolsey Hall, the first to be given by that organization in this city, was a tremendous one. The orchestra, contrary to the usual custom in traveling had not been reduced in size, and so had all the richness and breadth of tone of the large number of strings. Its playing was finished and thorough under the dominance of Mr. Gustav Mahler's baton.

On first glance, the conducting of Mr. Mahler appears erratic, a mere helter-skelter of zigzags, up, down, and across and around, now rapid, now slow, long and short. With a little study and watchfulness one finds that each and every motion carries a suggestion, a hint to the players. Keeping the tempo by beating time in the ordinary fashion is entirely unnecessary with a so well-trained organization as the Philharmonic

[123]MacDowell Chorus - named after the Irish-American composer, choral conductor and teacher, Edward Alexander MacDowell (1860-1908).

Society, so that the conductor has only to outline with suggestions, emphasizes here and there the things that are on the score before him. Mr. Mahler is a conductor with few equals and his power was well shown last night. Of course the mere details of his conducting are nothing compared with the immense learned conception of the great masterpieces which those details help to bring out.
[. . .]
Olga Samaroff, pianist, played by the Grieg concerto with distinction. To be sure, she seemed like a child playing under the benevolent, indulgent eye of a great master, because even in this number one could not get away from the potent spell of Mr. Mahler's stick. [. . .]

(*New Haven Evening Register*, February 24, 1910, p. 5)

387

Playing a concerto with the Philharmonic under Mahler's direction was a privilege I repeatedly enjoyed. The first time I was soloist in one of his concerts on tour was in New Haven. By that time he and I had become good friends, and I had conceived a great liking for his lovely wife who was one of the most beautiful women I have ever seen. She was not with him on this particular occasion and he felt the need of company at supper after the concert. [. . .]
Being in a university town, Mahler expected to find gay cafés filled with students in multicolored caps. When we had searched in vain for something more exciting than a corner drug store, and our hotel had refused to serve what we wanted at such a late hour, his dismay was pathetic.
"*Was für eine Stadt!*", he murmured bitterly. "What kind of students do they have here? No wine, no songs, and not yet midnight!"
It did not seem to comfort him at all when I assured him that Yale students did sing at other times and had pretty much what they wanted to drink on other occasions.
He only shook his head [. . .] and he remained pessimistic about the *joie de vivre* of the American university student. [. . .]

(Samaroff-Stokowski, *op. cit.*, pp. 160f.)

388

It was a paragon of concerts that the New York Philharmonic Society gave in Court Square Theatre last evening. A superb orchestra, a conductor of the "first force", [. . .], a stimulating programme - what more could be asked for? Those who were not present missed one of the finest performances heard here in many years. [. . .] With a noble orchestra of nearly one hundred men, and with a genius like Gustav Mahler to conduct, it was as striking a demonstration as could well be of the marvelous possibilities of the modern orchestra.

Especially striking was the extreme modernity of Hector Berlioz when put beside his successors. [. . .] He has had to wait long for adequate recognition, but now the twentieth century is claiming him for its own. [. . .]

There are gruesome passages [in the Fantastic Symphony]. [. . .] But there are beautiful scenes as well, and altogether it is an extraordinary, imaginative and impressive work. Mr. Mahler's reading of it was superb.

In some respects, it was unfortunate to have this duplicated by a modern work of so nearly the same genre as Richard Strauss's "Till Eulenspiegel." [. . .] Berlioz' symphony is tragedy [. . .] Strauss's is a burlesque, a jeu d'esprit, an immensely clever bit of fun, coupled with a strenuous technical effort. Inevitably it suffers in the comparison. [. . .]

If these were characteristic works, no less was the familiar "Meistersinger" overture. [. . .] What splendid sonorous effects [. . .] Wagner gets in this rich and eloquent overture, and how superbly it was played under Mr. Mahler's conducting. It made a triumphal close to the evening.

(*The Springfield Daily Republican*, February 25, 1910)

389

Springfield, February 24, 1910

[Dear Alma],

Things are becoming ever more 'old fashioned'. Oh, Savoy! What a nice, peaceful Tusculum you are. - Today I am in a hole (there is nothing else here), a roar of machinery, 'cars', and so on. My stomach is also no longer in order! Perhaps it is the butter again, which I will cut out from now on. It is very cold, and everything snowed in and icy! How good it is that I have the fur along. - This tour would not be for you at all! Negro service everywhere. Otherwise, here there are very pleasantly industrious and smart fellows.

Spiering as tour-guide is an operetta-character. - Conversation with him becomes more and more difficult. He considers each word for so long that in the meantime he thinks of something else, and then no longer knows what he is saying. In any case, New Haven is a nice little place

with a bad hotel. Springfield is a wretched hole with an impossible
hotel. [. . .]

(*ELM*, p. [908])[124]

390

The concert by the New York Philharmonic Orchestra in Infantry Hall
last evening was attended by an audience of moderate size only. This fact
signifies chiefly that a good many people lost the opportunity to hear one
of the best concerts of the kind, and certainly the most splendid
orchestral programme, which has ever been given here. It was most
unfortunate, of course, that the date of the orchestra's appearance in
Providence coincided with that of the Kreisler recital. Still, had the whole
Kreisler audience been transferred to Infantry Hall, it would scarcely
have sufficed to swell the attendance to the number commonly seen at the
regular appearances of the Boston Symphony. All of which tends to
prove what is, indeed, already pretty well known, that the patronage
which may be depended upon for concerts of the very highest class can
be reckoned within certain well-defined and rather narrow limits.
   [. . .]
The orchestra [. . .] is certainly a superb body of players, and under
the inspiring lead of Conductor Gustav Mahler, made a magnificent
showing. It is too much, perhaps, to hope for another visit from this
splendid organization after the poor attendance last night, but certainly
everyone who heard this concert would take some trouble, if necessary,
to hear another like it.

(*The Providence Journal*, February 26, 1910, p. 2)

391

At Symphony Hall[125] last night, the Philharmonic Society of New York,
Gustav Mahler conducting, gave its first concert in Boston. [. . .]
   Mahler's beat is exceedingly elastic. It may be said to cease altogether
during periods approaching some point of stress which is the more

---

[124]For the German text, see Appendix, A38.
[125]Replacing the old Music Hall (1852; now the Aquarius Theatre) as the home of
orchestral music, Symphony Hall opened in 1900, with a seating capacity of 2,645.
It was the first auditorium in America to incorporate acoustical engineering into the
building process.

accentuated at its resumption. Here is the impressive thing in his conducting. [...] He is a vital, magnetic and puissant conductor. [...]

Nothwithstanding limitations of the orchestra's technique which were impossible to conceal, Mr. Mahler infused into pages of Berlioz' symphony, the "Fantastic", an absorbing subtlety, and an enkindling glow, a breadth and sweep of passion, which made them luminous with the poetry and the terror of the work. [...]

The quality which makes Mr. Mahler a temperamental and an operatic conductor showed in the dignified yet essentially dramatic reading of Beethoven's "Leonore" overture No. 3. It is the same quality which makes his scale of values in "Till Eulenspiegel's Merry Pranks" cognizant of humour, sentiment and the mock heroic. Unfortunately, he was attempting to play upon an orchestra unequal to the exactions of Strauss's score.

(*The Boston Sunday Globe*, February 27, 1910, p. 15)

392

My first knowledge of Mahler as conductor was when the Berlioz Fantastic Symphony was played by him in Boston (for with him you felt that it was *he* that played, the orchestra being his instrument). That performance was enough to show that he was one of the greatest conductors of all time. Could he have lived, his "passion for perfection" in orchestra playing would have been a constant object-lesson to us; with our easy-going way of never caring to do the thing just the way it should be done, we need such teaching. [...]

(Arthur Foote[126] in *SFM*, p. 12)

393

The fact that the Board of Directors of the Metropolitan has deferred all public announcement of its plans until May 1 has paved the way for another deluge of rumors regarding future policies and appointments. The latest of these reports and one that is believed, by those well informed, to be based upon truth, states that Henry Russell, general manager of the Boston Opera Company, will succeed Giulio Gatti-Casazza at the close of the latter's contract in the autumn of 1911.

---

[126]Arthur William Foote (1853-1937) - Organist and composer, he was active chiefly in Boston. He was president of the American Guild of Organists from 1909 to 1912.

Plate 68. Arthur W. Foote, organist and composer. (*LCE*, Figure 54)

[...] there is a strong feeling that a man better acquainted with American ideas and conditions should have charge of the management [...] and the unquestioned success that has characterized Mr. Russell's administration of affairs in Boston has advanced him as the logical candidate for the position. [...]

(*MA* 11, no. 18, March 12, 1910, p. 1)

394

When ["The Queen of Spades"] is produced at the Metropolitan Opera House next Saturday afternoon it will be the first of [Tchaikowsky's] operas to have a stage production in America. [...] There will also be a special interest in it from the fact that it will be conducted by Mr. Gustav Mahler, who then will return to the conductor's stand at the opera house for the first time since he became the regular conductor of the Philharmonic Society's concerts, to which he has been devoting all his energies hitherto this season.

"Pique Dame" [...] is founded on a story by Pushkin, the Russian novelist.[127] [...] Pushkin's tale is one of Russian life, [...] a gruesome tale, with few points of relief. [...]

[It] was composed in blood and tears in little more than the single month of February, 1890, while Tchaikowsky was staying in Florence. His letters of that period bear evidence of his unhappiness, of his discouragement, of his general disgust with life. [...]

Tchaikowsky was no follower of the modern school of lyric drama, and wrote his operas in the general outline of the elder operatic forms. [...]

"Pique Dame" has also made its way to some opera houses outside of Russia, and Mr. Mahler conducted it in Vienna while he ruled at the Imperial Opera there.[128]

(*NYT*, February 27, 1910, Part Five, p. 15)

395

The fifth historical concert of the Philharmonic Society at Carnegie Hall last night reached what used to be called "the music of the future". This goes to show that in these days history is made very fast. Who is writing

---

[127]Alexander S. Pushkin (1799-1837) - One of the greatest figures in Russian literature, his position and significance is best compared to that of Goethe in German literature.
[128]Mahler produced the Viennese premiére of *Pique Dame* on December 9, 1902. He conducted the opera twelve times during that season alone.

the music of the future now? It must be Henry Hadley. [129] The programme last evening comprised the following historical numbers: The "Flying Dutchman" overture, "Lohengrin" and "Parsifal" preludes, Siegmund's love song from "Die Walküre", the prize song from "Die Meistersinger" and the funeral march from "Götterdämmerung". In addition to these were two of Liszt's symphonic poems, "Les Preludes" and "Mazeppa".

The singer of the evening was Carl Jörn of the Metropolitan Opera House, who went up as far as Fifty-seventh street to cause regret. Mr. Jörn came here with a fine, fresh, vibrant tenor voice and the promise of youth. He has unfortunately fallen into vicious vocal habits which may prove injurious to his voice if not corrected. He sang last evening with more vigor than discretion.

Mr. Mahler conducted the orchestra through some very dramatic readings.

[...]

(*NYS*, March 3, 1910, p. 9)

396

Years later I met him again in New York.

A tired, sick man.

We had *Pique Dame* - American première at the Metropolitan Opera House.

At the rehearsals he and I were mostly alone.

The others simply did not turn up.

He rarely got a whole ensemble together.

He sat there with me, resigned, a different man.

I sought in vain the fiery spirit of yesteryear. He had become mild and sad.

(Leo Slezak, *Meine sämtliche Werke*, Berlin, 1922, p. 256; translation in *BRM(E)*, p. 263)

397

Peter Ilitsch Tcshaikovsky's opera "Pique Dame" was performed at the Metropolitan Opera House yesterday afternoon for the first time in this

---

[129]Henry (Kimball) Hadley (1871-1937) - American composer and conductor, he was a significant figure in the growth of American music. He toured Germany with his own works between 1905 and 1909. Among other orchestras, he conducted the Seattle Symphony (1909) and the San Francisco Symphony (1911-1915).

Plate 69. Photograph of the stage for Act I, Scene 1 of *Pique Dame*. (Metropolitan Opera Archives)

country. [130] None of the famous Russian's lyric dramas had hitherto found their way to the American stage. One, "Eugene Onegin," had been given in concert form by Walter Damrosch. [...] Whether the work brought forward yesterday afternoon will suit the taste of this public remains to be seen. That it is a creation of singularly insinuating musical power was sufficiently demonstrated. [...]

Gustav Mahler made his first appearance in the conductor's chair and demonstrated his value by an intelligent and communicative reading of the score.

(*NYS*, March 6, 1910, p. 5)

398

"Pique Dame" in the excellent performance it received, presented itself as an opera above the level of many modern lyric dramas. It is a work of imagination, if not always of the most vigorous invention, supported by a skill in instrumentation, in graphic representation and plastic development of musical material, and with many pages of passionate and melancholy expression such as we have long known in Tcshaikovsky's music for the concert hall. [...]

The new opera is given a handsome and appropriate setting and is enacted with power and appreciation of its less obvious qualities by those chiefly concerned in it. The performance, under Mr. Mahler's direction, especially that of the orchestral score, has remarkable finish, delicacy, and finesse and a strong vitality.

(*NYT*, March 6, 1910, p. 4)

399

So smoothly proceeded the first representation in America of Tschaikowsky's opera "Pique Dame" at the Metropolitan Opera House on Saturday afternoon, March 5, as seen from the front of the house, that the casual observer could never have suspected the strained forces and circumstances which appear to have been masked by the event. Those within earshot of operatic rumors have heard it affirmed that Andreas Dippel has been making the most strenuous efforts to have the "Pique

---

[130]The complete cast was as follows: Hermann - Slezak; Count Tomsky - Didur; Prince Jeletzky - Forsell; Czekalinsky - Otto; Tsurin - Mühlmann; Tschaplitzky - Hall; Narumoff - Ludwig; Countess - Meitschik; Lisa - Destinn; Pauline - Wickham; Governess - Mattfeld; Mascha - Sparkes. Interlude characters: Chloe-Gluck; Daphnis - Wickham; Plutus - Didur. At the subsequent performances, the role of Narumoff was sung by Rehkopf.

Dame" performance a success, and that certain elements of the
"opposition" have been equally concerned that it should be otherwise.
Opera may be art, but it is sometimes forced upon one that it is also
politics and war.

It has also leaked out that there has been a very unpleasant atmosphere
at the rehearsals, and that the players have been loth to respond to Mr.
Mahler's direction.

[...]

(Arthur Farwell in *MA* 11, no. 18, March 12, 1910, p. 1)

400

Florence Wickham,[131] who sang in the Metropolitan's 1910 revival [sic]
of Tchaikovsky's "Pique Dame" under Mahler, recalled the conductor's
somber bearing as more like a minister than a conductor. She spoke of his
thoroughness in rehearsals and the length of them, as he strove for the
perfection he felt the music called for. These sessions were often a strain
on the artists involved. Miss Wickham remembers one young American
singer who cracked under Mahler's discipline and to whom Mahler said,
"If I ever had to conduct you again, I wouldn't be a conductor". Also
Miss Wickham recalled the extreme fear that Emmy Destinn felt towards
Mahler. At one rehearsal she was in such a state of nerves that the
session was broken up by her inability to sing any longer.

(Ardoin, *op. cit.*, p. 162)

401

New Orleans, February 27, 1910

[...] I am now writing a little analysis of *Turandot*[132] for Mahler. I
think I shall be able to hear the rehearsal and the idea refreshes
me. [...]

(Ferruccio Busoni, *Letters to his Wife*, tr. Rosamond Ley, New York,
Da Capo Press, 1975, p. 155 [reprint of the 1938 edition,
London, E. Arnold])

---

[131]Florence Wickham (1880?-1962) - American contralto, sang in England, Germany,
and at the Metropolitan from 1909 to 1912.
[132]Based on Carlo Gozzi's play (1763), Busoni's *Turandot Suite* (begun in 1904,
completed in 1906) was later turned into incidental music for the theatre, and
eventually into an opera (Zurich, 1917). - Krehbiel noted in the programme booklet
that his own comments were based on a free translation and amplification of notes
provided by Busoni.

402

The last of the Thursday evening concerts of the Philharmonic Society took place last evening at Carnegie Hall. The programme embraced Busoni's suite entitled "Turandot," the Brahms Violin Concerto, Debussy's "Afternoon of a Faun", and Strauss's tone poem, "Death and Transfiguration." The solo performer was Fritz Kreisler. The programme was altogether too long. Not even the skill of Gustav Mahler can make continuously interesting a concert which lasts over two hours. [...]

The Busoni suite was well worthy of production and it was very well played. Mr. Busoni modestly remained in the background while Mr. Mahler accepted a half a dozen calls then appeared to take two for himself. [...]

Mr. Kreisler played the [Brahms concerto] with breadth of style but with most communicative emotion. It was one of the truly eloquent readings of this concerto which this town has heard. [...]

The applause for this violin playing was such as it deserved. The accompaniment was good.

(*NYS*, March 11, 1910, p. 9)

403

Boston, March 12, 1910

[...]

What a pity that you did not hear *Turandot* under Mahler. In the end I remained there for the evening; it seemed to me to be unjust towards Mahler to go away. With what love and unerring instinct this man rehearsed! Artistically, and humanly, it was both gratifying and warming.

The performance was perfect, better than all the previous ones, and the success was great. It is true the papers did not wish to take it quite seriously, but the world is full of errors and misunderstandings.

(Busoni, *op. cit.*, p. 161)

404

[New York], March 15, 1910

[...] *Turandot* was a great success. Frau Mahler herself fetched me from the box in which I sat half hidden. "Do go, give Gustav the pleasure". And I went on the platform as shy and "unused to it" as if I had never stood in front of an audience before.

(Busoni, *op. cit.*, p. 162)

405

[New York, March 1910]

Dear Herr Gutmann!

[. . .]

One thing, however, I request of you already now and for all occasions. *Forego all* committee-nonsense and (completely superfluous) publicity. - One doesn't need a committee to mount a concert. And I hate all that and feel *prostituted* by such humbug.

[. . .] Once again, *no committee*! I forbid anything like that!

(Peter Revers, "Gustav Mahler und Emil Gutmann", in *MUB*, p. 75)[133]

406

Gustav Mahler will be the conductor of the music festival organized in his honour at Mannheim. The performance will begin with "Die Meistersinger," which Herr Mahler will conduct. It will be followed by concerts to include the Beethoven symphonies and compositions by the conductor.[134]

(*NYS*, March 13, 1910, 3. section, p. 8)

407

The New York Philharmonic Orchestra gave its second local concert for the season [. . .] last evening, when it was heard in a program consisting of Berlioz's "Symphonie Fantastique" and the "Tannhäuser" overture.

---

[133]This letter (concerning the première of the Eighth Symphony - see next chapter) shows Mahler's fanatical hatred of what to him were superfluous trappings of concert life and organizations. Soon, he was going to have his own problems with the Guarantors' Committee in New York.

[134]As may be seen from two recently published letters to William Ritter, postmarked February 4 and March 17, 1910 (*MUB*, pp. 152f.), a festival in Mannheim had, in fact, been planned, with Mahler clearly the central attraction. (The *MA* had been impressively well informed: already on February 5th [p. 4] it advised its readers that "Mahler has cabled formal acceptance" of the invitation from Mannheim.) The fact that he himself bowed out of such a prestigious event (second letter in *MUB*; see also **415** and **416**) shows the extent to which he must have been exhausted by his first season at the head of the New York Philharmonic.

This was rather an unfortunate selection. Berlioz's work has already been given here this season and as it is not the kind of thing one wants to hear very often, its repetition was in the nature of a superfluity, while the "Tannhäuser" overture has all seasons for its own. Presumably Mr. Mahler wanted to show how differently they would sound as played by him as compared with previous interpretations, but perhaps this demonstration was hardly worth while, and the difference did not prove to be so tremendously important, anyhow.

[. . .] The assisting artist of the evening was Mr. Fritz Kreisler, one of the greatest, if not the greatest absolutely, of living violinists, who was heard in a nobly eloquent interpretation of Beethoven's concerto.

The audience, although considerably larger than last time, was not all it should have been [. . .]

(*Philadelphia Inquirer*, March 15, 1910, p. 8)

408

For someone who had had the privilege of hearing a Philharmonic concert under Mahler in Vienna, the outward aspect of a concert in New York was heart-rending: the audience, the greater part of which came too late and ran off before the end of the concert, the clinical and graceless Carnegie Hall, the cool discipline and austere impersonality of the orchestra (I can with warmth register two exceptions: the outstanding leader Spiering and the excellent horn-player Reiter, who both really understood Mahler). And yet, for those with ears and hearts, performances which are unforgettable! For Mahler was resigned, but his temperament and his strength were untouched - indeed, perhaps even more concentrated and intense [. . .] Mahler still had what made his interpretations so irresistible: he identified himself with the work that he was conducting. I can remember how he positively discovered the "Romantic" Symphony of Bruckner that he was conducting in New York, how he spoke of it as though he had just seen the score for the first time. [. . .]

(Ernst Jokl,[135] "Gustav Mahler in Amerika," *Musikblätter des Anbruch*, vol. 2, no. 7/8 [1920] (Sonderheft Gustav Mahler), p. 290; tr. in *BRM(E)*, pp. 263f.)

---

[135]The identity of Jokl is somewhat of a mystery. In the Metropolitan Opera's prospectus for the 1909-1910 season, published in *MC* (October 6, 1909, p. 29), he is identified as a newly engaged Assistant Conductor. In *HLG3* (p. 677) he is described as a Berlin journalist. He is not listed in any reference work known to me.

409

The Metropolitan Opera Company offered a somewhat belated fulfillment of one of its promises made for last season by producing, last evening, Frederick S. Converse's opera, "The Pipe of Desire"[136]. [. . .] It was the first performance of it in New York, and there was an altogether unusual interest attaching to the occasion because it was the first time that an opera in English had ever been performed at the regular opera season at the Metropolitan Opera House, and also because it was the first opera by an American composer that had ever been set before the subscribers there.[137]

[. . .] Last evening's representation, which was under the direction of Mr. Hertz, counseled by the composer, may very likely have been the first that embodied in anything like completeness Mr. Converse's intentions. The performance was, in fact, an excellent one; it had been prepared with much pains and was carried through with real devotion by all who were concerned in it. [. . .] Everything, in fact, had been done for the opera to set it forth in the most advantageous way.

[. . .]
It was significant that all the members of the cast were American singers except Miss Leonora Sparkes, the first Sylph, who is English. They all entered upon their task with much sincerity, and the performance was excellent.

[. . .]
It was somewhat discouraging to the advocates of opera in English that these English-speaking singers had so little success in making their words understood. Mr. Whitehill achieved the best results in this way; there were long passages delivered by the other chief singers in which little or nothing of the text was intelligible. [. . .]

(*NYT*, March 19, 1910, p. 9)

---

[136]Frederick Shepherd Converse (1871-1940) was an American teacher and composer of neo-Romantic music; he wrote concert, stage and film music. *The Pipe of Desire*, a one-act opera, was composed in 1905, and performed for the first time on January 31, 1906 in Boston.

[137]The "dream" to produce opera in English, partly in order to "aid native American talent" (composers as well as singers), had been a long-standing one with Kahn and his fellow directors of the Metropolitan Opera Company. Although it took some time to make a start on fulfilling them, intentions of this nature were announced even before Gatti-Casazza's actual arrival in New York (see **75**).

410

28 May [sic - March?], 1910[138]

Dear Master and Friend,

I do not know at the moment what chance there is of our meeting again in America - fresh engagements prevent me from returning to New York. But I cannot let you go without taking any farewell [. . .] I thank you for the masterly performance of *Turandot*, for the pleasure it gave me, and for the repetition of it you plan in Rome.

[. . .]

I envy you the 1st of May in Rome. [. . .] But [. . .] I wish you all the joys life can offer. May these wishes accompany you on your voyage and beyond [. . .]

Yours very sincerely,
Ferruccio Busoni

(*AMM*, p. 339; original German in *AME*, p. 466)

411

The final historical concert of the Philharmonic Society took place last night at Carnegie Hall. The programme consisted entirely of orchestral numbers, which were Pfitzner's overture to "Das Christelflein," Anton Bruckner's "Romantic" Symphony in E Flat, the preludes to Act I and II of Richard Strauss's opera "Guntram", and the same composer's "Till Eulenspiegel." [. . .]

The symphony was superbly played and the reading was what might have been expected from Mr. Mahler, whose own music betokens him a sympathizer with the ways of Bruckner.

(*NYS*, March 31, 1910, p. 9)

412

Bruckner's Fourth Symphony [. . .] had not been heard in New York for many years. Anton Seidl first played it here in 1888. Yet last night's performance showed it to be considerably more worth re-hearing than the symphonies of Bruckner that have been played here in recent years. [. . .]

[138]Judging from this letter and from other available evidence, there can be little doubt that Alma had misread its date, and that it must have been written *prior* to the Mahlers' departure for Europe on April 5th. As is evident from his letters to his wife (Busoni, *op. cit.*), Busoni was on an extended tour of the United States at the end of March, and he himself will have returned to Europe by early May. - Mahler did not perform the *Turandot* suite at his concerts in Rome (see next chapter).

Some of this impression was no doubt due to the truly superb interpretation which the symphony received at the hands of Mr. Mahler - a performance that proclaimed even more unmistakably than they have been proclaimed before the mastery and the authority of the conductor. It showed his insight and entire sympathy with Bruckner's music, of which he is a chief exponent, and, as well, the fine skill of the orchestra, which is steadily gaining for itself the right to be called a virtuoso organization. The freedom, breadth, and brilliancy of last night's performance, its many sided eloquence, did much to carry conviction for the music. [. . .]

The instrumentation in this symphony is singularly fine, with effects that are new and striking. And yet it might easily be that this work, which seems so interesting and that really touched and thrilled, as it was played last evening might lose much of its effect in a performance less masterly than Mr. Mahler's.

(*NYT*, March 31, 1910, p. 11)

413

The interesting last historical concert of the Philharmonic Society of New York was given at Carnegie Hall on Wednesday evening, March 30, before what one New York critic called "the smallest audience at a Philharmonic concert in fifty years."

[. . .]

Altogether too little is known in America about Hans Pfitzner.

[. . .] his music does not make an immediate emotional appeal of the usual sort. He writes with a fine sense of the character of the separate instruments, and holds the interest both in this way and by the new and rather peculiar individuality which animates his music, the ideas of which are incisive, cleancut, and imaginative. He has a fine knowledge of development, although he appears sometimes to depend too greatly upon it, the music at places not appearing spontaneously continuous in its flow.

[. . .]

Bruckner has moments of authentic inspiration, true musical outpouring; but something of an old-world flavor is over it all. The wine of life which Bruckner offers has stood a moment too long in the glass. His fundamental ideas are poetic, but they are not of a sufficiently new sort to constitute him a great leader. Every great composer should be epochal in some sense, and as musicianly a composer as Bruckner is, it is still doubtful whether he arrives at this.

[. . .]

(Arthur Farwell in *MA* 11, no. 22, April 9, 1910, p. 25)

414

There were plenty of really perfect performances, and these of course gave [Mahler] great pleasure. [. . .] The Bruckner Symphony in particular Mahler prepared with remarkable care and love. Through a whole series of very skilfully worked-out cuts he relieved the work of its jerky, periodic nature; and he achieved a logical unity which brought out the work's many beauties to an unimaginable degree. The way he made this Bruckner Symphony, and the C major Symphony of Schumann, playable—that is to say, as enjoyable as possible for the listener—seems to be entirely justified [. . .]

(Spiering, *op. cit.*; *BRM(E)*, p. 261; original German in *BRM*, p. 267)

415

Having concluded his first season as the conductor of [the Philharmonic Society], Mahler will leave for Europe, where he hopes to get some rest before returning [. . .] for another season.

"I am much pleased with the results of my work here, " he said. "Things have been as satisfactory as could have been expected. The orchestra has improved from concert to concert, and the attitude of the New York public is always serious and attentive.

"I have made no plans as yet for my concerts for next season, [but] I shall divide the programmes more or less evenly between the classic and the modern schools, and I shall play good music of all nations. [. . .]

"For important novelties, one must turn exclusively to France and Germany, with occasional aid from Russia, Finland, and Bohemia. Debussy has just written something which I may produce next season, and Paul Dukas has almost completed a symphony, which he has promised to let me have as soon as it is done.

"Strauss has told me that henceforth he will write only operas. He said that he is done with symphonic works. [. . .]

"I have already cabled the authorities of the festival at Mannheim that I am too tired to conduct there. There was to have been a season of my works, [. . .] and some other things, but I have had a very hard winter, and a week of hard conducting in May would be too much for me now. I want rest.

"I shall probably not conduct next year at the Metropolitan Opera House. [. . .] There are enough other conductors there now. They do not need me anymore. [. . .]"

"Do you prefer to conduct operas or symphony orchestras?" Mr. Mahler was asked.

"I have no preference. I like to go from one to the other, it is a change."

"Will you write an opera?"

"No, never. I have been in the theatre all my life and have come too close to the operas of other men ever to care to write one. When I compose, I shall devote myself to symphonic works. But I shall not play too many of my compositions here myself. That might be misunderstood. I prefer to bring out the newer works of other composers."

(*NYT*, March 30, 1910, p. 8)

416

The Mahler festival, scheduled to be held at Mannheim this May, has been cancelled. Apropos, a Munich newspaper declares that Mahler is "tired of America," and said recently to a New York journalist: "Musical life in America has in it nothing to attract me permanently, nor to appeal to my artistic aims or principles. I am musically homesick for Germany." If Gustav Mahler ever made such statements to any of our metropolitan reporters, they failed to appear in the columns of the dailies here [. . .].

(*MC* 60, no. 14, April 6, 1910, p. 20)

417

Gustav Mahler, conductor of the New York Philharmonic Orchestra, has made some remarks to a representative of the New York TIMES, which were printed in a recent issue. [. . .]

One thing he said that will be of special interest to Americans is that so many of the modern composers have turned their attention exclusively to opera that the conductor of a symphony orchestra has a difficult time finding new works. If this is the case, was there ever a more divinely appointed moment for attention to the many unheard scores by American composers which are crying out for performance? If the conductor of a symphony orchestra in America is actually put to it to find new works, it would appear that the very first thing for him to do would be to explore the American field thoroughly. If the European conductor of an American orchestra thinks that the best American scores are going to come tumbling over themselves in their eagerness to reach him, and that if they are not brought to him and presented on bended knee they do not exist, he is making a vast mistake.

[. . .]

(Editorial, *MA* 11, no. 22, April 9, 1910, p. 18)

418

Andreas Dippel announced yesterday that he had resigned as administrative manager of the Metropolitan Opera Company and had become general manager of the new Chicago Opera Company [. . .] The executive directors of the Metropolitan Opera Company, in accepting the resignation, wrote in reply that [. . .] they believe that a single head is necessary for the success of any great operatic venture, and in this belief they have conferred complete control in the coming year upon Mr. Gatti-Casazza.

(*NYTrib*, April 2, 1910, p. 7)

419

BOSTON, April 3—That the professional relations of Arturo Toscanini, musical director of the Metropolitan Opera Company, and Leo Slezak, the tenor, are far from amicable developed during the visit of the company here last week.

Mr. Slezak was booked to appear last night in "Die Meistersinger" [. . .] However, he did not sing. [. . .]

It is well understood here, that Mr. Slezak's failure to appear was the culmination of certain difficulties in existence for some time between Mr. Slezak and Mr. Toscanini, and that, preceding last evening's performance Mr. Toscanini stated, simply but emphatically, that he would not conduct if Mr. Slezak sang.

It was also said to be the case that Mr. Toscanini refused to conduct when Miss Farrar sang on Tuesday evening.

[. . .]

(*MA* 11, no. 22, April 9, 1910, p. 1)

420

The Philharmonic Society's series of Beethoven concerts came to a conclusion yesterday afternoon at Carnegie Hall, when the "Choral Fantasia" and the Ninth Symphony were performed. The same compositions will be repeated tonight, and then the concerts of the organization's season will be completed. For yesterday's entertainment Mr. Mahler secured the services of Corinne Rider-Kelsey[139] and Viola

---

[139]Corinne Rider-Kelsey (1877-1947) - American soprano, active in opera and oratorio. She sang chiefly in England and in the United States.

Waterhouse, sopranos; Janet Spencer,[140] contralo; Dan Beddoe[141] and Paul Duffault, tenors, and Herbert Watrous, bass. The choral force was that of the Bach Choir of Montclair.

[. . .]

The piano part [in the "Choral Fantasia"] was played with lovely spirit, with finish of style, with richness and warmth of color and with find understanding by Ernest Hutcheson,[142] who has never given a better demonstration of his art in this city.

The orchestral part of the work was given with clarity, balance and precision and soloists and chorus contributed good singing to the ensemble. Mr. Mahler's reading was reposeful and continent and the impression left after the performance was one of beneficient beauty.

The playing of the symphony was less satisfactory. Here the conductor's fondness for accentuation of details and his originality in the regulation of tempi produced results not altogether grateful. Again, he called so insistently upon the brass and the wood for much tone that balance was often wanting. There were fine and inspiring moments in the performance, as in the coda of the first movement, but the general impression was disappointing.

In the choral movement Mr. Mahler showed a disposition to be considerate of his singers, and for this they doubtless were grateful. But whether Beethoven's intent is to be reached in this way is a matter which will at least admit of discussion. [. . .]

(*NYS*, April 2, 1910, p. 5)

421

Mr. Mahler's reading of the Ninth Symphony is remembered from the performance of it he gave at the close of last season at an extra concert of the Philharmonic Society. It is in many respects a deeply stirring performance, and it is in every measure profoundly interesting, keeping the listener's attention tense, beguiling him with its beauty and poetry, thrilling him with its dramatic power. It is marked by intensity of expression, and in many passages by a wonderful eloquence in the plastic

---

[140]Janet Spencer (1864?-1948) - American concert and oratorio singer (alto), Geraldine Farrar's close friend. She was one of the early recording artists for Victor.
[141]Dan Beddoe (1863?-1937) - Welsh-born tenor, chiefly active as an oratorio singer. He was a member of the Oratorio Society of New York from 1905 to 1933.
[142]Ernest Hutcheson (1871-1951) - Prominent Australian pianist and teacher; held leading positions at the Peabody Conservatory and the Juilliard School of Music. In 1910, he published a *Guide* for the first performance of *Elektra* in New York.

treatment of the phrase, the tracing of the melodic line, the pulsing rhythm. The most characteristic qualities of Mr. Mahler's interpretation are to be found in the last movement, in which he brings out the potent dramatic quality, the variety, and contrast of the music, at the same time preserving the unity of the idea that underlies it. [. . .]

Mr. Mahler's reading is unquestionably one that has certain excesses, at times of a tumultuous order; but they do not result from a seeking after sensation for its own sake. They are clearly intended to give what he considers to be the insistent, overpowering effect of Beethoven's music, even in their most uncompromising moments. Thus he uses for some passages two pairs of kettledrums, which make a noise that passes beyond the bounds of musical effect. Elsewhere he accentuates the stroke of the drums with nerve-racking results, as in the scherzo, especially at the very beginning, where the rhythm is marked as by the shots of a rifle. Nor does Mr. Mahler hesitate in many other places to revise and reinforce the orchestration of Beethoven, as it is the custom of conductors in these days to do. There may well be a question whether this is not carried to excess, though in not a few passages there are good reasons for doing it.

[. . .]

(*NYT*, April 2, 1910, p. 11)

422

It was my privilege to sing under Gustav Mahler's baton twice in performances of Beethoven's Ninth Symphony.

[. . .]

Mahler's keenly sensitive musical understanding and his broad comprehension of musical art were patent to any one who had the good fortune to be associated with him.

[. . .]

(Dan Beddoe in *SFM*, pp. 4f.)

423

Character Sketch of the
Philharmonic Orchestra's Conductor

To those who have attended the concerts of the Philharmonic Orchestra, or who have been present at one of the performances of "Pique Dame" at the Metropolitan Opera House, the figure of Gustav Mahler must have come to be the symbol of concentrated nervous energy. No one who has ever seen him at his position in the conductor's stand can forget his slight, almost emaciated, figure, his fine, dome-shaped head, his crown of black hair slightly tinged with grey, every strand of which, erect, self-supporting, appears charged with the full force of the energy which animates the man himself. Whether conducting the rehearsal of his orchestra, or in command of the ensemble of a Wagner opera performance, there can be no doubt as to who is absolute master both over the musicians and over the prima donnas on the stage. Gustav Mahler realizes that one mind, one spirit, must animate a performance; that a great work of art can be adequately expressed only by the complete unity of the exponent parts.

Yet what Mr. Mahler says regarding his conception of the place of a conductor may well be pondered on by those who confuse tyranny with authority.

"Of course," he says, "the conductor must always be the master mind of any performance, but he must always realize that he is only a part of a great whole. In opera especially, various singers have various peculiarities. [. . .] The conductor must be a man of broad sympathies, he must be able to look beyond his own personality and realize that we live in a world of limitations.

"A conductor's baton is not a club with which to chastise singers, but rather a wand to lead them in the proper paths." [. . .]

The energy that inspires Mr. Mahler was manifest last week, when a Tribune representative visited him in his apartment in the Hotel Savoy. Mr. Mahler was alone at the time, and he was forced to answer his doorbell a dozen times during the course of the interview. A father arrived who wished the conductor to hear his son play the cello; packages kept coming; telephone calls galore regarding rehearsals, and from persons who wanted interviews - yet, though he answered them all, he never seemed out of patience. [. . .]

Mr. Mahler does not believe in dogmatic criticism, and he says so emphatically. [. . .]

"I am absolutely opposed to dogma in criticism," he said. "You cannot limit anything absolutely. The radical of today is the conservative of tomorrow. What really counts is genuine self-expression. It is this that interests me. If a man writes a composition that is sincere, no matter if it breaks the old rules, that man must be admired."

In this connection, Mr. Mahler shows little patience with those who call much modern music, notably that of Richard Strauss, decadent.

"How can we tell what is decadent?" he said, rather heatedly. "When a man produces something new, something that surprises the conservatives, it is immediately branded as decadent. I admire Strauss, I admire Debussy. They have done something original. Fifty years from now perhaps we can tell whether or not they are decadent. But we are too near to that time to tell now." [. . .]

Mr. Mahler's own sincerity is proven by his remarks upon the music-loving public. He does not flatter, nor does he mince words.

"The truly musical section of the public is very small," he said. "After all, the public as a whole is, in all countries, uneducated, even stupid. The opera is patronised largely by people who want to make a noise, to be seen, to hear a song or two, to watch the ballet, and then to talk some more. The concert-going public is comparatively small. Yet I do not think the opera vitiates the taste of this public." [. . .]

Mr. Mahler is a good deal of a philosopher. His philosophy extends even to the way he looks upon his appellation of a Bohemian composer.

"I am always called a Bohemian," he said. "I read it everywhere. Yet I am not. I am a German. It is true that I was born in Bohemia, but of German parents. It is also true that I admire Smetana. Yet I admire also Debussy, and that does not make me a Frenchman. Still, I have [not] denied that I am a Bohemian. I have said to myself if people want to call me a Bohemian, why I shall let them call me a Bohemian! Yet I am really a German."

(NYTrib, April 3, 1910, Part Five, p. 2)

424

"[Mahler] spoke very little if any English, as I remember"', Reinshagen[143] says, "but of course at that time the orchestra was very largely German. He was a frail little man, about five foot seven I would guess. We used to say he was Mahler from the neck up because the rest of him was not very prepossessing. He would drag one leg a little and we liked to say he had a five/four walk. I must say this though, his wife was one of the most beautiful women I have ever seen".

(Roddy, op. cit., p.33)

425

The concluding concert of the sixty-eighth season of the Philharmonic Society took place last evening in Carnegie Hall, and another season there will be marked change in the policy and plans of this, the oldest organization of its kind in America. In place of thirty-three [sic] concerts—which were given in New York this year—there will be thirty-

---

[143]Herman Reinshagen was a double bass player with the Philharmonic.

one in future. Both the historical and the Beethoven cycles, begun this year by Gustav Mahler, are to be discontinued. There is a strong desire on the part of the directors of the Society to have fewer repetitions of compositions hereafter and to that end every effort will be bent on securing new musical material, and in so arranging the next season's programmes that there will be no unnecessary duplications.[144] [...]

Although the season brought a heavy deficit—the estimates being about $90,000—it was expected. With the changes to be installed and the artistic progress the orchestra made during its first year under Mr. Mahler, it is the belief of those in charge of the Philharmonic destinies that its future is bright. Felix F. Leifels is to be business manager next year, and he will be in entire control of the business affairs of the organization.[145] [...]

Said Manager Leifels yesterday: "[...] Our services are in demand out of New York. In consequence, the directors of the Philharmonic have decided to widen the scope of operations beginning next fall, and it is the present intention of giving several times the number of concerts out of the city than were held this year."

"[...] I am pleased with what we have accomplished this year, which is our first in our reconstructed form," said Mr. Mahler yesterday. "We have had many changes among our playing membership which were necessary, and that has acted as a sort of handicap in perfecting the orchestra as an instrument. Nevertheless, I am well-pleased with the progress the men have made, and I believe that the Philharmonic's rank, today, is one which we may point to with what you call pride. Still, in our endeavour to make the orchestra perfect, I shall make further changes another season. It is too early now to go into details about the plans for the coming season. There is plenty of time for that. For the present, I shall go away to Europe to spend the summer."

(*NYW*, April 3, 1910, Metropolitan Section, p. M5)

426

That important changes will be made in the policy of the New York Philharmonic Society by next season was learned when the society closed its season with a concert in Carnegie Hall, Saturday evening, April 2. The entire business management of the orchestra next year will be in the hands of Felix F. Leifels, who has been secretary of the society

---

[144]It is quite clear from this article that the meddling by the "directors of the Society" (*i.e.*, the Guarantors) in the purely musical decision making process was well under way at the end of the first season (s.a. Note 133).
[145]At least for the time being, this did not turn out to be the case (see **433**).

for several years. Richard Arnold, for twenty-five years concertmaster, and who has more recently divided the business management with Mr. Leifels, will discontinue his duties in this department.

[...]

The artistic results of the season were satisfactory to the directors, and the financial deficit was not more than expected. Nevertheless, the losses were heavy, reaching a total estimated at about $75,000.

(*MA* 11, no. 22, April 9, 1910, p. 1)

427

[April 3, 1910]

Dear Herr Leifels,

As I leave the day after tomorrow (Tuesday), it is quite important that we have another talk before then. Therefore, I should like to ask that you come to see me around 9:30 tomorrow morning. I have just received a definitive negative reply from the flautist in Chicago.

I have asked the Committee to agree to my leaving on the 18th on the Kaiser Wilhelm, so that I would arrive here only on the 24th. If the Committee is agreeable, I would ask you most kindly to secure for my return trip the same cabins I now have for the crossing.

With best regards
Mahler[146]

428

Gustav Mahler, the orchestral conductor of the Philharmonic Society, sailed yesterday on the steamship Kaiser Wilhelm II, of the North German Lloyd Line. He was accompanied by his wife and daughter. Mr. Mahler said that he would spend the summer with his family in the mountains, after visiting Paris, Rome, and Vienna. He expects, he said, to compose some music, which he hopes may be heard in Philharmonic concerts here this fall.

(*NYTrib*, April 6, 1910, p. 7)

429

THEODORE SPIERING has been signed for another year as concertmaster of the Philharmonic Society, a post he filled this winter

---

[146]For the German text, see Appendix, A39.

with uncommon mastery and success. The string section of the organization was one of its striking merits. Mr. Spiering assisted Gustav Mahler recently in selecting new string players for the Philharmonic, as substitutes for those not to be re-engaged. It is the ambition of the concertmaster to make the string part of the orchestra as nearly impeccable as possible.

(*MC* 60, no. 14, April 6, 1910, p. 20)

430

BERLIN, April 8—According to the *Boersen Zeitung*, Gustav Mahler, upon his return within a few days to Berlin, will sign a five years' contract with "The Grand Opera," a new private undertaking, the plans of which include the erection of an opera house at an early date. The paper adds that Mr. Mahler will complete his contract as director of the Philharmonic Orchestra of New York, and then settle permanently in Berlin.

(*MA* 11, no. 23, April 16, 1910, p. 1)

431

The report of the director of the New York Public Library for 1909, for the first time in the history of the institution, calls attention, through a carefully prepared table of statistics, to the circulation of its musical works. At present the library contains 6,919 volumes of scores, divided as follows: Operas, 3,180; oratorios and church music, 654; songs and choruses, 1,514; piano, 1,158; organ, 81; other instruments, 332. These figures are exclusive of the music reference library at the Lenox branch, which will be housed in the building now being erected at Forty-second street and Fifth avenue. [. . .]

The table showing total circulation of scores in 1909 by branches is of interest, and important in a study of artistic conditions in this country. [. . .]

At the Lenox branch 4,556 volumes of music and music literature were consulted for reference during 1909. [. . .] Only books on history, genealogy and law surpassed books on music in the figures showing consultation. [. . .]

(*MA* 11, no. 23, April 16, 1910, p. 15)

432

AN AGREEMENT, made and entered into as of this 26th day of April, in the year one thousand nine hundred and ten, between OSCAR HAMMERSTEIN, of the City of New York ([. . .] the "Vendor"), party of the first part; ARTHUR HAMMERSTEIN, of the same place, party of the second part, and EDWARD T. STOTESBURY,[147] of the City of Philadelphia [. . .] ([. . .] the "Purchaser"), party of the third part.

[. . .]

IT IS AGREED between the parties hereto as follows:

[. . .]

SECOND: For the purpose of assuring the good-will of said business unto the Purchaser and his assigns, the Vendor and the party of the second part hereby jointly and severally covenant with the purchaser and his assigns and with the Metropolitan Opera Company and its assigns [. . .] that they will not [. . .] at any time hereafter within ten years from this date hereof, be or become, directly or indirectly, engaged or interested in or connected with [. . .] in the cities of New York, Boston, Philadelphia or Chicago[148] [. . .] the business of producing grand opera or any of the operas named in Schedule "A" hereto annexed, in any language or any opera, operetta or comic opera that has ever been produced at the Metropolitan Opera House or the Manhattan Opera House in the City of New York, or any operetta or comic opera that may at any time hereafter have been first given at the Metropolitan Opera House or at any opera house in the City of New York, and that no opera, operetta or comic opera of the character described will be permitted or suffered to be produced upon the premises now occupied by the Manhattan Opera House within five years from the date hereof [. . .]

Nothing herein contained shall, however, be construed to prevent the Vendor or the party of the second part from engaging in the business of producing musical comedies [. . .]

[147]Edward Townsend Stotesbury (1849-1938) - Banker and patron of the arts, he was an officer and director of the Metropolitan in Philadelphia. He formed and headed a syndicate to buy out Hammerstein.

[148]In a power of attorney on April 15, 1910, Oscar Hammerstein authorized his son to extend his renouncing of opera production for 10 years to "any part of the United States". The final clause, and all other prohibitions and permissions in the signed agreement were negotiated by Arthur Hammerstein (Cone, *op. cit.*, p. 370). (S.a. **350** and **354**).

FOURTH: The Purchaser will pay to the Vendor and the party of the second part [. . .] the sum of One million two hundred thousand dollars [. . .]

SIXTH: [. . .] It is understood that the Metropolitan Opera Company is interested with the Purchaser in the subject-matter of this agreement, that all the covenants hereof [. . .] are intended to enure to the benefit of the Metropolitan Opera Company, and may be enforced by it as though it were named herein as a party hereto.

[. . .]

(Cone, *op cit.*, pp. 356-364)

433

The Philharmonic Society [. . .] announces the appointment of Loudon Charlton[149] as manager of the Philharmonic Orchestra. The object in view in placing this time-honored organization into professional and experienced hands is an immediate broadening of the scope of the orchestra's activities, both in New York and outside cities. [. . .]

The advent of Gustav Mahler as conductor, a year ago, and the re-establishment of the orchestra upon a permanent basis of twenty-three weeks of daily rehearsal or performance, has raised the organization to a standard that makes it possible for Mr. Charlton to assume executive control and establish a business system calculated to keep the Philharmonic well in the front rank of the great orchestras of the world.

(*MA* 11, no. 25, April 30, 1910, p. 5)

---

[149]Loudon Charlton (1869-1931) - Starting as a concert manager in 1899 in New York, Charlton went on to represent such celebrities as Nordica and Gabrilovitch (s.a. Note 74, Chapter II).

CHAPTER IV

The 1910-1911 Season

Commentary

For the second year in a row, the Mahlers' European holiday began with a brief sojourn in Paris. On this occasion, however, their visit was primarily for professional reasons: the first performance in France of the Second Symphony on April 17, 1910. The work, conducted by the composer himself, found considerable success with the public, and was reasonably well received by the critics. But as an omen of the upheavals to come in the summer, the occasion was seriously marred for Mahler when Debussy, Dukas and Gabriel Pierné[1] walked out of the concert.

From Paris Mahler travelled to Rome where he was scheduled to conduct three concerts. Because of difficulties with a less than adequate, and apparently highly uncooperative orchestra, only the first two concerts—on April 28th and May 1st—were given, while the third one, scheduled for May 5th, was cancelled.

Aside from brief absences for preparatory rehearsals in Vienna, Leipzig and Munich for the first performance of the Eighth Symphony,

---

[1]Henri Constant Gabriel Pierné (1863-1937) - French organist, conductor and composer; pupil of Massenet and Franck. He was conductor of the Concerts Colonne from 1910 to 1932.

Mahler spent most of the last summer of his life in Toblach, and celebrated his fiftieth birthday there. Early in the summer, Alma felt compelled once again to take a rest cure:

> I took Mahler to Toblach and then, following medical advice, I had to go to Tobelbad to cure my bad nerves. [...] I was very ill, and could simply not continue - the wear and tear of being driven on without respite by a spirit so intense as his had brought me to a complete breakdown.[2]

This rest cure was cut short, however, because of the dramatic impact on Alma of her first meeting with Walter Gropius, the architect who was to become her second husband. Gropius's pursuit of Alma, her initial resistance,[3] and Mahler's eventual involvement in the affair are amply chronicled in Alma's memoirs and elsewhere. Suffice it to say here that it was undoubtedly this episode that brought to Mahler the conscious realization that his marriage, which had been in one way or another troubled from the beginning, was on the brink of collapse. By August, Mahler was ready to seek the help of his famous compatriot, Sigmund Freud.

Although we do not know the precise extent of Mahler's familiarity with Freud's work, it is clear from at least one contemporary report that he did not hold it in high esteem.[4] But now, his desperation drove him to consult Freud on August 26th, during the latter's holiday at Leyden in Holland. Although the meeting was a brief one, it uncovered the expected springs of the couple's difficulties: Gustav's mother fixation, Alma's seeking of a father image, and so on.[5]

---

[2]*AMM*, p. 172, with additional translation by Z. Roman; original German text in *AME*, p. 210.

[3]The suspicion—always there—that Alma's "resistance" did not endure for long has been confirmed by the recent publication of the pertinent correspondence between he and Gropius (Reginald R. Isaacs, *Walter Gropius, der Mensch und sein Werk*, Volume 1, Berlin, Mann, 1983). For a detailed description of the affair, see *HLG3*, pp. 773ff. *et passim*.

[4]Klaus Pringsheim recorded a conversation from the summer of 1907 in which Freud's name was mentioned: "Mahler's reaction was a momentary silence; the subject of psychoanalysis did not interest him. Then he said, with a dismissive gesture, 'Freud . . . he attempts to cure everything from a single point'." (Quoted in *BRM(E)*, p. 266; original German text in *BRM*, p. 272.)

[5]A brief account of the encounter is in Ernest Jones, *Siegmund Freud - Life and Work*, Volume 2, London, The Hogarth Press, 1955, pp. 88f. For a selected list of the subsequent psychoanalytical literature, see *HLG3*, p. 754, Note 193.

Plate 70. Sigmund Freud. (*HLG3*, Illustration 55)

375

According to Alma her husband, while apparently able to gain a certain amount of relief from his interview with Freud, was skeptical about the particulars of the "diagnosis".[6] Both states of mind are evident in a telegram he sent to Alma from Leyden: "I am happy. The interview was interesting, mountains made out of molehills. [. . .]"[7]

The summer of 1910 appears to have been an unusually unproductive one for Mahler as concerns the writing of new music. In all likelihood, he worked only intermittently on the sketches and drafts of the Tenth Symphony. This was partly due to the work which resulted from a newly concluded, major publishing agreement with Universal Edition, and was no doubt exacerbated by the marital crisis. As is implied by his letter to Hertzka (see **440**), Mahler was also occupied with an apparently wide-ranging search of the musical literature for the Philharmonic programmes of the upcoming season. It is not unreasonable to conjecture, though, that an important cause of the relative lack of compositional activity lay in the mounting excitement and enormously complicated and time-consuming preparations for the première of the Eighth Symphony.

Mahler went to Munich at the beginning of September to take charge of the final rehearsals which brought together the 1,000-plus performers from three cities. His letters written from there to Alma (who was to follow him later) depict graphically the febrile state of mind, and the alternating bouts of elation and anxiety which characterized the last eight or nine days of preparation. Musical preparations had been going on for months, and were directed by such close friends and eminent musicians as Bruno Walter. The actual 'staging' of the performance was designed by Alfred Roller. Nevertheless, the sound of this overwhelming work was something that even the composer could not imagine completely but had to await in the realization. The moment of arrival at this point, that brief suspension of time that precedes the first public hearing of a much-discussed and eagerly awaited new work was admirably captured by the impresario Emil Gutmann, whose role in and contribution to this 'happening' was secondary only to Mahler's:

As Mahler stepped on the podium in the semidarkness of the enormous hall, where the black mass of the audience merged with the

[6]*AME*, p. 175.
[7]*ELM*, p. [905].

black and white mass of the performers, everyone sensed that a primordial, fully formed and vital being had just been given a heart which was about to start beating. In this moment, there were no singers and no listeners, no instruments and no sounding boards, only one single body, with many, many veins and nerves, that was waiting to have the blood and breath of art course through it. Under no one else has there been such a complete readiness of all for art, for the art work and the reception of art. The name and purpose of this body was the concept of the communality of art!

And Mahler began to beat with this baton - animating blood throbbed rhythmically through his body, and for the first time humanity, massed on the sacred heights, brought forth the ardent cry: "Veni creator spiritus!"[8]

The two performances on September 12th and 13th were heard not only by Mahler's close friends and colleagues, but also by many leading social, intellectual and artistic personalities of the day. Even though his reputation as a composer had been increasing gratifyingly for a number of years, the Eighth Symphony brought Mahler unprecedented public and critical acclaim.

It was almost inevitable that the emotional and physical strain associated with the triumph in Munich should exert its toll on Mahler's strength and health. While one may, perhaps, suspect Adler of exaggerating his report on Mahler's state prior to his final departure for America (see **449**), it is clear from Alma's memoirs and from his letters to her from there that Mahler was, in fact, in poor health in Munich. Concern about a throat infection—an especially serious ailment because of his heart condition—continued even after the Mahlers' return to Austria in mid-September. The impression of poor health created by Mahler in Munich is also confirmed by neutral observers who were present at the première of the Eighth Symphony.[9]

This autumn, the Mahlers departed from different ports: he sailed

---

[8]"Gustav Mahler als Organisator," in *MUB*, p. 91; Gutmann's essay—constituting a eulogy—was first published in *Die Musik* 10, no. 18 (June 1911), pp. 364-368.
[9]For example, Henry Ellis Wooldridge, the English writer on music, entered this in his diary in Munich: "M[ahler] looks so ill we hardly knew him. Alma says bad heart prognosis poor." (Quoted in David Wooldridge, *From the Steeples and Mountains - A Study of Charles Ives*, New York, Knopf, 1974, p. 206.)

Plate 71. Mahler rehearsing the Eighth Symphony in the Exhibition Hall in Munich, September 1910. (*HLG3*, Illustration 60)

from Bremen on October 18th, while she boarded the ship a day later at Cherbourg.[10] They arrived in New York on the 25th.

A number of press reports published in the spring had implied that the number of concerts played by the Philharmonic would be reduced for the 1910-1911 season (see **425**). It is clear from the extant documents, however, that now Mahler was faced with an even greater workload than before (see **437**). These documents also indicate that the pertinent decisions in this respect had been taken by the Philharmonic's management without consulting Mahler. The ill-feelings created by such actions, and the subsequent compromise mediated by Samuel Untermeyer, unquestionably contributed to what was a very rapid deterioration of the relationship between Mahler and the directors of the orchestra.[11]

As concerns Mahler's actual workload for the partial season that he was able to complete between November 1, 1910 and February 21, 1911, the available evidence yields the following statistics. Out of the scheduled 63 concerts, Mahler conducted a total of 46; 32 of these were given in New York, 5 in Brooklyn, and 9 on tours to Pittsburgh, Cleveland, Buffalo, Rochester, Syracuse, Utica, Philadelphia, Washington and Hartford. Once again, we have no indication of the number of rehearsals that were necessary in the course of the season. However, secondary information does not bear out Alma's implication that Mahler's workload was lighter this season because

---

[10]Today, this separate boarding no longer appears puzzling: it has been arranged, no doubt by Alma, to allow her to meet Gropius in Paris (in fact, already on the train there; see *HLG3*, as cited in Note 3 above).

[11]Documents **437**, **442** and **446** illustrate the successive stages of Mahler's disagreement with the new (business) management of the orchestra with respect to the number of concerts to be conducted by him during the 1910-1911 season, and the relationship of his contract to this disagreement. The final disposition of the matter is recorded in the Minutes of the Guarantors' Committee on January 4, 1911. The arbitrator (Samuel Untermeyer) ruled in favour of Mahler, awarding him the additional salary of $5,000 he had demanded as compensation for the concerts he would have to conduct in excess of the number stipulated in his contract. Having won, Mahler now accepted a compromise settlement, and "consented, at the suggestion of Mr. Untermeyer, to reduce his claim to $3,000. - This sum to be paid Mr. Mahler on March 1st and Mr. Mahler to be accorded the privilege of leaving for Europe on March 29th, or three days before the expiration of his contract." (The Minutes are in the ANYP; this excerpt is quoted with their kind permission.) Ironically, the last clause of the agreement (in the meantime changed to the 30th of March, probably because of the schedule of sailings) was to be rendered meaningless in a few weeks by the onset of Mahler's final illness.

"a new [programme] had only to be rehearsed every third week and more use was made of each."[12] By February 21st, Mahler had conducted 94 works by 38 composers, compared to 97 works and 33 composers for the entire 1909-1910 season. Moreover, no fewer than 73 works by 17 composers were new to Mahler's partial 1910-1911 season![13]

While the average number of concerts per week for the 16 weeks directed by Mahler was just under three, in this season, too, the distribution of the workload was uneven. In the period from January 3rd to February 3rd Mahler conducted 15 concerts; this amounted to nearly one third of his entire season, and considerably exceeded the workload of even the busiest period of the preceding year. The week of January 22nd, with concerts on Sunday and Friday in New York, and on Monday and Tuesday in Philadelphia and Washington, respectively, compares well with the busiest week of a year earlier. In the current season, however, one week (that of December 4th) saw no fewer than six concerts, all of them out of town and in different cities. As if to compensate for such an onerous schedule, for the rest of December (that is, between the 11th and the 31st) Mahler had to conduct only five more times, and only one concert was given during the week of the 18th. Nonetheless, in retrospect it appears inevitable that Mahler, in less than ideal condition after a physically and spiritually exhausting summer and autumn, would sooner or later succumb to an illness, the onset and rapid development of which was aided by his sustained exertions in an inhospitable climate.

As if they had also begun to suffer from overwork arising from the increased number of concerts, there was a gradual, and eventually quite noticeable, decline in the percentage of Philharmonic concerts reviewed in detail by the leading critics. Although there was a slight falling off in the number of new compositions introduced by Mahler in this season, and a slightly greater incidence of repeated performances of some works, it is unlikely that these two factors alone would have brought about this situation. For want of concrete evidence, we can only speculate that the decline was also due to a loss of novelty as concerned Mahler's personality, as well as to an

---

[12]*AMM*, p. 183; original German text in *AME*, pp. 223f.
[13]See Note 12, Chapter III.

alienating atmosphere resulting from the increasingly troubled relationship between conductor and management.

Three quarters of the programme of the season-opening pair of concerts on November 1 and 4, 1910 was made up of works new to the Philharmonic's repertoire under Mahler; in fact, one half of it was conducted by him for the first time at these concerts. The single exception was a work that was one of the most popular of the previous season: the concert opened with Mahler's Bach Suite, with "Mr. Mahler at the harpsichord". According to the programme notes (which now prominently featured the legend "Management Loudon Charlton"), this work was included in the programme "by request". Unlike that of the previous year, the critical reception of the first concert was decidedly mixed. Although the playing of the orchestra was praised, the concert was found to be too long and noisy (*Tribune*), while Mahler's interpretation of Schubert's C major Symphony was received with considerable skepticism (*Sun* and *Times*). However, from Krehbiel's summary of the week it appears that revamping the concert schedule would be to the benefit of the Philharmonic, as "a large and entirely new audience has been drawn to its support - one that evidently approves the idea of the increased number of concerts and is free and eager to attend them."

Mahler's own music was heard for the first time in this Philharmonic season at the third pair of the regular subscription concerts on November 22nd and 25th (having been previewed, as it were, on the 20th in Brooklyn): Alma Gluck sang the second of the *Lieder eines fahrenden Gesellen* and "Rheinlegendchen". These songs were accepted quite readily by the critics - even if Krehbiel deprecated them as a "delightful intermezzo". Perhaps for that reason, on this occasion he seemed satisfied to print only the song texts (in English) in the programme notes, without commenting on the fact. It is interesting to note that Aldrich, who had already heard "Rheinlegendchen" a month earlier with piano accompaniment (see **454**), was now expressing some doubt about the value of an orchestral accompaniment for "songs of this sort".

Not surprisingly, the intrigues evolving in Vienna around this time, precipitated by the untimely resignation of Felix Weingartner (who had been Mahler's immediate successor at the Imperial Opera), and the subsequent appointment of a non-conducting director, also touched Mahler. While it is clear from his letters to Moll and Freund that he was, at most, only remotely interested, the rumours linking him with the affair were duly reported in the New York musical press (see **443** and **469**).

The fourth pair of regular subscription concerts presented the audience with what Aldrich described as a "surprise". In point of fact, Mahler was simply continuing in the spirit of the previous season's "historical" series when he presented Mozart's G minor Symphony (K.V. 550) in an orchestration that he considered truer to its own period. Aldrich's review of the concert of November 29th provides not only an account of Mahler's alterations, but also a good insight into the generous nature of this broadminded—even if, in this instance, slightly skeptical—critic.

Alma tells us that Mahler intensely disliked the upheaval and discomfort associated with playing away from New York. Still, the six-day tour that opened on December 6th in Pittsburgh cannot but have had its moments of deep satisfaction for him. Critics and audiences alike received him in a manner befitting his reputation as one of the greatest orchestral conductors of the time.

Even though de Koven had bemoaned the "atmosphere of lassitude and depression"—caused, according to him, by the recent demise of the Manhattan Opera—at the opening of the new opera season in November (see **467**), New Yorkers were not, in fact, condemned to an entire year bereft of operatic excitement. While Mahler was on tour with the Philharmonic, the first major operatic world première in North America took place on December 10th at the Metropolitan with Puccini's *La fanciulla del West*. Although the capturing of such an event—typically reserved heretofore for the major European houses—by the Metropolitan was undoubtedly due in part to the presence there of such eminent artists as Toscanini and Caruso, it also testified to the increasing international respect commanded by New York as a musical city of importance. As if to reaffirm the promise of equality pledged by Gatti-Casazza to the German 'side' of the Metropolitan company in 1908, a second world première took place less than three weeks later, on December 28th. On this occasion, Humperdinck's *Königskinder* was given under the baton of Alfred Hertz, who had reassumed his position as the chief German conductor when Mahler left the Metropolitan.

It was early in the new year that rumours about the uncertainty of Mahler's position at the head of the Philharmonic began to circulate. Although the Society issued denials at regular intervals (a practice that was to continue until late March!), it is clear from the extant documents (*e.g.*, **499**) that discussions concerning his replacement had begun as early as December, 1910 - that is, around the time of Mahler's letter to Gutmann (see **497**), in which he expressed his certainty about another season in New York.

On January 17th and 20th, Mahler conducted one of his own works in New York for the last time. This pair of subscription concerts was devoted to an "All-Modern Programme" and presented Mahler's Fourth Symphony, flanked by Pfitzner's *Das Kätchen von Heilbronn* overture and Strauss's *Ein Heldenleben*. The Fourth Symphony had been Mahler's first work performed in New York in 1904. Yet this occasion—unremarked by the critics—was a première of sorts, even for the composer. He had thoroughly revised the orchestration during the summer and autumn, and the work was now heard for the first time in its new guise.[14]

Mahler was well pleased with the new sound of his Fourth Symphony (see **529**); so, apparently, was the audience. Most of the critics, however, found fault with one aspect or another of the work. De Koven's unhappiness moved him to mount a wholesale attack on "modern" (especially Germanic) music. Even Aldrich, in a column otherwise written with his accustomed combination of erudition and civility, appeared baffled by the "enigmatical qualities" (a description echoed by most of his colleagues) of the work: it is "one way" in which "it is hard to take this symphony seriously."

By this time of the season, declining attendance at some of the Philharmonic Society's concerts was once again becoming a matter for concern to the directors. Possibly to rekindle public interest, the back of the January 17/20th programme booklet carried a "Special Announcement", "Another Cycle within the regular series - Five National Programmes with Great Soloists". These were to be "English-American", "Romantic (Italian, Spanish and French)", "Living Composers", "Norse-Slavic", and "All-German" programmes; a soloist was named for all but the Romantic programme.

When the Special Announcement reappeared on the back of the programme booklet for February 5th (a Sunday concert, rather than one of the regular series), the "Romantic" concert had been changed

---

[14]For a history of the revisions of the Fourth Symphony, see the "Revisionsbericht" of the critical edition (*Gustav Mahler - Sämtliche Werke - Kritische Gesamtausgabe*, Volume 4, Vienna, Universal Edition and Internationale Gustav Mahler Gesellschaft, 1963).

to an "Italian" one, now with a soloist indicated. While we do not have direct evidence for this, such a change in programme plans already publicized may well prove Alma's contention (see **525** and **530**) that the Guarantors' Committee was now actively interfering with Mahler's programming. The case of the pair of regular subscription concerts on February 14th and 17th (in fact, the first one of the "Special" series, devoted to "English-American" music, although, curiously, this is not noted on the programme booklet) may be indicative of a tug-of-war between Mahler and the administration. According to Krehbiel in his review of the concert, Chadwick's "Melpomene" overture "was on the programme till a week ago, off when the house bills and descriptive notes were printed [it was not included in the programme previewed in the *Tribune* on February 12th], and on again by means of a special proclamation in red when the concert was given" (*NYTrib*, February 18, 1911, p. 7). The "special proclamation" appears added at the bottom of the programme booklet's front page; it announced that the addition—to an already overlong programme—of the overture, and of the fourth of Elgar's *Sea Pictures* to the three originally scheduled, was "in response to a general request." Whatever the truth may have been in specific instances of programme changes, it may be noted that on February 1st (that is, just before the first programme change mentioned above) it was decided by the Guarantors to form a "Programme Committee", to "supervise the selection of music to be played at the various concerts of the Society"!

Such an insult to a distinguished and proud conductor—hired less than two years earlier as *de facto* music director with virtually unlimited powers—was merely one symptom of the well-advanced malaise affecting Mahler's relationship with his employers. Around the middle of February Mahler was summoned to Mrs. Sheldon's residence; Alma's colourful description of the scene there conveys the impression of a veritable showdown between conductor and Guarantors (see **530**). In all likelihood, one of the main issues at this meeting was the pending dismissal of Mahler's 'spy' in the orchestra, the second violinist T. Johner. His activities, and Mahler's refusal to deprive himself of his 'services', had long been a cause for unrest in the ensemble (see also **492** and Note 46).

Over the past several years, numerous scientific analyses of Mahler's illnesses and cause of death have been published (see **547** and Note 86); some of these exclude psychological considerations altogether, while others assign a dominant role to them. On balance, though, it seems not unreasonable to suggest that his confrontation with the Philharmonic Committee, and its inevitably catastrophic nervous after-effects, acted as a catalyst in precipitating Mahler's final collapse. While there is evidence of a surprisingly active social life by the couple around this time (see **533** and **538**), there is no doubt that Mahler conducted his last concert (the first of a pair of regular subscription concerts) on February 21st in a fever from which he was, essentially, never to recover.

Following Mahler's collapse, the Philharmonic season continued uninterrupted, chiefly due to the resourcefulness of the concert master, Theodore Spiering. He and Busoni shared the podium for the repetition of the "Italian" concert on the 24th of February; Spiering then led the orchestra to the end of the season on April 2nd.

On the whole (and surprisingly to some observers), Spiering acquitted himself to the general satisfaction of critics and listeners, so much so that Busoni, for instance, was quite dismayed by what he perceived as callous indifference to Mahler's absence and illness on the part of many. In point of fact, the apparent attitude decried by Busoni was due more to a lack of precise information than to a want of interest, or even concern. While this appears somewhat surprising today—given the length of time between Mahler's last concert and their departure for Europe (more than six weeks)—we can only speculate about the reasons. Perhaps, at least for a while, there was hope that Mahler may return to the podium. Certainly, the periodic announcements to this effect (even though they were usually promptly denied) would seem to indicate this, as may the fact that, to the very end of the season, the programme booklets of the Philharmonic bore the legend, "Gustav Mahler, Conductor". On the other hand, a sufficiency of rumours published in the press indicates that the Guarantors' Committee was actively searching for Mahler's replacement already in March. The extant Minutes of the Committee confirm this.

In any case, certain preparations for the following year had to be made towards the end of the current season. Aside from the search for a new conductor—a non-public activity, so to speak—the most important concern was the schedule for the following season, and the associated need to build an audience. Accordingly, the programme for the March 21/24th concerts carried the subscription announcement for the 1911-1912 season. This shows that the management planned for the same number of concerts for the following year as had been originally scheduled for the current one. It also provides us with interesting information on the cost of attending a Philharmonic concert at this time. On the subscription basis, per concert, prices for the regular series ranged from 38 cents for the cheapest seats to $12.50 for a lower box. The cost of attending a concert at the Brooklyn Academy of Music was almost the same: it ranged from 35 cents to $12, the latter amount also for a lower box. Although the Sunday afternoon concerts in New York had been intended from the beginning to serve a broader, 'family' audience, substantial reductions in price were offered only to box holders!

The list of box holders, published for the first time in the programme booklets during Mahler's last year, shows some interesting changes for the 1911-1912 season. The turnover was considerable: 13 of the 88 box holders listed at the end of December, 1910 do not appear in the list for the opening concert of the following season. The most notable names missing are those of Mrs. Loudon Charlton, Mrs. William P. Draper, Mme. Johanna Gadski, Mrs. Samuel Untermeyer and Miss Dorothy P. Whitney.

Aside from Alma's relatively detailed, if somewhat impressionistic, account of the progress of Mahler's illness, we know practically nothing about his last six weeks in New York. While his condition seems to have changed quite frequently, a gradual deterioration apparently made it necessary to cancel the long-scheduled sailing date of March 30th.[15] During March Anna Moll arrived from Europe; the three of them left New York together on the 8th of April on the SS Amerika.

Following their arrival in France, Mahler was treated briefly and unsuccessfully in a clinic at Neuilly. When the final outcome was beyond doubt, he asked to be transported to his beloved Vienna. He died there on May 18, 1911, some seven weeks short of this 51st birthday.

The news of Mahler's death created unprecedented public interest on both sides of the Atlantic. The European press, in a sizeable number of obituary notices and eulogies, imputed a greater or lesser

---

[15]Although the last Philharmonic concert was played only on the 2nd of April, this had been a late addition to the season that was originally scheduled to end on March 30th (s.a. Note 11).

degree of blame to America for Mahler's untimely death; in a few cases, the alleged 'offences' bordered on the ludicrous (*e.g.*, see **575**). By the same token, and not unnaturally, many North American articles strike us today as at least faintly defensive in tone; some, such as Krehbiel's deplorable 'eulogy', smack of rampant paranoia. But the majority of American critics—whatever their basic predilections, and however much they may have differed in their appraisal of the various aspects of Mahler's activities in America—found it in themselves to pay homage to the man and to the artist who, in the course of four short seasons, left an indelible mark on their musical life.

Somewhat belatedly, the Philharmonic paid its own fitting tribute to the memory of the man who had given so much of himself to the making of it into a first-class orchestra. The season's third pair of regular subscription concerts on November 23 and 24, 1911 were officially dedicated to Mahler's memory. The programme, led by the orchestra's new permanent conductor Josef Stransky, consisted of the first movement of Mahler's Fifth Symphony, the Good Friday Spell, Prelude, and Glorification from *Parsifal*, and the "Eroica" Symphony. The programme notes were prefaced with a brief biography of Mahler; the section on the Fifth Symphony was limited, as the composer would have wished it, to factual data (performance directions, and the dates of the European and American first performances).

During the three decades following his death, Mahler's memory was kept alive in the United States chiefly through occasional performances under such eminent interpreters of his music as Willem Mengelberg and Leopold Stokowski. But the phenomenon of a full-fledged Mahler-renaissance in North America—dating from the Second World War, and stronger than ever today—is to the inestimable credit of two outstanding spiritual heirs to Mahler's art: Bruno Walter and Leonard Bernstein. Their dedication and achievement—carried on at the Philharmonic, 'Mahler's orchestra', by Pierre Boulez and Zubin Mehta—ensured that in the New World, too, Mahler's time has come.

Plates 72 and 73. The photograph above was taken on Mahler's last sailing to America (A. Roller, ed., *Die Bildnisse von Gustav Mahler*, Leipzig, Wien, E.P. Tal, 1922, Illustration 77); the one below is, in all likelihood, his last photograph, taken on the return voyage to Europe in April, 1911. (W.G.W. Kurz Collection)

388

1910 - 1911
Documents

434

ROME, May 7 - In a rage at the manner in which the orchestra for the concerts at the Corea performed under his conductorship, Gustav Mahler has abruptly shaken the dust of Rome from his feet and precipitated what looks like a pretty legal tangle. "Bootblacks" and "brigands" were some of the terms Mahler employed in referring to the musicians he was engaged to conduct.

"They want me to conduct those bootblacks, those brigands," he is quoted as saying after the first concert. "Never! I have never met such a set of undisciplined ignoramuses in my whole career, and I am going to leave. They may do what they like!"

Friends of the famous conductor remonstrated with him, but in vain. He left, presumably for Vienna. [. . .]

(*MA* 12, no. 1, May 14, 1910, p. 30)

435

An attempt to interfere with the giving of five Sunday concerts next Fall in the Brooklyn Academy of Music by the Philharmonic Society of New York, under Gustav Mahler, conductor, has been threatened by Canon William S. Chase, who has protested against the concerts in the name of the Sunday Observance Association.

[. . .] Canon Chase incidentally asserted that, although Manhattan might permit Sunday concerts, he would not allow them in Brooklyn.

Mr. Charlton, in reply paid his proper respects to the intolerance of the minister, asserting his surprise at "this Philistine attitude toward Sunday performances of a purely ethical, educational and uplifting character."

[. . .] He ended by saying that the Philharmonic begged to inform the Canon that its Brooklyn concerts would not be withdrawn.

(*MA* 12, no. 6, June 18, 1910, p. 8)

436

[. . .] Regarding the commercial side of [the] proposed Sunday concerts in Brooklyn, little [. . .] need be said. The objections raised are preposterous, particularly when it is recalled that the generous guarantors of the New York Philharmonic Society paid out last season $90,000 more than was taken in at the box offices. The concerts are not given for profit.

Artistically, the concerts by the New York Philharmonic Society are of the highest importance; the community would suffer if such concerts were abandoned. When Canon Chase wrote his letter he may have forgotten that Bach, Mozart, Haydn, Beethoven, Schubert, etc., composed some of the sublimest ecclesiastical music we have heard. When it comes to other works by these immortals, it may be, that looking at it from the angle of the Sunday Observance Association, that Beethoven's fifth symphony is meretricious; the Bach air, on the G string, degrading, and the Schubert-Liszt "Wanderer" fantasie unfit for polite ears. [. . .] If the Sunday Observance Association of Kings County has any power, let it bestir itself and put an end to the frightful noises at Coney Island on Sundays. [. . .] The music heard at Coney Island is an imaginative man's idea of a frightful nightmare or an inferno. Even devils must be arrayed against such vulgarity and uproar. Instead of benefiting the masses who flock to the island on Sundays, the music heard there transforms most of the listeners into nervous wrecks and must end by ruining their musical morals and destroying all taste for real tonal art. It may be wise also to inform Canon Chase and the Sunday Observance Association of Kings County, that nothing is free at Coney Island on Sundays, except a meagre strip of the beach, and the disagreeable odors of the cheap drinks and foods.

[. . .]

(*MC* 60, no. 25, June 22, 1910, p. 27)

437

[Postmark: Munich, June 21, 1910]

My dear Spiering,

[. . .]

I have had no news at all from America. As you know, after urging
from me a regular manager was appointed,[16] but to my considerable
dismay he proposes 65 concerts, maintaining that success cannot be
guaranteed without this vast increase in the workload. - For such a
colossal amount of extra work I then asked for a small increase in my fee
(by contract I am committed to no more than 45 concerts), but this
request was rejected by the committee,[17] so that I shall now simply have
to insist on the rights and obligations laid down in the contract.

I informed the committee of this intention, but I have heard nothing
from them since.

[. . .]

(*MSL*, pp. 358f.; original German in *GMB*, p. 385.)

438

Loudon Charlton, who will be business manager of the New York
Philharmonic Society next year, is enthusiastic over the extent of musical
appreciation in this country and believes that too much stress has been
laid upon the encouragement given music by the foreign element in
America. "It has been my experience," he says, "that the native born are
the ones who support and appreciate music. Even in a German city like
Milwaukee, it is not the Germans who turn out to the best concerts. This
is largely due, no doubt, to the fact that the foreign element is largely of
the lower classes."

(*MA* 12, no. 7, June 25, 1910, p. 16)

439

GUSTAV MAHLER, conductor of the New York Philharmonic
Orchestra, is in Torpach [sic] Tyrol, at work in sketching the proposed
programs of next season's concerts. There are to be more rehearsals for
each concert than last season, and this will enforce rehearsals on our

[16]See **433**, and Notes 74, Chapter II and 149, Chapter III.
[17]See Note 11.

other orchestral performances. The claim of rehearsing indulged in by certain New York orchestras is merely an advertising item and would not be thought of had this paper not compelled the question of rehearsing to be considered as foremost.

(MC 60, no. 26, June 29, 1910, p. 20)

440

[Toblach, July 3, 1910]

Dear Herr Director [Hertzka],[18]

And so here I sit in my solitude, enjoying it very much. (Even the bowels are quite in order.) But, in the turmoil of the departure this time, I forgot to bring with me any music at all.

I have already wired the publisher. Still, I would like to waste no time, and would ask you, dear Director, in the meantime to send me *immediately* some cantatas by Bach, the B-minor Mass, also by him, the Walpurgisnight by Mendelssohn, and a few things by *Reger*, in so far as they are published by the [Universal] Edition. Have you, perhaps, published the Masses of *Haydn*, Mozart or Schubert? Then I should also like a few of those. - *Cherubini, Requiem? Beethoven, Battle of Waterloo?* (or whatever the thing is called), *Liszt*, Christus. -

[. . .]

With cordial greetings, your devoted
Mahler

Incidentally, in case you have any interesting novelties, I should like to receive them now, as well as regularly in the future, as I would be happy to find something new for my programmes.[19]

(Original German in Hans Moldenhauer, "Unbekannte Briefe
Gustav Mahlers an Emil Hertzka", Neue Zeitschrift für Musik 135, no. 9
[September 1974], pp. 547f.)

[18]Emil Hertzka (1869-1932) - Hungarian-born Austrian music publisher. It was under his guidance that Univeral Edition developed into one of the leading European firms in the field of music publishing.

[19]Aside from the evidence provided by some of his programmes in New York, Mahler's interest in the music of his contemporaries is also clear from such letters as this, as well as from anecdotal reports. For example, it seems fairly well established that he had seriously occupied himself with Ives's Third Symphony during the summer of 1910, possibly considering it for performance in New York (Wooldridge, *op. cit.*, pp. 150f.)

441

It cost the ladies [...] who conducted the affairs of the New York Philharmonic Society, about $100,000 last season; but they and all of us had the pleasure of Gustav Mahler's learned and inspired readings by means of a controlled orchestra under systematic rehearsing. When this paper called for a business manager for this and the future seasons, it reflected the desire of these ladies, who found, after a few months, that management under experienced hands was essential if they wanted audiences. It did not occur to me that a manager would be selected who had a bureau of his own with his own artists, for that would, at once, create an unnecessary conflict [...].

However, [...] as these ladies are willing to pay such a large loss, it seems a supererogation to advise them [...]. I am not condemning the selection, but the selection of the type [...]. There are many men competent to manage the Philharmonic who are not handicapped for such a position by having a successful business of their own, as Mr. Charlton has. The Boston Symphony has such a one. The New York Symphony Society is even better off, for its own conductor is its business head, and is far more successful in the latter than in the former position. [...]

The finale of this will be an ultimatum which Mr. Charlton will one day put to himself, and that will be that it must be either the Philharmonic or his own bureau, and his own bureau will win. [...]

("Reflections", *MC* 61, no. 2, July 13, 1910, p. 6)

442

[Alt-Schluderbach, July 15, 1910]

Dear [Emil],[20]

[...]

I posted the letter to Flinsch[21] without making any alterations. - I do not think Charlton played a hand; it is the quite naive, brutal egoism of these people, who simply do not consider their opponents point of view at all. - No, *vederemo*, the answer.[22]

[...]

(*MSL*, p. 364; original German in *GMB*, p. 393.)

---

[20]Emil Freund - See Note 38, p. 274.
[21]Rudolf Flinsch (1867-1948) - Born in Germany, Flinsch emigrated to America in 1892, and became wealthy as an engineer and a banker. He was a member of the Guarantors' Committee.
[22]See Note 11.

443

VIENNA, July 14 - The departure of Felix Von Weingartner from his position as director of the Vienna Royal Court Opera is now recognized on all sides as an established fact. The only question left is the "when," which depends upon the securing of a suitable successor for this, one of the most important positions in operatic life in Europe.

[...]

Among possible successors who have been mentioned are Felix Mottl, of the Munich Royal Opera; Ernst von Schuch of the Dresden Opera; Richard Strauss and Karl Muck, of Berlin, and Gustav Mahler.

[...]

Mahler might be induced to return to his old love, although he is at present bound by his concert-conducting and "definite artistic plans which he must bring to completion."

(*MA* 12, no. 12, July 30, 1910, p. 5)

444

I last saw him last summer at Tobelbad. At the time the rumour was that they wanted him back at the Vienna Court Opera; but for this he had only a smile. He had just come back from America and spoke a lot of the American orchestras' conditions. In general he felt that the English [sic] nation had too little temperament, too little artistic talent, but said that the 96 musicians that he had to conduct followed him better than any previous orchestra because he had them to himself.

(Ernst Decsey,[23] "Stunden mit Mahler",
Die Musik 10, no. 21, p. 151, quoted in *BRM(E)*,
pp. 265f.; original German in *BRM*, p. 272.)

445

Mahler has given it out that under no circumstances will he reconsider his decision not to renew his contract with the New York Philharmonic [...]. The modest little Mahler also must have shown more of the contract, for the papers state that he receives 140,000 marks, which means $35,000 for the season and a sum per annum of that extent is rather contemptuously and disdainfully rejected. The Mahlers are our pets. The greater the contumely and contempt exhibited toward us the

---

[23]Ernst Decsey (1870-1941) - An Austrian critic and prolific writer on music, he was an early champion of Mahler's.

better we like it and the more do we admire the exhibitor. There is no nation today [. . .] that will endure the insults heaped upon it by those who draw their revenues from it; and those are the people we admire because we are snobs. [. . .] The Damrosches are Polanders from Posen, which has much to do with their success in New York [. . .]. Under a peculiar inspiration, [. . .] we are always convinced that a man, if he is a Pole, must be a fervid and gifted musician [. . .].

[. . .] Mr. Mahler will not return to New York after the conclusion of the next season; what will he do next season? Help along in losing about $100,000 more money of those ladies whose sentiments are also so ruggedly and sternly pushed aside with the usual tactless behavior of the imported boor? After all Mr. Mahler's money drawing record, I mean his record as an attraction that draws money from the public, is no greater than Damrosch's, for there were just about as few people to hear the one as to hear or see the other conducting of Philharmonic concerts. Then why not amalgamate the New York Symphony and the Philharmonic and create a real Permanent proposition to meet the tremendous operatic competition and put one of the Damrosches in, or both, as conductors? [. . .]

("Reflections", *MC* 61, no. 7, August 17, 1910, p. 5)

446

Toblach, 29th September [sic - August] [1910][24]

Dear Herr Untermyer!

I just received your kind letter of August 24th, from which it appears to me that they had committed the faux paux of somehow informing you one-sidedly. - The matter in which I had proposed you as a referee[25] (merely to avoid time- and energy-consuming controversies, and truly only to indicate my position) is of a very insignificant nature, and should it be in the least uncomfortable for you, I shall withdraw my proposal without further ado.

As you are sailing from Cherbourg on the 14th of September, it will not be possible for you and your wife to attend the première of my Eighth Symphony which is to take place in Munich on the 12th of September. Since, however, you will obviously be travelling via Munich, perhaps it will interest your wife to attend one of the full rehearsals which will be held on the 10th and 11th of September. In that case it would give me great pleasure to arrange admission for you and anyone else you wish; all

---

[24]As is clear from the contents, Mahler meant to write "August," not "September."
[25]See Note 11.

I need is timely notice. I will be at the Hotel Continental in Munich from the 5th of September on, and my wife and I would be very happy to be able to shake your hand during those days.

With cordial greetings from both of us to you and Mrs. Untermyer,

Your most devoted

Gustav Mahler[26]

447

[Postmark: Vienna, September 26, 1910]

Dear friend Mengelberg!

I am sailing on *October 18th* with the Kaiser Wilhelm II (North-German Lloyd) from *Bremen*.

[. . .]

(Original German in Reeser, *op. cit.*, p. 102)

448

A new schedule of salaries for musicians, members of the Musical Protective Union of New York, went into effect on September 2, and the possible effects of its operations have caused considerable apprehension in symphony orchestra circles. The increase in the rate is large, particularly in the prices charged for rehearsals, and this, it is said by officers of several New York symphony societies, will place a heavy burden upon their organization. [. . .]

The former price per man for symphony concerts was $7 a concert and $2 for each rehearsal. The new schedule raises this to $8 a concert and $4 for each rehearsal.

[. . .]

Felix Leifels, of the Philharmonic Orchestra, said that the new rule would not affect the Philharmonic this season as the contracts had been made before the increase went into effect.

[. . .]

The New York union has a membership of six thousand, and is affiliated with the American Federation of Musicians.

Of the large musical organizations of the country, only the Boston Symphony Orchestra is free of union control.

(*MA* 12, no. 21, October 1, 1910, p. 9)

---

[26]For the German text, see Appendix, A40.

449

Before the day of his last, disastrous voyage to America—how his most intimate friends shuddered at the prospect of it, with what grief they saw him depart into the land that could bring him none of the genuine, artistic joy that he longed for, into which the almost mortally exhausted man was driven by others for the sake of the mammon that he scorned—he came to me, pale, with weary eyes [. . .] From sure signs, which I could not unravel until later, influences may well have increased that were aimed at his spiritual separation from the 'old world', and were intended to lead to the luxuriant mode of life of the 'new world' and new, something less than sympathetic circles. [. . .] At that time I obtained his promise: 'Gustav, you must never again go to America.' He promised, and kept it, as in life every promise was sacred to him.

(From Guido Adler's unpublished epilogue to his *Gustav Mahler*
[1916]; quoted in Reilly, *op. cit.*, p. 112)

450

I saw him for the last time six months before his death. He was about to go to America. On the way there, between Berlin and Hamburg, he visited me at Nikolassee. But not a word was spoken of either his or my plans for the future. He merely played in the garden with my child.

(Oskar Fried,[27] "Errinnerungen an Mahler",
Musikblätter des Anbruch 1, no. 1, p. 18,
quoted in *BRM (E)*, p. 268; original German in *BRM*, p. 275)

451

We met on board the boat at Cherbourg early in November, 1910, for our last outward voyage, he coming from Bremen and I from Paris. The voyage to America had no terrors for us now. We sailed on the 15th and arrived at New York on the 25th.[28] It was child's play. We used the ten days to have a complete rest. They were wonderful days - every time!

(*AMM*, p. 182; additional translation by Z. Roman;
original German in *AME*, p. 223)

---

[27]Oscar Fried (1871-1941) - German conductor and composer. A faithful interpreter of Mahler's music, he was active in Berlin until 1926.
[28]Although the Mahlers did arrive in New York on the 25th, it was October, rather than November; the ship, with Mahler aboard, had sailed from Bremen on the 18th.

Plate 74. Gustav Mahler in 1911. (*RSM*, "Bilder," p. 14)

452

Those persons who about a year ago were waiting in silent expectancy to see just how the reform of the venerable Philharmonic Orchestra under Gustav Mahler would result now feel that they may openly exult and point to it with pardonable pride as a dangerous rival of the unsurpassable Boston Symphony. The present season—the organization's sixty-ninth of existence—opens with prospects of bountiful prosperity from every point of view. A notable difference this year, however, is the fact that the orchestra is under the business management of Loudon Charlton - its first experiment in submitting to the direction of a professional manager. The wisdom of the move is not to be gainsaid.
[. . .]
The Philharmonic's programs are to be somewhat longer than last year, and will provide for a short intermission. A number of novelties will be offered, including one or two of Mr. Mahler's own compositions, among them his Fourth Symphony, with soprano solo. A number of works which made a deep impression last year will be repeated.

(*MA* 12, no. 22, October 8, 1910, p. 7)

453

Although the musical manager deals largely in "publicity" he himself is often a retiring, exceedingly modest man. For this reason it has been difficult to obtain as satisfactory portraits of them as could be desired.
In the case of Loudon Charlton it was necessary to call in the services of a confederate who obtained the accompanying portrait without Mr. Charlton's knowledge or consent. Apologies to Mr. Charlton are offered herewith. [. . .]
"With such an avalanche of work as is now sliding down upon us, and with all hands working days, nights, and Sundays and holidays, it is difficult for me to stop even for a moment to give you my impressions of concert matters present and prospective," said Loudon Charlton. [. . .].
"The working out of a new and broad scheme, calculated to multiply and extend the usefulness of that time-honored organization, the Philharmonic Orchestra, is a managerial problem of great interest. Evidences of our ultimate success in this direction are already apparent, and the one thing which we are now directly aiming for is to put the Philharmonic next season on a basis of one hundred concerts a year, which will permit it to be self-supporting. [. . .]"

(*MA* 12, no. 22, October 8, 1910, p. 9)

454

Miss Alma Gluck[29] is remembered gratefully as one of the younger
recruits at the Metropolitan Opera House last season. [. . .] [Her]
recital, given last evening in Mendelssohn Hall [had] an exceedingly
interesting program. It was a program, indeed, such as few newcomers on
the concert stage would have either the courage or the knowledge of the
modern song literature to present; for it was significant of curious
searching in some little known by-paths of that literature.

[. . .] Her second group comprised some most attractive modern
German songs by Robert Kahn,[30] Strauss, Wolf, Schillings,[31] and
Mahler. [. . .]

In his "Rheinlegendchen" Mahler shows that characteristic fondness
for the note of folk-song sophisticated with modern harmonic subtleties
that has been heard in some of his larger compositions. In it he manages
to impart a most alluring charm and grace which Miss Gluck truly
denoted in her singing, and she was made to repeat it.

[. . .] Mr. Kurt Schindler [. . .] played her accompaniments not as a
perfunctory adjunct to the performance but with the nicest sense of
artistic fitness and balance and with an exquisitely musical feeling [. . .]

(*NYT*, October 19, 1910, p. 11)

455

The Philharmonic Society opened its sixty-ninth season brilliantly last
night - one might say very brilliantly if the reader were to limit the
statement to such elements as the quality of the band's finest utterances,
some of the features of Mr. Mahler's reading of the familiar works on the
programme, and the appearance of the audience.

[. . .] The end [. . .] came after more than two hours of music,
considerably too much, especially when weary listeners were compelled
to go home with the cacophonous concluding measures of Richard
Strauss's "Also sprach Zarathustra" haunting the ear and outraging the
aesthetic sense and fancy. [. . .]

The orchestra seemed to be in excellent condition and the fine stringed
tone—muscular is the favourite descriptive word—was of thrilling effect

---

[29]Alma Gluck [Reba Fiersohn] (1884-1938) - Rumanian-born American soprano.
Following a brief stint at the Metropolitan Opera (debut in 1909), she concentrated
on a concert career.
[30]Robert Kahn (1865-1951) - German pianist and composer (chiefly of chamber
and vocal music), Otto H. Kahn's brother.
[31]Max von Schillings (1868-1933) - German composer and conductor, music
director of the Stuttgart Court Theatre 1908-1918.

when not overwhelmed by the brass and the fairly ear-splitting kettle drums. This happened frequently in the [Schubert C Major] symphony and the Symphonic Poem.

(*NYTrib*, November 2, 1910, p. 7)

456

The performance of the Schubert Symphony was planned on a large scale. There were many variations of tempo, there was plentiful emphasizing of heavily instrumented passages, and there were portentous nuances. These are the days of grandiose effects, and we must expect to find them injected into readings of Schubert, especially by a conductor like Mr. Mahler, who is fond of painting in vivid colours. The only question which arises at times like last evening is whether the work under presentation lends itself readily to this kind of treatment.

Again, these are the days of personal equations in conducting, and if Mr. Mahler feels the symphony in this way, then in this way he must read it, and the public must, and probably does, gladly take it thus.

(*NYS*, November 2, 1910, p. 7)

457

[Mahler] treated Schubert's symphony from the same subjective point of view and with the same freedom that has marked so much of what he has done. It cannot be denied that it was in many respects an exceedingly interesting, even a captivating performance, however much it may have wrenched old time memories and deep-rooted conceptions of how Schubert's music ought to sound - and how he probably thought it would sound. It is not everybody who could have played fast and loose with the letter of the score and brought forth a result that went so far to carrying conviction to it. There were, for instance, almost incessant and sometimes very far-reaching modifications of tempo, of accent and rhythm, even of orchestral colour. There were also numerous passages of exquisite poetical insight. Mr. Mahler apparently did not exercise the prerogative which he has sometimes claimed, of cutting and shortening some of those "heavenly lengths" in Schubert's music. Instead he seemed to wish to impart to them so much variety, interest, and diversity of expression that the burden of their length would seem to be relieved.

(*NYT*, November 2, 1910, p. 7)

458

The success of the Philharmonic Society's opening concert in Carnegie Hall on Tuesday night points unmistakably to a broadened sphere of usefulness for this fine old organization. A large and entirely new audience has been drawn to its support - one that evidently approves the idea of the increased number of concerts and is free and eager to attend them. The management has expressed itself as well pleased with the spontaneous public response to its plans, the goal of which is to establish the orchestra on a permanent basis that will increase its importance many fold.

(*NYTrib*, November 6, 1910, Part Four, p. 2)

459

Since last season much improvement has been made in the personnel of the orchestra; this is especially marked in the woodwind and brass choirs.[32] The new management which has shown itself alert, succeeded in bringing a large audience to Carnegie Hall for the opening concert, but there were seats for all late comers, and the work of selling the boxes for the season is going on with zest. Gustav Mahler received a hearty welcome when he appeared to conduct.

[. . .]

The names of the boxholders were published on the program notes and this innovation calls attention to the increased interest which society is taking in the reorganized Philharmonic Society. [. . .]

(*MC* 61, no. 19, November 9, 1910, p. 30)

460

Franz Schubert was a gentle soul. No one ever charged him with being cast in the heroic mold. [. . .] [He] was never overwhelmed with a consciousness of his own identity. It never occured to him that he was a priest or a prophet. He just sang out his soul and was content. [. . .]

However, Schubert composed some symphonies and sometimes philharmonic societies play them. It is always a joy to hear a Schubert symphony. [. . .]

When he sat down to compose a symphony, Schubert was not in the habit of providing himself with a programme. He was content to write

---

[32]For a detailed discussion of personnel changes, see the introductory essay to the 1909-1910 season.

symphonies as Haydn and Mozart did, just to make beautiful music and let it indicate in its own indeterminate language moods almost as subtle and elusive as the atmosphere. Schubert was satisfied with the apparatus of the symphonic orchestra of his day. [. . .] He did not [. . .] write for four horns, three trumpets, three trombones, and a tuba, as later masters did. [. . .] Schubert painted in quiet tones, and his scoring shows that he never thought of seeking for brilliant effects for their own sake.

With such considerations as these in mind, the concert-goer cannot help regretting all attempts to bring Schubert "up-to-date." Schubert is going to be up to much later dates than this present year of grace, 1910, but not by force of orchestral main strength. Pure, serene and flawless beauty will continue to hold its position in the world of art, despite the larger disturbance caused by problem music and exercises in the contrapuntal double cross.

Accepting the conditions as they are, to wit, that Schubert wrote for two horns, two trumpets, and three trombones, why should anyone seek to make this aggregation of brass sound like that employed by Strauss? [. . .]

It is a pity to treat trombones rudely in a score like that of the C Major Symphony in which the composer used them with so much respect for their character and with so much resource in enlarging their field of expressiveness. [. . .] Surely it never occurred to Schubert to use stopped trumpets when he desired a pianissimo effect. If he wrote "pianissimo" under his trumpet parts, he probably desired a trumpet pianissimo. [. . .]

It may be respectfully submitted at this time that this practice of writing three or four F's or P's in the hope of inciting players to the extreme measures in force or softness had not originated in the day of Schubert.

(*NYS*, November 6, 1910, 3. section, p. 8)

461

Mr. Mahler will [. . .] freshen up the programmes of the Philharmonic Society [this season] but oftener, it seems likely, by presenting old works in new garbs than by giving a hearing to unfamiliar compositions, though these are not to be neglected. What startling results can be achieved in this direction was proved at the first two concerts by the brass ornaments added to Schubert's Symphony in C.

(*NYTrib*, November 7, 1910, p. 7)

462
THE TRUTH ABOUT THE NEW YORK PHILHARMONIC

A woman, forceful as well as tender, with a consuming love of art and a deep love for humanity, has, by the aid of a few friends and her own determination, provided New York with a great orchestra, a thing that never existed until this new combination took matters in hand. Like almost every one who does something extraordinary for the world, this woman, outside of her immediate circle of friends and acquaintances, has not received the appreciation due her. Mrs. George R. Sheldon [. . .] is the lady who has wrought this marvel, and it is high time the American musical public was convinced of the fact.

Mrs. Sheldon does not appear to want the credit for all that has been done, but without her zeal and her labors in season and out of season, there would probably be a different story to tell, or no story at all, for things would be the same with the old Philharmonic.

[. . .]

A representative of THE MUSICAL COURIER called upon Mrs. Sheldon last Thursday morning at her home in the old aristocratic section of Murray Hill. All the while the interview went on Mrs. Sheldon was called up on the telephone by friends who wished her to reserve boxes or give other information about the concerts. [. . .]

First of all, Mrs. Sheldon complained of the manner in which certain newspapers had treated the society. She said: "There has been much misinformation published about us. We have given New York one of the best orchestras ever heard here or anywhere, and if the musical public does not support this work, the orchestra will be disbanded; but we are receiving encouragement and the concerts will not lose money. Should Mr. Mahler return to Europe next season this country will find out what it has lost. He is a wonderful organizer and a great conductor. New Yorkers never heard such programs as Mr. Mahler has planned for the season."

Mrs. Sheldon was asked to give further details about the road tour of the Philharmonic and with a forced smile and quickened phrase, replied:

"Why, certainly; I will give any and all information about the plans of the Philharmonic Society; we have nothing to conceal [. . .]."

When Mrs. Sheldon was questioned about the soloists she seemed anxious to defend Loudon Charlton, who was appointed manager of the orchestra for this season. [. . .] Mrs. Sheldon explained with some emphasis, that Mr. Charlton has absolutely nothing to do with the engaging of artists for the Philharmonic concerts. This is a matter that rests with the artistic committee and the musical director. She requested the interviewer to make this fact public.

"Mr. Charlton," Mrs. Sheldon added, "attends merely to the managerial work, and he has no hand in the regulation of the artistic side. The artists from his bureau who have been engaged as soloists for the Philharmonic concerts would have been engaged if we had chosen another manager."

[...]

While discussing certain sections of the reorganized orchestra, Mrs. Sheldon stated that, in Mr. Mahler's opinion, no orchestra in the world has a finer body of cellists, and this season new men are playing in the woodwind and brass sections. [...]

(*MC* 61, no. 19, November 9, 1910, p. 35)

463

[George] Braun[33] noticed that Mahler seemed to have trouble breathing whenever he got excited. "He couldn't stand the cold weather here," he remembers. Early in his second season at the Philharmonic, Mahler told Braun privately that he could not return the next year, but that he would like to have the young musician come to Europe and be the timpanist in any orchestra he led. "I thought it would be a great opportunity to study conducting," Braun says. He never saw Alma, but he [...] heard from the men around him that she was a beautiful woman. Mahler, at the time, seems to have been as noted for his wife as for his music.

(Roddy, *op. cit.*, p. 85)

464

Mr. Mahler did not worry himself to procure either a soloist or an orchestral novelty for the first Sunday concert of the Philharmonic Society at Carnegie Hall yesterday afternoon. [...]

After hearing the Boston Orchestra, one realizes how indifferent much of the Philharmonic material is, and how rough and explosive their playing often is [...] while the compact, mellow sonority which distinguishes Mr. Fiedler's organization is noticeably absent. This is not Mr. Mahler's fault; for my part, I think he works wonders with the material at his command. Still, it always irks me to have to admit that orchestrally New York must take a back seat to Boston, and I wonder if it would not be possible—even with the union regulations as they are—to

[33]George Braun, Jr.'s name first appears in the list of orchestral players during the 1909-1910 season.

improve the present personnel of the Philharmonic Orchestra. There is surely enough wealth among its guarantors to effect this desirable end, if only money be needed.

(*NYW*, November 14, 1910, p. 7)

465

[Autumn-Winter, 1910?][34]

Dear [Mrs. Untermyer],

Please forgive me that it is only today that I am getting around to replying to your kind lines. Also, I had hoped to do so in person. I miss your presence very much at the rehearsals and performances; the invisible ties between me and the profoundly discerning, kind listener endure, and I long for the opportunity to reknot them. The orchestra is much advanced this season, especially the double basses—thanks to your generous intervention—are a truly magnificent sight. I believe that you will be pleased.

Hoping to be able to greet you soon in our midst in all your former liveliness and capacity for enthusiasm, I am your

sincerely devoted
Gustav Mahler

May I ask that you remember me to Mr. Untermyer.[35]

466

The second Tuesday evening concert of the Philharmonic Society at Carnegie Hall last night was the occasion of the production of a new composition by Claude Debussy [. . .] The title of this work is "Rondes de Printemps". It was published in the present year and is therefore an expression of Debussy's imagination in its latest phase. It was received with generous applause by a liberal minded audience.

[. . .]

The incisive rhythm of the chief motive suggests the exuberant open air dance of the vernal festival, and the tumultuous character of the polyphony and instrumentation well colors the picture. But it must be

---

[34]Mahler's phrase concerning the double basses points to the relatively early origin of this letter during the 1910-1911 season. The Untermeyers' absence from New York in the late autumn would also explain why the settling of Mahler's differences with the Guarantors' Committee over his salary had to wait until January (see Note 11). (S.a. **530** and Note 69)

[35]For the German text, see Appendix, A41.

confessed that the plentiful provision of acrid harmonies makes little for musical beauty, while the spasmodic treatment of many phrases and the overladen method of the scoring produces a confusion of sound which frequently suggests the mud of spring thaws rather than anything more agreeable. But old fashioned music lovers must perhaps be content to give heed to the preachments of those who discover mystic and wonderful meanings in all this sort of thing.

[. . .] Josef Hofmann[36] was the solo performer, and was heard in the C minor piano concerto of Saint-Saens.

(*NYS*, November 16, 1910, p. 9)

467

At the opening night [of the Metropolitan Opera] one felt an atmosphere of lassitude and depression everywhere the moment one entered the house, which was due, I think, to the fact that with the departure of Mr. Hammerstein operatic excitement has died out. The air is no longer electrical with operatic wars and rumours of war, and the strife of competing managers. There is no further doubt or uncertainty as to what may happen in the way of operatic developments, everything is now cut and dried, and we know exactly what we have to expect. The Metropolitan remains in undisturbed possession of the former battlefield and backed by its present enormous subscription is practically independent of any necessity to consult or concede to popular taste or inclination, and can give us just what kind of opera it sees fit.

[. . .]

Speaking of novelties, operatic or otherwise, what is modern music coming to? I had reason to refer to several new orchestral compositions heard of late as "pepperbox music." For the benefit of those who might consider this term either too jaunty or obscure, I would explain that to me "pepperbox music" is music that sounds as if its composer had plentifully and indiscriminately sprinkled his scorepaper with a haphazard collection of notes from a pepperbox or ordinary flour sifter, so little meaning do they express and so scant apparent relation do they bear to one another. A case in point was a new Debussy orchestral number, "Rondes de Printemps" or "Spring Songs," played at the last Philharmonic concerts, which for willful mad eccentricity transcends anything in the shape of ultramodern music I have yet heard. Spring

---

[36]Josef (Casimir) Hofmann [Jozef Kazimierz] (1876-1957) - Polish-born American pianist, pupil of Anton Rubinstein. Hofmann was one of the greatest Romantic pianists of the earlier 20th century; he became director of the Curtis Institute of Music in 1926.

songs, perhaps, but from the way in which the orchestra groaned, grunted and cackled with topsy-turvy instrumentation, trombones playing piccolo parts and the character of every instrument inverted in like fashion, one might be led to suppose that these songs were sung by dogs, cats and fowls in a barnyard. If this be modern music, I for one have no patience with it. [. . .] It is only those composers really lacking in the divine melodic gift who deliberately attempt to cover up their paucity of melodic invention by a discordant volume of tumultuous sound and empirical instrumentation. We may in time come to a revision of our present chromatic scale, a goal toward which Strauss's dissonances are leading us, but the time is not yet; and meanwhile, oh, modernly ambitious composers, spare, oh, spare our tortured ears.

(*NYW*, November 20, 1910, Metropolitan Section, p. M5)

468

Humanity, its hopes and fears, joys and sorrows, struggles and triumphs, was the blood-red thread that ran through the warp of the musical texture woven by the New York Philharmonic Society in its second recital of the season, at the Brooklyn Academy of Music, yesterday afternoon, with Gustav Mahler, expert, at the weaving loom. [. . .]

Humanity in Brahms? Yes; in spite of the opinion of many that he is somber and gray, in the Brahms first symphony, opus 68, in C minor, that was gloriously interpreted by the conductor and played with devotion by the men, is a soul's life history. [. . .]

Alma Gluck of the Metropolitan Opera House was the solo-soprano artist of the day. She sang, for the first time, with the orchestra, in German, a Bohemian "Cradle Song" from the opera "Hubicka",[37] arranged by Kurt Schindler; also "Morning in the Fields" and "A Tale of the Rhine", by Gustav Mahler. Miss Gluck's voice is wonderful for purity of tone. It is honey. With breadth, simplicity and sympathetic feeling she delivered the berceuse, but for art and maturity of method she surpassed it in her singing of Mr. Mahler's exceedingly difficult and syncopated "Morning in the Fields". She was joyous and objective in the opening, hailing the day and the sunlight, and then sorrowful and subjective in recurring to the woe in her heart, oppressed with lover's troubles. A pretty story was unfolded in "A Tale of the Rhine", and it

[37]Smetana's *Hubicka* [The Kiss], a popular 2-act opera, was first performed in Prague in 1876.

was sung rougishly and archly. A most promising artist is Miss Gluck. She is yet young and has already gone far.

(Brooklyn Daily Eagle, November 21, 1910, p. 4)

469

VIENNA, Oct. 26 - In Berlin, the loss of Hans Gregor,[38] of the Comic Opera, as the result of his selection as successor to Felix von Weingartner, director of the Vienna Imperial Opera, has aroused mixed feelings of regret at his departure and pride at his being summoned to so important a post as the Vienna Hofoper. At the latter institution some unpleasantness has already been called forth by Gregor's remark to a Berlin interviewer anent the solution of the conductor problem at the Vienna opera. Gregor, it must be explained, is most efficient as technical manager, and he proposes, now that Weingartner will be lost to the Hofoper, to endeavor to make some arrangement with Gustav Mahler, if only for part of every year, though such excellent men as Franz Schalk and Bruno Walter remain as conductors. Schalk and Walter have protested on the ground that the inference might be that hitherto only second rate conductors have officiated at the Vienna opera. Both Schalk and Walter are orchestra leaders of the highest rank.

(MA 13, no. 2, November 19, 1910, p. 15)

470

[New York, November (?), 1910]

My dear Karl,

[...]

As for Gregor's splended plans, I have so far received no communication of any kind. But I am by no means inclined to link my destiny for the immediate future in any way with the personality of a man of whom I have never heard anything that was not highly unfavourable.

I do not feel under the least obligation to Montenuovo, since I have always emphasized that I can only make a decision when I have a clear view of the situation from the artistic standpoint. We were overjoyed to hear that you [are] now fully reconciled to dear little Mama's coming to stay with us here for a while. God bless you for it, dear Karl. Perhaps we

---

[38]Hans Gregor (1866-1945) - German actor, and theatre and opera director. He founded the Komische Oper in Berlin in 1905; from 1911 to 1918, he was director of the Imperial Opera in Vienna.

can arrange it so that Mama goes to fetch Almschi, who wants to go off about the 1st of March 'in order to supervision [sic] "affaires etrangers" over there' [. . .]

[P.S.] Alma is now for the first time really doing something sensible about her health, and I am *very* satisfied with her progress. She is also in very good spirits and full of hope.

(*MSL*, p. 368; original German [incomplete][39] in *GMB*, pp. 399f.)

471

[New York, November 21, 1910]

Dear Emil,

[. . .] You will have been able to read between the lines of the newspaper hoax about my return to the Court Opera. In fact, it had never even occurred to me to work with a person I do not even know and one who, from all accounts, seems thoroughly unlikable.

[. . .]

I am pretty well at the moment, with a frantic amount of work, which I am coping with very well. Alma and Gucki are, I'm afraid, not in the best of health.

[. . .]

(*MSL*, p. 369; original German in *GMB*, pp. 398f.)

472

It has now been definitely arranged that Gustav Mahler will retire from the conductorship of the New York Philharmonic Society at the end of this season.

(*MC* 61, no. 21, November 23, 1910, p. 20)

473

The Philharmonic Society gave the third of its regular evening concerts yesterday in Carnegie Hall. [. . .] The symphony performed was Schumann's in C Major; Mr. Mahler's reading of it was intensely vital and plastic, insistent in its reproduction of characteristic rhythms, sonorous, brilliant in the scherzo, which was taken at an exceedingly rapid pace. [. . .] There were a few rearrangements of Mr. Mahler's own

---

[39]The last complete sentence of the letter is missing from *GMB*, while the postscript is attached to another letter there (Letter 395, p. 343).

devising in the orchestration; but from that nobody is safe, especially not a composer who has to bear a reputation for unskillfulness in scoring. The performance of the Symphony was truly impressive. [. . .]

Mme. Alma Gluck was the soloist. She sang [. . .] two songs by Mr. Mahler, "Morning in the Fields" and "A Tale of the Rhine." [. . .]

The folk song character, dear to Mr. Mahler as a composer, is notable in them, especially in the second. It hardly seems as if songs of this sort receive much additional value by being set to an orchestral accompaniment. Mme. Gluck [. . .] was much applauded and several times recalled, when, with some difficulty, she got Mr. Mahler to share the plaudits with her.

(NYT, November 23, 1910, p. 11)

474

Schumann's Symphony in C [. . .] disclosed some unwanted features due to the revision which it has received at the hands of Mr. Mahler. Nearly all the symphonies, symphonic poems and overtures which figure in the Society's programme nowadays should be accepted as the works of the composers plus emendations, alterations and additions made by Mr. Mahler. It is all one whether the original author be Bach, Beethoven, Schubert, Schumann, or even Tschaikovsky, the modernizing hand of Mr. Mahler has touched his creations. The effect of these revisions has generally been felt pleasurably by the audiences (the most notable example being the Schubert symphony in C some weeks ago). [. . .]

A question of what might be called moral aesthetics is involved, of course. [. . .] The Schumann Symphony sounded very well indeed, and perhaps if somebody had pointed out to the composer that the "motto theme," as it may be called, might have been used once again where Mr. Mahler interpolated it last night in the last movement, he would have accepted the suggestion, though while composing the work he probably thought he had used it as often as he thought necessary for his purposes. It is also undoubtedly true that Mr. Mahler is a greater adept at orchestration in the modern sense than Schumann was, and could add brilliancy to the work by re-writing it *ab initio*. The only question is [. . .] - ought Schumann be permitted to utter his thoughts in his own language? [. . .]

The songs which Mme. Gluck sang, though of a character which never before had a place in a Philharmonic programme, were accepted as a delightful intermezzo by the audience. [. . .] Mr. Mahler [. . .] has a strong feeling toward the romantic element in music which such songs exemplify, and his utterances are of singular eloquence when not too

411

sophisticated by the harmonic and instrumental habiliments with which he is prone to clothe them.

(*NYTrib*, November 23, 1910, p. 7)

475

From having long been a day of next to nothing in music (outside of the churches, of course, and church music has never been more than half-religious, half-artistic sentimentality), Sunday has become a day of much, too much, music. [...] Too frequently two or more concerts are given together which all lovers of the higher class of music ought to hear, but are prevented by the restrictions of time and space. [...] Conductors still remain absolutely deaf to the suggestion that they establish an intelligence exchange bureau, and so it happens only too often that at the same stroke of the hour two or more things are going on [...] Yesterday was a case in point. Did one want to hear Mr. Hadley's symphony at The New Theatre it could only be done by a sacrifice of Mr. Xaver Scharwenka's[40] new pianoforte concerto, which was played at the same moment by the composer in Carnegie Hall. [...]

[...] The new concerto [...] was the centre of gravity in the second Sunday concert of the Philharmonic Society, being preceded by Rimsky-Korsakow's "Scheherezade" (which has often been played more picturesquely and brilliantly) and followed by Chabrier's scintillant Spanish Rhapsody, also an old acquaintance, but a composition which makes a more elemental appeal to Mr. Mahler's love for color and sonority. Mr. Scharwenka, though he had conducted performances of his work in Europe when the solo part was in the hands of another virtuoso, played the music for the first time, and the concerto had its first performance in America. Had a younger player been at the pianoforte the audience might have missed some of the authoritativeness which went out from the performance (though even this was a little obscured by evidence of insufficient co-operation between solo player, conductor and the band), but it might also have heard a brilliancy in the work which was not fully brought out yesterday. But never mind that. Let us stop in the mad onrush into which the supposed "tendency of the times" is trying to force us to give honor due to a musician who manifests his reverence for old idioms, not only by employing them when he feels so inclined, but also by making them exert their old charm on every mind that still is willing

---

[40](Franz) Xaver Scharwenka (1850-1924) - Polish-German pianist, composer, teacher and conductor, especially admired as a Chopin-interpreter. His fourth and last piano concerto was composed in 1908.

Plate 75. Henry Hadley, composer and conductor. (*LCE*, Figure 55)

413

Plate 76. Charles W. Cadman, critic of the *Pittsburgh Dispatch* between 1908 and 1910. (*LCE*, Figure 104)

414

and capable (the terms are by no means synonymous in this period of affectation) of appreciating beauty in music for its own sake. [. . .] [Mr. Scharwenka] writes pianoforte music for the pianoforte and makes no effort to solve any cosmic riddles or give expression to cosmic sorrows in his music. His composition is addressed to the imagination, to the emotions and to a taste for the beautiful - and these faculties it holds in an amiable thrall from beginning to end. [. . .]

(*NYTrib*, November 28, 1910, p. 7)

476

CHICAGO, Nov. 29 - Following the official criticism from the Chicago Police Department, [. . .] the production of "Salome", in which Mary Garden had twice appeared here, was withdrawn from the Grand Opera programme for Friday night.

The Chief of Police informed the management that "offensive" features, particularly the "head scene", should be toned down. Miss Garden strenuously objected to eliminating any of her lines or poses, and accordingly the production for Friday evening was withdrawn.

[. . .]

"If they touch it or try to cut any of my performance they can get some one else to dance it. I won't", said Miss Garden, "I won't do anything by halves. I suppose they want me to stand behind a screen and timidly speak the lines".

After the announcement that "Salome" would not be presented Friday night it was further declared by the Grand Opera management that other artists had refused to substitute their productions for the withdrawn opera and in consequence the stage would be dark that night.

(*NYT*, November 30, 1910, p. 11)

477

The fourth of the Philharmonic Society's evening concerts was given yesterday in Carnegie Hall. [. . .] Mr. Mahler began with Sir Edward Elgar's "Variations on an Original Theme" for orchestra. [. . .]

Such a performance as Mr. Mahler gave of them last evening, richly elaborated in detail, delicate, and strong in nuance, is needed to show forth their intrinsic interest. They have been played here when they sounded dull. [. . .]

The symphony was Mozart's in G minor; and in this Mr. Mahler gave the audience a surprise. He had it played by a much reduced number of orchestral players, on the basis of eight first violins instead of the sixteen that make up the normal number of the orchestra. The other stringed instruments were reduced in proportion; some of the wind instruments were also lessened in number, but there were four flutes, though they did not always all play. The intention obviously was to give, as far as might be, the effect of such an orchestra as Mozart had in mind when he composed the symphony - an effect in which the wind instruments have a larger share than they have in performance of such works by the modern orchestra.

But it may be doubted whether the results falling upon the ears of auditors in Carnegie Hall were such as were heard by listeners of Mozart's time; for they were those of a small orchestra in a large hall, instead of a small orchestra in a hall suited to its number. They were interesting results, however. The sonority was greater than was to be expected, and the quality of the orchestral color, with the increased proportion of the wind instruments, was no doubt new to many to whom the symphony has been a lifelong friend. It may be questioned whether this attempt was convincing to those who know the symphony as it is usually played in these days, or whether many will wish to hear Mozart's symphonic music hereafter in no other guise.

The performance was not so finished as most that have been heard recently from the Philharmonic; and Mr. Mahler made more free with tempo and phrasing than he did with a memorable performance of Mozart's C major symphony last season. [. . .]

(NYT, November 30, 1910, p. 11)

478

An audience that filled practically every seat in the great auditorium [. . .] welcomed the famous New York Philharmonic Orchestra on its first visit to Pittsburgh last night. [. . .]

[. . .] the Orchestra with the invincible Mahler at its head made music at Memorial Hall,[41] the quality of which has scarcely been equalled in this city. [. . .] Interest of course centered in the appearance of the great conductor. A thrill of curiosity ran through the large audience as a striking figure, small of stature, but absolutely individual in looks, walked to the front of the stage with quick, nervous strides and perching himself in a high chair with his back to the audience, directed the orchestra in the Bach Suite, while he looked after a part assigned in his arrangement [to] the harpsichord. [. . .]

---

[41]Memorial Hall, completed in 1910, seated 2,600 people. It was hailed from the beginning for its excellent acoustics.

Soldiers Memorial Hall

Pittsburgh Orchestra
Association

Presenting

New York Philharmonic Orchestra

Monday Evening, December 5, 1910

GUSTAV MAHLER Conductor

Management
Mr. Loudon Charlton, New York

Resident Assistant
Miss May Beegle

Pittsburgh Orchestra Association Offices, 1516-1517 Farmers Bank Building
Telephone, 1897 Grant

Plate 77. Title page of the Philharmonic's program booklet in Pittsburgh.

417

Beethoven's "Pastorale" Symphony, [. . .] while poetically expressing the composer's fancy and sentiment in a "Hymn to subtle Nature", it is strictly in the realm of absolute music. That is, it was in this realm until last night, when Mr. Mahler and his players made of it such a living, breathing, material thing that even the most staid absolutist was almost ready to desert the shrine of his Beethoven idealism and rush pall mall over to Mahler's fascinating materialism.

We wager that the original score has been considerably modernized and Mahlerized. [. . .] Yet no matter what was done to the Symphony, it was simply great music, and everybody had to gasp for breath and admire such a virile reading.

(*The Pittsburgh Dispatch*, December 6, 1910)

479

Little Mahler with the big brain.

Little Mahler with the mighty force.

Little Mahler with the great musical imagination.

Little Mahler, whose gigantic power makes the other conductors seem like pygmies.

It is this Herculean little Mahler who directs the New York Philharmonic orchestra which furnished the second concert of the symphony series at Grays armory[42] last night.

His strength, his mastery over his instrument, were obvious from the first beat of the first measure of the Bach suite. There was no getting ready, no working up, no preliminary warming process before the orchestra found itself, as is so often the case. [. . .] When it had anything to do, it did it at once, and did it bravely and forcibly and effectively. There was no vacillation, no weakening, no hesitancy, no drag. Everything was firm, decided, certain, secure.

And this from little Gustav Mahler, that mere wisp of a man, with the slight frame, the long slender hands, the loose shock of black hair standing away in all directions from the delicate, ascetic face. Little Mahler, the giant!

[. . .]

And how that suite did dance along! For Bach was not only the Wagner and Puccini and Richard Strauss of his time. He was the Sousa as well, a fact not always appreciated. He had the merry rhythmic swing,

---

[42]Grays' Armory, seating 5,000, was built in 1893.

the gay melody. And Mahler got them in his mind, and just poured them out of that orchestra in a torrent.

[...]

(*Cleveland Plain Dealer*, December 7, 1910, p. 2)

480

Engelbert Humperdinck, the German composer [...] arrived yesterday [...] to superintend the production of his new opera, "Königskinder". [...]

"I love the simple, naive folk tales, and am no admirer of blood and murder," said Mr. Humperdinck. "I even hated to burn the Witch in 'Hänsel und Gretel'. Music in Germany today has two tendencies, a radical and a reactionary one. I think a middle ground will be found that in the end will prevail. Richard Strauss in his latest opera, "The Rose Cavalier",[43] has returned to melody and simple harmonies, and in the future I believe that he will have a large following. [...]

(*NYTrib*, December 8, 1910, p. 9)

481

[Mahler] left with his orchestra for Springfield[44] on 7th December, and on the 9th I joined him at Buffalo. [...] I found Mahler at the hotel, and after a short rest we took the train to Niagara and drove from there in an antediluvian carriage to the Falls.[45]

(*AMM*, p. 183; original German in *AME*, p. 224)

---

[43]Strauss composed *Der Rosenkavalier* between May, 1909 and September, 1910; it was first given at Dresden on January 26, 1911.

[44]Alma's memory evidently juxtaposed the Philharmonic's tours of the two seasons: the orchestra played in Springfield in February of 1910 (see **389**).

[45]In 1960, Alma recalled the incident thus:

"Mahler was to conduct in Buffalo, New York, and we took advantage of the trip to visit Niagara Falls. We spent hours near and even under the roaring falls—they were even greater at that time than they are today, you know—and then with that roar still in his ears Mahler went to conduct Beethoven's 'Pastorale'. I was waiting for him as he stepped off the podium. 'Endlich ein fortissimo!', he said, 'At last a fortissimo!' "

(From an interview with Howard Shanet - for full details, see **100**) (S.a. **483**)

482

Buffalonians had last evening a real opportunity to hear for the first time in this city one of the famous orchestras of the country and to become somewhat acquainted with the personality and methods of a conductor who is one of the conspicuous figures in the music world today. [. . .]

[Mahler's] readings are marked by abounding vitality, by bold daring effects rather than by suavity. The large outline is never lost sight of, and while detail is not overlooked, it is quite apparent that Mr. Mahler's natural feeling is for effect of colossal grandeur rather than for the poetic. The intellectual far outweighs the emotional in his interpretations. [. . .]

The Beethoven "Pastorale" Symphony was given a remarkable reading by the conductor. There was a rhythmic surety which constantly impressed, and raising into prominence certain inner voices which seemed never to have been heard before. A more tremendously realistic portrayal of the thunderstorm has certainly never been given, and the conductor himself seemed like the very genius of the storm, driving his forces on to fiercer and yet fiercer outbursts. Wonderful climaxes were built up in this movement, and also in the *Tristan and Isolde* prelude and finale which followed the Beethoven. [. . .]

The Orchestra itself, although sometimes lacking in the mellowness and beauty of tonal quality which marks the work of some other orchestral bodies in the land, yet was compact and well-blended. Except in the beginning of the Bach overture, the playing was marked by unity, generally good balance and by splendid attack.

(*The Buffalo Express*, December 8, 1910, p. 5)

483

[Mahler] came straight back after the concert in high spirits to a simple and belated meal. "I have realized today", he said, "that articulate art is greater than inarticulate nature." He had been conducting the *Pastoral* symphony and had found it more tremendous than all the Niagara Falls.

(*AMM*, p. 184; original German in *AME*, p. 225)

484

Convention Hall was well filled last night by an audience that gave a most cordial reception to Mr. Gustav Mahler and his splended organization of men. [. . .] But three composers were represented, Bach, Beethoven and Wagner, each the greatest in his own line of work, and all equally great in the musicianly interpretation of his work by Mr. Mahler. [. . .] [He] showed himself equally at home in the operatic music as in the other two styles, the programme giving ample scope for his versatility. [. . .]

(*The [Rochester] Union and Adviser*, December 9, 1910, p. 16)

485

Gustav Mahler's control over the men of the Philharmonic Orchestra, which appears at the Majestic tomorrow night, has been widely commented upon, but to understand it one has only to see him at rehearsal. Mr. Mahler seems to throw himself heart and soul into the spirit of the music, striving by voice and gesture to convey to his players his conception of the composition. He keeps up a running fire of comment and instruction, addressing the men in German. Often he breaks off and sings the bars he wishes to emphasize, his voice ringing clear and true above the instruments. In concert Mr. Mahler's manner is more reserved, but his men respond with equal enthusiasm. On tour the work of the orchestra is conducted with the same scrupulous care, so that no ragged edges may creep in and mar the beauty of the perfect ensemble. [. . .]

(*Utica Observer*, December 9, 1910, p. 4)

486

A group of New York musicians were praising the compositions of Gustav Mahler, who is conductor of the Philharmonic Orchestra which will be heard at the Majestic tonight. "From every sound in nature he learns something", said one. "He and I went walking one summer day. In a wood he suddenly seized my arm. 'Hush!' he said, and pointed to a huge beetle that went droning by. 'I wanted' he explained afterwards, 'to hear how its note would die away'. And one day the next winter he showed me a passage where the 'cello modulated in the chord of the seventh of the descending scale from B minor to F sharp minor. 'There is our beetle of last summer's walk', he said."

(*Utica Daily Press*, December 10, 1910, p. 15)

487

Giacomo Puccini's latest opera, "La fanciulla del West", was performed for the first time on any stage at the Metropolitan Opera House last evening, with all the circumstances denoting great success. [. . .]

Every effort had been made not only to achieve this success but as well to make the performance a notable one in the history of the house. The composer had come from Italy to superintend the rehearsals and to assure the realization of his intentions in the music; David Belasco, the master of stagecraft, upon whose drama, "The girl of the golden West", the opera is founded, had spent days and nights in directing the stage management and securing the perfect co-operation and interplay of all the factors that count for a perfect ensemble - such an ensemble as New York has often had occasion to admire in his own theatre and such as the authorities of the Opera House, with all their resources, have not often been able to equal. And the Opera House had itself provided the finest talent it has in its service to interpret the work - Mr. Toscanini to conduct it, Mme. Destinn and Messrs. Caruso and Amato, and a host of its lesser and many of its most excellent singers in the minor parts. It was the first time that a new work by one of the most distinguished and popular of European composers had had its first representation in New York, and it is not likely that any finer or more authoritative presentation of this most difficult opera will be given on the other side of the water.

(*NYT*, December 11, 1910, p. 2)

488

Add to an ability to interpret with feeling the work of master musicians, an influence which can bring three score and more artists to act as one, and a personality which has its influence upon its audience instantly, and you have a picture of Gustav Mahler. Hypnotic is scarcely an exaggeration in characterizing his work in conducting the New York Philharmonic Orchestra. This organization appeared Saturday night at the Majestic, and though an audience of music lovers was in attendance, the number deserved by the program was not in evidence. [. . .]

The selections [. . .], difficult as they are, lost none of their effectiveness in their rendition Saturday evening. The fact that a great percentage of the organization is German may have something to do with the spirit manifested throughout the evening, but that, of course, is insignificant in comparison with the fact that the members of the orchestra are musicians, and that their conductor is Gustav Mahler.

(*Utica Daily Press*, December 12, 1910, p. 5)

489

The committee supporting the New York Philharmonic Society met a real want when it fixed upon Sunday afternoons as the time for its Brooklyn concerts. The increase in attendance at the first concert this year over the largest evening audience drawn by Mr. Mahler and his superb orchestra last winter proved that there is a public in Brooklyn for the best orchestral music on Sunday afternoons.

But although that audience was a great gain upon those drawn during the Philharmonic's first season here, there is room for a still larger attendance. If the great Philharmonic Orchestra is to become a regular feature in Brooklyn, adding greatly to the richness and variety of our life, the Academy should be crowded for these concerts.

It is not a question of one concert or one programme, but of making the Philharmonic a fixture in Brooklyn. That is a result valuable enough to justify the enthusiastic support of all music lovers.

(Editorial in the *Brooklyn Daily Eagle*, December 14, 1910)

490

Theodore Spiering, concertmaster of the New York Philharmonic Orchestra, is an ardent admirer of Gustav Mahler. Said Mr. Spiering anent the recent tour: "It was marvelous to see the way in which Mahler infused spirit in the men after a long day's travel and made them play even better at the last concert than at the first. His will is indomitable and a second performance of a work under his direction is always an improvement."

(*MA* 13, no. 7, December 24, 1910, p. 20)

491

Did you usually go to rehearsals?

Oh yes, most of the time. Not always for the entire rehearsal - sometimes I went for the last part of it and took him home afterwards in order to save him. *(What do you mean, "save him"?)* You see, Mahler had a peculiarity, a special characteristic - he listened to the gossip and intrigues of the orchestra men. It was so in Vienna, and it was so here in New York, too. In every orchestra there is at least one musician who lives on such plots, and Mahler would listen to him and become upset about some real or imagined injury. If I were there at the end of the rehearsal, the troublemakers couldn't do anything, but if bad weather or some other reason kept me away, he would be sure to come home angry from some poison they had put in his ear. The greatest men are sometimes like children, they have no weapons to defend themselves. And Mahler was so insecure (not musically—no one was more secure there—but personally) that he was ready to listen to anyone. But in all this, you must understand, he was an innocent, a complete innocent.

(Shanet, "Notes on the Programs", p. 3)

492

Mahler had a tale-bearer at his service in the orchestra in New York as, unfortunately, he used also to have in Vienna. His name was J[ohner].[46] He wormed his way into Mahler's confidence by describing his sufferings as a consumptive; but soon he talked more about the orchestra than his ailment and kept Mahler informed of everything that was said against him. J[ohner] was always at his elbow, and Mahler used to come back at the end of the morning feeling thoroughly annoyed. The orchestra also were indignant when they realized that he made use of J[ohner] as a spy, and so ill-will increased on both sides. J[ohner] may have been inspired by devotion to Mahler, but the results could not have been worse. Mahler was insulting with the orchestra, irritable and intolerant.[47] Several of the orchestra complained to the ladies of the Committee and all demanded J[ohner]'s dismissal. Mahler refused. I advised him to give his unqualified consent, but he would not listen. J[ohner], he said, was his only friend. If he lost him he would be alone among enemies, for the whole orchestra hated him.

J[ohner] had done his work well.

> (*AMM*, pp. 184f., with additional translation by Z. Roman;
> original German in *AME*, p. 226)

493

An "all-Tchaikowsky" programme was one of the distinguishing features of the concert of the Philharmonic Society given in Carnegie Hall last night under the direction of Gustav Mahler. Another still more distinguishing feature was that, except the solo number, the compositions

---

[46]A violinist listed as Th. E. Yohner appears among the second violins beginning with the first programme booklet for the 1909-1910 season. A T. Johner appears as leader of the second violins in the list for the first concert of the 1910-1911 season; he is still so listed in the programme for the concerts on February 26 and March 5, 1911, but does not appear in the programme for March 14 and 17 (the booklet for March 7 and 10 does not include an orchestral list). Although Alma identifies him as "Jonas" in *AME* (and his first name is given as Walter in the Biographical List in *AMM* [p. 348]), Yohner/Johner was, in all likelihood, Mahler's 'spy'.

[47]Unaccountably, this sentence was omitted by the editor and/or translator of *AMM*, as was the second clause of the first sentence. This results in a considerable toning down of the entire passage. In some respects, this continues a process begun by Alma: at this point, *ELM*, (p. [254]) has the added sentence, "As once upon the time with the musicians of the Vienna Philharmonic."

belonged in the category of the least interesting, or, at any rate, the least valuable music which ever found its way into print from the Russian composer's pen. The exception was the violin concerto, which Mr. Edouard Dethier[48] played with so much elegance and distinction in its first and second movements (not an easy matter, considering the nature of the music) as to make the feature wholly worthy of the Philharmonic Society and its traditions. The other numbers (played in the reverse order of their announcement - and wisely) were the first suite and second symphony. [. . .] It was not a musically elevating evening: rather a grievous one, indeed, for the old patrons of the institution, and consequently not a pleasant one for detailed discussion.

(*NYTrib*, December 28, 1910, p. 7)

494

For the second time this season the operatic public of New York was invited to witness the first performance of a new opera by one of the foremost of European composers, when Engelbert Humperdinck's "Königskinder" was given at the Metropolitan Opera House last evening.[49] It was clear that the occasion was regarded as a notable one and that the new opera made a deep impression. The audience was very large, and its applause so generous as to indicate emphatically that it had received great pleasure. The composer [. . .] was called before the curtain repeatedly to acknowledge the enthusiasm that his work aroused.

The management of the Metropolitan had been generous in its provision for the new opera and had done much to insure its proper presentation. [. . .] The scenic pictures were unusually beautiful and the choral scenes remarkably well developed.

[. . .]

The performance of "Königskinder" was in almost every respect admirable, and presented Prof. Humperdinck's work in its true spirit. It showed at every point the energy and mastery of Mr. Hertz, his understanding of the composer's intentions, which came to him through personal counsel, and his zeal in carrying them out.

[. . .]

The composer of "Königskinder" is still the composer of "Hänsel und Gretel", but the amiable qualities of that work are raised to a far higher

---

[48]Édouard Déthier (1886-1962) - Belgian violinist. After settling in the United States in 1906, he concertized and taught (Juilliard) there.
[49]Apparently, the première of *Königskinder* had been planned for the New Theatre, and in English, for the previous season (Kolodin, *The Metropolitan Opera*, p. 224).

power in the newer. "Königskinder" has the same roots punched deeply into the sound and fertile soil of the German folk song and the German folk tale. [. . .] There is a similar relation in it to the art of Wagner.

[. . .]

The vocal parts of "Königskinder" are chiefly declamatory, in the Wagnerian manner. They vivify the spoken word and enhance its potency, but with an essentially musical quality that is not lost in crass and unvocal intervals such as some of the most modern musical dramatists, as Strauss, assign to the speech of their characters, with utter disregard for the powers and rights of singers. Mr. Humperdinck has nowhere sacrificed the human voice. The orchestra unceasingly expounds and illustrates, but it never overwhelms and never fails to support.

[. . .]

Such orchestration as that of "Königskinder" is a delight and a joy unceasing in these days. It is incredibly skillful in its delicacy and lightness of touch, in the precision and subtle differentiation of coloring that the composer has attained. [. . .]

Mr. Humperdinck's modernity stops short with Wagner. He has naught to do with that which is now regarded as "modern" in music. So far as this opera shows, he might never have heard of the "whole tone scale" or of the harmonies associated with it, of augmented intervals and the dissonances of the highest degrees.

[. . .] Very few who have adopted Wagner's method or who have drunk so deep at the spring of his inspiration have been able to write with so much naturalness and charm, nay, with so much real power; few have been able to assimilate that method so thoroughly, or to attain results of such pure beauty. But for the very reasons that are implied in this praise, it is impossible to attribute the highest qualities to the opera or to its composer. He has bestowed delight and a pleasure that may be richly enjoyed; a pleasure that is likely to last long. And for this he is entitled to much gratitude; but he cannot be put among the daring or the original spirits. These are few in any age; and they are not always enjoyed when they appear.

(*NYT*, December 29, 1910, pp. 1f.)

495

With "Hoch - dreimal hoch!" and clinking of glasses, Engelbert Humperdinck was greeted last night by the Bohemians, who gave a dinner for him at the Hotel Astor. Behind a golden lyre and a wealth of roses and under the German and American flags the composer of

"Koenigskinder" sat beaming while the speakers threw bouquets of German polysyllables at his gentle head. [. . .]

Herr Humperdinck said, half in English and half in German, that he was glad that the first performance of "Koenigskinder" was in the Metropolitan Opera House, which he hoped some day would be the opera centre of the world.

"All are coming here," he said. "First it was the great artists, and now the composers begin to see that you love music, and know it." [. . .][50]

(*NYTrib*, December 31, 1910, p. 7)

496

Fränkel was with us on New Year's Night - our last. New York stretched on out of sight in a milk-white haze. Sirens opened up at five minutes to twelve from every factory in the city and from every boat in the harbour. The bells of all the churches united in an organ-note of such awful beauty that we three who loved each other joined hands without a word and wept. Not one of us—then—knew why.

(*AMM*, p. 187; original German in *AME*, p. 229)

497

[New York, December 1910-January 1911]

Dear Gutmann,

I beg to have from 1 June to 1 October always strictly regarded as the 'close season'. Barring extraordinary circumstances I should like to have peace and quiet for physical recuperation and for creative work during these months. [. . .] It is as good as certain that I shall return here next season. [. . .]

(*MSL*, p. 370; original German in *GMB*, p. 400)

---

[50]Although the partial guest-list published in the *Tribune* does not include the Mahlers, the two composers had been warm admirers of each other for some years. Mahler was enchanted by *Hänsel und Gretel* when he saw it in Weimar in 1894 (*KBM(E)*), pp. 110f.), while Humperdinck's sentiments are eloquently expressed in **274**. As Humperdinck had been in New York for over three weeks by this time (see **480**), there can be little doubt that the two would have met.

It may be recalled that Mahler himself had been fêted by the Bohemians nearly two years earlier, at the time of the New York première of *The Bartered Bride* (see **218**).

498

There were three novelties on the programme of modern French music presented by Mr. Mahler at the Philharmonic Concert at Carnegie Hall last night - a suite for orchestra by Georges Enesco, a young Franco-Roumanian composer, "Iberia", the second of three "Images pour Orchestre" by Debussy, and Chabrier's "Ode a la Musique" for women's chorus, tenor solo and orchestra. [. . .] Clement,[51] with all his usual finish and elegance of style sang [airs by Lalo and Massenet], besides the solo part in the "Ode", and was rapturously applauded.

A like fate did not befall the Enesco Suite, which, [. . .] though well written and not aggressively modern, did not impress me. [. . .]

Debussy's "Iberia" proved an extravagant bit of impressionistic orchestra painting, without harmonic design or real melodic thought, although a Spanish atmosphere in rhythm is definitely suggested, and the orchestral tints are resplendently varied. [. . .] Clever it may be, but is it music?

[. . .] Chabrier's "Ode" [. . .] was a tenderly melodious composition, elegiac in feeling, purely musical and vocal, without taint of yearning modernity [. . .] Mahler conducted the not over typical programme with much real appreciation and the orchestra did excellent work throughout. [. . .]

(*NYW*, January 4, 1911, p. 11)

499

The question of engaging a conductor for next season was discussed.

A letter from Mr. Franz Kneisel, who has been unofficially requested to state if his services for the position of Conductor are available, was received and read. Mr. Kneisel stating at length that he would feel highly honoured to accept the position, that, however, he can not leave his present field of activity for a contract of one year only.

It was resolved that Mr. Charlton be instructed to unofficially inquire from Mr. Mahler his attitude regarding the acceptance of the position of conductor for next season and also his terms.

(Excerpt from the Minutes of the Guarantors' Committee, January 4, 1911; in the ANYP, quoted with permission)

---

[51]Edmond Clément (1867-1928) - French operatic tenor. Following a career of some 20 years with the Opéra Comique in Paris, he made several highly successful tours of America beginning in 1910.

500

Rumours were current yesterday that the directors of the Philharmonic Society had offered the leadership of the Philharmonic Orchestra to Franz Kneisel, the well-known violinist. It has been understood that Gustav Mahler will not return next year, and the backers of the Orchestra have recently been casting about for a new director. [...]

Mrs. George R. Sheldon, who has been one of the chief supporters of the Philharmonic, said last night that those in control of the Orchestra had sent no official request to Mr. Kneisel to become the director next season.

"Whatever may have been discussed privately is our own affair," said Mrs. Sheldon. "We do not feel called upon to give private matters to the public. We are continually trying to interest new people in the Orchestra, in order to place it on a permanent basis."

(NYTrib, January 10, 1911, p. 7)

501

Every year, remarks Ouida, the roses bloom, and every year men love. She neglected to add: and every year conductors give Wagner concerts. There are several reasons for this, but the most pointed one is that a concert of Wagner music almost invariably attracts a large audience. Last night it was the Philharmonic Society's turn to play a Wagner programme, and consequently there had to be a Wagnerian prima donna as the solo singer. This singer was Mme. Johanna Gadski, who has been roaming up and down the "weite, weite welt" singing songs for all sorts and conditions of men and getting thereby much glory and abundant lucre.

[...] Last night she was heard in four of Wagner's songs; lyrics forever to be associated with the name of that remarkable woman who inspired so much of his best thought. Mathilde Wesendonck wrote the text of the four songs heard last night. [...]

Mme. Gadski sang the songs in a reverential spirit [...] Later in the programme she was heard in the last words of *Isolde*. [...] In the closing measures there was a splendor of utterance well worthy of the noble music.

[...]

It was a good concert and the musicians of the Philharmonic orchestra played with more style than they showed in several of the earlier concerts of this same season.

(NYS, January 11, 1911, p. 7)

429

Plate 78. Alma Gluck. (*COS*, Illustration 201)

Plate 79. Johanna Gadski. (*COS*, Illustration 110)

Both Gluck (previous page) and Gadski appeared with the Philharmonic
during Mahler's final season.

502

Gustav Mahler was undoubtedly one of the greatest orchestra leaders of our time. More than that, he was also a great musician of wonderfully fine and subtle characteristics. [. . .]

I am proud to have enjoyed his personal friendship, and I shall never forget the time of our contemporaneous engagement at the Metropolitan Opera and also later at some memorable concerts of the New York Philharmonic Orchestra.

(Johanna Gadski-Tauscher in *SFM*, p. 15)

503

The action of the Société des Auteurs, Compositeurs et Editeurs de Musique through its recently appointed American representative, Ovide Robillard, in setting out to enforce the copyright laws in regard to the performance of musical compositions, yesterday seemed likely to have results little looked for by the French society. [. . .] It seemed likely that if M. Robillard was successful in his endeavors he would simply eliminate the works of his clients from American programmes.

Dr. Frank Damrosch said yesterday, regarding the society's attempt:

"I think the enforcement of the foreign copyright laws in exacting royalties on the performance of modern works an excellent thing for musical development, and a very bad thing for the good modern composers. I think it will have the result of keeping off our programmes the many would-be original compositions of modern composers who are trying to develop new schools of composition by artificial methods, or who try to cover up their lack of inventive power and inspiration by complexity of technical treatment.

[. . .]

"On the other hand, the best works of modern composers, which should be heard frequently in order that the public may learn to appreciate them, will also be left off the programmes, because the public does not pay for its musical entertainment or education."

[. . .]

Walter Damrosch felt similarly, though he said that as yet he had received no notice from Mr. Robillard. [. . .]

Loudon Charlton, manager of the Philharmonic Orchestra, said that Mr. Robillard had informed him that certain works on the next French programme of the orchestra would have to be paid for.

"I told Mr. Robillard [. . .] that I would show him our next programme, and that if we could not reach an understanding I should simply eliminate all the disputed works."

"This will be bad for the French composers, but good for the young Americans, who will then get a chance. [. . .]"

[. . .]

Mr. Robillard himself said that he did not believe that his action would affect the performance of modern French works.

[. . .]

"I do not believe that the small percentage demanded by us will affect the various orchestras. It has not in France, and I don't see why it should here. We want to be perfectly fair in this, but we think the composers should be protected."

It was thought probable that the French society would insist only on the payment of royalties on compositions copyrighted since the passage of the new copyright law on July 1, 1909, as the courts have repeatedly held, as in the case of "Parsifal", that before that date foreign composers had no jurisdiction over the performance of their works, provided those works had been published.

(*NYTrib*, January 11, 1911, p. 7)

504

Ovide Robillard [. . .] said yesterday that he would take immediate steps to prevent further [copyright] violations. There has been some question as to whether or not it is possible to hold persons liable for playing compositions copyrighted prior to the law of July 1, 1909, but Mr. Robillard said he believed all copyrights taken out since the law of 1891 would hold.

[. . .]

"As to the case of Wagner's 'Parsifal', in which the courts upheld Mr. Conried against Frau Wagner, I do not think this will affect the present question. [. . .]"

Victor Herbert said yesterday that he thought the French society's action an excellent one, and that if asked to join the organization he would gladly do so.

"If I could get royalties for all my works that are played it would mean to me thousands of dollars," he said. "Any movement to protect the composer should be encouraged."

(*NYTrib*, January 12, 1911, p. 7)

505

Resolved that the Chairman [Mrs. Sheldon] appoint a Committee of
three to form a plan for the subdivision of Committees within the
Guarantors' Committee.

[...]

The Chairman reported that in response to Mr. Charlton's unofficial
inquiry of Mr. Mahler, regarding Mr. Mahler's acceptance of the
Conductorship for next season, Mr. Mahler has expressed his willingness
to conduct 90 to 100 concerts for $30,000. -

(Excerpt from the Minutes of the Guarantors' Committee,
January 11, 1911; in the ANYP, quoted with permission)

506

Rumors have been rife concerning the directorship of the New York
Philharmonic Society for the next season. It will be recalled that at the
end of last year's concerts it was reported that Gustav Mahler, the
present director, would remain in Europe and would not return, but the
opening of the season found Mr. Mahler again at his post.

The latest report is that Franz Kneisel, the well-known violinist, and
founder of the Kneisel Quartet, has been slated to succeed Mr. Mahler.

[...]

While it may be that Mr. Mahler will see fit to accept important posts
which have been offered him abroad, he has not yet definitely announced
his refusal to direct the Philharmonic for the coming year. It is generally
considered certain, however, that the society will present its concerts
next season under a new director.

It is known that at least half a dozen eminent conductors have been
approached unofficially, but that matters have not reached the dignity of
definite negotiations. [...]

It has been reported that there is some dissension among the orchestral
authorities regarding the choice of a new director should Mr. Mahler
decide to remain in Europe next season. [...]

The crux of the whole situation is that, after next year, when the
present guarantee fund will have been completed, the society will find
itself in the position of being compelled to raise a guarantee fund for a
succeeding series of years, and that such a guarantee can be raised only
with the aid which a conductor of great prestige will give. [...]

(*MA* 13, no. 10, January 14, 1911, p. 1)

507

As THE MUSICAL COURIER goes to press this paper is reliably informed that Gustav Mahler has been offered the conductorship of the New York Philharmonic Orchestra for another year, but he has not accepted as yet.

(*MC* 62, no. 3, January 18, 1911, p. 23)

508

Resolved that Mr. Charlton be instructed to secure from Mr. Mahler, in writing, the terms and conditions on which he will accept the Conductorship for next season.

(Excerpt from the Minutes of the Guarantors' Committee, January 18, 1911; in the ANYP, quoted with permission)

509

The Philharmonic concert at Carnegie Hall last night began with Hans Erich Pfitzner's overture to Heinrich von Kleist's drama, "Das Kätchen von Heilbronn". Pfitzner's music was composed in 1905, and up to last night none of it had fallen upon New York. [. . .] The overture heard last evening is plainly intended to be a detailed prelude to the drama.
[. . .]
The second number on the list was the fourth symphony of Gustave[sic] Mahler, a contemporaneous German composer, who chances also to be at present the conductor of the Philharmonic Society. Mr. Mahler enjoys no small distinction in Germany and kind things have been said about him by Richard Strauss and Felix Weingartner.
[. . .]
All four of the movements have idyllic feelings as their basis. The trouble is that these idyllis moods are continually interrupted by the rude invasion of acrid modern harmonies and the bleating of stopped trumpets. So persistent are these stopped trumpets that one wonders whether they are imitations of some abundant vegetables, for we all recall the directions given to the Englishman about catching a rabbit: "Go behind a fence and make a noise like a turnip."
Four movements of the dancing of the blessed might have been too much even for Gluck to set to music, but Mr. Mahler seems never to have tired of it. [. . .]
Mr. Mahler has composed other symphonies, and some of them are more varied in character and more interesting in content than this. The

last stanza of the folk song tells that the 11,000 virgins of Cologne were dancing to the measures entrancing. [. . .] But a dance of 11,000 blessed virgins from any such discouraging suburb of the Rhine as Cologne is too much for music, even though she is a heavenly maid. [. . .]

After Mr. Mahler's symphony, in which Bella Alten of the Metropolitan Opera House sang the solo part from a position abreast of the busy kettle drums, the concert came to a resounding finish with the autobiographic "Heldenleben" of Richard Strauss, the canny composer, who said many nice things of Mr. Mahler but who cautiously avoided the composition of 11,000 virgins and devoted his attention to the "Salome" of Oscar Wilde.

(*NYS*, January 18, 1911, p. 9)

510

In the course of the special series of concerts[52] which Mr. Mahler is giving with the Philharmonic Orchestra at present, he arrived last night at what was called a "modern" programme, which included his own Fourth Symphony. [. . .]

Mr. Mahler's Fourth Symphony was already known to New York, when it was performed here [. . .] with the New York Symphony Orchestra on November 6, 1904. It was the first of the composer's works to be played here, and to many it will still seem the most interesting and individual. It has not the grandeur and vast ambition of the Second Symphony; it is more accessible, and, to tell the truth, has more real musical substance than the Fifth, and assuredly stands considerably higher than the First which Mr. Mahler played here last season. It has its enigmatical qualities, like those others, and it shows certain of the remarkable power of an original and individual talent that goes its own way.

Mr. Mahler's familiarity with the resources of the modern orchestra, with the refinements of modern technique, with the most daring of modern harmonic combinations and manipulation of thematic material is joined to an unmistakable predilection for the naive, the folktune, the simplicity and sometimes the bareness of the archaic. This fondness for the folktune element has been observed in many of his compositions. He also, as he has said, when he conceives a great musical picture, often

---

[52]It seems that the "special cycle" of concerts inaugurated in December, of which this was the last one, was intended to be "especially attractive to those not already Philharmonic subscribers" (*NYTrib*, December 11, 1910, Part Five, p. 2). (S.a. the introductory essay to this season).

arrives at the point where he must employ the human voice as the bearer of his musical idea. [. . .]

It is a work of power and mastery; but in one way it is hard to take this symphony seriously. It is what the painters would call "amusing," when they speak of a dexterously and masterfully painted canvas. It has an undeniable fascination, it is certainly entirely characteristic of the composer. [. . .]

The performance of the symphony by Mr. Mahler and his men was an exceedingly brilliant one, and after it was finished the applause of the audience burst out in force, and Mr. Mahler was called forward many times.

(*NYT*, January 18, 1911, p. 6)

511

Mr. Mahler's Symphony [. . .] is more or less an enigma. The composer has not given titles to the different movements, nor to the symphony as a whole, yet by the device of community of theme between the movements, and still more emphatically by introducing a vocal part in the last movement, which brings the text of an old German folksong into association with the melodies of the earlier portions of the work, Mr. Mahler willingly, or unwillingly, confesses that his music is of the programmatic kind. [. . .]

We have had other instances of Mr. Mahler's fondness of the folksong, and, indeed, his characteristic penchant for melodies of a folksong character is one of the most amiable traits of his musical nature; but also the most troublesome to explain, because it is associated with so much modern sophistication in harmony, modulation and orchestration that the charm of simplicity and naturalness which ought to accompany it is lost, and a general effect of fragmentariness and disjointedness is conveyed instead.

(*NYTrib*, January 18, 1911, p. 7)

512

Gustav Mahler is likely to remain in his present position at the head of the Philharmonic Orchestra of New York for three more years. The idea of appointing Franz Kneisel as conductor is said to have been abandoned. There has been a discussion this week of the possibility of a merger of the Philharmonic with the Symphony Orchestra, of which

Walter Damrosch is conductor, but the interests behind the two
orchestras are not likely to agree to such a move for a long time to come.

(*MA* 13, no. 11, January 21, 1911, p. 1)

513

What with the new Max Reger quartet played by the Kneisel Quartet,
and the two all modern music concerts of the Philharmonic Society, the
music lover and amateur has had an opportunity during the past week to
get in close touch with musical thought in its most modern expression.

It may be, as his ardent adherents claim, that Reger is the greatest
living composer; it may be that Richard Strauss is another great
composer, and Gustav Mahler a third. It may be, too, that critics of a
later day in reviewing the work of these composers and turning over the
pages of their complicated scores may exclaim at their simplicity, and
comment with admiration on the great effects produced by the small
means at their command. Heeding the lesson of oral [sic] assimilation taught
by the Wagner scores, and granting that the human ear may in time be
accustomed to anything, it again may be that rustic lovers of a future
generation may accept as divine melody sounds like the rasping of a saw
or the squeakings of guinea pigs, but if they do, will it be necessary, will it
be art, which after all in its ultimate intent means the expression of the
beautiful?

[...]

I must contend that to the average music lover the all modern
programmes presented by the Philharmonic last week were distinctly and
decidedly dull and often unbeautiful. In the opening overture by a modern
German composer and would-be follower of Richard Strauss, one
Pfitzner, we had what I must hold to be an excellent example of the
maleficent influences of the Strauss theory of orchestral expression. Dull
in melodic content, fragmentary in construction, uncouth in harmonies
and strained and forced in effect, the work bore all the earmarks of the
ultra-modern methods which attempt to conceal paucity of invention
beneath an overladen, empirical and unlovely orchestral expression.
[...] As Mr. Mahler has taken a definite stand among the adherents of
the ultra-modern in musical thought and expression, his fourth
symphony, heard for the first time under its composer's direction at these
concerts, obtained an interest and importance quite apart from the
personal interest naturally attaching to a work by our foremost New York
conductor.

It was stated in the programme notes that it was Mr. Mahler's wish
that no attempt at an analysis or description of his symphony should be

Plate 80. The Kneisel Quartet. (*LCE*, Figure 28)

made.[53] The reason for this I fail to grasp, for the work is so evidently programmatic in intent that without some hint of the composer's meaning it seemed obscure and even fantastic. A distinguishing feature of the symphony is the vocal solo written to the text of a quaint old German folk-song, which forms the last of the four movements. There may be a time when the human voice becomes a necessity to give to a thought expressed symphonically its fullest emotional meaning. The necessity in this symphony for such departure from established symphonic norm was not apparent; neither do I believe, with all due deference to Beethoven and the immortal "Ninth", that vocal effects can ever be properly engrafted on the symphonic form as such. [. . .]

(*NYW*, January 22, 1911, Metropolitan Section, p. M5)

514

After a third and fourth hearing of the work last week the compiler of this report sees no reason to change his opinion expressed seven years ago, for he found Mahler's fourth symphony to have gained nothing in coherence of meaning, definiteness of expression, or distinctiveness of melody and orchestral characterization. A heaven such as the Bavarian poem describes so naively must be a queer place at best [. . .].

It must be that Mahler mistook the literary pleasure he derived from the perusal of the lines as sufficient prompting wherewith to invite the tonal muse, but that lady failed to bless the composer with any noticeable inspiration, and in many arid places of his work seems to have turned her back upon him altogether. The pleasantest parts of the symphony were the several gentle little episodes in unadorned folk tune style and manner. However, that is not symphony and does not become such merely by being decked out with that title and with pretentious orchestration.

Mahler is right; he does not resemble Richard Strauss in the least, as the program proved when it came the turn of "Heldenleben" [. . .]. In the face of such glorious boldness of musical utterance as Strauss's and such original tonal terms in which to clothe it, the Mahler talent as revealed in his fourth symphony seems puny and futile.

---

[53]Once again, Krehbiel was obliged to state that "in deference to Mr. Mahler's wishes there shall be no attempt at an analysis or description here of his symphony [. . .]"; accordingly, the programme booklet contains for this item only the headings of the movements, and an English translation of the text of the soprano solo.

As a conductor, however, the concerts of last week revealed Mahler to be a master second to none, and that is glory of no inconsiderable order. [...]

(*MC* 62, no. 4, January 25, 1911, p. 19)

515

[...]

What, in all sincerity, can be said of [Mahler's Fourth Symphony]? What can be said of musical qualities where none can be detected, and why should one go into detail concerning the orchestral mask, when there is nothing behind it? With the most sincere search it seems impossible to find anything in this symphony, except a series of unrelated orchestral effects, fairly clever as far as a knowledge of the instruments goes, but wholly superficial, and which have nothing whatsoever to offer the music-hungry spirit.

The themes of folk character seem de-humanized, mere dry imitations of similar themes of a previous epoch. Nowhere does a creative force seize upon the current of the work and expand it with emotional exaltation. There is abundance of orchestral cleverness throughout the work, but it seems all spent to no purpose, as the hearer is left unmoved.

(Arthur Farwell in *MA* 13, no. 12, January 28, 1911, p. 23)

516

A regular feast was spread for the delectation of the Wagnerites at the Academy of Music yesterday afternoon, when the Philharmonic Society of New York, with the assistance of Madame Gadski, and under the direction of Mr. Gustav Mahler, was heard in a program exclusively derived from the works of the Bayreuth master. To other than Wagner enthusiasts the arrangement was a somewhat formidable one. It comprised no fewer than five overtures - it had been originally intended to make the number six, but at the last moment more merciful counsels prevailed, and the "Rienzi" number was omitted. [...]

There is no doubt that the concert from first to last was very much enjoyed. The orchestra itself is nothing extraordinary, not so good in some important respects as our own, but Mr. Mahler is an exceptionally magnetic and masterful conductor, who is a recognized specialist in the interpretation of Wagner's scores, and his reading of the program was exceedingly luminous, lucid, eloquent, emphatic and impressive. [...]

The upper parts of the house were well filled, but downstairs the audience was small.

(*The Philadelphia Inquirer*, January 24, 1911, p. 8)

517

The matter of sub committees was now taken up [. . .] and it was resolved: that Mrs. Sheldon, Mr. Choate,[54] Mr. Flinsch and Mr. Leifels be appointed as an Executive Committee with powers to be defined by a resolution to be drafted by them which is to contain a proposition for an auditing and finance and a program committee [. . .].

(Excerpt from the Minutes of the Guarantors' Committee, January 25, 1911; in the ANYP, quoted with permission)

518
THE INFLUENCE OF THE FOLK-SONG ON GERMAN MUSICAL ART
From an Interview with the Eminent Composer and Director
GUSTAV MAHLER
Secured expressly for THE ETUDE

Mr. Mahler gave his opinions to our interviewer partly in German and partly in English. Consequently it has been impossible to employ his exact phraseology

[Editor's Note - Gustav Mahler (. . .) is now recognized as one of the very foremost composers and directors of our time (. . .) In 1880 he started his career as a conductor, which has made him one of the most renowned musicians of our time. Success followed success (. . .) and (he) eventually came to New York as conductor of the German Grand Opera at the Metropolitan, later taking his recently resigned position as director of America's oldest orchestra, the "New York Philharmonic." (. . .) THE ETUDE feels that it is exceedingly fortunate in securing an interview such as the following from Herr Mahler since he has refrained from giving similar interviews upon subjects of this kind for many years.]

The influence of the folk-song upon the music of the nations has been exhibited in many striking forms. At the very root of the whole matter lies a great educational truth which is so powerful in its effects, and so obvious to all, that one can almost make an axiom: "As the child is, so will the man be." [. . .] What occurs in childhood makes an indelible impression. The depth of this psychological impression must ever be the

---

[54]Joseph Hodges Choate, Jr. (1876-1968) - Prominent American lawyer.

rock upon which all educational systems are founded. So it is in music, that the songs which a child assimilates in his youth will determine his musical manhood.

[. . .] I have said assimilated – you will notice that I did not say appropriated. That is quite a different matter. The music is absorbed and goes through a process of mental digestion until it becomes a part of the person. [. . .]

I have often heard composers who claim to seek individuality above all things state that they purposely avoid hearing too much music above all other composers, fearing that their own originality will be affected. They also avoid hearing the songs of the street or folk-songs for a similar reason. What arrant nonsense! [. . .]

In some cases we find that the great composers have actually taken folk-melodies as themes for some of their works. In most cases of this kind they have given the source of the theme all possible publicity. In some cases where they may not have done this a few critics with limited musical knowledge and no practical ability in composition have happened to find these instances, and being at a loss to write anything more intelligent, they have magnified these deliberate settings of folk-themes into disgraceful thefts. The cry of plagiarism is in most cases both cruel and unjustified. [. . .] After all, the handling of the theme is even more significant than the evolution of the theme. Consider for one moment the incalculable benefits to the literature of the world brought about by the Shakespeare treatment of plots, which otherwise would have been absolutely forgotten [. . .], all of them plagiarised, but gloriously plagiarised.

[. . .]

The early composers also realised that in order to make their work understandable and more readily received, it behooved them to employ folk-themes as the basis for some of their more complicated works, so that the public that heard them could grasp the significance of the work more readily.

One does not have to delve very deep into the works of Haydn to realise what a keen appreciation he had for the beauty and simplicity of the folk-song. [. . .] When he came to produce his great works, he was so thoroughly imbued with the musical language of the people that the folk-song character and influence keeps cropping up all the time. This is, perhaps, not quite so much the case with Mozart, whose musical father, Leopold Mozart, took every pains to have his phenomenal son surrounded with the very best music of the day. Notwithstanding this, one cannot help feeling that the folk-songs which the wonderful child must have heard from his little playmates were assimilated, although their influence is not so pronounced as in the case of Haydn. [. . .]

Although the actual instances where Beethoven used real folk-songs as themes or as suggestions for his works are limited, it is nevertheless the fact that this gigantic genius conceived in his most exquisite and moving melodies thematic designs which when analyzed are really very simple and often of the character of folk-songs. [. . .]

I do not think that the tendency to use the idiom of the people will ever die out, and I do believe that music which has the true melodic characteristics will exist long after the furies of cacophony have worn themselves out of existence.

All this I have said as a composer, but as a director I am thoroughly eclectic. I am tremendously curious about all new music, and seek to give each new work, regardless of type, the interpretation nearest that which the composer intended. This is my duty to myself, to my art and to the public which attends my concerts.

Since my residence in America [. . .] I have observed [. . .] that a musical condition exists in this country which makes it extremely difficult for the American composer to work with the same innate feeling which characterises the work of some of his European contemporaries. [. . .] The subject of the folk-song bears such a direct relation to this matter that I cannot fail to avail myself of this opportunity to discuss the matter.

[. . .] When I am asked whence the future American composer will come I am forced to inquire: "Where is the American folk-song?" I cannot be quoted as an authority on American music, but depending upon the information received from friends whom I consider keen observers, and upon what I have heard myself, it seems to me that the popular music of America is not American at all, but rather that kind of music which the African negro transplanted to American soil has chosen to adopt. [. . .]

That the negroes in America have accomplished so much is truly amazing. [. . .] But to expect that they would evolve a new, distinct and original folk-song is preposterous in itself. They are great imitators, I am told, but that is no reason why the American composer should imitate their distorted copies of European folk-songs. The syncopations introduced in negro songs under the name of "rag-time" are not original, but may be found in the folk-songs of Hungary and other European nations. [. . .]

Just why the American composer should feel that he is doing something peculiarly American when he employs negro folk-songs is difficult to tell. Hungarian composers are prone to employ gypsy themes, and the music of Hungary has become marked in this way so that it has become gypsy music and not Hungarian music. Surely American music based upon crude themes of the red-skinned aborigines, or upon the appropriated European type of folk-song which the African Americans

444

have produced, is not any more representative of the great American people of today than are those swarthy citizens of the New World representative of all Americans.

So long as young Americans have to content themselves with the kind of trashy popular songs which are ground out by the thousand every year and howled mercilessly in the music halls of the country, just so long will America be forced to wait for its great master in music. But I am told by educators, America is awakening to this condition, and American children are being furnished with ever-increasing opportunities to hear good music [. . .], the music of all nations played by performers from all nations. One does not have to be a prophet to see that some day [. . .] America may look for results in music far beyond the fairest dreams of the most optimistic.

(*The Etude* [Philadelphia], May, 1911, pp. 301f.)[55]

519

After more than half a century of honorable achievement in the world of music, the New York Philharmonic Society made its debut in Washington at the National Theatre yesterday afternoon [. . .]

Although Mr. Mahler is noted in New York and in other centers of population which he visits frequently, for the breadth of poetic fire of his Wagnerian readings, it was questionable judgment to announce an all-Wagner program for an unheard organization's initial concert, as there are still many music lovers who are unregenerate enough, even in this pro-Wagnerian age, to hesitate before committing themselves to an entire afternoon amid the aural cyclones of the master Teuton. [. . .]

There are both distinction and charm in the beat of the Mahler baton. The director has a wealth of temperament [. . .] The Philharmonic Society as a body, however, lacks something of that homogeneity which is one of the chief charms of the Boston Symphony Orchestra and which Dr. Pohlig[56] is succeeding so admirably in developing in the Philadelphia Orchestra. [. . .]

(*The Washington Post*, January 25, 1911, p. 9)

---

[55]The interview in question was probably given during Mahler's last appearance with the Philharmonic in Philadelphia, on January 23, 1911.
[56]Carl Pohlig (1858-1928) - German conductor and pianist (Liszt's pupil). He was conductor of the Philadelphia Orchestra from 1907 to 1913.

520

[Postmark: January 27, 1911]

HOTEL SAVOY

My dear Herr Ritter!

[. . .]

As the dice appear to have fallen here, I may well become my own successor next season. - With their love and determination, the people here are making it virtually impossible for me to leave them in a bind. - And thus I am half decided to return here next winter. [. . .]

Just exactly what is it that the little birds have been chirping in my ear about Casella[57] lately [?] It would pain me greatly to find myself disappointed in this case. I had, and have a great deal of sympathy for the young man, and also expect rectitude from him.

The matter itself - that is, "being in" in Paris or where ever, is to me, as you know, quite unimportant. For all I care, Paris can live with or without me. [. . .]

(Eleanore and Bruno Vondenhoff, *op. cit.*, pp. 153f.)

521

When Gustav Mahler conducted Tschaikowsky's "Pathetique" symphony for the first time at one of the concerts of the Philharmonic last year his treatment of the work was such as to call forth a chorus of disapproval from even his devoted admirers. New York entertains an especial fondness for this music, and there was no small amount of indignation when it was hinted that Mr. Mahler's perfunctory reading of it was due to his abiding dislike for the Russian composer. At all events the unfavorable comments set him thinking and a few weeks later he conducted it again, this time in a much more satisfactory style, albeit not

[57]Alfredo Casella (1883-1947) - Eminent Italian composer, pianist, conductor and writer on music. He was an early and eloquent champion of Mahler's music (s.a. **569**).

The context in which Casella's name appears more than once around this time (s.a. **529**) is baffling and, for now, unexplained. The programmes of the New York Philharmonic for the 1909-1910 and the following two seasons contain no evidence of Casella's planned or actual appearance as either soloist or composer.

approaching the standard set by his predecessor, Safonoff.[58] At the concert given by the Philharmonic in Carnegie Hall last Sunday afternoon the "Pathetique" figured on the program for the first time this Winter and as the *pièce de résistance* of the occasion. There was a fair amount of applause after each movement, though the truth of the matter is that Mr. Mahler, while giving a better performance than the first last year, did not rise to the level of his second. [. . .]

(MA 13, no. 12, January 28, 1911, p. 15)

522

HOTEL SAVOY

January 31, 1911

Dear Herr Gutmann!

[. . .]

4. As concerns next year, it is, as I had foreseen it, difficult to leave here. The people are making every effort, and will probably capture me again. I think that once I will have to run away secretly, otherwise I will not get away from here. [. . .]

(Revers, op. cit., pp. 85f.)

523

[New York, January-February 1911]

My dear little Mama,

For some time your letters have made no mention of your coming, which we are *all* looking forward to so much. [. . .] We have our posh cabins on the finest ship in the German merchant navy, the *George Washington*, for 20 [30?][59] March, and you will be sure to arrange your

---

[58]This is a highly subjective and somewhat fanciful account of past events. While some critics had, in fact, disliked Mahler's first performances of the "Pathétique" on January 20 and 21, 1910, these had not given rise to a "chorus of disapproval" (see, for example, **365**). On the second occasion (March 6, 1910: the day after the American première of *Pique Dame* under Mahler - hardly evidence of an "abiding dislike" for the composer!), the all-Tchaikovsky (!) programme caused the *Times'* critic (not Aldrich in this instance) to write: "[Mahler] has previously been instrumental in producing the works of the greatest Russian composer at Vienna, and it is probable that he feels strongly in sympathy with them" (March 7, 1910, p. 9).

[59]In another letter, written to Emil Gutmann around the same time, Mahler referred to the 30th of March (*GMB*, Letter 462, p. 402). In any case, the Philharmonic's season was to close only at the end of March. (S.a. Note 11 and **554**)

journey in such a way that the three of us can return together, won't you? That will be wonderful. When are you coming?

This time I can give you the best of news about Almscherl. She is really blossoming - is keeping to a splendid diet, and has entirely given up alcohol,[60] looking younger every day. She is hard at work and has written a few delightful new songs that mark great progress. This, of course, also contributes to her well-being.

Her published songs are causing a furore here and will soon be sung by two different singers.[61] [. . .] I shall probably be returning here for another year. [. . .]

Thank God I can now sense the first breaths of spring. (I mean, I too have kept very fit this year, but I am tremendously looking forward to being back.)

[. . .]

(*MSL*, pp. 370f.; original German [incomplete] in *GMB*, p. 401)

524

As forecasted exclusively in THE MUSICAL COURIER a fortnight ago, Gustav Mahler has been signed for another year as conductor of the New York Philharmonic Sociey, a wise and proper move on the part of the orchestra's executive committee.

(*MC* 62, no. 5, February 1, 1911, p. 20)

525

When the Committee was first formed I warned Mahler not to allow these ladies too free a hand in the choice of the programmes. He laughed and said he did not at all mind being relieved of the burden. It would give him less to do. But he was to pay dearly for this.

(*AMM*, p. 184; original German in *AME*, pp. 225f.)

---

[60]It is hardly surprising to find that the clause referring to "alcohol" is missing in *GMB*.

[61]Five of Alma's songs were published by Universal Edition late in 1910, but only one of these was performed while the Mahlers were still in New York (see **546**). (For more information on Alma's songs, see Susan M. Filler, "A composer's wife as composer: The songs of Alma Mahler," *Journal of Musicological Research* 4, no. 3-4 [1983], pp. 427-441.)

526

Resolved that the Executive Committee appointed at the last meeting be continued as a permanent standing committee.

[...]

Resolved that the General Committee forthwith appoint a Finance Committee which shall consist of three persons elected by the General Committee from among its members. [...]

Resolved that the General Committee forthwith appoint a Program Committee which shall be composed of six persons to be elected by the General Committee from among its members, and the Chairman of the General Committee, Ex-Officio [...]. The Program Committee shall supervise the selection of music to be played at the various concerts of the Society. It shall submit the minutes of its meetings at the regular meetings of the [General] Committee for approval by that body.[62]

[...]

Committees elected:

[...]

Program Committee:

Mrs. Untermeyer, Mrs. Roosevelt, Mrs. Cheney, Miss Draper, Mr. Arnold and Mr. Schmitt.[63]

(Excerpt from the Minutes of the Guarantors' Committee, February 1, 1911; in the ANYP, quoted with permission)

527

No orchestral project in the past two seasons has aroused more interest or comment than the reorganization and establishment on a permanent basis of the New York Philharmonic Society.

[...] Said Mrs. Sheldon to a MUSICAL AMERICA representative this week:

"It has always been my intention and the intention of the committee working for me in taking hold of the Philharmonic Orchestra to provide an organization for New York and the entire country that would have as its ideal the giving of the best concerts that money could provide.

[...]

"The Philharmonic Orchestra is not an orchestra maintained for the exploitation of Gustav Mahler and he would be the first man to deny such an assertion. It makes no difference whether the conductor is Mr.

[62]Regrettably, none of the minutes of the Program Committee seem to have been preserved.
[63]Thus, with Richard Arnold and Henry P. Schmitt (also a violinist; s.a. **228**), the Program Committee had two musician-members against four laymen.

Mahler or somebody else, as long as he is a musician of Mr. Mahler's caliber. The idea is not to exploit a certain man, but to present in the best possible way the music of the great composers. Of course, to do this it is absolutely necessary that the conductor be a man, not necessarily of renown, but of great ability, and in Mr. Mahler we have such a man.

"Personally, I feel that Mr. Mahler is the greatest conductor, either in Europe or America, today, and I feel further that we have been most fortunate in keeping him as long as we have. While it is not settled absolutely, I believe that he will remain with us at least another year.

"Of course, we have not been entirely fortunate in the attitude of the critics toward the orchestra. Certain of the critics are entirely free, that is, they have no other interests which prevent them from writing what they think and can criticise a program favorably, or adversely, merely upon the music's merits. On the other hand, there are critics in this city whose interests in other institutions and organizations are so great that they cannot afford to write as they must feel concerning the magnificent work of the orchestra.

[...]

"[...] when the Philharmonic makes a slip of any sort most of the critics are very alert and seize upon the opportunity to call attention to trivial things, magnifying them until, if the public were to accept their dicta, the Philharmonic would have no support whatever. Fortunately, the public has developed a mind of its own and, in this case, seems to have used its judgement to very good advantage.

[...]

"I read in your paper the other day an interview given you by Alexander Lambert, that as long as the direction of musical affairs remained in the hands of women music in this country would be in a barbaric state.

[...]

"[...] Mr. Lambert at one time had remarked to me that no woman in America has done so much for music, or had advanced the standing of the art so much as I had, and that if it were not for us women music in this country would be in a parlous state. It is very evident that he has had a remarkable change of sentiment since his failure to be engaged, either as business manager or as soloist, with the orchestra."

(*MA* 13, no. 13, February 4, 1911, p. 37)

528

No. 792 LEXINGTON AVENUE, NEW YORK, Feb. 4, 1911.
To the Editor of MUSICAL AMERICA:
I read in your issue of February 4 a statement on me by Mrs. Sheldon

which requires correction. I met Mrs. Sheldon two years ago at a dinner and was immediately approached by her to interest myself in the proposed reorganization of the Philharmonic Society. Being an old friend and admirer of Mr. Mahler, I was glad and ready to help in any way possible. I was asked to become a member of the committee and in that capacity attended several meetings, and, in fact, was one of the signers of the first agreement made between Mr. Mahler and the reorganized orchestra.

Mrs. Sheldon, whom I saw at several of the meetings, often made some remarks about my old friend Walter Damrosch, conductor of the Symphony Society, that I felt in honor bound to withdraw from further active participation in the affairs of the Philharmonic Society[64] and thereby invoked Mrs. Sheldon's displeasure.

As to the extraordinary assertion that I applied for the position of manager of the society, I can only say that it is the invention of a very imaginative mind. The Philharmonic Society, with all its endowment, is not rich enough to engage me for such a position. For several years past I have been repeatedly asked by such men as Mahler and Damrosch to appear as soloist with their respective organizations, but I have always and positively declined to appear! I am in the happy position to be able to sit among the audience and watch other pianists agonize over the keyboard. My remarks about "Women and Music" in your paper of January 21 were general, and not intended to be personal. I regret that Mrs. Sheldon should feel that the cap fits her.

Believe me to be

Yours very sincerely,
ALEX. LAMBERT.

(*MA* 13, no. 14, February 11, 1911, p. 2)

529

[Received in Vienna on February 21, 1911][65]
HOTEL SAVOY

Dear Herr Director [Hertzka],

First of all, please excuse the "trouble" with Novak-Suk; it is

---

[64]See **160**.

[65]As this is Mahler's last known letter, it is given here in its entirety. Less than three months before his death, and already seriously ill, he is seen here in a good frame of mind, and planning assiduously for the summer and beyond.

attributable to a misunderstanding by the uncommonly stupid office of the manager. - I have set back the performance of both works (because I wish to give a "Bohemian" evening among the upcoming concerts),[66] and the clerk translated this as - I am sending it back to the publisher. - Naturally, everything is 'All right' now - I am most grateful to you for advising me. I have had not a moment's doubt that you had acted loyally towards me.[67] But do not take it amiss if I reiterate that I do not consider the inventor or contriver of the plan loyal to me. So then, now we can forget it. And in future you will, indeed, know how I feel about such things. Above all, I ask once again that *unconditional* discretion should be exercised with everyone with respect to the works I hand over to you for publication, until the day of publication. This is extremely important to me for 1000 reasons. - I have received the proofs of the 4. [Symphony]. Not yet the score of the 8. In April I am conducting in Paris, and will be in Vienna in May. There we will then talk about everything in detail.

The business with Casella[68] was downright unpleasant for me. I had already taken him off the programme twice. Now I am postponing him definitely until next season - which I will, unfortunately, have to spend here again. I could not yet free myself from here. But this time it is definitely the last time.

Please, dear friend, just watch very carefully that my symphonies are published *only* with the corrections. Those in the IV. proved their worth brilliantly here. The work had a great success. - Now heartiest greetings and many thanks from your

most devoted
Gustav Mahler

The errors in the parts of the IV. are unbelievable! I believe that a new edition *is unavoidable!*

(Moldenhauer, *op. cit.*, pp. 548f.)

---

[66]Mahler probably meant the concerts in the special cycle of national programmes that had been announced as a "Norse-Slavic" evening (see the introductory essay). These concerts were eventually given under Spiering on March 14th and 17th.
[67]The reference here is to tentative plans for the première of a "new work" by Mahler (presumably the Ninth Symphony) that were communicated to him by Hertzka, and to which Mahler had reacted angrily in a letter written at the end of December, 1910 (Moldenhauer, *op. cit.*, p. 548).
[68]See Note 57.

530

Storms were brewing in the Philharmonic Committee, and Mahler paid no attention. They were now dictating programmes he had no wish to perform and they did not like it when he declined. J[ohner] had set the whole orchestra by the ears and they were so refractory that Mahler no longer felt secure in his position. His habit of shutting his eyes to what was unpleasant prevented him seeing his danger, until one day in the middle of February, he was required to attend at Mrs. Sheldon's house. She was chairman of the Executive. He found several of the male members of the Committee there and was severely taken to task. The ladies had many instances to allege of conduct which in their eyes was mistaken. He rebutted these charges, but now at a word from Mrs. Sheldon a curtain was drawn aside and a lawyer, who (as came out later) had been taking notes all the time, entered the room. A document was then drawn up in legal form, strictly defining Mahler's powers. He was so taken aback and so furious that he came back to me trembling in every limb; and it was only by degrees that he was able to take pleasure in his work. He decided to ignore all these ladies in the future. The only exception was Mrs. Untermeyer, his guardian angel. She was away at this time;[69] otherwise nothing of all this could have happened.

(*AMM*, pp. 188f. [tr. revised by Z. Roman]; original German in *AME*, pp. 230f.)

531

Count Albert Apponyi,[70] the Hungarian statesman and peace advocate, spoke last night in Carnegie Hall on "Some Practical Difficulties of the Peace Problem in Europe." He told a large audience, which included many figures that are well known in the peace movement in this country, that Americans were leaders in the enthusiasm for peace and that it was their duty to spread their ideas through Europe. He compared the energetic advocacy of peace in America with the languid acceptance of

[69]Although it is a very remote possibility, the reference to the Untermeyers' absence from New York in **465** could perhaps place that letter in this period (but see Note 34).

[70]Count Albert Apponyi (1846-1933) was generally considered the leading Hungarian statesman between 1880 and 1920. He had been Mahler's friend and ardent supporter during his directorship of the Royal Hungarian Opera (1888-1891), and brought his considerable influence at the Austrian Court into play to ensure Mahler's appointment to the Imperial Opera in 1897. The lack of documentary evidence notwithstanding, it is more than likely that the two of them met during Apponyi's stay in New York.

the desirability of peace by Europeans and said that the time appeared still far away when the demand for permanent peace will become a factor of political power in Europe.

(*NYTrib*, February 16, 1911, p. 5)

532

Marked interest is manifested in the first performance in America of Chabrier's opera "Briseis"[71] which will be given in Carnegie Hall on Friday evening, March 3rd, by a competent cast of well-known operatic artists with the MacDowell Chorus, under Kurt Schindler, assisted by the Philharmonic Society, under Gustav Mahler.

(*NYTrib*, February 19, 1911, Part Five, p. 2)

533

Nahan Franko,[72] the musician, gave a reception and supper last night at his home, 296 West Ninety-second Street, to a number of his friends. Among those present were Mr. and Mrs. Victor Herbert, Mr. and Mrs. Gustav Mahler, Franz Kneisel, Baron von Wolzogen, Mr. and Mrs. A.J. Webber, Reuben Goldmark, Rafael Joseffy, Mrs. Randolph Guggenheim, Mr. and Mrs. F. Lewisohn, Mr. and Mrs. William Guard, and Signors Campanari and de Segurola from the Metropolitan Opera House.

(*NYT*, February 19, 1911, p. 11)

---

[71](Alexis) Emmanuel Chabrier's (1841-1894) lyric drama remained unfinished at the composer's death. Although, to the best of my knowledge, Mahler had not performed any music by this French composer until his years with the New York Philharmonic, he had presented the world première of Goldmark's opera *Der Kriegsgefangene*—a work based on the same story as *Briséis*—in Vienna in 1899.
[72]Nahan Franko (1861-1930) - American violinist and conductor. He was concertmaster of the Metropolitan Opera orchestra from 1883 to 1905, following which he had a brief and unspectacular career there as a conductor. There are two notes preserved from Mahler to him in the Archives of the New York Philharmonic Society, both undated. In one of them (most likely written after Mahler had assumed the conductorship of the Philharmonic), Mahler asks to borrow "his" harpist "again". An explanation for this curious request may be provided by the fact that for several years beginning in 1905, Franko was the conductor of a popular civic orchestra in the summers.
  Among the distinguished list of musical guests, perhaps the most distinguished one was Baron Hans (Paul) von Wolzogen (1848-1938), the German writer on music, Wagner's friend and foremost early champion.

534

On 20th February he was suffering once more from the inflammation of the throat and fever. On the 21st he was to conduct and insisted on doing so. Fränkel, he said, would pull him through. Fränkel warned him not to attempt it, but Mahler insisted that he had conducted time after time with a temperature and Fränkel had to give way. We wrapped him up carefully and drove to Carnegie Hall. Among other works he conducted that night was the first performance in public of Busoni's *Cradlesong at the Grave of my Mother.*[73]

He felt very exhausted when the interval came, and his head was aching. But he pulled himself together and conducted the rest of the concert. His last concert. We drove back, taking all possible precautions, accompanied by Fränkel, who examined him as soon as we arrived. His temperature was normal again and Mahler was very merry about conducting himself back to health.

(*AMM*, p. 189; original German in *AME*, pp. 231f.)

535

First steps for the reorganization of the "Society for the Promotion of Opera in English"[74] were taken yesterday at No. 1425 Broadway. The purpose as set forth is "to advocate and maintain the principle that opera-goers should be enabled to understand and more fully enjoy opera by hearing it sung clearly to them as frequently as possible in their own language."

A committee composed of Horatio Parker,[75] director of music at Yale; Walter Damrosch, David Bispham,[76] Charles Henry Meltzer,[77] Reginald

---

[73]The full title of Busoni's Op. 42, composed in 1903, is *Berceuse élégiaque - Des Mannes Wiegenlied am Sarge seiner Mutter.*

[74]For earlier references to the questions of opera in English, see **75, 409**, and Note 137, Chapter III.

[75]Horatio William Parker (1863-1919) - Eminent American composer, organist and educator. He studied composition with Chadwick and Rheinberger, and was professor of music at Yale University from 1894 to his death.

[76]David Bispham (1857-1921) - Eminent operatic baritone, one of the first American male singers to attain international fame. He was highly influential in establishing English-language opera performances in North America.

[77]Charles Henry Meltzer (1852-1936) - Born in England, he settled in the United States in 1888; foreign correspondent for a number of New York papers, he also translated many opera libretti.

de Koven and Alfred Mildenberg called a regular meeting of the new society for two weeks from yesterday.

(*NYW*, February 20, 1911, p. 9)

536

A symphony concert devoted to the music of Italy is such an extraordinary event that it really deserves more than ordinary mention. When Gustav Mahler announced that he would devote one of the Philharmonic concerts to such a purpose, curiosity was aroused as to where he would go for his material. For Italian composers of late years, and in fact, in the past, have devoted their attention almost exclusively to the composition of opera. The Italians seem to care for no other form of music, and the composers' ambition seems to be to satisfy this public.

The Philharmonic Society's Italian programme was performed by the Orchestra last evening in Carnegie Hall, and it surprised no one to find that Mr. Mahler had resorted to a clever strategy and introduced as a symphony Mendelssohn's fourth work in that form, known as the "Italian." It would be difficult to find an Italian symphony, written by an Italian, and probably still more difficult to listen to it.

The other names on the programme [Sinigaglia,[78] Martucci,[79] Bossi,[80] and Busoni] were more or less unfamiliar to symphony concertgoers, one of them wholly so. The programme was interesting as an experiment, perhaps, but it is not likely that the Italian composers will reign in New York anywhere but in the Opera House, where they are given full sway. [. . .]

This performance [of Busoni's "Berceuse Elegiaque"] was the first which the work had received anywhere. [. . .] Its harmonic and instrumental combinations were singular to a degree. It is a gruesome work in a modern composer's most modern manner. However, it was applauded, and Mr. Busoni, who sat in a box with Mr. Toscanini, rose to bow his thanks.

(*NYT*, February 22, 1911, p. 9)

---

[78]Leone Sinigaglia (1868-1944) - Italian composer, studied with Dvorak. In his later works, he frequently utilized the folk melodies of his native Piedmont.
[79]Giuseppe Martucci (1856-1909) - Italian composer and conductor, he directed the conservatories of Bologna and, later on, of Turin. He endeavored to raise symphonic and chamber music in Italy to the level and rank of opera.
[80]Marco Enrico Bossi (1861-1925) - Italian composer, organist and pianist, he shared Martucci's aspirations (see above). He directed music schools in Venice and Bologna.

Plate 81. Title page of the Philharmonic program booklet
for Mahler's last concert.

457

537

We are a courteous people. Mr. Busoni's compatriots, Sinigaglia, Martucci, and Bossi, disclosed in their music a respect for all the things which Mr. Busoni took laborious pains to condemn. They adhered to some old-fashioned notions touching tonality as well as melody, which in a little book in which he outlines a new system of musical aesthetics he seeks to brush aside as old-fashioned rubbish.[81] He could not introduce his new scale of third-tone intervals, but he could, and did, introduce enough cacophony to make the audience wish he had never perpetrated his "Berceuse Elegiaque," or if he had, he had not honoured New York with its first performance. It is not always possible to escape a first performance, but it is easy to avoid a second. It is not likely that the New York public will be aggrieved by the "Berceuse Elegiaque" again.

(*NYTrib*, February 22, 1911, p. 7)

538

New York, February 22, 1911

The day before yesterday [...] at Schirmer's[82] [...] at dinner Mahler said something very good. "I have found", he said, "that people in general are better (more kindly) than one supposes." "You are an optimist", here interposed a fat American woman. "And more stupid", Mahler concluded, quickly, addressing the lady.

The first performance of the Berceuse took place yesterday. Toscanini came.

[...] The Berceuse belongs to a type of music which does *not* suit Mahler so well as the rhythm and drums of Turandot. [...]

(Busoni, *op. cit.*, pp. 181f.)

539

The Philharmonic Society yesterday afternoon repeated its Italian programme that it gave on Tuesday evening. Mr. Mahler was indisposed and did not conduct. He is said to have had a light attack of grippe. His

---

[81]The reference here is to Busoni's *Entwurf einer neuen Ästhetik der Tonkunst* (1907; 2/1910), published in English in 1911 as *Sketch of a New Aesthetic of Music.*

[82]Presumably the home of Ernest Charles Schirmer (1865-1958), who at this time headed the music publishing firm founded by his father in 1861. Schirmer's published Mahler's 'Bach Suite' in 1910 (see Note 68, p. 297).

place on the conductor's stand was taken by Theodore Spiering, the concert-master of the Orchestra, who fulfilled his task with competence. Ferruccio Busoni conducted his number on the programme, a "Berceuse Elegiaque," which he did not do last Tuesday. [. . .]

(*NYT*, February 25, 1911, p. 11)

540

New York, February 25, 1911

[. . .] Yesterday I had much to do, and yet too little. You will soon understand why.

At two o'clock I was asked to conduct the Berceuse myself, Mahler ill and absent.

The concert began at 2.30, but it was almost four o'clock before it was my turn to stand on the platform for those ten minutes. [. . .]

(Busoni, *op. cit.*, p. 183)

541

While there was evidence of deep disappointment on the part of the audience assembled at the National Theater yesterday afternoon when it was learned that Gustav Mahler would be unable to conduct the New York Philharmonic Society for the second concert in Washington, the leadership of Theodore Spiering, the concert master, was so scholarly as to cause the music lovers to forget the fact that Mr. Mahler's illness not only prevented his direction of the orchestra, but caused a change in the program.

Instead of the Bach suite for orchestra, with the distinguished director at the harpsichord, Ernest Hutcheson appeared as the soloist, playing MacDowell's concerto in D minor, for pianoforte and orchestra.

[. . .]

Mr. Spiering conducts with quiet dignity, having his musicians always under complete control. He conveys an impression of fine sincerity, which is not marred by the fantastic or sensational, either in personal mannerisms or in reading.

(*The Washington Post*, March 1, 1911, p. 3)

542

Chicago, March 30, 1911

[. . .] Mahler has not conducted since the 21st February. Spiering took his place on the 24th and remained and will remain until the end of the season. It was very creditable that an averagely good violinist should show so much *présence d'esprit*, and was able to carry through the performance fairly well. But—! The behaviour of the New York audience and the critics over the matter will remain in my memory as one of the most painful experiences.

The sensation made by a leader of an orchestra being able to conduct unprepared, has made a greater impression on them than Mahler's whole personality was ever able to do! Spiering has been exalted to the position of one of the greatest conductors, and they have spoken quite seriously about his continuing to fill the post. *Not one word of regret has fallen about Mahler's absence!!* One reads of such things happening in history, but when it is a personal experience, one is filled with despair. [. . .]

(Busoni, *op. cit.*, p. 194)

543

Besides owing thanks for the results obtained through his system of drilling an orchestra, the musical community of New York City is under obligations to Gustav Mahler also for having selected as concertmaster of the Philharmonic Theodore Spiering, who during the last two weeks while Mr. Mahler has been ill [. . .] has conducted the Philharmonic concerts in New York and other cities [. . .]. Mr. Spiering has been competent to do this work without disturbing the Philharmonic equilibrium, and, in fact, curious to relate, the concerts of Sunday a week ago and last Sunday (particularly the last one), both under Mr. Spiering's direction, represented the largest receipts of any Philharmonic concerts for a long time past.

There are statements made by authority that Mr. Mahler has not signed for next season and shows the usual disinclination of the European of mature age, who comes here and who cannot find himself capable of assimilating our conditions, having been born and having developed and lived the better part of his life in Europe.

In many circles it is looked upon as desirable for Mr. Mahler to continue, but if he should retire, [. . .] under the present conditions, an American might be sought in place of a foreigner again.

[. . .] It behooves those who are the stockholders or the owners of the Philharmonic [. . .] to look to some kind of a reformation that will enable the Philharmonic Orchestra [. . .] to consider this question of conductorship more seriously than at any other period in the history of this society.

Should Mr. Mahler's successor be a European conductor, brought here temporarily without any other foothold and without any interests in

American musical development, merely as a kind of star conductor to attract people through the semi-sensational spirit of such an engagement, or should he be [...] any one of the number of Americans who have reached that development of a musician indicative of the knowledge to conduct [...] the kind of a repertory which is embraced in the scheme of the Philharmonic?

The fact that Mr. Spiering bears relations to Mr. Mahler that might make his engagement impossible[83] under these delicate conditions now prevailing [...] does not signify that we should again search Europe for a conductor. [...] The Philharmonic [...] should secure a conductor, if Mr. Mahler does not continue, who is identified with [...] a feeling of permanent interest in the organization and in music in New York and America [...].

(*MC* 62, no. 10, March 8, 1911, p. 25)

544

The Executive Committee reported its negotiations with Mr. Mahler, the Committee having received Mr. Mahler's terms in a letter to Mr. Flinsch. It was moved to reject the proposition contained in the writing received by Mr. Flinsch and it was resolved that the Executive Committee have power to negotiate and contract with Mr. Weingartner[84] on substantially the terms as set forth by the Committee in its cable to his agent and in case of failure to contract with Mr. Weingartner the Committee to have power to reopen negotiations and to contract with Mr. Mahler.

(Excerpt from the Minutes of the Guarantors' Committee, March 8, 1911; in the ANYP, quoted with permission)

---

[83]Although in the end Spiering decided to return to Berlin to live (see **562**), it is reasonable to think that his considerable success in conducting the Philharmonic during Mahler's illness may have given him the aspiration to succeed him permanently. There is also evidence enough to show that he had a fair amount of support in some quarters. The *MA*, for instance, published a full page of New York, Brooklyn and Washington press excerpts on April 1st (p. 8), with the heading "Theodore Spiering [in outsized bold print] / Conducts One-fourth of the Season's Philharmonic Concerts / What the Papers Say Concerning His Work as Conductor." It looks suspiciously similar to an editor's (or an agent's) 'campaign' leaflet.

[84]It illustrates the inefficacy of the rumour-mill well that among the many published lists of supposed successors to Mahler, Weingartner's name does not turn up in a single instance known to me (for example, see **557**). At any rate, it would have been rather ironic to have Weingartner succeed Mahler for the second time in just four years, in two positions literally a world apart.

545

I had a visit from the singer, Alda Gatti-Casazza.[85] [. . .] She had seen my volume of songs and wanted to sing one of them at her next recital. Mahler [. . .] urged her to sing all the five songs in the volume. This she could not do, as her programme was already settled. [. . .] the conclusion was that Mahler agreed to rehearse this one song ["Laue Sommernacht"] with her.

— — — — — — — — — —

One day Schindler, who was to accompany Alda Casazza, came to ask me about the tempi of the song of mine she was going to sing. Mahler who was in bed in the next room was enraged at the dilettante way he went to work [. . .]
One afternoon Fränkel came for me unexpectedly. This was very opportune, as it was the afternoon of Alda Casazza's recital and I had a ticket for the back of the gallery. Mahler and I came to a secret understanding that Fränkel should take me. [. . .] Mahler was awaiting my return in the keenest suspense. He said he had never been in such a state of excitement over any performance of his own works. When I told him it had been encored he said, "Thank God", over and over again. He was quite beside himself for joy.

(*AMM*, pp. 188 and 190f.; original German in *AME*, pp. 230 and 233)

546

A song recital was given yesterday afternoon in Mendelssohn Hall by Mme. Frances Alda, formerly of the Metropolitan Opera Company. [. . .] Mme. Alda's programme was long and interesting [. . .] Among her modern songs was a charming and characteristic one by Alma Maria Mahler, who is the wife of the conductor of the Philharmonic Society [. . .] Mme. Alda's voice is unpleasant in quality [. . .] Her vocal style is frequently imperfect, and this was revealed with special cruelty in the old music that she sang [. . .] She was more at home in some of the modern songs.

(*NYT*, March 4, 1911, p. 11)

[85]Frances Alda [Davies] (1883-1952) - Celebrated American soprano, born in New Zealand. She was a member of the Metropolitan ensemble from 1908 to 1930; married Gatti-Casazza.

Plate 82. Dr. Joseph Fränkel, Mahler's friend and physician in New York.
(*BRM*, Illustration 203)

Plate 83. The soprano Frances Alda-Casazza sang Alma Mahler's songs
in New York. (*COS*, Illustration 193)

During the winter, he had several attacks of what his biographers call "angina"; in February 1911 he had a bout of pharyngitis—he had had frequent sore throats—and despite fever, conducted a concert on February 21. He collapsed and worked no more. [. . .]

The most probable diagnosis is rheumatic heart disease with superimposed subacute bacterial endocarditis. [. . .] The authors are able to give here an accurate technical recital of [the evidence for endocarditis] based on the very detailed recollections of Dr. George Baehr, formerly Chief of Medicine at Mt. Sinai Hospital, New York, who was in 1911 Fellow in Pathology and Bacteriology in Libman's laboratory. Dr. Baehr's vivid account, extracted from his personal communication to us, follows:

"Sometime in February 1911, Dr. Emanuel Libman was called in consultation by Mahler's personal physician, Dr. Fraenkel, to see the famous composer and director. Apparently Dr. Fraenkel had suspected that Mahler's prolonged fever and physical debility might be due to subacute bacterial endocarditis and therefore called Libman, Chief of the First Medical Service and Associate Director of Laboratories at the Mt. Sinai Hospital, in consultation. Libman was at that time the outstanding authority on the disease. [. . .] Libman confirmed the diagnosis clinically by finding a loud systolic-presystolic murmur over the pericardium characteristic of chronic rheumatic mitral disease, a history of prolonged low grade fever, a palpable spleen, characteristic petechiae on the conjunctivae and skin and slight clubbing of fingers. To confirm the diagnosis bacteriologically, Libman telephoned me to join him at the hotel and bring the paraphernalia and culture media required for a blood culture.

On arrival I withdrew 20 c.cm. of blood from an arm vein with syringe and needle, squirted part of it into several bouillon flasks and mixed the remainder with melted agar media which I then poured into sterile Petri dishes. After 4 or 5 days of incubation in the hospital laboratory, the Petri dishes revealed numerous bacterial colonies and all the bouillon flasks were found to show a pure culture of the same organism which was subsequently identified as *streptococcus viridans*.

As this was long before the days of antibiotics, the bacterial findings sealed Mahler's doom. [. . .] The diagnosis and prognosis were reconfirmed [in Paris]."

Mahler's death has been seriously attributed, at least indirectly, to psychosomatic causes. On the basis of the foregoing evidence, this idea is untenable.[86]

(Nicholas P. Christy, M.D., Beverly M. Christy, and Barry G. Wood, M.D., "Gustav Mahler and his Illnesses", *Transactions of the American Clinical and Climatological Association* 82 (1970), pp. 207, 211f.)

548

Concertmeister Theodore Spiering again conducted the concert given by the Philharmonic Society yesterday afternoon in Carnegie Hall. Gustav Mahler, the conductor of these concerts, has been absent from his post for two weeks now and last evening well-defined rumors were afloat that he has no intention of conducting again until some matters between him and the Directors of the society are arranged.

It is said that he has had difficulty in making out his programmes this season, that in almost every instance his programmes have been changed for some reason or other by members of the Board of Directors. Mr. Mahler has submitted to this under protest until recently, it was said by a friend of the conductor last evening, but now he has decided that unless affairs are arranged more to his liking he will not continue with the society.

Gustav Mahler has been conductor of the Philharmonic Society now for two seasons, and it was recently announced that he was engaged for a third; his next season here, however, will doubtless depend on the outcome of his present dispute. It was announced some time ago that he was ill and that he could not conduct at a certain concert. Since then he has not appeared.

On one occasion, it was said, he wanted to perform the overture to Cornelius's "Barber of Bagdad", but took it off the programme because some one connected with the society did not like the work.

(*NYT*, March 11, 1911, p. 13)

---

[86] Among studies known to me, a more or less opposite point of view is represented by William E. Mooney's "Gustav Mahler - A Note of Life and Death in Music," *Psychoanalytical Quarterly* 37, no. 1 (1968), pp. 80-102. An excellent study of more recent vintage, at the same time summarizing earlier research and attempting to steer a 'middle course', is Stuart Feder's "Gustav Mahler, Dying", *International Review of Psycho-Analysis* 5 (1978), pp. 125-148.

549

Loudon Charlton writes to THE TIMES to contradict the rumors printed in Saturday's issue that Gustav Mahler's absence from his post was due to differences between himself and the management of the Philharmonic Society. "Mr. Mahler," Mr. Charlton writes, "has been confined to his bed since Feb. 21, suffering with a severe attack of grip. Last Monday he expected to resume rehearsals and conduct last week's performances, but the effort proved beyond his strength, and his physician forbade him to leave his room". He goes on to say that "Mr. Mahler and the management are now, and have been throughout the season, working in perfect harmony. There have been no differences as to programmes or policy".

(*NYT*, March 13, 1911, p. 9)

550

A letter from Mr. Mahler was read: Mr. Mahler requested that the balance of his salary be forwarded to him, after a pro rata reduction for the concerts he has failed to conduct on account of illness.

(Excerpt from the Minutes of the Guarantors' Committee, March 15, 1911; in the ANYP, quoted with permission)

551

Not very long since, a reorganized Philharmonic Orchestra was announced for New York. The services of a great conductor were engaged, the personnel of the orchestra was improved, and it was given out that no effort would be spared in bringing the orchestra up to the condition of the first orchestras of the world.

This line of advance has proved not so easy to follow as was anticipated. There have been wars and rumors of wars, most of them concentrating about the conflict between two forces, one represented by the province over which the conductor is supposed to have control, and the other by that province whose management belongs with the board of directors.

Mr. Mahler has now been absent from his post for several weeks, his place being filled by Concert-master Theodore Spiering. This circumstance led to the publication in the New York *Times* of March 11 of an article giving the rumored reasons for this absence, and subsequently to a reply from Loudon Charlton, manager of the Philharmonic Orchestra, denying that there had been any differences between himself and Mr. Mahler. [. . .]

[...]

In the absence of exact knowledge as to the ultimate causes of the present circumstances, and without any desire to be over-hasty in placing the blame, it is plain that all is not running smoothly within the Philharmonic Society. It is much to Mr. Charlton's credit in his connection with the society that he has popularized it to a degree unknown in the past and has procured greatly increased returns at the box office.

That there is division somewhere within the Philharmonic Society would appear to be evident. It is well known what happens to a house that is divided against itself. Until the Philharmonic Society awakens to the true nature of these difficulties there is no possibility that it can succeed in the high enterprise upon which it ventured forth at the time of its reorganization.

[...]

It is hoped that the Philharmonic Society will be capable of rising far enough above the mists of the struggle to see the source and the greatness of its danger, and that it will be able to prevail against the forces of disintegration and degeneration which threaten it.

(Editorial, *MA* 13, no. 19, March 18, 1911, p. 20)

552

Despite denials made by those interested, it may be stated on the highest authority that Gustav Mahler, conductor of the Philharmonic Society's orchestra will not return to New York next season as director of that organization, nor will he again appear in that capacity during the remainder of the present season.

Although strained relations have existed between Mr. Mahler and the committee, the management of the orchestra has announced his illness as the reason for his failure to appear at the concerts given in New York, Newark, Washington, Princeton and other cities. It is well known that were Mr. Mahler physically able to conduct he would have appeared at the final concerts this season.

The difficulty is said to have had its origin when Mr. Mahler, believing that certain members of the orchestra were not playing as he wished them to, received damaging evidence against the offenders through a second violinist's reports.[87] Those affected by this criticism demanded the discharge of Mr. Mahler's informant and were supported in their

[87]See **492**, Note 46, and **530**.

demands by some of the women of the board. This disagreement is said
to have affected Mr. Mahler to such an extent that he was on the verge of
a nervous breakdown when he fell victim to an attack of the
grippe. [. . .]

(*MA* 13, no. 20, March 25, 1911, p. 1)

553

Mr. Flinsch was apponted as a Committee of one to visit Mr. Mahler and
to express the sympathy of the Committee in Mr. Mahler's illness.

(Excerpt from the Minutes of the Guarantors' Committee, March 22,
1911; in the ANYP, quoted with permission)

554

Gustav Mahler was too weak to sail for Europe this week, and passage
which has been engaged for him on the *George Washington* for Thursday
[March 30th] had to be canceled. His condition has improved but
slightly.

(*MA* 13, no. 21, April 1, 1911, p. 5)

555

I met Mengelberg but once and he talked chiefly about Mahler, who, he
tried to persuade me, was the Beethoven of our time. However that may
be, he certainly was a giant among conductors. Yet when he was in New
York he was so pitilessly hounded that he wrote me on the eve of his
departure for Vienna, where he was idolized as few musicians ever have
been: "Let me take this occasion to press your hand warmly for your
repeated energetic championing of my ideals. Your sympathy and
support have been among the few experiences that have made New York
worth while for me."

(Henry T. Finck, *My Adventures in the Golden Age of Music*,
New York, Da Capo Press, 1971, p. 424 [originally published by
Funk & Wagnalls, 1926])

556

The story published in a New York morning paper to the effect that
Frank Van der Stucken will be the next conductor of the New York
Philharmonic Society is absurd and utterly without foundation. No such

contract has been entered into by the organization and every executive connected with it denies emphatically the existence of negotiations to that end. [. . .]

(*MC* 62, no. 14, April 5, 1911, p. 20)

557

Gustav Mahler's successor as conductor of the Philharmonic Society of New York is likely to be Henry J. Wood, the English conductor. [. . .]

Mr. Wood at present leads the Queen's Hall Orchestra in London. [. . .]

The one other man whose name has been most prominently mentioned as a likely successor to Mr. Mahler is Frank van der Stucken, of Cincinnati, musical director of the Cincinnati May Festival, and former conductor of the Cincinnati Orchestra. [. . .] The names of Ernst Kunwald, assistant director of the Berlin Philharmonic, and of Wilhelm Gericke, former conductor of the Boston Orchestra, have also been brought forward. [. . .] Henry Hadley, conductor of the Seattle Orchestra, has been suggested as still another candidate, and the fact that he is an American has won over to him a certain amount of support.

[. . .]

(*MA* 13, no. 22, April 8, 1911, p. 1)

558

(By Cable). Moscow, April 10, 1911.
To the Musical Courier:

Report here that if New York daily papers indorse Safonoff he will become Mahler's successor as conductor of the New York Philharmonic Society.

Q.[88]

(*MC* 62, no. 15, April 12, 1911, p. 20)

559

Our cabin was booked, the packing was done, and Mahler was dressed. A stretcher was waiting, but he waived it aside. He looked as white as a

---

[88]In light of Blumenberg's antagonistic attitude towards the daily press (see Note 51, Chapter I), and his inclination to ridicule them (see **34**), it is difficult to see this "report" as anything other than a hoax.

sheet as he walked unsteadily to the lift, leaning on Fränkel's arm. The lift-boy kept out of the way until the last moment, to hide his tears, and then took him down for the last time. The huge hotel lounge was deserted. Mrs. Untermeyer's automobile was waiting at a side entrance; Fränkel helped him in and drove to the quay with him. I went back to the office to pay the bill and to thank the office staff for all they had done for us without a thought for themselves during those weeks. They all came out and shook hands. "We cleared everyone out of the lounge - we knew Mr. Mahler wouldn't like to be looked at."

Blessed America! We never met with any such proof of true sensibility during our subsequent weeks in Europe.

(*AMM*, pp. 193f.; original German in *AME*, p. 237)

560

Though still a very sick man, Gustav Mahler, conductor of the Philharmonic Society of New York, sailed for Europe last Saturday on the *Amerika* of the Hamburg-American line. Mrs. Mahler accompanied him. It is their plan to go to the Austrian Tyrol as soon as Mr. Mahler's health will allow.

(*MA* 13, no. 23, April 15, 1911, p. 1)

561

Previous to Gustav Mahler's departure for Europe last Saturday morning, THE MUSICAL COURIER received a piece of paper on which was a typewritten, unsigned eulogy on the departing conductor and his work in New York during the past two seasons. The document began: "The Guarantors' Committee of the Philharmonic Society has issued the following statement," and the commendatory phrases followed. If the communication came from the Guarantors' Committee, it should have been signed by them; if it came from the press agent, and was unauthorized, then nothing more need be said about the matter by THE MUSICAL COURIER; and if it came from Mrs. Sheldon, president of the Philharmonic Society, then that fact should have appeared in some way in connection with the paper praises. This journal cannot and will not print anonymous communications. There is no reason for any one to be ashamed to praise Gustav Mahler. Why this secrecy?

(*MC* 62, no. 15, April 12, 1911, p. 20)

Plate 84. This was probably the last photograph of Mahler
taken in New York. (Roller, *op. cit.*, Illustration 79)

472

562

Theodore Spiering [. . .] has announced that he has severed his relations with the Philharmonic Society.

Mr. Spiering will return to Berlin, from which city he will go as a guest conductor to several of the great European orchestras the coming season. [. . .] In addition to his guest conducting he will again establish his school for violin in Berlin.

[. . .]

(*MA* 13, no. 23, April 15, 1911, p. 3)

563

In these days of the establishment and growth of symphony orchestras, America should be thoroughly awakened to the fact that money alone does not make a symphony orchestra. [. . .]

After a year of experience in which the Philharmonic Society of New York should have learned this lesson, even if it has not, a year threateningly disintegrating in its results, the society is ransacking Europe to find a conductor to succeed Mr. Mahler. The Philharmonic Society can pay the price asked by any conductor whom it solicits. This, however, is not saying that it can get any conductor that it wants. Most of the desirables are tied up by contracts of longer or shorter duration. It is possible that others, casting an inquiring and retrospective glance over the affairs of the past year, might be apt to decline the proffered honor. A firm position at less money in one of the cities of Europe is more desirable than a position of doubtful security and artistic discouragement in New York. [. . .]

What any symphony orchestra in New York or anywhere else needs first is not a conductor, but an ideal. It needs a clear, definite, practical artistic ideal, to which every person connected with the organization shall subscribe, and for which everyone shall work. [. . .] No working plan which does not recognize this fact, and which is not founded first of all upon a definite program of artistic progress, can carry a symphony orchestra to success and supremacy. [. . .]

Before true progress is possible the artistic purpose for which the symphony orchestra stands should be plain to the management of the orchestra, the conductor and the public. Everyone should know whether the orchestra exists for the performance of the classics, to represent modern progress in composition, to present works which are already known to appeal to concert-goers, or for whatever blending of these or other purposes.

[. . .]

These remarks are of a general nature, and applicable to every symphony orchestra in America. They may indicate, in a manner, why the Boston Symphony Orchestra has arisen to its position of supremacy. If the Philharmonic Society of New York wishes to find its way out of Egypt into the Promised Land it could do nothing better than to postpone the engagement of any conductor until it had promulgated a well-conceived artistic ideal, and a promise of adherence to it.

(Editorial, *MA* 13, no. 24, April 22, 1911, p. 18)

564

Paris, 21 April [. . .]

Mahler wants the world to know that it is by no means overwork in America that has shattered his health: "I have worked really hard for decades and have borne the exertion wonderfully well. I have never worked as little as I did in America. I was not subjected to an excess of either physical or intellectual work in America."

(*Neue Freie Presse*, April 11, 1911, quoted in *BRM*, p. 279; translation in *BRM(E)*, p. 272)

565

Mahler is probably the foremost synthetic conductor we have had in America, outside of Arthur Nikisch, although in the final evidences of a thorough analysis, not only of detail in execution, but in the sense of poetical testimony, he is not equal to Nikisch. But he is unquestionably an artist of first quality with the baton and none of the old line of directors ever approached him. [. . .] Mahler is an artist and his production of Berlioz, the first time New York actually heard Berlioz, all former productions of Berlioz having been travesties in comparison, places us under obligation to this erudite musician, particularly considering the material he had at his disposal.

And this brings us to the issue. The Philharmonic nonagenarian players insist upon occupying their places. Mahler, with the assistance of one of the violinists, attempted a *coup de théâtre*, but failed, and that led to his illness [. . .]. Mahler could not reform orchestral New York. Add to this his lack of tact [. . .] and we see quickly why he could not maintain himself [. . .]. As a personality Mahler is so completely self-centered that he loses his own personality; it is consumed within himself. [. . .] As a conductor he is remarkably gifted, as a man he has no gifts; he accepts every compliment as a truth. As a musician he is conscientiousness itself; as a personality he is too conscious of himself. These are all

contradictions that constitute a bar to practical and purposive success
[...].

("Reflections", *MA* 62, no. 17, April 26, 1911, p. 22)

566

The process of selecting a conductor for the New York Philharmonic
Society to succeed Gustav Mahler, goes merrily on, and the office of
Loudon Charlton, manager of the orchestra, was besieged this week by
those who desired to confirm reports received by cable from Europe,
where Felix Leifels, acting in the interests of the committee, is
approaching a number of prospective candidates.

A new name, that of Joseph Stransky, of Berlin, entered the lists on
Monday.

[...]

Negotiations with Sir Henry Wood, of London, are also under
way. [...]

(*MA* 13, no. 26, May 6, 1911, p. 1)

567

Paris, May 5. - Gustav Mahler, the composer and former conductor of
the Philharmonic Society of New York, is desperately ill at a sanitarium
at Neuilly, near the Bois de Boulogne. He is suffering from a nervous
disorder which, it is said, has been aggravated by his differences with
members of the Philharmonic, and his trouble is complicated by angina
pectoris. His life seems in grave danger, and it is said that, even if he
recovers, it will be a long time before he is able to resume work as
composer or conductor.

According to information obtained by the New York critic, Charles
Henry Meltzer, now in Paris, in an interview with the wife of the
composer, the latter's illness is directly attributable to his unfortunate
relations with the backers of the New York organization. Mr. Meltzer
quotes Mme. Mahler as follows:

"You cannot imagine what Mr. Mahler has suffered. In Vienna my
husband was all powerful. Even the Emperor did not dictate to him, but
in New York, to his amazement, he had ten ladies ordering him about like
a puppet. He hoped, however, by hard work and success to rid himself of
his tormentors. Meanwhile he lost health and strength. Then, after an
excursion to Springfield, he contracted angina. At his last concert in New
York, rather than disappoint the public, he conducted when he was in

high fever. Now the angina has been complicated by blood poisoning. My husband cannot read or work. Heaven only knows how it all will end."

Leading members of the Philharmonic Society deny that Mr. Mahler's illness is the result of his relations with that organization, insisting that those relations were always agreeable, and that the illness of the conductor came about through his extreme nervousness.

(*MA* 14, no. 1, May 13, 1911, p. 1)

568

Two cablegrams from distinct sources received in New York on Tuesday confirmed the appointment [of Joseph Stransky, of Berlin, as conductor of the New York Philharmonic Society] and it is believed that an official statement to this effect will be made before the end of the week.

[. . .]

A cablegram from London on Wednesday announced Sir Henry J. Wood's decision to decline the offer made to him by the Philharmonic committee.

(*MA* 14, no. 1, May 13, 1911, p. 1)

569

For years I had been enthusiastic about the personality of Gustav Mahler, who was totally unknown in France. I had studied all of his symphonies and knew them practically by memory. He came through Paris on his return from New York in April, 1909, and a Viennese woman friend obtained an appointment with him for me. He was a rather small man, of a somewhat Schubertian Viennese-Czech type. He was very nervous and could not remain quiet for a second. He was quite friendly, and seemed sincerely moved when he discovered that I knew so much of his music from memory.

At the beginning of May, 1911, I learned that Mahler had returned from America gravely ill and was a patient in a clinic at Neuilly. His illness was the result of overwork and, above all, of the incomprehension and hostility which he met in America, a world which was certainly not for him. [. . .] I had not been able to see him again because of his weakened condition. [. . .] his memory remains sacred for me. He was one of the noblest and finest musicians I have ever known.

(Alfredo Casella, *Music in My Time* [tr. and ed. Spencer Norton], Norman [Okl], University of Oklahoma Press, 1955, pp. 92, 101)

570

Vienna, May 17. - It is feared that the condition of Gustav Mahler, the noted composer and conductor, is hopeless. He is suffering from inflammation of the lungs, and although the attending physicians today reported their patient a trifle better, they announced also that the inflammation was spreading and they did not believe it could be checked.

Dr. Joseph Fraenkel [. . .] who was Mr. Mahler's physician in America [. . .] states that Mr. Mahler was taken ill at his last rehearsal of the Philharmonic Orchestra, but insisted on conducting the concert the next day. Since then he has been constantly under a physician's care.

(*NYTrib*, May 18, 1911, p. 9)

571

After much upheaval, search, and negotiation, the New York Philharmonic Society, it has been confirmed, has engaged Joseph Stransky of Berlin, as its conductor. Without disrespect to Mr. Stransky, there are reasons which cause this circumstance to remind one of Aesop's fable of the mountain in labor which finally brought forth a mouse.

What was the reason given by the Philharmonic Society for not retaining Theodore Spiering as its leader? It was because he could not be regarded as a sufficiently "international figure." Accordingly, the society went on a hunt for an international figure, and after the proffered honor of the society's baton had been declined in at least one quarter, as is understood, Stransky was finally settled upon.

After refusing to consider Theodore Spiering on these very grounds of international significance, the Philharmonic Society will have considerable difficulty justifying its final choice. Herr Stransky is unquestionably a good conductor. He holds an honorable post in Berlin as conductor of the Bluthner Orchestra[89] in a series of concerts for the Berliner Concert Verein.

However, if the Philharmonic Society recedes from its position of requiring an "international figure," it should at least have sufficient dignity and initiative not to fall into the stale, time worn and outworn attitude that, other things being equal, a European is better than an American. To get a leader who is as little of an international figure as Stransky in a country where we have a Hadley, a Van der Stucken, and others, is a procedure scarcely likely to appeal strongly to Americans.

---

[89]The Blüthner Orchestra, bearing the name of the famous German firm of piano makers, was founded in 1907.

The Philharmonic Society is behind the times. American advance has overridden it and left it surrounded by the stale atmosphere of dead traditions. America wants live organizations, musical enterprises which, if not brilliantly international in their affiliations, are at least electrically in touch with the affairs and personalities of American life.

(Editorial, *MA* 14, no. 2, May 20, 1911, p. 20)

572

Gustav Mahler, lately conductor of the Philharmonic Orchestra of this city, died in Vienna last night, after an illness which has prostrated him for the last eight weeks. He was taken to Vienna from Paris early in May, when his condition was realized to be hopeless, in response to his urgently expressed wish to die in his native country.

(*The [N.Y.] Evening Post*, May 19, 1911, p. 9)

573

Anton Seidl was forty-eight years old when he passed away, and this morning's cable brings the sad news that his pupil and successor, Gustav Mahler, had died only three years older. While there are plenty of cases of longevity among musicians, both creative and interpretative, it nevertheless does seem as if in the majority of cases death sought its early victims too often in their ranks. [. . .] Nor is this to be wondered at. Music is the most emotional of the arts, and the most intoxicating; unless its devotees cultivate moderation, it is apt to lead them to excesses. [. . .]

Gustav Mahler [. . .] worked and fought too hard, and now he is no more. He was both a creator and a conductor, and it was this dual capacity, combined with his pronounced individuality, that put a special stamp on everything he did. [. . .] Mahler re-created whatever he interpreted. He made a Bach suite the sensation of a musical season; he conducted the "Flying Dutchman" overture so that one could smell the salt breezes of the stormy sea and hear the whistling of the wind in the masts; he made Beethoven's hackneyed symphonies seem new, and was the first conductor who revealed the full grandeur of the funeral march in the "Eroica"; and he brought out all that is best in the works of the contemporary German composers, notably his friend Richard Strauss. His creative impulse sometimes made him retouch the orchestral coloring of the music of former epochs so as to make it sound as it would if the respective composers had lived today. For this he was violently abused, though he left the scores unaltered for others to follow the letter instead of the spirit.

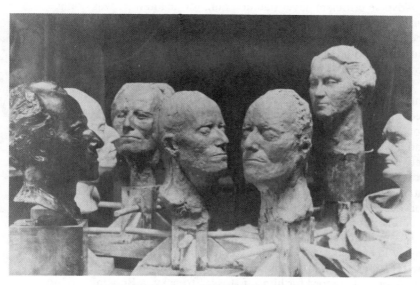

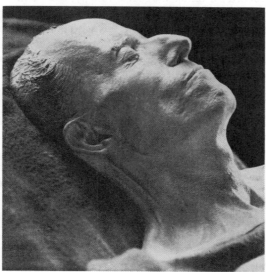

Plate 85. *Above*, This unidentified photograph, probably taken in Carl Moll's studio, shows some versions of Mahler's death-mask, and a copy of Rodin's Mahler-bust. (W.G.W. Kurz Collection)

Plate 86. *Below*, Mahler's death-mask, made by Carl Moll.
(W.G.W. Kurz Collection)

Adverse criticism never daunted him, for he knew he was doing missionary work for masterpieces. Once his patience gave way; being accused of having come across the Atlantic to teach Americans how music should be peformed, he demurred, but added that neither had he come over here to be taught.

It so happened that on the very day Mahler died came the official announcement of the engagement of his successor. The situation was a peculiarly difficult one for the directors and sponsors of the Philharmonic Society. Up to the time when Mahler's illness assumed an acute form, it had been hoped that he would return for another year. The differences between him and those at the head of affairs have been grossly exaggerated; there were mistakes on both sides; he had been too much interfered with, but he also had done some very queer things in his nervous excitement; but all that had been smoothed over and the contract was ready for him to sign. [...]

Under the circumstances, the Philharmonic directors doubtless acted wisely in engaging a young man who, while not yet named among what are facetiously called "prima donna conductors," nevertheless had made an honourable record for himself. Josef Stransky, a Bohemian of not quite forty years, is one of the best-known orchestral and operatic conductors in Berlin, and there are not a few who consider him the coming conductor - an interpretor of the emotional Seidl-Mahler type. [...]

The death of Mahler calls attention to one of the most significant changes in the musical world. His emoluments—$30,000 for five month's work—were the highest ever paid an orchestral leader. [...] The conductor's importance is being more and more appreciated, and so long as great orchestral interpreters are as scarce as great operatic tenors or sopranos, they can virtually make their own terms; yet if they are wise they will observe moderation in their demands, lest the sponsors who make their engagement possible conclude that first-class orchestras are too expensive playthings for them.

(*The [N.Y.] Evening Post*, May 19, 1911, p. 8)

574

"It is easy to kill a man through witchcraft; provided it be helped out by a little arsenic." So said Voltaire. "Nobody dies of a broken heart," say we, unconvinced when we are not able to find the germ or "bug."

There were some expressions of derision when it was reported that Gustav Mahler, late of this city, was dying in Europe of "worry." His wife was the authority for the statement. A prejudiced witness, of course, and without the scientific authority that would attach, say, to the family doctor.

Well, as to the seriousness of the composer's condition, it turns out that there was no exaggeration. The man is dead. It is probable that no postmortem examination, conducted by the cleverest surgeon of Vienna, would show whether or not his death was due to the willingness of the Metropolitan in letting him go to the Philharmonic Society, or the fussiness of the Philharmonic in arranging his work for him.

Geniuses, or men of great talent, are strange creatures. They are sometimes absurdly thin skinned. We pay them huge salaries, and yet they are not satisfied. They have a way of refusing to consider what they have for sale as a commodity worth so much. Mahler, Tschaikowsky, Dvorak and Richard Strauss were the most distinguished men to conduct in our Carnegie Hall. Perhaps if the first had had some amiable peculiarities, if he had used no baton in conducting, or had had a huge family, or had gone to afternoon teas, he would have been more popular, and would be alive today.

(*The [N.Y.] Evening Sun*, May 19, 1911, p. 8)

575

[Mahler's] death, in all likelihood, was caused (or at least hastened) by his sojourn in America. [. . .] So many irritations awaited him in America that it is not surprising that the fatal illness developed and overcame him in short order. First of all, he had to take a *pro forma* oath that in time he will acquire American citizenship; his second trial consisted of having to take—before an America music jury—formal examinations in piano playing and music theory. [. . .]

(*Egyetèrtès* [Budapest], May 19, 1911, p. 7)

576

BERLIN, May 20. - The death of Gustav Mahler induces the Mittag Zeitung, one of Berlin's most popular newspapers, to publish a "casualty list" of German artists who have succumbed to the "nerve-wracking and peculiar demands of American art."

The Mittag Zeitung heads the list "Victims of the Dollar."
[. . .]
The Mittag Zeitung says that no German artist who has not the reserve

and strength of a Schumann-Heink can hope to survive the "killing demands of American artistic life".

(NYT, May 21, 1911, Part Three, p. 4)

577

[. . .] Against the few in the [Mittag] Zeitung's list who may have shortened their lives by the hard work they did in this country we may place a list including the names of MARIE SEEBACH, FRIEDRICH HAASE, ADOLF SONNENTHAL, ERNST POSSART, AGNES SORMA, MARCELLA SEMBRICH, MATERNA, LILLI LEHMANN, WASILY SAFONOFF, who won great fame and much money here with no impairment of health. MAHLER was never a strong man, and he was, to be sure, an overstrenuous worker, always battling against the conventional, the stupid, and the commercial obstacles to artistic progress. Vienna, Hamburg and Munich would have worn him out as quickly as New York. His fame was vastly increased in America, where his untimely death is greatly deplored. Nevertheless, the Mittag Zeitung's argument, which is summarized in the special cable dispatches from Berlin to THE SUNDAY TIMES, reveals a curious point of view. The theory that the activity of the artistic life in this country, the brisk competition, and the climatic conditions combine to make the lot of the virtuoso difficult is quite comprehensible. But the Mittag Zeitung fails to make the point in regard to MAHLER.

(Editorial, NYT, May 21, 1911, p. 10)

578

[. . .] The news of his demise was received all over the musical world with genuine sorrow, for Mahler represented a singularly high type of modern musician and in many respects served as a model often held up as an example to other chiefs of the baton, who regard themselves as of more importance than the works they interpret and the composers who wrote them. Nikisch, Strauss, Kreisler, Mottl, Richter, Toscanini, Gericke are among the living musical authorities who admired Mahler tremendously, and of lesser known adherents he had thousands in every city where he has led performances of operas and symphonic works.

Some of his staunch partisans in New York are moved to connect his untimely death with certain circumstances that arose here as Mahler's second season with the Philharmonic was running to a close.

[. . .]

Of course THE MUSICAL COURIER heard reports of all kinds

482

about Mahler and the Philharmonic directorate, and now and then read disparaging notices about him here and there, but until the present rather open references in the daily newspaper obituary notices, THE MUSICAL COURIER had no idea that there was any serious foundation to all the rumors that came into this office. Our news editor telephoned at the time to several persons high in the executive councils of the Philharmonic, but was informed that all stories afloat about differences between its leader and those in control were unqualifiedly false.

In the interests of everyone concerned (not the least, those of the newly engaged Philharmonic conductor and his possible successors under the present executives) a full explanation should be forthcoming if there is anything to explain. Already the Berlin newspapers are using Mahler's death as the text for sermons on our musical methods, and the cable reports that the Mittag Zeitung of that city without much ado calls the deceased "another victim of dollarland."

(*MC* 62, no. 21, May 24, 1911, pp. 22f.)

579

Vienna, May 22. - In the presence of a great gathering composed of the leading members of musical and artistic circles Gustav Mahler, the eminent composer, who died May 18 of angina pectoris, was buried in the Grinzing Cemetery here this afternoon.

At the express wish of the composer the ceremony was of the simplest character. There were no speeches at the graveside. The musical portion of the service was rendered by the chorus of the Imperial Opera.

(*NYT*, May 23, 1911, p. 11)

580

Gustav Mahler is dead, and his death was made to appear in some newspaper accounts as the tragic conclusion of unhappy experiences in New York. As a matter of fact, though his American career, which endured three years, was more productive of disappointment to him, and also to others, than of delight, there was nothing that happened to him here which could by any stretch of the imagination be construed as even a remote cause of the disease which brought about his death. He was a sick man when he came to New York three years ago. His troubles with the administration of the Philharmonic were of his own creation, for he might have had the absolute power which he enjoyed for a space in Vienna had he desired it. He was paid a sum of money which ought to

483

have seemed to him fabulous from the day on which he came till the day when his labours ended, and the money was given to him ungrudgingly, though the investment was a poor one for the opera company which brought him to America and the concert organizations which kept him here. He was looked upon as a great artist, and possibly he was one, but he failed to convince the people of New York of the fact, and therefore his American career was not a success. His influence was not helpful but prejudicial to good taste. It is unpleasant to say such things, but a sense of duty demands that they be said. [. . .]

When he first went to Vienna Mahler introduced many changes, some of which were not looked upon in the light of reforms, but he adhered to them and built up a party which has made itself troublesome to all his successors since. [. . .]

He was brought [to New York] as one of the conductors of the Metropolitan Opera House [. . .], effecting his first appearance as a conductor [. . .] in Wagner's "Tristan und Isolde." [. . .] Mahler's work was greatly admired by the reviewers for the newspapers and the public, but it was in no sense revolutionary, and there was even disappointment in the circumstance that there was nothing except things with which the cognoscenti were only too familiar in the stage management - a department which needed reformation. [. . .] [In Mahler's "Don Giovanni"] some novel elements were noticeable, most of them generally conceded to be excellent, some of them of a kind that caused more than a little headshaking. There were changes of tempo which ran counter not only to long accepted tradition the world over, but which could not be reconciled with a conviction that Mr. Mahler was familiar with the original text, which is Italian, or its spirit. [. . .]

Much ado was made over [. . .] his production of "Fidelio," with [. . .] the changes he had introduced in the score in Vienna, but they were not accepted here as inspired revelations, because it was recognized that the personal equation in them was so large as to compel the raising of aesthetic questions which every honest and intelligent musician felt went to the very heart of artistic purity.

[. . .] Thus, he did not scruple to change the orchestration of the introduction to the second act, and give it a distinctly latter-day cast, simply because he thought, or professed to think, that Beethoven would have orchestrated the number in a different manner if he had had his perfect hearing - meaning, if it meant anything, if he heard and desired as Mr. Mahler heard and desired, nearly a hundred years later. This disposition to meddle with the classics grew upon him later and had much to do with the disappointment which he brought as a conductor of the Philharmonic Society.

It was not long before the local musical authorities, those of the operatic and concert field, found that Mr. Mahler was an expensive and unprofitable proposition. [. . .] This [. . .] did not prevent a committee of women [. . .] from carrying out a plan for the reorganization of the Philharmonic Society, so that Mr. Mahler may be secured permanently for the musical evangelization of New York. [. . .]

To pursue an orderly course in the story of Mr. Mahler's life something ought now to be said about his compositions, because it was as a composer as well as a conductor that his friends, a well defined party, or clique, sought to impress the world with a sense of his greatness. [. . .] After Mr. Mahler began to attract attention as a composer, as was plainly proved in an article printed in this journal after the performance of his fourth symphony, he professed to cut loose from the programmatic school, and though his early symphonies are utterly inexplicable without the titles, mottoes and sub-titles which he gave them, he insisted on their acceptance as absolute music. It is a harsh thing to say of a dead man, but the truth demands that it be said that in one instance he denied in a letter to this writer that he had ever written a letter quoted in an analysis of one of his symphonies written by a warm admirer and friend, and made believe that he could not understand it at all, though the symphony demanded some such a programme as was suggested. In other cases he insisted that he had written as freely and unconstrainedly as Mozart and Schubert, though his symphonies bore titles and sub-titles. [. . .]

It was a singular paradox in Mahler's artistic nature that while his melodic ideas were of the folksong order, his treatment of them was of the most extravagant kind, harmonically and orchestrally. He attempted in argument to reconcile the extremes by insisting that folksong was the vital spark of artistic music, but in his treatment of the simple melodies of his symphonies (some of them borrowed without acknowledgement) he was utterly inconsiderate of their essence, robbing them of their characteristics and elaborating them to death. He should have been an ingenuous musician - a musician, had he the genius, like Dvorak. Instead, he tried to out-Strauss Strauss and out-Reger Reger, and not having the native force of either of them he failed. We cannot see how any of his music can long survive him. There is no place for it between the old and the new schools.

There remains much to be said about his activity for two years in connection with the Philharmonic Society. A very large endeavor was made by the management, especially during the season which has just closed, to arouse popular interest in the concerts of the venerable society. It failed. Not only did the general public fail to respond to the loud appeal, but the subscription list steadily grew smaller. For this no one was to blame except Mr. Mahler. It is a famous notion of foreigners that Americans know nothing about music in its highest forms. Only of late years have the European newspapers begun to inform their readers that the opera in New York has some significance. Had their writers on music been students they would have known that for nearly a century New Yorkers have listened to singers of the highest class - singers that the people of the musical centres of the European continent never were permitted to hear. Mr. Mahler early learned a valuable lesson at the opera, but he never learned it in the concert room. He never discovered that there were Philharmonic subscribers who had inherited not only their seats from their parents and grandparents, but also their appreciation of good music. He never knew, or if he knew he was never willing to acknowledge, that the Philharmonic audience would be as quick to resent an outrage on the musical classics as a corruption of the Bible or Shakespeare. He did not know that he was doing it, or if he did he was willing wantonly to insult their intelligence and taste by such things as multiplying the voices in a Beethoven symphony (an additional kettle-drum in the "Pastoral," for instance), by cutting down the strings and doubling the flutes in Mozart's G minor, by fortifying the brass in Schubert's C major until the sweet Vienna singer of nearly a century ago seemed a modern Malay running amuck, and—most monstrous of all his doings—starting the most poetical and introspective of all Schumann's overtures—that to "Manfred"—with a cymbal clash like that which set Mazeppa's horse on his wild gallop in Liszt's symphonic poem. And who can ever forget the treatment of the kettledrums which he demanded of his players? Wooden-headed sticks, not only in Beethoven's ninth symphony, but even in Weber's "Oberon" overture! But the man is dead and the catalogue might as well be closed. Of the unhappy relations which existed between him and the Philharmonic Society's promoters it would seem to be a duty to speak; but the subject is unpleasant; those most interested know the facts; the injury that has been done cannot be undone, and when it becomes necessary the history may be unfolded in its entirety. It were best if it could be forgotten.

(*NYTrib*, May 21, 1911, Part Five, p. 2)

581

An Open Letter to the Music Critic of the
New York Tribune

Sir:

When, after a long agony of suffering, Gustav Mahler died in Vienna, you published an article in the *New York Tribune*, where, in language full of hatred, you insulted the memory of that great artist.

The time has come when it seems necessary to disclose the true character of your attitude towards the Philharmonic Society's late conductor.

When during Mahler's lifetime you took every occasion to attack and abuse him, you at least tried to make believe (and maybe some simple-hearted people did believe) that yours was 'bona fide' criticism, not prompted by any personal animosity. But when Mahler died and on the very next day you piled up in the columns of your paper every possible columny that could be invented against the man and the artist - then you showed your cards. No *critic* would be so eager to throw a pail of mud on a fresh grave. Only an enemy would do that.

It does not occur to me to discuss with you the value of Mahler as an artist, or to 'defend' him against you. This would be ridiculous. In fact I would consider it a lack of reverence to the memory of the great deceased master. But as this letter is to be published and will be read by many, I should like to mention a few facts which may not be known to every reader.

Gustav Mahler in the last two decades was recognized by the whole musical world as one of the greatest orchestra leaders of modern times, and was by many regarded as the greatest conductor of our time. The years of his directorship at the Vienna Court Opera—the most dignified operatic institution in Europe—formed an era not only in the artistic life of that city, but in the history of musical and dramatic production in general.

In Mahler's day people traveled from all parts of Europe to Vienna to hear his interpretations - just as they traveled to Bayreuth for Wagner's operas. The world's greatest composer of that time—Brahms—declared Mahler's productions of opera to be a *revelation*. The same is to be said of Mahler's activity on the concert platform. In Vienna, in Berlin, in Paris, in St. Petersburg—whatever difference of opinion may have existed as to his compositions—the verdict was unanimous that as an interpreter of Beethoven, Mozart, Wagner, Schubert, he was unsurpassed.

How far Mahler's popularity extended in Europe was clearly shown at the time of his fatal illness and of his death. Then the newspapers of all European countries and languages daily brought whole columns of news about his condition. Cable dispatches appeared and were eagerly read everywhere - a fact singularly significant in Europe where little attention, if any, is ever given by the press to anything concerning the private life of an artist. When Mahler died the newspapers and periodicals gave as much space and attention to him as is usually given only to kings. He was recognized as king in the realm of art. Of the glowing tributes paid to Mahler's memory after his death it would be easy to quote enough to fill volumes. The key note of all these tributes is best formulated in one

487

sentence, a sentence by which the leading European musical publication, *Die Musik*, opened its pages after Mahler's death:

"The world has lost its greatest artist. Gustav Mahler is dead."

It was this artist whom Mr. Krehbiel denounced as "prejudicial to the good taste of the American people," and to whom he undertook to give lessons as to the interpretation of musical classics.

In 1907 Mahler came to New York. The American public—always genuinely responsive and with a keen sense of appreciation for the work of a true genius—received him enthusiastically. But one day it was discovered by the music critic of the *New York Tribune* that Gustav Mahler was a very poor conductor. The 'discovery' was immediately announced to the public and fault after fault was pointed out to the surprised readers. Mr. Mahler was indeed very severely criticized in the *Tribune*. We find a characteristic sample of these criticisms in the *Tribune*'s 'post mortem' article.

"Mahler was willing wantonly to insult the people's intelligence and taste by such things as multiplying the voices in a Beethoven Symphony (additional kettledrums in the 'Pastorale', for instance) by cutting down the strings, and doubling the flutes in Mozart's G-minor."

This sentence is characteristic of the way the *Tribune*'s critic listened to Mahler's interpretations. He never noticed or mentioned the dramatic power of Mahler's conceptions, the rhythmical and dynamic perfection, the beauty of tone he drew from the orchestra - all these great and beautiful things, which made Mahler's interpretations unique in their picturesque suggestive power. But he carefully noted every 'double flute' and every 'additional kettledrum'. Imagine an art critic incapable of feeling the beauties of a picture but carefully criticizing the picture's frame and mentioning every speck of dust on it!

Oh, Richard Wagner! Of all the wonderful creations there is none more genuinely alive than Beckmesser in the 'Meistersinger von Nürnberg'. This specimen—the hater of genius, the faultfinder, the man miserably small in his attacks on everything great—this specimen exists! He always has existed and always will exist. He is indeed immortal. And here in the *Tribune*'s music 'critic' we have a most perfect sample of his type.

Now then, Mr. Beckmesser-Krehbiel, let me inform you that such items, in the editing of the classics, as you reproach Mahler with, were first introduced by no less a man than Richard Wagner himself and that since then they have been and are being used by every prominent conductor. Perhaps you have never read Wagner's essay on the Symphonies of Beethoven; for if you had read it, you would have known the facts. As a conductor, Wagner was the first to double the horn parts in the Ninth Symphony. After that von Bülow added two horns in the

Seventh Symphony, augmented the brass in the Coriolan Overture, changed the division of strings in the third 'Leonore' Overture and introduced innumerable other changes. Most of these alterations have since then become a tradition. Such facts are known nowadays to every professional musician and I daresay to every conservatory pupil. Sadly enough they are not know to the music 'critic' of the *New York Tribune.*

(Ossip Gabrilovich,[90] quoted in Clara Clemens, *My Husband Gabrilowitsch*, New York, Harper, 1938, pp. 131-135)

582

Very naturally, there is a great deal of interest in the new conductor of the Philharmonic. The future of the society is in question; every wise man knows that, and therefore he would be as big an ass who should try to obstruct its progress as he would be a scoundrel who would try to ruin it because some things in its history were distasteful to him. The muddle-headed and ugly-minded cattle who can never distinguish between honest criticism based on devotion to art and fetich worship we always have with us, and nobody has ever spent a few years in the critical department of a newspaper without hearing from them periodically. The Tribune's writer did not expect for a moment that even so liberal, tolerant and kindly a review of the late Mr. Mahler's career as appeared last Sunday would be permitted to pass without some ignoramus, too cowardly to sign his name and vile enough to send a postal card (as if any carrier was going to read it and set about it to hurt the reputation of the reviewer) containing his protest. Since he seems to be a reader of this newspaper (we don't know why, inasmuch as he obviously has no appreciation of its principles) his lucubration might as well be printed, not for what it was intended to be, but as a commendation of the article of last Sunday - for it is an honor to offend such fools:

"Congratulate you on your clever bit of Jackalism in re Mahler. You guarded your interests all right and if one is self-centered enough it does make the world turn. We should not expect a man who has no respect for the (illegible word) Hapsburgs and their environment to appreciate the great value of having (or being) a father or grandfather. But then he's dead and you will be some day too. R.I.P.

A-Flat."

[...]

(*NYTrib*, May 28, 1911, Part Four, p. 2)

---

[90]Ossip Gabrilovich (1878-1936) - Born in Russia, he gained fame as a pianist and conductor chiefly in the United States.

583

The period of Mahler's tenure tested the Philharmonic as a modern American orchestra with a long season addressed to a broad public. It is true that each of these elements was in an early stage of development - the Philharmonic was only slightly more modern, slightly more American, with a somewhat longer season, addressed to a relatively broader public, than in the days before 1909. Nor were the special features of the new regime original either with Mahler or with the Guarantors' Committee - Jullien,[91] Bergmann,[92] Thomas, and a number of conductors and orchestras in cities other than New York had long ago explored the mysteries of extended seasons, historical concerts, famous-composer programs, popular concerts, and out-of-town tours. But Mahler's two years represented the first time that the conservative Philharmonic, which formerly had stood like a great rock in the midst of the swirling waters of change, had made an effort to move with the currents and even to influence their course. For Mahler the experiment had often been a stormy experience, but for the orchestra there was no question that it had begun to succeed. In the first year of the reorganization the number of concerts was three times as great as it had ever been before, and in the second year it was four times as great. The deficit was very large, it is true, but there were generous citizens not only willing to pay it, but also to give their time and skills to the cause, and in the second year they had narrowed considerably the gap between the orchestra's expenses and its earned income. The expressed policy of the Guarantors' Committee was "to reconcile the commercially possible with the artistically desirable," and the Committee now knew, after its two instructive years with Mahler, that an expanding Philharmonic was compatible with the most exacting artistic standards.

[. . .]

In the life story of the Philharmonic, Mahler's brief term marks a moment of great historic significance - the moment when the new rubbed abrasively against the old, clearing a path for the future. But Mahler did *not*, as is generally supposed, sweep aside with one brusque gesture the shaky structure of an old Philharmonic to begin his work with an orchestra built entirely of new materials and on new principles. His period of service can better be seen as a period of transition and he as an

[91]Louis Antoine Jullien (1812-1860) - French conductor, composer and impresario. He led his own large and excellent orchestra in New York and on tours in 1853-54.
[92]Karl Bergmann (1821-1876) - German-born conductor and cellist. He conducted the New York Philharmonic from 1855 to his death, and was especially devoted to the music of Liszt and Wagner.

instrument of change - a change that had been gradually prepared, inside and outside the Philharmonic, for many years before he appeared on the scene.

(Shanet, *Philharmonic*, pp. 218f.)

584

The death of Gustav Mahler removes from the musical world one of its commanding figures. Whatever may have been the consensus of critical opinion as to the manner in which Mr. Mahler interpreted certain masterpieces, there was never any doubt as to the high level on which he carried on his artistic efforts. His conducting of the Mozart works and Beethoven's "Fidelio" at the Metropolitan Opera House will live long in the memories of those who had the good fortune to be present.

The present writer has no disposition to discuss the causes which led to Mr. Mahler's retirement from the post of the conductor of the Philharmonic. Persons of no importance whatever in this community have already obtained too much cheap notoriety from such discussions. The whole unhappy story will probably get an airing, for the conductor's wife evinced no hesitation in the statements which she made, before she departed from New York and after she landed in Europe.

It is more pleasant to take note of the fact that as a composer Mr. Mahler was accepted very seriously in Europe. His eighth symphony, performed last year in Munich, created a profound impression, and it is to be hoped that at some time not too far off it may be heard here.[93]

(*NYS*, May 21, 1911, Morning edition, 2. section, p. 12)

585

In Gustav Mahler music loses one of its most potent and picturesque figures - potent because Mahler undoubtedly was one of the best operatic and orchestral conductors of the past two decades, and picturesque because he composed symphonies of unusual form and content, and possessed a personality of such force that, although he seemed shy and reserved and almost taciturn by nature, nevertheless wherever his career led him he at once became the center of discussion and controversy. Some men loved Mahler and others hated him, but no one connected in

---

[93]Henderson's wish was to be fulfilled in less than five years: the Eighth was performed in New York on April 9, 1916, under Leopold Stokowski; the document *SFM* was issued for that occasion.

any way with him or his music could remain indifferent. The little man with the piercing eyes, black shock of hair, strongly hooked nose and defiant carriage was a musical power not to be overlooked or ignored.

[. . .]

The world is a poorer place for the passing of Gustav Mahler, a truly great man who did things worthwhile during his stay on earth, and he will be remembered with pride and gratitude by those he leaves behind.

(*MC* 62, no. 21, May 24, 1911, p. 36)

586

The untimely death of Gustav Mahler takes from the musical world one of its most notable personalities, and one who, by common consent, is ranked among the world's greatest orchestral conductors. By many he has also been very highly regarded as a composer, although despite the enthusiasm aroused on several occasions by the performance of his symphonies it cannot be said that his success in this field is as world-convincing as in the field of conducting.

Mr. Mahler has had a long and honorable career in Europe and America as a conductor of both opera and symphony. His devotion to high artistic ideals has been at all times unquestionable, a fact which must be recognized even by those whose ideals were sometimes at variance with his own. It was, in fact, this very quality of uncompromising directness in striving for his ideals that lent to his own achievements a sternness and hardness sometimes disturbing to the realization of more sympathetic qualities.

Mr. Mahler was not a virtuoso conductor in the sense in which that term is understood to-day. If he exacted much from the orchestra it was not for the purpose of making a show either of the orchestra or himself, but to gain the artistic ends deemed necessary by him. Economy of motion was one of his characteristics as a conductor. His intellectuality was of a nature to make him realize that with proper rehearsing and slight signals greater results were to be had from the orchestra with less expenditure than by extravagance of physical motion in conducting.

Among his chief qualities as a conductor were incisiveness in an unusual degree, and force. Above all he realized the great outlines of the works which he conducted. His sense of form was epic. His commanding and uncompromising nature as an artist led, perhaps, in a general way, to an obscuring of the tenderer qualities of music by the more forceful and severe. Whatever the degree of one's sympathy with Mr. Mahler as an artist, the recognition of his well established artistic attitude has been spontaneous and, in fact, imperative.

As a clearly defined individuality in the musical world Mr. Mahler has claimed a place with the foremost of those achieving this distinction. His loss will be deeply felt by the musical world.

(Editorial, *MA* 14, no. 3, May 27, 1911, p. 18)

587

As Mahler was getting ready to leave last year, he took me to his room to say good-bye. "During the winter, you have asked me often enough how I spend my free time. Now you will see." Then he laid before me the completed manuscript of his ninth symphony, which now needed only the final touching up of the orchestration. Like Beethoven and Bruckner, Mahler was not to get beyond his Ninth. As he told me about it at that time, it was to be something entirely new, reflecting the essence of a perception of life, in which his sojourn in America played a not insignificant part.

Even if Mahler had railed against the banality and snobs of New York often enough in sharp terms, he did not blind himself to the greatness and uniqueness of the city. He loved the sun in New York with a virtual passion. From the corner window of his drawing room in the Hotel Savoy, he had a wide view of the green of Central Park. Quite entranced, he could sit for hours and stare at the life bussling below him. "Wherever I am, the longing after this blue sky, this resplendent sun, this pulsating activity accompanies me." Slowly, he had also learned to trust the artistic earnestness of New York. During the first half of the winter, before people had begun to spoil his work for him through petty interference, we had often talked about his mission of developing precisely in New York a musical understanding of a higher kind. He had questioned the possibility for that for a long time. But as he began to sense how the public was starting to warm to his truly holy earnestness, how steadily, from concert to concert, there was a growth from what he was attempting to sow with all his might, he was determined to return and to complete his work here. How then later people tortured this thoroughly generous man with all sorts of petty things, how a righteous incomprehension began to see the only worthwhile success in dollars, rather than in his ultimate intentions, how people tore apart and destroyed his sensitive nerves—something that can, of course, be denied easily, but cannot be undone—until the day of that sudden collapse which happened to coincide with the onset of his fatal illness - all that must be only hinted at here. Should there have come days of improvement, Mahler (who then had not yet comprehended that he was doomed) had no other thought but to return to the concert hall. Only fourteen days before his departure, out of bed for the first time, and having called a rehearsal for the next day, he decided with us on the programme of the concert in which he wanted to take leave of New York for the current season.

It was the final flaring up of a completely exhausted force. Already the next day brought the severe attack which left no further doubt that his weeks were numbered. [. . .]

While notices were still being published in the papers that Mahler would conduct on this or that day, while there were people in New York who would see nothing more behind his illness than a sulking against the powers at the Philharmonic, he languished in the face of certain death. Sundered by a mysterious, unconquerable fever, like the hero Tristan. I said good-bye to him on the afternoon before his departure. Like in earlier days, he lay on his couch, wrapped in warm blankets, in front of the open window, gazing at that New York which always accompanied him in his memories. The short interval in which I had not seen him, had been sufficient to wreak a veritable destruction on his features. The always active one, who was endowed with the richest facial expressions, lay tired and emaciated, almost as if already on the bier. Whether Mahler sensed that it was a farewell for ever, I don't know. [. . .] Just as we have already often had the impression that Mahler was somewhere else in spirit (that he "was on a journey", as we came to say), so now in the hour of parting I felt explicitly that I was being spoken to by someone who retreated farther from us with each hour. [. . .]

Art has suffered an incalculable loss with Mahler's death. Mankind, however, even more. For he was one of the few greats who could give with both hands from an inexhaustible store of riches. The extent to which one man leaves his imprint on his time can never be expressed in words. But now that Mahler's voice has been silenced for ever, thousands will begin to notice what is missing, what they failed to appreciate while it lay all around them, carelessly strewn in the fullness of its wealth. His tones will continue to speak to us, but that which was the very essence of his being—the titanesque humanity, the infinite wisdom, borne of goodness and understanding, with which he was able to see beyond the limits of our own time—is no more. Very few had truly understood him. But for those, not merely a brilliant musician has died, but a truly great man.

(Maurice Baumfeld in the *Sonntagsblatt der New-Yorker Staats-Zeitung*, May 21, 1911, p. 2)

Appendix

A 1.
Konzert Direktion
Chas. Loewenstein

Gründer der s. Z.
Waldorf-Astoria Subs. Konzerte
  New-York
    and
The Permanent Orchestra
  of New-York   Berlin, den 25. Mai 1907.
Anton Seidl, Dirigent   Jaegerstrasse 47/48
New-York Addresse:
Waldorf-Astoria Hotel
Fifth Avenue 34. Str.
  An den
  Direktor der k.k. Hofoper in Wien,
    Herrn Gustav Mahler   Wien
Sehr geehrter Herr Direktor!

Ich hoffe, dass Sie sich unserer Korrespondenz entsinnen, als ich Sie
vor Jahren ersuchte, an die Spitze meiner seinerzeitigen hiesigen grossen
Subskriptions-Konzerte zu treten, woran Sie durch die Krankheit und
den Tod Ihres Herrn Kapellmeister Dr. Fuchs verhindert wurden. Wie
Sie sich erinnern werden, verdankte ich auch Frau Lilli Lehmanns
Mitwirkung, dass Sie Ihre bereitwilligkeit erklärten. Ich musste freilich
die Konzerte nachher fallen lassen.

Heute komme ich Ihnen, sehr geehrter Herr Direktor, mit ein
Offerte, die über alle Massen sämtliche Sachen, welche in dem Bereich
Ihrer Tätigkeit bis jetzt gelegen haben mögen, bei weitem übertreffen

495

wird. Ich bin an die Spitze eines Komités berufen worden, welches binnen kurzer Zeit in der Reichshauptstadt unter der Aegide Sr. Majestät des Deutschen Kaisers einen grossen Konzert-Theaterbau aufführen wird und möchte nun keinen Schritt vorwärtsgehen, bevor ich nicht mit Ihnen, was die musikalische Leitung dieses Unternehmens anbelangt, eine kurze Rücksprache gehabt habe. Es ist mir leider unmöglich, in diesem Schreiben auf die näheren Details des Gesamt-Unternehmens einzugehen, nur soviel sei hier gesagt, dass ein grosses Konsortium die Finanzierung übernommen hat. Die auf die Sache bezgl. Prospekte sind bereits im Druck, so dass ich bald imstande sein werde, Ihnen einen solchen Prospekt einzusenden. Es sei nur noch erwähnt, dass sowohl was das Aeussere wie die innere Ausstattung dieses Konzert-Theaters das Grossartigste und Vornehmste sein wird, was wohl der Kontinent aufzuweisen wird.

Zur ferneren Orientierung teile ich Ihnen mit, dass die Fassungskapazität des Hauses in Parkett, Logen und Rangen mehr als 3000 Personen beträgt, das Orchester-Podium resp. die Bühne fast 800 Personen, das versenkte Orchester ca. 150 Personen.

Ausserdem ist im Hause eine grosse Konzertorgel, so dass allen künstlerischen Intentionen genügt werden kann.

Nun, verehrter Herr Direktor, ich glaube hiermit auch Ihren Intentionen zu entsprechen, wenn ich Ihnen als Allerersten Mitteilung mache, wohl wissend, dass es keinen berufeneren Meister gibt, der einem derartigen musikalischen Unternehmen voll und ganz, so wie es sein soll, vorstehen kann.

Die einzige Bitte, die ich an diese Mitteilung knüpfe, ist, dass Sie über die Angelegenheit Diskretion währen wollen.

Könnten Sie mir postwendend mitteilen, wann und wo ich Sie recht bald in dieser Sache persönlich sprechen kann? Ich wäre gern bereit, evtl. nach Wien zu kommen und bitte um diesbezgl. Nachrichten.

Hochachtungsvoll
Ch. Loewenstein

A 2.

Lieber Salter!

Es ist möglich, daß ich mich mit Conried nicht einige! Reflektiert *Hammerstein* tatsächlich auf mich? In diesem Falle bitte ich um ein präcises Angebot! *Womöglich telegrafisch.*

Eiligst
Mahler

(The manuscript of this letter is in the Bayerische Staatsbibliothek,

Munich; the complete German text and English translation are published here for the first time with their kind permission.)

A 3.

[May 1907]

Mahler wäre einverstanden zweijähriger Vertrag für jährlich vier Monate Dollars fünftausend per Monat. [. . .] Ersucht wenn einverstanden sofortige Sie bindende Depesche während er sich zur definitiven Annahme [. . .] bis 8. Juni Bedenkzeit erbittet. [. . .]

A 4.

[May 1907]

Mir liegt natürlich unendlich viel daran Mahler zu engagieren [. . .] für sechs Monate. [. . .] Sollte ihm Amerika nicht behagen oder Verhältnisse nicht konvenieren, bin ich bereit gegenseitige Kündigung bei zu vereinbarender Kündigungsfrist zu gewähren. Bin bereit Konzerte in denen seine Werke zur Aufführung gelangen zu arrangieren. [. . .] Sollte Mahler ein vier bis sechs wöchentliches Gastspiel vorziehen bin ich auch hierzu bereit. Dieses Gastspiel könnte sich alljährlich wiederholen.

Conried

A 5.

[May 1907]

Mahlers definitive Proposition lautet acht Wochen [. . .]. Mahler käme für diese acht Wochen auch für den Fall als er seine Entlassung hier nicht bekäme. Falls er seine Entlassung bekommt behält er sich vor nochmals auf Ihre erste Offerte bezüglich sechs Monaten zurückzukommen [. . .].

A 6.

[May 26 or 27, 1907]

Erkläre unsere Vereinbarung hiemit perfekt. Bitte nochmals Geheimhaltung bis offizielle Entlassung erfolgt. Freue mich aufrichtig dass wir uns gefunden haben, hoffe mit Ihnen zusammen Grosses zu wirken. Komme Anfang Juni mit Winternitz zu Ihnen nach Berlin um Feldzugsplan zu entwerfen. [. . .]

Mahler

A 7.

10/6 [1907]

[. . .] Mahler muss fühlen, dass er der musikalische Kopf des Ganzen ist und ich Verfügungen nur nach gemeinsamer Beratung mit ihm treffen werde. Zur offiziellen Bekanntgabe Engagement Mahler muss ich dem Wunsche des Fürsten entsprechend warten bis seine Entlassung genehmigt, bis dahin muss es Gerücht bleiben. [. . .]

Conried

A 8.

18/6 [1907]

[. . .] Habe an Fürsten telegrafiert um Bewilligung Engagement Veröffentlichung. Erwarte seine Zustimmung. [. . .]

Conried

A 9.
UEBEREINKOMMEN,

welches am unten angesetzten Tage zwischen Herrn Direktor GUSTAV MAHLER in Wien einerseits und Herrn Direktor HEINRICH CONRIED, Präsidenten der CONRIED METROPOLITAN OPERA COMPANY andererseits verabredet und abgeschlossen wurde, wie folgt:

I.

Herr Direktor HEINRICH CONRIED engagiert hiemit Herrn Direktor GUSTAV MAHLER für die VEREINIGTEN STAATEN von NORDAMERIKA als Dirigenten für Oper und Konzerts auf die Dauer von je 3, d.i. drei Monate in den Jahren 1908 (acht) bis 1911 (elf).

Die dreimonatliche Tätigkeit des Herrn Direktor GUSTAV MAHLER in jedem Jahr der genannten vier Jahre beginnt am zweiten Tag nach seiner Ankunft in New York und läuft sohin ununterbrochen durch 90 (neunzig) Tage fort.

Herr Direktor GUSTAV MAHLER ist verpflichtet, die Reise in jedem Jahr so rechtzeitig anzutreten, dass er zwischen dem 20. und 25. Januar in New York ankommen kann.

II.

Während des im Artikel I festgesetzten Zeitraumes verpflichtet sich Herr Direktor GUSTAV MAHLER in dem in Artikel I bezeichneten vier Jahren, Opern und Konzerte in den VEREINIGTEN STAATEN von NORDAMERIKA dort, wo Herr Direktor HEINRICH CONRIED dies anordnet, zu dirigieren, jedoch nur unter der Bedingung, dass die bezüglichen Veranstaltungen künstlerischen Charakter tragen. Herr Direktor GUSTAV MAHLER ist jedoch nicht verpflichtet, öfters als wöchentlich dreimal zu dirigieren. Sollte jedoch Herr Direktor GUSTAV MAHLER, durch in den Vereinigten Staaten von Nordamerika vorausgegangene Tätigkeit übermüdet, nicht öfters als zweimal zu dirigieren im Stande sein, dann wird für diesen Fall die Herabsetzung der Verpflichtung auf zweimal in der betreffenden Woche konzediert. Andererseits erklärt sich Herr Direktor Gustav MAHLER bereit, wenn er sich hiezu im Stande fühlt, auch öfters als dreimal zu dirigieren, ohne hiefür eine separate Vergütung in Anspruch zu nehmen.

III.

Herr Direktor Gustav MAHLER verpflichtet sich vom Tage der Unterzeichnung dieses Uebereinkommen bis zum Ablauf der Vertragsdauer, d.i. bis zum Ablauf des im Artikel I zu berechnenden dreimonatlichen Zeitraumes im Jahre 1911 in den VEREINIGTEN STAATEN von Nordamerika für niemand anderen als die CONRIED METROPOLITAN OPERA COMPANY tätig zu sein und weder an öffentlichen, noch an privaten Orten als musikalisch ausübender Künstler ohne besondere Einwilligung des Herr Direktor HEINRICH CONRIED zu wirken.

In allen andern Ländern ist Herr Direktor Gustav MAHLER in Bezug auf seine Tätigkeit keiner Beschränkung unterworfen.

IV.

Herr Direktor Gustav MAHLER hat für seine im Artikel II näher bezeichnete dreimonatliche Tätigkeit in jedem Jahre ein Honorar von je 75.000 K., d.i. fünfundsiebzigtausend Kronen, zusammen daher in vier Jahren 300.000 K., d.i. dreihunderttausend Kronen zu erhalten. Ausserdem sind Herrn Direktor GUSTAV MAHLER in jedem Jahr die Reisespese, von und nach New York und zwar erste Kajüte, beziehungsweise Eisenbahn erster Klasse Schlaf- oder Salonwagen, weitere Wagenspesen von und zur Bahn zu ersetzen. Das Gleiche gilt von den Reisespesen innerhalb der Vereinigten Staaten von Nordamerika, wenn und soweit Herr Direktor Gustav MAHLER ausserhalb New York's zu dirigieren haben wird.

Weiters sind Herrn Direktor Gustav MAHLER die gesamten Kosten seines erstklassigen Aufenthaltes in den Vereinigten Staaten von Nordamerika, also die einer normalen Lebensführung entsprechenden Kosten der Wohnung und Verpflegung zu ersetzen und zwar die Kosten des Aufenthaltes in Hotels ersten Ranges.

Ferner wird Herr Direktor Gustav MAHLER das Recht haben, in einem der vier Jahre und zwar nach seiner Wahl, den Ersatz der Reise- und Aufenthaltskosten auch für seine Frau in Anspruch zu nehmen.

V.

Das jedesmalige Honorar des Herrn Direktor Gustav MAHLER per je
75.000 K., ist spätestens am 1. Dezember seiner Tätigkeit
vorangehenden Jahres, also das erste Mal am 1. Dezember 1907, das
zweite, dritte und vierte Mal am 1. Dezember 1908, beziehungsweise
1909, beziehungsweise 1910, bei der k.k. priv. österreichischen Boden-
Kredit-Anstalt in Wien oder einem andern von Herr Direktor Gustav
MAHLER akzeptierenden Bankinstitut in der Weise sicherzustellen,
dass das betreffende Bankinstitut für den Honoraranspruch des Herrn
Direktor Gustav MAHLER in gleicher Höhe die solidarische Mithaftung
übernimmt.

Spätestens am 1. Dezember des seiner Tätigkeit vorangehenden Jahres
ist Herrn Direktor Gustav Mahler ein Vorschuss auf sein Honorar, und
zwar jedesmal in der Höhe von 25.000 K., d.i. fünfundzwanzigtausend
Kronen auszubezahlen, wodurch die Haftung der Bank um den gleichen
Betrag sich vermindert. Der nach Abzug des Vorschusses per 25.000 K.,
erübrigende Honorarrest ist in drei gleichen Teilbeträgen und zwar nach
Ablauf je eines Monates an Herrn Direktor Gustav Mahler zu bezahlen,
vorausgesetzt, dass Herr Direktor Gustav MAHLER der in Artikel II
übernommenen Verpflichtung nachgekommen ist, oder nachzukommen
bereit war.

Gleichzeitig mit dem Honorarrest sind Herrn Direktor Gustav
MAHLER die im Artikel IV erwähnten Barauslagen zu ersetzen,
insoweit sie nicht direkt von der CONRIED METROPOLITAN
OPERA COMPANY bestritten worden sind.

VI.

Im Falle einer Erkrankung innerhalb des in Artikel I bezeichneten
Zeitraumes hat Herr Direktor Gustav MAHLER für die Zeit, während
welcher seine Tätigkeit aus diesem Grunde unterbleibt, keinen Anspruch
auf das in Artikel IV zugesicherte Honorar, beziehungsweise den pro rate
entfallenden Teil des Honorars, und ist der bezügliche Teil des Honorars
in der Auszahlung in Abzug zu bringen. Doch hat Herr Direktor Gustav
MAHLER auch in diesem Falle den Anspruch auf vollen Ersatz seiner
Reise- und Aufenthaltskosten im Sinne der Bestimmungen des Artikel IV
und zwar einschliesslich der Rückreise sowie selbstverständlich, soferne
er vor oder nach der krankheit tätig war, auch auf den entsprechenden
Teil des honorars.

VII.

Herr Direktor Heinrich CONRIED und die CONRIED
METROPOLITAN OPERA COMPANY gelten zusammen als ein
Vertragsteil und sind aus diesem Vertrage solidarisch berechtigt und
verpflichtet.

VIII.

Es wird vereinbart, dass die Rechtsverhältnisse aus diesem Uebereinkommen durchwegs nach österreichischem Rechte zu beurteilen sind.

IX.

Die von diesem Vertrage zu bemessenden Gebühren hat die CONRIED METROPOLITAN OPERA COMPANY beziehungsweise Herr Direktor HEINRICH CONRIED zu tragen, eventuell Herrn Direktor Gustav Mahler zu ersetzen.

X.

Dieser Vertrag wird in einem Originalexemplar errichtet, welches beiden Teilen gemeinschaftlich gehört und bei einem gemeinschaftlichen Vertrauensmann verwahrt wird. Beide Teile erhalten beglaubigte Abschriften dieses Vertrages.

XI.

Sollte Herr Direktor Heinrich CONRIED aus irgendwelchem Grunde von der Leitung der METROPOLITAN OPERA zurücktreten, so steht Herrn Direktor Gustav MAHLER das Recht zu diesen Vertrag in allen seinen Teilen zu lösen.

XII.

Herr Direktor Gustav MAHLER ist nicht verpflichtet "Parsifal" von Richard Wagner zu dirigieren.

Durch Unterfertigung dieses Vertrages werde alle vorherigen Abmachungen, insoferne sie mit diesem vorliegenden Vertrage in Widerspruch stehen, hinfällig.
NAUHEIM

WIEN, 21. Juni 1907

Direktor Heinrich Conried	Gustav Mahler m.p.
Präsident der Conried Metro-	
politan Opera Co., New York	
Ernest Goerlitz, als Zeuge	Alfred Roller, als Zeuge
I.C. Coppicus, als Zeuge	Rudolf Winternitz, als Zeuge

A 10.

27. September 07

Mein sehr verehrter Herr Direktor,

501

[...]

Herr Direktor werden erst einsehen, was für künstlerischen Wert die Tatsache haben wird, dass Direktor Mahler vier Wochen früher nach Amerika kommt. Dies ist heute gar nicht voraus zu schildern, und wird sich in der Qualität der Vorstellungen nach dieser künstlerischen Vorarbeit ausdrücken.

Einen materiellen Erfolg will sich Direktor Mahler gewiss durch die vier Wochen, die er früher hingeht, nicht sichern. Er erklärt ganz aufrichtig, dass er bei einem Honorar von K 25.000 für diese vier Wochen ungefähr fl. 2000 mehr bekommt, als er in Russland und Amsterdam verdient hätte.

Ganz abgesehen nun davon, dass Direktor Mahler sagt, dass jeder Künstler in Amerika mindestens das Doppelte in derselben Zeit verdienen will, fällt noch die Tatsache in die Wagschale, dass er ja durch die Konzerte in Russland und Holland ein wichtiges Arbeitsfeld für seine Zukunft sich eröffnet hätte, doch verzichtet er auf die Vorteile gerne im Interesse Ihrer gemeinsamen Sache und will nur Grosses und Vollkommenes erreichen.

[...]

Er geht mit grossem Enthusiasmus an die Arbeit für Ihre gemeinsame Sache, studiert mit Frau Fremstad die "Isolde" in der Form, dass Fräulein von Mildenburg am Vormittage mit Mahler und Fremstad zusammen in Direktor Mahlers Probezimmer studieren. Er ist von der Fremstad ganz entzückt und lässt Ihnen sagen, dass "Tristan" ganz gewiss ein grosser Erfolg sein wird.

Auch mit Fräulein La Fornia studiert Herr Direktor Mahler.

Der neue Tenor Martin hat ihn sehr interessiert und gefällt ihm ausserordentlich und beglückwünscht er Sie zu dieser Acquisition. Auch mit diesem Herrn studiert Herr Direktor Mahler sehr fleissig. Er sagt, Herr Direktor werden staunen, wie erleichtert durch diese künstlerischen Vorarbeiten die Arbeit drüben sein wird.

Endlich bittet Sie Direktor Mahler ihm zu bestätigen, dass es bei dem aufgestellten Programm verbleibt und zwar: 1. Vorstellung "Tristan", 2. Vorstellung "Fidelio". Trotzdem er vier Wochen früher kommt, möchte er sehr dafür, diese Reihenfolge einzuhalten.

[...]

A 11.

NACHTRAG

Im Nachhange zu dem zwischen der CONRIED METROPOLITAN OPERA COMPANY durch deren Präsidenten Herrn HEINRICH

CONRIED einerseits und Herrn Direktor GUSTAV MAHLER andererseits unter dem 21. Juni 1907 abgeschlossenen Vertrage wird noch Folgendes vereinbart:

Herr Direktor GUSTAV MAHLER tritt seine Reise um circa 4 (vier) Wochen früher als im Vertrage festgesetzt war, an und zwar wird sich Herr Direktor MAHLER am 12. Dezember von Cherbourg aus nach Amerika einschiffen.

Für diese Prolongation von vier Wochen erhält Herr Direktor Gustav MAHLER ein Honorar von K 25.000 (Kronen fünfundzwanzigtausend) und übernimmt dafür die Verpflichtung, während der vier Wochen 2 (zwei) mal wöchentlich zu dirigieren.

Diese Nachtragsbestimmungen werden alle unter der selbstverständlichen Voraussetzung festgesetzt, dass es Herrn Direktor Gustav MAHLER gelingt, seine Verpflichtungen, welche er für diese Zeit in Russland und Holland eingegangen ist, zu lösen, wozu Herr Direktor Gustav MAHLER sofort die erforderlichen Schritte eingeleitet hat.

Dieser Nachtragspunkt wurde wieder in einem Exemplar ausgefertigt, welches von beiden Teilen gefertigt und für beide Teile gemeinsam ist und bei einem Vertrauensmann im Original hinterlegt bleibt, während beide der kontrahierten Teile eine Abschrift des Nachtrages erhalten.

Im Uebrigen gelten für diesen Nachtrag alle im Hauptvertrage festgesetzten Bestimmungen ohne Ausnahme (auch bezüglich der Verpflegung etc.) und wird dieses Honorar von K 25.000 (Kronen fünfundzwanzigtausend) Herrn Direktor MAHLER nach Ablauf dieser ersten VIER Wochen ausbezahlt.

WIEN, den 27. September 1907   Gustav Mahler m.p.
    als Zeuge: Alfred Roller m.p.
      "   "   Rudolf Winternitz m.p.

A 12.
HOTEL MAJESTIC, NEW YORK

Sonntag 16. Feber 1908

Mein lieber Karl!

Hab Dank für Deinen lieben Brief. Mein Gewissen schlägt mir täglich, daß ich ihn noch nicht beantwort [sic] - Du wirst es aber verstehen, wenn ich Dir sage, daß ich hier gar keine Zeit habe; denn ich faulenze fortwährend. - Das ist eine Arbeit, mit der man nie fertig wird. Mein Arbeitsprogramm ist ungemein einfach. Wenn ich aufstehe, dann frühstüke ich. Hierauf schlägt mir mein Gewissen eine Zeit lang (je nach

503

dem Wetter). Nachher lenze ich mein Pensum faul. Dann kommt der
Lunch. Hierauf muß ich auf ärtzliches Gebot einige Stunden ruhen.
Wenn ich aufstehe ist Jausenzeit. Von da ab bis zum Dinner hätte ich
nun etwas Zeit. Aber die leidige Gewohnheit ist so schwer zu besiegen.
Richtig - ab und zu dirigiere [ich] auch und halte Proben. -

Wenn ein Brief von Mama oder von Dir kommt ist es ein Fest für uns
(für mich bloß etwas getrübt, durch die Hiebe [?] die ich vom Gewissen
bekomme). -

Über Amerika wollen wir im Sommer viel plauschen. Ich sehe es jetzt
als unartigen Jungen an, dem man selbst seine Roheiten, als Überschuß
drängender Lebenskraft gerne verzeiht. - Ob aus dem reizenden Jungen
später nicht ein ekelhafter Philister [wird], lasse ich dahin gestellt sein.
Aber sicherlich findest Du hier wie in Europa jenes winzige Häuflein von
Menschen, um derentwillen einem das Leben wert erscheint. - Wir
speciell lernen übrigens Alles nur von der angenehmsten Seite kennen,
die man dem ausgezeichneten Fremden unwillkürlich zeigt. - Jedes Jahr
einige Wochen hier zuzubringen, wird mir, wenn es mir beschieden ist,
immer angenehm sein; und ich habe es fest vor, daß auch Ihr einmal
dieses für einen Europäer außerordentlich mitreißendes und
erfrischendes Leben in der Nähe ansehen müßt. - Wie alles junge Volk,
sind die Amerikaner außerordentlich dankbar (leider schlingen sie Alles,
wie die Kinder kritiklos genießend, hinunter - d.h. genau gesagt es gibt für
Alles hier Abnehmer, für das Gute wie das Schlechte.) - Wäre ich noch
theaterfreudig, so hätte ich hier, wie nirgends das Arbeitsfeld für meine
nie rastenden Kräfte gefunden. Nun muß ich mich aber damit
bescheiden, für Almschi und Gucki "in die Scheune" [zu]tragen, was ich
kann. - Über diese Dinge seid Ihr wohl durch Almsch am Laufenden.

Ganz neu ist es mir—nach der Wiener Wüstenei—überall Wohlwollen
und Dankbarkeit vorzufinden, für das Wenige was ich zu leisten im
Stande bin. Ich lebe wie eine Primadonna, denke in einen fort an mein
liebes Ich, und so hoffe ich, daß mir dieses gefürchtete Amerika keinen
Schaden zufügen wird. -

Die neue Entwicklung der Verhältniße am Metropolitan-Theatre wird
vielleicht auch Roller herüberwehen. Der würde ein Arbeitsfeld
vorfinden, wie er sich es in seinen kühnsten Träumen nicht hätte
vorstellen können. Alle Erzählungen, die bei uns über Amerika im
Umlauf sind, rühren von diesen ekelhaften Sorte von Deutschen her, die
Du ebenso kennst, wie ich. Der Abhub unserer Gesellschaft, die allen
Mißerfolge, der aus ihrer eigenen Unfähigkeit und Indolenz herrührt, den
"Verhältnißen" in die Schuhe schieben, und zugleich allen
Nachkommenden die Sache dadurch erschweren, daß sie das Mißtrauen
gegen die Fremden immer höher anwachsen machen. - Dieß scheinen mir
auch hauptsächlich die Gefahren zu sein, die das junge Wesen hier am

meisten bedrohen. - Ein wirklich *nativ* [sic] Amerikaner ist ein *vornehmer* und *tüchtiger* Mensch. Dieß merke Dir unter allen Umständen, lieber Freund. Was Dir da draußen unter dieser Marke lächerlich gemacht wird, ist immer auf Rechnung der Eingewanderten zu setzen, die hier Alles Bodenständige unausgesetzt in Faulniß setzt. - Noch ist abert der Boden kräftig genug, alles Fremde zu überwinden. Wie lange? - kann ich nicht beurteilen. - Almschi, die die ersten 4 Wochen nach allen Richtungen ziemlich elend war, fängt Gott sei Dank seit 2 Wochen an, sich ganz zu erholen und ist—*unberufen*—recht frisch; und ich will auch dafür sorgen, daß sie es bleibt.

Die Elizza kann ich hier nicht unterbringen. Es sind alle Fächer überfüllt. Es tut mir recht leid.

Jetzt muß ich zur Probe. - Vielleicht überwinde ich nächstens meine Faulheit, und schreibe weiter. Für heute Dir und Mama tausend Grüße und Dank für Euere Liebe.

Euer alter
Gustav

(The manuscript of this this letter is in the Pierpont Morgan Library. Part of the letter has been published in English translation in J. Rigbie Turner, "Musical Manuscripts and Letters" in Charles Ryskamp, ed., *Nineteenth Report to the Fellows of the Pierpont Morgan Library*, New York, 1981, pp. 237f. The complete German text and English translation are published here for the first time with the kind permission of the Library.)

A 13.
William and Pine Streets

Kuhn, Loeb & Co.   New York, 18. März 1908
Geehrter Herr Mahler!

Besten Dank für Ihren Brief vom 16. ds. Ich habe denselben unserem Executive Comitee vorgelegt, welches mit den proponierten Vereinbarungen vollkommen übereinstimmt und den von Ihnen erwähnten Kontraktpunkten nur folgende verhältnismässig unwichtige Ergänzungen beifügen möchte:

1. Die Staatskabine ist in Ihrer Wahl, doch soll die Auslage, zu welcher wir hierfür verpflichtet sind, den Höchstbetrag von $500. für die Reise hierher und den gleichen Betrag für die Rückreise nicht übersteigen (wie ich höre, hat die Kabine, welche Conried Ihnen für Ihre Hierherreise besorgt hat, unter $200. gekostet).

2. Um unerquickliche Diskussionen, was unter "Kosten des New-Yorker Aufenthalts" im Sinne des Vertrags zu verstehen ist, zu vermeiden, schlagen wir vor, eine definitive Summe zu fixieren, die wir

Ihnen zur Bestreitung dieser Kosten zahlen, und zwar würde uns $200. per Woche angenehm erscheinen.

3. Während der drei Monate Ihres Engagements sollen wir das Recht haben, Sie einige Male in Konzerten zu plazieren, ebenso wie dies Conried'schen Kontrakte vorgesehen war. Auch hoffen wir Sie damit einverstanden, dass Sie vor dem 1/7. Januar nirgends in Amerika dirigieren; nach dem 1/7. April wären Sie natürlich vollkommen frei.

Sobald ich Ihre Rückäusserungen betreffs dieser Punkte erhalten habe, werde ich den Kontrakt in legale Form bringen lassen. Vielleicht haben Sie die Freundlichkeit, mir Ihren bestehenden Kontrakt zu übersenden, damit ich denselben als Modell benützen kann.

Es ist uns Allen eine grosse Befriedigung von Ihnen zu hören, dass Sie "mit Zuversicht der Gestaltung der Dinge unter der neuen Leitung entgegensehen". Aus Allem was die beiden italienischen Herren gesagt und getan haben, geht hervor, wie aufrichtig und hoch sie Ihr grosses Künstlertum würdigen. Eine wie freudige Genugtuung es mir ist, Ihr geniales Können weiterhin im Dienste unserer Sache zu wissen, brauche ich Ihnen nicht zu sagen.

Mit besten Grüssen,

Ihr sehr ergebener,
Otto Kahn

Herrn Gustav Mahler
Hotel Majestic
Central Park West & 72nd St., City.

A 14.
William and Pine Streets

Kuhn, Loeb & Co.   New York, den 23. März 1908
Verehrter Herr Mahler!

Entschuldigen Sie, bitte, die Verzögerung in der Beantwortung Ihres Briefes vom 18. März. Der Grund ist, dass ich betreffs der beiden von Ihnen berührten Punkte die Ansicht unseres Executive Committee's einholen musste, welches ich nicht früher zusammenbringen konnte.

Ad 1. - Wir hatten gedacht, dass $200. per Woche, für Wohnung, Verpflegung, etz., angemessene Kompensation sei; das Executive Committee ist jedoch bereit, diese Summe auf $225. per Woche zu erhöhen. Persönlich füge ich bei, wenn Sie indessen auf $250. per Woche bestehen, ich diese Summe, ohne ein weiteres Wort darüber zu verlieren, in Ihren Kontrakt setzen lassen und die Verantwortlichkeit für die Sanktion des Executive Committees auf mich nehmen werde.

Ad 2. - Bei allem Kunstenthusiasmus müssen wir sehen, unsere Ausgaben in den Grenzen unserer Einnahmen zu halten, und als das

Executive Committee bei unserer ersten Diskussion des Gegenstandes
vor der Idee einer Kompensation erschrak, welche, inklusive Verpflegung
und Reisekosten, sich·auf über $22,000. für dreimonatliche Tätigkeit
beläuft, wurde dagegen hervorgehoben, dass wir voraussichtlich durch
Ihr Dirigieren in Konzerten $3,000. bis $5,000. von dieser Ausgabe
wieder würden einbringen können. Nun denkt sich das Executive
Committee, dass, wenn Sie vor dem 1. Januar mehrere Konzert
Engagements auf eigene Rechnung machen, Ihre Plazierung in
Konzerten für uns wesentlich erschwert werden und von ihrem
kommerziellen Werte einbüssen würde. Andererseits sehen wir das
Berechtigte Ihres Argumentes vollkommen ein. Wir möchten daher,
womit beiden Teilen Gerechtigkeit erwiesen scheint, vorschlagen, dass
Sie die Anzahl Ihrer Konzerte *vor dem 1. Januar* auf zwei beschränken.
Beiläufig wurde bei unserer Diskussion die Frage aufgeworfen, ob Sie
willens sein würden, wenn Sie vor dem 1. Januar doch in New-York sind,
und *falls Sie Zeit frei haben*, einen Teil dieser Zeit zu vorbereitenden
Proben für Ihre Opern Saison zu verwenden - ohne weitere finanzielle
Gegenleistung unsererseits, aber auch ohne jede Verpflichtung Ihrerseits,
und nur insoweit es Ihnen selbst passt, im Interesse des künstlerischen
Resultates.

Falls Sie vorziehen, diesen Brief mündlich anstatt schriftlich zu
beantworten, wird es mir ein Vergnügen sein, Sie Mittwoch nachmittags
zu besuchen.

Es hat mir sehr leid getan, dass mein dummer Chauffeur Sie letzten
Samstag hat warten lassen; ich hatte ihn instruiert, um 2.30 bein Ihnen
zu sein, er behauptet aber, 3.30 verstanden zu haben.

Mit besten Grüssen,

Ihr sehr ergebener
Otto H. Kahn

Herrn Gustav Mahler
Hotel Majestic, City.

A 15.

Hotel Majestic
West Seventy-Second Street
   at
Central Park   New-York, d. 15. April 1908
Lieber Herr Director!

Ich habe noch über eine Lösung der schwebenden Zeitfrage Ihr
Engagement betreffend, nachgedacht, welche es uns ersparen würde,
Herrn Kahn nochmals zu incommodieren und die abermalige Vorlage der
Angelegenheit an den Board zu vermeiden. Es ist und bleibt ja nur eine

Geldfrage und es ist mir schon peinlich dass wir durch
Zeitverschwendung an diese leidige Affaire gar nicht dazu kommen, uns
über gewisse notwendige künstlerische Fragen ausführlich
auszusprechen. Nachdem man mir freigestellt hatte, betreffs des Datums
Ihres Engagementsantritts mich mit Ihnen zu verständigen, wollte ich
Ihren Wunschen voll und ganz entsprechen, nur stosse ich auf
Schwierigkeiten wegen des Repertoiren der "Festival-Performances".
Kommen Sie daher mir auf halbem Wege entgegen und willigen Sie ein,
Ihren Vertrag am 17. Dezember beginnen und am 16. März endigen zu
lassen. In diesem Fälle könnte ich mir vielleicht bei Bildung des
Repertoires helfen und die ganze neue Aufrollung der Frage würde
vermieden. Sie hätten da nur drei freie Tage im Dezember nach Ihrem
Konzert. Am 14. sollten Sie sich ohnedies ausruhen; 15. ist Philadelphia
und Sie wissen ja selbst, dass man da nicht ordentlich probieren kann.

Betreffs der Differenz von 3 & 4 Tagen Urlaub für Konzertzwecke
setzen wir vielleicht den Passus: "Drei, eventuell vier Tage" in den
Kontrakt, das schliesst auch jede weitere Diskussion aus und da Sie nun
einmal in Ihrem Schreiben vom 16. März freie Reise für Ihre Frau (mit
ihrem Kammermädchen) und sich selbst von Wien nach New-York und
zurück sowie Ersatz der sonstigen Reisespesen verlangen, ist es wohl
auch tunlicher, wenn Sie später über diese Kosten eine
Pauschalrechnung einreichen, anstatt jetzt auf ein Fixum zu bestehen,
was wiederum Weitläufigkeiten im Gefolge hätte.

Da ich den ganzen Tag über stark beschäftigt bin, so möchte ich Sie
freundlichst bitten, mir baldmöglichst zu bestätigen, ob Sie mit der
gemachten Proposition einverstanden sind.

Mit bestem Gruss

Ihr ergebener
A. Dippel

A 16.
K.k. conc. Theater- und Conzert-Agentur
Wilhelm Minkus und Rudolf Bratmann
Wien

Telegramm-Adresse: Telegramm-Adresse:
Theateragent Minkus Wien.   Theateragent Bratmann, Wien.
VI. Millöckergasse 2.

Engagements und Gastspiele
1898-1907

Comm. Aless. Bonci
    "   Fernando de Luccia
    "   Francesco Tamagno
    "   Pietro Mascagni
    "   Ermete Novelli
    "   Ermete Zacconi
    "   Tommaso Salvini
K.k. Kammersängerin Gemma Bellincioni
    "   "   Marie Gutheil-Schoder
    "   "   Lucie Weidt
K.k. Hofschauspieler
    Adolf Ritter v. Sonnenthal
Sarah Bernhardt
Hans Melms etz etz

                    Wien, am 10. Juni 1908.
Hochwohlgeboren
    Herrn Direktor Gustav Mahler,

                          z.Z. Wien.
Hochgeschätzter Herr Direktor!
Im vergangenen Jahre konnte die Impresa des Theater Colon in
Buenos Aires mit Ihnen aus folgenden Gründen nicht einigen:
I. weil die Salome und der Ring ausgeschaltet wurden und erst
Sommer 1909 gegeben werden;
II. weil das Theater zu spät fertig wurde und keine Zeit übrig blieb,
zwischen New-York und Europa zu verhandeln.
Nunmehr beauftragt mich die Impresa, jetzt schon Ihnen geschätzter
Herr Direktor Offerte für 1909 zu machen, welche Ende August a.c.
beim Eintreffen der Impresa perfektuiert werden sollen.
Das Theater gibt in italienischer Sprache im nächsten Jahre folgende
Opern, die dem deutschen Dirigenten vorbehalten bleiben und zwar.
Parsifal - Tristan - Tannhäuser - Lohengrin - Salome - Elektra -
Rheingold - Siegfried - Walküre - Götterdämmerung und noch einige
andere Opern. Sie verlangten für die drei Monate 20.000 Dollar und die
Impresa wird Ihnen gerne 80.000 Frs oder Dollar 16.000 bewilligen.
Abreise 28. April, Retourkunft in Europa Mitte September. Nachdem
heute die Reise von Genua nach Buenos Aires 15-16 Tage und von
New-York nach Cherbourg 6 Tage beläuft, so is es vorteilhafter über
Europa die Hin- und Retourreise zu machen.
              Erbitte Ihre geehrte gefällige Willensäusserung.
              Mit aller Hochachtung ganz ergebenst
                          Ihr getreuer
                          Wilh. Minkus

A 17.

Kaltenleutgeben, Rudolfshof
d. 9. Juli 1908.

Lieber Herr Director!

Ich bin von meiner Reise zurückgekehrt und hatte gehofft, dass ich innerhalb der nächsten Woche Gelegenheit haben würde, Sie in Ihrer Sommerfrische aufzusuchen und persönlich über verschiedene die kommende Saison betreffende Fragen mit Ihnen Rücksprache zu nehmen. Leider habe ich noch eine Menge dringende Arbeiten zu erledigen, auch noch ein paar geschäftliche Reisen zu unternehmen, so dass ich zu meinem grossen Bedauern meinen geplanten Ausflug zu Ihnen noch für einige Zeit verschieben muss. Ich war mit Gatti-Casazza in Wien sechs Tage zusammen und haben wir in gemeinsamer Arbeit das Repertoire der Saison in zum Teil bestimmten, zum Teil allgemeinen Zügen entworfen. Wir haben auch an die Zeitungen ein kurzes Communiqué ausgegeben, welches allerdings durch einige Privatbemerkungen, die verschiedene Blätter aus eigener Initiative hinzuzufügen beliebten, ziemlich entstellt wurde. Ich halte es daher für angemessen, Ihnen den Wortlaut mitzuschicken in Gestalt der Notiz des Neuen Wiener Tagblatt, welche den genauen Wortlaut unserer Bekanntmachung enthält. Sie sehen daraus, dass ich Ihrem Wunsche betreffs Engagements Spetrino sogleich entgegengekommen bin, indem ich nach Ihrem letzten Besuche Herrn Gatti sofort depeschierte und ihn von Ihrer Fürsprache verständigte. Ich hatte auch gehofft, Ihnen betreffs Ihres Wunsches bezüglich Tristan in vollständig neuer Inscenierung nach Professor Roller günstigen Bescheid geben zu können, doch bin ich da insofern auf Hindernisse gestossen, als Herr Gatti einen Teil des Mailänder Fundus käuflich erworben hat, bei welchem sich auch der Tristan befindet. Obwohl ich meiner gerechten Besorgnis Ausdruck gab, dass durch dieses Experiment die Dekorationsfrage des Tristan für New-York nicht endgiltig gelöst würde, glaubte ich doch in Anbetracht des Umstandes, dass ich vor einer vollendeten Tatsache stand, nicht weiter protestieren zu sollen. Da eine Trennung der deutschen Oper von der italienischen in dem Sinne, wie wir beide es ursprünglich annahmen, unter dem geschaffenen Regime nicht stattfindet, entspricht es der Ansicht des Aufsichtsrates (Board of Directors) und ist auch nicht mehr als recht und billig, dass Herrn Gatti die Chance gegeben wird, zu zeigen, was er zu leisten vermag. Ich selbst habe dies Privileg für mich auch in Anspruch genommen und ist mir beispielsweise betreffs der Novitäten "Tiefland", "Verkaufte Braut", "Königskinder" (die wir als erste Oper in englischer Sprache herausbringen und zwar als Uraufführung) vollständige Aktionsfreiheit kontraktlich zugesichert. Nachdem Sie mir sagten, dass Sie gern die "Verkaufte Braut" dirigieren möchten, lege ich

510

ganz speziellen Wert darauf, dass alle Ihre Wünsche und Ansprüche zur Geltung kommen und bitte ich mir nur baldmöglichst mitzuteilen, was ich meinerseits noch Besonderes tun kann, um Ihren Intentionen gerecht zu werden. Ich habe die Dekorationen bei Kautsky, die Kostüme bei Blaschke bestellt, alle Stoffe nach Leflers Figurinen unter seiner persönlichen Assistenz selbst ausgesucht, so dass ich sicher bin, dass wir in diesem Falle die gewöhnliche Theaterschablone vermeiden und stilvolle Bühnenbilder schaffen werden. Für die Rolle des Hans habe ich eigens Herrn Joern von Berlin engagiert, die Destinn wird die Marie singen und betreffs Goritz als Kezel hatten wir uns ja schon verständigt. Die übrigen Rollen werden wir von Anbeginn doppelt und dreifach besetzen und können Sie sich ja die besten Vertreter selbst wählen. Das Material habe ich bei Bote & Bock in Berlin bestellt und da Sie mir sagten, Sie wollten die Overture in einem Ihrer Konzerte aufführen, habe ich von vorherein die Streicher in genügender Anzahl Bestellt (10 erste Violinpulte etz), so dass Sie gleich das richtige Material für das Konzert zur Verfügung haben.

Betreffs "Pique Dame", die wir gleichfalls mit Ihnen herausbringen möchten, haben Sie wohl selbst zu bestimmen, ob Sie den Regisseur der italienisch-französischen Oper, Herrn Speck (übrigens ein guter deutscher Name) mit der Regie betrauen oder sich mit mir verständigen wollen, in welchem Falle wir mit Hilfe Schertel's und mehrerer Inspizienten die Sache schon nach Ihrem Gefallen herauszubringen uns anheischig machen. Ich erwähne der Ordnung wegen, dass ich diese Frage mit Herrn Gatti noch nicht erörtert habe und dieselbe auch heute nur aufwerfe, um Ihre prinzipielle Meinung zu hören. Einstweilen habe ich für die Sache nur insofern gearbeitet, als ich die Dekorationen in Wien bei Burghart, die Kostüme (circa 200 neu; der Rest dürfte wohl aus dem Fundus ergänzt werden) bei Blaschke bestellt habe; alles unter Beihilfe und nach persönlicher Angabe Leflers, der mir überdies noch alle wichtigen Details der Vorstellung, soweit er sich erinnert, angeben wird. Wir geben die Oper italienisch, da wir sie in dieser Sprache am besten besetzen können und weil wir hauptsächlich auf Caruso in der Tenorpartie rechnen. Glauben Sie, dass sich die Morena für die Lisa eignen möchte? Wir möchten ihr gerne eine neue Rolle zuteilen, um sie zu beschäftigen. Als Gräfin käme in erster Linie Maria Gay in Betracht, ausserdem hätten wir noch die Fremstad und Homer, sowie Madame Flauhaut. Ich schicke Ihnen übrigens in allernächster Zeit den vollständigen Besetzungsvorschlag für beide Opern. Um Beschaffung des Notenmaterials bin ich bemüht. Die Sache ist nicht so einfach. Italienische Klavierauszüge existieren nur in Russland; von dort wird wieder nach Deutschland nicht ausgeliefert und die deutsche Partitur ist wiederum nur in Leipzig zu haben. Ich versuche jetzt über Riga das

Material von Moskau zu bekommen, weil wir doch, da das Werk in Amerika nicht geschützt ist, die Zahlung der Tantième vermeiden wollen. Ueberhaupt bin ich der Ansicht, dass Tantièmen nur dem Komponisten und nicht dem Verleger zufliessen sollten.

Ich habe mit Herrn Schmid in der Hofoper gesprochen: derselbe wird das Material nach der Wiener Einrichtung in Ordnung bringen. Wenn Sie noch spezielle Anordnungen treffen wollen, müsste ich Sie bitten, mir dies ehestens mitzuteilen.

"Figaro's Hochzeit." Nach dem Repertoire-Entwurf dürfte dies die erste neue Oper sein, welche Sie dirigieren und zwar ist die Première für den 19. Dezember angesetzt. Besetzung, wie wir sie s.Z. besprochen haben: Eames - Gräfin (Gadski kommt erst im Februar), Sembrich - Susanne, Farrar - Cherubin, Sparkes (eine junge Amerikanerin mit prächtiger Stimme) Bärbchen, Amato oder Scotti - Graf (eventuell auch Feinhals, München, den ich jüngst engagiert habe, wenn er die Rolle italienisch lernen kann), Campanari oder Didur - Figaro, Marcelline - Frau Matja van Niessen oder Woehning, Basilio und Don Curzio - Reiss-Delvary-Tecchi-Bada, Bardolo - Paterna, Antonio - Missinao [sic] etz. etz. Sie finden eine Reihe neuer Namen, aber Sie werden sehen, es wird eine glänzende Besetzung und die Auffürung selbst wird Ihnen Freude machen und künstlerische befriedigung gewähren. Wenn nun noch die Dekorations- und Kostümfrage zur Zufriedenheit erledigt werden könnte, würde ich mich ausserordentlich freuen. Leider macht mir da Herr Professor Roller einen grossen Strich durch die Rechnung: ganz abgesehen davon, dass er behauptet, die Skizzen und Figurinen nicht mehr liefern zu können (welcher Punkt ja sehr einfach dadurch erledigt werden könnte, dass uns die Wiener Hofoper mit Roller's Bewilligung die Sachen zur Verfügung stellte) stellt Roller die geradezu unerhörte Forderung von 6000 Kronen für Skizzen, Figurinen etz. etz. Die Verantwortung für ein solches finanzielles Opfer kann ich unserem Verwaltungsrat gegenüber nicht übernehmen, umsomehr als beispielsweise Professor Lefler für die drei Skizzen und die Figurinen für Humperdincks "Königskinder" die Summe von 1000 Kronen verlangt, die möglicherweise noch von dem Verleger bezahlt wird. Ich hätte geglaubt, dass Roller erstens um Ihnen, der Sie doch persönlich sehr viel für ihn getan haben, gefällig zu sein und zweitens um wirklich mit der Metropolitan Oper in Kontakt zu kommen, einigermassen diskutierbare Ansprüche gestellt hatte. Aber es scheint, dass Künstler jeglicher Kategorie ihr klares Begriffsvermögen verlieren, sobald das Wort "Amerika" fällt. Dass ich Wien treu bleibe, habe ich durch die Aufträge bewiesen, die ich den hiesigen Ateliers zugewandt habe und mit deren Ausführung ich Ehre einlegen muss, um der in diesem Jahr besonders stark hervortretenden Konkurrenz zu begegnen. Ich hätte es daher nur

mit Freuden begrüsst, wenn wir uns heuer auch der künstlerischen
Mitwirkung des Herrn Prof. Roller hätten rühmen können. Unter den
somit vorliegenden Verhältnissen muss ich natürlich mir die grösste
Mühe geben, auch ohne Herrn Prof. Roller eine möglichst stylechte
Vorstellung in dekorativer Beziehung zu Stande zu bringen. Herr Lefler
ist mit dem grössten Vergnügen bereit mir mit Rat und Tat zur Seite
zustehen, auch ist seine wöchentlich mehrmalige Anwesenheit in Wien
und der Umstand, dass ich mit ihm in regelmässigem Verkehr stehe, von
höchster Wichtigkeit. Ausserdem kommt die Tatsache hinzu, dass wir
bereits heute für die nächste Saison ein enormes Defizit voraussehen und
somit nicht auf's Gerate wohl hin bestellen können, sondern mit den
Budgetmitteln rechnen müssen. Da wir für Pique Dame, wenn die Oper
ein Erfolg haben soll, Alles aufbieten müssen, um eine glänzende
Ausstattung zu bieten, legte mir Herr Prof. Lefler nahe, dass man wohl
mit Figaro Verschiedenes sparen könnte, wenn man für Pique Dame viel
anschafft. Beispielsweise ist auch in der Wiener Hofoper der Festsaal
von Pique Dame für den Figaro verwendet worden, was mir auch
Brioschi bestätigt. Die von Ihnen eingelegte Szene im 3. Akt (ich meine
die Gartendekoration, in welcher das Briefduett spielt) könnte—sofern
Sie darauf nicht besonderen Wert legen—vielleicht gespart werden und
dann blieben absolut neu anzufertigen: das Zimmer der Gräfin, das
Zimmer des ersten Aktes und die Schlusszene. Das Zimmer des ersten
Aktes müssten wir für New-York jedenfalls ändern, das befürworteten
Sie ja gelegentlich unserer letzten Begegnung selbst, dagegen glaube ich,
sollten wir für den letzten Akt die Idee, dass der Schauplatz der
Handlung auf eine Terrasse verlegt wird, von der man auf das Schloss
herabsieht, festhalten. Das Zimmer der Gräfin ist nur eine Geldfrage: das
kann man teurer oder billiger herstellen und bin ich persönlich dafür,
etwas wirklich Gediegenes machen zu lassen, selbst wenn wir in
Anbetracht der New-Yorker Bühnen- und Lagerraumverhältnisse mit
plastischen Dekorationen sehr vorsichtig sein müssen. Das Zimmer lässt
sich übrigens ähnlich wie in Wien arrangieren und werde ich auch die
entsprechenden Möbel etz in Wien bestellen. Haben Sie noch besondere
Wünsche für Figaro, so möchte ich Sie bitten, mir dieselben
baldmöglichst mitzuteilen, denn einstweilen ist immer noch Zeit,
dieselben zu berücksichtigen, wozu es möglicherweise nach ein paar
Wochen zu spät sein dürfte.
   Fidelio und Don Giovanni kommen später in der Saison dran und
zwar aller Wahrscheinlichkeit nach im Rahmen besonderer
Vorstellungen ausserhalb des Abonnements, um zu erreichen, dass diese
Vorstellungen nich von einem Publikum besucht werden, welches in der
Oper nur eine Zerstreuung und kein künstlerische Anregung sucht. Ich
glaube übrigens, dass wir in Don Giovanni und Nozze di Figaro unter

Umständen sehr gut unseren deutschen Chor, der ohnedies nicht viel zu tun hat, in italienischer Sprache singen lassen könnten und wenn Sie diesen Vorschlag gutheissen, spreche ich gelegentlich meiner nächsten Begegnung mit Gatti-Casazza hierüber.

Des Weiteren muss ich noch eine Frage an Sie richten, zu der Sie sich zunächst prinzipiell aussern müssten, bevor wir unsererseits definitive Pläne entwerfen. Sie haben sich in zuvorkommendster Weise bereit erklärt, sich in die Wagner-Opern mit Toscanini und Hertz zu teilen und glaubten wir das so auslegen zu sollen, dass Sie nichts dagegen einzuweden haben, wenn vor Ihnen einer der anderen Dirigenten die eine oder andere Wagneroper leitet. Wir werden sogar gezwungen sein, drei bis vier Wagner-Opern herauszubringen, ehe Sie Ihr Engagement antreten und werden aller Wahrscheinlichkeit nach die Opern zuerst herauskommen, welche für den neuen deutschen Chor, der erst tüchtig gedrillt werden muss, nicht in Betracht kommen. Am 26. November soll überdies am Thanksgiving Day Parsifal herauskommen, worauf wir die ganze Kraft des neuen Chors konzentrieren müssen. Lohengrin werden wir die Saison gar nicht geben und Tannhäuser, Meistersinger und Götterdämmerung erst später in der Saison. Walküre ist gleich die erste Woche mit Hertz und ich glaube, Sie werden auch keine Cabinetsfrage daraus machen, wenn vor Antritt Ihres Engagements Toscanini ein paar Tristan-Aufführungen in der von ihm von Mailand gewohnten Mise-en-scene dirigiert. Man hat geltend gemacht, dass es gerade für einen Ausländer, der zeigen will, dass er ausser dem italienischen Repertoire auch Wagner dirigieren kann, leichter sei, mit dem Tristan zu debutieren, als mit einer andern Oper und zwar der Solisten wegen, mit denen in einem solchen Werke immerhin eine verhältnismässig leichte Verständigung möglich sei. Auch ist Tristan im Vergleich mit Siegfried, Walküre etz ein komplettes Werk, während die anderen Musikdramen nur Teile eines grossen Ganzen bilden. Dass es Ihnen während der Dauer Ihres Engagements freisteht, den Tristan zu dirigieren, wann Sie wollen, ist dabei selbstverständlich, auch bitte ich Sie, Ihrerseits zu bestimmen, ob, resp. welche der anderen in Frage kommenden Werke, wie Götterdämmerung, Tannhäuser oder Meistersinger Sie übernehmen wollen, oder ob Sie mit dem angeführten Arbeitsprogramm zur Genüge beschäftigt sind. Ich habe übrigens gelegentlich unserer Konferenz die Frage berührt, dass es Ihnen, der Sie doch stets eine grosse Vorliebe für die Spieloper bekundet haben, vielleicht nicht uninteressant sein dürfte, ein Werk wie Elisir d'Amore oder Don Pasquale einzustudieren. Wollen Sie mich gefälligst wissen lassen, ob Sie auf ein derartiges Werk reflektieren? Wir wählen dann natürlich dasjenige, welches wir am Besten besetzen können.

Ich bitte Sie um Entschuldigung, dass ich Sie in der Sommerfrische mit einem so langen Schreiben bombardiere: ich hätte mich, wie schon erwähnt, viel lieber mündlich über Alles ausgesprochen.

Somit sehe ich einer bald gefl. Antwort der gestellten Fragen mit grosser Freude entgegen und verbleibe mit den herzlichsten Grüssen von Haus zu Haus

Ihr ergebener
A. Dippel

A 18.

[Toblach, Summer 1908]

Lieber Herr Lambert!

Vielen Dank für Ihre lieben Zeilen. Wir haben in Toblach ein Bauernhaus gemietet, und hoffen sehr, Sie vor Ihrer Abreise da begrüßen zu können. -

Der Oper des Herrn Mildenberg werde ich mit größtem Wohlwollen nähertreten. Wenn Sie mit Wolfsohn reden, lassen Sie sich ja *nichts* davon [an]merken, daß wir für die kommenden Jahre nicht *ihn* als Manager in's Auge gefaßt haben. Er rechnet sehr darauf, und würde heuer sich gewiß an den Intriguen beteiligen, wenn er erführe, wie die Sachen stehen.

[Mit] herzlichsten Grüßen und hoffentlich auf baldiges Wiedersehen in Toblach.

Ihr ergebenster
Mahler

(The manuscript of this letter is in NALT; it is published here for the first time with their kind permission.)

A 19.

[October 1908]

Lieber Freund!

Nur einen kurzen Gruß und die Anzeige, daß wir [uns] am 12. November mit der "Amerika" einzuschiffen, und ungefähr am 20-21. in New York anzukommen gedenken. Hätten Sie die Liebe, *Mr. Damrosch* (beiden Brüdern) meine Ankunft anzuzeigen, und da Sie ja doch gelegentlich im Hotel Savoy verkehren, es auch Herrn Ries wissen zu lassen, damit er unsere Wohnung zu unserem Empfang bereit hält.

Wir freuen uns schon sehr, wieder bald mit Ihnen zu plaudern und grüßen Sie herzlichst.

Ihr ergebener
Gustav Mahler

(The manuscript of this letter is in NALT; it is published here for the first time with their kind permission.)

A 20.
HOTEL SAVOY

Lieber Herr Kosmann [sic]!

Verzeihen Sie, daß ich erst heute Ihre freundlichen Zeilen vom 19. Nov. beantworte. Aber ich wollte Ihnen gleich etwas Definitives sagen können.

Die Angelegenheir ist hier so gut als geordnet. Vom nächsten Jahr ab tritt hier ein permanentes Orchester unter meiner Leitung zusammen. Die Saison soll ungefähr 6 Monate dauern. Die andere Zeit des Jahres wären Sie frei! Ich soll nun bei Ihnen anfragen, welche Bedingungen Sie zum Eintritt in unsere Vereinigung als 1. Conzertmeister stellen würden. Ich bitte um eine möglichst umgehende und präcise Antwort, da eine schnelle Entscheidung hier erforderlich ist. Für Ihre Talente würde sich hier jedenfalls ein reiches Arbeitsfeld und für Sie gewiß auch Befriedigung finden. - Ich schreibe in aller Eile, und werde, wenn ich Ihre Antwort in Händen habe, auch in der Lage sein, Ihnen Näheres über die Details mitzuteilen zu können [sic].

Mit herzlichsten Grüßen
Ihr ergebenster
Mahler

(The manuscript of this letter is in the Archive of the Gesellschaft der Musikfreunde, Vienna. An excerpt from it was published in Otto Biba, "Neue Mahleriana im Archiv der Gesellschaft der Musikfreunde in Wien", *Nachrichten zur Mahler-Forschung* 18 [October, 1987], p. 8; the complete German text and English translation are published here for the first time with the kind permission of the Gesellschaft.)

A 21.
HOTEL SAVOY, NEW YORK

[April 8, 1909]

Verehrter Herr Morris!

Darf ich Sie um Intervention in folgender Sache bitten?

In meinem Vertrage wurde mir eine "*Staatscabine*" zur Überfahrt bewilligt. Eine solche besteht aus einem Schlaf- und einem Wohnraum und Bad. - Hr. Schelling der beauftragt war für meine Oktoberreise die nötigen Vorkehrungen zu treffen hat für mich und meine Frau eine *Luxuscabine* genommen. Ich muß dieß, als der Abmachung widersprechend, ablehnen und ersuchen, meinem Contrakte gemäß für mich und meine Frau eine Staatscabine (auf dem *Kaiser Wilhelm* Suite gennant) und für Miss Turner eine Cabine 1. Class zu nehmen. Ich möchte die Tickets gerne *vor meiner Abreise* in Empfang nehmen.

2. Ich gestern in einem Meeting den Vorschlag gemacht, um dem Commitee gefällig zu sein, mit Hr. Dippel das Arrangement zu treffen, daß die Metropolitan Oper die Kosten meiner Oktoberreise übernimmt, wofür ich mich anheischig machte 2 Vorstellungen im Metropolitan zu übernehmen. Da aber die Zeit schon zu vorgeschritten ist, und ich meine Oktoberfahrt in kürzester Frist geordnet wünsche, so möchte ich meinen Antrag gerne dahin modifizieren daß dieses Abkommen für meine *Rückreise nach Europa* im nächsen April angenommen würde. Wir hätten dann den ganzen Winter Zeit, das Arrangement mit der Metropolitan zu treffen.

Ich wiederhole nochmals mein Anerbieten, zu Gunsten des Garantiefonds im Metropolitan nächsten Winter 2 Vorstellungen zu dirigieren. - Da ich schon Samstag abreise, so wäre ich Ihnen unedlich Verbunden, wenn Sie beide Punkte noch im Laufe des heutigen und morgigen Tages erledigen wollten. Mit herzlichstem Danke

Ihr ergebenster
Mahler

Die Suiten, die mir passend erscheinen sind unter nachfolgenden
    130, 131, 132, 129
    125, 126.-
Die Cabine für Miss Turner sollte in der Nähe sein.
Meine Adresse in Europa ist:
    Direktor Mahler
    Wien
    III. Rennweg 5   *bis 1.* Juni
    nach dem 1. Juni
    Toblach a.d. Südbahn
    Tyrol

(The manuscript of this letter is in ANYP; it is published here for the first time with their kind permisison. My translation is based on one appended to the manuscript.)

A 22.

Quarantäne N[ew] Y[ork] 10 April [1909]

Mrs. Untermyer, 675 5th Ave. N[ew] Y[ork]

Tausend Dank und Liebe, unvergängliche Liebe. Sie sind der einzige Mensch der uns den Abschied schwer macht. Wir umarmen Sie.

Gustav und Alma Mahler

(The original copy of this telegram (probably in the hand of the receiving clerk, and containing numerous errors) is in NALT; the complete German text and English translation are published here for the first time with their kind permission.)

A 23.

[Summer 1909]

Lieber Herr Arnold!

Ich habe bis jetzt noch immer keine Nachricht von Ihnen, wie es sich mit der Besetzung von Flöte und Pauke verhält. Meine *Cables* scheinen nicht anzukommen; denn anders kann ich mir es nicht erklären, daß sie gewöhnlich unbeantwortet bleiben. - Da ich nächste Woche Wien verlasse, um mich an meinen Sommerort zu begeben, so weiß ich nicht ob ich Herrn van Leeuwen engagieren kann oder nicht. - Auch daß der Pauker noch nicht gesichert ist, setzt mich in höchste Unruhe. - Meine Schiffsbillete, die Herr Leifels in Ordnung zu bringen versprach, sind auch noch nicht in meine Hände gelangt. Auf eine direkte Anfrage bei German Lloyd erfuhr ich daß nicht eine *Staatscabine* für mich und eine solche 1. Classe für die Governesse meines Kindes genommen ist - wie der Contrakt *ausdrücklich* vorschreibt, sondern eben jene Cabine, die ich schon vor meiner Abreise aus Newyork [sic] bemängelte.

Sie begreifen, daß mich auch dieß verstimmen muß. Ich bitte in dieser Angelegenheit freundlichst das Nötige veranlassen zu wollen und dafür zu sorgen, daß die Bestimmungen meines Vertrages eingehalten werden.

Ich habe nach unglaublich schwierigen Verhandlungen mit einer Menge von Bewerbern

Hr. *Theodor [sic] Spiering*

geborenen Amerikaner und **Mitglied** der *Chicagoer* Union, als Conzertmeister engagiert. Die Bedingungen erfahren Sie aus beifolgendem Vertrage. Wollen Sie, bitte, auch freundlichst dafür Sorge tragen, daß für Hr. *Spiering* am *Kaiser* Wilhelm II. der am *12.* Oktober von Bremen abfahrt ein erste Classe Cabine für H. Sp. belegt wird.

Es ist dasselbe Schiff mit dem ich und meine Familie am *13.* von Cherbourg abfahren wird.

Da ich für den Conzertmeisterposten ein *Unionsmitglied* engagiert habe und die Union mir für diesen *Posten* einen Ausländer zu importieren erlaubt hat; - ferner uns beiden zugesagt worden ist, daß wir für Flöte einen Ausländer engagieren können, und den Pauker in Amerika nehmen können, wo wir ihn finden; so wird doch die **Union** keine Schwierigkeiten machen, den **Flötisten** zu importieren, und einen

518

Pauker aus einer anderen Stadt als Newyork zu engagieren? Stellen Sie doch den Herren dies alles vor! Und auch welche Schwierigkeiten wir schon in unseren Aprilconzerten mit dem Pauker gehabt. -
Meine Sommeradresse ist
Toblach
Tyrol
Villa Altschluderbach.
Wollen Sie freundlichst Ihre Antwort und alle ferneren Nachrichten dahin richten. - Die Programme werde ich Ihnen in den nächsten Tagen zuschicken. -
Ein ganz famoser Geiger Herr Hammer, ein Amerikaner und Unionmitglied reiste wieder nach Amerika zurück. Bitte, wenn es möglich engagieren Sie ihn. - Bitte, seien Sie in Ihrer Antwort recht ausführlich.
Herrn Leifels grüßen Sie von mir. Er möchte entschuldigen, daß ich seinen Brief nicht separat beantworte. Er findet alles in diesem Brief an Sie. -
Mit den Gast-Solisten, die er mir angegeben:
Hr. Busoni
Hr. Wüllner
Frn Tilly Koenen
bin ich einverstanden. Nur bitte ich um genaue *Angabe* **des Datums** und eines Programmvorschlags, damit ich meine Programme danach einrichten kann. Bloß die Mrs *Powell* von der er schreibt, kenne ich nicht! Wenn sie wirklich *hervorragend* ist, so können Sie sie ja engagieren!
Mit herzlichen Grüßen, und die Bitte die Sache mit meiner Überfahrt in Gemeinschaft mit Hr. Leifels ordnen zu wollen. Ihr ganz ergebenster
Gustav Mahler

(The manuscript of this letter is in ANYP; the complete German text and English translation are published here for the first time with their kind permission.)

A 24.

26 Mai 1909

Verehrtes Fräulein!
Darf ich Sie bitten, mir anzuzeigen am welchen Datum ich Sie [sic] Ihr erstes Auftreten festsetzen darf? Und ferner bitte ich, mir freundlichst einen Programmvorschlag zu machen. Ich freue mich schon sehr, wieder

einmal mit Ihnen wirken zu können, und hoffe daß die Amerikaner Ihre
große Kunst ebenso verständig würdigen werden, wie die Europäer.

Ihr ganz ergebenster
Gust[av] Mahler

A 25.

[Summer 1909]

Lieber Herr Leifels!

Soeben habe ich mit Herrn Schnellar (Hofmusiker, Wien) bezüglich
der Pauken alles abgemacht.

Er schickt sofort 2 Paar seiner neuen Pauken an die Adresse des H.
Arnold nach Newyork [sic]. Haben Sie die Güte, wenn Sie dieselben
angekommen sind, das Nötige wegen der Zollbehandlung und der
Abholung zu veranlaßen, und dem dortigen Pauker (der bis dahin
hoffentlich schon vorhanden sein wird) zur näheren Kenntnißnahme der
Behandlung dieselben vorzulegen. - Sie kosten: *2.700 Kronen* (d. ist 540
Dollars) und ich bitte freundlichst veranlaßen zu wollen, daß der Betrag
nach Ankunft der Instrumente an Herrn Hofmusiker Hans Schnellar

    Wien

I k.k. Hofoper

abgesendet werde.

Wie Sie wissen, hat Mrs. Scheldon [sic] diesen freundlichst zur
Verfügung gestellt. - Die Transport- und Zollkosten übernimmt doch,
wie recht und billig, die Philharmonie?! Leider bin ich noch immer ohne
Antwort auf mein letztes Cablegramm. - Ich kann mir dies absolut nicht
erklären. Ich hoffe, daß ich nunmehr an meine Sommeradresse:

    Toblach a.d. Südbahn

    Tyrol

einen ausführlichen Bericht über alles erhalte. Die Programme werde ich
noch im Verlaufe dieses Monats fertig stellen und Ihnen zusenden.

Mit herzlichsten Grüßen an Sie und Herrn Arnold

Ihr ergebenster
Mahler

Wo befindet sich gegenwärtig Frau Scheldon und wie lautet ihre
Adresse? - Was ist mit meiner Überfahrt? Und wann bekomme ich meine
Billete?

(An excerpt from this letter is published in BRM, p. 265. - The manuscript is in ANYP; the complete German text and English translation
are published here for the first time with their kind permission.
The translation of the published excerpt is in BRM(E), p. 259.)

A 26.

Toblach, Juni 1909

[...] Wegen Buenos-Ayres [sic] werde ich also die Handlungen beginnen und die mindestens bis zu Deiner Rückkunft hinausziehen, damit wir alles persönlich gut besprechen können. - Jetzt wird bald der New-Yorker Arnold kommen; ich bin neugierig, was er zu erzählen hat. *Der Pauker aus Pittsburg* [sic], den sie acquiriert zu haben scheinen, ist ganz gut. [...]

A 27.

Toblach, 17. Juni 1909

[...] Ich mache hier fleissig Programme - denn wegen der Proben ist das doch nicht so einfach; damit wenn Mr. Arnold aus New-York kommt, alles schon klappt. [...]

A 28.

Toblach, [18.] Juni 1909

Eben gehe ich zur Post, um mir Deine Briefe zu holen - da kommt Arnold daher direkt aus New-York - ganz gemütlich - ich komme also keinesfalls mehr zum Schreiben heute [...]

A 29.

Toblach, [19.] Juni 1909

Die unendliche Langeweile des amerikanischen Ehepaares hat sich auf diese Landschaft herabgesenkt. Im ersten Moment, als ich die schönere Hälfte meines Managements erblickte, war es mir klar, dass ich einer der ungastfreundlichsten Menschen bin un liess der "Germania" alle Ehren und Freuden, die die Beherbergung unserer distinguished foreigners bietet. Heute Abend kommt Freund [...]

Ich bin momentan also wieder einmal ganz Orchesterangelegenheit, das haben die Arnolde einmal an sich. Es gibt auch eine ganze Menge zu tun. - Arnolds haben auch generöser Weise ihren Aufenthalt in der Germania bis Donnerstag ausgedehnt. - Morgen (Sonntag) habe ich sie zu einem Lunch eingeladen. [...]

Deckners Schreiben habe ich dahin beantwortet, dass ich folgende Forderungen stelle:

18000 Dollars, Staatscabine, Engagement des assistant conductor, der mit mir sich ins Dirigieren zu teilen hat, Engagement van Rooys. - [...]

521

A 30.

Wien, 18.6. 1909
13./2 Matznergasse 44.III.

Sr. Wohlgeboren, Herrn Director Gustav Mahler
z. Z. in Toblach.

Hochverehrter Herr!

Beehre mich zur gfl. Kentniss zu bringen, dass ein Paar Pauken (solche wie Ew. W. in München gesehen) fertig geworden und, was mich besonders mitzuteilen freut, ganz famos ausgefallen sind. Es ging so rasch, da alle Bestandteile vorrätig waren. Dagegen wird das 2.te Paar (Pedalpauk.) lange erfordern, weil zu diesem Paar von Haus aus Alles erst besorgt werden muss, besonders die hier unvermeidlichen "Temper"-Gussteile von der Fabrik aus (St. Pölten) erst nach Wochen mit Mühe erhätlich sind. Selbstredend werde ich Alles daransetzen, dass die Instrumente zur Zeit in New York sind. -

Transport: Bis Hamburg empfehle ich unbedingt Eilgut. Die Schiffsladung nach *Raum* berechnet, per Eildampfer (7 Tage Laufzeit) per m³ 8 Dollar; Frachtendampfer nur 6 Dollar, doch 12-14 Tage Laufzeit, Hamburg-New York. Ganz nach Ordre.

Zoll: Will nach dem Werte bemessen, ca. 20%; der Sendung sind obligator. 2 gleichlautende, von einem hiesig. Notar u. dem amerikanisch. Konsulat vidierte Facturen beizuschliessen.

Ich möchte hierin der edlen Paukenstifterin gerne entgegenkommen, pro forma einen niedrigern Preis in den amtlichen Rechnungen notieren; doch könnte unter Umständen ein Irrtum, oder sonst etwas herauskommen, wodurch ich dann tatsächlich nur auf den Scheinpreis Anspruch erheben könnte. Diesbetreff bitte Ew. W. ditto um Directive.

Reserve-Felle sind bereits zur Stelle, in Rolle eingepackt. *Wann* und *wohin* soll ich sie bringen (senden)?—

Eine hfl. Bitte, mit deren Erfüllung mir Ew. W. eine grosse Sorge abnähmen: Die aufgelaufenen Spesen (Arbeitslöhne, Material) muss ich meist wöchentlich auszahlen. Die bereits *fertigen* Pauken (1200 K.) mein (bis jetzt unzureichendes) Betriebskapital fast erschöpft. So ungern ich Ew. W. mit dergleichen belästige, bitte ich recht herzlich um eine a conto Zahlung von 600 K; dieselbe ist durch das Vorhandensein der bereits fertigen, zur Verfügung stehenden Pauken gedeckt. -

Das geplante Engagement muss ja nicht gerade 3000 Dollar tragen; wenigstens mache ich hieraus keine Bedingung; für einen Pauker (!) werden die Herrschaften dies vielleicht doch nicht ausgeben wollen, obschon ich über das ausgeben "können" keinen Augenblick zweifle. Wenn *Herr Director* wollen, dann ist der obige Betrag so gut wie bewilligt. -

Lebhaft wünschend, Herr Director möchten sich zum Zwecke der bevorstehenden grossen künstlerischen Taten den ganzen Sommer über *recht wohl* befinden, harre ich Ihrer güt. Antwort u. zeichne mit Versicherung meiner Ergebenheit hochachtungsvoll!

Hans Schnellar.

(Obige Adresse gilt; bin heuer nicht in Bayreuth.)

(The manuscript of this letter is in ANYP; the German text and English translation are published here for the first time with their kind permission.)

A 31.

Toblach, [21.] Juni 1909

[. . .] In das Gemüt von Frau *Arnold* habe ich unterdessen—es war gestern beim Ansichtskartenschreiben an Freund Leifels—tiefe Blicke getan. - Ich dachte früher, sie ist ein Strunk! Aber nein! Sie ist ein Schäker. Neckisch ist der Grundzug ihres Wesens. Gestern, als ich ihre Begeisterung für die Natur—hauptsächlich liebt die illustrierte Ansichten— kam mir plötzlich wieder eine Idee, merkwürdiger Weise wieder mit einer Kalesche. Sie gehen morgen (Dienstag statt Donnerstag) mit einem Wagen die neue Dolomitenstrasse, um sich sämtliche hier befindliche Gegenden anzusehen. - War das nicht genial?

[. . .]

A 32.

Toblach, 25. Juni 1909

[. . .] Das Ehepaar Arnold sind nun gestern fort. - Jetzt aber war es höchste Zeit. Diese Leute sind mir an die Nerven gegangen - ich habe es wirklich *nicht* länger ausgehalten. - Freund bleibt bis Samstag. [. . .]

A 33.

Soviel ich glaube, hat Hr. Spiering seinerseits auch eine Cabine schon belegt - ich bitte also freundlichst diese Sache zu ordnen.

[Toblach, 25. Juni 1909?]

Mein lieber Herr Leifels!

Durch einem Irrtum öffnete ich Ihren Brief an H. Arnold (der gestern nach Leipzig abgereist ist) und nahm Einsicht in den Inhalt desselben. -

Das Programm habe ich an Hr Krehbiels Sommeradresse abgeschickt. H. Arnold hat eine Copie desselben mitgenommen. - Bitte, laßen Sie mich wissen ob Hr Krehbiel meine Sendung empfangen, und haben Sie die Güte, alle seine Wünsche im Bezug auf die Programme zu erfüllen. -

Die Adresse des *H. Spiering* lautet:
Mr. Th. Spiering
Heppenheim
Germany Bergstrasse
Recommandieren Sie jedoch die Sendungen an ihn.

Mit H. Dippel habe ich noch kein Arrangement getroffen; jedoch besprochen, daß wenn es meine Zeit ohne Schädigung der Philharmonie erlaubt, ich einige Vorstellungen am neuen Theater dirigieren werde. In diesem Falle hätte die Metropolitan-compagnie meine **Rückreise** zu bezahlen. Die *Hinreise* muß also jedenfalls die Philharmonie übernehmen. Es war aber auch *zu fatal*, daß Hr. Schelling, der doch meinen Vertrag am besten gekannt hat, nicht gleich die mir gebührende Staatscabine genommen hat. - Da hatten wir vielleicht ein vorteilhafteres Arrangement treffen können. Vergessen Sie, bitte, nicht, daß ich außer der Staatscabine noch eine Cabine I. Classe für meine Governess brauche. -

Wenn wir nur zu allerletzt nicht mit Herrn *Friese* Schwierigkeiten bekommen? [!sic] Glauben Sie, daß er sicher in Pittsburg [sic] frei kommt? Und wenn nich - was geschieht dann? - Der Flötist Scheers ist *mittelmäßig* wie mir Hr Mengelberg aus Amsterdam mitteilt! Auch fatal!

Herzlichst grüße ich Sie

ergebenst
Gustav Mahler

(The manuscript of this letter is in ANYP; it is published here for the first time with their kind permission.)

A 34.

Toblach, 11. Juli 1909

[...] Denke Dir, Leifels hat schon die Staatscabine - sie kostet aber *1800 Dollars!* An die Scheldon [sic] habe ich einen netten Brief und sämtliche Programme geschickt. Das wird sie mich hoch anrechnen. [...]

A 35.

[Late Summer 1909]

Verehrteste Frau!

Vom Wiener Lieferanten unserer neuen Pauken (selbst ein ganz unbemittelter Orchestermusiker) bekomme ich schon zum 3ten Male einen (diesmal ziemlich unhöflichen) Mahnbrief. Er hat sein Geld noch immer nicht erhalten. Auf was für einer Confusion die Sache beruht,

weiß ich nicht. Ich habe Arnold unzähligemahl gebeten, die Sache in
Ordnung zu bringen. Ich wende mich nun an Sie, gnädige Frau, unseren
"Schutzengel", und bitte Sie freundlichst einzugreifen. - Wir Beide
(meine Frau, die leider wieder an einer Angina zu Bett liegt, und ich)
sehnen uns schon sehr nach einem Wiedersehen mit Ihnen. Meine
Recherchen nach guten Musiker[n] schreiten fort, und hoffe Ihnen bald
günstige Resultate vorlegen zu können. Mit herzlichsten Empfehlungen

Ihr sehr ergebener
Gustav Mahler

(The manuscript of this letter is in NALT; it is published here for the first
time with their kind permission.)

A 36.
[New York, Winter 1909-1910?]

Mein lieber Karl!

[. . .]

Im Ganzen geht es uns recht gut. - Bezüglich meine Ernährung habt
gar keine Sorge. Ich sehe blühend aus, habe ein normales Gewicht, und
halte die starke Arbeit prachtvoll aus. Auch Almschl geht es heuer **viel**
besser. In den letzten Tagen hatte sie wieder (zum 1. Mal heuer) diese
gewissen Schwächezustände. Aber bei weitem nicht so arg wie voriges
Jahr. Die Kleine ist jetzt verkühlt, aber im Ganzen auch
zufriedenstellend. Mein Erfolg als Dirigent ist ganz nach Wunsch.
(Vielleicht sogar über Wunsch - denn je erfolgreicher ich bin, desto
schwerer komme ich hier weg.) [. . .]

(The manuscript of this letter is in the Austrian National Library; the
German text and English translation of this excerpt are published here
for the first time with their kind permission.)

A 37.
[Winter 1909-1910?]

Verehrte gnädige Frau!

Eine Äußerung, die Sie gestern getan ("ich tue Nights als [anderes?],
als Geld geben") ist mir im Ohr geblieben. Ich verstand gestern die
Tragweite nicht. Aber es ist mir ein Bedürfnis, Ihnen zu sagen, daß Sie
sehr viel mehr tun, als "Geld zu geben". (Was allerdings uns auch sehr
nottut) - Ich bedarf Ihrer sehr, und die Philharmonie weiß Ihrer steten
warmen Fürsorge in allen kleinen und großen Sorgen des Tages großen
Dank. Sie schätzen sich und Ihre Dienste im Interesse unserer Sache zu

tief ein, und ich sage Ihnen das vor Ihrer Abreise nach dem Süden mit meinen herzlichsten Wünschen für eine schöne Zeit.

Ihr herzlichst ergebener
Gustav Mahler

(The manuscript of this letter is in NALT; the complete German text and English translation are published here for the first time with their kind permission.)

A 38.

Springfield, 24. Febr. 1910

Liebste! Das wird immer old-fashioneder. O Savoy! Was bist Du für ein ruhiges, neices Tusculum. - Heute bin ich in einem L[och?] (es gibt hier keine anderen) ein Gebrüll von Maschinen, Cars, etc. Mein Magen ist auch nicht mehr in Ordnung! Vielleicht ist es wieder die Butter, die ich von jetzt an ausscheiden will. Sehr kalt und Alles beschneit und vereist! Wie gut, dass ich den Pelz mithabe. - Es wäre gar nichts für Dich diese Tour! Ueberall Negerbedienung. Hier übrigens sehr angenehme dienststeifrige und bescheidene Burschen.

Spiering als Reisemarschall Operettenfigur. - Ein Conversation mit ihm wird immer schwieriger. Er überlegt sich jedes Wort so lange, dass indessen immer was Anderes denkt, und dann nicht mehr weiss, was er sagt. Jedenfalls ist New-Haven ein liebes Oertchen, mit einem schlechten Hotel. Springfield ist ein ekelhaftes Nest mit einen unmöglichen Hotel. [...]

A 39.

[April 3, 1910]

Lieber Herr Leifels!

Da ich übermorgen (Dienstag) verreise, so ist es wohl nötig, daß wir uns vorher noch sprechen. Ich bitte Sie daher, mich morgen gegen 1/2-10 Uhr aufzusuchen. Der Flötist von Chicago hat eben definitiv abgeschrieben.

Ich habe an das Comité die Bitte gerichtet, zuzustimmen, daß ich am 18. mit dem Kaiser Wilh. abfahre, so daß ich also erst am 24.ten hier eintreffe. Falls das Comité damit einverstanden ist, so bitte ich mir freundlichst für meine Rückreise dieselben Cabinen zu belegen, die ich jetzt bei meiner Überfahrt inne habe.

Mit besten Grüßen ergebenst
Mahler

APPENDIX

(The manuscript of this letter is in ANYP; the complete German text and English translation are published here for the first time with their kind permission.)

A 40.

Toblach, 29. September [sic - August] [1910]

Verehrter Herr Untermyer!

Ich empfang eben Ihr freundliches Schreiben vom 24th Aug. aus dem ich entnehme, daß man den faux pas gemacht hat, Sie irgendwie einseitig zu informieren. - Die Angelegenheit in der ich Sie zum Schiedsrichter vorgeschlagen (lediglich um Zeit- und Stimmung-raubenden Controversen zu entgehen, und wirklich bloß um meinem Standpunkt zu markieren) ist sehr geringfügiger Natur, und falls es Ihnen auch nur im geringsten unsympathisch ist, werde ich meinen Vorschlag ohne Weiteres zurückziehen.

Da Sie am 14ten September von Cherburg [sic] abfahren, so wird es Ihnen und Ihrer Frau Gemahlin wohl nicht möglich sein, der Uraufführung meiner 8. Symphonie in München, die am 12. September stattfindet, beizuwohnen. Da Sie jedoch offenbar über München fahren müssen, so wird es Ihre Gemahlin vielleicht interessieren, einer der großen Proben, die am 10. und 11. September stattfinden, beizuwohnen. In diesem Falle wird es mir ein großes Vergnügen sein, Ihnen und wem Sie sonst wünschen den Eintritt zu denselben zu ermöglichen, und ich bitte nur seinerzeit um eine Benachrichtigung. Ich werde vom 5. September an in München im Hotel Continental wohnen, und sowohl meine Frau als auch ich würden uns sehr freuen, Ihnen in diesen Tag[en] die Hand drücken zu können.

Mit herzlichsten Grüßen von uns Beiden an Sie und Mrs. Untermyer

Ihr sehr ergebener
Gustav Mahler

(The manuscript of this letter is in NALT; the complete German text and English translation are published here for the first time with their kind permission.)

A 41.

[Autumn-Winter, 1910?]

Verehrte gnädige Frau!

Entschuldigen Sie, daß ich erst heute dazu komme, Ihre lieben Zeilen zu beantworten. Auch hoffte ich immer, dies persönlich tun zu können.

Ich vermisse Ihre Gegenwart bei den Aufführungen und Proben sehr; die unsichtbaren Fäden zwischen mir und der verständnisinnigen liebenswürdigen Zuhörerin bestehen noch immer und ich harre nur des Moments sie wieder anzuknüpfen. Das Orchester ist heuer um ein gutes Stück weiter, und besonders die Contrabässe - dank Ihres hochherzigen Eingreifens ein wahrer Staat. Ich denke, Sie werden Ihre Freude daran haben.

Mit dem Wünsche, Sie bald in Ihrer alten Frische und Begeisterungsfähigkeit wieder in unserer Mitte zu begrüßen, bin ich Ihr

herzlichst ergebener
Gustav Mahler

Darf ich Sie bitten, mich Mr. Untermyer zu empfehlen.

(The manuscript of this letter is in NALT; the complete German text and English translation are published here for the first time with their kind permission.)

Index

(Page numbers followed by "n" indicate entries that appear in footnotes only, and those followed by "(i)" appear in illustration captions. The Index also serves as a bibliographic locator.)

531